*The Editor*

MARGARET REYNOLDS is Reader in English and Contemporary Culture at Queen Mary, University of London, and a Life Member of Clare Hall, Cambridge. She is the editor of the variorum *Aurora Leigh*, *Erotica*, and *The Penguin Book of Lesbian Short Stories*. She is co-editor (with Angela Leighton) of *Victorian Women Poets: An Anthology*; editor of *The Sappho Companion*; and series editor of Vintage Living Texts. Her next book, *The Sappho History*, is forthcoming.

W. W. NORTON & COMPANY, INC.
*Also Publishes*

THE NORTON ANTHOLOGY OF AFRICAN AMERICAN LITERATURE
*edited by Henry Louis Gates Jr. and Nellie Y. McKay et al.*

THE NORTON ANTHOLOGY OF AMERICAN LITERATURE
*edited by Nina Baym et al.*

THE NORTON ANTHOLOGY OF CONTEMPORARY FICTION
*edited by R. V. Cassill and Joyce Carol Oates*

THE NORTON ANTHOLOGY OF ENGLISH LITERATURE
*edited by M. H. Abrams and Stephen Greenblatt et al.*

THE NORTON ANTHOLOGY OF LITERATURE BY WOMEN
*edited by Sandra M. Gilbert and Susan Gubar*

THE NORTON ANTHOLOGY OF MODERN AND CONTEMPORARY POETRY
*edited by Jahan Ramazani, Richard Ellmann, and Robert O'Clair*

THE NORTON ANTHOLOGY OF POETRY
*edited by Margaret Ferguson, Mary Jo Salter, and Jon Stallworthy*

THE NORTON ANTHOLOGY OF SHORT FICTION
*edited by R. V. Cassill and Richard Bausch*

THE NORTON ANTHOLOGY OF THEORY AND CRITICISM
*edited by Vincent B. Leitch et al.*

THE NORTON ANTHOLOGY OF WORLD LITERATURE
*edited by Sarah Lawall et al.*

THE NORTON FACSIMILE OF THE FIRST FOLIO OF SHAKESPEARE
*prepared by Charlton Hinman*

THE NORTON INTRODUCTION TO LITERATURE
*edited by Jerome Beaty, Alison Booth, J. Paul Hunter, and Kelly J. Mays*

THE NORTON INTRODUCTION TO THE SHORT NOVEL
*edited by Jerome Beaty*

THE NORTON READER
*edited by Linda H. Peterson, John C. Brereton, and Joan E. Hartman*

THE NORTON SAMPLER
*edited by Thomas Cooley*

THE NORTON SHAKESPEARE, BASED ON THE OXFORD EDITION
*edited by Stephen Greenblatt et al.*

For a complete list of Norton Critical Editions, visit
www.wwnorton.com/college/english/nce_home.htm

A NORTON CRITICAL EDITION

# Elizabeth Barrett Browning
# AURORA LEIGH

AUTHORITATIVE TEXT
BACKGROUNDS AND CONTEXTS
CRITICISM

*Edited by*

MARGARET REYNOLDS
UNIVERSITY OF LONDON

W. W. NORTON & COMPANY *New York London*

Printed in the United States of America
First Edition

The text of this book is composed in Electra
with the display set in Bernhard Modern
Composition and manufacturing by The Maple-Vail
Book Manufacturing Group

Library of Congress Cataloging-in-Publication Data
Browning, Elizabeth Barrett, 1806–1861.
Aurora Leigh : authoritative text, backgrounds and contexts, criticism / Elizabeth Barrett Browning ; edited by Margaret Reynolds.
p. cm.—(A Norton critical edition)
Bibliographical references.
1. Browning, Elizabeth Barrett, 1806–1861. Aurora Leigh.
I. Reynolds, Margaret. II. Title.
PR4185.A2R49 1995
821′.8—dc20 94-4511
r95

ISBN 0-393-96298-9

W. W. Norton & Company, Inc., 500 Fifth Avenue, New York, N.Y. 10110
W. W. Norton & Company Ltd., Castle House, 75/76 Wells Street,
London W1T 3QT

5 6 7 8 9 0

# Contents

# Preface

At the heart of *Aurora Leigh* there is a book. It's the book that Aurora sits down to write when she begins her story (1.1–9). It's the new and brave book that she attempts in the center of the poem (5.351–357). It's the manuscript book that she leaves with her publisher before setting out for Italy (5.1212–1213 and 5.1261–1266). It's the book that Romney reads and that makes him realize, ten years too late, that Aurora really is a poet (8.261–262 and 8.278–297).

This imagined book is the pattern for *Aurora Leigh* itself. The real verse-novel published by Elizabeth Barrett Browning at the end of 1856 mirrors the made-up poem written by the fictional Aurora. Both books tell the story of a woman poet that is, and is not, her own story. Both books aspire to a new poetic form, both deal with the topical questions of the day, both appear in England while the author travels to Italy. So much is true of both Aurora's book and Barrett Browning's. The part that Barrett Browning had to make up, because it hadn't yet happened, is the story of what became of the book that is and is not *Aurora Leigh*.

Fantasizing about the reception of her own book, Barrett Browning tells us how the critics admired Aurora's book, how they exclaimed over this unlooked-for triumph from a woman, how they accorded Aurora respect and fame (7.551–571). In the event, it didn't work out quite like this for *Aurora Leigh*. Some reviewers were amazed because the work was so big and bold; some deemed it cumbersome and excessive. But they all agreed that it was important for two reasons. First, it tackled with enthusiasm the pressing contemporary issues of socialism and the position of women. Second, it outlined the model for the successful working woman poet. Readers from Queen Victoria to the art critic John Ruskin, from the historian Thomas Carlyle, to the poet Christina Rossetti found *Aurora Leigh* riveting because of its politics; because of its passionate defense of individual, as opposed to collective, enterprise; because of its eager championing of the "fallen" woman and the single mother. The book had a huge success with a wide general public. The first edition sold out in a fortnight, and it was reprinted five times before Elizabeth Barrett Browning's death in 1861. By the end of the nineteenth century it had been reprinted more than twenty times in Britain and nearly as often in the United States. It became one of the books that everyone knew and read. Oscar Wilde loved it, the poet Algernon

Charles Swinburne wrote a gushing preface for it, the novelist Rudyard Kipling borrowed the plot for *The Light That Failed* (1890), and, in America, the feminist activist Susan B. Anthony presented her treasured copy to the Library of Congress in 1902 and wrote on the flyleaf:

> This book was carried in my satchel for years and read & re-read. The noble words of Elizabeth Barrett . . . sink deep into my heart. I have always cherished it above all other books. I now present it to the Congressional Library Washington D.C. With the hope that Women may more & more be like "Aurora Leigh".

This one aspect of Barrett Browning's feminist politics remained urgent and relevant throughout the nineteenth century: how was the writing woman to make her life? and where could she look for a role-model? This, too, Barrett Browning wrote into her imagined version of what happened to Aurora's book. When Vincent Carrington writes to tell Aurora of the book's success he also tells her how she has acquired a disciple in the person of his young fiancée, Kate Ward. Vincent paints Kate's portrait, but she insists on appearing in an old cloak just like one that Aurora herself had worn. Kate insists too upon being represented holding a copy of Aurora's book, and in using Aurora's arguments to quarrel with her future husband:

> She has your books by heart more than my words
> And quotes you up against me. . . . (7.603–604)

Barrett Browning's imagined Kate Ward was only the first of any number of real writing and thinking women who made Aurora, and Barrett Browning herself, their special heroines. George Eliot was one of these. She reviewed *Aurora Leigh* when it was first published and admired it deeply. She borrowed images from the novel-poem for *The Mill on the Floss* and *Middlemarch*, and in her verse-drama about an artist/opera singer, *Armgart* (1871), she too quoted arguments derived from Barrett Browning. But it was the women poets of the latter nineteenth century who formed Aurora's most dedicated band of acolytes. Dora Greenwell wrote two love sonnets to the older poet; the activist Bessie Rayner Parkes wrote her a hesitant dedication ("Indeed I should not dare—but that this love,/Long nursed, demands expression, and alone/Speaks by love's dear strength—to approach near you/In words so weak and poor beside your own"; the Irish poet Emily Hickey adapted the verse-novel form in her poem *Michael Villiers: Idealist* (1891) to mix public questions about colonial domination and personal questions of individual development; Katherine Bradley and Edith Cooper, who together wrote the extraordinary poems published under the name Michael Field, used pseudonyms—"Isla" and "Arran Leigh"—that reflected their admiration, and they traveled to Italy to stay with Elizabeth's son, Pen Browning, and to commune with the spirit of their predecessor; and the Modernist poet Charlotte Mew, whose taut controlled work is so different from Barrett Browning's extravagance, nevertheless reworked many of her subjects and managed, to some extent, to live the independent working life imagined for the woman poet in *Aurora Leigh*.

The verse-novel form of Barrett Browning's work had many poetic successors, but it was the model of Aurora's independent life that made the fictional heroine so precious to the writers and scholars that came afterwards. One young disciple, Kate Field, really did have a picture of herself painted, in the manner of Kate Ward, as an homage to *Aurora Leigh*. In the portrait, which she commissioned from Elihu Vedder, she is shown in half profile, wearing classical drapery and posed against the skyline of Florence. Field donated the picture to the Boston Art Gallery, and though the original is now lost, a version of the portrait appears on the cover of this Norton Critical Edition of *Aurora Leigh*. The icon once would have been recognized by thousands of young intellectual women. At Wellesley College in Massachusetts, for instance, at the end of the nineteenth century, stained glass windows representing scenes from Barrett Browning's work were installed for the edification of the women educated there. These windows too have gone, destroyed by fire.

And for a time in the twentieth century *Aurora Leigh* itself also disappeared. It's a curious critical history. After nearly half a century of being read, discussed, and revered, *Aurora Leigh* came off the bookshelves, and Barrett Browning, that stalwart of women's independence, dwindled into the sofa-dwelling invalid portrayed in Rudolph Besier's well-known play *The Barretts of Wimpole Street* (1930). It's hard to say why it happened, but happen it certainly did. Perhaps the lush hagiography coming from Browning critics such as Lilian Whiting was too much for the new and lean Modernist sensibility. Certainly, as the extract included in this Norton Critical Edition from Marjory Bald makes plain, Barrett Browning seemed too strident, too self-conscious, too angry, to appear sympathetic to the cooler, more refined, version of early-twentieth-century feminism. Even Virginia Woolf—who, after all, was born a Victorian and knew the ubiquitous influence of Barrett Browning in her own youth—found *Aurora Leigh*, with all its many good points, too long, too heavy, too dated, too roundly upholstered with facts and dates and times and arguments. So that was that. Elizabeth Barrett Browning became an odd little aside in the life of her much-greater-poet-husband, and there was no more *Aurora Leigh*.

And then. And then in the 1960s . . . feminism happened. It took a while, of course, to percolate into literary studies, but when it did, it was *Aurora Leigh* that became the heroine-text. First Ellen Moers took it up in her astonishingly forward-thinking book *Literary Women* (1977). In *Aurora Leigh* she found all the metaphors (the caged bird, the need to stride out, the improvisatrice, Italy as mother-country) that were important to women writers of the nineteenth century and that have become topics for numerous theses since. Then Cora Kaplan reprinted *Aurora Leigh* with the radical Women's Press in Britain. And in the States, Sandra Gilbert and Susan Gubar restored this neglected text to the canon of nineteenth century women's writing by including it in their monumental book *The Madwoman in the Attic*. In the 1980s and 1990s *Aurora Leigh* has become the central text of nineteenth-century women's writing in academic circles; it competes with Christina Rossetti's ever-popular *Goblin Market* for first place as the most written-on text of Victorian women's poetry. In Britain it has even found its way out to a more general audience. In the early 1980s a stage version by Michelene Wandor appeared at the National Theatre and was broadcast by the BBC's Radio 3. More recently, an audiotape of the poem has been published, with the well-known actress Diana Quick reading the part of Aurora. I see no plans yet for a Hollywood movie, but who knows?

The reasons for Aurora's current popularity are clear, and curiously they are exactly the same reasons that made her popular in the nineteenth century. She is bold, she is brave, she is independent and liberated and, above all, she gets everything she wants in the end. In the nineteenth century *Aurora Leigh* told contemporary readers a great deal about their own time. Today the poem can still tell us a great deal about that time. In that sense *Aurora Leigh* is a historical document more than a poem. But it's also a significant literary document and, as such, it works both for then and for now. In the nineteenth century, women writers were only just beginning to come to terms with the exclusions and prohibitions that hedged about their aspirations. *Aurora Leigh* spoke to those anxieties and said things would be all right. In the late twentieth century, when we are only just beginning to understand the subtle history of women's invisibility in literature, *Aurora Leigh* helps to explain how it happened in a particular place and time.

At the heart of *Aurora Leigh* there is a book. When Aurora starts to write that book she knows that her work is necessary for herself, and for others—writing women into a literary history that had left them out:

> Of writing many books there is no end;
> And I who have written much in prose and verse
> For others' uses will write now for mine . . .
> (1.1–3)

This is why Aurora's book is important. And because Aurora's book and Barrett Browning's book are one and the same thing, *Aurora Leigh* is important. *Aurora Leigh* may not figure in Harold Bloom's canon, for he privileges the aesthetic, and charts only the cultures and the texts that have made Western civilization the way it is. But *Aurora Leigh* makes the canon for a new culture. For women are a civilization still in the making. A country without history, without art. A country making its laws, its myths, its histories. *Aurora Leigh* is one of those myths. When its uses are no longer so urgent, it will fade into history. But until then *Aurora Leigh* speaks to us, because it is empowering, because it is encouraging and cheerful, because it is necessary.

# The Text of
# AURORA LEIGH

Reprinted by arrangement with Ohio University Press.

Fanny Smith

June 1859

# AURORA LEIGH.

BY

ELIZABETH BARRETT BROWNING.

FOURTH EDITION.

*REVISED.*

LONDON:

CHAPMAN AND HALL, 193 PICCADILLY.

1859.

*Title page for the revised edition published by Chapman and Hall, 1859.*

# To
# John Kenyon, Esq.

The words 'cousin' and 'friend' are constantly recurring in this poem, the last pages of which have been finished under the hospitality of your roof, my own dearest cousin and friend;—cousin and friend, in a sense of less equality and greater disinterestedness than 'Romney' 's

Ending, therefore, and preparing once more to quit England, I venture to leave in your hands this book, the most mature of my works, and the one into which my highest convictions upon Life and Art have entered; that as, through my various efforts in literature and steps in life, you have believed in me, borne with me, and been generous to me, far beyond the common uses of mere relationship or sympathy of mind, so you may kindly accept, in sight of the public, this poor sign of esteem, gratitude, and affection from

your unforgetting
E.B.B.

39, Devonshire Place,
October 17, 1856.

# Aurora Leigh

## First Book

Of writing many books there is no end;[1]
And I who have written much in prose and verse[2]
For others' uses, will write now for mine,-
Will write my story for my better self[3]
As when you paint your portrait for a friend,
Who keeps it in a drawer and looks at it
Long after he has ceased to love you, just
To hold together what he was and is.

I, writing thus, am still what men call young;
I have not so far left the coasts of life
To travel inland, that I cannot hear
That murmur of the outer Infinite[4]
Which unweaned babies smile at in their sleep
When wondered at for smiling; not so far,
But still I catch my mother at her post
Beside the nursery-door, with finger up,
'Hush, hush - here's too much noise!' while her sweet eyes
Leap forward, taking part against her word
In the child's riot. Still I sit and feel
My father's slow hand, when she had left us both,
Stroke out my childish curls across his knee,
And hear Assunta's[5] daily jest (she knew
He liked it better than a better jest)
Inquire how many golden scudi[6] went

1. See Ecclesiastes 12.12.
2. This applies as much to Elizabeth Barrett Browning (hereafter referred to as EBB) as to Aurora herself.
3. Aurora is writing her life story retrospectively at the age of 26 or 27. Her past catches up with her present (briefly) at the beginning of book 3 and again in book 5. Thereafter the poem takes on the form of journal entries and is, in effect, written while it is being lived.
4. Cf. Wordsworth, "Ode: Intimations of Immortality from Recollections of Early Childhood" (1807), lines 71–74 and 165–71.
5. A common name in nineteenth-century Italy. It suggests an homage to the Virgin Mary and means, literally, "Our Lady, received into Heaven."
6. The scudo was no longer current in mid-nineteenth-century Florence, but the word continued in popular use as a general term for any large amount of money. The association of golden hair and gold coin is a familiar one in the world of fairytale and was often exploited for its

To make such ringlets. O my father's hand,
Stroke heavily, heavily the poor hair down,
Draw, press the child's head closer to thy knee!
I'm still too young, too young, to sit alone.

I write. My mother was a Florentine,[7]
Whose rare blue eyes were shut from seeing me
When scarcely I was four years old, my life
A poor spark snatched up from a failing lamp
Which went out therefore. She was weak and frail;
She could not bear the joy of giving life,
The mother's rapture slew her.[8] If her kiss
Had left a longer weight upon my lips[9]
It might have steadied the uneasy breath,
And reconciled and fraternised my soul
With the new order. As it was, indeed,
I felt a mother-want about the world,
And still went seeking, like a bleating lamb
Left out at night in shutting up the fold,-
As restless as a nest-deserted bird
Grown chill through something being away, though what
It knows not. I, Aurora Leigh, was born
To make my father sadder, and myself
Not overjoyous, truly. Women know
The way to rear up children, (to be just)
They know a simple, merry, tender knack
Of tying sashes, fitting baby-shoes,
And stringing pretty words that make no sense,
And kissing full sense into empty words,
Which things are corals[1] to cut life upon,
Although such trifles: children learn by such,
Love's holy earnest in a pretty play
And get not over-early solemnised,
But seeing, as in a rose-bush, Love's Divine

---

criticism of public versus private value by nineteenth-century women writers; see especially George Eliot's *Silas Marner* (1861), ch. 12, and Christina Rossetti's *Goblin Market* (1862). The fairytale context of Aurora's childhood is further emphasized in manuscript by the reference to "my uncle captain, fresh from Spain" who speaks not of scudi, but *moidores*, a gold coin of Portugal that was current in England in the first half of the eighteenth century. See textual note.

7. A native of Florence, where the Brownings lived from 1847. Her mother's blue eyes were "rare," because one would expect them to be dark, as they were in the drafts for the poem. See textual note.

8. The tensions surrounding EBB's conceit on labor and childbirth are based as much on her own mixed experience of miscarriage and birth as on her memory of her mother's long years of childbearing.

9. Cf. EBB, *Sonnets from the Portuguese* 18 (1850), lines 13–14, wherein the speaker (EBB) gives her beloved, Robert Browning (hereafter referred to as RB), a lock of hair, saying, "Take it thou, finding pure from all those years,/The kiss my mother left here when she died."

1. A toy made of polished coral, given to infants to assist teething (OED).

Which burns and hurts not,[2] - not a single bloom, -
Become aware and unafraid of Love.
Such good do mothers. Fathers love as well
- Mine did, I know, - but still with heavier brains,[3]
And wills more consciously responsible,
And not as wisely, since less foolishly;
So mothers have God's licence to be missed.

My father was an austere Englishman,
Who, after a dry life-time spent at home
In college-learning, law, and parish talk,
Was flooded with a passion unaware,
His whole provisioned and complacent past
Drowned out from him that moment.[4] As he stood
In Florence, where he had come to spend a month
And note the secret of Da Vinci's drains,[5]
He musing somewhat absently perhaps
Some English question . . whether men should pay
The unpopular but necessary tax
With left or right hand[6] - in the alien sun
In that great square of the Santissima[7]
There drifted past him (scarcely marked enough
To move his comfortable island scorn)
A train of priestly banners, cross and psalm,
The white-veiled rose-crowned maidens holding up
Tall tapers, weighty for such wrists, aslant
To the blue luminous tremor of the air,
And letting drop the white wax as they went
To eat the bishop's wafer at the church;[8]

2. See Exodus 3.2. The rose is the traditional symbol of love.
3. Nineteenth-century students of anatomy noticed that men tend to have brains that weigh more than women's—not surprising, given the relative difference in average body weight. Unfortunately, this evidence was cited by some psychologists in support of their theory that the male possessed a higher intellect than the female. Similarly, responsibility was taken to be a masculine characteristic, and spontaneity a feminine trait (see lines 62–63).
4. Cf. *Aurora Leigh* 8.34–61.
5. Vasari makes scant reference to Leonardo's engineering skills, but he does mention his suggestion for "the formation of a canal from Pisa to Florence, by means of certain changes to be effected on the river Arno." EBB's allusion to Da Vinci's drains, when he is much better known for more noble artistic activity, is a joke about the prosaic character of Leigh's imagination.
6. An ironic allusion to Matthew 6.3, "But when thou doest alms, let not thy left hand know what thy right hand doeth."
7. The church of the Santissima Annunziata in Florence stands on the north side of the square called the Piazza Santissima Annunziata.
8. The procession described here is probably that held to celebrate the nativity of the Virgin on September 8. Events for that occasion, and particularly the youth of the participants, are noted in *Murray's Handbook for Travellers in Northern Italy* (London, 1847). As the Santissima Annunziata is a church of the Servite order, and the special symbol of that order is the image of the Virgin stabbed with seven swords (see lines 160–61), it is fairly certain that this is the same as the Servite procession described by RB in "Up at a Villa, Down in the City" (1855) 9.59–62: "Look, two and two go the priests, then the monks with cowls and sandals,/And the penitents dressed in white shirts a-holding the yellow candles; /One, he carries a flag up straight, and another a cross with handles."

From which long trail of chanting priests and girls,
A face flashed like a cymbal on his face
And shook with silent clangour brain and heart,
Transfiguring him to music. Thus, even thus,
He too received his sacramental gift
With eucharistic meanings;[9] for he loved.

And thus beloved, she died. I've heard it said
That but to see him in the first surprise
Of widower and father, nursing me,
Unmothered little child of four years old,
His large man's hands afraid to touch my curls,
As if the gold would tarnish, - his grave lips
Contriving such a miserable smile
As if he knew needs must, or I should die,
And yet 'twas hard, - would almost make the stones
Cry out for pity.[1] There's a verse he set
In Santa Croce[2] to her memory, -
'Weep for an infant too young to weep much
When death removed this mother' - stops the mirth
To-day on women's faces when they walk
With rosy children hanging on their gowns,
Under the cloister[3] to escape the sun
That scorches in the piazza. After which
He left our Florence and made haste to hide
Himself, his prattling child, and silent grief,
Among the mountains above Pelago;[4]
Because unmothered babes, he thought, had need
Of mother nature more than others use,
And Pan's white goats,[5] with udders warm and full
Of mystic contemplations, come to feed
Poor milkless lips of orphans like his own -
Such scholar-scraps he talked, I've heard from friends,
For even prosaic men who wear grief long
Will get to wear it as a hat aside

9. As Aurora's mother goes to take communion in the (Catholic) church, celebrating the sacrament of the Eucharist by eating the wafer (see line 1.85) and drinking the wine (which represent the body and blood of Christ through the miraculous process of transubstantiation), so EBB takes over Catholic doctrine, applying that nexus of ideas to the discovery of sexual love, which also encompasses body and spirit. Cf. *Aurora Leigh* 5.14–16.
1. See Luke 19.40.
2. The church of Santa Croce (begun 1294) was known as the Westminster Abbey of Florence because of the number of eminent men buried there.
3. *Murray's Handbook for Travellers in Northern Italy* for 1842 notes that the memorials in the cloisters of Santa Croce are "turgid and affected in sentiment" and that "the youth of a large proportion of the deceased, is remarkable."
4. The Brownings passed through the village of Pelago in 1847 on their way to the monastery at Vallombrosa. See *Letters of EBB* 1.333, 336, and 340.
5. Used here as the embodiment of nature, the god Pan chose not to live on Olympia but preferred the rural pleasures of earth and lived in Arcadia tending his flocks and beehives, taking part in the revels of the mountain nymphs, and assisting hunters to pursue their quarry.

With a flower stuck in't.[6] Father, then, and child,
We lived among the mountains many years,
God's silence on the outside of the house,
And we who did not speak too loud within,
And old Assunta to make up the fire,
Crossing herself whene'er a sudden flame
Which lightened from the firewood, made alive
That picture of my mother on the wall.

The painter drew it after she was dead,[7]
And when the face was finished, throat and hands,
Her cameriera[8] carried him, in hate
Of the English-fashioned shroud, the last brocade
She dressed in at the Pitti;[9] 'he should paint
No sadder thing than that,' she swore, 'to wrong
Her poor signora.'[1] Therefore very strange
The effect was. I, a little child, would crouch
For hours upon the floor with knees drawn up,
And gaze across them, half in terror, half
In adoration, at the picture there, -
That swan-like supernatural white life
Just sailing upward from the red stiff silk[2]
Which seemed to have no part in it nor power
To keep it from quite breaking out of bounds.
For hours I sate and stared. Assunta's awe
And my poor father's melancholy eyes
Still pointed that way. That way went my thoughts
When wandering beyond sight. And as I grew
In years, I mixed, confused, unconsciously,
Whatever I last read or heard or dreamed,
Abhorrent, admirable, beautiful,
Pathetical, or ghastly, or grotesque,
With still that face . . . which did not therefore change,
But kept the mystic level of all forms
Hates, fears, and admirations, was by turns
Ghost, fiend, and angel, fairy, witch, and sprite,

6. Ruskin declared EBB's image here to be silly and insufficiently serious (John Ruskin to RB, November 27, 1856, in *The Works of John Ruskin*, ed. E. T. Cook and Alexander Wedderburn, vol. 36 [London, 1903–12], 247). Ruskin lacked EBB's sense of humor.
7. EBB knew of the portrait of Lady Blanche Georgiana Burlington by the artist John Lucas, which was painted under similar circumstances.
8. An Italian waiting woman.
9. The Pitti Palace, which stands diagonally opposite Casa Guidi where the Brownings lived from 1847, was the official residence of the grand dukes of Tuscany during the nineteenth century. The grand duke held weekly balls at the Pitti that were enthusiastically attended by many members of the English and American communities in Florence.
1. Lady.
2. Cf. this portrait of Aurora's mother with the description of Lady Waldemar's appearance in *Aurora Leigh* 5.611–24.

A dauntless Muse[3] who eyes a dreadful Fate,[4]
A loving Psyche who loses sight of Love,[5]
A still Medusa[6] with mild milky brows
All curdled[7] and all clothed upon with snakes
Whose slime falls fast as sweat will; or anon
Our Lady of the Passion, stabbed with swords
Where the Babe sucked;[8] or Lamia[9] in her first
Moonlighted pallor, ere she shrunk and blinked
And shuddering wriggled down to the unclean;
Or my own mother, leaving her last smile
In her last kiss upon the baby-mouth
My father pushed down on the bed for that, -
Or my dead mother, without smile or kiss,
Buried at Florence. All which images,
Concentred on the picture, glassed themselves
Before my meditative childhood, as
The incoherencies of change and death
Are represented fully, mixed and merged,
In the smooth fair mystery of perpetual Life.

And while I stared away my childish wits
Upon my mother's picture, (ah, poor child!)
My father, who through love had suddenly
Thrown off the old conventions, broken loose

3. According to Greek mythology, nine Muses preside over the arts. They are the daughters of Zeus and Memosyne, and their names are Calliope, Clio, Thalia, Melpomene, Euterpe, Terpsichore, Erato, Polyhymnia, and Urania.
4. The three Fates robed in white were the daughters of Erebus and Night. They are Clotho ("the spinner"), Lachesis ("the measurer"), and Atropos ("she who cannot be avoided"). Of these, Atropos is the most terrible.
5. Eros, or Cupid, the god of love, married the mortal woman Psyche. Wishing to keep his identity a secret, he visited her only at night and in the dark. When her sisters suggested that she had probably married a monster, Psyche resolved to smuggle in a light to view her beloved. As she did so, a drop of wax fell on his sleeping form, and he awoke to leave her forever in punishment for her lack of trust. See Lucius Apuleis, *Metamorphoses* 4.28ff. See also EBB's translations from Apuleis in *The Poetical Works of Elizabeth Barrett Browning* (Boston, 1974), 472–76.
6. The most notorious of the three Gorgons, Medusa was transformed by Athene into a snake-haired monster, and her glance turned men to stone. See Ovid, *Metamorphoses* 4.790–803.
7. Cf. *Casa Guidi Windows* 2.104–5: "lest a doubt/Should curdle brows of gracious sovereigns, white." This elaborate metaphor describing a frown gave EBB some trouble in the composition of *Casa Guidi Windows*. See Julia Markus's edition (New York, 1977), 128, for preceding variants.
8. See Luke 2.35. The image of the Virgin, stabbed with seven swords representing seven sorrows, is the special icon of the Servite order, or Servants of Mary, whose Florentine church is the Santissima Annunziata. RB describes a similar statue in "Up at a Villa, Down in the City" (1855) 9.51–52.
9. In Greek mythology Lamia ruled in Libya and was the mistress of Zeus, by whom she had several children. Most of these were killed by Hera, Zeus' jealous wife, and Lamia thereafter took her revenge by seeking out and killing the children of others, behaving so wickedly that her face took on a nightmarish mask. EBB's allusion owes more to John Keats' poem of the same name, where Lamia is a serpent who transforms herself into the shape of a woman in order to seduce the innocent Lycius. At their wedding feast the philosopher Apollodorus recognizes her serpent nature and denounces her. Cf. Keats' *Lamia* (1820), lines 272–76: "In the bride's face, where now no azure vein/Wandered on fair-spaced temples; no soft bloom/Misted the cheek; no

From chin-bands[1] of the soul, like Lazarus,[2]
Yet had no time to learn to talk and walk
Or grow anew familiar with the sun, -
Who had reached to freedom, not to action, lived,
But lived as one entranced, with thoughts, not aims, -
Whom love had unmade from a common man
But not completed to an uncommon man, -
My father taught me what he had learnt the best
Before he died and left me, - grief and love.
And, seeing we had books among the hills,
Strong words of counselling souls confederate
With vocal pines and waters, - out of books
He taught me all the ignorance of men,
And how God laughs in heaven when any man
Says 'Here I'm learned; this, I understand;
In that, I am never caught at fault or doubt.'
He sent the schools to school, demonstrating
A fool will pass for such through one mistake,
While a philosopher will pass for such,
Through said mistakes being ventured in the gross
And heaped up to a system.[3]
I am like,
They tell me, my dear father. Broader brows
Howbeit, upon a slenderer undergrowth
Of delicate features, - paler, near as grave;
But then my mother's smile breaks up the whole,
And makes it better sometimes than itself.

So, nine full years, our days were hid with God
Among his mountains: I was just thirteen,
Still growing like the plants from unseen roots
In tongue-tied Springs, - and suddenly awoke
To full life and life's needs and agonies
With an intense, strong, struggling heart beside
A stone-dead father. Life, struck sharp on death,
Makes awful lightning. His last word was, 'Love -'
'Love, my child, love, love!' - (then he had done with grief)
'Love, my child.' Ere I answered he was gone,
And none was left to love in all the world.

---

passion to illume/The deep-recessèd vision. All was blight;/Lamia, no longer fair, there sat a deadly white."

1. A winding cloth or shroud.
2. See John 11.1–53. Cf. Robert Browning's "An Epistle containing the Strange Medical Experience of Karshish, the Arab Physician" (1855), of which EBB wrote, "The way in which Lazarus is described as living his life after his acquaintance with the life beyond death, strikes me as entirely sublime" (*EBB: Letters to Her sister,* 236). EBB herself had once considered Lazarus as a possible subject for a poem (*Letters of EBB* 1.82).
3. Cf. *Aurora Leigh* 6.40–48.

There, ended childhood. What succeeded next
I recollect as, after fevers, men
Thread back the passage of delirium,
Missing the turn still, baffled by the door;
Smooth endless days, notched here and there with knives;
A weary, wormy darkness, spurred i' the flank
With flame, that it should eat and end itself
Like some tormented scorpion.[4] Then at last
I do remember clearly, how there came
A stranger with authority, not right,
(I thought not) who commanded, caught me up
From old Assunta's neck; how, with a shriek,
She let me go, - while I, with ears too full
Of my father's silence, to shriek back a word,
In all a child's astonishment at grief
Stared at the wharf-edge where she stood and moaned,
My poor Assunta, where she stood and moaned!
The white walls, the blue hills, my Italy,
Drawn backward from the shuddering steamer-deck,
Like one in anger drawing back her skirts
Which suppliants catch at. Then the bitter sea
Inexorably pushed between us both,
And sweeping up the ship of my despair
Threw us out as a pasture to the stars.

Ten nights and days we voyaged on the deep;
Ten nights and days without the common face
Of any day or night; the moon and sun
Cut off from the green reconciling earth,
To starve into a blind ferocity
And glare unnatural; the very sky
(Dropping its bell-net down upon the sea
As if no human heart should 'scape alive,)
Bedraggled with the desolating salt,
Until it seemed no more that holy heaven
To which my father went. All new and strange;
The universe turned stranger, for a child.

Then, land! - then, England! oh, the frosty cliffs
Looked cold upon me. Could I find a home
Among those mean red houses through the fog?
And when I heard my father's language first
From alien lips which had no kiss for mine
I wept aloud, then laughed, then wept, then wept,

4. In extreme heat, a scorpion will thrash about in a violent manner. The popular belief that it stings itself suicidally by plunging its tail into its head has no basis in fact.

And some one near me said the child was mad
Through much sea-sickness. The train swept us on.
Was this my father's England? the great isle?
The ground seemed cut up from the fellowship
Of verdure, field from field, as man from man;
The skies themselves looked low and positive,
As almost you could touch them with a hand,
And dared to do it they were so far off
From God's celestial crystals;[5] all things blurred
And dull and vague. Did Shakspeare and his mates
Absorb the light here? - not a hill or stone
With heart to strike a radiant colour up
Or active outline on the indifferent air.

I think I see my father's sister stand
Upon the hall-step of her country-house
To give me welcome. She stood straight and calm,
Her somewhat narrow forehead braided tight
As if for taming accidental thoughts
From possible pulses; brown hair pricked with grey
By frigid use of life, (she was not old
Although my father's elder by a year)
A nose drawn sharply yet in delicate lines;
A close mild mouth, a little soured about
The ends, through speaking unrequited loves
Or peradventure niggardly half-truths;
Eyes of no colour, - once they might have smiled,
But never, never have forgot themselves
In smiling; cheeks, in which was yet a rose
Of perished summers, like a rose in a book,
Kept more for ruth than pleasure,[6] - if past bloom,
Past fading also.
She had lived, we'll say,
A harmless life, she called a virtuous life,
A quiet life, which was not life at all,
(But that, she had not lived enough to know)
Between the vicar and the county squires,
The lord-lieutenant[7] looking down sometimes
From the empyrean[8] to assure their souls

5. Milton refers to the crystalline sphere that lies beyond the stars of the firmament. See *Paradise Lost* 3.482.
6. Cf. the image of the prostitute in Dante Gabriel Rossetti's "Jenny" (1870): "Like a rose shut in a book/In which pure women may not look" (*The Complete Works of Dante Gabriel Rossetti*, ed. William Michael Rossetti [London, 1903], 110).
7. The luminaries in middle-class provincial English life. The lord-lieutenant was the official governor of a county, but his function was almost entirely ceremonial.
8. A classical designation for heaven.

Against chance-vulgarisms, and, in the abyss
The apothecary,[9] looked on once a year
To prove their soundness of humility.
The poor-club[1] exercised her Christian gifts
Of knitting stockings, stitching petticoats,
Because we are of one flesh[2] after all
And need one flannel (with a proper sense
Of difference in the quality) - and still
The book-club,[3] guarded from your modern trick
Of shaking dangerous questions from the crease,
Preserved her intellectual. She had lived
A sort of cage-bird life,[4] born in a cage,
Accounting that to leap from perch to perch
Was act and joy enough for any bird.
Dear heaven, how silly are the things that live
In thickets, and eat berries!

I, alas,
A wild bird scarcely fledged, was brought to her cage,
And she was there to meet me. Very kind.
Bring the clean water, give out the fresh seed.

She stood upon the steps to welcome me,
Calm, in black garb. I clung about her neck, -
Young babes, who catch at every shred of wool
To draw the new light closer, catch and cling
Less blindly. In my ears, my father's word
Hummed ignorantly, as the sea in shells,
'Love, love, my child.' She, black there with my grief,
Might feel my love - she was his sister once,
I clung to her. A moment she seemed moved,
Kissed me with cold lips, suffered me to cling,
And drew me feebly through the hall into
The room she sate in.

There, with some strange spasm
Of pain and passion, she wrung loose my hands

9. The apothecary, who dispensed medicines for minor ailments, was at the bottom of the social scale.
1. Many middle-class Victorian women occupied their time with charitable activities, often centered on the local poor-club, which got together to collect clothes or funds for the needy.
2. See Ephesians 5.9–30.
3. A local reading circle, which lent books to members before the advent of the circulating libraries.
4. Cf. Mary Wollstonecraft, *Vindication of the Rights of Woman* (1792), ed. Miriam Brody (Harmondsworth Middlesex, 1975), 146: "Confined, then, in cages like the feathered race they have nothing to do but to plume themselves, and stalk with mock majesty from perch to perch. It is true they are provided with food and raiment, for which they neither toil nor spin; but health, liberty and virtue are given in exchange." The image of the caged bird is a distinctively female metaphor in literature of the nineteenth century. See Ellen Moers, *Literary Women* (London, 1978), 250–51.

Imperiously, and held me at arm's length,
And with two grey-steel naked-bladed eyes
Searched through my face, - ay, stabbed it through and through,
Through brows and cheeks and chin, as if to find
A wicked murderer in my innocent face,
If not here, there perhaps. Then, drawing breath,
She struggled for her ordinary calm
And missed it rather, - told me not to shrink,
As if she had told me not to lie or swear, -
'She loved my father and would love me too
As long as I deserved it.' Very kind.

I understood her meaning afterward;
She thought to find my mother in my face,
And questioned it for that. For she, my aunt,
Had loved my father truly, as she could,
And hated, with the gall of gentle souls,
My Tuscan mother[5] who had fooled away
A wise man from wise courses, a good man
From obvious duties, and, depriving her,
His sister, of the household precedence,[6]
Had wronged his tenants,[7] robbed his native land,
And made him mad, alike by life and death,
In love and sorrow. She had pored for years
What sort of woman could be suitable
To her sort of hate, to entertain it with,
And so, her very curiosity
Became hate too, and all the idealism
She ever used in life, was used for hate,
Till hate, so nourished, did exceed at last
The love from which it grew, in strength and heat,
And wrinkled her smooth conscience with a sense
Of disputable virtue (say not, sin)
When Christian doctrine was enforced at church.

And thus my father's sister was to me
My mother's hater. From that day, she did
Her duty to me, (I appreciate it
In her own word as spoken to herself)
Her duty, in large measure, well-pressed out,[8]
But measured always. She was generous, bland,

5. Florence is in Tuscany.
6. A strict code of precedence operated in Victorian society. Men came first in the household without regard to age (Aurora's aunt is older than her father), and the wife of the head of the household takes priority over unmarried sisters; as does his daughter (see lines 365–66).
7. In that he lived abroad and was no longer at home to look after the interests of his estate.
8. See Luke 6.38: "Give and it shall be given unto you; good measure, pressed down, and shaken together and running over, shall men give into your bosom."

More courteous than was tender, gave me still
The first place, - as if fearful that God's saints
Would look down suddenly and say, 'Herein
You missed a point, I think, through lack of love.'
Alas, a mother never is afraid
Of speaking angerly[9] to any child,
Since love, she knows, is justified of love.

And I, I was a good child on the whole,
A meek and manageable child. Why not?
I did not live, to have the faults of life:
There seemed more true life in my father's grave
Than in all England. Since *that* threw me off
Who fain would cleave, (his latest will, they say,
Consigned me to his land) I only thought
Of lying quiet there where I was thrown
Like sea-weed on the rocks, and suffering her
To prick me to a pattern with her pin
Fibre from fibre, delicate leaf from leaf,
And dry out from my drowned anatomy
The last sea-salt left in me.[1]

So it was.
I broke the copious curls upon my head
In braids, because she liked smooth-ordered hair.
I left off saying my sweet Tuscan words
Which still at any stirring of the heart
Came up to float across the English phrase
As lilies, *(Bene* or *Che che,)*[2] because
She liked my father's child to speak his tongue.
I learnt the collects and the catechism,[3]
The creeds, from Athanasius back to Nice,[4]
The Articles, the Tracts *against* the times,[5]

9. An archaic term for "angrily."
1. An image drawn from the popular study of natural history and biology as practiced by many amateur collectors in the nineteenth century. Aurora uses her "saltiness" as evidence of the wildness that her aunt aims to tame by restriction and classification.
2. "Good" or "Well well."
3. Popular manual of Christian doctrine arranged in the form of question and answer for the purpose of instructing those to be confirmed; a short form of prayer, adapted from medieval sources and included in the *Book of Common Prayer* (1611).
4. The Athanasian creed, with the Apostles' and Nicene creeds, formulates the basic tenets of faith in the liturgy of the Church of England (see Article 8 of the thirty-nine articles in the *Book of Common Prayer*). As a nonconformist, EBB was not sympathetic to the dogma of the creeds: "The Athanasian way of stating opinions, between a scholastic paradox and a curse, is particularly distasteful to me" (*Letters of EBB* 2.150). See also Frederic Kenyon's account of EBB's apparent ignorance of the exact words of the Athanasian creed (*Letters of EBB* 1.74–75).
5. Alludes to *Tracts for the Times*, published between 1833 and 1841 by an Oxford High Church group led by John Henry Newman. The publication was part of an effort to warn against a popular movement toward the secularization of the church and to reaffirm the reliance of the

(By no means Buonaventure's 'Prick of Love,')[6]
And various popular synopses of
Inhuman doctrines never taught by John,[7]
Because she liked instructed piety.
I learnt my complement of classic French
(Kept pure of Balzac and neologism)[8]
And German also, since she liked a range
Of liberal education, - tongues, not books.[9]
I learnt a little algebra, a little
Of the mathematics, - brushed with extreme flounce
The circle of the sciences, because
She misliked women who are frivolous.
I learnt the royal genealogies
Of Oviedo,[1] the internal laws
Of the Burmese empire,[2] - by how many feet
Mount Chimborazo outsoars Teneriffe,[3]
What navigable river joins itself
To Lara,[1] and what census of the year five

---

Anglican church on Catholic principles; the thirty-nine articles, which summarize Anglican doctrine, are included in the *Book of Common Prayer*.

6. *Stimulus Divini Amoris (The Prick, or Goad, of Love)* is a composite devotional work, incorrectly attributed to St. Bonaventure. The first section, by an unidentified author, consists of a series of meditations on the Passion. The second and third sections contain a treatise on the spiritual life by James of Milan and some anonymous prayers and meditations. The whole is characterized by an affective, rather than rational, approach to the mysteries.
7. The Gospel according to John is characterized as the "spiritual" Gospel. Alternately this reference may be to St. John of the Cross, who was the author of *Llama de amor viva (The Living Flame of Love)* written c. 1583–84.
8. Honoré de Balzac (1799–1850) was generally condemned in England both for his impropriety and for his experiments with language. EBB, however, admired both his style—"His French is another language—he throws new metals into it . . malleable metals, which fuse with the heat of his genius"—and his content—"He is a writer of most wonderful faculty—with an overflow of life everywhere—with the vision and the utterance of a great seer" (April 28, 1846, *The Letters of Robert Browning and Elizabeth Barrett Barrett*, ed. Elvan Kintner [Cambridge, Mass., 1969], 2 vols., 2.663).
9. Compare EBB to Isa Blagden, spring 1855: "I believe that nothing helps the general faculties so little as the study of languages" (*PMLA* 66 [June–Dec. 1951]: 601).
1. Gonzalo Fernandez de Oviedo y Valdes (1478–1557), Spanish garrison commander and historian. His principal work, and the one to which EBB refers, "Las Quincuagenas de los generosos e ilustres e no menos famosos Reyes, principes, duques, marquesas y condes et cabelleros et personas notables de Espana . . . ," written c. 1550–56, was never published. The manuscript is, however, described in William H. Prescott's *History of the Reign of Ferdinand and Isabella the Catholic of Spain* (London, 1838), (1.220n): "This very curious work is in the form of dialogues, in which the author is the chief interlocutor. It contains very full and, indeed, prolix notice of the principal persons in Spain, their lineage, revenues, arms, with an inexhaustible fund of private anecdote. The author, who was well acquainted with most of the individuals of note in his time, amused himself, during his absence in the New World, with keeping alive the images of home by this minute record of early reminiscences. In this mass of gossip there is a good deal, indeed, of very little value."
2. The first Burmese empire flourished from the eleventh to the thirteenth century, and the second existed in the sixteenth century. The reference, like many others here, is a joke.
3. Chimborazo, a peak in the Andes, rising to 20,561 feet, was long thought to be the highest mountain in the world. Cf. the first edition reading "Mount Chimborazo outsoars Himmeleh" (see textual note). Teneriffe, in the Canary Islands, rises to 12,198 feet.
4. Unidentified. It probably does not exist.

Was taken at Klagenfurt,[5] - because she liked
A general insight into useful facts.
I learnt much music, - such as would have been
As quite impossible in Johnson's day[6]
As still it might be wished - fine sleights of hand
And unimagined fingering, shuffling off
The hearer's soul through hurricanes of notes
To a noisy Tophet;[7] and I drew . . costumes
From French engravings, nereids[8] neatly draped,
(With smirks of simmering godship) - I washed in
Landscapes from nature (rather say, washed out).
I danced the polka and Cellarius,[9]
Spun glass, stuffed birds, and modelled flowers in wax,
Because she liked accomplishments in girls.
I read a score of books on womanhood
To prove, if women do not think at all,
They may teach thinking, (to a maiden-aunt
Or else the author) - books that boldly assert
Their right of comprehending husband's talk
When not too deep, and even of answering
With pretty 'may it please you,' or 'so it is,' -
Their rapid insight and fine aptitude,
Particular worth and general missionariness,
As long as they keep quiet by the fire
And never say 'no' when the world says 'ay,'
For that is fatal, - their angelic reach
Of virtue, chiefly used to sit and darn,
And fatten household sinners, - their, in brief,
Potential faculty in everything
Of abdicating power in it:[1] she owned

5. Klagenfurt, in the federal state of Kärnten (Carinthia) in southern Austria, was founded in the twelfth century. Another joke.
6. See Sir John Hawkins, *The Life of Samuel Johnson* (London, 1787), 319n: "Upon his once hearing a celebrated performer go through a hard composition, and hearing it remarked that it was very difficult, Johnson said, 'I would it had been impossible.' "
7. A site in the valley of Hinnom, defiled by Moloch-worship, mentioned several times in the Old Testament (see Isaiah 30.33 and Jeremiah 7.31–32). In general use, synonymous with chaos or hell.
8. Nymphs of the sea. They are more usually depicted naked and not as here "neatly draped."
9. Henri Cellarius described the polka and the waltz-mazurka named for him in *La Danse des Salons* (Paris, 1846), translated as *The Drawing Room Dances* (London, 1847). The former he introduced, the latter he devised. Both dances were a sensation in the 1840s. See RB to EBB, April 15, 1845 and EBB to RB, April 17, 1845, *RB/EBB Letters* 1.45 and 48.
1. Although numerous books of moral and practical advice for women were published in the 1830s and 1840s—sample titles include *Woman as She Is and as She Should Be* (1835), *Women's Rights and Duties* (1840), *Woman's Worth, or Hints to Raise the Female Character* (1844)—it would appear that EBB had the works of a female author in mind, and the most likely candidate is Sarah Stickney Ellis (1812–72). EBB knew of her series of didactic volumes—"twelve editions of instructions to the 'Women', 'Wives', 'Daughters' (and 'Grandmothers' says *Punch*) of our common England"—and, while proposing Sarah Ellis for inclusion in Horne's *New Spirit of the Age* (1844), suggested that "the race of Mrs. Ellis's disciples runs the risk of being model-women of the most abominable virtue" (*Letters of Elizabeth Barrett Browning addressed to Richard Hengist Horne*, ed. S. R. Townshend Mayer [London, 1877], 2.154).

She liked a woman to be womanly,
And English women, she thanked God and sighed,
(Some people always sigh in thanking God)
Were models to the universe. And last
I learnt cross-stitch, because she did not like
To see me wear the night with empty hands
A-doing nothing. So, my shepherdess
Was something after all, (the pastoral saints
Be praised for't) leaning lovelorn with pink eyes
To match her shoes, when I mistook the silks;
Her head uncrushed by that round weight of hat
So strangely similar to the tortoise-shell
Which slew the tragic poet.[2]
By the way,
The works of women are symbolical.
We sew, sew, prick our fingers, dull our sight,
Producing what? A pair of slippers, sir,
To put on when you're weary - or a stool
To stumble over and vex you . . 'curse that stool!'
Or else at best, a cushion, where you lean
And sleep, and dream of something we are not
But would be for your sake. Alas, alas!
This hurts most, this - that, after all, we are paid
The worth of our work, perhaps.
In looking down
Those years of education (to return)
I wonder if Brinvilliers[3] suffered more
In the water-torture, . . flood succeeding flood
To drench the incapable throat and split the veins. .
Than I did. Certain of your feebler souls
Go out in such a process; many pine
To a sick, inodorous light; my own endured:
I had relations in the Unseen, and drew
The elemental nutriment and heat
From nature, as earth feels the sun at nights,
Or as a babe sucks surely in the dark.
I kept the life thrust on me, on the outside
Of the inner life with all its ample room

2. Aeschylus (c. 525–456 BC) was reputed to have died when an eagle dropped a tortoise on his bald head (mistaking it for a stone) in order to break the shell (Aelian, *Variae Historiae* 8.16).

3. Marie Marguerite d'Aubray, marquise de Brinvilliers (1630–76) was executed for the poisoning of her father and two brothers. Mme. de Sévigné's *Letters* (1726)—which EBB read in 1818—give a full account of the detention and death of Mme. Brinvilliers, including the story of her ordeal in undergoing the water torture. See de Sévigné, *Lettres* (La Haye, 1726), letter no. 131 to Mme. de Grignan, July 22, 1676, 2.136. See also EBB to RB, March 3, 1846: "Tie up your drinker under the pour of his nine gallons, & in two minutes he will moan & writhe (as you perfectly know) like a Brinvilliers under the water-torture" (*RB/EBB Letters* 1.513).

For heart and lungs, for will and intellect,
Inviolable by conventions. God,
I thank thee for that grace of thine!
At first
I felt no life which was not patience, - did
The thing she bade me, without heed to a thing
Beyond it, sate in just the chair she placed,
With back against the window, to exclude
The sight of the great lime-tree on the lawn,
Which seemed to have come on purpose from the woods
To bring the house a message, - ay, and walked
Demurely in her carpeted low rooms,
As if I should not, harkening my own steps,
Misdoubt I was alive. I read her books,
Was civil to her cousin, Romney Leigh,[4]
Gave ear to her vicar, tea to her visitors,
And heard them whisper, when I changed a cup,
(I blushed for joy at that) - 'The Italian child,
For all her blue eyes and her quiet ways,
Thrives ill in England: she is paler yet
Than when we came the last time; she will die.'

'Will die.' My cousin, Romney Leigh, blushed too,
With sudden anger, and approaching me
Said low between his teeth, 'You're wicked now?
You wish to die and leave the world a-dusk
For others, with your naughty light blown out?'

I looked into his face defyingly;
He might have known that, being what I was,
'Twas natural to like to get away
As far as dead folk can: and then indeed
Some people make no trouble when they die.
He turned and went abruptly, slammed the door
And shut his dog in.
Romney, Romney Leigh.
I have not named my cousin hitherto,
And yet I used him as a sort of friend;
My elder by few years, but cold and shy
And absent . . tender, when he thought of it,
Which scarcely was imperative, grave betimes,
As well as early master of Leigh Hall,
Whereof the nightmare sate upon his youth
Repressing all its seasonable delights
And agonising with a ghastly sense

4. In the draft manuscript, EBB originally conceived the hero's name as "Percy Vane." See textual note.

Of universal hideous want and wrong
To incriminate possession. When he came
From college to the country, very oft
He crossed the hill on visits to my aunt,
With gifts of blue grapes from the hothouses,
A book in one hand, - mere statistics, (if
I chanced to lift the cover,) count of all
The goats whose beards grow sprouting down toward hell
Against God's separative judgement-hour.[5]
And she, she almost loved him, - even allowed
That sometimes he should seem to sigh my way;
It made him easier to be pitiful,
And sighing was his gift. So, undisturbed
At whiles she let him shut my music up
And push my needles down, and lead me out
To see in that south angle of the house
The figs grow black as if by a Tuscan rock,
Or some light pretext. She would turn her head
At other moments, go to fetch a thing,
And leave me breath enough to speak with him,
For his sake; it was simple.
                                        Sometimes too
He would have saved me utterly, it seemed,
He stood and looked so.
                                    Once, he stood so near
He dropped a sudden hand upon my head
Bent down on woman's work, as soft as rain -
But then I rose and shook it off as fire,
The stranger's touch that took my father's place
Yet dared seem soft.
                            I used him for a friend
Before I ever knew him for a friend.
'Twas better, 'twas worse also, afterward:
We came so close, we saw our differences
Too intimately. Always Romney Leigh
Was looking for the worms, I for the gods.
A godlike nature his; the gods look down,
Incurious of themselves; and certainly
'Tis well I should remember, how, those days,
I was a worm too, and he looked on me.

A little by his act perhaps, yet more
By something in me, surely not my will,
I did not die. But slowly as one in swoon,
To whom life creeps back in the form of death,

5. Matthew 25.32–33.

With a sense of separation, a blind pain
Of blank obstruction, and a roar i' the ears
Of visionary chariots which retreat
As earth grows clearer[6] . . slowly, by degrees,
I woke, rose up . . where was I? in the world;
For uses therefore I must count worth while.

I had a little chamber in the house,
As green as any privet-hedge a bird
Might choose to build in, though the nest itself
Could show but dead-brown sticks and straws; the walls
Were green, the carpet was pure green, the straight
Small bed was curtained greenly, and the folds
Hung green about the window which let in
The out-door world with all its greenery.
You could not push your head out and escape
A dash of dawn-dew from the honeysuckle,
But so you were baptized into the grace
And privilege of seeing . . .
First, the lime,
(I had enough there, of the lime, be sure, -
My morning-dream was often hummed away
By the bees in it;) past the lime, the lawn,
Which, after sweeping broadly round the house,
Went trickling through the shrubberies in a stream
Of tender turf, and wore and lost itself
Among the acacias, over which you saw
The irregular line of elms by the deep lane
Which stopped the grounds and dammed the overflow
Of arbutus and laurel. Out of sight
The lane was; sunk so deep, no foreign tramp
Nor drover of wild ponies out of Wales[7]
Could guess if lady's hall or tenant's lodge
Dispensed such odours, - though his stick well-crooked
Might reach the lowest trail of blossoming briar
Which dipped upon the wall. Behind the elms,
And through their tops, you saw the folded hills
Striped up and down with hedges, (burly oaks
Projecting from the line to show themselves)
Through which my cousin Romney's chimneys smoked
As still as when a silent mouth in frost
Breathes, showing where the woodlands hid Leigh Hall;
While, far above, a jut of table-land,[8]

6. Possibly a reference to the assumption of the prophet Elijah, who was carried to Heaven in a fiery chariot; see 2 Kings 2.9–12.
7. Hope End, EBB's childhood home, is very close to the border with Wales, which can be seen clearly from the hill behind the house.
8. The spine of the Malvern Hills clearly visible from Hope End.

A promontory without water, stretched, -
You could not catch it if the days were thick,
Or took it for a cloud;[9] but, otherwise,
The vigorous sun would catch it up at eve
And use it for an anvil till he had filled
The shelves of heaven with burning thunderbolts,
Protesting against night and darkness: - then,
When all his setting trouble was resolved
To a trance of passive glory, you might see
In apparition on the golden sky
(Alas, my Giotto's background!)[1] the sheep run
Along the fine clear outline, small as mice
That run along a witch's scarlet thread.[2]

Not a grand nature. Not my chesnut-woods
Of Vallombrosa,[3] cleaving by the spurs
To the precipices. Not my headlong leaps
Of waters, that cry out for joy or fear
In leaping through the palpitating pines,
Like a white soul tossed out to eternity
With thrills of time upon it. Not indeed
My multitudinous mountains, sitting in
The magic circle, with the mutual touch
Electric, panting from their full deep hearts
Beneath the influent[4] heavens, and waiting for
Communion and commission. Italy
Is one thing, England one.
On English ground
You understand the letter, - ere the fall
How Adam lived in a garden.[5] All the fields
Are tied up fast with hedges, nosegay-like;
The hills are crumpled plains, the plains parterres,
The trees, round, woolly, ready to be clipped,
And if you seek for any wilderness

9. This picture of the house, grounds, and landscape of Aurora's childhood home is based on Hope End near Ledbury in Herefordshire, the estate that belonged to her father from 1809 to 1832 and where EBB spent most of her youth.
1. Vasari emphasizes the reliance of Giotto di Bondone (1276–1336) on nature as model and inspiration, in contrast to the stylized efforts of contemporary artists. In "A Face" (1864), Robert Browning also refers to Giotto's gold background: "If one could have that little head of hers/Painted upon a background of pale gold,/Such as the Tuscan's art prefers!"
2. In German folklore, witches are said to make mice by shaping a piece of cloth into the form of a mouse and saying, "Run along and come back," whereat the mouse runs away alive. The scarlet thread is possibly a reminiscence of Joshua 2.18.
3. The Brownings stayed at the monastery at Vallombrosa for five days in July 1847. Influenced not a little by Milton's reference to Vallombrosa (*Paradise Lost* 1.302), EBB was much impressed by the mountain scenery, which she described in *Casa Guidi Windows* 1.1148–54 and in her letters (see *Letters of EBB* 1.337, 340,343).
4. Exercising celestial or astral influence or occult power (OED).
5. A play on 2 Corinthians 3.6: "The letter killeth, but the spirit giveth life." For Adam living in the Garden of Eden see Genesis 2.15.

You find, at best, a park. A nature tamed
And grown domestic[6] like a barn-door fowl,
Which does not awe you with its claws and beak
Nor tempt you to an eyrie too high up,
But which, in cackling, sets you thinking of
Your eggs to-morrow at breakfast, in the pause
Of finer meditation.
Rather say,
A sweet familiar nature, stealing in
As a dog might, or child, to touch your hand
Or pluck your gown, and humbly mind you so
Of presence and affection,[7] excellent
For inner uses, from the things without.

I could not be unthankful, I who was
Entreated thus and holpen.[8] In the room
I speak of, ere the house was well awake,
And also after it was well asleep,
I sate alone, and drew the blessing in
Of all that nature. With a gradual step,
A stir among the leaves, a breath, a ray,
It came in softly, while the angels made
A place for it beside me. The moon came,
And swept my chamber clean of foolish thoughts.
The sun came, saying, 'Shall I lift this light
Against the lime-tree, and you will not look?
I make the birds sing - listen! but, for you,
God never hears your voice, excepting when
You lie upon the bed at nights and weep.'

Then, something moved me. Then, I wakened up
More slowly than I verily write now,
But wholly, at last, I wakened, opened wide
The window and my soul, and let the airs
And out-door sights sweep gradual gospels in,
Regenerating what I was. O Life,
How oft we throw it off and think, - 'Enough,
Enough of life in so much! - here's a cause
For rupture; - herein we must break with Life,
Or be ourselves unworthy; here we are wronged,
Maimed, spoiled for aspiration: farewell Life!'
And so, as froward[9] babes, we hide our eyes

6. EBB often made this kind of comparison between English and Italian scenery; see *Letters of EBB* 2.135 and 139.
7. Cf. the conclusion to EBB's "Flush or Faunus" (1850).
8. Helped.
9. Forward, precocious.

And think all ended. - Then, Life calls to us
In some transformed, apocalyptic[1] voice,
Above us, or below us, or around:
Perhaps we name it Nature's voice, or Love's,[2]
Tricking ourselves, because we are more ashamed
To own our compensations than our griefs:[3]
Still, Life's voice! - still, we make our peace with Life.

And I, so young then, was not sullen. Soon
I used to get up early, just to sit
And watch the morning quicken in the grey,
And hear the silence open like a flower
Leaf after leaf, - and stroke with listless hand
The woodbine through the window, till at last
I came to do it with a sort of love,
At foolish unaware: whereat I smiled, -
A melancholy smile, to catch myself
Smiling for joy.
                Capacity for joy
Admits temptation. It seemed, next, worth while
To dodge the sharp sword set against my life;
To slip down stairs through all the sleepy house,
As mute as any dream there, and escape
As a soul from the body, out of doors,
Glide through the shrubberies, drop into the lane,
And wander on the hills an hour or two,
Then back again before the house should stir.

Or else I sate on in my chamber green,
And lived my life, and thought my thoughts, and prayed
My prayers without the vicar; read my books,
Without considering whether they were fit
To do me good. Mark, there. We get no good
By being ungenerous, even to a book,
And calculating profits, - so much help
By so much reading. It is rather when
We gloriously forget ourselves and plunge
Soul-forward, headlong, into a book's profound,

1. EBB experimented with words derived from "apocalypse," especially in her youthful works. "The Development of Genius" included the lines "as they who wept/A watch on ruined Babylon, and wept,/In Apocalyptic vision," and an early version of the poem "Sounds" included "As erst in Patmos apolyptic John." In "A Sea-Side Meditation" (written before 1833) EBB used "apocryphal" for "apocalyptic" as she did in the first edition of *Aurora Leigh*: "Hell's angel (saith a scroll apocryphal)/Shall, when the latter days of earth have shrunk/Before the blast of God . . . ," etc. Realizing her error when revising *Aurora Leigh*, EBB noted that this was "a mistake of importance." See textual note.
2. The argument here about the return to life and enthusiasm is reminiscent of the experiences that EBB describes in *Sonnets from the Portuguese*, which were written during her courtship.
3. Compare *Aurora Leigh* 6.862.

Impassioned for its beauty and salt of truth -
'Tis then we get the right good from a book.

I read much. What my father taught before
From many a volume, Love re-emphasised
Upon the self-same pages: Theophrast[4]
Grew tender with the memory of his eyes,
And Ælian[5] made mine wet. The trick of Greek
And Latin, he had taught me, as he would
Have taught me wrestling or the game of fives[6]
If such he had known, - most like a shipwrecked man
Who heaps his single platter with goats' cheese
And scarlet berries; or like any man
Who loves but one, and so gives all at once,
Because he has it rather than because
He counts it worthy. Thus, my father gave;
And thus, as did the women formerly
By young Achilles, when they pinned a veil
Across the boy's audacious front,[7] and swept
With tuneful laughs the silver-fretted rocks,
He wrapt his little daughter in his large
Man's doublet, careless did it fit or not.

But, after I had read for memory,
I read for hope. The path my father's foot
Had trod me out, (which suddenly broke off
What time he dropped the wallet of the flesh
And passed) alone I carried on, and set
My child-heart 'gainst the thorny underwood,
To reach the grassy shelter of the trees.
Ah babe i' the wood,[8] without a brother-babe!
My own self-pity, like the red-breast bird,
Flies back to cover all that past with leaves.

Sublimest danger, over which none weeps,
When any young wayfaring soul goes forth
Alone, unconscious of the perilous road,
The day-sun dazzling in his limpid eyes,

4. Theophrastus of Eresus (c. 371–287 BC). EBB read his *Ethical Characters* in 1831.
5. Claudius Ælianus (c. 170–235), whose *Variae Historiae* relates strange anecdotes of men and animals. EBB alluded to this work in her essay, "Some Account of the Greek Christian Poets" (1842).
6. A game in which a ball is struck by the hand against the wall of a three-sided court, the aim being to force the opponent into error. Eton built their first fives courts in 1840, though the game had long been popular, especially in debtor's prisons.
7. Thetis, the mother of Achilles, having been warned of her son's death before the walls of Troy, tried to prevent him going to the war by hiding him among the women at the court of Lycomedes, king of Scyros (Hyginus, *Fabulae*, 96; and Statius, *Achilleid* 2.200ff).
8. An old folktale of a brother and sister who, lost in the wood, are covered over with leaves by the sympathetic birds.

To thrust his own way, he an alien, through
The world of books! Ah, you! - you think it fine,
You clap hands - 'A fair day!' - you cheer him on,
As if the worst, could happen, were to rest
Too long beside a fountain. Yet, behold,
Behold! - the world of books is still the world,
And worldlings in it are less merciful
And more puissant.[9] For the wicked there
Are winged like angels; every knife that strikes
Is edged from elemental fire to assail
A spiritual life; the beautiful seems right
By force of beauty, and the feeble wrong
Because of weakness; power is justified
Though armed against Saint Michael;[1] many a crown
Covers bald foreheads.[2] In the book-world, true,
There's no lack, neither, of God's saints and kings,
That shake the ashes of the grave aside
From their calm locks and undiscomfited
Look stedfast truths against Time's changing mask.
True, many a prophet teaches in the roads;
True, many a seer pulls down the flaming heavens
Upon his own head in strong martyrdom
In order to light men a moment's space.
But stay! - who judges? - who distinguishes
'Twixt Saul and Nahash justly, at first sight,[3]
And leaves king Saul precisely at the sin,
To serve king David?[4] who discerns at once
The sound of the trumpets, when the trumpets blow
For Alaric as well as Charlemagne?[5]
Who judges wizards, and can tell true seers
From conjurors? the child, there? Would you leave
That child to wander in a battle-field
And push his innocent smile against the guns;
Or even in the catacombs, - his torch

9. Powerful.
1. The first of God's seven archangels, Michael is the lawgiver, the heavenly scribe, and the protector and champion of Israel. Possibly an allusion to Revelation 12.7–9.
2. Julius Caesar was said to wear the laurel wreath, an honor granted him by the Senate, on all occasions in order to hide his baldness. See Suetonius, *De Vita Caesarum 1*, "Divus Julius," 45.
3. See 1 Samuel 11. When Israel begged Samuel to nominate a king, he reluctantly anointed Saul. Nevertheless, the people of Jabesh-Gilead offered to serve Nahash, the Ammonite who besieged their city. Nahash refused their offer and Saul routed the Ammonites soon afterward. This satisfactory resolution did not expiate the faithlessness of the Israelites in asking for a king at all. In the event, Saul and Nahash proved indistinguishable in that both lacked God's favor.
4. Saul's "sin" was to spare the life of Agag, king of the Amalekites, in defiance of God's command that they should be utterly destroyed. See 1 Samuel 16.8–11.
5. King of the Franks, crowned Emperor by Pope Leo III in 800, Charlemagne (c. 742–814) was considered the prototype of a Christian king throughout medieval Europe; Alaric (c. 370–410) leader of the Visigoths, represents the idea of the pagan barbarian at his most ignorant and violent.

Grown ragged in the fluttering air, and all
The dark a-mutter round him? not a child.

I read books bad and good - some bad and good
At once; (good aims not always make good books:
Well-tempered spades turn up ill-smelling soils
In digging vineyards even) books that prove
God's being so definitely, that man's doubt
Grows self-defined the other side the line,
Made atheist by suggestion; moral books,
Exasperating to license; genial books,
Discounting from the human dignity;
And merry books, which set you weeping when
The sun shines, - ay, and melancholy books,
Which make you laugh that anyone should weep
In this disjointed life for one wrong more.

The world of books is still the world, I write,
And both worlds have God's providence, thank God,
To keep and hearten: with some struggle, indeed,
Among the breakers, some hard swimming through
The deeps - I lost breath in my soul sometimes
And cried, 'God save me if there's any God,'[6]
But, even so, God saved me; and, being dashed
From error on to error, every turn
Still brought me nearer to the central truth.

I thought so. All this anguish in the thick
Of men's opinions . . press and counterpress,
Now up, now down, now underfoot, and now
Emergent . . all the best of it, perhaps,
But throws you back upon a noble trust
And use of your own instinct, - merely proves
Pure reason stronger than bare inference
At strongest. Try it, - fix against heaven's wall
The scaling-ladders of school logic - mount
Step by step! - sight goes faster; that still ray
Which strikes out from you, how, you cannot tell,
And why, you know not, (did you eliminate,
That such as you indeed should analyse?)
Goes straight and fast as light, and high as God.

6. EBB found this prayer in Dr. William King's *Political and Literary Anecdotes of His Own Times* (London, 1818), 8: "Sir William Wyndham told us, that the shortest prayer he had ever heard was the prayer of a common soldier just before the battle of Blenheim, 'O God, if there be a God, save my soul, if I have a soul!' " EBB said that as a child this prayer . . . "took my fancy & met my general views exactly" (January 15, 1846, *RB/EBB Letters* 1.392).

The cygnet finds the water, but the man
Is born in ignorance of his element
And feels out blind at first, disorganised
By sin i' the blood,[7] - his spirit-insight dulled
And crossed by his sensations. Presently
He feels it quicken in the dark sometimes,
When, mark, be reverent, be obedient,
For such dumb motions of imperfect life
Are oracles of vital Deity
Attesting the Hereafter.[8] Let who says
'The soul's a clean white paper,' rather say,
A palimpsest,[9] a prophet's holograph
Defiled, erased and covered by a monk's, -
The apocalypse, by a Longus![1] poring on
Which obscene text, we may discern perhaps
Some fair, fine trace of what was written once,
Some upstroke of an alpha and omega[2]
Expressing the old scripture.
Books, books, books!
I had found the secret of a garret-room
Piled high with cases in my father's name,
Piled high, packed large, - where, creeping in and out
Among the giant fossils of my past,
Like some small nimble mouse between the ribs
Of a mastadon, I nibbled here and there
At this or that box, pulling through the gap,
In heats of terror, haste, victorious joy,
The first book first. And how I felt it beat
Under my pillow, in the morning's dark,
An hour before the sun would let me read!
My books! At last because the time was ripe,
I chanced upon the poets.
As the earth
Plunges in fury, when the internal fires
Have reached and pricked her heart, and, throwing flat
The marts[3] and temples, the triumphal gates
And towers of observation, clears herself
To elemental freedom - thus, my soul,

7. A reference to the concept of original sin.
8. As in Wordsworth's "Ode: Intimations of Immortality from Recollections of Early Childhood" (see notes to lines 10–12), Aurora interprets moments of vision and power as presentiments of eternal life.
9. A parchment or other writing material written on twice, the original writing having been erased or rubbed out to make place for the second (OED).
1. Greek sophist, around the fourth or fifth century, and author of an erotic prose romance, the *Pastoral of Daphnis and Chloe*; the Revelation of St. John the Divine.
2. Revelation 1.8 and 11.
3. Markets.

At poetry's divine first finger-touch,
Let go conventions and sprang up surprised,
Convicted[4] of the great eternities
Before two worlds.
What's this, Aurora Leigh,
You write so of the poets, and not laugh?
Those virtuous liars, dreamers after dark,
Exaggerators of the sun and moon,
And soothsayers in a tea-cup?
I write so
Of the only truth-tellers now left to God,
The only speakers of essential truth,
Opposed to relative, comparative,
And temporal truths;[5] the only holders by
His sun-skirts, through conventional grey glooms;
The only teachers who instruct mankind
From just a shadow on a charnel-wall
To find man's veritable stature out
Erect, sublime, - the measure of a man,
And that's the measure of an angel, says
The apostle.[6] Ay, and while your common men
Lay telegraphs, gauge railroads, reign, reap, dine,
And dust the flaunty carpets of the world
For kings to walk on or our president,
The poet suddenly will catch them up
with his voice like a thunder,[7] - 'This is soul,
This is life, this word is being said in heaven,
Here's God down on us! what are you about?'
How all those workers start amid their work,
Look round, look up, and feel, a moment's space,
That carpet-dusting, though a pretty trade,
Is not the imperative labour after all.
My own best poets, am I one with you,
That thus I love you, - or but one through love?

4. Convinced.
5. Compare EBB's letter to RB of February 27, 1845, where she discusses Carlyle's achievement: "He fills the office of a poet—does he not?—by analyzing humanity back into its elements, to the destruction of the conventions of the hour. That is—strictly speaking . . the office of the poet" (*RB/EBB Letters* 1.29).
6. See Revelation 21.17: "And he measured the wall thereof, an hundred and forty-four cubits, according to the measure of a man, that is, of the angel." The American artist William Page devised a theory of human proportion based on this verse from Revelation, which he propounded to Robert Browning in 1853 while the Brownings were living in Rome. Page gave an account of his discovery in an article in *Scribner's Monthly* where he says, "I may here mention that my friend Robert Browning, was the first one to whom I had the pleasure of communicating my discovery and its use. Subsequently he advised me to publish it in some English periodical, and assisted me in recollecting the date of my first observations by saying: 'I put it in "Cleon," and my wife in "Aurora Leigh" ' " (*Scribner's Monthly* 17 [April 1879]: 894–98). The lines to which Robert Browning referred are "Cleon" 55–56: "I know the true proportions of a man,/And woman also, not observed before," and *Aurora Leigh* 1.864–69.
7. See Revelation 3.5, 6.1, 10.4, etc.

Does all this smell of thyme about my feet
Conclude my visit to your holy hill[8]
In personal presence, or but testify
The rustling of your vesture through my dreams
With influent odours? When my joy and pain,
My thought and aspiration, like the stops
Of pipe or flute, are absolutely dumb
Unless melodious, do you play on me
My pipers, - and if, sooth, you did not blow,
Would no sound come? or is the music mine,
As a man's voice or breath is called his own,
Inbreathed by the Life-breather? There's a doubt
For cloudy seasons!
But the sun was high
When first I felt my pulses set themselves
For concord; when the rhythmic turbulence
Of blood and brain swept outward upon words,
As wind upon the alders, blanching them
By turning up their under-natures till
They trembled in dilation. O delight
And triumph of the poet, who would say
A man's mere 'yes,' a woman's common 'no,'
A little human hope of that or this,
And says the word so that it burns you through
With a special revelation, shakes the heart
Of all the men and women in the world,
As if one came back from the dead and spoke,
With eyes too happy, a familiar thing
Become divine i' the utterance! while for him
The poet, speaker, he expands with joy;
The palpitating angel in his flesh
Thrills inly with consenting fellowship
To those innumerous spirits who sun themselves
Outside of time.
O life, O poetry,
- Which means life in life! cognisant of life
Beyond this blood-beat, passionate for truth
Beyond these senses! - poetry, my life,
My eagle, with both grappling feet still hot
From Zeus's thunder, who hast ravished me
Away from all the shepherds, sheep, and dogs,[9]
And set me in the Olympian roar and round
Of luminous faces for a cup-bearer,

8. Mount Parnassus, sacred to Apollo, patron of poetry, and the Muses.
9. When Zeus fell in love with Ganymede the shepherd boy, he transformed himself into an eagle and seized the boy in his talons, carrying him away to Olympia, the mountain home of the gods, to make him the cupbearer who serves the gods with nectar. See Virgil, *Aeneid* 5.254–257.

To keep the mouths of all the godheads moist
For everlasting laughters,[1] - I myself
Half drunk across the beaker with their eyes!
How those gods look!
Enough so, Ganymede,
We shall not bear above a round or two.
We drop the golden cup at Heré's[2] foot
And swoon back to the earth, - and find ourselves
Face-down among the pine-cones, cold with dew,
While the dogs bark, and many a shepherd scoffs,
'What's come now to the youth?' Such ups and downs
Have poets.
Am I such indeed? The name
Is royal, and to sign it like a queen,
Is what I dare not, - though some royal blood
Would seem to tingle in me now and then,
With sense of power and ache, - with imposthumes[3]
And manias usual to the race. Howbeit
I dare not: 'tis too easy to go mad
And ape a Bourbon in a crown of straws;[4]
The thing's too common.
Many fervent souls
Strike rhyme on rhyme, who would strike steel on steel
If steel had offered, in a restless heat
Of doing something. Many tender souls
Have strung their losses on a rhyming thread,
As children, cowslips: - the more pains they take,
The work more withers. Young men, ay, and maids,
Too often sow their wild oats in tame verse,
Before they sit down under their own vine[5]
And live for use. Alas, near all the birds
Will sing at dawn, - and yet we do not take
The chaffering swallow for the holy lark.[6]

1. *ασβεστος γελως*, inextinguishable, or unquenchable laughters, an attribute Homer accords to the Olympian gods. See *Iliad* 1.599 and *Odyssey* 8.326.
2. Hera, wife of Zeus and queen of the gods.
3. Abscesses or swellings; figuratively used with reference to moral corruption (OED).
4. An allusion to Henri, comte de Chambord (1820–83), the last representative of the elder branch of the Bourbon line. The rule of the house of Bourbon ended in France with the deposition of Charles X and the rise of Louis-Philippe of the house of Orleans. Legitimists continued, however, to hope for the restoration of the Bourbon line in the person of the comte de Chambord, the grandson of Charles X, who had lived in exile since 1830, surrounded by his adherents and holding court at Frohsdorf, near Vienna. The revolution in France in 1848 incited many observers to review the chances of "Henri Cinq," who was, in EBB's opinion, "as much out of the question as Henri Quatre himself" (*Letters of EBB* 1.360; see also 1.387). In 1851, during the unrest following Louis Napoleon's coup d'etat, the possible restoration of the Bourbon line was again under discussion ("Aunt Jane [Hedley] groans for the comte de Chambord" [EBB to Mrs. Martin, December 11, 1851, Kenyon Typescript]), but neither occasion was seized for effecting the legitimist restoration.
5. See 1 Kings 4.25 and Micah 4.4.
6. The lark is "holy" because it flies and sings high in the heavens.

In those days, though, I never analyzed,
Not even myself. Analysis comes late.
You catch a sight of Nature, earliest,
In full front sun-face, and your eyelids wink
And drop before the wonder of't; you miss
The form, through seeing the light. I lived, those days,
And wrote because I lived - unlicensed else;
My heart beat in my brain. Life's violent flood
Abolished bounds, - and, which my neighbour's field,
Which mine, what mattered? it is thus in youth!
We play at leap-frog over the god Term;[7]
The love within us and the love without
Are mixed, confounded; if we are loved or love,
We scarce distinguish: thus, with other power;
Being acted on and acting seem the same:
In that first onrush of life's chariot-wheels,
We know not if the forests move or we.

And so, like most young poets, in a flush
Of individual life I poured myself
Along the veins of others, and achieved
Mere lifeless imitations of live verse,
And made the living answer for the dead,
Profaning nature. 'Touch not, do not taste,
Nor handle,'[8] - we're too legal, who write young:
We beat the phorminx[9] till we hurt our thumbs,
As if still ignorant of counterpoint;[1]
We call the Muse, - 'O Muse, benignant Muse,' -
As if we had seen her purple-braided head,[2]
With the eyes in it, start between the boughs
As often as a stag's. What make-believe,
With so much earnest! what effete results
From virile efforts! what cold wire-drawn[3] odes,
From such white heats! - bucolics,[4] where the cows
Would scare the writer if they splashed the mud

7. A Roman divinity presiding over boundaries and frontiers.
8. Colossians 2.21.
9. An ancient stringed instrument, like a cither or a lyre, and played, according to Homer, by Apollo (*Iliad* 1.603) and Achilles (*Iliad* 9.186, 194).
1. The practice of weaving different harmonies together in complicated patterns. Here it represents sophisticated later styles over primitive early ones.
2. The epithet "violet-tressed" or "violet-haired" (ιοπλοκαμοι) is borrowed from Pindar. See *Pythian Odes* 1.3 and *Isthnian Odes* 7.23. In 1828 EBB discussed at length the exact meaning of the term in a letter to Hugh Stuart Boyd: "Perhaps . . . the *darkness and gloss* of the violet,—not its distinctive colouring,—are meant to be apprehended" January 12, 1828, *The Brownings' Correspondence*, ed. Philip Kelley and Ronald Hudson (Winfield, KS, 1984), 2.103. See also *Sonnets from the Portuguese* 19: "As purply black, as erst to Pindar's eyes/The dim purpureal tresses gloomed athwart/The nine white Muse-brows," lines 5–7.
3. Drawn to a great length, or with subtle ingenuity (OED).
4. A rustic and pastoral form of poetry.

In lashing off the flies, - didactics, driven
Against the heels of what the master said;
And counterfeiting epics, shrill with trumps
A babe might blow between two straining cheeks
Of bubbled rose, to make his mother laugh;
And elegiac griefs, and songs of love,
Like cast-off nosegays picked up on the road,
The worse for being warm: all these things, writ
On happy mornings, with a morning heart,
That leaps for love, is active for resolve,
Weak for art only. Oft, the ancient forms
Will thrill, indeed, in carrying the young blood.
The wine-skins, now and then, a little warped,
Will crack even, as the new wine gurgles in.
Spare the old bottles! - spill not the new wine.[5]

By Keats's soul, the man who never stepped
In gradual progress like another man,
But, turning grandly on his central self,
Ensphered himself in twenty perfect years[6]
And died, not young, (the life of a long life
Distilled to a mere drop, falling like a tear
Upon the world's cold cheek to make it burn
For ever;) by that strong excepted soul,
I count it strange and hard to understand
That nearly all young poets should write old,
That Pope was sexagenary at sixteen,[7]
And beardless Byron academical,[8]
And so with others. It may be perhaps
Such have not settled long and deep enough
In trance, to attain to clairvoyance, - and still
The memory mixes with the vision, spoils,
And works it turbid.

5. Matthew 9.17 and Luke 5.37–38.
6. The English poet John Keats (1795–1821), who, though living a bit more than the twenty years named here, produced an impressive body of work, and who, by virtue of his work's quality and his youth and early death, is sometimes taken to represent the epitome of the popular idea of the Romantic poet.
7. Alexander Pope (1688–1744). Pope's *Pastorals*—four short poems on the seasons, in the manner of Virgil—though first published in 1709 (in *Poetical Miscellanies: The Sixth Part*), were actually composed, according to Pope's own notes to his *Letters* (1735), in 1704 when he was 16. See *The Correspondence of Alexander Pope*, ed. George Sherburn (Oxford, 1956), 1.7–8.
8. George Gordon, Lord Byron (1788–1824). See Thomas Moore, *Letters and Journals of Lord Byron with Notices of his Life* (London, 1830), 1.35: "My first dash into poetry (he says) was as early as 1800. It was an ebullition of a passion for my first cousin Margaret Parker . . . one of the most beautiful of evanescent beings. I have long forgotten the verses . . . I was then about twelve—she rather older, perhaps a year. She died about a year or two afterwards . . . Some years after, I made an attempt at an elegy—a very dull one." The elegy to which Byron refers—"On the Death of a Young Lady, Cousin to the Author, and Very Dear to Him"—was composed in 1802 when the author was 14, and privately printed in 1806.

Or perhaps, again,
In order to discover the Muse-Sphinx,
The melancholy desert must sweep round,
Behind you as before.[9] -
For me, I wrote
False poems, like the rest, and thought them true
Because myself was true in writing them.
I peradventure have writ true ones since
With less complacence.
But I could not hide
My quickening inner life from those at watch.
They saw a light at a window now and then,
They had not set there: who had set it there?
My father's sister started when she caught
My soul agaze in my eyes. She could not say
I had no business with a sort of soul,
But plainly she objected, - and demurred
That souls were dangerous things to carry straight
Through all the spilt saltpetre of the world.
She said sometimes, 'Aurora, have you done
Your task this morning? have you read that book?
And are you ready for the crochet here?' -
As if she said, 'I know there's something wrong;
I know I have not ground you down enough
To flatten and bake you to a wholesome crust
For household uses and proprieties,
Before the rain has got into my barn
And set the grains a-sprouting. What, you're green
With out-door impudence? you almost grow?'
To which I answered, 'Would she hear my task,
And verify my abstract of the book?
Or should I sit down to the crochet work?
Was such her pleasure? Then I sate and teased
The patient needle till it spilt the thread,
Which oozed off from it in meandering lace
From hour to hour. I was not, therefore, sad;
My soul was singing at a work apart
Behind the wall of sense, as safe from harm
As sings the lark when sucked up out of sight
In vortices of glory and blue air.[1]

9. Possibly a reminiscence of Homer, *Iliad* 3.108–10: "Ever unstable are the hearts of young; but in whatsoever an old man taketh part, he looketh both before and after, that the issue may be far the best for either side" (Loeb translation).

1. Compare Wordsworth's "To a Skylark" (1827), lines 8–11: "A privacy of glorious light is thine;/ Whence thou dost pour upon the world a flood / Of harmony, with instinct more divine;/Type of the wise who soar, but never roam." See also EBB's reference, presumably to this poem, in *Letters of EBB* 1.110.

And so, through forced work and spontaneous work,
The inner life informed the outer life,
Reduced the irregular blood to a settled rhythm,
Made cool the forehead with fresh-sprinkling dreams,
And, rounding to the spheric soul the thin,
Pined body, struck a colour up the cheeks
Though somewhat faint. I clenched my brows across
My blue eyes greatening in the looking-glass,
And said, 'We'll live, Aurora! we'll be strong.
The dogs are on us - but we will not die.'

Whoever lives true life, will love true love.
I learnt to love that England. Very oft,
Before the day was born, or otherwise
Through secret windings of the afternoons,
I threw my hunters off and plunged myself
Among the deep hills, as a hunted stag
Will take the waters, shivering with the fear
And passion of the course. And when at last
Escaped, so many a green slope built on slope
Betwixt me and the enemy's house behind,
I dared to rest, or wander, in a rest
Made sweeter for the step upon the grass,
And view the ground's most gentle dimplement,[2]
(As if God's finger touched but did not press
In making England) such an up and down
Of verdure, - nothing too much up or down,
A ripple of land; such little hills, the sky
Can stoop to tenderly and the wheatfields climb;
Such nooks of valleys lined with orchises,[3]
Fed full of noises by invisible streams;
And open pastures where you scarcely tell
White daisies from white dew, - at intervals
The mythic oaks and elm-trees standing out
Self-poised upon their prodigy of shade, -
I thought my father's land was worthy too
Of being my Shakspeare's.
Very oft alone,
Unlicensed; not unfrequently with leave
To walk the third with Romney and his friend
The rising painter, Vincent Carrington,
Whom men judge hardly as bee-bonnetted,
Because he holds that, paint a body well,

2. A dimpling. The word is apparently peculiar to EBB; the OED gives only two examples—*Aurora Leigh* 1.1079 and EBB's "A False Step" (1862), 4.4: "Where the smile in its dimplement was."
3. Orchids.

You paint a soul by implication,[4] like
The grand first Master.[5] Pleasant walks! for if
He said, 'When I was last in Italy,'
It sounded as an instrument that's played
Too far off for the tune - and yet it's fine
To listen.
Ofter we walked only two
If cousin Romney pleased to walk with me.
We read, or talked, or quarrelled, as it chanced.
We were not lovers, nor even friends well-matched:
Say rather, scholars upon different tracks,
And thinkers disagreed, he, overfull
Of what is, and I, haply, overbold
For what might be.
But then the thrushes sang,
And shook my pulses and the elms' new leaves;
At which I turned, and held my finger up,
And bade him mark that, howsoe'er the world
Went ill, as he related, certainly
The thrushes still sang in it. At the word
His brow would soften, - and he bore with me
In melancholy patience, not unkind,
While breaking into voluble ecstasy
I flattered all the beauteous country round,
As poets use..the skies, the clouds, the fields,
The happy violets hiding from the roads
The primroses run down to, carrying gold;
The tangled hedgerows, where the cows push out
Impatient horns and tolerant churning mouths
'Twixt dripping ash-boughs, - hedgerows all alive
With birds and gnats and large white butterflies
Which look as if the May-flower had caught life
And palpitated forth upon the wind;
Hills, vales, woods, netted in a silver mist,
Farms, granges, doubled up among the hills;
And cattle grazing in the watered vales,
And cottage-chimneys smoking from the woods,
And cottage-gardens smelling everywhere,
Confused with smell of orchards. 'See', I said,
'And see! is God not with us on the earth?
And shall we put Him down by aught we do?
Who says there's nothing for the poor and vile
Save poverty and wickedness? behold!'

4. Cf. RB's "Fra Lippo Lippi" (1855), lines 205–8: "Why can't a painter . . . Make his flesh liker and his soul more like" and lines 212–14: "Suppose I've made her eyes all right and blue/Can't I take breath and try to add life's flash/And then add soul and heighten them threefold?"
5. God.

And ankle-deep in English grass I leaped
And clapped my hands, and called all very fair.

In the beginning when God called all good,
Even then was evil near us, it is writ;[6]
But we indeed who call things good and fair,
The evil is upon us while we speak;
Deliver us from evil,[7] let us pray.

6. Genesis 1.31 and 2.17.
7. Matthew 6.13.

## Second Book

Times followed one another. Came a morn
I stood upon the brink of twenty years,
And looked before and after,[1] as I stood
Woman and artist, - either incomplete,
Both credulous of completion. There I held
The whole creation in my little cup,
And smiled with thirsty lips before I drank
'Good health to you and me, sweet neighbour mine,
And all these peoples.'
                                        I was glad, that day;
The June[2] was in me, with its multitudes
Of nightingales all singing in the dark,
And rosebuds reddening where the calyx split.
I felt so young, so strong, so sure of God!
So glad, I could not choose be very wise!
And, old at twenty, was inclined to pull
My childhood backward in a childish jest
To see the face of't once more, and farewell!
In which fantastic mood I bounded forth
At early morning, - would not wait so long
As even to snatch my bonnet by the strings,
But, brushing a green trail across the lawn
With my gown in the dew, took will and way
Among the acacias of the shrubberies,
To fly my fancies in the open air
And keep my birthday, till my aunt awoke
To stop good dreams. Meanwhile I murmured on
As honeyed bees keep humming to themselves,
'The worthiest poets have remained uncrowned
Till death has bleached their foreheads to the bone;
And so with me it must be unless I prove
Unworthy of the grand adversity,
And certainly I would not fail so much.
What, therefore, if I crown myself to-day[3]

1. Like the two-headed god Janus, who gives his name to the first month of the year, Aurora looks back over her past and forward to her future. This image of "double vision," looking back to analyze and forward to new experiment and experience, is one that runs throughout the verse-novel: see 1.4–8; 5.183–88; and books 8 and 9 passim.
2. It may be relevant that Queen Victoria's birthday falls in June.
3. Ellen Moers argues, in *Literary Women* (London, 1977), that the scene of Aurora's self-crowning invokes recollection of Mme. de Stael's *Corinne, or Italy* (Paris, 1807), bk. 2, ch. 4, in which the poet-heroine is crowned with a wreath of bay and myrtle in a great ceremony at the Capitol in Rome. EBB knew *Corinne* well, and declared it "an immortal book, [which] . . . deserves to be read three score and ten times—that is, once every year in the age of man" (June 9, 1832, *Elizabeth Barrett Browning to Hugh Stuart Boyd*, ed. Barbara P. McCarthy [London, 1955], 176). EBB remembers just such an episode when she crowned herself with leaves in

In sport, not pride, to learn the feel of it,
Before my brows be numb as Dante's[4] own
To all the tender pricking of such leaves?
Such leaves! what leaves?'
I pulled the branches down
To choose from.
'Not the bay![5] I choose no bay,
(The fates deny us if we are overbold)
Nor myrtle - which means chiefly love;[6] and love
Is something awful which one dares not touch
So early o' mornings. This verbena[7] strains
The point of passionate fragrance; and hard by,
This guelder-rose,[8] at far too slight a beck
Of the wind, will toss about her flower-apples.
Ah - there's my choice, - that ivy on the wall,
That headlong ivy! not a leaf will grow
But thinking of a wreath. Large leaves, smooth leaves,
Serrated like my vines, and half as green.
I like such ivy, bold to leap a height
'Twas strong to climb; as good to grow on graves
As twist about a thyrsus;[9] pretty too,
(And that's not ill) when twisted round a comb.'
Thus speaking to myself, half singing it,
Because some thoughts are fashioned like a bell
To ring with once being touched, I drew a wreath
Drenched, blinding me with dew, across my brow,
And fastening it behind so, turning faced
. . My public! - cousin Romney[1] - with a mouth
Twice graver than his eyes.
I stood there fixed, -
My arms up, like the caryatid,[2] sole
Of some abolished temple, helplessly
Persistent in a gesture which derides

---

*Sonnets from the Portuguese* (1850), xviii; "My day of youth went yesterday;/My hair no longer bounds to my foot's glee,/Nor plant I it from rose or myrtle-tree,/As girls do, any more."

4. Dante Alighieri (1265–1321), the chief of Italian poets, and author of the *Vita Nuova* and the *Divina Commedia*.
5. The bay, or laurel crown, was an attribute of Apollo, god of poetry and song. Cf. Ovid, *Metamorphoses* 1.557–59.
6. Myrtea or Murcia, thought to be derived from myrtus, a myrtle, was a surname of Venus, the goddess of love.
7. The sweet-scented plant vervain. It was grown as a sacred plant in the Capital at Rome.
8. Common name for viburnum opulus, which bears globular bunches of white flowers. Also known as the snowball-tree.
9. A staff or spear tipped with an ornament, wreathed with ivy or vine-branches, and borne by Dionysius (Bacchus) and his votaries. Cf. Ovid, *Metamorphoses* 4.7. See also *Letters of EBB* 1:143.
1. "Arthur Duncomb" (later corrected to "Harry Vaughan") in the first draft manuscript; cousin "Percy" in the "fair copy" manuscript—see textual note.
2. An architectural form representing a nymph holding up the roof, very widely employed in the temples of classical Greece.

A former purpose. Yet my blush was flame,
As if from flax, not stone.[3]
'Aurora Leigh,[4]
The earliest of Auroras!'
Hand stretched out
I clasped, as shipwrecked men will clasp a hand,
Indifferent to the sort of palm. The tide
Had caught me at my pastime, writing down
My foolish name too near upon the sea[5]
Which drowned me with a blush as foolish. 'You,
My cousin!'
The smile died out in his eyes
And dropped upon his lips, a cold dead weight,
For just a moment, 'Here's a book I found!
No name writ on it - poems, by the form;
Some Greek upon the margin, - lady's Greek
Without the accents.[6] Read it? Not a word.
I saw at once the thing had witchcraft in't,
Whereof the reading calls up dangerous spirits:
I rather bring it to the witch.'
'My book.
You found it' . .
'In the hollow by the stream
That beech leans down into - of which you said
The Oread in it has a Naiad's[7] heart
And pines for waters.'
'Thank you.'
'Thanks to *you*
My cousin! that I have seen you not too much
Witch, scholar, poet, dreamer, and the rest,
To be a woman also.'
With a glance
The smile rose in his eyes again and touched

3. Flax will burn, as stone (taken from the caryatid image) will not.
4. "Aurora Vaughan" in the first draft manuscript.
5. Cf. the epitaph John Keats composed for himself: "Here lies one whose name was writ in water."
6. Neither EBB nor RB used accents in writing Greek. In 1828, while reading with Hugh Stuart Boyd, EBB argued against the use of accents, partly because of possible confusion with other necessary marks and partly because of the doubts that had been expressed by scholars as to their authenticity. See EBB to Boyd, December 24, 1827, and January 12, 1828, *The Brownings' Correspondence* 2.101–2. In spite of EBB's own reasoned rejection of accents, Romney's comment in this instance must be read as indicative of his scorn for Aurora's attempt to infiltrate the male preserve of the classics. Compare George Eliot's *Middlemarch* (1871–72), ch. 7, where Casaubon's dismissive reply to Dorothea's questions about Greek accents leads to Dorothea acquiring "a painful suspicion that here indeed there might be secrets not capable of explanation to a woman's reason."
7. The naiad is a spirit inhabiting lakes, rivers, and springs. An oread inhabits hills, mountains, or grottos. Apparently an error on EBB's part: in Greek mythology a tree-nymph is a dryad or hamadryad. The original manuscript reading "nereid" is also incorrect, for the nereid inhabits the sea.

The ivy on my forehead, light as air.
I answered gravely, 'Poets needs must be
Or men or women - more's the pity'
'Ah,
But men, and still less women, happily,
Scarce need be poets. Keep to the green wreath,
Since even dreaming of the stone and bronze
Brings headaches, pretty cousin, and defiles
The clean white morning dresses.'
'So you judge!
Because I love the beautiful I must
Love pleasure chiefly, and be overcharged
For ease and whiteness! well, you know the world,
And only miss your cousin, 'tis not much.
But learn this; I would rather take my part
With God's Dead, who afford to walk in white[8]
Yet spread His glory, than keep quiet here
And gather up my feet from even a step
For fear to soil my gown in so much dust.
I choose to walk at all risks. - Here, if heads
That hold a rhythmic thought, must ache perforce,
For my part I choose headaches - and to-day's
My birthday.'
'Dear Aurora, choose instead
To cure them. You have balsams.'[9]
'I perceive.
The headache is too noble for my sex.
You think the heartache would sound decenter,[1]
Since that's the woman's special, proper ache,
And altogether tolerable, except
To a woman.'
Saying which, I loosed my wreath,
And swinging it beside me as I walked,
Half petulant, half playful, as we walked,
I sent a sidelong look to find his thought, -
As falcon set on falconer's finger may,
With sidelong head, and startled, braving eye,
Which means, 'You'll see - you'll see! I'll soon take flight,
You shall not hinder.' He, as shaking out
His hand and answering 'Fly then,' did not speak,
Except by such a gesture. Silently

8. See Revelation 3.4. "Thou hast a few names even in Sardis which have not defiled their garments; and they shall walk with me in white: for they are worthy."
9. An aromatic resin from plant sources, used as a salve to heal wounds or sooth pain.
1. The commonplaces of nineteenth-century gender characteristics dictated that the head, intellect, and reason were associated with man, while the heart, feeling, and sentiment were associated with woman.

We paced, until, just coming into sight
Of the house-windows, he abruptly caught
At one end of the swinging wreath, and said
'Aurora!' There I stopped short, breath and all.

'Aurora, let's be serious, and throw by
This game of head and heart. Life means, be sure,
Both heart and head, - both active, both complete,
And both in earnest. Men and women make
The world, as head and heart make human life.
Work man, work woman, since there's work to do
In this beleaguered earth, for head and heart,
And thought can never do the work of love:
But work for ends, I mean for uses, not
For such sleek fringes[2] (do you call them ends,
Still less God's glory?) as we sew ourselves
Upon the velvet of those baldaquins[3]
Held 'twixt us and the sun. That book of yours,
I have not read a page of; but I toss
A rose up - it falls calyx down, you see!
The chances are that, being a woman, young
And pure, with such a pair of large, calm eyes,
You write as well . . and ill . . upon the whole,
As other women. If as well, what then?
If even a little better, . . still, what then?
We want the Best in art now, or no art.
The time is done for facile settings up
Of minnow gods, nymphs here and tritons there;[4]
The polytheists[5] have gone out in God,
That unity of Bests. No best, no God!
And so with art, we say. Give art's divine,
Direct, indubitable, real as grief,
Or leave us to the grief we grow ourselves
Divine by overcoming with mere hope
And most prosaic patience. You, you are young
As Eve[6] with nature's daybreak on her face,
But this same world you are come to, dearest coz,[7]
Has done with keeping birthdays, saves her wreaths
To hang upon her ruins, - and forgets

2. Used here for the idea of an end or finish to a garment or piece of cloth, but also for the idea of a decorative item that is unnecessary and useless in terms of function.
3. A canopy of rich material suspended over an altar or throne.
4. Lesser deities in Greek mythology—the nymphs were spirits of the trees, groves, and rivers; the tritons, monstrous sons of Poseidon and Amphitrite, inhabited the sea.
5. Those who believe in many gods, rather than in the one god of Christianity, Judaism, and Islam.
6. According to the book of Genesis, Eve was created from Adam's rib to be his companion and helpmeet in the Garden of Eden, Genesis 2.18–23.
7. An archaic term for "cousin."

To rhyme the cry with which she still beats back
Those savage, hungry dogs that hunt her down
To the empty grave of Christ.[8] The world's hard pressed;
The sweat of labour in the early curse[9]
Has (turning acrid in six thousand years)[1]
Become the sweat of torture. Who has time,
An hour's time . . think! - to sit upon a bank
And hear the cymbal tinkle[2] in white hands?
When Egypt's slain,[3] I say, let Miriam sing! -
Before - where's Moses?'
'Ah, exactly that.
Where's Moses? - is a Moses to be found?
You'll seek him vainly in the bulrushes,[4]
While I in vain touch cymbals. Yet concede,
Such sounding brass[5] has done some actual good
(The application in a woman's hand,
If that were credible, being scarcely spoilt,)
In colonising[6] beehives.'
'There it is! -
You play beside a death-bed like a child,
Yet measure to yourself a prophet's place
To teach the living. None of all these things,
Can women understand. You generalise
Oh, nothing, - not even grief! Your quick-breathed hearts,
So sympathetic to the personal pang,
Close on each separate knife-stroke, yielding up
A whole life at each wound, incapable
Of deepening, widening a large lap of life
To hold the world-full woe. The human race
To you means, such a child, or such a man,
You saw one morning waiting in the cold,
Beside that gate, perhaps. You gather up
A few such cases, and when strong sometimes
Will write of factories and of slaves,[7] as if

8. A reference to the disappearance of Christ's body from the tomb of Joseph of Arimithea, where it was laid after the crucifixion, used here to suggest the disappearance of faith and consolation in the modern world.
9. Genesis 3.19.
1. In the nineteenth century the traditional date of the creation and the expulsion from Eden was 4004 BC.
2. 1 Corinthians 13.1.
3. See Exodus 15.20.
4. Exodus 2.3.
5. 1 Corinthians 13.1. See also note to line 170 above.
6. Achieving very little.
7. EBB makes a joke against herself. She had written on the evils of child labor in "The Cry of the Children" (*Blackwood's Edinburgh Magazine* [August 1843]) and on the inhumanity of slavery in "The Runaway Slave at Pilgrim's Point" (*The Liberty Bell* [1848]). The first was a poem addressed to a prevalent abuse in England, reported on by EBB's friend R. H. Horne. The second was a criticism directed toward America, where slavery continued in the South until the American Civil War. These two poems were published consecutively in EBB's *Poems*

Your father were a negro, and your son
A spinner in the mills. All's yours and you,
All, coloured with your blood, or otherwise
Just nothing to you. Why, I call you hard
To general suffering. Here's the world half blind
With intellectual light, half brutalised
With civilisation, having caught the plague
In silks from Tarsus,[8] shrieking east and west
Along a thousand railroads, mad with pain
And sin too! . . does one woman of you all
(You who weep easily) grow pale to see
This tiger shake his cage? - does one of you
Stand still from dancing, stop from stringing pearls,
And pine and die because of the great sum
Of universal anguish? - Show me a tear
Wet as Cordelia's,[9] in eyes bright as yours,
Because the world is mad. You cannot count,
That you should weep for this account, not you!
You weep for what you know. A red-haired child
Sick in a fever, if you touch him once,
Though but so little as with a finger-tip,
Will set you weeping; but a million sick . .
You could as soon weep for the rule of three[1]
Or compound fractions. Therefore, this same world
Uncomprehended by you, must remain
Uninfluenced by you. - Women as you are,
Mere women, personal and passionate,
You give us doating[2] mothers, and perfect wives,
Sublime Madonnas, and enduring saints!
We get no Christ from you, - and verily
We shall not get a poet, in my mind.'

'With which conclusion you conclude' . .
'But this:

That you, Aurora, with the large live brow
And steady eyelids, cannot condescend
To play at art, as children play at swords,

(1850) because she wished "to appear impartial as to national grievances" (*Letters of EBB* 1.462). Note that Romney's formulation, "as if/Your father were a negro, and your son/A spinner in the mills," makes the female poet only the passive recorder of man's active experience.

8. Tarsus is on the plain of Galicia in Turkey and is used here as an example of a backward and uncivilized city whose products, coveted and exploited by modern commercial enterprize, are contaminated with the infections of barbarism.
9. See *King Lear* 4.7.71.
1. The rule of proportion, or "golden rule," enables a fourth number to be discovered in any given sequence of three where the first number is in the same proportion to the third as the third is to the unknown fourth.
2. Archaic spelling for "doting."

To show a pretty spirit, chiefly admired
Because true action is impossible.
You never can be satisfied with praise
Which men give women when they judge a book
Not as mere work but as mere woman's work,
Expressing the comparative respect
Which means the absolute scorn. 'Oh, excellent!
'What grace, what facile turns, what fluent sweeps
'What delicate discernment . . almost thought!
'The book does honour to the sex, we hold.
'Among our female authors we make room
'For this fair writer, and congratulate
'The country that produces in these times
'Such women, competent to' . . spell.'[3]
'Stop there,'
I answered, burning through his thread of talk
With a quick flame of emotion, - 'You have read
My soul, if not my book, and argue well
I would not condescend . . we will not say
To such a kind of praise, (a worthless end
Is praise of all kinds) but to such a use
Of holy art and golden life. I am young,
And peradventure weak - you tell me so -
Through being a woman. And, for all the rest,
Take thanks for justice. I would rather dance
At fairs on tight-rope,[4] till the babies dropped
Their gingerbread for joy, - than shift the types[5]
For tolerable verse, intolerable
To men who act and suffer. Better far
Pursue a frivolous trade by serious means,
Than a sublime art frivolously.'
'You,
Choose nobler work than either, O moist eyes
And hurrying lips and heaving heart! We are young
Aurora, you and I. The world, - look round, -
The world, we're come to late, is swollen hard

3. Romney's account of the reaction of male reviewers to the work of a female poet is a fairly accurate parody of the condescending critical treatment that EBB's poetry too often received from her contemporaries.

4. In choosing tight-rope dancing as an example of a frivolous trade to be contrasted with the business of serious writing, EBB shares the metaphor with Carlyle, who used it in a letter addressed to RB dated June 23, 1847: "Surely, I say, men called 'of genius,'—if genius be anything but a paltry toybox fit for Bartholomew Fair,—are commissioned, and commanded under pain of death, to throw their whole 'genius,' however great or small it be, into the remedy; . . . And they spend their time in traditionary rope-dancings and mere Vauxhall gymnastics . . . Dickens writes a *Dombey and Son,* Thackeray a *Vanity Fair;* . . . In fact the business of rope-dancing goes to a great height" (*Letters of Thomas Carlyle to John Stuart Mill, John Sterling, and Robert Browning,* ed. Alexander Carlyle [London, 1923], 284. Also, see textual note to *Aurora Leigh* 3.240, where EBB used the same metaphor in manuscript.

5. Print books.

With perished generations and their sins:
The civiliser's spade grinds horribly
On dead men's bones, and cannot turn up soil
That's otherwise than fetid. All success
Proves partial failure; all advance implies
What's left behind; all triumph, something crushed
At the chariot-wheels; all government, some wrong:
And rich men make the poor, who curse the rich,
Who agonise together, rich and poor,
Under and over, in the social spasm
And crisis of the ages. Here's an age
That makes its own vocation! here we have stepped
Across the bounds of time! here's nought to see,
But just the rich man and just Lazarus,
And both in torments, with a mediate gulph,
Though not a hint of Abraham's bosom.[6] Who
Being man, Aurora, can stand calmly by
And view these things, and never tease his soul
For some great cure? No physic for this grief,
In all the earth and heaven too?'
'You believe
In God, for your part? - ay? that He who makes,
Can make good things from ill things, best from worst,
As men plant tulips upon dunghills when
They wish them finest?'
'True. A death-heat is
The same as life-heat, to be accurate,
And in all nature is no death at all,
As men account of death, so long as God
Stands witnessing for life perpetually,
By being just God. That's abstract truth, I know,
Philosophy, or sympathy with God:
But I, I sympathise with man, not God,
(I think I was a man for chiefly this)
And when I stand beside a dying bed
'Tis death to me. Observe, - it had not much
Consoled the race of mastodons to know,
Before they went to fossil, that anon
Their place would quicken with the elephant:[7]
They were not elephants but mastodons;
And I, a man, as men are now and not
As men may be hereafter, feel with men

6. See Luke 16.19–26.
7. EBB's reference makes it clear that she was familiar with contemporary evolutionary theory as expressed in the work of Charles Lyell (1797–1875) in his *Principles of Geology* (1830–33) and Charles Darwin (1809–82). Darwin's famous work, *On the Origin of Species By Means of Natural Selection* (1830–33) was not published until 1859, but his theories were widely disseminated before that date.

In the agonising present.'
'Is it so,'
I said, 'my cousin? is the world so bad,
While I hear nothing of it through the trees?
The world was always evil, - but so bad?'

'So bad, Aurora. Dear, my soul is grey
With poring over the long sum of ill;
So much for vice, so much for discontent,
So much for the necessities of power,
So much for the connivances of fear,
Coherent in statistical despairs
With such a total of distracted life, . .
To see it down in figures on a page,
Plain, silent, clear, as God sees through the earth
The sense of all the graves, - that's terrible
For one who is not God, and cannot right
The wrong he looks on. May I choose indeed
But vow away my years, my means, my aims,
Among the helpers, if there's any help
In such a social strait? The common blood
That swings along my veins, is strong enough
To draw me to this duty.'
Then I spoke.
'I have not stood long on the strand of life,
And these salt waters have had scarcely time
To creep so high up as to wet my feet:
I cannot judge these tides - I shall, perhaps.
A woman's always younger than a man
At equal years, because she is disallowed
Maturing by the outdoor sun and air,
And kept in long-clothes[8] past the age to walk.
Ah well, I know you men judge otherwise!
You think a woman ripens as a peach,
In the cheeks, chiefly. Pass it to me now;
I'm young in age, and younger still, I think,
As a woman. But a child may say amen
To a bishop's prayer and feel the way it goes,
And I, incapable to loose the knot
Of social questions, can approve, applaud
August compassion, christian thoughts that shoot
Beyond the vulgar white[9] of personal aims.
Accept my reverence.'

8. Strictly speaking, "long-clothes" is descriptive of the elaborate long dresses worn by babies of both sexes in the nineteenth century, but here Aurora is making an ironic comparison with the long, full skirts that all women wore.
9. In archery, the central portion of the target.

There he glowed on me[1]
With all his face and eyes. 'No other help?'
Said he - 'no more than so?'
'What help?' I asked.
'You'd scorn my help, - as Nature's self, you say,
Has scorned to put her music in my mouth
Because a woman's. Do you now turn round
And ask for what a woman cannot give?'

'For what she only can, I turn and ask,'
He answered, catching up my hands in his,
And dropping on me from his high-eaved brow
The full weight of his soul, - 'I ask for love,
And that, she can; for life in fellowship
Through bitter duties - that, I know she can;
For wifehood - will she?'
'Now,' I said, 'may god
Be witness 'twixt us two!' and with the word,
Meseemed I floated into a sudden light
Above his stature, - 'am I proved too weak
To stand alone, yet strong enough to bear
Such leaners on my shoulder? poor to think,
Yet rich enough to sympathise with thought?
Incompetent to sing, as blackbirds can,
Yet competent to love, like HIM?'[2]
I paused;
Perhaps I darkened, as the light-house will
That turns upon the sea. 'It's always so.
Anything does for a wife.'
'Aurora, dear,
And dearly honoured,' - he pressed in at once
With eager utterance, - 'you translate me ill.
I do not contradict my thought of you
Which is most reverent, with another thought
Found less so. If your sex is weak for art,
(And I who said so, did but honour you
By using truth in courtship) it is strong
For life and duty. Place your fecund heart
In mine, and let us blossom for the world
That wants love's colour in the grey of time.
My talk, meanwhile, is arid to you, ay,
Since all my talk can only set you where
You look down coldly on the arena-heaps
Of headless bodies, shapeless, indistinct!

1. Gazed with glowing eyes. This instance of the verb is the only example given in the OED.
2. Christ, presumably.

The Judgment-Angel[3] scarce would find his way
Through such a heap of generalised distress
To the individual man with lips and eyes,
Much less Aurora. Ah my sweet, come down,
And hand in hand we'll go where yours shall touch
These victims, one by one! till, one by one,
The formless, nameless trunk of every man
Shall seem to wear a head with hair you know,
And every woman catch your mother's face
To melt you into passion.'
'I am a girl,'
I answered slowly; 'you do well to name
My mother's face. Though far too early, alas,
God's hand did interpose 'twixt it and me,
I know so much of love as used to shine
In that face and another. Just so much;
No more indeed at all. I have not seen
So much love since, I pray you pardon me,
As answers even to make a marriage with
In this cold land of England. What you love,
Is not a woman, Romney, but a cause:
You want a helpmate, not a mistress, sir,
A wife to help your ends, - in her no end!
Your cause is noble, your ends excellent,
But I, being most unworthy of these and that,
Do otherwise conceive of love. Farewell.'

'Farewell, Aurora? you reject me thus?'
He said.
'Sir, you were married long ago.
You have a wife already whom you love,
Your social theory. Bless you both, I say.
For my part, I am scarcely meek enough
To be the handmaid of a lawful spouse.
Do I look a Hagar[4] think you?'
'So you jest.'

'Nay, so I speak in earnest,' I replied.
'You treat of marriage too much like, at least,
A chief apostle: you would bear with you

3. An allusion to Revelation 20.4: "And I saw thrones, and they sat upon them, and judgement was given unto them: and I saw the souls of them that were beheaded for the witness of Jesus, and the word of God. . . ."
4. See Genesis 16. Hagar was the serving maid of Sarah, wife of Abraham. When Sarah realized that she was too old to bear a son, she suggested that Abraham take Hagar as his concubine, which he did, and Hagar bore a son named Ishmael. The point is that Hagar was never raised to the status of a true wife.

A wife . . a sister[5] . . shall we speak it out?
A sister of charity.'
'Then, must it be
Indeed farewell? And was I so far wrong
In hope and in illusion, when I took
The woman to be nobler than the man,[6]
Yourself the noblest woman, in the use
And comprehension of what love is, - love,
That generates the likeness of itself
Through all heroic duties? so far wrong,
In saying bluntly, venturing truth on love,
'Come, human creature, love and work with me,' -
Instead of, 'Lady, thou art wondrous fair,
'And, where the Graces walk before, the Muse
'Will follow at the lighting of their eyes,
'And where the Muse walks, lovers need to creep:
'Turn round and love me, or I die of love."

With quiet indignation I broke in.
'You misconceive the question like a man,
Who sees a woman as the complement
Of his sex merely.[7] You forget too much
That every creature, female as the male,
Stands single in responsible act and thought
As also in birth and death. Whoever says
To a loyal woman, 'Love and work with me,'
Will get fair answers if the work and love,
Being good themselves, are good for her - the best
She was born for. Women of a softer mood,
Surprised by men when scarcely awake to life,
Will sometimes only hear the first word, love,
And catch up with it any kind of work,
Indifferent, so that dear love go with it.
I do not blame such women, though, for love,

5. The "chief apostle" is St. Paul. See 1 Corinthians 9.5: "Have we not power to lead about a sister, a wife, as well as other apostles." Paul's recommendation here generally has been taken to mean that women and wives should not be treated as equals, but should be used in chaste or even celibate marriage, as assistants in missionary life. This is the interpretation EBB uses, though it has recently been disputed. It often has been noted that this scene and the proposal that Romney makes to Aurora is very similar to that made to Jane Eyre by St. John Rivers in Charlotte Brönte's *Jane Eyre* (1847). When a friend pointed out that the denouement of *Aurora Leigh* also resembled *Jane Eyre* EBB said that she had forgotten all about the book; see EBB to Anna Jameson, December 26, 1856, *Letters of EBB* 2.246.

6. It was a common Victorian proposition that woman was the repository of elevated moral and spiritual values.

7. Probably a reply to Tennyson's *The Princess* (1847), 7.283–86: "either sex alone/Is half itself, and in true marriage lies/Nor equal, nor unequal: each fulfils/Defect in each." EBB was wary of Tennyson's "implied under-estimate of women" and professed herself disappointed in *The Princess* (see *Letters of EBB* 1.345).

They pick much oakum;[8] earth's fanatics make
Too frequently heaven's saints. But *me* your work
Is not the best for, - nor your love the best,
Nor able to commend the kind of work
For love's sake merely. Ah, you force me, sir,
To be over-bold in speaking of myself:
I too have my vocation, - work to do,
The heavens and earth have set me since I changed
My father's face for theirs, and, though your world
Were twice as wretched as you represent,
Most serious work, most necessary work
As any of the economists'. Reform,
Make trade a Christian possibility.
And individual right no general wrong;
Wipe out earth's furrows of the Thine and Mine,
And leave one green for men to play at bowls,
With innings for them all! . . what than, indeed,
If mortals are not greater by the head
Than any of their prosperities? what then,
Unless the artist keep up open roads
Betwixt the seen and unseen, - bursting through
The best of your conventions with his best.
The speakable, imaginable best
God bids him speak, to prove what lies beyond
Both speech and imagination? A starved man
Exceeds a fat beast: we'll not barter, sir,
The beautiful for barley. - And, even so,
I hold you will not compass your poor ends
Of barley-feeding and material ease,
Without a poet's individualism
To work your universal. It takes a soul,
To move a body: it takes a high-souled man,
To move the masses,[9] even to a cleaner stye:
It takes the ideal, to blow a hair's-breadth off
The dust of the actual. - Ah, your Fouriers[1] failed,

8. Untwisting and picking old rope used in caulking ships' seams; convicts and inmates of workhouses were employed in picking oakum.

9. Cf. EBB to Isa Blagden, Sunday [no date], 1850: "in every advancement of the work hitherto, the individual has led the masses. . . . Now, in these new theories [Christian socialism, Fourierism], the individual is ground down into the multitude, and society must be 'moving all together' if it moves at all;—restricting the very possibility of progress by the use of the lights of genius. Genius is *always individual*" (*Letters of EBB* 1.467). EBB's theories, of course, owe a great deal to Carlyle, particularly his *On Heroes, Hero-Worship, and the Heroic in History* (1840), vol. 6 of *The Collected Works of Thomas Carlyle* (London, 1858).

1. Charles François-Marie Fourier (1772–1837), social theorist, who advocated the reconstruction of society through the establishment of communal associations of producers call "phalanges" or "phalanxes." His major works were *Théorie des quatre mouvements et des destinees generales* (1808) and *Le nouveau monde industriel* (1829–30). EBB's letters frequently refer to her disbelief in the viability of Fourier's theories (e.g., *Letters of EBB* 1.467), her chief

Because not poets enough to understand
That life develops from within. - For me,
Perhaps I am not worthy, as you say,
Of work like this: perhaps a woman's soul
Aspires, and not creates: yet we aspire,
And yet I'll try out your perhapses, sir,
And if I fail . . why, burn me up my straw[2]
Like other false works - I'll not ask for grace;
Your scorn is better, cousin Romney. I
Who love my art, would never wish it lower
To suit my stature.[3] I may love my art.
You'll grant that even a woman may love art,
Seeing that to waste true love on anything
Is womanly, past question.'
                                        I retain
The very last word which I said that day,
As you the creaking of the door, years past,
Which let upon you such disabling news
You ever after have been graver. He,
His eyes, the motions in his silent mouth,
Were fiery points on which my words were caught,
Transfixed for ever in my memory
For his sake, not their own. And yet I know
I did not love him[4] . . nor he me . . that's sure . .
And what I said, is unrepented of,
As truth is always. Yet . . a princely man! -
If hard to me, heroic for himself!
He bears down on me through the slanting years,
The stronger for the distance. If he had loved,
Ah, loved me, with that retributive face, . .
I might have been a common woman now
And happier, less known and less left alone,
Perhaps a better woman after all,
With chubby children hanging on my neck
To keep me low and wise. Ah me, the vines
That bear such fruit, are proud to stoop with it.
The palm stands upright in a realm of sand.

---

objection being the loss of individuality that she felt his creed demanded: "I would rather (for *me*) live under the absolutism of Nicholas of Russia than in a Fourier machine, with all my individuality sucked out of me by a social air-pump" (*Letters of EBB* 1.452).

2. A reference to the practice of burning down the stubble in the wheatfield after the completion of the harvest.
3. Cf. EBB to H. F. Chorley, January 7, 1845: "And though I in turn . . . may be turned out 'Arcadia', and told that I am not a poet, still, I should be content, I hope, that the divineness of poetry be proved in my human-ness, rather than lowered to my uses" (*Letters of EBB* 1.232).
4. Aurora is narrating at this point from the perspective she has reached in book 5 when she is 26 or 27 and not from the overall perspective of her maturity as reached in books 8 and 9, when she is 30.

And I, who spoke the truth then, stand upright,
Still worthy of having spoken out the truth,
By being content I spoke it though it set
Him there, me here. - O woman's vile remorse,
To hanker after a mere name, a show,
A supposition, a potential love!
Does every man who names love in our lives,
Become a power for that? is love's true thing
So much best to us, that what personates love
Is next best? A potential love, forsooth!
I'm not so vile. No, no - he cleaves, I think,
This man, this image, - chiefly for the wrong
And shock he gave my life, in finding me
Precisely where the devil of my youth
Had set me, on those mountain-peaks of hope
All glittering with the dawn-dew,[5] all erect
And famished for the noon, - exclaiming, while
I looked for empire and much tribute, 'Come,
I have some worthy work for thee below.
Come, sweep my barns and keep my hospitals,
And I will pay thee with a current coin
Which men give women.'
As we spoke, the grass
Was trod in haste beside us, and my aunt,
With smile distorted by the sun, - face, voice
As much at issue with the summer-day
As if you brought a candle out of doors,
Broke in with, 'Romney, here! - My child, entreat
Your cousin to the house, and have your talk,
If girls must talk upon their birthdays. Come.'

He answered for me calmly, with pale lips
That seemed to motion for a smile in vain.
'The talk is ended - madam, where we stand.
Your brother's daughter has dismissed me here;
And all my answer can be better said
Beneath the trees, than wrong by such a word
Your house's hospitalities. Farewell.'

With that he vanished. I could hear his heel
Ring bluntly in the lane, as down he leapt
The short way from us. - Then a measured speech
Withdrew me. 'What means this, Aurora Leigh?
My brother's daughter has dismissed my guests?'
The lion in me felt the keeper's voice

5. Possibly a reference to Psalms 110.3 ("thou has the dew of thy youth") and certainly a play on the name Aurora ("dawn of day").

Through all its quivering dewlaps; I was quelled
Before her, - meekened[6] to the child she knew:
I prayed her pardon, said, 'I had little thought
To give dismissal to a guest of hers,
In letting go a friend of mine who came
To take me into service as a wife, -
No more than that, indeed.'
'No more, no more?
Pray Heaven,' she answered, 'that I was not mad.
I could not mean to tell her to her face
That Romney Leigh had asked me for a wife,
And I refused him?'
'Did he ask?' I said;
'I think he rather stooped to take me up
For certain uses which he found to do
For something called a wife. He never asked.'

'What stuff!' she answered; 'are they queens, these girls?
They must have mantles, stitched with twenty silks,
Spread out upon the ground, before they'll step
One footstep for the noblest lover born'

'But I am born,' I said with firmness, 'I,
To walk another way than his, dear aunt.'

'You walk, you walk! A babe at thirteen months
Will walk as well as you,' she cried in haste,
'Without a steadying finger. Why, you child,
God help you, you are groping in the dark,
For all this sunlight. You suppose, perhaps,
That you, sole offspring of an opulent man,
Are rich and free to choose a way to walk?
You think, and it's a reasonable thought,
That I, beside, being well to do in life,
Will leave my handful in my niece's hand
When death shall paralyse these fingers? Pray,
Pray, child, albeit I know you love me not,
As if you loved me, that I may not die
For when I die and leave you, out you go,
(Unless I make room for you in my grave)
Unhoused, unfed, my dear poor brother's lamb,
(Ah, heaven, - that pains!) - without a right to crop
A single blade of grass beneath these trees,
Or cast a lamb's small shadow on the lawn,
Unfed, unfolded! Ah, my brother, here's

6. To be made, or to become, meek.

The fruit you planted in your foreign loves!-
Ay, there's the fruit he planted! never look
Astonished at me with your mother's eyes,
For it was they who set you where you are,
An undowered orphan.[7] Child, your father's choice
Of that said mother, disinherited
His daughter, his and hers. Men do not think
Of sons and daughters, when they fall in love,
So much more than of sisters; otherwise
He would have paused to ponder what he did,
And shrunk before that clause in the entail
Excluding offspring by a foreign wife,
(The clause set up a hundred years ago
By a Leigh who wedded a French dancing-girl
And had his heart danced over in return);
But this man shrank at nothing, never thought
Of you, Aurora, any more than me -
Your mother must have been a pretty thing,
For all the coarse Italian blacks and browns,
To make a good man, which my brother was,
Unchary of the duties to his house;
But so it fell indeed. Our cousin Vane,
Vane Leigh,[8] the father of this Romney, wrote
Directly on your birth, to Italy,
'I ask your baby daughter for my son[9]
'In whom the entail now merges by the law.
'Betroth her to us out of love, instead
'Of colder reasons, and she shall not lose
'By love or law from henceforth' - so he wrote;
A generous cousin, was my cousin Vane.
Remember how he drew you to his knee
The year you came here, just before he died,
And hollowed out his hands to hold your cheeks,
And wished them redder, - you remember Vane?
And now his son who represents our house
And holds the fiefs and manors in his place,
To whom reverts my pittance when I die,
(Except a few books and a pair of shawls)

7. As a woman, Aurora would not necessarily have been the natural inheritor of her father's rights and titles, but EBB makes the circumstances of Aurora's disinheritance more entire by introducing an extra and particular legal barrier in "that clause in the entail/Excluding offspring by a foreign wife."
8. "Ralph Duncombe" in the first draft; see textual note.
9. In Tennyson's *Maud* (1855) the same thing happens when her father agrees with the father of the speaker-hero that the two children should be betrothed; see *Maud* 19.4. EBB read the poem in 1855 and heard Tennyson read it aloud in October of that year, but her first draft manuscript was completed by then, so she did not derive this circumstance from Tennyson. Rather, it is, for both poems, a generalized fairytale reference useful for its relevance to concepts of duty and patriarchal authority.

The boy is generous like him, and prepared
To carry out his kindest word and thought
To you, Aurora. Yes, a fine young man
Is Romney Leigh; although the sun of youth
Has shone too straight upon his brain, I know,
And fevered him with dreams of doing good
To good-for-nothing people. But a wife
Will put all right, and stroke his temples cool
With healthy touches' . .
I broke in at that.
I could not lift my heavy heart to breathe
Till then, but then I raised it, and it fell
In broken words like these - 'No need to wait.
The dream of doing good to . . me, at least,
Is ended, without waiting for a wife
To cool the fever for him. We've escaped
That danger, - thank Heaven for it.'
'You,' she cried,
'Have got a fever. What, I talk and talk
An hour long to you, - I instruct you how
You cannot eat or drink or stand or sit
Or even die, like any decent wretch
In all this unroofed and unfurnished world,
Without your cousin, - and you still maintain
There's room 'twixt him and you, for flirting fans
And running knots in eyebrows? You must have
A pattern lover sighing on his knee?
You do not count enough, a noble heart
(Above book-patterns) which this very morn
Unclosed itself in two dear fathers' names
To embrace your orphaned life? fie, fie! But stay,
I write a word, and counteract this sin.'

She would have turned to leave me, but I clung.
'O sweet my father's sister, hear my word
Before you write yours. Cousin Vane did well,
And cousin Romney well, - and I well too,
In casting back with all my strength and will
The good they meant me. O my God, my God!
God meant me good, too, when he hindered me
From saying 'yes' this morning. If you write
A word, it shall be 'no.' I say no, no!
I tie up 'no' upon His altar-horns,[1]
Quite out of reach of perjury! At least

1. Projections, resembling horns, at each corner of the altar in the Jewish temple. See Exodus 27.2. The horns were used to bind the sacrifice to the altar (Exodus 38.1–2 and Psalms 118.27). They were also seized by criminals claiming sanctuary (1 Kings 1.50–51 and 2.28).

My soul is not a pauper; I can live
At least my soul's life, without alms from men;
And if it must be in heaven instead of earth,
Let heaven look to it, - I am not afraid.'

She seized my hands with both hers, strained them fast,
And drew her probing and unscrupulous eyes
Right through me, body and heart. 'Yet, foolish Sweet,
You love this man. I've watched you when he came,
And when he went, and when we've talked of him:
I am not old for nothing; I can tell
The weather-signs of love: you love this man.'

Girls blush sometimes because they are alive,
Half wishing they were dead to save the shame.
The sudden blush devours them, neck and brow;
They have drawn too near the fire of life, like gnats,
And flare up bodily, wings and all. What then?
Who's sorry for a gnat . . or girl?
I blushed.
I feel the brand upon my forehead now
Strike hot, sear deep, as guiltless men may feel
The felon's iron,[2] say, and scorn the mark
Of what they are not. Most illogical
Irrational nature of our womanhood,
That blushes one way, feels another way,
And prays, perhaps, another! After all,
We cannot be the equal of the male
Who rules his blood a little.
For although
I blushed indeed, as if I loved the man,
And her incisive smile, accrediting
That treason of false witness in my blush,
Did bow me downward like a swathe of grass
Below its level that struck me, - I attest
The conscious skies and all their daily suns,
I think I loved him not, - nor then, nor since,
Nor ever. Do we love the schoolmaster,
Being busy in the woods? much less, being poor,
The overseer of the parish?[3] Do we keep
Our love to pay our debts with?
White and cold

2. A reference to the medieval practice of branding criminals as a mark, a punishment, and a warning.
3. The office of overseer was created by the 1601 Poor Law Act, for administrative duties connected with the relief of the poor, such as finding work for the able-bodied poor, apprenticing children, and distributing the poor rate. The office was much abused, and the overseer was feared and hated in many districts.

I grew next moment. As my blood recoiled
From that imputed ignominy, I made
My heart great with it. Then, at last, I spoke,
Spoke veritable words but passionate,
Too passionate perhaps . . ground up with sobs
To shapeless endings. She let fall my hands
And took her smile off, in sedate disgust,
As peradventure she had touched a snake, -
A dead snake, mind! - and turning round, replied,
'We'll leave Italian manners, if you please.
I think you had an English father, child,
And ought to find it possible to speak
A quiet 'yes' or 'no,' like English girls,
Without convulsions. In another month
We'll take another answer - no, or yes.'
With that, she left me in the garden-walk.

I had a father! yes, but long ago -
How long it seemed that moment. Oh, how far,
How far and safe, God, dost thou keep thy saints
When once gone from us! We may call against
The lighted windows of thy fair June-heaven
Where all the souls are happy, - and not one,
Not even my father, look from work or play
To ask, 'Who is it that cries after us,
Below there, in the dusk?' Yet formerly
He turned his face upon me quick enough,
If I said 'father.' Now I might cry loud;
The little lark reached higher with his song
Than I with crying. Oh, alone, alone, -
Not troubling any in heaven, nor any on earth,
I stood there in the garden, and looked up
The deaf blue sky that brings the roses out
On such June mornings.
                    You who keep account
Of crisis and transition in this life,
Set down the first time Nature says plain 'no'
To some 'yes' in you, and walks over you
In gorgeous sweeps of scorn. We all begin
By singing with the birds, and running fast
With June-days, hand in hand: but once, for all,
The birds must sing against us, and the sun
Strike down upon us like a friend's sword caught
By an enemy to slay us, while we read
The dear name on the blade which bites at us! -
That's bitter and convincing: after that,
We seldom doubt that something in the large

Smooth order of creation, though no more
Than haply a man's footstep, has gone wrong.
Some tears fell down my cheeks, and then I smiled,
As those smile who have no face in the world
To smile back to them. I had lost a friend
In Romney Leigh; the thing was sure - a friend,
Who had looked at me most gently now and then,
And spoken of my favourite books, 'our books,'
With such a voice! Well, voice and look were now
More utterly shut out from me I felt,
Than even my father's. Romney now was turned
To a benefactor, to a generous man,
Who had tied himself to marry . . me, instead
Of such a woman, with low timorous lids
He lifted with a sudden word one day,
And left, perhaps, for my sake. - Ah, self-tied
By a contract, male Iphigenia bound
At a fatal Aulis for the winds to change,[4]
(But loose him, they'll not change), he well might seem
A little cold and dominant in love!
He had a right to be dogmatical,
This poor, good Romney. Love, to him, was made
A simple law-clause. If I married him,
I should not dare to call my soul my own
Which so he had bought and paid for: every thought
And every heart-beat down there in the bill;
Not one found honestly deductible
From any use that pleased him! He might cut
My body into coins[5] to give away
Among his other paupers; change my sons,
While I stood dumb as Griseld,[6] for black babes
Or piteous foundlings; might unquestioned set
My right hand teaching in the Ragged Schools,[7]
My left hand washing in the Public Baths,[8]

4. Iphigenia, the daughter of Agamemnon, was demanded as a sacrifice by the goddess Diana, who had caused the Greek fleet, headed for Troy, to be becalmed at Aulis. Compare to Ovid, *Metamorphoses* 2.27–34.
5. Possibly a reminiscence of *Julius Caesar* 4.3, 72–73: "By heaven, I had rather coin my heart,/ And drop my blood for drachmas. . . ."
6. See Boccaccio, *Decameron*, tenth day, tenth story, and Chaucer, *The Canterbury Tales*, "The Clerk's Tale." Gualtieri (Walter, in Chaucer), the Marquis of Saluzzo, married Griselda, a girl of humble birth, having obtained from her a promise that she would obey him in all things. The long-suffering Griselda kept her vow, and uttered no word of recrimination, even when Gualtieri had first her daughter, and then her son, taken away and apparently murdered.
7. The first "Ragged School" was opened at Field Lane, Saffron Hill, in 1842. It opened initially three times a week and offered religious instruction and elementary education to those children and adults who cared to attend.
8. The first public baths were opened in Goulston Square, Whitechapel, in 1847.

What time my angel of the Ideal stretched
Both his to me in vain. I could not claim
The poor right of a mouse in a trap, to squeal,
And take so much as pity from myself.

Farewell, good Romney! if I loved you even,
I could but ill afford to let you be
So generous to me. Farewell, friend, since friend
Betwixt us two, forsooth, must be a word
So heavily overladen. And, since help
Must come to me from those who love me not,
Farewell, all helpers - I must help myself,
And am alone from henceforth. - Then I stooped
And lifted the soiled garland from the earth,
And set it on my head as bitterly
As when the Spanish monarch crowned the bones
Of his dead love.[9] So be it. I preserve
That crown still, - in the drawer there! 'twas the first.
The rest are like it; - those Olympian crowns,
We run for, till we lose sight of the sun
In the dust of the racing chariots![1]
After that,
Before the evening fell, I had a note,
Which ran, - 'Aurora, sweet Chaldean, you read
My meaning backward like your eastern books,[2]
While I am from the west, dear. Read me now
A little plainer. Did you hate me quite
But yesterday? I loved you for my part;
I love you. If I spoke untenderly
This morning, my beloved, pardon it;
And comprehend me that I loved you so
I set you on the level of my soul,

9. Alludes to Pedro I of Portugal (1320–67), whom EBB had confused with Pedro the Cruel of Spain (1334–69). While heir to the Portuguese throne Pedro secretly married Inez de Castro, who was murdered at the instigation of Pedro's father, King Alphonse IV, when the union was discovered. Pedro succeeded his father in 1357 and, in 1361, six years after the death of Inez, he had her body exhumed and public honors paid to her remains, as to the queen of Portugal. The story is told in Luiz de Camoes' *Os Lusidas* (1572), canto 3, stanzas 118–35. See textual note, which includes a manuscript reference to "Inez."
1. The crown of wild olive was the traditional prize awarded to the victors in the Olympic games, which were held every four years at Olympia in Elis (the West Peloponnese) from the eighth century BC to the fourth century AD. See also Horace, *Carmina* (Odes) 1, 1.3–6: "some there are whose one delight is to gather Olympic dust upon the racing car, and whom the turning post cleared with glowing wheel and the glorious palm exalt as masters of the earth to the very gods" (Loeb translation).
2. In the Babylonian tradition, the people of Chaldee were renowned for their skills in astrology, magic, and occult learning (see Daniel 2.2). Syriac, or Aramaic, script is read from right to left. In March 1846, EBB wrote to RB that her father could not understand love "any more than he understands Chaldee" (*RB/EBB Letters* 1.514).

And overwashed you with the bitter brine
Of some habitual thoughts. Henceforth, my flower,
Be planted out of reach of any such,
And lean the side you please, with all your leaves!
Write woman's verses and dream woman's dreams;
But let me feel your perfume in my home
To make my sabbath after working-days.
Bloom out your youth beside me - be my wife.'

I wrote in answer - 'We Chaldeans discern
Still farther than we read. I know your heart,
And shut it like the holy book it is,
Reserved for mild-eyed saints to pore upon
Betwixt their prayers at vespers. Well, you're right,
I did not surely hate you yesterday;
And yet I do not love you enough to-day
To wed you, cousin Romney. Take this word,
And let it stop you as a generous man,
From speaking farther. You may tease, indeed,
And blow about my feelings, or my leaves,
And here's my aunt will help you with east winds
And break a stalk, perhaps, tormenting me;
But certain flowers grow near as deep as trees,
And, cousin, you'll not move my root, not you,
With all your confluent storms. Then let me grow
Within my wayside hedge, and pass your way!
This flower has never as much to say to you
As the antique tomb which said to travellers, 'Pause,'
'Siste, viator."[3] Ending thus, I signed.

The next week passed in silence, so the next,
And several after: Romney did not come
Nor my aunt chide me. I lived on and on,
As if my heart were kept beneath a glass,
And everybody stood, all eyes and ears,
To see and hear it tick. I could not sit,
Nor walk nor take a book, nor lay it down,
Nor sew on steadily, nor drop a stitch,
And a sigh with it, but I felt her looks
Still cleaving to me, like the sucking asp
To Cleopatra's breast,[4] persistently
Through the intermittent pantings. Being observed,
When observation is not sympathy,
Is just being tortured. If she said a word,

3. "Pause, traveler"; a popular invocation on tombstones before the story of the deceased; designed to halt the traveler.
4. See *Antony and Cleopatra* 5.2, 309–11.

A 'thank you,' or an 'if it please you, dear,'
She meant a commination,[5] or, at best,
An exorcism against the devildom[6]
Which plainly held me. So with all the house.
Susannah could not stand and twist my hair,
Without such glancing at the looking-glass
To see my face there, that she missed the plait.
And John, - I never sent my plate for soup;
Or did not send it, but the foolish John
Resolved the problem, 'twixt his napkined thumbs,
Of what was signified by taking soup
Or choosing mackerel. Neighbours who dropped in
On morning visits, feeling a joint wrong,
Smiled admonition, sate uneasily,
And talked with measured, emphasised reserve,
Of parish news, like doctors to the sick,
When not called in, - as if, with leave to speak,
They might say something. Nay, the very dog
Would watch me from his sun-patch on the floor,
In alternation with the large black fly
Not yet in reach of snapping. So I lived.

A Roman died so; smeared with honey, teased
By insects, stared to torture by the noon:[7]
And many patient souls 'neath English roofs
Have died like Romans. I, in looking back,
Wish only, now, I had borne the plague of all
With meeker spirits than were rife at Rome.

For, on the sixth week, the dead sea broke up,
Dashed suddenly through beneath the heel of Him
Who stands upon the sea and earth and swears
Time shall be nevermore.[8] The clock struck nine
That morning too, - no lark was out of tune,
The hidden farms among the hills breathed straight
Their smoke toward heaven, the lime-tree scarcely stirred
Beneath the blue weight of the cloudless sky,
Though still the July air came floating through
The woodbine at my window, in and out,
With touches of the out-door country-news
For a bending forehead. There I sate, and wished

5. A threatening of divine punishment or vengeance. In the *Book of Common Prayer*, the "Commination Service," read at the beginning of Lent, consists of a proclamation of God's anger and judgment against sinners.
6. The dominion, rule, or sway of the devil (OED).
7. Cf. Boccaccio, *Decameron*, second day, ninth story, where Ambrogiulo of Piacenza is executed in this manner. Cf. also Shakespeare, *The Winter's Tale* 4.3, 816–25.
8. See Revelation 10.5–6.

That morning-truce of God would last till eve,
Or longer. 'Sleep,' I thought, 'late sleepers, - sleep,
And spare me yet the burden of your eyes.'
Then, suddenly, a single ghastly shriek
Tore upward from the bottom of the house.
Like one who wakens in a grave and shrieks,
The still house seemed to shriek itself alive,
And shudder through its passages and stairs
With slam of doors and clash of bells. - I sprang,
I stood up in the middle of the room,
And there confronted at my chamber-door,
A white face, - shivering, ineffectual lips.

'Come, come,' they tried to utter, and I went:
As if a ghost had drawn me at the point
Of a fiery finger through the uneven dark,
I went with reeling footsteps down the stair,
Nor asked a question.
There she sate, my aunt, -
Bolt upright in the chair beside her bed,
Whose pillow had no dint! she had used no bed
For that night's sleeping, yet slept well. My God,
The dumb derision of that grey, peaked face
Concluded something grave against the sun,
Which filled the chamber with its July burst
When Susan drew the curtains ignorant
Of who sate open-eyed behind her. There
She sate . . it sate . . we said 'she' yesterday . .
And held a letter with unbroken seal
As Susan gave it to her hand last night:
All night she had held it. If its news referred
To duchies or to dunghills, not an inch
She'd budge, 'twas obvious, for such worthless odds:
Nor, though the stars were suns and overburned
Their spheric limitations, swallowing up
Like wax the azure spaces, could they force
Those open eyes to wink once. What last sight
Had left them blank and flat so, - drawing out
The faculty of vision from the roots,
As nothing more, worth seeing, remained behind?

Were those the eyes that watched me, worried me?
That dogged me up and down the hours and days,
A beaten, breathless, miserable soul?
And did I pray, a half-hour back, but so,
To escape the burden of those eyes . . those eyes?
'Sleep late' I said? -

Why now, indeed, they sleep.
God answers sharp and sudden on some prayers,
And thrusts the thing we have prayed for in our face,
A gauntlet with a gift in't. Every wish
Is like a prayer, with God.
I had my wish,
To read and meditate the thing I would,
To fashion all my life upon my thought,
And marry or not marry. Henceforth none
Could disapprove me, vex me, hamper me.
Full ground-room, in this desert newly made,
For Babylon or Balbec,[9] - when the breath,
Now choked with sand, returns for building towns.

The heir came over on the funeral day,
And we two cousins met before the dead,
With two pale faces. Was it death or life
That moved us? When the will was read and done,
The official guests and witnesses withdrawn,
We rose up in a silence almost hard,
And looked at one another. Then I said,
'Farewell, my cousin.'
But he touched, just touched
My hatstrings tied for going, (at the door
The carriage stood to take me) and said low,
His voice a little unsteady through his smile,
'Siste, viator.'
'Is there time,' I asked,
'In these last days of railroads, to stop short
Like Caesar's chariot (weighing half a ton)
On the Appian road[1] for morals?'
'There is time,'
He answered grave, 'for necessary words,
Inclusive, trust me, of no epitaph
On man or act, my cousin. We have read
A will, which gives you all the personal goods
And funded monies[2] of your aunt.'
'I thank
Her memory for it. With three hundred pounds
We buy in England even, clear standing-room
To stand and work in. Only two hours since,
I fancied I was poor.'
'And, cousin, still

9. Both Biblical cities that represent triumphs of early civilization.
1. The construction of this simile suggests that EBB had a particular incident in mind, but the allusion is unidentified.
2. A debt or stock that has been made part of the permanent debt of the state, with the provision for the regular payment of interest at a fixed rate (OED).

You're richer than you fancy. The will says,
*Three hundred pounds, and any other sum*
*Of which the said testatrix dies possessed.*
I say she died possessed of other sums.'

'Dear Romney, need we chronicle the pence?
I'm richer than I thought - that's evident.
Enough so.'
'Listen rather. You've to do
With business and a cousin,' he resumed,
'And both, I fear, need patience. Here's the fact.
The other sum (there *is* another sum,
Unspecified in any will which dates
After possession, yet bequeathed as much
And clearly as those said three hundred pounds)
Is thirty thousand. You will have it paid
When? . . where? My duty troubles you with words.'

He struck the iron when the bar was hot;
No wonder if my eyes sent out some sparks
'Pause there! I thank you. You are delicate.
In glosing[3] gifts; - but I, who share your blood,
Am rather made for giving, like yourself,
Than taking, like your pensioners.[4] Farewell.'

He stopped me with a gesture of calm pride.
'A Leigh,' he said, 'gives largesse and gives love,
But gloses never: if a Leigh could glose,
He would not do it, moreover, to a Leigh,
With blood trained up along nine centuries
To hound and hate a lie from eyes like yours.
And now we'll make the rest as clear; your aunt
Possessed these monies.'
'You will make it clear.
My cousin, as the honour of us both,
Or one of us speaks vainly! that's not I.
My aunt possessed this sum, - inherited
From whom, and when? bring documents, prove dates.'

'Why now indeed you throw your bonnet off
As if you had time left for a logarithm!
The faith's the want. Dear cousin, give me faith,
And you shall walk this road with silken shoes,
As clean as any lady of our house

3. Palliating or extenuating (OED).
4. Romney's dependants.

Supposed the proudest. Oh, I comprehend
The whole position from your point of sight.
I oust you from your father's halls and lands
And make you poor by getting rich - that's law;
Considering which, in common circumstance,
You would not scruple to accept from me
Some compensation, some sufficiency
Of income - that were justice; but, alas,
I love you, - that's mere nature; you reject
My love, - that's nature also; and at once,
You cannot, from a suitor disallowed,
A hand thrown back as mine is, into yours
Receive a doit,[5] a farthing, - not for the world!
That's woman's etiquette, and obviously
Exceeds the claim of nature, law, and right,
Unanswerable to all. I grant, you see,
The case as you conceive it, - leave you room
To sweep your ample skirts of womanhood,
While, standing humbly squeezed against the wall,
I own myself excluded from being just,
Restrained from paying indubitable[6] debts,
Because denied from giving you my soul.
That's my misfortune! - I submit to it
As if, in some more reasonable age,
'Twould not be less inevitable. Enough.
You'll trust me, cousin, as a gentleman,
To keep your honour, as you count it, pure,
Your scruples (just as if I thought them wise)
Safe and inviolate from gifts of mine.'

I answered mild but earnest. 'I believe
In no one's honour which another keeps.
Nor man's nor woman's. As I keep, myself,
My truth and my religion, I depute
No father, though I had one this side death,
Nor brother, though I had twenty, much less you,
Though twice my cousin, and once Romney Leigh,
To keep my honour pure. You face, to-day,
A man who wants instruction, mark me, not
A woman who wants protection. As to a man,
Show manhood, speak out plainly, be precise
With facts and dates. My aunt inherited
This sum, you say -'
'I said she died possessed

5. Small Dutch coin, formerly in use, worth the eighth part of a stiver, or half an English farthing—hence, chiefly in a negative phrase, as the type of a very small or trifling sum (OED).
6. Undoubted.

Of this, dear cousin.'
'Not by heritage.
Thank you: we're getting to the facts at last.
Perhaps she played at commerce with a ship
Which came in heavy with Australian gold?[7]
Or touched a lottery with her finger-end,
Which tumbled on a sudden into her lap
Some old Rhine tower or principality?[8]
Perhaps she had to do with a marine
Sub-transatlantic railroad, which pre-pays
As well as pre-supposes? or perhaps
Some stale ancestral debt was after-paid
By a hundred years, and took her by surprise? -
You shake your head my cousin; I guess ill.'

'You need not guess, Aurora, nor deride;
The truth is not afraid of hurting you.
You'll find no cause, in all your scruples, why
Your aunt should cavil at a deed of gift
'Twixt her and me.'
'I thought so - ah! a gift.'

'You naturally thought so,' he resumed.
'A very natural gift.'
'A gift, a gift!
Her individual life being stranded high
Above all want, approaching opulence,
Too haughty was she to accept a gift
Without some ultimate aim: ah, ah, I see, -
A gift intended plainly for her heirs,
And so accepted . . if accepted . . ah,
Indeed that might be; I am snared perhaps
Just so. But, cousin, shall I pardon you,
If thus you have caught me with a cruel springe?'[9]

He answered gently, 'Need you tremble and pant
Like a netted lioness? is't my fault, mine,
That you're a grand wild creature of the woods

7. Gold was discovered at Lewis Ponds Creek, New South Wales, in February 1851. See E. H. Hargraves, *Australia and its Goldfields* (London, 1855). The discovery attracted much attention in England, especially after April 1852, when the first shiploads of gold arrived from Australia, and many people set out to the colony in the hope of making their fortune.
8. See RB to EBB, February 15, 1846: "Did you ever hear of the plain-speaking of some of the continental lottery-projectors? An estate on the Rhine, for instance, is to be disposed of, and the holder of the lucky ticket will find himself suddenly owner of a mediaeval castle with an unlimited number of dependencies, vineyards, woods, pastures and so forth . . ." *(RB/EBB Letters* 1.466).
9. A noose fastened to an elastic body and drawn close with a sudden spring to catch a bird or other animal; figuratively, any snare or trap.

And hate the stall built for you? Any way,
Though triply netted, need you glare at me?
I do not hold the cords of such a net;
You're free from me, Aurora!'
'Now may God
Deliver me from this strait! This gift of yours
Was tendered . . when? accepted . . when?' I asked.
'A month . . a fortnight since? Six weeks ago
It was not tendered; by a word she dropped
I know it was not tendered nor received.
When was it? bring your dates.'
'What matters when?
A half-hour ere she died, or a half-year,
Secured the gift, maintains the heritage
Inviolable with law. As easy pluck
The golden stars from heaven's embroidered stole
To pin them on the grey side of this earth,
As make you poor again, thank God.'
'Not poor
Nor clean again from henceforth, you thank God?
Well, sir - I ask you - I insist at need, -
Vouchsafe the special date, the special date.'
'The day before her death-day,' he replied,
'The gift was in her hands. We'll find that deed,
And certify that date to you.'
As one
Who has climbed a mountain-height and carried up
His own heart climbing, panting in his throat
With the toil of the ascent, takes breath at last,
Looks back in triumph - so I stood and looked.
'Dear cousin Romney, we have reached the top
Of this steep question, and may rest, I think.
But first, - I pray you pardon, that the shock
And surge of natural feeling and event
Had made me oblivious of acquainting you
That this, this letter, (unread, mark, still sealed)
Was found enfolded in the poor dead hand:
That spirit of hers had gone beyond the address,
Which could not find her though you wrote it clear, -
I know your writing, Romney, - recognise
The open-hearted A, the liberal sweep
Of the G. Now listen, - let us understand:
You will not find that famous deed of gift,
Unless you find it in the letter here,
Which, not being mine, I give you back. - Refuse
To take the letter? well then - you and I,
As writer and as heiress, open it

Together, by your leave.—Exactly so:
The words in which the noble offering's made,
Are nobler still, my cousin; and, I own,
The proudest and most delicate heart alive,
Distracted from the measure of the gift
By such a grace in giving, might accept
Your largesse without thinking any more
Of the burthen of it, than King Solomon
Considered, when he wore his holy ring
Charactered over with the ineffable spell,[1]
How many carats of fine gold made up
Its money-value: so, Leigh gives to Leigh!
Or rather, might have given, observe, - for that's
The point we come to. Here's a proof of gift,
But here's no proof, sir, of acceptancy,
But rather, disproof. Death's black dust, being blown,
Infiltrated through every secret fold
Of this sealed letter by a puff of fate,
Dried up for ever the fresh-written ink,
Annulled the gift, disutilised[2] the grace,
And left these fragments.'
As I spoke, I tore
The paper up and down, and down and up
And crosswise, till it fluttered from my hands,
As forest-leaves, stripped suddenly and rapt
By a whirlwind on Valdarno,[3] drop again,
Drop slow, and strew the melancholy ground
Before the amazèd hills . . . why, so, indeed,
I'm writing like a poet,[4] somewhat large
In the type of the image, and exaggerate
A small thing with a great thing, topping it: -
But then I'm thinking how his eyes looked, his,
With what despondent and surprised reproach!
I think the tears were in them as he looked;
I think the manly mouth just trembled. Then
He broke the silence.
'I may ask, perhaps,
Although no stranger . . only Romney Leigh,
Which means still less . . than Vincent Carrington,

1. Solomon's ring is not mentioned in the Bible, but Rabbinic legend tells of a seal or ring with the name of God engraved on it, given to Solomon by the archangel and by means of which Solomon wielded power over demons. The ring is mentioned in the *Talmud* (Gittin 68a and 68b), but the most circumstantial account of the powers of the ring is to be found in a group of early manuscripts, falsely attributed to the king and called *The Testament of Solomon*.
2. To deprive of utility, render useless.
3. The valley of the river Arno, which flows through Florence.
4. The poet that Aurora is imitating here is Milton. Compare his description of the legion armies of Satan "who lay intrans't/Thick as Autumnal Leaves that strow the Brooks/In Vallombrosa," etc. The image is extended for a lengthy section in Milton, *Paradise Lost*, 1.283–330.

Your plans in going hence, and where you go.
This cannot be a secret.'
'All my life
Is open to you, cousin. I go hence
To London, to the gathering-place of souls,
To live mine straight out, vocally, in books;
Harmoniously for others, if indeed
A woman's soul, like man's, be wide enough
To carry the whole octave[5] (that's to prove)
Or, if I fail, still purely for myself.
Pray God be with me, Romney.'
'Ah, poor child,
Who fight against the mother's 'tiring[6] hand,
And choose the headsman's![7] May God change his world
For your sake, sweet, and make it mild as heaven,
And juster than I have found you.'
But I paused.
'And you, my cousin?' -
'I,' he said, - 'you ask?
You care to ask? Well, girls have curious minds
And fain would know the end of everything,
Of cousins therefore with the rest. For me,
Aurora, I've my work; you know my work;
And, having missed this year some personal hope,
I must beware the rather that I miss
No reasonable duty. While you sing
Your happy pastorals of the meads and trees,
Bethink you that I go to impress and prove
On stifled brains and deafened ears, stunned deaf,
Crushed dull with grief, that nature sings itself,
And needs no mediate poet, lute or voice,
To make it vocal. While you ask of men
Your audience, I may get their leave perhaps
For hungry orphans to say audibly
'We're hungry, see,' - for beaten and bullied wives
To hold their unweaned babies up in sight,
Whom orphanage[8] would better, and for all
To speak and claim their portion . . by no means
Of the soil, . . but of the sweat in tilling it;
Since this is now-a-days turned privilege,
To have only God's curse[9] on us, and not man's.

5. A musical reference. The eight tones of the octave form the basic scale in Western music.
6. That is, attiring, dressing.
7. The executioner's. Romney argues that Aurora's choice of independence means that she is choosing the ministrations of the executioner over the tender preparation for life offered by the nurturing mother.
8. Orphaning; being orphaned.
9. Genesis 3.17–19.

Such work I have for doing, elbow-deep
In social problems, - as you tie your rhymes,
To draw my uses to cohere with needs
And bring the uneven world back to its round,
Or, failing so much, fill up, bridge at least
To smoother issues some abysmal cracks
And feuds of earth, intestine heats have made
To keep men separate, - using sorry shifts
Of hospitals, almshouses, infant schools,
And other practical stuff of partial good
You lovers of the beautiful and whole
Despise by system.'
'*I* despise? The scorn
Is yours, my cousin. Poets become such
Through scorning nothing. You decry them for
The good of beauty sung and taught by them,
While they respect your practical partial good
As being a part of beauty's self. Adieu!
When God helps all the workers for his world,
The singers shall have help of Him, not last.'

He smiled as men smile when they will not speak
Because of something bitter in the thought;
And still I feel his melancholy eyes
Look judgment on me. It is seven years since:[1]
I know not if 'twas pity or 'twas scorn
Has made them so far-reaching: judge it ye
Who have had to do with pity more than love
And scorn than hatred. I am used, since then,
To other ways, from equal men. But so,
Even so, we let go hands, my cousin and I,
And, in between us, rushed the torrent-world
To blanch our faces like divided rocks,
And bar for ever mutual sight and touch
Except through swirl of spray and all that roar.

1. One of the points where EBB makes her time scale clear. Aurora is writing retrospectively here at the age of 27.

# Third Book

'To-day thou girdest up thy loins thyself[1]
And goest where thou wouldest: presently
Others shall gird thee,' said the Lord, 'to go
Where thou would'st not.' He spoke to Peter thus,
To signify the death which he should die[2]
When crucified head downward.[3]
                                        If He spoke
To Peter then, He speaks to us the same;
The word suits many different martyrdoms,
And signifies a multiform of death,
Although we scarcely die apostles, we,
And have mislaid the keys of heaven and earth.[4]

For 'tis not in mere death that men die most,
And, after our first girding of the loins
In youth's fine linen and fair broidery[5]
To run up hill and meet the rising sun,
We are apt to sit tired, patient as a fool,
While others gird us with the violent bands
Of social figments, feints, and formalisms,
Reversing our straight nature, lifting up
Our base needs, keeping down our lofty thoughts,
Head downward on the cross-sticks of the world.
Yet He can pluck us from that shameful cross.
God, set our feet low and our forehead high,
And show us how a man was made to walk!

Leave the lamp, Susan,[6] and go up to bed.
The room does very well; I have to write

1. In the first draft manuscript (now at Wellesley) book 3 opens with a deleted and largely illegible passage about the lark, leading directly into a similar passage, which appears in this text as 3.151–155. When EBB came to transcribe the poem into the fair copy manuscript (now at Harvard), she used some lengthy passages from the original opening of the first draft manuscript as the introduction to book 3. Thus, draft versions of lines 1–21, 25–35, 41–50, 53–57, and 59–101 are to be found on the pages of the first draft manuscript numbered 1–5.
2. See John 21.18–19: "When thou wast young, thou girdest thyself, and walkest whither thou wouldest; but when thou shalt be old, thou shalt stretch forth thy hands and another shalt gird thee, and carry thee whither thou wouldest not. Thus spake he, signifying by what death he should glorify God."
3. The tradition of Peter's upside-down crucifixion (c. 64–65) is of early date. Eusebius of Caesarea (265–340) quotes a statement by Origen (185–254) to the effect that Peter requested that he might suffer in this way. See Eusebius, *Ecclesiastical History*, 3.i.2
4. Peter is traditionally the keyholder for heaven and is often represented carrying a set of keys. This is why he is always the first to greet new arrivals in the kingdom of heaven. See Matthew 16.19.
5. Embroidery.
6. "Agnes" in the first draft manuscript. "Mabel," then "Susan," in the fair copy manuscript. "Susan" is apparently the same maid that served Aurora while she lived with her aunt.

Beyond the stroke of midnight. Get away;
Your steps, for ever buzzing in the room,
Tease me like gnats. Ah, letters![7] throw them down
At once, as I must have them, to be sure,
Whether I bid you never bring me such
At such an hour, or bid you. No excuse;
You choose to bring them, as I choose perhaps
To throw them in the fire. Now get to bed,
And dream, if possible, I am not cross.

Why what a pettish, petty thing I grow, -
A mere, mere woman, a mere flaccid nerve,
A kerchief left out all night in the rain,
Turned soft so, - overtasked and overstrained
And overlived in this close London life!
And yet I should be stronger.
Never burn
Your letters, poor Aurora! for they stare
With red seals[8] from the table, saying each,
'Here's something that you know not.' Out alas,
'Tis scarcely that the world's more good and wise
Or even straighter and more consequent
Since yesterday at this time - yet, again,
If but one angel spoke from Ararat[9]
I should be very sorry not to hear:
So open all the letters! let me read.
Blanche Ord, the writer in the 'Lady's Fan,'[1]
Requests my judgment on . . that, afterwards.
Kate Ward desires the model of my cloak,
And signs, 'Elisha to you.'[2] Pringle Sharpe
Presents his work on 'Social Conduct,' craves
A little money for his pressing debts . .
From me, who scarce have money for my needs;
Art's fiery chariot[3] which we journey in
Being apt to singe our singing-robes[4] to holes

7. In the mid-nineteenth century, mail was delivered at least twice a day—in the morning and in the evening.
8. Sealing wax was the only way of ensuring the privacy of a letter before the introduction of sticky self-sealing envelopes.
9. The mountains of Ararat, where Noah's ark landed after the flood.
1. There was no periodical of this name in the nineteenth century, but it is clearly an ironic reference to such real titles as *The Keepsake* annual or the *Forget-me-Not*, which were aimed at a polite female audience.
2. See 2 Kings 2.1–15. When the prophet Elijah was carried away into heaven, his cloak fell to his disciple Elisha, who thenceforth was invested with the spirit of the prophet. EBB alluded to this story in 1845 when RB wished to lend her a cloak. See *RB/EBB Letters* 1.219, 222.
3. See 2 Kings 2.11. A fiery chariot separated Elijah and Elisha.
4. EBB frequently refers to the poet's "singing-robes" or "singing clothes." See John Milton's *The Reason of Church Government Urged against Prelaty* (1641), introduction to bk. 2: "a Poet in the high region of his fancies with his garland and singing robes about him."

Although you ask me for my cloak, Kate Ward!
Here's Rudgely knows it, - editor and scribe;
He's 'forced to marry where his heart is not,
Because the purse lacks where he lost his heart.'
Ah,—lost it because no one picked it up;
That's really loss, - (and passable impudence.)
My critic Hammond flatters prettily,
And wants another volume like the last.
My critic Belfair wants another book
Entirely different, which will sell, (and live?)
A striking book, yet not a startling book,
The public blames originalities, -
(You must not pump spring-water unawares
Upon a gracious public full of nerves:)
Good things, not subtle, new yet orthodox,
As easy reading as the dog-eared page
That's fingered by said public fifty years,
Since first taught spelling by its grandmother,
And yet a revelation in some sort:
That's hard, my critic Belfair. So - what next?
My critic Stokes objects to abstract thoughts;
'Call a man, John, a woman, Joan,' says he,
'And do not prate so of *humanities:*'
Whereat I call my critic simply, Stokes.
My critic Jobson recommends more mirth
Because a cheerful genius suits the times,
And all true poets laugh unquenchably
Like Shakspeare and the gods.[5] That's very hard.
The gods may laugh, and Shakspeare; Dante[6] smiled
With such a needy heart on two pale lips
We cry, 'Weep rather, Dante.' Poems are
Men, if true poems: and who dares exclaim
At any man's door, 'Here, 'tis understood
The thunder fell last week and killed a wife
And scared a sickly husband - what of that?
Get up, be merry, shout and clap your hands,
Because a cheerful genius suits the times - '?
None says so to the man, and why indeed
Should any to the poem? A ninth seal;
The apocalypse is drawing to a close.[7]
Ha, - this from Vincent Carrington,[8] - 'Dear friend,
I want good counsel. Will you lend me wings

5. See textual notes to lines 86–90 and note to *Aurora Leigh* 1.925.
6. See note to *Aurora Leigh* 2.84–85. Dante was conventionally regarded as the type of the solemn poet.
7. See Revelation 5.1: "And I saw on the right hand of him that sat on the throne a book written within and on the backside, sealed with seven seals."
8. "Gerald Webster" in the first draft manuscript.

To raise me to the subject, in a sketch
I'll bring to-morrow - may I? at eleven?
A poet's only born to turn to use:
So save you! for the world . . and Carrington.'
'(Writ after.) Have you heard of Romney Leigh,
Beyond what's said of him in newspapers,
His phalansteries[9] there, his speeches here,
His pamphlets, pleas, and statements, everywhere?
He dropped *me* long ago, but no one drops
A golden apple[1] - though indeed one day
You hinted that, but jested. Well, at least
You know Lord Howe who sees him . . whom he sees
And *you* see and I hate to see, - for Howe
Stands high upon the brink of theories,
Observes the swimmers and cries 'Very fine,'
But keeps dry linen equally, - unlike
That gallant breaster, Romney. Strange it is,
Such sudden madness seizing a young man
To make earth over again, - while I'm content
To make the pictures. Let me bring the sketch.
A tiptoe Danae,[2] overbold and hot,
Both arms a-flame to meet her wishing Jove
Halfway, and burn him faster down; the face
And breasts upturned and straining, the loose locks
All glowing with the anticipated gold.
Or here's another on the self-same theme.
She lies here - flat upon her prison-floor,
The long hair swathed about her to the heel
Like wet sea-weed. You dimly see her through
The glittering haze of that prodigious rain,
Half blotted out of nature by a love
As heavy as fate. I'll bring you either sketch.
I think, myself, the second indicates
More passion.'
                    Surely. Self is put away,

9. From the French "Phalanstére" (coined by Fourier in the 1840s) and denoting a set of buildings occupied by a "phalanx" or socialist community (see note to *Aurora Leigh* 2.482). Ruskin complained to the Brownings that he could not find "phalanstery" in Johnson's *Dictionary*, and did not know what the word meant (John Ruskin to RB, November 27, 1856, *The Works of John Ruskin*, ed. E. T. Cook and Alexander Wedderburn, [London, 1903–12], 36.247).

1. Possibly an allusion to the golden apples of Hera that were guarded by the nymphs called the Hesperides. Cf. RB to EBB, January 17, 1846: "And am I not grateful to your sisters . . . they do not see me, know me—and must moreover be jealous of you, chary of you, as the daughters of Hesperus, of wonderers and wistful lookers up at the gold apple—yet . . . they are indulgent" (*RB/EBB Letters* 1.397).

2. The daughter of Acrisius of Argos. An oracle foretold that Danae's son would kill her father, and Acrisius, to prevent the fulfilment of the prophecy, imprisoned Danae in a brazen tower or chamber. But Danae was visited by Zeus in the form of a shower of golden rain (Apollodorus, *The Library*, 2.4.1; Ovid, *Metamorphoses* 4.610). Danae conceived Perseus, and the prophecy of the oracle was eventually realized (Apollodorus, *The Library*, 2.4.4).

And calm with abdication. She is Jove,
And no more Danae - greater thus. Perhaps
The painter symbolises unaware
Two states of the recipient artist-soul,
One, forward, personal, wanting reverence,
Because aspiring only. We'll be calm,
And know that, when indeed our Joves come down,
We all turn stiller than we have ever been.[3]

Kind Vincent Carrington. I'll let him come.
He talks of Florence, - and may say a word
Of something as it chanced seven years ago,
A hedgehog in the path, or a lame bird,
In those green country walks, in that good time
When certainly I was so miserable . .
I seem to have missed a blessing ever since.

The music soars within the little lark,
And the lark soars. It is not thus with men.
We do not make our places with our strains, -
Content, while they rise, to remain behind
Alone on earth instead of so in heaven.
No matter; I bear on my broken tale.[4]

When Romney Leigh and I had parted thus,
I took a chamber up three flights of stairs
Not far from being as steep as some larks climb,
And there, in a certain house in Kensington,[5]
Three years I lived and worked. Get leave to work
In this world - 'tis the best you get at all;
For God, in cursing, gives us better gifts
Than men in benediction. God says, 'Sweat
For foreheads,'[6] men say 'crowns,' and so we are crowned,
Ay, gashed by some tormenting circle of steel
Which snaps with a secret spring. Get work, get work;
Be sure 'tis better than what you work to get.

Serene and unafraid of solitude
I worked the short days out, - and watched the sun
On lurid morns or monstrous afternoons

3. Cf. this passage with the introduction to the scenes between Romney and Aurora at the beginning of book 7. See also *Aurora Leigh* 7.1296–311.
4. A clear reference to the interruption of the narrative that has occurred with Aurora's present-tense episode in lines 1–156. Now she resumes her story at the point seven years ago, soon after her twentieth birthday, when she parted from Romney.
5. A district in London that was respectable in the nineteenth century and is still fashionable because of its proximity to Hyde Park and the royal residence of Kensington Palace.
6. Genesis 3.19.

(Like some Druidic idol's fiery brass
With fixed unflickering outline of dead heat,
From which the blood of wretches pent inside[7]
Seems oozing forth to incarnadine[8] the air)
Push out through fog with his dilated disk,
And startle the slant roofs and chimney-pots
With splashes of fierce colour. Or I saw
Fog only, the great tawny weltering fog,
Involve the passive city, strangle it
Alive, and draw it off into the void,
Spires, bridges, streets, and squares, as if a spunge
Had wiped out London,[9] - or as noon and night
Had clapped together and utterly struck out
The intermediate time, undoing themselves
In the act. Your city poets see such things
Not despicable. Mountains of the south,
When drunk and mad with elemental wines
They rend the seamless mist and stand up bare,
Make fewer singers, haply. No one sings,
Descending Sinai: on Parnassus-mount[1]
You take a mule to climb and not a muse
Except in fable and figure: forests chant
Their anthems to themselves, and leave you dumb.
But sit in London at the day's decline,
And view the city perish in the mist
Like Pharaoh's armaments in the deep Red Sea,[2]
The chariots, horsemen, footmen, all the host,
Sucked down and choked to silence - then, surprised
By a sudden sense of vision and of tune,
You feel as conquerors though you did not fight,
And you and Israel's other singing girls,
Ay, Miriam with them,[3] sing the song you choose.

7. Caesar gives an account of the ritual human sacrifice supervised by the Druids, but he describes the huge idol in which the victims were burnt as being made of woven twigs, not brass (*De Bello Gallico* 6.16).
8. To make red, or to make bloody.
9. See Aeschylus, *Agamemnon*, 1326–29: "Alas for human fortune? When prosperous, a mere shadow can overturn it; if calamitous, the dash of a wet sponge blots out the drawing" (Loeb translation). EBB used the metaphor in "Some Account of the Greek Christian Poets" (1842): "the obliterative sponge, we hear of in Aeschylus" (*Poetical Works of EBB*, 523). She also used it in a letter to Mrs. Martin: "I wonder you have not wiped me out with a sponge by this time. . . ." (Kenyon Typescript).
1. See note to *Aurora Leigh* 1.884. The point here is that Moses' experience on Sinai was very serious and his mood on descending, somber; Moses spent forty days and nights on Mount Sinai (Exodus 24.15–18), where God appeared to him. He descended with directions for building the ark of the covenant and the two tables of stone bearing the ten commandments (Exodus 32.15)
2. When the enslaved Israelites fled the kingdom of Egypt they were pursued by Pharaoh's armies to the shores of the Red Sea. There the Lord parted the waves of the Red Sea in order to allow the Israelites to pass safely to the other side. When the army similarly attempted to follow in their path, the waters closed over them and they were drowned. See Exodus 15.19.
3. Exodus 15.20–21. See also *Aurora Leigh* 2.171.

I worked with patience, which means almost power:
I did some excellent things indifferently,
Some bad things excellently. Both were praised,
The latter loudest. And by such a time
That I myself had set them down as sins
Scarce worth the price of sackcloth, week by week
Arrived some letter through the sedulous post,
Like these I've read, and yet dissimilar,
With pretty maiden seals, - initials twined
Of lilies, or a heart marked *Emily*
(Convicting Emily of being all heart);
Or rarer tokens from young bachelors,
Who wrote from college with the same goosequill,
Suppose they had just been plucked of,[4] and a snatch
From Horace, 'Collegisse juvat,'[5] set
Upon the first page. Many a letter, signed
Or unsigned, showing the writers at eighteen
Had lived too long, although a muse should help
Their dawn by holding candles, - compliments
To smile or sigh at. Such could pass with me
No more than coins from Moscow circulate
At Paris: would ten roubles[6] buy a tag
Of ribbon on the boulevard, worth a sou?[7]
I smiled that all this youth should love me, - sighed
That such a love could scarcely raise them up
To love what was more worthy than myself;
Then sighed again, again, less generously,
To think the very love they lavished so,
Proved me inferior.[8] The strong loved me not,
And he . . my cousin Romney . . did not write.
I felt the silent finger of his scorn
Prick every bubble of my frivolous fame
As my breath blew it, and resolve it back
To the air it came from. Oh, I justified
The measure he had taken of my height:
The thing was plain - he was not wrong a line;
I played at art, made thrusts with a toy-sword,

4. They were geese too, i.e., foolish, in Aurora's estimation.
5. Horace, *Carmina* (Odes), 1.1.3–4; "Sunt quos curriculo pulverem Olympicum/collegisse iuvat" ("some there are whose one delight it is to gather Olympic dust upon the racing car"; (Loeb translation). The author goes on to say that while others may desire to succeed in various enterprizes, his only ambition is to be a lyric poet. Cf. also *Aurora Leigh* 2.814 where EBB alludes to the same passage.
6. The currency of Russia.
7. With the franc, one of the denominations of French currency.
8. Cf. EBB to RB, March 20, 1846: "The writer doesn't see anything 'in Browning and Turner,' she confesses . . . only has wide-open eyes of admiration for EBB . . . now isn't it satisfactory to me . . . to be praised by somebody who sees nothing in Shakespeare?—to be found on the level of somebody so flat? Better the bad-word of the Britannia, ten times over! And best, to take no thought of bad or good words. . . ! (*RB/EBB Letters* 1.547).

Amused the lads and maidens.
Came a sigh
Deep, hoarse with resolution, - I would work
To better ends, or play in earnest. 'Heavens,
I think I should be almost popular
If this went on!' - I ripped my verses up,
And found no blood upon the rapier's point;
The heart in them was just an embryo's heart
Which never yet had beat, that it should die;
Just gasps of make-believe galvanic life;[9]
Mere tones, inorganised[1] to any tune.

And yet I felt it in me where it burnt,
Like those hot fire-seeds of creation held
In Jove's clenched palm before the worlds were sown, -[2]
But I - I was not Juno[3] even! my hand
Was shut in weak convulsion, woman's ill,
And when I yearned to loose a finger - lo,
The nerve revolted. 'Tis the same even now:
This hand may never, haply, open large,
Before the spark is quenched, or the palm charred,
To prove the power not else than by the pain.

It burns, it burnt - my whole life burnt with it,
And light, not sunlight and not torchlight, flashed
My steps out through the slow and difficult road.
I had grown distrustful of too forward Springs,
The season's books in drear significance
Of morals, dropping round me. Lively books?
The ash has livelier verdure than the yew;
And yet the yew's green longer, and alone
Found worthy of the holy Christmas time:
We'll plant more yews if possible, albeit
We plant the graveyard[4] with them.
Day and night

9. Animal electricity; from *De viribus electricitatis in motu musculari commentarius* (1791). Electricity applied to a corpse stimulates the nerves and produces an appearance of life. Carlyle also calls apparent, or spurious animation, "galvanic life." See *Sartor Resartus*, bk. 3, ch. 5, "The Phoenix," and *Past and Present*, bk. 2, ch. 15.
1. Not ordered, not organized.
2. Compare RB's essay on Shelley: "Not what man sees, but what God sees—the Ideas of Plato, seeds of creation lying burningly on the Divine Hand—it is toward these that he [the subjective poet] struggles" (*Letters of Percy Bysshe Shelley with an introductory essay by Robert Browning* [London, 1852], 7.)
3. The wife of Jove and the queen of the gods. Juno is her Roman name as Jupiter or Jove is the Roman form. They are called Zeus and Hera in their Greek manifestation.
4. Yews are traditionally grown in the graveyards of Europe. Some explanations for this are mystic and concern the supposed magic properties of the tree; others are practical and concern their use in making bows when the people of the village would, in emergency, retreat to the sanctuary of the church.

I worked my rhythmic thought, and furrowed up
Both watch and slumber with long lines of life
Which did not suit their season. The rose fell
From either cheek, my eyes globed luminous
Through orbits of blue shadow, and my pulse
Would shudder along the purple-veined wrist
Like a shot bird. Youth's stern, set face to face
With youth's ideal: and when people came
And said, 'You work too much, you are looking ill,'[5]
I smiled for pity of them who pitied me,
And thought I should be better soon perhaps
For those ill looks. Observe - 'I,' means in youth
Just *I*, the conscious and eternal soul
With all its ends, and not the outside life,
The parcel-man, the doublet of the flesh,[6]
The so much liver, lung, integument,
Which make the sum of 'I' hereafter when
World-talkers talk of doing well or ill.
*I* prosper if I gain a step, although
A nail then pierced my foot: although my brain
Embracing any truth froze paralysed,
*I* prosper: I but change my instrument;
I break the spade off, digging deep for gold,
And catch the mattock up.
I worked on, on.
Through all the bristling fence of nights and days
Which hedges time in from the eternities,
I struggled, - never stopped to note the stakes
Which hurt me in my course. The midnight oil
Would stink sometimes; there came some vulgar needs:
I had to live that therefore I might work,
And, being but poor, I was constrained, for life,
To work with one hand for the booksellers
While working with the other for myself
And art: you swim with feet as well as hands,
Or make small way. I apprehended this, -
In England no one lives by verse that lives;
And, apprehending, I resolved by prose
To make a space to sphere my living verse.
I wrote for cyclopaedias, magazines,
And weekly papers, holding up my name

5. EBB may be recalling her own experience of strenuous study during the long years of illness in her adolescence. Her doctors and her family were always quick to attribute her weakness to her intensive application, but illness and study served its purpose in allowing her private time and inviolable regimentation of the otherwise extensive demands of family and social life.
6. Doublet is used for its simple meaning of "clothing," but also for its suggestion of "double to" the flesh.

To keep it from the mud. I learnt the use
Of the editorial 'we' in a review
As courtly ladies the fine trick of trains,
And swept it grandly through the open doors
As if one could not pass through doors at all
Save so encumbered. I wrote tales beside,
Carved many an article on cherry-stones
To suit light readers, - something in the lines
Revealing, it was said, the mallet-hand,[7]
But that, I'll never vouch for: what you do
For bread, will taste of common grain, not grapes,
Although you have a vineyard in Champagne;
Much less in Nephelococcygia[8]
As mine was, peradventure.
Having bread
For just so many days, just breathing room
For body and verse, I stood up straight and worked
My veritable work. And as the soul
Which grows within a child makes the child grow, -
Or as the fiery sap, the touch from God,
Careering through a tree, dilates the bark
And roughs with scale and knob, before it strikes
The summer foliage out in a green flame -
So life, in deepening with me, deepened all
The course I took, the work I did. Indeed
The academic law convinced of sin;
The critics cried out on the falling off,
Regretting the first manner. But I felt
My heart's life throbbing in my verse to show
It lived, it also - certes incomplete,
Disordered with all Adam in the blood,[9]
But even its very tumours, warts and wens
Still organised by and implying life.

A lady called upon me on such a day.
She had the low voice of your English dames,
Unused, it seems, to need rise half a note
To catch attention, - and their quiet mood,
As if they lived too high above the earth
For that to put them out in anything:
So gentle, because verily so proud;
So wary and afraid of hurting you,

7. The hand of the sculptor who works in stone with a mallet.
8. "Cloud-cuckoo-land," the city in the clouds in Aristophanes' comedy *The Birds*.
9. Not true and pure, because the sin of Adam, the original sin of disobedience, means that each individual must find his or her own way to salvation.

By no means that you are not really vile,
But that they would not touch you with their foot
To push you to your place; so self-possessed
Yet gracious and conciliating, it takes
An effort in their presence to speak truth:
You know the sort of woman, - brilliant stuff,
And out of nature. 'Lady Waldemar.'
She said her name quite simply, as if it meant
Not much indeed, but something, - took my hands,
And smiled as if her smile could help my case,
And dropped her eyes on me and let them melt.
'Is this,' she said, 'the Muse?'[1]
'No sybil[2] even,'
I answered, 'since she fails to guess the cause
Which taxed you with this visit, madam.'
'Good,'
She said, 'I value what's sincere at once.
Perhaps if I had found a literal Muse,
The visit might have taxed me. As it is,
You wear your blue so chiefly in your eyes,
My fair Aurora, in a frank good way,
It comforts me entirely for your fame,
As well as for the trouble of ascent
To this Olympus.'[3]
There, a silver laugh
Ran rippling through her quickened little breaths
The steep stair somewhat justified.
'But still
Your ladyship has left me curious why
You dared the risk of finding the said Muse?'

'Ah, - keep me, notwithstanding, to the point,
Like any pedant? Is the blue in eyes
As awful as in stockings after all,[4]
I wonder, that you'd have my business out
Before I breathe - exact the epic plunge
In spite of gasps? Well, naturally you think
I've come here, as the lion-hunters go
To deserts, to secure you with a trap

1. The writer of poetry.
2. A wise woman and oracle of the future.
3. Lady Waldemar's joke about the height of Aurora's apartment is based on a reference to Mount Olympus, the home of the gods in ancient Greek mythology.
4. Another one of Lady Waldemar's complicated and affected jokes. Aurora has blue eyes, but she also has a reputation as a "bluestocking," that is, an intellectual woman. The wearing of blue stockings was adopted by Benjamin Stillingfleet, who attended the salon of educated ladies at the houses of Mrs. Montague, Mrs. Vesey, and Mrs. Ord in about 1750.

For exhibition in my drawing-rooms
On zoologic soirées?[5] not in the least.
Roar softly at me; I am frivolous,
I dare say; I have played at wild-beast shows
Like other women of my class, - but now
I meet my lion simply as Androcles[6]
Met his . . when at his mercy.'
So, she bent
Her head, as queens may mock, - then lifting up
Her eyelids with a real grave queenly look,
Which ruled and would not spare, not even herself, -
'I think you have a cousin: - Romney Leigh.'[7]

'You bring a word from *him?*' - my eyes leapt up
To the very height of hers, - 'a word from *him?*'

'I bring a word about him, actually.
But first,' (she pressed me with her urgent eyes)
'You do not love him, - you?'
'You're frank at least
In putting questions, madam,' I replied;
'I love my cousin cousinly - no more.'

'I guessed as much. I'm ready to be frank
In answering also, if you'll question me,
Or even for something less. You stand outside,
You artist women, of the common sex;
You share not with us, and exceed us so
Perhaps by what you're mulcted[8] in, your hearts
Being starved to make your heads: so run the old
Traditions of you. I can therefore speak
Without the natural shame which creatures feel
When speaking on their level, to their like.
There's many a papist[9] she, would rather die

5. Compare EBB's own experience with a literary "lionhunter," when a Mrs. Paine from Farnham came to see her: "with the sort of face which a child might take to see a real, alive lioness in the Zoological Gardens . . . she just sat down on a chair, & stared" (April 3, 1846, *RB/EBB Letters* 2.586). To describe a celebrity as a "lion" was common parlance in the nineteenth century.
6. One day in the forest Androcles met a lion that was wounded by a thorn in its foot. Androcles removed the thorn and allowed the lion to depart. As an outlawed Christian, Androcles was later arrested and taken to Rome where, along with other Christians, he was thrown to the lions in the arena of the Coliseum. But one of the lions was that once rescued by Androcles, and the beast, much to the amazement of the onlookers, fawned on him and was tame. The story of Androcles and the lion is to be found in Aulus Gellius' *Attic Nights* 5.14 and Aelian's *On the Characteristics of Animals* 7.48. It is also one of Aesop's *Fables*. Aulus Gellius records that Androcles, on reencountering the lion but not recognizing the animal, was, at first, terrified by its approach.
7. "Walter Vane" throughout this passage in the first draft manuscript.
8. Punished by a fine, deprived or divested of something (OED).
9. Roman Catholic.

Than own to her maid she put a ribbon on
To catch the indifferent eye of such a man,
Who yet would count adulteries on her beads
At holy Mary's shrine and never blush;
Because the saints are so far off, we lose
All modesty before them. Thus, to-day.
'Tis *I*, love Romney Leigh.'
'Forbear,' I cried.
'If here's no Muse, still less is any saint;
Nor even a friend, that Lady Waldemar
Should make confessions' . .
'That's unkindly said.
If no friend, what forbids to make a friend
To join to our confession ere we have done?
I love your cousin. If it seems unwise
To say so, it's still foolisher (we're frank)
To feel so. My first husband left me young,
And pretty enough, so please you, and rich enough,
To keep my booth in May-fair[1] with the rest
To happy issues. There are marquises
Would serve seven years to call me wife,[2] I know,
And, after seven, I might consider it,
For there's some comfort in a marquisate
When all's said, - yes, but after the seven years;
I, now, love Romney. You put up your lip,
So like a Leigh! so like him! - Pardon me,
I'm well aware I do not derogate[3]
In loving Romney Leigh. The name is good,
The means are excellent, but the man, the man -
Heaven help us both, - I am near as mad as he,
In loving such an one.'
She slowly swung
Her heavy ringlets till they touched her smile,
As reasonably sorry for herself,
And thus continued.
'Of a truth, Miss Leigh,
I have not, without struggle, come to this.
I took a master in the German tongue,
I gamed a little, went to Paris twice;
But, after all, this love! . . . you eat of love,
And do as vile a thing as if you ate
Of garlic - which, whatever else you eat,

1. A fashionable and expensive district in London. The allusion to the "booth" in Mayfair is yet another of Lady Waldemar's extravagant plays with words, pivoting here on the idea of the fair.
2. Genesis 29.18–20. Jacob served Laban for seven years in order to earn his daughter as a wife. Laban then gave Jacob his elder daughter Leah, so that Jacob had to work for another seven years to earn Rachel, whom he really wanted.
3. Condescend.

Tastes uniformly acrid, till your peach
Reminds you of your onion. Am I coarse?
Well, love's coarse, nature's coarse - ah, there's the rub!
We fair fine ladies, who park out our lives
From common sheep-paths, cannot help the crows
From flying over, - we're as natural still
As Blowsalinda.[4] Drape us perfectly
In Lyons' velvet,[5] - we are not, for that,
Lay-figures, look you: we have hearts within,
Warm, live, improvident, indecent hearts,
As ready for outrageous ends and acts
As any distressed sempstress[6] of them all
That Romney groans and toils for. We catch love
And other fevers, in the vulgar way:
Love will not be outwitted by our wit,
Nor outrun by our equipages: -[7] mine
Persisted, spite of efforts. All my cards
Turned up but Romney Leigh; my German stopped
At germane Wertherism;[8] my Paris rounds
Returned me from the Champs Elysées just
A ghost, and sighing like Dido's.[9] I came home
Uncured, - convicted rather to myself
Of being in love . . . in love! That's coarse you'll say
I'm talking garlic.'

Coldly I replied.
'Apologise for atheism, not love!
For me, I do believe in love, and God.
I know my cousin: Lady Waldemar
I know not: yet I say as much as this;
Whoever loves him, let her not excuse
But cleanse herself, that, loving such a man,

4. Shepherdess in John Gay's *Shepherd's Week* (1714), a series of six pastorals in which the characters are portrayed with grotesque realism.
5. In the nineteenth century, Lyons was a major center of silk manufacture. Mechlin (see textual note) is a fine lace made at the town of Mechlin in Belgium.
6. The plight of Victorian seamstresses was notorious. They were very poorly paid, and the trade was much oversupplied with workwomen, while few other opportunities of employment for women were available. Many of their number took to prostitution to supplement their income; so much so that simply to be a seamstress was enough to compromise a woman's virtue in the eyes of some.
7. The equipment for stylish traveling, horses, carriage, footmen, coachmen.
8. From Goethe's *Die Leiden des jungen Werther* (1774). See Carlyle's essay "Goethe" (1828) for an influential account of the significance and popularity of the work. "*Werter*, infusing itself into the core and whole spirit of Literature, gave birth to a race of Sentimentalists, who have raged and wailed in every part of the world" (*Works of Thomas Carlyle* 2.165). In *Alton Locke* (1850), ch. 9, Charles Kingsley refers to "that peculiar melancholy of intellectual youth, which Mr. Carlyle has christened for ever by one of his immortal nicknames—'Wertherism.' "
9. Virgil, *Aeneid*, 6.450–76. Aeneas, visiting the underworld with the Sibyl, met the shade of Dido, the Phoenician queen whom he had unwillingly deserted and who had subsequently committed suicide. Although this encounter takes place in the Lugentes campi (fields of mourning), Lady Waldemar intends a pun on Champs Elysées, for the virtuous dead inhabit the Elysian Fields. The Champs Elysées is the principal street in the center of Paris.

She may not do it with such unworthy love
He cannot stoop and take it.'
                    'That is said
Austerely, like a youthful prophetess,
Who knits her brows across her pretty eyes
To keep them back from following the grey flight
Of doves between the temple-columns.[1] Dear,
Be kinder with me; let us two be friends.
I'm a mere woman, - the more weak perhaps
Through being so proud; you're better; as for him,
He's best. Indeed he builds his goodness up
So high, it topples down to the other side
And makes a sort of badness; there's the worst
I have to say against your cousin's best!
And so be mild, Aurora, with my worst,
For his sake, if not mine.'
                    'I own myself
Incredulous of confidence like this
Availing him or you.'
                    'And I, myself,
Of being worthy of him with any love:
In your sense I am not so - let it pass.
And yet I save him if I marry him;
Let that pass too.'
                    'Pass, pass! we play police
Upon my cousin's life, to indicate
What may or may not pass?' I cried. 'He knows
What's worthy of him; the choice remains with *him*;
And what he chooses, act or wife, I think
I shall not call unworthy, I, for one.'
' 'Tis somewhat rashly said,' she answered slow;
'Now let's talk reason, though we talk of love.
Your cousin Romney Leigh's a monster; there,
The word's out fairly, let me prove the fact.
We'll take, say, that most perfect of antiques
They call the Genius of the Vatican,[2]
(Which seems too beauteous to endure itself
In this mixed world,) and fasten it for once

1. In ancient Greece the priestess who served her particular god or goddess in the temple might use various methods of supernatural divination to see into the future. One such method was the release and observation of a flock of doves.
2. Also known as the contemplative Amor, the Eros of Centocelle, or Thanatos. The statue, which was thought to be a copy of a work by Praxiteles, stood during the 1850s in the Gallery of Statues at the Vatican Museum. In *The Ruins and Museums of Rome*—a copy of which work was sent to EBB (see *Letters of EBB* 2.195)—Emil Braun gives a lengthy description of the statue that accords with EBB's allusion, for he speaks of "sublime enthusiasm," "gentle and tender melancholy," and a "mild, serious expression which displays that peculiar melting of the soul, usually the result of the more deep and serious emotions of love" (*The Ruins and Museums of Rome* [Brunswick, 1854], 202–3).

Upon the torso of the Dancing Fawn,
(Who might limp surely, if he did not dance,)
Instead of Buonarroti's mask:[3] what then?
We show the sort of monster Romney is,
With god-like virtues and heroic aims
Subjoined to limping possibilities
Of mismade human nature. Grant the man
Twice godlike, twice heroic, - still he limps,
And here's the point we come to.'
'Pardon me,
But, Lady Waldemar, the point's the thing
We never come to.'
'Caustic, insolent
At need! I like you' - (there, she took my hands)
'And now my lioness, help Androcles,
For all your roaring. Help me! for myself
I would not say so - but for him. He limps
So certainly, he'll fall into the pit
A week hence, - so I lose him - so he is lost!
For when he's fairly married, he a Leigh,
To a girl of doubtful life, undoubtful birth,
Starved out in London till her coarse-grained hands
Are whiter than her morals, - even you
May call his choice unworthy.'
'Married! lost!
He, . . . Romney!'
'Ah, you're moved at last,' she said.
'These monsters, set out in the open sun,
Of course throw monstrous shadows: those who think
Awry, will scarce act straightly. Who but he?
And who but you can wonder? He has been mad,
The whole world knows, since first, a nominal man,
He soured the proctors, tried the gownsmen's[4] wits,
With equal scorn of triangles and wine,[5]
And took no honours,[6] yet was honourable.

3. The statue of the Dancing Faun is (and was, in the mid-nineteenth century) housed in the Tribune of the Uffizi Gallery in Florence, which EBB visited soon after the Brownings' arrival in Florence in 1847 (see *Letters of EBB* 1.326, 331). The faun is represented as playing simultaneously the "crotala" (an instrument similar to cymbals) and the "scabellum" or "croupezion" under his right foot. The position of the latter instrument can be imagined as giving the figure the appearance of limping. The faun was popularly supposed to have been restored by Michelangelo, who was thought to have sculpted the arms and the head of the figure (see *Murray's Handbook for Travellers in Northern Italy* [1852], 520), hence EBB's allusion to "Buonarroti's mask." Buonarroti was Michelangelo's surname.
4. The students and scholars at the university; that is, those who wore the formal university dress of cap and gown; the official university police, still called Proctors, at Oxford.
5. The usual subjects of conversation at the colleges of the university, mathematics and vintage wine. Romney did not involve himself in either the studious life of the scholarly community or the social and pastoral life of the college.
6. Did not take a degree.

They'll tell you he lost count of Homer's ships[7]
In Melbourne's poor-bills, Ashley's factory bills,[8] -
Ignored the Aspasia[9] we all dare to praise,
For other women, dear, we could not name
Because we're decent.[1] Well, he had some right
On his side probably; men always have,
Who go absurdly wrong. The living boor
Who brews your ale, exceeds in vital worth
Dead Caesar who 'stops bungholes'[2] in the cask;
And also, to do good is excellent,
For persons of his income, even to boors:
I sympathise with all such things. But he
Went mad upon them . . madder and more mad
From college times to these, - as, going down hill,
The faster still, the farther. You must know
Your Leigh by heart: he has sown his black young curls
With bleaching cares of half a million men
Already. If you do not starve, or sin,
You're nothing to him: pay the income-tax[3]
And break your heart upon't, he'll scarce be touched;
But come upon the parish,[4] qualified
For the parish stocks, and Romney will be there
To call you brother, sister, or perhaps
A tenderer name still. Had I any chance
With Mister Leigh, who am Lady Waldemar
And never committed felony?'
'You speak
Too bitterly,' I said, 'for the literal truth.

7. See *Iliad* 2.493–760. Homer catalogues details of the 1,186 Greek ships that set out for Troy.
8. Antony Ashley Cooper, seventh earl of Shaftesbury (1801–85). From 1833 to 1846 Ashley supported many bills in the House of Commons designed to ameliorate working conditions in factories and mines. Two major acts were passed in 1833 and 1844 that limited the employment of children and women, prohibited night work, and established an inspectorate. Ashley also strove with successive amendments and failed bills to establish a ten-hour working day for all factory workers (see note to line 601); William Lamb, second viscount Melbourne (1779–1848). In 1832, while Melbourne was home secretary in Lord Grey's cabinet, a commission was appointed to inquire into the operation of the laws for the relief of the poor. The measures suggested in their report were implemented in the Poor Law Amendment Act of 1834. It was intended that this act should relieve the crippling burden on the parishes by ending outdoor relief and sending all paupers to the workhouse. Moreover, in order to encourage paupers to seek diligently for work in the free market, conditions in the workhouse were designed to be as uncongenial as possible.
9. Aspasia of Miletus (fl. fifth century BC), mistress of Pericles. Her intellect and political influence with Pericles earned her a prominent place in Athenian society. See Plutarch, *Lives*, "Pericles," 24.
1. Women of loose morals who are not to be noticed in polite society because they do not have the support of an eminent man.
2. See *Hamlet* 5.1, 196–207.
3. Direct taxation on income had been introduced in Great Britain as an emergency measure to raise funds for the French Revolutionary and Napoleonic Wars but was abolished in 1816. In 1842, Peel reintroduced income tax at 7 pence on the pound in order to facilitate financial reform.
4. Claim poor relief.

'The truth is bitter. Here's a man who looks
For ever on the ground! you must be low,
Or else a pictured ceiling overhead,
Good painting thrown away. For me, I've done
What women may, we're somewhat limited,
We modest women, but I've done my best.
- How men are perjured when they swear our eyes
Have meaning in them! they're just blue or brown,
They just can drop their lids a little. And yet
Mine did more, for I read half Fourier[5] through,
Proudhon, Considerant, and Louis Blanc,[6]
With various others of his socialists,
And, if I had been a fathom less in love,
Had cured myself with gaping. As it was,
I quoted from them prettily enough
Perhaps, to make them sound half rational
To a saner man than he whene'er we talked,
(For which I dodged occasion) - learnt by heart
His speeches in the Commons[7] and elsewhere
Upon the social question; heaped reports
Of wicked women and penitentiaries
On all my tables, (with a place for Sue)[8]
And gave my name to swell subscription-lists[9]
Toward keeping up the sun at nights in heaven,

5. See note to *Aurora Leigh* 2.483.
6. Jean Joseph Charles Louis Blanc (1811–82). Like Fourier, Louis Blanc advocated the establishment of community workshops regulated by the workers. His *L'Organisation du travail* was published in 1839. Victor-Prosper Considérant (1808–93). After the death of Fourier in 1837, Considérant became the acknowledged leader of the Fourierist movement and took charge of its journal, *La phalange*. His *Destinée sociale* was published in 1834–38. Pierre-Joseph Proudhon (1809–65), libertarian socialist, whose most influential works were *Qu'est-ce que la proprieté* (1840) and *Systéme des contradictions economiques ou philosophie de la misére* (1846). Unlike the other authors on Lady Waldemar's list, Proudhon did not subscribe to systems of Utopian socialism but believed in the free development of the individual.
7. The British Parliament is made up of two houses, the Lords and the Commons. Seats in the Lords are held by right of heritage (or, later, appointment), but most of the work is done in the House of Commons, whose seats are held by election. After the reforming bills of 1832, the procedure at the House of Commons began to resemble the processes of modern democracy. The basic instrument of this process, and the one copied by most parliaments in the modern age, is the concept of individual speeches given in public both on issues of personal interest and according to party lines.
8. Joseph Marie Eugene Sue (1804–57), author of sensationalist novels including *Mathilde* (1841), *Mystéres de Paris* (1842–43), and *Le juif errant* (1844–45). Sue's reputation as a social critic earns him a place on Lady Waldemar's table. The misfortunes of Fleur de Marie in *Mystéres de Paris,* which EBB read in 1851 (*Letters of EBB* 2.31), may have provided a source for the circumstances of Marian's sufferings in *Aurora Leigh*. See textual note on allusion to French historian Jules Michelet (1798–1874). Appointed to a chair in history at the Collége de France, Michelet gave a series of lectures that expounded his socialist and antisacerdotal views. These were published in 1845 as *Du Prêtre, de la femme, de la famille* and translated into English in the same year.
9. Much charity fundraising in the nineteenth century was effected by raising money through public subscription where individuals undertook to pay money into the fund for a named cause.

And other possible ends. All things I did,
Except the impossible . . such as wearing gowns
Provided by the Ten Hours' movement:[1] there,
I stopped - we must stop somewhere. He, meanwhile,
Unmoved as the Indian tortoise 'neath the world,[2]
Let all that noise go on upon his back:
He would not disconcert or throw me out,
'Twas well to see a woman of my class
With such a dawn of conscience. For the heart,
Made firewood for his sake, and flaming up
To his face, - he merely warmed his feet at it:
Just deigned to let my carriage stop him short
In park or street, - he leaning on the door
With news of the committee which sate last
On pickpockets at suck.'

'You jest - you jest.'

'As martyrs jest, dear, (if you read their lives)[3]
Upon the axe which kills them. When all's done
By me, . . for him - you'll ask him presently
The colour of my hair - he cannot tell,
Or answers 'dark' at random; while, be sure,
He's absolute on the figure, five or ten,
Of my last subscription. Is it bearable,
And I a woman?'
'Is it reparable,
Though *I* were a man?'
'I know not. That's to prove.
But first, this shameful marriage?'
'Ay?' I cried,
'Then really there's a marriage?'
'Yesterday
I held him fast upon it. 'Mister Leigh,'

1. As early as 1831, legislation was called for to limit the working day to ten hours of daylight. During debates on the factory bills, Lord Ashley tried repeatedly to introduce the principle of a ten-hour working day and his efforts were at length rewarded in 1847 with the passing of the Factory Act, which restricted the working day for women and young persons to ten hours falling between 6 a.m. and 6 p.m. (Ashley had at this time resigned his seat and the bill was seen through by John Fielden.) However, the legislation did not extend to children, or to men, and unscrupulous mill owners continued to keep men at work through the night, assisted by relays of children. An amending act was eventually passed in 1853, which extended the 1847 act to regulate the employment of children, and this effectively secured a ten-and-a-half-hour day for all factory workers.
Presumably Lady Waldemar would not wear gowns provided by the Ten Hours' movement because they would prove insufficiently fashionable.
2. According to Indian mythology, the world is supported on the shell of a giant tortoise.
3. Lady Waldemar is apparently referring to John Foxe's account of the lives of the primitive and protestant martyrs, *Rerum in ecclesia gestarum* . . . (Strasberg, 1559), popularly known as *Foxe's Book of Martyrs*.

Said I, 'shut up a thing, it makes more noise.
'The boiling town keeps secrets ill; I've known
'Yours since last week. Forgive my knowledge so:
'You feel I'm not the woman of the world
'The world thinks; you have borne with me before,
'And used me in your noble work, our work,
'And now you shall not cast me off because
'You're at the difficult point, the *join*. 'Tis true
'Even I can scarce admit the cogency
'Of such a marriage . . where you do not love,
'(Except the class) yet marry and throw your name
'Down to the gutter, for a fire-escape
'To future generations! 'tis sublime,
'A great example, a true Genesis
'Of the opening social era. But take heed,
'This virtuous act must have a patent weight,
'Or loses half its virtue. Make it tell,
'Interpret it, and set it in the light,
'And do not muffle it in a winter-cloak
'As a vulgar bit of shame, - as if, at best,
'A Leigh had made a misalliance and blushed
'A Howard[4] should know it.' Then, I pressed him more:
'He would not choose,' I said, 'that even his kin, . .
'Aurora Leigh, even . . should conceive his act
'Less sacrifice, more fantasy.' At which
He grew so pale, dear, . . to the lips, I knew
I had touched him. 'Do you know her,' he inquired,
'My cousin Aurora?' 'Yes,' I said, and lied,
(But truly we all know you by your books)
And so I offered to come straight to you,
Explain the subject, justify the cause,
And take you with me to St. Margaret's Court[5]
To see this miracle, this Marian Erle,[6]
This drover's daughter (she's not pretty, he swears)
Upon whose finger, exquisitely pricked
By a hundred needles, we're to hang the tie
'Twixt class and class in England, - thus indeed
By such a presence, yours and mine, to lift
The match up from the doubtful place. At once
He thanked me sighing, murmured to himself
'She'll do it perhaps, she's noble.' - thanked me twice,

4. The ancient family name of the duke of Norfolk, first duke of the realm, and hereditary earl marshal of England.
5. The precise address cannot be identified, but EBB might have placed St. Margaret's Court notionally in the parish of St. Margaret's, Westminster, which was the site of one of London's most notorious slums.
6. "Mabel Gray" in the first draft manuscript.

And promised, as my guerdon,[7] to put off
His marriage for a month.'
I answered then.
'I understand your drift imperfectly.
You wish to lead me to my cousin's betrothed,
To touch her hand if worthy, and hold her hand
If feeble, thus to justify his match.
So be it then. But how this serves your ends,
And how the strange confession of your love
Serves this, I have to learn - I cannot see.'

She knit her restless forehead. 'Then, despite,
Aurora, that most radiant morning name,[8]
You're dull as any London afternoon.
I wanted time, and gained it, - wanted *you*,
And gain you! you will come and see the girl
In whose most prodigal eyes the lineal pearl
And pride of all your lofty race of Leighs
Is destined to solution.[9] Authorised
By sight and knowledge, then, you'll speak your mind,
And prove to Romney, in your brilliant way,
He'll wrong the people and posterity,
(Say such a thing is bad for me and you,
And you fail utterly,) by concluding thus
An execrable marriage. Break it up,
Disroot it - peradventure presently
We'll plant a better fortune in its place.
Be good to me, Aurora, scorn me less
For saying the thing I should not. Well I know
I should not. I have kept, as others have,
The iron rule of womanly reserve
In lip and life, till now: I wept a week
Before I came here.' - Ending, she was pale;
The last words, haughtily said, were tremulous.
This palfrey pranced in harness, arched her neck,
And, only by the foam upon the bit,
You saw she champed against it.
Then I rose.
'I love love: truth's no cleaner thing than love.
I comprehend a love so fiery hot,
It burns its natural veil of august shame,
And stands sublimely in the nude, as chaste

7. Reward.
8. Aurora is the goddess of the dawn.
9. Cleopatra, in contest with Antony to provide the most extravagant banquet, was said to have consumed pearls of fabulous worth dissolved in vinegar. Pliny, *Natural History* 9.58. RB referred to this story in a letter to EBB. See *RB/EBB Letters* 2.833, 835.

As Medicean Venus.[1] But I know,
A love that burns through veils will burn through masks
And shrivel up treachery. What, love and lie!
Nay - go to the opera! your love's curable.'

'I love and lie?' she said - 'I lie, forsooth?'
And beat her taper foot upon the floor,
And smiled against the shoe, - 'You're hard, Miss Leigh.
Unversed in current phrases. - Bowling-greens
Of poets are fresher than the world's highways:
Forgive me that I rashly blew the dust
Which dims our hedges even, in your eyes,
And vexed you so much. You find, probably,
No evil in this marriage, - rather good
Of innocence, to pastoralise in song:
You'll give the bond your signature, perhaps,
Beneath the lady's mark, - indifferent
That Romney chose a wife, could write her name,
In witnessing he loved her.'
'Loved!' I cried;
'Who tells you that he wants a wife to love?
He gets a horse to use, not love, I think:
There's work for wives as well, - and after, straw,
When men are liberal. For myself, you err
Supposing power in me to break this match.
I could not do it, to save Romney's life,
And would not, to save mine.'
'You take it so,'
She said, 'farewell then. Write your books in peace,
As far as may be for some secret stir
Now obvious to me, - for, most obviously,
In coming hither I mistook the way.'
Whereat she touched my hand and bent her head,
And floated from me like a silent cloud
That leaves the sense of thunder.
I drew breath,
Oppressed in my deliverance. After all
This woman breaks her social system up
For love, so counted - the love possible
To such, - and lilies are still lilies, pulled
By smutty hands, though spotted from their white;
And thus she is better haply, of her kind,
Than Romney Leigh, who lives by diagrams,
And crosses out the spontaneities
Of all his individual, personal life

1. The figure known as the Venus de Medici, in the Tribune of the Uffizi at Florence. EBB visited the Tribune soon after her arrival in Florence in 1847 (*Letters of EBB* 1.331).

With formal universals. As if man
Were set upon a high stool at a desk
To keep God's books for Him in red and black,[2]
And feel by millions! What, if even God
Were chiefly God by living out Himself
To an individualism of the Infinite,
Eterne, intense profuse - still throwing up
The golden spray of multitudinous worlds
In measure to the proclive[3] weight and rush
Of His inner nature, - the spontaneous love
Still proof and outflow of spontaneous life?
Then live, Aurora.
Two hours afterward,
Within St. Margaret's Court I stood alone,
Close-veiled. A sick child, from an ague-fit,[4]
Whose wasted right hand gambled 'gainst his left
With an old brass button in a blot of sun,
Jeered weakly at me as I passed across
The uneven pavement; while a woman, rouged
Upon the angular cheek-bones, kerchief torn,
Thin dangling locks, and flat lascivious mouth,
Cursed at a window both ways, in and out,
By turns some bed-rid creature and myself, -
'Lie still there, mother! liker the dead dog
You'll be to-morrow. What, we pick our way,
Fine madam, with those damnable small feet!
We cover up our face from doing good,
As if it were our purse! What brings you here,
My lady? is't to find my gentleman
Who visits his tame pigeon in the eaves?
Our cholera catch you with its cramps and spasms,
And tumble up your good clothes, veil and all,
And turn your whiteness dead-blue.'[5] I looked up;
I think I could have walked through hell that day,
And never flinched. 'The dear Christ comfort you,'
I said, 'you must have been most miserable,
To be so cruel,' - and I emptied out
My purse upon the stones: when, as I had cast
The last charm in the cauldron, the whole court
Went boiling, bubbling up, from all its doors
And windows, with a hideous wail of laughs
And roar of oaths, and blows perhaps . . I passed
Too quickly for distinguishing . . and pushed

2. In debt and credit.
3. Leaning, rushing forward.
4. Fever-fit.
5. Poor sanitation in cities led to frequent outbreaks of cholera during the first half of the nineteenth century.

A little side-door hanging on a hinge,
And plunged into the dark, and groped and climbed
The long, steep, narrow stair 'twixt broken rail
And mildewed wall that let the plaster drop
To startle me in the blackness. Still, up, up!
So high lived Romney's bride. I paused at last
Before a low door in the roof, and knocked;
There came an answer like a hurried dove -
'So soon? can that be Mister Leigh so soon?'
And, as I entered, an ineffable face
Met mine upon the threshold. 'Oh, not you,
Not you!' - the dropping of the voice implied,
'Then, if not you, for me not any one.'
I looked her in the eyes, and held her hands,
And said, 'I am his cousin, - Romney Leigh's;
And here I come to see my cousin too.'
She touched me with her face and with her voice,
This daughter of the people. Such soft flowers,
From such rough roots? the people, under there,
Can sin so, curse so, look so, smell so . . . faugh!
Yet have such daughters?
No wise beautiful
Was Marian Erle. She was not white nor brown,
But could look either, like a mist that changed
According to being shone on more or less:
The hair, too, ran its opulence of curls
In doubt 'twixt dark and bright, nor left you clear
To name the colour. Too much hair perhaps
(I'll name a fault here) for so small a head,
Which seemed to droop on that side and on this,
As a full-blown rose uneasy with its weight
Though not a wind should trouble it. Again,
The dimple in the cheek had better gone
With redder, fuller rounds; and somewhat large
The mouth was, though the milky little teeth
Dissolved it to so infantine a smile.[6]
For soon it smiled at me; the eyes smiled too,
But 'tis as if remembering they had wept,
And knowing they should, some day, weep again.

We talked. She told me all her story out,
Which I'll re-tell with fuller utterance,[7]
As coloured and confirmed in aftertimes

6. This description of Marian Erle's appearance is a very good likeness of EBB herself.
7. This is the answer to those critics who feel that Marian's is not the authentic voice of the people. It isn't. The only voice heard throughout *Aurora Leigh* is that of Aurora herself, and here she makes it plain that she retells Marian's story so that Marian speaks only through her.

By others and herself too. Marian Erle
Was born upon the ledge of Malvern Hill[8]
To eastward, in a hut built up at night
To evade the landlord's eye, of mud and turf,
Still liable, if once he looked that way,
To being straight levelled, scattered by his foot,
Like any other anthill. Born, I say;
God sent her to his world, commissioned right,
Her human testimonials fully signed,
Not scant in soul - complete in lineaments;
But others had to swindle her a place
To wail in when she had come. No place for her,[9]
By man's law! born an outlaw, was this babe;
Her first cry in our strange and strangling air,
When cast in spasms out by the shuddering womb,
Was wrong against the social code, - forced wrong: -
What business had the baby to cry there?

I tell her story and grow passionate.
She, Marian, did not tell it so, but used
Meek words that made no wonder of herself
For being so sad a creature. 'Mister Leigh
'Considered truly that such things should change.
'They *will*, in heaven - meantime, on the earth,
'There's none can like a nettle as a pink,
'Except himself. We're nettles, some of us,
'And give offence by the act of springing up;
'And, if we leave the damp side of the wall,
'The hoes, of course, are on us.' So she said.

Her father earned his life by random jobs
Despised by steadier workmen - keeping swine
On commons, picking hops, or hurrying on
The harvest at wet seasons, or, at need,
Assisting the Welsh drovers, when a drove
Of startled horses plunged into the mist
Below the mountain-road, and sowed the wind[1]
With wandering neighings. In between the gaps
Of such irregular work, he drank and slept,
And cursed his wife because, the pence being out,
She could not buy more drink. At which she turned,
(The worm) and beat her baby in revenge
For her own broken heart. There's not a crime

8. EBB's early home, Hope End, near Ledbury in Herefordshire, is in the Malvern Hills.
9. The first draft manuscript reading (see textual note to line 840) suggests that these words are a reminiscence of Luke 2.7.
1. Hosea 8.7: "They have sown the wind, and they shall reap the whirlwind. . . ."

But takes its proper change out still in crime
If once rung on the counter of this world:
Let sinners look to it.
                                    Yet the outcast child,
For whom the very mother's face forewent
The mother's special patience, lived and grew;
Learnt early to cry low, and walk alone,
With that pathetic vacillating roll
Of the infant body on the uncertain feet,
(The earth being felt unstable ground so soon)
At which most women's arms unclose at once
With irrepressive instinct. Thus, at three,
This poor weaned kid would run off from the fold,
This babe would steal off from the mother's chair,
And, creeping through the golden walls of gorse,
Would find some keyhole toward the secresy
Of Heaven's high blue, and, nestling down, peer out -
Oh, not to catch the angels at their games,
She had never heard of angels, - but to gaze
She knew not why, to see she knew not what,
A-hungering outward from the barren earth
For something like a joy. She liked, she said,
To dazzle black her sight against the sky,
For then, it seemed, some grand blind Love came down,
And groped her out, and clasped her with a kiss;
She learnt God that way, and was beat for it
Whenever she went home, - yet came again,
As surely as the trapped hare, getting free,
Returns to his form. This grand blind Love, she said,
This skyey father and mother both in one,
Instructed her and civilised her more
Than even Sunday-school[2] did afterward,
To which a lady sent her to learn books
And sit upon a long bench in a row
With other children. Well, she laughed sometimes
To see them laugh and laugh and maul their texts;
But ofter she was sorrowful with noise
And wondered if their mothers beat them hard
That ever they should laugh so. There was one
She loved indeed, - Rose Bell,[3] a seven years' child
So pretty and clever, who read syllables
When Marian was at letters; *she* would laugh
At nothing - hold your finger up, she laughed,
Then shook her curls down over eyes and mouth

2. Often the only form of schooling received by the children of the poor, Sunday schools usually were run as philanthropic efforts on the part of clergymen's wives or daughters.
3. This character might be named for the heroine of William Bell Scott's poem "Rosabell" (1837).

To hide her make-mirth from the schoolmaster:
And Rose's pelting[4] glee, as frank as rain
On cherry-blossoms, brightened Marian too,
To see another merry whom she loved.
She whispered once (the children side by side,
With mutual arms entwined about their necks)
'Your mother lets you laugh so?' 'Ay,' said Rose,
'She lets me. She was dug into the ground
Six years since, I being but a yearling wean.[5]
Such mothers let us play and lose our time,
And never scold nor beat us! don't you wish
You had one like that?' There, Marian breaking off
Looked suddenly in my face. 'Poor Rose,' said she,
'I heard her laugh last night in Oxford Street.[6]
I'd pour out half my blood to stop that laugh.
Poor Rose, poor Rose!' said Marian.
She resumed.
It tried her, when she had learnt at Sunday-school
What God was, what he wanted from us all,
And how in choosing sin we vexed the Christ,
To go straight home and hear her father pull
The Name down on us from the thunder-shelf[7]
Then drink away his soul into the dark
From seeing judgment. Father, mother, home,
Were God and heaven reversed to her: the more
She knew of Right, the more she guessed their wrong;
Her price paid down for knowledge, was to know
The vileness of her kindred: through her heart,
Her filial and tormented heart, henceforth,
They struck their blows at virtue. Oh, 'tis hard
To learn you have a father up in heaven
By a gathering certain sense of being, on earth,
Still worse than orphaned: 'tis too heavy a grief,
The having to thank God for such a joy!

And so passed Marian's life from year to year.
Her parents took her with them when they tramped,
Dodged lane and heaths, frequented towns and fairs,
And once went farther and saw Manchester,[8]

4. Figuratively, violently passionate, or hot (OED).
5. A dialect contraction of "wee ane," or little one (OED).
6. A large and important thoroughfare in London, newly constructed in the nineteenth century and very close to St. Giles, which was a notoriously poor district and the haunt of prostitutes and thieves. Rose has become a prostitute.
7. According to the law of Moses, the ineffable name of the Lord should never be taken in vain, or uttered lightly. This regulation is frequently taken simply as a prohibition against swearing, but obviously its implications are larger than that. See Exodus 20.7.
8. A large city in Lancashire that grew considerably as a center of industrial production in the nineteenth century.

And once the sea, that blue end of the world,
That fair scroll-finis of a wicked book, -
And twice a prison, - back at intervals,
Returning to the hills. Hills draw like heaven,
And stronger sometimes, holding out their hands
To pull you from the vile flats up to them.
And though perhaps these strollers still strolled back,
As sheep do, simply that they knew the way,
They certainly felt bettered unaware
Emerging from the social smut of towns
To wipe their feet clean on the mountain turf.
In which long wanderings, Marian lived and learned,
Endured and learned. The people on the roads
Would stop and ask her why her eyes outgrew
Her cheeks, and if she meant to lodge the birds
In all that hair; and then they lifted her,
The miller in his cart, a mile or twain,
The butcher's boy on horseback. Often too
The pedlar stopped, and tapped her on the head
With absolute forefinger, brown and ringed,
And asked if peradventure she could read,
And when she answered 'ay,' would toss her down
Some stray odd volume from his heavy pack,[9]
A Thomson's Seasons, mulcted of the Spring,[1]
Or half a play of Shakspeare's torn across,
(She had to guess the bottom of a page
By just the top sometimes,-as difficult,
As, sitting on the moon, to guess the earth!)
Or else a sheaf of leaves (for that small Ruth's
Small gleanings)[2] torn out from the heart of books,
From Churchyard Elegies and Edens Lost,[3]
From Burns, and Bunyan, Selkirk, and Tom Jones,[4] -
'Twas somewhat hard to keep the things distinct,
And oft the jangling influence jarred the child
Like looking at a sunset full of grace

9. In 1829, at Hope End, EBB lost some books belonging to her and to Hugh Stuart Boyd, the blind scholar with whom she read. The books were recovered from a "strolling Pedlar" with a bribe of sixpence (*The Brownings' Correspondence* 2.219).
1. James Thomson (1700–48). *The Seasons*, published between 1726 and 1730, was an instant success and remained, at least until 1850, a widely popular poem.
2. Ruth 2.3.
3. John Milton's *Paradise Lost* (1677); "Elegy Written in a Country Churchyard" (1751), by Thomas Gray (1716–71).
4. *The History of Tom Jones, A Foundling* (1749) by Henry Fielding (1707–54). EBB was forbidden to read *Tom Jones* by her father. See *RB/EBB Letters* 1.392; Robert Burns (1759–96); John Bunyan (1628–88). Doubtless EBB is thinking of *Pilgrim's Progress* (1678). See textual note, which includes a reference to "Christian"; Alexander Selkirk (1676–1721). The Scottish sailor was the prototype of Daniel Defoe's *Robinson Crusoe* (1719).

Through a pothouse[5] window while the drunken oaths
Went on behind her. But she weeded out
Her book-leaves, threw away the leaves that hurt,
(First tore them small, that none should find a word)
And made a nosegay of the sweet and good
To fold within her breast, and pore upon
At broken moments of the noontide glare,
When leave was given her to untie her cloak
And rest upon the dusty highway's bank
From the road's dust: or oft, the journey done,
Some city friend would lead her by the hand
To hear a lecture at an institute.[6]
And thus she had grown, this Marian Erle of ours,
To no book-learning, - she was ignorant
Of authors, - not in earshot of the things
Out-spoken o'er the heads of common men
By men who are uncommon, - but within
The cadenced hum of such, and capable
Of catching from the fringes of the wind
Some fragmentary phrases, here and there,
Of that fine music, - which, being carried in
To her soul, had reproduced itself afresh
In finer motions of the lips and lids.

She said, in speaking of it, 'If a flower
Were thrown you out of heaven at intervals,
You'd soon attain to a trick of looking up, -
And so with her.' She counted me her years,
Till *I* felt old; and then she counted me
Her sorrowful pleasures, till I felt ashamed.
She told me she was fortunate and calm
On such and such a season, sate and sewed,
With no one to break up her crystal thoughts,
While rhymes from lovely poems span around
Their ringing circles of ecstatic tune,
Beneath the moistened finger of the Hour.
Her parents called her a strange, sickly child,
Not good for much, and given to sulk and stare,
And smile into the hedges and the clouds,
And tremble if one shook her from her fit
By any blow, or word even. Out-door jobs
Went ill with her, and household quiet work
She was not born to. Had they kept the north,

5. A (somewhat disreputable) public house.
6. Working men's institutes and other benevolent foundations were widely set up for the education of the poor.

They might have had their pennyworth out of her
Like other parents in the factories,[7]
(Your children work for you, not you for them,
Or else they better had been choked with air
The first breath drawn;) but, in this tramping life,
Was nothing to be done with such a child
But tramp and tramp. And yet she knitted hose
Not ill, and was not dull at needlework;
And all the country people gave her pence
For darning stockings past their natural age,
And patching petticoats from old to new,
And other light work done for thrifty wives.

One day, said Marian, - the sun shone that day -
Her mother had been badly beat, and felt
The bruises sore bout her wretched soul,
(That must have been): she came in suddenly,
And snatching in a sort of breathless rage
Her daughter's headgear comb, let down the hair
Upon her like a sudden waterfall,
Then drew her drenched and passive by the arm
Outside the hut they lived in. When the child
Could clear her blinded face from all that stream
Of tresses . . there, a man stood, with beast's eyes
That seemed as they would swallow her alive
Complete in body and spirit, hair and all, -
And burning stertorous breath[8] that hurt her cheek,
He breathed so near. The mother held her tight,
Saying hard between her teeth - 'Why wench, why wench,
The squire speaks to you now - the squire's too good;
He means to set you up, and comfort us.
Be mannerly at least.' The child turned round
And looked up piteous in the mother's face,
(Be sure that mother's death-bed will not want
Another devil to damn, than such a look)[9] . .
'Oh, mother!' then, with desperate glance to heaven,
'God, free me from my mother,' she shrieked out,
'These mothers are too dreadful.' And, with force
As passionate as fear, she tore her hands

7. EBB was aware of the conditions of child labor in the textile factories of the industrial north of England, as reported by the royal commission investigating the employment of children (1842). In 1861, another Royal Commission on the Employment of Children noted that "against no persons do the children of both sexes require so much protection as against their own parents."
8. Loud breathing; snoring or snorting.
9. *Othello* 5.2.274–76: "when we shall meet at count,/This look of thine will hurl my soul from heaven,/And fiends will snatch at it."

Like lilies from the rocks, from hers and his,
And sprang down, bounded headlong down the steep,
Away from both - away, if possible,
As far as God, - away! They yelled at her,
As famished hounds at a hare. She heard them yell;
She felt her name hiss after her from the hills,
Like shot from guns. On, on. And now she had cast
The voices off with the uplands. On. Mad fear
Was running in her feet and killing the ground;
The white roads curled as if she burnt them up,
The green fields melted, wayside trees fell back
To make room for her. Then her head grew vexed;
Trees, fields, turned on her and ran after her;
She heard the quick pants of the hills behind,
Their keen air pricked her neck: she had lost her feet,
Could run no more, yet somehow went as fast,
The horizon red 'twixt steeples in the east
So sucked her forward, forward, while her heart
Kept swelling, swelling, till it swelled so big
It seemed to fill her body, - when it burst
And overflowed the world and swamped the light;
'And now I am dead and safe,' thought Marian Erle -
She had dropped, she had fainted.
As the sense returned,
The night had passed - not life's night. She was 'ware
Of heavy tumbling motions, creaking wheels,
The driver shouting to the lazy team
That swung their rankling bells against her brain,
While, through the waggon's coverture and chinks,
The cruel yellow morning pecked at her
Alive or dead upon the straw inside, -
At which her soul ached back into the dark
And prayed, 'no more of that.' A waggoner
Had found her in a ditch beneath the moon.
As white as moonshine save for the oozing blood.
At first he thought her dead; but when he had wiped
The mouth and heard it sigh, he raised her up,
And laid her in his waggon in the straw,
And so conveyed her to the distant town
To which his business called himself, and left
That heap of misery at the hospital.

She stirred; - the place seemed new and strange as death;
The white strait bed, with others strait and white,
Like graves dug side by side at measured lengths,
And quiet people walking in and out

With wonderful low voices and soft steps
And apparitional[1] equal care for each,
Astonished her with order, silence, law.
And when a gentle hand held out a cup,
She took it, as you do at sacrament,
Half awed, half melted, - not being used, indeed,
To so much love as makes the form of love
And courtesy of manners. Delicate drinks
And rare white bread, to which some dying eyes
Were turned in observation. O my God,
How sick we must be, ere we make men just!
I think it frets the saints in heaven to see
How many desolate creatures on the earth
Have learnt the simple dues of fellowship
And social comfort, in a hospital,
As Marian did. She lay there, stunned, half tranced,
And wished, at intervals of inflowing sense,
She might be sicker yet, if sickness made
The world so marvellous kind, the air so hushed,
And all her wake-time quiet as a sleep;
For now she understood (as such things were)
How sickness ended very oft in heaven
Among the unspoken raptures:- yet more sick,
And surelier happy. Then she dropped her lids,
And, folding up her hands[2] as flowers at night,
Would lose no moment of the blessed time.

She lay and seethed in fever many weeks,
But youth was strong and overcame the test;
Revolted soul and flesh were reconciled
And fetched back to the necessary day
And daylight duties. She could creep about
The long bare rooms, and stare out drearily
From any narrow window on the street,
Till some one who had nursed her as a friend
Said coldly to her, as an enemy,
'She had leave to go next week, being well enough,'
(While only her heart ached.) 'Go next week,' thought she,
'Next week! how would it be with her next week,
Let out into that terrible street alone
Among the pushing people, . . to go . . where?'

1. It seems clear that EBB here intended the unusual, but quite correct, meaning of "pertaining to service or attendance, ministering." After her death the question of her sense for the word was discussed by RB with James Murray and Alfred Erlebach, who were working on the first Oxford English Dictionary. See K. M. E. Murray, *Caught in the Web of Words* (New Haven and London, 1977), 235.
2. Proverbs 6.10: "Yet a little sleep, a little slumber, a little folding of the hands to sleep."

One day, the last before the dreaded last,
Among the convalescents, like herself
Prepared to go next morning, she sate dumb,
And heard half absently the women talk, -
How one was famished for her baby's cheeks,
'The little wretch would know her! a year old
And lively, like his father!' - one was keen
To get to work, and fill some clamorous mouths;
And one was tender for her dear goodman
Who had missed her sorely, - and one, querulous . .
'Would pay backbiting neighbours who had dared
To talk about her as already dead,' -
And one was proud . . 'and if her sweetheart Luke
Had left her for a ruddier face than hers,
(The gossip would be seen through at a glance)
Sweet riddance of such sweethearts - let him hang!
'Twere good to have been sick for such an end.'

And while they talked, and Marian felt the worse
For having missed the worst of all their wrongs,
A visitor was ushered through the wards
And paused among the talkers. 'When he looked
It was as if he spoke, and when he spoke
He sang perhaps,' said Marian; 'could she tell?
She only knew' (so much she had chronicled,
As seraphs might the making of the sun)
'That he who came and spake, was Romney Leigh,
And then and there she saw and heard him first.'

And when it was her turn to have the face
Upon her, all those buzzing pallid lips
Being satisfied with comfort - when he changed
To Marian, saying 'And *you?* you're going, where?' -
She, moveless as a worm beneath a stone
Which some one's stumbling foot has spurned aside,
Writhed suddenly, astonished with the light,
And breaking into sobs cried, 'Where I go?
None asked me till this moment. Can I say
Where *I* go, - when it has not seemed worth while
To God himself, who thinks of every one,
To think of me and fix where I shall go?'

'So young,' he gently asked her, 'you have lost
Your father and your mother?'
'Both,' she said,
'Both lost! my father was burnt up with gin
Or ever I sucked milk, and so is lost.

My mother sold me to a man last month,
And so my mother's lost, 'tis manifest.
And I, who fled from her for miles and miles,
As if I had caught sight of the fire of hell
Through some wild gap, (she was my mother, sir)
It seems I shall be lost too, presently,
And so we end, all three of us.'
'Poor child,'
He said - with such a pity in his voice,
It soothed her more than her own tears, - 'poor child!
'Tis simple that betrayal by mother's love
Should bring despair of God's too. Yet be taught,
He's better to us than many mothers are,
And children cannot wander beyond reach
Of the sweep of his white raiment. Touch and hold![3]
And if you weep still, weep where John was laid
While Jesus loved him.'[4]
'She could say the words,'
She told me, 'exactly as he uttered them
A year back, since in any doubt or dark
They came out like the stars, and shone on her
With just their comfort. Common words, perhaps;
The ministers in church might say the same;
But *he*, he made the church with what he spoke, -
The difference was the miracle,' said she.

Then catching up her smile to ravishment,
She added quickly, 'I repeat his words,
But not his tones: can any one repeat
The music of an organ, out of church?
And when he said 'poor child,' I shut my eyes
To feel how tenderly his voice broke through,
As the ointment-box broke on the Holy feet
To let out the rich medicative nard.'[5]

She told me how he had raised and rescued her
With reverent pity, as, in touching grief,
He touched the wounds of Christ, - and made her feel
More self-respecting. Hope, he called, belief
In God, - work, worship, - therefore let us pray!
And thus, to snatch her soul from atheism,

3. Matthew 14.35–36: "And when the men of that place had knowledge of him, they sent out into all that country round about, and brought unto him all that were diseased; And besought him that they might only touch the hem of his garment: and as many as touched were made perfectly whole."
4. John 13.23: "Now there was leaning on Jesus' bosom one of his disciples, whom Jesus loved."
5. Luke 7.37–38. Referring to the story of the woman (called later Mary Magdalen) who anointed Jesus's feet with a precious ointment.

And keep it stainless from her mother's face,
He sent her to a famous sempstress-house
Far off in London, there to work and hope.

With that, they parted. She kept sight of Heaven,
But not of Romney. He had good to do
To others: through the days and through the nights
She sewed and sewed and sewed. She drooped sometimes,
And wondered, while along the tawny light
She struck the new thread into her needle's eye,
How people without mothers on the hills
Could choose the town to live in! - then she drew
The stitch and mused how Romney's face would look,
And if 'twere likely he'd remember hers
When they two had their meeting after death.

# Fourth Book

They met still sooner. 'Twas a year from thence
That Lucy Gresham, the sick sempstress girl,
Who sewed by Marian's[1] chair so still and quick,
And leant her head upon its back to cough
More freely, when, the mistress turning round,
The others took occasion to laugh out,
Gave up at last. Among the workers, spoke
A bold girl with black eyebrows and red lips;
'You know the news? Who's dying, do you think?
Our Lucy Gresham. I expected it
As little as Nell Hart's wedding. Blush not, Nell,
Thy curls be red enough without thy cheeks,[2]
And, some day, there'll be found a man to dote
On red curls. - Lucy Gresham swooned last night,
Dropped sudden in the street while going home;
And now the baker says, who took her up
And laid her by her grandmother in bed,
He'll give her a week to die in. Pass the silk.
Let's hope he gave her a loaf too, within reach,
For otherwise they'll starve before they die,
That funny pair of bedfellows! Miss Bell,
I'll thank you for the scissors. The old crone
Is paralytic - that's the reason why
Our Lucy's thread went faster than her breath,
Which went too quick, we all know. Marian Erle!
Why, Marian Erle, you're not the fool to cry?
Your tears spoil Lady Waldemar's new dress,
You piece of pity!'
                    Marian rose up straight,
And, breaking through the talk and through the work,
Went outward, in the face of their surprise,
To Lucy's home, to nurse her back to life
Or down to death. She knew, by such an act,
All place and grace were forfeit in the house,
Whose mistress would supply the missing hand
With necessary, not inhuman haste,
And take no blame. But pity, too, had dues:
She could not leave a solitary soul
To founder in the dark, while she sate still

1. "Mabel Gray" throughout this passage in the first draft manuscript.
2. Red hair was very unfashionable in the mid nineteenth century, and girls unlucky enough to have red hair were considered plain. Contrary to popular opinion today, the pre-Raphaelite models were not redheads; Jane Morris was dark, and Elizabeth Siddal and Fanny Cornforth were blonde. Effie Ruskin, later Millais, seems to have had reddish gold hair.

And lavished stitches on a lady's hem
As if no other work were paramount.
'Why, God,' thought Marian, 'has a missing hand
This moment; Lucy wants a drink, perhaps.
Let others miss me! never miss me, God!'

So Marian sate by Lucy's bed, content
With duty, and was strong, for recompense,
To hold the lamp of human love arm-high
To catch the death-strained eyes and comfort them,
Until the angels, on the luminous side
Of death, had got theirs ready. And she said,
If Lucy thanked her sometimes, called her kind,
It touched her strangely. 'Marian Erle, called kind!
What, Marian, beaten and sold, who could not die!
'Tis verily good fortune to be kind.
Ah you,' she said, 'who are born to such a grace,
Be sorry for the unlicensed class, the poor,
Reduced to think the best good fortune means
That others, simply, should be kind to them.'

From sleep to sleep when Lucy had slid away
So gently, like the light upon a hill,[3]
Of which none names the moment that it goes
Though all see when 'tis gone, - a man came in
And stood beside the bed. The old idiot wretch
Screamed feebly, like a baby overlain,[4]
'Sir, sir, you won't mistake me for the corpse?
Don't look at *me*, sir! never bury *me!*
Although I lie here I'm alive as you,
Except my legs and arms, - I eat and drink
And understand, - (that you're the gentleman
Who fits the funerals up, Heaven speed you, sir,)
And certainly I should be livelier still
If Lucy here . . sir, Lucy is the corpse . .
Had worked more properly to buy me wine;
But Lucy, sir, was always slow at work,
I shan't lose much by Lucy. Marian Erle,
Speak up and show the gentleman the corpse.'

And then a voice said, 'Marian Erle.' She rose;
It was the hour for angels - there, stood hers!
She scarcely marvelled to see Romney Leigh.[5]

3. Lucy means "light."
4. Because babies from poorer homes frequently slept in beds shared with a number of people, "overlying" or squashing the baby by lying on it accidentally was a hazard and quite a common cause of infant mortality.
5. "Walter Vane" throughout this passage in the first draft manuscript.

As light November snows to empty nests,
As grass to graves, as moss to mildewed stones,
As July suns to ruins, through the rents,
As ministering spirits to mourners, through a loss,
As heaven itself to men, through pangs of death,
He came uncalled wherever grief had come,
'And so,' said Marian Erle, 'we met anew,'
And added softly, 'so, we shall not part.'

He was not angry that she had left the house
Wherein he placed her. Well - she had feared it might
Have vexed him. Also, when he found her set
On keeping, though the dead was out of sight,
That half-dead, half-live body left behind
With cankerous[6] heart and flesh, which took your best
And cursed you for the little good it did,
(Could any leave the bedrid wretch alone,
So joyless she was thankless even to God,
Much more to you?) he did not say 'twas well,
Yet Marian thought he did not take it ill, -
Since day by day he came, and every day
She felt within his utterance and his eyes
A closer, tenderer presence of the soul,
Until at last he said, 'We shall not part.'

On that same day, was Marian's work complete:
She had smoothed the empty bed, and swept the floor
Of coffin sawdust,[7] set the chairs anew
The dead had ended gossip in, and stood
In that poor room so cold and orderly,
The door-key in her hand prepared to go
As *they* had, howbeit not their way. He spoke.
'Dear Marian, of one clay God made us all,[8]
And though men push and poke and paddle in 't
(As children play at fashioning dirt-pies)
And call their fancies by the name of facts,
Assuming difference, lordship, privilege,
When all's plain dirt, - they come back to it at last,
The first grave-digger proves it with a spade,
And pats all even. Need we wait for this,
You, Marian, and I, Romney?'
                                        She, at that,
Looked blindly in his face, as when one looks
Through driving autumn-rains to find the sky.

6. Cancerous, diseased.
7. Most preparations for the burial of the dead were carried out at home, including the swift making of the coffin, and the corpse was carried out directly for burial.
8. Genesis 2.7.

He went on speaking.
'Marian, I being born
What men call noble, and you, issued from
The noble people, - though the tyrannous sword
Which pierced Christ's heart,[9] has cleft the world in twain
'Twixt class and class, opposing rich to poor,
Shall *we* keep parted? Not so. Let us lean
And strain together rather, each to each,
Compress the red lips of this gaping wound
As far as two souls can, - ay, lean and league,
I from my superabundance, - from your want
You, joining in a protest 'gainst the wrong
On both sides.'
All the rest, he held her hand
In speaking, which confused the sense of much.
Her heart against his words beat out so thick,
They might as well be written on the dust
Where some poor bird, escaping from hawk's beak,
Has dropped[1] and beats its shuddering wings, - the lines
Are rubbed so, - yet 'twas something like to this,
- 'That they two, standing at the two extremes
Of social classes, had received one seal,[2]
Been dedicate and drawn beyond themselves
To mercy and ministration, - he, indeed,
Through what he knew, and she, through what she felt,
He, by man's conscience, she, by woman's heart,
Relinquishing their several 'vantage posts
Of wealthy ease and honourable toil,
To work with God at love. And since God willed
That putting out his hand to touch this ark[3]
He found a woman's hand there, he'd accept
The sign too, hold the tender fingers fast,
And say, 'My fellow-worker, be my wife?' '
She told the tale with simple, rustic turns, -
Strong leaps of meaning in her sudden[4] eyes
That took the gaps of any imperfect phrase
Of the unschooled speaker: I have rather writ
The thing I understood so, than the thing
I heard so. And I cannot render right

9. Apparently an allusion conflating Luke 2.34–35 and John 19.33–37.
1. Aurora's metaphor here and that about the "autumn rain" (at lines 117–19) make it clear that Marian is as much Romney's victim, because she fails to understand the need to consider her own individual needs, as she is his dependant.
2. Had been given by the authority (of God) the same kind of task.
3. See 2 Samuel 6.6–7: "And when they came to Nachon's threshing-floor, Uzzah put forth his hand to the ark of God, and took hold of it; for the oxen shook it. And the anger of the Lord was kindled against Uzzah; and God smote him there for his error; and there he died by the ark of God."
4. The OED gives the adjective "sudden"—of the eye, glancing quickly—as an obsolete word.

Her quick gesticulation, wild yet soft,
Self-startled from the habitual mood she used,
Half sad, half languid, - like dumb creatures (now
A rustling bird, and now a wandering deer,
Or squirrel 'gainst the oak-gloom flashing up
His sidelong burnished head, in just her way
Of savage spontaneity,) that stir
Abruptly the green silence of the woods,
And make it stranger, holier, more profound;
As Nature's general heart confessed itself
Of life, and then fell backward on repose.

I kissed the lips that ended. - 'So indeed
He loves you, Marian?'
'Loves me!' She looked up
With a child's wonder when you ask him first
Who made the sun - a puzzled blush, that grew,
Then broke off in a rapid radiant smile
Of sure solution. 'Loves me! he loves all, -
And me, of course. He had not asked me else
To work with him for ever and be his wife.'

Her words reproved me. This perhaps was love -
To have its hands too full of gifts to give,
For putting out a hand to take a gift;
To love so much, the perfect round of love
Includes, in strict conclusion, being loved;
As Eden-dew went up and fell again,
Enough for watering Eden.[5] Obviously
She had not thought about his love at all:
The cataracts of her soul had poured themselves,
And risen self-crowned in rainbow:[6] would she ask
Who crowned her? - it sufficed that she was crowned.

With women of my class 'tis otherwise:
We haggle for the small change of our gold,
And so much love accord for so much love,
Rialto-prices.[7] Are we therefore wrong?
If marriage be a contract, look to it then,
Contracting parties should be equal, just,
But if, a simple fealty[8] on one side,
A mere religion, - right to give, is all,
And certain brides of Europe duly ask

5. Genesis 2.6: "[t]here went up a mist from the earth, and watered the whole face of the ground."
6. Cf. the angel in Revelation 10.1: "and a rainbow was upon his head."
7. At market rate. The Venetian exchange was situated in the Rialto quarter, the commercial center of the city.
8. Loyalty; subservient allegiance.

To mount the pile as Indian widows do,[9]
The spices of their tender youth heaped up,
The jewels of their gracious virtues worn,
More gems, more glory, - to consume entire
For a living husband: as the man's alive,
Not dead, the woman's duty by so much,
Advanced in England beyond Hindostan.

I sate there musing, till she touched my hand,
With hers, as softly as a strange white bird
She feared to startle in touching. 'You are kind.
But are you, peradventure, vexed at heart
Because your cousin takes me for a wife?
I know I am not worthy - nay, in truth,
I'm glad on 't, since, for that, he chooses me.
He likes the poor things of the world the best;
I would not therefore, if I could, be rich.
It pleasures him to stoop for buttercups,
I would not be a rose upon the wall
A queen might stop at, near the palace-door,
To say to a courtier, 'Pluck that rose for me,
'It's prettier than the rest.' O Romney Leigh!
I'd rather far be trodden by his foot,
Than lie in a great queen's bosom.'
                                        Out of breath
She paused.
                    'Sweet Marian, do you disavow
The roses with that face?'
                                        She dropt her head
As if the wind had caught that flower of her
And bent it in the garden, - then looked up
With grave assurance. 'Well, you think me bold!
But so we all are when we're praying God.
And if I'm bold - yet, lady, credit me,
That, since I know myself for what I am,
Much fitter for his handmaid than his wife,
I'll prove the handmaid and the wife at once,
Serve tenderly, and love obediently,
And be a worthier mate, perhaps, than some
Who are wooed in silk among their learned books;
While I shall set myself to read his eyes,
Till such grow plainer to me than the French
To wisest ladies. Do you think I'll miss
A letter, in the spelling of his mind?

9. *Suttee*, the practice of widow's self-immolation on the funeral pyre of her husband, was forbidden in British India in 1829, but instances continued to occur.

No more than they do when they sit and write
Their flying words with flickering wild-fowl tails,
Nor ever pause to ask how many *ts*,
Should that be *y* or *i*, they know 't so well:
I've seen them writing, when I brought a dress
And waited, - floating out their soft white hands
On shining paper. But they're hard sometimes,
For all those hands! - we've used out many nights,
And worn the yellow daylight into shreds
Which flapped and shivered down our aching eyes
Till night appeared more tolerable, just
That pretty ladies might look beautiful,
Who said at last . . 'You're lazy in that house!
'You're slow in sending home the work, - I count
'I've waited near an hour for 't.' Pardon me,
I do not blame them, madam, nor misprize;[1]
They are fair and gracious; ay, but not like you,
Since none but you has Mister Leigh's own blood
Both noble and gentle, - and, without it . . well,
They are fair, I said; so fair, it scarce seems strange
That, flashing out in any looking-glass
The wonder of their glorious brows and breasts,
They're charmed so, they forget to look behind
And mark how pale we've grown we pitiful
Remainders of the world. And so perhaps
If Mister Leigh had chosen a wife from these,
She might, although he's better than her best
And dearly she would know it, steal a thought
Which should be all his, an eye-glance from his face,
To plunge into the mirror opposite
In search of her own beauty's pearl; while *I* . .
Ah, dearest lady, serge[2] will outweigh silk
For winter-wear when bodies feel a-cold,
And I'll be a true wife to your cousin Leigh.'

Before I answered he was there himself.
I think he had been standing in the room
And listened probably to half her talk,
Arrested, turned to stone, - as white as stone.
Will tender sayings make men look so white?
He loves her then profoundly.
'You are here,
Aurora? here I meet you!' - We clasped hands.

1. To condemn, despise or scorn (OED).
2. A woollen fabric favored by the poor because of its durability.

'Even so, dear Romney. Lady Waldemar[3]
Has sent me in haste to find a cousin of mine
Who shall be.'

'Lady Waldemar is good.'

'Here's one, at least, who is good,' I sighed, and touched
Poor Marian's happy head, as doglike she
Most passionately patient, waited on,
A-tremble for her turn of greeting words;
'I've sate a full hour with your Marian Erle,
And learnt the thing by heart, - and from my heart
Am therefore competent to give you thanks
For such a cousin.'

'You accept at last
A gift from me, Aurora, without scorn?
At last I please you?' - How his voice was changed.

'You cannot please a woman against her will,
And once you vexed me. Shall we speak of that?
We'll say, then, you were noble in it all
And I not ignorant - let it pass. And now
You please me, Romney, when you please yourself;
So, please you, be fanatical in love,
And I'm well pleased. Ah, cousin! at the old hall,
Among the gallery portraits of our Leighs,
We shall not find a sweeter signory[4]
Than this pure forehead's.'

Not a word he said.
How arrogant men are! - Even philanthropists,
Who try to take a wife up in the way
They put down a subscription-cheque, - if once
She turns and says, 'I will not tax you so,
Most charitable sir,' - feel ill at ease
As though she had wronged them somehow. I suppose
We women should remember what we are,
And not throw back an obolus inscribed
With Caesar's image, lightly.[5] I resumed.

3. "Lady Waldegrave" throughout this passage in the first draft manuscript.
4. Authority or supremacy expressed in looks or bearing (OED).
5. In ancient Greece the obolus was a silver coin of little worth. EBB's allusion is to the story of the Roman general Belisarius (c. 505–65), who was dismissed by Justinian on suspicion of complicity in a plot against the life of the emperor. Legend adds that the general's eyes were put out and that he lived in the streets of Constantinople begging of passersby with the words, "Date obolum Belisario."

'It strikes me, some of those sublime Vandykes[6]
Were not too proud to make good saints in heaven;
And if so, then they're not too proud to-day,
To bow down (now the ruffs are off their necks)
And own this good, true, noble Marian, yours,
And mine, I'll say! - For poets (bear the word)
Half-poets even, are still whole democrats, -
Oh, not that we're disloyal to the high,
But loyal to the low, and cognisant[7]
Of the less scrutable[8] majesties. For me,
I comprehend your choice, I justify
Your right in choosing.'
'No, no, no' he sighed,
With a sort of melancholy impatient scorn,
As some grown man who never had a child
Puts by some child who plays at being a man,
'You did not, do not, cannot comprehend
My choice, my ends, my motives, nor myself:
No matter now; we'll let it pass, you say.
I thank you for your generous cousinship
Which helps this present; I accept for her
Your favourable thoughts. We're fallen on days,
We two who are not poets, when to wed
Requires less mutual love than common love
For two together to bear out at once
Upon the loveless many. Work in pairs,
In galley-couplings[9] or in marriage-rings,
The difference lies in the honour, not the work, -
And such we're bound to, I and she. But love,
(You poets are benighted[1] in this age,
The hour's too late for catching even moths,
You've gnats instead,) love! - love's fool-paradise
Is out of date, like Adam's. Set a swan
To swim the Trenton,[2] rather than true love
To float its fabulous plumage safely down
The cataracts of this loud transition-time,[3] -
Whose roar for ever henceforth in my ears

6. Anthony Van Dyck (1599–1641), a Flemish painter, was appointed "principalle Paynter in ordinary of their Majesties" by Charles I in 1632 and was well known in England for his portraits of leading members of society.
7. Aware of; knowing about.
8. The less obvious; less visible.
9. Slaves rowing in the galley ships of early days were chained together in pairs and expected to exert themselves in unison.
1. In the dark.
2. The six cataracts of the Trenton Falls on West Canada Creek, near Utica, New York.
3. Thomas Carlyle, along with a number of other contemporary commentators, had frequently described the nineteenth century as an age of "transition," because many felt that the imperatives of progress—industrial, economic, and colonial—meant that society in Britain was changing its character in the world.

Must keep me deaf to music.'
There, I turned
And kissed poor Marian, out of discontent.
The man had baffled, chafed me, till I flung
For refuge to the woman, - as, sometimes,
Impatient of some crowded room's close smell,
You throw a window open and lean out
To breathe a long breath in the dewy night
And cool your angry forehead. She, at least,
Was not built up as walls are, brick by brick,
Each fancy squared, each feeling ranged by line,
The very heat of burning youth applied
To indurate[4] forms and systems! excellent bricks,
A well-built wall, - which stops you on the road,
And, into which, you cannot see an inch
Although you beat your head against it - pshaw!
'Adieu,' I said, 'for this time, cousins both,
And, cousin Romney, pardon me the word,
Be happy! - oh, in some esoteric sense
Of course! - I mean no harm in wishing well.
Adieu, my Marian: - may she come to me,
Dear Romney, and be married from my house?
It is not part of your philosophy
To keep your bird upon the blackthorn?'
'Ay,'
He answered, 'but it is. I take my wife
Directly from the people, - and she comes,
As Austria's daughter to imperial France,[5]
Betwixt her eagles,[6] blinking not her race,
From Margaret's Court[7] at garret-height, to meet
And wed me at St. James's,[8] nor put off
Her gown of serge for that. The things we do,
We do: we'll wear no mask, as if we blushed.'
'Dear Romney, you're the poet,' I replied,
But felt my smile too mournful for my word,
And turned and went. Ay, masks, I thought, - beware
Of tragic masks we tie before the glass,
Uplifted on the cothurn half a yard
Above the natural stature![9] we would play

4. Hard; unyielding.
5. Marie-Louise (1791–1847), the daughter of Francis I of Austria, married Napoleon in 1810, shortly after his divorce from Josephine.
6. The two-headed eagle was the emblem of the Habsburgs, the royal family of Austria.
7. See note to *Aurora Leigh* 3.657.
8. The church of St. James, Piccadilly, built by Christopher Wren from 1676–1684, served a fashionable and eminent congregation.
9. The mask and the cothurn (or buskin), worn by the actors of ancient Greece, are the characteristics of tragedy. The size and significance of the tragic apparatus seem to have been exaggerated in the nineteenth century (see *Aurora Leigh* 5.325–34).

Heroic parts to ourselves, - and end, perhaps,
As impotently as Athenian wives
Who shrieked in fits at the Eumenides.[1]

His foot pursued me down the stair. 'At least
You'll suffer me to walk with you beyond
These hideous streets, these graves, where men alive
Packed close with earthworms, burr[2] unconsciously
About the plague that slew them; let me go.
The very women pelt their souls in mud
At any woman who walks here alone.
How came you here alone? - you are ignorant.'

We had a strange and melancholy walk:
The night came drizzling downward in dark rain,
And, as we walked, the colour of the time,
The act, the presence, my hand upon his arm,
His voice in my ear, and mine to my own sense,
Appeared unnatural. We talked[3] modern books
And daily papers, Spanish marriage-schemes[4]
And English climate - was 't so cold last year?
And will the wind change by to-morrow morn?
Can Guizot[5] stand? is London full? is trade
Competitive?[6] has Dickens turned his hinge

1. *The Eumenides* is the final play in the *Oresteia* trilogy by Aeschylus (c. 525–c.456 BC) and deals with the pursuit of Orestes by the Furies. The play was first performed in 458 BC, and on that occasion the appearance of the Erinyes, or Furies, described as black and lothly, dripping blood and slime from their eyes (*Eumenides*, 50–54), was said to have struck terror in the spectators: "some say that the bringing in of the chorus scattered about at the performance of the Eumenides so frightened the public that they were struck dumb, and some miscarried" (the *Vita* of Aeschylus § 9).
2. To speak inarticulately or indistinctly (OED).
3. The conversation related in this passage may, in light of the topics discussed, be dated to the autumn of 1846—the period of the Brownings' secret marriage and departure for Italy.
4. The deleted reference to "Isabella" in the first draft manuscript (see textual note) illuminates EBB's allusion. In August 1846 it was announced that the marriage of Isabella, queen of Spain, would take place simultaneously with that of her sister, the Infanta Maria Luisa. Isabella was to marry the duke of Cadiz, and her sister, the duc de Montpensier, son of Louis-Philippe of France. The English government reacted angrily to the announcement, fearing that if Isabella should die childless, Spain might thus come under the influence of France. Indignation increased when it was revealed that Louis-Philippe had, some time previously, "spontaneously" promised Queen Victoria that he would make no attempt to place his son on the Spanish throne. Throughout September 1846, *The Times* carried articles on the marriages that grew increasingly hysterical. Nonetheless, the double wedding was duly solemnized in Madrid on October 10, 1846.
5. Français Pierre Guillaume Guizot (1787–1874), French minister for Foreign Affairs (1840–47). Conservative and nationalist in outlook, Guizot was influential in the affair of the Spanish marriages (see note to line 3.399) and persisted in regarding that alliance as "the first grand thing that we have effected completely single-handed in Europe since 1830." In fact, Guizot was not to "stand" for long; his authoritarian approach to government and his reluctance to introduce parliamentary reform precipitated the revolution of 1848. Louis-Philippe dismissed him from office in February 1848 in a belated attempt to salvage the situation, but he was too late to save the monarchy.
6. Probably a reference to the Free Trade movement of the 1840s. See note to line 405.

A-pinch upon the fingers of the great?[7]
And are potatoes to grow mythical[8]
Like moly?[9] will the apple die out too?
Which way is the wind to-night? south-east? due east?[1]
We talked on fast, while every common word
Seemed tangled with the thunder at one end,[2]
And ready to pull down upon our heads
A terror out of sight. And yet to pause
Were surelier mortal: we tore greedily up
All silence, all the innocent breathing-points,
As if, like pale conspirators in haste,
We tore up papers where our signatures
Imperilled us to an ugly shame or death.

I cannot tell you why it was. 'Tis plain
We had not loved nor hated: wherefore dread
To spill gunpowder on ground safe from fire?
Perhaps we had lived too closely, to diverge
So absolutely: leave two clocks, they say,
Wound up to different hours, upon one shelf,
And slowly, through the interior wheels of each,
The blind mechanic motion sets itself
A-throb to feel out for the mutual time.[3]

7. In the "Hungry Forties" Charles Dickens' social criticism was regarded, in some quarters, as seditious. *The Chimes*, Dickens' Christmas book for 1844, in particular, satirized upper-class attitudes to the poor, exposing social injustice and neglect.
8. Potato blight, a parasitic fungus, caused the Irish potato crop to fail for a second consecutive year in 1846. Since the 1830s, Free Traders and the Anti-Corn Law League (formed 1838–39) had been campaigning for the repeal of the Corn Laws, which placed severe restrictions on the importation of foreign corn to Britain.
9. A plant described by Homer as a white flower on a black root. The herb was uprooted by Hermes and given to Odysseus as an antidote to the enchantments of Circe, enabling him to return his companions to human form (*Odyssey* 10.302–6).
1. In Biblical terms, the east wind is the harbinger of evil. See Exodus 10.13, Psalms 48.7, Ezekiel 19.12, and Hosea 12.1.
2. In September 1846, thunder was literally in the air. See *RB/EBB Letters* 2.1054. Moreover, the reference to thunder, which occurs three times in the first draft manuscript, may have been prompted by EBB's personal memories of the crucial period, August–September 1846, for at least twice in her correspondence with Robert Browning, EBB uses thunder as an image representing her father's domination: once in describing her mother ("A sweet, gentle nature, which the thunder a little turned from its sweetness" [*RB/EBB Letters* 2.1012]) and once in describing her own position ("Think of my being let loose upon a common, just when the thunderclouds are gathering" [*RB/EBB Letters* 2.1036]).
3. EBB alludes to the example used by Gottfried Wilhelm Leibniz (1646–1715) to explain his theories of the universal governing influence of preestablished harmony. He employed the example first in 1696, in the second and third "Explanations" of his "New System of the Nature and Communication of Substances, As Well As of the Union Existing between the Soul and the Body," which had been published in 1695. See Leibniz, *Opera Philosphica*, ed. Joannes Eduardus Erdmann (Berlin, 1840), 134.

EBB's reference is drawn from Leibniz's remarks on natural influence: "Imagine two clocks or watches which are in perfect agreement. Now this agreement may come about *in three ways*. *The first* consists of a natural influence. This is what M. Huygens tried with a result that surprised him. He suspended two pendulums from the same piece of wood; the continual strokes of the pendulums communicated similar vibrations to the particles of wood; but since these different vibrations could not well persist independently and without interfering with one

It was not so with us, indeed: while he
Struck midnight, I kept striking six at dawn,
While he marked judgment, I, redemption-day;[4]
And such exception to a general law
Imperious upon inert matter even,
Might make us, each to either, insecure,
A beckoning mystery or a troubling fear.

I mind me, when we parted at the door,
How strange his good-night sounded, - like good-night
Beside a deathbed, where the morrow's sun
Is sure to come too late for more good-days:
And all that night I thought . . ' 'Good-night,' said he.'

And so, a month passed. Let me set it down
At once, - I have been wrong, I have been wrong.
We are wrong always when we think too much
Of what we think or are: albeit our thoughts
Be verily bitter as self-sacrifice,
We're no less selfish. If we sleep on rocks
Or roses, sleeping past the hour of noon
We're lazy. This I write against myself.
I had done a duty in the visit paid
To Marian, and was ready otherwise
To give the witness of my presence and name
Whenever she should marry. - Which, I thought,
Sufficed. I even had cast into the scale
An overweight of justice toward the match;
The Lady Waldemar had missed her tool,
Had broken it in the lock as being too straight
For a crooked purpose, while poor Marian Erle
Missed nothing in my accents or my acts:
I had not been ungenerous on the whole,
Nor yet untender; so, enough. I felt
Tired, overworked: this marriage somewhat jarred;
Or, if it did not, all the bridal noise,
The pricking of the map of life with pins,
In schemes of . . 'Here we'll go', and 'There we'll stay,'
And 'Everywhere we'll prosper in our love,'
Was scarce my business: let them order it;
Who else should care? I threw myself aside,

another, unless the pendulums were in agreement, it happened by some sort of miracle that even when their strokes had been purposely disturbed, they soon went back to swinging together. . . ." (*Leibniz: Philosophical Writings*, ed. G. H. R. Parkinson [London, 1973], 130–31).

4. They are the same day, of course, but much depends on whether one emphasizes the retributive or the redemptory character of the occasion.

As one who had done her work and shuts her eyes.
To rest the better.
I, who should have known,
Forereckoned mischief! Where we disavow
Being keeper to our brother we're his Cain.[5]

I might have held that poor child to my heart
A little longer! 'twould have hurt me much
To have hastened by its beats the marriage-day,
And kept her safe meantime from tampering hands
Or, peradventure, traps. What drew me back
From telling Romney plainly the designs
Of Lady Waldemar, as spoken out
To me . . me? had I any right, ay, right,
With womanly compassion and reserve
To break the fall of woman's impudence? -
To stand by calmly, knowing what I knew,
And hear him call her *good?*
Distrust that word.
'There is none good save God,' said Jesus Christ,[6]
If He once, in the first creation-week,
Called creatures good,[7] - for ever, afterward,
The Devil only has done it, and his heirs,
The knaves who win so, and the fools who lose;
The word's grown dangerous. In the middle age,
I think they called malignant fays[8] and imps
Good people. A good neighbour, even in this,
Is fatal sometimes, - cuts your morning up
To mince-meat of the very smallest talk,
Then helps to sugar her bohea[9] at night
With your reputation. I have known good wives,
As chaste, or nearly so, as Potiphar's;[1]
And good, good mothers, who would use a child
To better an intrigue; good friends, beside,
(Very good) who hung succinctly[2] round your neck

5. Genesis 4.9.
6. See Matthew 19.17: "there is none good but one, that is, God"; and Luke 18.19: "none is good, save one, that is, God."
7. Genesis 1.21,25.
8. Fairies.
9. Originally the name given at the beginning of the eighteenth century to the finest kinds of black tea, but the quality later known as "bohea" was the worst, being the last crop of the season (OED).
1. Not chaste at all. She was the wife of the man who employed Joseph after he was sold into slavery by his brothers. Potiphar's wife desired Joseph, and when he rebuffed her advances, she told her husband that Joseph had attempted to rape her. He was subsequently imprisoned on the accusation. See Genesis 39.6–10.
2. Closely, as in close-fitting garments.

And sucked your breath, as cats are fabled to do
By sleeping infants.[3] And we all have known
Good critics who have stamped out poet's hopes,[4]
Good statesmen who pulled ruin on the state,
Good patriots who for a theory risked a cause,[5]
Good kings who disembowelled for a tax,[6]
Good popes who brought all good to jeopardy,[7]
Good Christians who sate still in easy chairs
And damned the general world for standing up. -
Now may the good God pardon all good men!

How bitterly I speak, - how certainly
The innocent white milk in us is turned,
By much persistent shining of the sun! -
Shake up the sweetest in us long enough
With men, it drops to foolish curd,[8] too sour
To feed the most untender of Christ's lambs.

I should have thought, - a woman of the world
Like her I'm meaning, centre to herself,
Who has wheeled on her own pivot half a life
In isolated self-love and self-will,
As a windmill seen at distance radiating
Its delicate white vans[9] against the sky,
So soft and soundless, simply beautiful,
Seen nearer, - what a roar and tear it makes,
How it grinds and bruises! - if she loves at last,
Her love's a re-adjustment of self-love,
No more, - a need felt of another's use
To her one advantage, as the mill wants grain,

3. The myth of the cat that sucks the breath of a sleeping baby is probably derived from the tendency of a cat to seek out a warm spot, thereby suffocating the child.
4. Possibly an allusion to Byron's well-known, if inaccurate, account of Keats' death as a reaction to John Croker's scathing review of *Endymion* in the *Quarterly Review*. See "John Keats" (1821): "Who kill'd John Keats/'I,' says the Quarterly,/So savage and Tartarly;/'Twas one of my feats' "; and *Don Juan* (1819–24), 11.60: "John Keats who was killed off by one critique,/Just as he really promised something great,/. . . 'Tis strange the mind, that very fiery particle,/ Should let itself be snuff'd out by an article."
5. Compare EBB's remarks on the Italian patriot, Giuseppe Mazzini (1805?–1872): "I . . . am initiated against him down to the roots of my understanding. He would risk Italy in the toss of a paul" (EBB to Isa Blagden, n.d. [c. 1850], [Fitzwilliam Museum]). Mazzini was the most romantically fiery of the three leaders for Italian unity in the mid nineteenth century.
6. The reference is general of course, but disembowelling was a common method of execution in Europe up to the seventeenth and eighteenth centuries. It was usually meted out for some more serious crime, such as treason or regicide.
7. In 1846, the newly elected Pope Pius IX began his reign by granting freedom of the press and amnesty to political prisoners. His liberal actions prompted many observers to hope that Italy might be united under the papal throne. But, finding himself unable to control the political agitation to which the atmosphere of liberalism gave birth in Italy, he fled in 1848, to the protection of Ferdinand II, King of the Two Sicilies, leaving Italy to the domination of Austria.
8. *Macbeth* 1.5, 17: "th' milk of human kindness."
9. The spines of the windmill.

The fire wants fuel, the very wolf wants prey,
And none of these is more unscrupulous
Than such a charming woman when she loves.
She'll not be thwarted by an obstacle
So trifling as . . her soul is, . . much less yours! -
Is God a consideration? - she loves you,
Not God; she will not flinch for Him indeed:
She did not for the Marchioness of Perth,
When wanting tickets for the fancy ball.[1]
She loves you, sir, with passion, to lunacy,
She loves you like her diamonds . . almost.
Well,
A month passed so, and then the notice came,
On such a day the marriage at the church.
I was not backward.
Half St. Giles in frieze
Was bidden to meet St. James in cloth of gold,[2]
And, after contract at the altar, pass
To eat a marriage-feast on Hampstead Heath.[3]
Of course the people came in uncompelled,
Lame, blind, and worse - sick, sorrowful, and worse,
The humours of the peccant[4] social wound
All pressed out, poured down upon Pimlico,
Exasperating the unaccustomed air
With hideous interfusion. You'd suppose
A finished generation, dead of plague,
Swept outward from their graves into the sun,

1. Apparently a reference to the fancy dress balls that Queen Victoria gave at Buckingham Palace during the 1840s. Cf. the first draft manuscript reading, "the queen's mask-ball" (see textual note). In May 1842 a grand ball was planned to enact a meeting between the courts of Edward III and Anne de Bretagne. In June 1845, twelve hundred people attended a "Georgian" ball and were entertained with eighteenth-century dances.
2. Frieze is a coarse woollen cloth. The contrast between the parish of St. Giles, the poorest quarter of the city, and the parish of St. James, the center of fashionable society, was a standard proverbial juxtaposition in the nineteenth century. For the "cloth of frieze/cloth of gold" contrast, cf. *EBB to MRM* 1.48: "Cloth of frieze be not too bold,/Tho' thou'rt matched with cloth of gold"; and *RB/EBB Letters* 7.372. "Cloth of frieze, be not too bold/Though thou'rt matched with cloth of gold!—. . . that, beloved, was written for *me*." EBB's quotation is part of an epigram on the discrepancy in rank between Mary Tudor, daughter of Henry VII and widow of the King of France, and her second husband, Charles Brandon, duke of Suffolk. The complete verse is "Cloth of gold do not despise/Thô thou'rt matched to cloth of frieze/Cloth of frieze be not too bold/Thô thou'rt matched to cloth of gold." These lines are inscribed on a portrait of Mary and Suffolk at Brocklesby Park and were quoted by Horace Walpole, *Anecdotes of Painting in England* . . . (1762), vol. 1, ch. 4.54.
3. A large expanse of green, now a park, to the north of London and a popular resort then and now. EBB's old friend from Hope End days, Hugh Stuart Boyd, lived in Hampstead in the 1840s, and it was to his house that she went immediately after her secret marriage to Robert Browning in Marylebone church in September 1846. The visit was a ruse to cover her absence from home, and a necessary breathing space before she went back home to Wimpole Street with her secret, to stay there for another week before departing finally for Italy. Under the circumstances, it seems clear that EBB is putting a little private allusion in here.
4. Causing disorder of the system, morbid, unhealthy, corrupt. Used especially in the humoral pathology (OED).

The moil[5] of death upon them. What a sight!
A holiday of miserable men
Is sadder than a burial-day of kings.

They clogged the streets,[6] they oozed into the church
In a dark slow stream, like blood. To see that sight,
The noble ladies stood up in their pews,
Some pale for fear, a few as red for hate,
Some simply curious, some just insolent,
And some in wondering scorn, - 'What next? what next?'
These crushed their delicate rose-lips from the smile
That misbecame them in a holy place,
With broidered hems of perfumed handkerchiefs;
Those passed the salts, with confidence of eyes
And simultaneous shiver of moiré silk:
While all the aisles, alive and black with heads,
Crawled slowly toward the altar from the street,
As bruised snakes crawl and hiss out of a hole
With shuddering involution,[7] swaying slow
From right to left, and then from left to right,
In pants and pauses. What an ugly crest
Of faces rose upon you everywhere
From the crammed mass! you did not usually
See faces like them in the open day:
They hide in cellars, not to make you mad
As Romney Leigh is. - Faces! O my God,
We call those, faces? men's and women's . . ay,
And children's; - babies, hanging like a rag
Forgotten on their mother's neck, - poor mouths,
Wiped clean of mother's milk by mother's blow
Before they are taught her cursing. Faces? . . phew,
We'll call them vices, festering to despairs,
Or sorrows, petrifying to vices: not
A finger-touch of God left whole on them,
All ruined, lost - the countenance worn out
As the garment, the will dissolute as the act,
The passions loose and draggling in the dirt
To trip a foot up at the first free step!
Those, faces? 'twas as if you had stirred up hell
To heave its lowest dreg-fiends uppermost
In fiery swirls of slime, - such strangled fronts,

5. Spot or taint (OED).
6. Aurora's (and EBB's) unflattering picture of the mass of the poor has attracted a great deal of criticism from modern liberal critics who accuse them both of lack of sympathy. But this view does not allow for the stated fact that Aurora is troubled and disturbed here by her own unacknowledged erotic impulses, nor the very obvious fact that part of her "lesson" includes losing her own artistic arrogance and acquiring a more generalized capacity for understanding.
7. Wavering, snaking, coiling.

Such obdurate jaws were thrown up constantly
To twit you with your race, corrupt your blood,
And grind to devilish colours all your dreams
Henceforth, - though, haply, you should drop asleep
By clink of silver waters, in a muse
On Raffael's mild Madonna of the Bird.[8]
I've waked and slept through many nights and days
Since then, - but still that day will catch my breath
Like a nightmare. There are fatal days, indeed,
In which the fibrous years have taken root
So deeply, that they quiver to their tops
Whene'er you stir the dust of such a day.

My cousin met me with his eyes and hand
And then, with just a word, . . that 'Marian Erle
Was coming with her bridesmaids presently,'
Made haste to place me by the altar-stair
Where he and other noble gentlemen
And high-born ladies, waited for the bride.

We waited. It was early: there was time,
For greeting and the morning's compliment,
And gradually a ripple of women's talk
Arose and fell and tossed about a spray
Of English ss, soft as a silent hush,
And, notwithstanding, quite as audible
As louder phrases thrown out by the men.
- 'Yes, really, if we need to wait in church
We need to talk there.' - 'She? 'tis Lady Ayr,
In blue - not purple! that's the dowager.'
- 'She looks as young' - 'She flirts as young, you mean.
Why if you had seen her upon Thursday night,
You'd call Miss Norris modest.' - '*You* again!
I waltzed with you three hours back. Up at six,
Up still at ten; scarce time to change one's shoes:
I feel as white and sulky as a ghost,
So pray don't speak to me, Lord Belcher.' - No,
I'll look at you instead, and it's enough
While you have that face.' 'In church, my lord! fie, fie!'
- 'Adair, you stayed for the Division?'[9] - 'Lost
By one.' 'The devil it is! I'm sorry for 't.

8. In the first draft manuscript (see textual note), a note in the author's hand identifies this painting as the "Virgin of the golden finch." The Madonna del Cardinello was hung in the Tribune of the Uffizi, which EBB visited in 1847. See *Letters of EBB* 1.331.

9. The "division" is the splitting into yes and no votes when the House of Commons decides an issue. This speaker absented himself from the vote, because he had promised "Mistress Grove" that he would not vote for the proposal.

And if I had not promised Mistress Grove' . .
'You might have kept your word to Liverpool.'
- 'Constituents[1] must remember, after all,
We're mortal.' - 'We remind them of it.' - 'Hark,
The bride comes! here she comes, in a stream of milk!'
- 'There? Dear, you are asleep still; don't you know
The five Miss Granvilles? always dressed in white
To show they're ready to be married.' - 'Lower!
The aunt is at your elbow.' - 'Lady Maud,
Did Lady Waldemar tell you she had seen
This girl of Leigh's?' 'No, - wait! 'twas Mistress Brookes,
Who told me Lady Waldemar told her -
No, 'twasn't Mistress Brookes.' - 'She's pretty?' - 'Who?
Mistress Brookes? Lady Waldemar?' - 'How hot!
Pray is't the law to-day we're not to breathe?
You're treading on my shawl - I thank you, sir.'
- 'They say the bride's a mere child, who can't read,
But knows the things she shouldn't, with wide-awake
Great eyes. I'd go through fire to look at her.'
- 'You do, I think,' - 'And Lady Waldemar
(You see her; sitting close to Romney Leigh.
How beautiful she looks, a little flushed!)
Has taken up the girl, and methodised
Leigh's folly. Should I have come here, you suppose,
Except she'd asked me?' - 'She'd have served him more
By marrying him herself.'
'Ah - there she comes,
The bride, at last!'
'Indeed, no. - Past eleven.
She puts off her patched petticoat to-day
And puts on May-fair manners,[2] so begins
By setting us to wait.' - 'Yes, yes, this Leigh
Was always odd; it's in the blood, I think;
His father's uncle's cousin's second son
Was, was . . you understand me; and for him,
He's stark, - has turned quite lunatic upon
This modern question of the poor - the poor.
An excellent subject when you're moderate;
You've seen Prince Albert's model lodging-house?[3]
Does honour to his Royal Highness. Good!

1. The people whom he is supposed to represent in his constituency (Liverpool here), who voted for him to act as their representative in the House of Commons.
2. She starts to be rude and selfish like other fashionable ladies who think nothing of keeping others waiting.
3. The Society for Improving the Condition of the Labouring Classes built its first model lodging-house for 104 working men in George Street, Bloomsbury, in 1848. Albert, as president of the society, addressed a meeting on May 18, 1848. In 1851 Albert personally financed the erection of four model dwelling houses for families in Cavalry Barrack Yard, opposite the Great Exhibition in Hyde Park. The cottages were later moved and can still be seen in Kennington Park.

But would he stop his carriage in Cheapside[4]
To shake a common fellow by the fist
Whose name was . . Shakspeare? no. We draw a line.
And if we stand not by our order, we
In England, we fall headlong. Here's a sight, -
A hideous sight, a most indecent sight!
My wife would come, sir, or I had kept her back.
By heaven, sir, when poor Damiens' trunk and limbs
Were torn by horses,[5] women of the court
Stood by and stared, exactly as to-day
On this dismembering of society,
With pretty, troubled faces.'
'Now, at last.
She comes now.'
'Where? who sees? you push me, sir,
Beyond the point of what is mannerly.
You're standing, madam, on my second flounce
I do beseech you . . . '
'No, - it's not the bride.
Half-past eleven. How late. The bridegroom, mark,
Gets anxious and goes out.'
'And as I said
These Leighs! - our best blood running in the rut!
It's something awful. We had pardoned him
A simple misalliance got up aside
For a pair of sky-blue eyes; the House of Lords
Has winked at such things, and we've all been young.
But here's an inter-marriage reasoned out,
A contract (carried boldly to the light
To challenge observation, pioneer
Good acts by a great example) 'twixt the extremes
Of martyrised society, - on the left
The well-born, on the right the merest mob,
To treat as equals! - 'tis anarchical;
It means more than it says; 'tis damnable.
Why, sir, we can't have even our coffee good,
Unless we strain it.'
'Here, Miss Leigh!'
'Lord Howe,
You're Romney's friend. What's all this waiting for?

'I cannot tell. The bride has lost her head
(And way, perhaps!) to prove her sympathy

4. An area in the City of London and part of the business and financial district.
5. Robert François Damiens (1715–57) attempted to assassinate Louis XV in 1757 and was condemned to die by "écartélement"—being torn apart by four horses. François Ravaillac (see textual note) also suffered this punishment in 1610 for his part in the assassination of Henry IV.

With the bridegroom.'
'What, - you also disapprove!'

'Oh, *I* approve of nothing in the world.'
He answered, 'not of you, still less of me,
Nor even of Romney, though he's worth us both.
We're all gone wrong. The tune in us is lost;
And whistling down back alleys to the moon
Will never catch it.'
Let me draw Lord Howe.
A born aristocrat, bred radical,
And educated socialist, who still
Goes floating, on traditions of his kind,
Across the theoretic flood from France,[6]
Though, like a drenched Noah on a rotten deck,
Scarce safer for his place there. He, at least,
Will never land on Ararat,[7] he knows,
To recommence the world on the new plan:
Indeed, he thinks, said world had better end,
He sympathises rather with the fish
Outside, than with the drowned paired beasts within
Who cannot couple again or multiply, -
And that's the sort of Noah he is, Lord Howe.
He never could be anything complete,
Except a loyal, upright gentleman,
A liberal landlord, graceful diner-out,
And entertainer more than hospitable,
Whom authors dine with and forget the hock.
Whatever he believes, and it is much,
But nowise certain, now here and now there,
He still has sympathies beyond his creed
Diverting him from action. In the House,[8]
No party counts upon him, while for all
His speeches have a noticeable weight.
Men like his books too, (he has written books)
Which, safe to lie beside a bishop's chair,
At times outreach themselves with jets of fire
At which the foremost of the progressists[9]
May warm audacious hands in passing by.
Of stature over-tall, lounging for ease;

6. For EBB's attitude to the French socialist movement, see *Aurora Leigh* 6.56–66. EBB was familiar with the works of Fourier, Blanc, Proudhon, Comte, and Cabet, but she did not believe their theories to be either practical or desirable. See *Letters of EBB* 1.452, 467.
7. After the flood that lasted forty days and forty nights, Noah's ark landed on Mount Ararat (now in modern Turkey), and a rainbow in the sky signalled the end of the flood and the beginning of a new covenant between God and man. See Genesis 8.4.
8. The House of Lords, presumably.
9. A term coined in the 1840s for one who favors or advocates progress, especially in social or political matters (OED).

Light hair, that seems to carry a wind in it,
And eyes that, when they look on you, will lean
Their whole weight, half in indolence and half
In wishing you unmitigated good,
Until you know not if to flinch from him
Or thank him. - 'Tis Lord Howe.
'We're all gone wrong,'
Said he, 'and Romney, that dear friend of ours,
Is nowise right. There's one true thing on earth,
That's love! he takes it up, and dresses it,
And acts a play with it, as Hamlet did,
To show what cruel uncles we have been,[1]
And how we should be uneasy in our minds
While he, Prince Hamlet, weds a pretty maid
(Who keeps us too long waiting, we'll confess)
By symbol, to instruct us formally
To fill the ditches up 'twixt class and class,
And live together in phalansteries.[2]
What then? - he's mad, our Hamlet! clap his play,
And bind him.'
'Ah Lord Howe, this spectacle
Pulls stronger at us than the Dane's.[3] See there!
The crammed aisles heave and strain and steam with life.
Dear Heaven, what life!'
'Why, yes, - a poet sees;
Which makes him different from a common man.
I, too, see somewhat, though I cannot sing;
I should have been a poet, only that
My mother took fright at the ugly world,
And bore me tongue-tied. If you'll grant me now
That Romney gives us a fine actor-piece
To make us merry on his marriage-morn,
The fable's worse than Hamlet's I'll concede.
The terrible people, old and poor and blind,
Their eyes eat out with plague and poverty
From seeing beautiful and cheerful sights,
We'll liken to a brutalised King Lear,[4]
Led out, - by no means to clear scores with wrongs -
His wrongs are so far back, he has forgot,

1. In Shakespeare's *Hamlet*, 3.2, the young prince, suspecting his uncle, now his stepfather, to have been guilty of the murder of his father, persuades a troop of traveling players to perform a play that mirrors the murder, in order to test his uncle's conscience.
2. See note to *Aurora Leigh* 3.108.
3. Hamlet is prince of Denmark.
4. In Shakespeare's *King Lear* the old king gives away his kingdom to his daughters, leaving himself poor and dependent on their good will. When he does not receive the treatment that is his due, he exiles himself to beggary, living among paupers and madmen. It is, however, Lear's loyal courtier Gloucester who is blinded by the daughters for showing support for the king.

(All's past like youth;) but just to witness here
A simple contract, - he, upon his side,
And Regan with her sister Goneril[5]
And all the dappled courtiers and court-fools
On their side. Not that any of these would say
They're sorry, neither. What is done, is done,
And violence is now turned privilege,
As cream turns cheese, if buried long enough.
What could such lovely ladies have to do
With the old man there, in those ill-odorous rags,
Except to keep the wind-side of him?[6] Lear
Is flat and quiet, as a decent grave;
He does not curse his daughters in the least;
*Be* these his daughters? Lear is thinking of
His porridge chiefly . . is it getting cold
At Hampstead? will the ale be served in pots?
Poor Lear, poor daughters! Bravo, Romney's play!'

A murmur and a movement drew around,
A naked whisper touched us. Something wrong.
What's wrong? The black crowd, as an overstrained
Cord, quivered in vibration, and I saw . .
Was that *his* face I saw? . . his . . Romney Leigh's . .
Which tossed a sudden horror like a spunge[7]
Into all eyes, - while himself stood white upon
The topmost altar-stair and tried to speak,
And failed, and lifted higher above his head
A letter, . . as a man who drowns and gasps.

'My brothers, bear with me! I am very weak.
I meant but only good. Perhaps I meant
Too proudly, and God snatched the circumstance
And changed it therefore. There's no marriage - none.
She leaves me, - she departs, - she disappears,
I lose her. Yet I never forced her 'ay,'
To have her 'no' so cast into my teeth
In manner of an accusation, thus.
My friends, you are dismissed. Go, eat and drink
According to the programme, - and farewell!'

He ended. There was silence in the church.
We heard a baby sucking in its sleep
At the farthest end of the aisle. Then spoke a man,

5. Two of Lear's daughters.
6. Avoid standing where the wind blows over the old man thus bringing his bad smell to their nostrils.
7. A reference to Cassandra's vision of approaching slaughter in Aeschylus's *Agamemnon* 1.232–33. See note to *Aurora Leigh* 3.182–83.

'Now, look to it, coves,[8] that all the beef and drink
Be not filched[9] from us like the other fun,
For beer's spilt easier than a woman's lost!
This gentry is not honest with the poor;
They bring us up, to trick us.' - 'Go it, Jim,'
A woman screamed back, - 'I'm a tender soul,
I never banged a child at two years old
And drew blood from him, but I sobbed for it
Next moment, - and I've had a plague of seven.
I'm tender; I've no stomach even for beef,
Until I know about the girl that's lost,
That's killed, mayhap. I did misdoubt,[1] at first,
The fine lord meant no good by her or us.
He, maybe, got the upper hand of her
By holding up a wedding-ring, and then . .
A choking finger on her throat last night,
And just a clever tale to keep us still,
As she is, poor lost innocent. 'Disappear!'
Who ever disappears except a ghost?
And who believes a story of a ghost?
I ask you, - would a girl go off, instead
Of staying to be married? a fine tale!
A wicked man, I say, a wicked man!
For my part I would rather starve on gin
Than make my dinner on his beef and beer.'[2] -
At which a cry rose up - 'We'll have our rights.
We'll have the girl, the girl! Your ladies there
Are married safely and smoothly every day,
And *she* shall not drop through into a trap
Because she's poor and of the people: shame!
We'll have no tricks played off by gentlefolks;
We'll see her righted.'
                                        Through the rage and roar
I heard the broken words which Romney flung
Among the turbulent masses, from the ground
He held still with his masterful pale face, -
As huntsmen throw the ration to the pack,[3]
Who, falling on it headlong, dog on dog
In heaps of fury, rend it, swallow it up
With yelling hound-jaws, - his indignant words,

8. Slang term for fellows or chaps (OED).
9. Slang term meaning to take away surreptitiously, to pilfer (OED).
1. Doubt, suspect; *Mayhap*: perhaps.
2. A proverbial coupling. Gin was the cheap spirit drunk by the poor, often with disastrous consequences to health, as much due to the adulteration of the drink as to the effects of drunkenness itself. Beer, on the other hand, was considered a traditional and healthful drink for the lower classes.
3. At the end of the hunt, after the fox has been killed, part of the carcass is thrown to the pack of hounds as their reward.

His suppliant words, his most pathetic words,
Whereof I caught the meaning here and there
By his gesture . . torn in morsels, yelled across,
And so devoured. From end to end, the church
Rocked round us like the sea in storm, and then
Broke up like the earth in earthquake. Men cried out
'Police' - and women stood and shrieked for God,
Or dropt and swooned; or, like a herd of deer,
(For whom the black woods suddenly grow alive,
Unleashing their wild shadows down the wind
To hunt the creatures into corners, back
And forward) madly fled, or blindly fell,
Trod screeching underneath the feet of those
Who fled and screeched.
The last sight left to me
Was Romney's terrible calm face above
The tumult! the last sound was 'Pull him down!
Strike - kill him!' Stretching my unreasoning arms,
As men in dreams, who vainly interpose
'Twixt gods and their undoing, with a cry
I struggled to precipitate myself
Head-foremost to the rescue of my soul
In that white face, . . till some one caught me back,
And so the world went out, - I felt no more.

What followed was told after by Lord Howe,
Who bore me senseless from the strangling crowd
In church and street, and then returned alone
To see the tumult quelled. The men of law
Had fallen as thunder on a roaring fire,
And made all silent, - while the people's smoke
Passed eddying slowly from the emptied aisles.

Here's Marian's letter, which a ragged child
Brought running, just as Romney at the porch
Looked out expectant of the bride. He sent
The letter to me by his friend Lord Howe
Some two hours after, folded in a sheet
On which his well-known hand had left a word.
Here's Marian's letter.
'Noble friend, dear saint,
Be patient with me. Never think me vile,
Who might to-morrow morning be your wife
But that I loved you more than such a name.
Farewell, my Romney. Let me write it once, -
My Romney.
' 'Tis so pretty a coupled word,

I have no heart to pluck it with a blot.
We say 'my God' sometimes, upon our knees,
Who is not therefore vexed: so bear with it . .
And me. I know I'm foolish, weak, and vain;
Yet most of all I'm angry with myself
For losing your last footstep on the stair
That last time of your coming, - yesterday!
The very first time I lost step of yours,
(Its sweetness comes the next to what you speak)
But yesterday sobs took me by the throat
And cut me off from music.
'Mister Leigh,
You'll set me down as wrong in many things.
You've praised me, sir, for truth, - and now you'll learn
I had not courage to be rightly true.
I once began to tell you how she came,
The woman . . and you stared upon the floor
In one of your fixed thoughts . . which put me out
For that day. After, some one spoke of me,
So wisely, and of you, so tenderly,
Persuading me to silence for your sake . . .
Well, well! it seems this moment I was wrong
In keeping back from telling you the truth:
There might be truth betwixt us two, at least,
If nothing else. And yet 'twas dangerous.
Suppose a real angel came from heaven
To live with men and women! he'd go mad,
If no considerate hand should tie a blind
Across his piercing eyes. 'Tis thus with you:
You see us too much in your heavenly light;
I always thought so, angel, - and indeed
There's danger that you beat yourself to death
Against the edges of this alien world,
In some divine and fluttering pity.
'Yes,
It would be dreadful for a friend of yours,
To see all England thrust you out of doors
And mock you from the windows. You might say,
Or think (that's worse), 'There's some one in the house
I miss and love still.' Dreadful!
'Very kind,
I pray you mark, was Lady Waldemar.
She came to see me nine times, rather ten -
So beautiful, she hurts one like the day
Let suddenly on sick eyes.
'Most kind of all,
Your cousin! - ah, most like you! Ere you came

She kissed me mouth to mouth: I felt her soul
Dip through her serious lips in holy fire.
God help me, but it made me arrogant;
I almost told her that you would not lose
By taking me to wife: though ever since
I've pondered much a certain thing she asked . .
'He loves you, Marian?' . . in a sort of mild
Derisive sadness . . as a mother asks
Her babe, 'You'll touch that star, you think?'
'Farewell!
I know I never touched it.
'This is worst:
Babes grow and lose the hope of things above;
A silver threepence sets them leaping high -
But no more stars! mark that.
'I've writ all night
Yet told you nothing. God, if I could die,
And let this letter break off innocent
Just here! But no - for your sake . .
'Here's the last:
I never could be happy as your wife,
I never could be harmless as your friend,
I never will look more into your face
Till God says, 'Look!' I charge you, seek me not,
Nor vex yourself with lamentable thoughts
That peradventure I have come to grief;
Be sure I'm well, I'm merry, I'm at ease,
But such a long way, long way, long way off,
I think you'll find me sooner in my grave,
And that's my choice, observe. For what remains,
An over-generous friend will care for me
And keep me happy . . happier . .
'There's a blot!
This ink runs thick . . we light girls lightly weep . .
And keep me happier . . was the thing to say,
Than as your wife I could be. - O, my star,
My saint, my soul! for surely you're my soul,
Through whom God touched me! I am not so lost
I cannot thank you for the good you did,
The tears you stopped, which fell down bitterly,
Like these - the times you made me weep for joy
At hoping I should learn to write your notes
And save the tiring of your eyes, at night;[4]

4. EBB referred to this remark of Marian's in defending herself against the charge of plagiarizing *Jane Eyre* for the circumstances of Romney's blinding: "the eyes, the visual nerve perished showing no external stain—perished as Milton's did. I believe that a great shock on the nerves might produce such an effect in certain constitutions, and the reader on referring as far back as Marian's letter (when she avoided the marriage) may observe that his eyes had never been

And most for that sweet thrice you kissed my lips
Saying 'Dear Marian.'
' 'Twould be hard to read,
This letter, for a reader half as learn'd;
But you'll be sure to master it in spite
Of ups and downs. My hand shakes, I am blind;
I'm poor at writing at the best, - and yet
I tried to make my *gs* the way you showed.
Farewell. Christ love you. - Say 'poor Marian' now.'

Poor Marian! - wanton Marian! - was it so,
Or so? For days, her touching, foolish lines
We mused on with conjectural fantasy,
As if some riddle of a summer-cloud
On which one tries unlike similitudes
Of now a spotted Hydra-skin[5] cast off,
And now a screen of carven ivory
That shuts the heavens' conventual secrets up
From mortals[6] over-bold. We sought the sense:
She loved him so perhaps (such words mean love,)
That, worked on by some shrewd perfidious tongue,
(And then I thought of Lady Waldemar)
She left him, not to hurt him; or perhaps
She loved one in her class, - or did not love,
But mused upon her wild bad tramping life
Until the free blood fluttered at her heart,
And black bread[7] eaten by the road-side hedge
Seemed sweeter than being put to Romney's school
Of philanthropical self-sacrifice
Irrevocably. - Girls are girls, beside,
Thought I, and like a wedding by one rule.
You seldom catch these birds except with chaff:
They feel it almost an immoral thing
To go out and be married in broad day,
Unless some winning special flattery should
Excuse them to themselves for 't, . . 'No one parts
Her hair with such a silver line as you,
One moonbeam from the forehead to the crown!'

---

strong, that her desire had been to read his notes at night, and save them. For it was necessary, I thought, to the bringing-out of my thought, that Romney should be mulcted in his natural sight" (*Letters of EBB* 2.246).

5. The Hydra, a nine-headed serpent living in the Lernaean swamp, ravaged the country of Argos. Hercules's second labor was the execution of this beast, which he accomplished with the help of his servant, Iolaus (Apollodorus, *The Library*, 2.5.2). The idea EBB uses here is of the seven-headed serpent shedding its skin.
6. The public room at a convent, where nuns would be able to receive visitors from the outside world, would be divided by a screen allowing the nuns to see out, but preventing the visitors from looking in.
7. Rough bread or rye bread made from unrefined flour and therefore cheaper than expensive white bread.

Or else . . 'You bite your lip in such a way,
It spoils me for the smiling of the rest,'
And so on. Then a worthless gaud[8] or two
To keep for love, - a ribbon for the neck,
Or some glass pin, - they have their weight with girls.

And Romney sought her many days and weeks:
He sifted all the refuse of the town,
Explored the trains, inquired among the ships,
And felt the country through from end to end;
No Marian! - Though I hinted what I knew, -
A friend of his had reasons of her own
For throwing back the match - he would not hear:
The lady had been ailing ever since,
The shock had harmed her. Something in his tone
Repressed me; something in me shamed my doubt
To a sigh repressed too. He went on to say
That, putting questions where his Marian lodged,
He found she had received for visitors,
Besides himself and Lady Waldemar
And, that once, me - a dubious woman dressed
Beyond us both;[9] the rings upon her hands
Had dazed the children when she threw them pence;
'She wore her bonnet as the queen might hers,
To show the crown,' they said, - 'a scarlet crown
Of roses that had never been in bud.'

When Romney told me that, - for now and then
He came to tell how the search advanced,
His voice dropped: I bent forward for the rest:
The woman had been with her, it appeared,
At first from week to week, then day by day,
And last, 'twas sure . .
                    I looked upon the ground
To escape the anguish of his eyes, and asked
As low as when you speak to mourners new
Of those they cannot bear yet to call dead,
'If Marian had as much as named to him
A certain Rose, an early friend of hers,
A ruined creature.'
                    'Never.' - Starting up
He strode from side to side about the room,
Most like some prisoned lion sprung awake,
Who has felt the desert sting him through his dreams.

8. Trifle; cheap and showy item.
9. A woman whose ostentatious and extravagant costume allowed the observers to take her for a fallen woman, a kept woman, or a prostitute.

'What was I to her, that she should tell me aught?
A friend! was *I* a friend? I see all clear.
Such devils would pull angels out of heaven,
Provided they could reach them; 'tis their pride;
And that's the odds 'twixt soul and body-plague!
The veriest slave who drops in Cairo's street,[1]
Cries, 'Stand off from me,'[2] to the passengers;
While these blotched souls are eager to infect,
And blow their bad breath in a sister's face
As if they got some ease by it.'
                                        I broke through.
'Some natures catch no plagues. I've read of babes
Found whole and sleeping by the spotted breast
Of one a full day dead. I hold it true,
As I'm a woman and know womanhood,
That Marian Erle, however lured from place,
Deceived in way, keeps pure in aim and heart
As snow that's drifted from the garden-bank
To the open road.'
                        'Twas hard to hear him laugh.
'The figure's happy. Well - a dozen carts
And trampers will secure you presently
A fine white snow-drift. Leave it there, your snow!
'Twill pass for soot ere sunset. Pure in aim?
She's pure in aim, I grant you, - like myself,
Who thought to take the world upon my back
To carry it o'er a chasm[3] of social ill,
And end by letting slip through impotence
A single soul, a child's weight in a soul,
Straight down the pit of hell! yes, I and she
Have reason to be proud of our pure aims.'
Then softly, as the last repenting drops
Of a thunder-shower, he added, 'The poor child,
Poor Marian! 'twas a luckless day for her,
When first she chanced on my philanthropy.'

He drew a chair beside me, and sate down;
And I, instinctively, as women use
Before a sweet friend's grief, - when, in his ear,
They hum the tune of comfort though themselves
Most ignorant of the special words of such,
And quiet so and fortify his brain
And give it time and strength for feeling out

1. Outbreaks of the plague were fairly common in Egypt until the last years of the nineteenth century.
2. A reminiscence of Leviticus 13.45, where a leper is required to cry "Unclean, unclean."
3. A reminiscence of St. Christopher, who carried the Christ child over a river on his back.

To reach the availing sense beyond that sound, -
Went murmuring to him what, if written here,
Would seem not much, yet fetched him better help
Than peradventure if it had been more.
I've known the pregnant thinkers of our time,
And stood by breathless, hanging on their lips,
When some chromatic sequence[4] of fine thought
In learned modulation[5] phrased itself
To an unconjectured harmony of truth:
And yet I've been more moved, more raised, I say,
By a simple word . . a broken easy thing
A three-years infant might at need repeat,
A look, a sigh, a touch upon the palm,
Which meant less than 'I love you,' than by all
The full-voiced rhetoric of those master-mouths.

'Ah dear Aurora,' he began at last,
His pale lips fumbling for a sort of smile,
'Your printer's devils[6] have not spoilt your heart:
That's well. And who knows but, long years ago
When you and I talked, you were somewhat right
In being so peevish with me? You, at least,
Have ruined no one through your dreams. Instead,
You've helped the facile youth to live youth's day
With innocent distraction, still perhaps
Suggestive of things better than your rhymes.
The little shepherd-maiden, eight years old,
I've seen upon the mountains of Vaucluse,[7]
Asleep i' the sun, her head upon her knees,
The flocks all scattered, - is more laudable
Than any sheep-dog trained imperfectly,
Who bites the kids through too much zeal.'
                                        'I look
As if I had slept, then?'
                        He was touched at once
By something in my face. Indeed 'twas sure
That he and I, - despite a year or two
Of younger life on my side, and on his
The heaping of the years' work on the days,
The three-hour speeches from the member's seat,[8]

4. A musical reference to the chromatic scale, which includes every tone and semitone in the scale moving directly from one to the other, leaving no note out.
5. Another musical term; resolution, or movement from one mode or key to another.
6. The "printer's devil" was the assistant who inked the typeface so that the impression would mark the paper. These assistants were popularly called devils, apparently because the nature of their job meant that they were permanently covered in black ink.
7. The valley of Vaucluse, not far from Avignon in Provence. The Brownings made a "pilgrimage" to Vaucluse in 1846 for the sake of the poet Petrarch (see note to 4.1150).
8. In the House of Commons.

The hot committees in and out of doors,
The pamphlets, 'Arguments,' 'Collective Views,'
Tossed out as straw before sick houses,[9] just
To show one's sick and so be trod to dirt
And no more use, - through this world's underground
The burrowing, groping effort, whence the arm
And heart come torn, - 'twas sure that he and I
Were, after all, unequally fatigued;
That he, in his developed manhood, stood
A little sunburnt by the glare of life,
While I . . it seemed no sun had shone on me,
So many seasons I had missed my Springs.
My cheeks had pined and perished from their orbs,
And all the youth-blood in them had grown white
As dew on autumn cyclamens; alone
My eyes and forehead answered for my face.
He said, 'Aurora, you are changed - are ill!'

'Not so, my cousin, - only not asleep,'
I answered, smiling gently. 'Let it be.
You scarcely found the poet of Vaucluse[1]
As drowsy as the shepherds. What is art
But life upon the larger scale, the higher,
When, graduating up in a spiral line
Of still expanding and ascending gyres,[2]
It pushes toward the intense significance
Of all things, hungry for the Infinite?
Art's life, - and where we live, we suffer and toil.'

He seemed to sift[3] me with his painful eyes.
'You take it gravely, cousin; you refuse
Your dreamland's right of common,[4] and green rest.
You break the mythic turf where danced the nymphs,
With crooked ploughs of actual life,[5] - let in
The axes to the legendary woods,

9. Refers to the practice of laying straw in the street before the house where a person lay ill, in order to muffle the din of wheels rattling over the stones. The practice continued well into the twentieth century.
1. Francesco Petrarca (1304–74), the Italian poet who lived chiefly at Avignon, near Vaucluse. Petrarch loved the solitude of Vaucluse and retreated to the valley to write and work. His most famous work, the poems to Laura, or *Canzoniere*, were composed here, but he also began his unfinished Latin poem, *Africa*—an epic on Scipio Africanus, modeled on Virgil's *Aeneid*—while he was staying at Vaucluse.
2. Ascending spirals, but the word has a special mystic significance as the path of aspiration that links earth and heaven.
3. To examine closely, to scrutinize narrowly, so as to find out the truth (OED).
4. The right to use common pasture, notionally belonging to all with freedom of access and use.
5. You turn the happy pastoral ways of life that characterized the early mythical days of the world into the harsher and more rigorous agricultural patterns of existence. The idea is parallel to the fall of Adam, where he was turned out of the Garden of Eden, and forced to till the land to grow food.

To pay the poll-tax.[6] You are fallen indeed
On evil days, you poets, if yourselves
Can praise that art of yours no otherwise;
And, if you cannot, . . better take a trade
And be of use: 'twere cheaper for your youth.'

'Of use!' I softly echoed, 'there's the point
We sweep about for ever in argument,
Like swallows[7] which the exasperate, dying year
Sets spinning in black circles, round and round,
Preparing for far flights o'er unknown seas.
And we, where tend we?'
                    'Where?' he said, and sighed.
'The whole creation, from the hour we are born,
Perplexes us with questions. Not a stone
But cries behind us, every weary step,[8]
'Where, where?' I leave stones to reply to stones.
Enough for me and for my fleshly heart
To harken the invocations[9] of my kind,
When men catch hold upon my shuddering nerves
And shriek, 'What help? what hope? what bread i' the house,
'What fire i' the frost?' There must be some response,
Though mine fail utterly. This social Sphinx[1]
Who sits between the sepulchres and stews,[2]
Makes mock and mow[3] against the crystal heavens,
And bullies God, - exacts a word at least
From each man standing on the side of God,
However paying a sphinx-price for it.

6. A tax levied on every person, a capitation or head tax (OED). An unpopular tax in the Middle Ages, recently reintroduced in Britain amid much controversy, and eventually rescinded.
7. The swallows that live in Britain during the summer months emigrate as a group to Egypt and warmer climates during the winter.
8. An allusion to the story of the Princess Periezade (or Perizadah) and the Speaking Bird, the Singing Tree, and the Golden Water, from the *Tales of the Arabian Nights.* As Periezade ascends the mountain in search of the Speaking Bird, she is constantly assailed by disembodied voices crying taunts and insults. The numerous Black Stones that litter the mountainside are all that remains of the questors who have preceded her, among them her own brothers, and who failed in their attempt to reach the summit.
   The story is often referred to in the 1845–46 correspondence of the Brownings—see for example EBB on Mary Russell Mitford's probable reaction to her marriage: "She is one of the Black Stones, which, when I climb up towards my Singing Tree & Golden Water, will howl behind me and call names" (*RB/EBB Letters* 2.1018).
9. Prayers.
1. The Sphinx was a monster, half woman and half beast, which terrorized the inhabitants of Thebes by standing at a crossroads near the city and forbidding any traveler to pass without attempting her riddles. If they failed to answer correctly, they died. Oedipus solved the riddle, killed the Sphinx, and was crowned king by a grateful Thebes. The image of human life and social problems as a Sphinxine enigma whose riddle none could read was not unique to EBB. Compare Thomas Carlyle's reference in *Sartor Resartus* (1833–34), bk. 2, ch. 4: " 'The Universe,' he says, 'was a mighty Sphinx-riddle, which I knew so little of, yet must rede, or be devoured" (*Works of Thomas Carlyle* 6.78).
2. Whorehouses.
3. Makes mocking gestures and grimaces.

We pay it also if we hold our peace,
In pangs and pity. Let me speak and die.
Alas, you'll say I speak and kill instead.'

I pressed in there. 'The best men, doing their best,
Know peradventure least of what they do:
Men usefullest i' the world are simply used;
The nail that holds the wood, must pierce it first,
And He alone who wields the hammer sees
The work advanced by the earliest blow. Take heart.'

'Ah, if I could have taken yours!' he said,
'But that's past now.' Then rising, - 'I will take
At least your kindness and encouragement.
I thank you. Dear, be happy. Sing your songs,
If that's your way! but sometimes slumber too,
Nor tire too much with following, out of breath,
The rhymes upon your mountains of Delight.
Reflect, if Art be in truth the higher life,
You need the lower life to stand upon
In order to reach up unto that higher;
And none can stand a-tiptoe in the place
He cannot stand in with two stable feet.
Remember then! - for Art's sake, hold your life.'

We parted so. I held him in respect.
I comprehended what he was in heart
And sacrificial greatness. Ay, but he
Supposed me a thing too small, to deign to know:
He blew me, plainly, from the crucible
As some intruding, interrupting fly,
Not worth the pains of his analysis[4]
Absorbed on nobler subjects. Hurt a fly!
He would not for the world: he's pitiful
To flies even. 'Sing,' says he, 'and tease me still,
If that's your way, poor insect.' That's your way!

4. The image used here is that of the scientist or chemist who collects material in a crucible in order to conduct an experiment on the matter contained there.

## Fifth Book

Aurora Leigh, be humble. Shall I hope
To speak my poems in mysterious tune
With man and nature? - with the lava-lymph[1]
That trickles from successive galaxies
Still drop by drop adown the finger of God[2]
In still new worlds? - with summer-days in this
That scarce dare breathe they are so beautiful?
With spring's delicious trouble in the ground,
Tormented by the quickened blood of roots,
And softly pricked by golden crocus-sheaves
In token of the harvest-time of flowers?
With winters and with autumns, - and beyond
With the human heart's large seasons, when it hopes
And fears, joys, grieves, and loves? - with all that strain
Of sexual passion, which devours the flesh
In a sacrament of souls?[3] with mother's breasts
Which, round the new-made creatures hanging there,
Throb luminous and harmonious like pure spheres? -
With multitudinous life, and finally
With the great escapings of ecstatic souls,
Who, in a rush of too long prisoned flame,
Their radiant faces upward, burn away
This dark of the body, issuing on a world,
Beyond our mortal? - can I speak my verse
So plainly in tune to these things and the rest,
That men shall feel it catch them on the quick,
As having the same warrant over them
To hold and move them if they will or no,
Alike imperious as the primal rhythm
Of that theurgic nature?[4] - I must fail,
Who fail at the beginning to hold and move
One man, - and he my cousin, and he my friend,
And he born tender, made intelligent,
Inclined to ponder the precipitous sides
Of difficult questions; yet, obtuse to *me*,
Of *me*, incurious! likes me very well,

1. Meaning the creative essence. Lava from the volcano is an image of elemental upheaval, and "lymph" is derived from descriptions of bodily fluids.
2. EBB seems to have been much influenced in her picture of creation by Michelangelo's image of God creating Adam, painted in the Sistine chapel in the Vatican in Rome, where God is shown in the act of animating Adam's clay.
3. Cf. the use of the same concept linking spiritual and sexual love in *Aurora Leigh* 1.89–91.
4. Theurgy is the operation of a divine or supernatural agency in human affairs.

And wishes me a paradise of good,
Good looks, good means, and good digestion, - ay,
But otherwise evades me, puts me off
With kindness, with a tolerant gentleness, -
Too light a book for a grave man's reading! Go,
Aurora Leigh: be humble.
There it is,
We women are too apt to look to One,[5]
Which proves a certain impotence in art.
We strain our natures at doing something great,
Far less because it's something great to do,
Than haply that we, so, commend ourselves
As being not small, and more appreciable
To some one friend. We must have mediators
Betwixt our highest conscience and the judge;
Some sweet saint's blood must quicken in our palms[6]
Or all the life in heaven seems slow and cold:
Good only being perceived as the end of good,
And God alone pleased, - that's too poor, we think,
And not enough for us by any means.
Ay, Romney, I remember, told me once
We miss the abstract when we comprehend.
We miss it most when we aspire, - and fail.

Yet, so, I will not. - This vile woman's way
Of trailing garments, shall not trip me up:
I'll have no traffic with the personal thought
In art's pure temple. Must I work in vain,
Without the approbation of a man?
It cannot be; it shall not. Fame itself,
That approbation of the general race
Presents a poor end, (though the arrow speed,
Shot straight with vigorous finger to the white,)[7]

5. Aurora rehearses here one of the platitudes of sexual difference that were common in the nineteenth century. The notion that a woman could be inspired only by the personal and the sentimental appears also in Aurora's argument with Romney in book 2, reappears here and in book 6, and is discussed again in her revised debate with Romney in books 8 and 9.

6. A revised reminiscence of a famous passage from Shakespeare's *Romeo and Juliet* 1.5.97–114: "If I profane with my unworthiest hand/This holy shrine, the gentle sin is this;/My lips, two blushing pilgrims, ready stand/To smooth that rough touch with a tender kiss." Juliet: "Good pilgrim, you do wrong your hand too much,/Which mannerly devotion shows in this;/ For saints have hands that pilgrims' hands do touch,/And palm to palm is holy palmer's kiss. . . ," etc.

7. The "white" is the center of the target on the archery board. EBB here remembers the exact terms of a compliment paid to her by RB quite early in their correspondence: "Let me say how perfect, absolutely perfect, are those three or four pages in the Vision ["A Vision of Poets" by EBB (1844)] which present the Poets; a line, a few words and the man there—one twang of the bow and the arrow head in the white . . ." (RB to EBB, August 4, 1845, *RB/EBB Letters* 1.142).

And the highest fame was never reached except
By what was aimed above it.[8] Art for art,
And good for God Himself, the essential Good!
We'll keep our aims sublime, our eyes erect,
Although our woman-hands should shake and fail;
And if we fail . . But must we? -
Shall I fail?
The Greeks said grandly in their tragic phrase,
'Let no one be called happy till his death.'[9]
To which I add, - Let no one till his death
Be called unhappy. Measure not the work
Until the day's out and the labour done,
Then bring your gauges. If the day's work's scant,
Why, call it scant; affect no compromise;
And, in that we have nobly striven at least,
Deal with us nobly, women though we be.
And honour us with truth if not with praise.

My ballads prospered; but the ballad's race
Is rapid for a poet who bears weights
Of thought and golden image. He can stand
Like Atlas, in the sonnet,[1] - and support
His own heavens pregnant with dynastic[2] stars;
But then he must stand still, nor take a step.

In that descriptive poem called 'The Hills,'
The prospects were too far and indistinct.
'Tis true my critics said, 'A fine view, that!'
The public scarcely cared to climb my book
For even the finest, and the public's right;
A tree's mere firewood, unless humanised, -
Which well the Greeks knew when they stirred its bark
With close-pressed bosoms of subsiding nymphs,[3]
And made the forest-rivers garrulous

8. Cf. RB's essay on Shelley: "We may learn from the biography whether his spirit invariably saw and spoke from the last height to which it had attained. . . . Did the poet ever attain to a higher platform than where he rested and exhibited a result? Did he know more than he spoke of?" (*Letters of Percy Bysshe Shelley* [1852], 17).
9. The last line of Sophocles's tragedy *Oedipus Tyrannus* (1528–30). See also Euripedes, *Andromache*, 100–101.
1. This simile seems to be derived from a reading of John Keats' verse-epistle "To Charles Cowden Clark" (1817): "Who read for me the sonnet swelling loudly/Up to its climax and then dying proudly?/Who found for me the grandeur of the ode./Growing, like Atlas, stronger from its load . . ." (lines 60–67).
2. Ruskin, who frequently found cause to quarrel with the vocabulary used by the Brownings, declared that "Dynastick hurts me like a stick" (John Ruskin to RB, November 27, 1856, *The Works of John Ruskin*, 36.248).
3. A reference to the story of Daphne, who, fleeing from Apollo, was changed into a laurel tree (Ovid, *Metamorphoses* 1.548–52).

With babble of gods.[4] For us, we are called to mark
A still more intimate humanity
In this inferior nature, or ourselves
Must fall like dead leaves trodden underfoot
By veritable artists. Earth (shut up
By Adam, like a fakir in a box[5]
Left too long buried) remained stiff and dry,
A mere dumb corpse, till Christ the Lord came down,[6]
Unlocked the doors, forced open the blank eyes,
And used his kingly chrism[7] to straighten out
The leathery tongue turned back into the throat;
Since when, she lives, remembers, palpitates
In every limb, aspires in every breath,
Embraces infinite relations. Now
We want no half-gods, Panomphæan Joves,[8]
Fauns, Naiads, Tritons, Oreads and the rest,[9]
To take possession of a senseless world[1]
To unnatural vampire-uses.[2] See the earth,

4. EBB's argument in this passage is very similar to that propounded by Ruskin in his chapter "Of Classical Landscape" (*The Works of John Ruskin: Modern Painters* 3.1856). Ruskin points out that the Greeks invested all the constituents of the natural world with an animating superhuman spirit: "What sympathy and fellowship he had, were always for the spirit *in* the stream, not for the stream; always for the dryad *in* the wood, not for the wood. Content with this human sympathy, he approached the actual waves and woody fibres with no sympathy at all . . . they, without their spirit, were dead enough" (*The Works of John Ruskin*, 5.232).
5. The practice of being buried alive *(samadh)* was rare among Hindu religious devotees, but if a fakir survived it, the practice conferred great sanctity on him. A well-known case was reported by J. M. Honigberger in 1852. He was told, in 1839, of a certain "faqueer" named Haridas who, at the invitation of Runjeet Sing, the maharajah of Lahore, had submitted to being locked in a chest and buried for forty days. When he was exhumed, Haridas was discovered "cold and stiff," still in the state of asphyxiation that he had willingly induced forty days earlier. Honigberger goes on to explain that the practitioners of samadh loosen their tongue as much as possible, by surgery and by exercise, "in order that they may be able to lay back the tongue at the time that they are about to stop respiration, so as to cover the orifice of the hinder part of the *fosses nasales*, and thus . . . keep the air shut up in the body and head." On the exhumation of the fakir, "one of the first operations is to draw his tongue into its natural position," a warm aromatic paste is applied to his head, plugs of wax are removed from the ears and nose, and strenuous friction is applied to the body (J. M. Honigberger, *Thirty-Five Years in the East* [London, 1852], 126–30).
   EBB's circumstantial description of samadh and her allusion to other Hindu ascetic practices (see note to *Aurora Leigh* 7.1212), suggest that she must have read a work on the mystics and ascetics of India.
6. Adam's was the first sin and the first fall, which was redeemed by the death of Christ.
7. Oil mingled with balm, consecrated for use as an unguent in the administration of certain sacraments in the eastern and western churches.
8. See EBB's "The Dead Pan" (1844), where she argues that the advent of Christian salvation abolished the need for the ancient conception of the inhabitation of the physical world by minor gods, by investing the natural world with a superior spiritual significance as the type of the invisible supernatural world.
9. Panomphaeus, "the author of all signs and omens," is a surname of Zeus.
1. A faun, half man, half animal, lives in the woods. The naiad is the spirit who lives in the water; a triton is an attendant of Neptune and lives in the sea; an oread is a spirit of the woods. They are all spirits according to the conventions of ancient mythology.
2. The point here is that if spirits are needed to animate the body of the earth, then the body of the earth is otherwise dead and needs to be made alive by the supernatural activities of the "vampire" spirits. Aurora argues that, in fact, the earth itself is alive, and does not need this supernatural agency to make it animated.

The body of our body, the green earth,
Indubitably human like this flesh
And these articulated veins through which
Our heart drives blood. There's not a flower of spring
That dies ere June, but vaunts itself allied
By issue and symbol, by significance
And correspondence, to that spirit-world
Outside the limits of our space and time,[3]
Whereto we are bound. Let poets give it voice
With human meanings, - else they miss the thought,[4]
And henceforth step down lower, stand confessed
Instructed poorly for interpreters,
Thrown out by an easy cowslip in the text.

Even so my pastoral[5] failed; it was a book
Of surface-pictures - pretty, cold, and false
With literal transcript, - the worse done, I think,
For being not ill-done: let me set my mark
Against such doings, and do otherwise.

This strikes me. - If the public whom we know
Could catch me at such admissions, I should pass
For being right modest. Yet how proud we are,
In daring to look down upon ourselves!

The critics say that epics have died out[6]
With Agamemnon[7] and the goat-nursed gods;[8]
I'll not believe it. I could never deem
As Payne Knight[9] did, (the mythic mountaineer

3. EBB derives this concept from the doctrine of Emmanuel Swedenborg (1688–1772), who argued that every manifestation of the earth has its spiritual counterpart in a heavenly or spiritual world and that the equation worked as a kind of mirror signified by symbolic representation that, if correctly read, could give a picture of that higher world. See particularly Swedenborg's *Arcana Cœlestia: The Heavenly Mysteries Contained in the Holy Scriptures* (1749–56).
4. Part of EBB's argument for a new kind of poetry expressed in new forms. Compare EBB to RB March 20, 1845: "I am inclined to think that we want new *forms* . . as well as thoughts. The old gods are dethroned. Why should we go back to the antique moulds . . classical moulds, as they are so improperly called? If it is a necessity of Art to do so, why then those critics are right who hold that Art is exhausted and the world too worn out for poetry. I do not, for my part, believe this: & I believe the so-called necessity of Art to be the mere feebleness of the artist. Let us all aspire rather to *Life*—& let the dead bury their dead . . . For there is poetry *everywhere* . . . then Christianity is a worthy *myth*, & poetically acceptable" (*RB/EBB Letters* 1.43).
5. A poem celebrating the pleasures of the country life.
6. A well-known critical commonplace of the 1830s and 1840s.
7. Agamemnon, king of Mycenae, was the brother of Menelaus, king of Sparta and husband to Helen. When Menelaus went to war with Troy over the abduction of Helen by Paris, Agamemnon was one of the great generals who joined in the siege of Troy. He was murdered by his wife Clytemnestra on his return to Mycenae.
8. Zeus was said to have been nursed by a goat called Amalthea (Hyginus, *Poetica Astronomica* 2.13).
9. Richard Payne Knight (1750–1824), connoisseur and collector of bronzes, coins, and gems. EBB's antipathy to Payne Knight can be traced to a number of causes, but chief among them was her discovery in 1831, when she was reading Payne Knight's edition of Homer, that he

Who travelled higher than he was born to live,
And showed sometimes the goitre in his throat[1]
Discoursing of an image seen through fog,)
That Homer's heroes measured twelve feet high.[2]
They were but men: - his Helen's[3] hair turned grey
Like any plain Miss Smith's who wears a front;[4]
And Hector's infant whimpered at a plume[5]
As yours last Friday at a turkey-cock.
All actual heroes are essential men,
And all men possible heroes: every age,
Heroic in proportions, double-faced,
Looks backward and before,[6] expects a morn
And claims an epos.
Ay, but every age
Appears to souls who live in't (ask Carlyle)
Most unheroic.[7] Ours, for instance, ours:
The thinkers scout it, and the poets abound
Who scorn to touch it with a finger-tip:
A pewter age, - mixed metal, silver-washed;[8]
An age of scum, spooned off the richer past,
An age of patches for old gaberdines,[9]
An age of mere transition,[1] meaning nought

---

had excised a number of lines from the *Iliad* and the *Odyssey*; "If I made no mistake, about 2,500 lines are left out of his Iliad, and 1,926, out of his Odyssey. Is this not atrox [atrocious]?" (*Elizabeth Barrett to Mr. Boyd*, ed. Barbara P. MacCarthy [London, 1955], 163).

1. Bronchocele, an enlargement of the thyroid gland. Because the complaint was very common among the inhabitants of mountainous regions, it was long thought to be caused by drinking snow water.
2. Payne Knight's edition of Homer, *Carmina Homerica Ilias et Odyssea . . . cum notis ac prolegomenis. . .* , was published in 1820. His prolegomena and notes were published without the text in 1808. In 1831, EBB read Payne Knight's edition, which she had borrowed from H. S. Boyd (see note to *Aurora Leigh* 5.142.)
3. Helen was the daughter of Leda by the god Zeus, who appeared to her in the form of a swan. Helen married Menelaus of Sparta but was carried off by Paris, son of Priam of Troy, thus beginning the famous Trojan War. She was, in ancient and modern times, considered to be the ideal of feminine beauty.
4. A band or bands of false hair or a set of false curls, worn on the forehead (OED).
5. Hector was one of Priam's sons and a valiant warrior on the Trojan side during the seige of Troy. Homer, *Iliad* 6.466–70: "Thus Hector spake, and stretched his arms to his child./Against the nurse's breast, the childly cry,/The boy clung back, and shunned his father's face,/And feared the glittering brass and waving hair/Of the high helmet, nodding horror down" (EBB's translation, *Poetical Works of EBB*, 480).
6. Cf. *Aurora Leigh* 2.3–17
7. A proposition frequently reiterated by Thomas Carlyle. See particularly the introduction to the first lecture, "The Hero as Divinity," of his *On Heroes*, and his essay "The Diamond Necklace." "Depend upon it, for one thing, good Reader; no age ever seemed the Age of Romance to *itself*" (*Works of Thomas Carlyle* 5.3–4).
8. Made of base metal, or alloy, or a base metal "washed" or plated with silver and not made of precious metals and intrinsically valuable.
9. Gaberdine is a serviceable woollen cloth that, in this case, is envisioned covered with patches and no longer whole.
1. See note to *Aurora Leigh* 5.155–57. See also John Stuart Mill's essay "The Spirit of Age" (*The Examiner*, January–May 1831): "The first of the leading peculiarities of the present age is, that it is an age of transition. Mankind have outgrown old institutions and old doctrines, and have not yet acquired new ones" (*Mill's Essays on Literature and Society*, ed. J. B. Schneewind [New York and London, 1965], 30).

Except that what succeeds must shame it quite
If God please. That's wrong thinking, to my mind,
And wrong thoughts make poor poems.
Every age,
Through being beheld too close, is ill-discerned
By those who have not lived past it. We'll suppose
Mount Athos carved, as Alexander schemed,
To some colossal statue of a man.[2]
The peasants, gathering brushwood in his ear,
Had guessed as little as the browsing goats
Of form or feature of humanity
Up there, - in fact, had travelled five miles off
Or ere the giant image broke on them,
Full human profile, nose and chin distinct,
Mouth, muttering rhythms of silence up the sky
And fed at evening with the blood of suns;
Grand torso, - hand, that flung perpetually
The largesse of a silver river down
To all the country pastures. 'Tis even thus
With times we live in, - evermore too great
To be apprehended near.
But poets should
Exert a double vision;[3] should have eyes
To see near things as comprehensively
As if afar they took their point of sight,
And distant things as intimately deep
As if they touched them. Let us strive for this.
I do distrust the poet who discerns
No character or glory in his times,[4]

2. See Plutarch's *Lives*, "Alexander," 72. "This man [the artist Stasicrates], indeed, had said to him at a former interview that of all mountains the Thracian Athos could most readily be given the form and shape of a man; if, therefore, Alexander should so order, he would make out of Mount Athos a most enduring and most conspicuous statue of the king, which in its left hand should hold a city of ten thousand inhabitants, and with its right should pour forth a river running with generous current into the sea. This project, it is true, Alexander had declined. . . ." (Loeb translation).

The first edition allusion to Xerxes (see textual note) seems to have been based on EBB's imperfect recollection of Herodotus' *Histories* 7.22–24, which recounts how Xerxes, having been shipwrecked in attempting to sail round the promontory of Mount Athos, directed that a canal should be built across the isthmus, thus allowing his fleet to pass from sea to sea without danger.

3. Cf. RB's remarks on the capacity of the "objective poet" in his essay on Shelley (1852): "the poet's double faculty of seeing external objects more clearly, widely, and deeply than is possible to the average mind, at the same time that he is so acquainted and in sympathy with its narrower comprehension as to be careful to supply it with no other materials than it can combine into an intelligible whole" (*Letters of Percy Bysshe Shelley*, 1).

4. The argument that follows was recognized by Tennyson as an elaboration of the dispute in his poem "The Epic" (published 1842, among "English Idyls," and later used as a frame to "Morte d'Arthur"). See particularly lines 27–37: " 'You know,' said Frank, 'he burnt/His epic, his King Arthur, some twelve books'—/And then to me demanding why? 'Oh sir,/He thought that nothing new was said, or else/Something so said 'twas nothing—that a truth/Looks freshest in the fashion of the day:/God knows: he has a mint of reasons: ask,/It pleased me well enough,'

And trundles back his soul five hundred years,
Past moat and drawbridge,[5] into a castle-court,
To sing - oh, not of lizard or of toad
Alive i' the ditch there, - 'twere excusable,
But of some black chief, half knight, half sheep-lifter,
Some beauteous dame, half chattel and half queen,
As dead as must be, for the greater part,
The poems made on their chivalric bones;
And that's no wonder: death inherits death.
Nay, if there's room for poets in this world
A little overgrown, (I think there is)
Their sole work is to represent the age,[6]
Their age, not Charlemagne's,[7] - this live, throbbing age,
That brawls, cheats, maddens, calculates, aspires,
And spends more passion, more heroic heat,
Betwixt the mirrors of its drawing-rooms,[8]
Than Roland with his knights at Roncesvalles.[9]
To flinch from modern varnish, coat or flounce,
Cry out for togas and the picturesque,[1]
Is fatal, - foolish too. King Arthur's self
Was commonplace to Lady Guenever;[2]

---

'Nay, nay,' said Hall,/'Why take the style of those heroic times?/For nature brings not back the Mastodon,/Nor we those times. . . .' " An 1889 edition of the works of Tennyson, which was interleaved with Tennyson's own annotations, cut up from a printed copy (British Library 11645.c.61), included Tennyson's note on "The Epic": "Mrs. Browning wanted me to continue this, she has put my answer in *Aurora Leigh.*" (See *The Poems of Tennyson*, ed. Christopher Ricks [London, 1969], 583).

5. EBB ridicules the contemporary fashion of the 1840s and 1850s for all things medieval. Its influence can be seen in the poems, paintings, and architecture of the period. Its apogee, just beginning when EBB was writing, was found in the work of the pre-Raphaelites and the school of William Morris.
6. Ruskin approved EBB's theory on the proper stuff of modern poetry, saying of *Aurora Leigh*, "It is the first also perfect poetical expression of the Age, according to her own principles. But poor Scott! and the sellers of old armour in Wardour St!" (*Works of John Ruskin* 36.248).
7. See note to *Aurora Leigh* 1.771.
8. Compare EBB's description of the conception that was to become *Aurora Leigh*: "a poem as completely modern as 'Geraldine's Courtship,' running into the midst of our conventions, and rushing into drawing-rooms and the like, 'where angels fear to tread'; and so, meeting face to face without mask the Humanity of the age, and speaking the truth as I conceive of it out plainly" (*RB/EBB Letters* 1.31).
9. The historical Roland, comte de la Marche de Bretagne, died in 778 in the valley of Roncesvalles (more correctly Roncevaux), when the battalions of Charlemagne's army that he was commanding were attacked by the Basques. The epic poem *La Chanson de Roland* (written around 1100–25) elevates this incident to the status of a holy war and represents Roland as the type of the chivalric Christian hero.
1. The toga was the official garb of the citizen of Rome. The fashion for the "picturesque" began in the late eighteenth century, but continued well into the nineteenth. It usually meant anything that was foreign, dirty, poverty-stricken, ruined, or colorful. Charles Dickens was particularly critical of lovers of the picturesque, one of whom is his horrible Mrs. Skewton (the name is relevant) in *Dombey and Son* (1846–47).
2. Possibly a remark prompted by Tennyson's "Morte d'Arthur" (1842). King Arthur was the legendary king of early Britain and leader of the Round Table of chivalric knights. His Christian fellowship broke up when his wife, Guinevere, fell in love with Lancelot, his friend and leader of the knights.

And Camelot[3] to minstrels seemed as flat
As Fleet Street[4] to our poets.
Never flinch,
But still, unscrupulously epic, catch
Upon the burning lava of a song
The full-veined, heaving, double-breasted Age:[5]
That, when the next shall come, the men of that
May touch the impress with reverent hand, and say
'Behold, - behold the paps we all have sucked!
This bosom seems to beat still, or at least
It sets ours beating: this is living art,
Which thus presents and thus records true life.'

What form is best for poems? Let me think
Of forms less, and the external. Trust the spirit,
As sovran[6] nature does, to make the form;
For otherwise we only imprison spirit
And not embody. Inward evermore
To outward, - so in life, and so in art
Which still is life.
Five acts to make a play.[7]
And why not fifteen? why not ten? or seven?
What matter for the number of the leaves,
Supposing the tree lives and grows? exact
The literal unities of time and place,[8]
When 'tis the essence of passion to ignore
Both time and place? Absurd. Keep up the fire,
And leave the generous flames to shape themselves.

'Tis true the stage requires obsequiousness
To this or that convention; 'exit' here
And 'enter' there; the points for clapping, fixed,
Like Jacob's white-peeled rods before the rams,[9]

3. The site of King Arthur's court.
4. An important thoroughfare in London running from St. Paul's to the Strand. It was traditionally the home of the newspaper offices. The allusion to "Regent Street" (see textual notes) was presumably discarded as inappropriate, given that the street, built by John Nash in 1813, was considered "The most handsome street in the metropolis" (*Murray's Handbook for Modern London* [London, 1851], 264).
5. This juxtaposition of images attracted a great deal of negative comment when *Aurora Leigh* was first published. Critics could not cope with the idea of lava and a woman's breast in the same simile, but it is typical of EBB's determination to challenge and shock through poetry, as well as bravely to defend the claims for women's poetry.
6. Milton's spelling of "sovereign," chiefly poetical (OED)
7. According to the conventions of drama.
8. The "unities" of ancient drama set down that there should be unity of time, in that a play should cover no more than twenty-four hours of real time, and unity of place, in that all the action should occur in the same place.
9. Genesis 30.37–38. "And Jacob took him rods of green poplar, and of the hazel and chestnut tree; and pilled white strakes in them, and made the white appear which was in the rods. And he set the rods which he had pilled before the flocks in the gutters in the watering troughs when the flocks came to drink, that they should conceive when they came to drink."

And all the close-curled imagery clipped
In manner of their fleece at shearing-time.
Forget to prick the galleries[1] to the heart
Precisely at the fourth act, - culminate
Our five pyramidal acts with one act more, -
We're lost so: Shakspeare's ghost could scarcely plead
Against our just damnation. Stand aside;
We'll muse for comfort that, last century,
On this same tragic stage on which we have failed,
A wigless Hamlet would have failed the same.[2]
And whosoever writes good poetry,
Looks just to art. He does not write for you
Or me, - for London or for Edinburgh;[3]
He will not suffer the best critic known
To step into his sunshine of free thought
And self-absorbed conception and exact
An inch-long swerving of the holy lines.
If virtue done for popularity
Defiles like vice, can art, for praise or hire,
Still keep its splendor and remain pure art?
Eschew such serfdom. What the poet writes,
He writes: mankind accepts it if it suits,
And that's success: if not, the poem's passed
From hand to hand, and yet from hand to hand,
Until the unborn snatch it, crying out
In pity on their fathers' being so dull,
And that's success too.
I will write no plays;
Because the drama, less sublime in this,
Makes lower appeals, depends more menially,
Adopts the standard of the public taste
To chalk its height on, wears a dog-chain round
Its regal neck, and learns to carry and fetch
The fashions of the day to please the day,[4]

1. The ranked seats of the audience, but especially those occupying the cheaper seats higher up in the theater.
2. In the eighteenth century, Shakespeare was played in contemporary dress. David Garrick (1717–79) played Hamlet in a powdered wig and Macbeth in the scarlet of the King's livery. Early in the nineteenth century, however, the fashion for realistic "historic" costuming was introduced by the actor Charles Kemble (1775–1854).
3. Many of the major literary periodicals were published in London, including *The Athenaeum, The Quarterly Review*, and *The Westminster Review*. *Blackwood's Edinburgh Magazine, The Edinburgh Review* and *The North British Review* were published in Edinburgh.
4. Compare EBB to RB, February 17, 1845: "I have wondered at you sometimes, not for daring, but for bearing to trust your noble works into the great mill of the 'rank, popular' playhouse, to be ground to pieces between the teeth of vulgar actors and actresses. I, for one, would as soon have 'my soul among lions.' . . . Publics in the mass are bad enough; but to distil the dregs of the public & baptise oneself in that acrid moisture, where can be the temptation [?]" (*RB/EBB Letters* 1.22).

Fawns close on pit and boxes,[5] who clap hands
Commending chiefly its docility
And humour in stage-tricks, - or else indeed
Gets hissed at, howled at, stamped at like a dog,
Or worse, we'll say. For dogs, unjustly kicked,
Yell, bite at need; but if your dramatist
(Being wronged by some five hundred nobodies
Because their grosser brains most naturally
Misjudge the fineness of his subtle wit)
Shows teeth an almond's breadth, protests the length
Of a modern phrase, - 'My gentle countrymen,
'There's something in it haply of your fault,' -
Why then, besides five hundred nobodies,
He'll have five thousand and five thousand more
Against him, - the whole public, - and all the hoofs
Of King Saul's father's asses,[6] in full drove,
And obviously deserve it. He appealed
To these, - and why say more if they condemn,
Than if they praise him? - Weep, my Æschylus,
But low and far, upon Sicilian shores!
For since 'twas Athens (so I read the myth)
Who gave commission to that fatal weight
The tortoise, cold and hard, to drop on thee
And crush thee, - better cover thy bald head;[7]
She'll hear the softest hum of Hyblan bee[8]
Before thy loudest protestation!
Then
The risk's still worse upon the modern stage:
I could not, for so little, accept success,
Nor would I risk so much, in ease and calm,

5. The pit is the main body of the audience seated in the floor of the theater. These were often cheaper seats for standing room only. The boxes were reserved for private occupation and offered more comfortable accommodation for theatergoers.
6. See 1 Samuel 9. Saul was seeking his father's lost herd of asses when he went to the priest Samuel to ask for help, and Samuel recognized him as God's chosen king.
7. Aeschylus died at Gela in Sicily when an eagle dropped a tortoise on his bald head, mistaking it for a stone (see note to *Aurora Leigh* 1.454–55). He had left Athens some time previously, though differing accounts exist as to the reason for his exile; Plutarch recounts how Aeschylus left Athens in distress and indignation after Sophocles was declared victorious in the dramatic contest (*Lives*, "Cimon," 8.7–8). The *Vita* of Aeschylus mentions this version but also tells how the terrifying representation of the Furies in *The Eumenides* contributed to his unpopularity at Athens (*Vita* § 9: also see note to *Aurora Leigh* 4.383–84).

   EBB wrote an unfinished poem on Aeschylus' last hours, the so-called "Aeschylus' Soliloquy," which has long been mistakenly attributed to RB (see *Index* 4.107). The extant draft of the poem suggests that EBB may have intended to use her theory regarding Athens' revenge in that earlier monologue: "I who did not die/That day in Athens when the people's scorn/Hissed toward the sun as if to darken it/Over my head because I spoke my Greek/Too deep down in my soul to suit their ears/Who did not die to see the solemn vests/Of my white chorus around the thymele/Flutter like doves, & sweep back like a cloud/Before the shrill lipped people . . . [wd not die At this time, by the crushing of a house] but stood calm,/ & cold, & felt the theatre wax hot/With mouthing whispers . . ." (manuscript at the Huntington Library).
8. Hybla is a mountain in Sicily, famous for the honey bees that worked its abundance of thyme and flowering plants. See Ovid, *Tristia* 5.13, 22, and Virgil, *Eclogues* 1.54.

For manifester gains: let those who prize,
Pursue them: I stand off. And yet, forbid,
That any irreverent fancy or conceit
Should litter in the Drama's throne-room where
The rulers of our art, in whose full veins
Dynastic[9] glories mingle, sit in strength
And do their kingly work, - conceive, command,
And, from the imagination's crucial heat,
Catch up their men and women all a-flame
For action, all alive and forced to prove
Their life by living out heart, brain, and nerve,
Until mankind makes witness, 'These be men
As we are,' and vouchsafes the greeting due
To Imogen and Juliet[1] - sweetest kin
On art's side.
'Tis that, honouring to its worth
The drama, I would fear to keep it down
To the level of the footlights. Dies no more
The sacrificial goat, for Bacchus, slain,[2]
His filmed eyes fluttered by the whirling white
Of choral vestures, - troubled in his blood,
While tragic voices that clanged keen as swords,
Leapt high together with the altar-flame[3]
And made the blue air wink. The waxen mask,[4]
Which set the grand still front of Themis' son[5]
Upon the puckered visage of a player, -
The buskin,[6] which he rose upon and moved,
As some tall ship first conscious of the wind
Sweeps slowly past the piers, - the mouthpiece, where
The mere man's voice with all its breaths and breaks
Went sheathed in brass,[7] and clashed on even heights

9. See note to line 88.
1. See Shakespeare's *Cymbeline* and *Romeo and Juliet*. Beatrice (see textual note) refers to *Much Ado about Nothing*.
2. Describing the dithyramb, a Greek choral lyric, anciently connected with the worship of Dionysius (or Bacchus). In classical myth, Dionysius was the personification of the "life-urge" and was worshipped with preeminently sacred rites practiced by the women of Delphi, and the Thyiads of Athens, on Mount Parnassus. In the orgiastic Thraco-Phrygian rites, the Dionysian winter-dance culminated in omophagia—a sacrificial animal was torn to pieces and the living flesh consumed by the dancers in order to become "Bacchoi," or god-possessed (cf. textual notes to lines 5.321–23).
3. In recognition of the ancient religious origins of the drama, the thymele, an altar to Dionysius, was situated in the middle of the orchestra in the Greek theater.
4. The mask worn by the actors in classical drama.
5. Prometheus is called "Themis' son" in Aeschylus' play *Prometheus Bound*. See EBB's translation (1850), lines 19 and 251–53 (*Poetical Works of EBB*, 451, 454).
6. The cothurnus, a boot worn by the actors in classical tragedy that came high up the calf. In later Hellenistic and imperial Roman periods, a thick sole of eight to ten inches was added, but the buskin was probably never quite as tall as EBB imagined (see note to *Aurora Leigh* 4.379–81).
7. The mouthpiece of the masks worn in classical drama almost certainly was not designed to serve as a means of amplification.

Its phrasèd thunders, - these things are no more,
Which once were. And concluding, which is clear,
The growing drama has outgrown such toys
Of simulated stature, face, and speech,
It also peradventure may outgrow
The simulation of the painted scene,
Boards, actors, prompters, gaslight, and costume,
And take for a worthier stage the soul itself,[8]
Its shifting fancies and celestial lights,
With all its grand orchestral silences
To keep the pauses of its rhythmic sounds.

Alas, I still see something to be done,
And what I do, falls short of what I see,
Though I waste myself on doing. Long green days,
Worn bare of grass and sunshine, - long calm nights,
From which the silken sleeps were fretted out,
Be witness for me, with no amateur's
Irreverent haste and busy idleness
I set myself to art! What then? what's done?
What's done, at last?
Behold, at last, a book.
If life-blood's necessary, which it is, -
(By that blue vein athrob on Mahomet's brow,[9]
Each prophet-poet's book must show man's blood!)
If life-blood's fertilising, I wrung mine
On every leaf of this, - unless the drops

8. Early in the course of their friendship, EBB had exclaimed at RB's willingness to submit to popular fashion and prejudice by writing plays for production on the London stage (see note to lines 5.267–73). Later, she continued, "you are not to think that I blaspheme the Drama, dear Mr. Browning; or that I ever thought of exhorting you to give up the 'solemn robes' & tread of the buskin. It is the theatre which vulgarizes these things; the modern theatre in which we see no altar!—where the thymele is replaced by the caprice of a popular actor. And also I have a fancy that your great dramatic power would work more clearly & audibly in the less definite mould . . ." (*RB/EBB letters* 1.29–30).

RB's intention of writing "poetry always dramatic in principle" (preface to the 1868 edition of his *Works*), while focusing on internal, rather than external action—taking the soul itself as a stage—was declared by RB on several occasions. See, for instance, the preface to *Paracelsus* (1835) and the introduction to *Strafford* (1837). See also RB's dedication to *Sordello* (1840): "The historical decoration was purposely of no more importance than a background requires; and my stress lay on the incidents in the development of a soul: little else is worth study. I, at least, always thought so. . . ." (*The Poetical Works of Robert Browning*, ed. Ian Jack and Margaret Smith, [Oxford, 1984], 2.194).

9. In his biography of Mohammed, Aloys Sprenger gives a description of the Prophet based on the Shamáyil of Tirmidzy, including mention of the vein on Mohammed's forehead: "his fine and long but narrow eyebrows were separated by a vein, which you could see throbbing if he was angry" (*The Life of Mohammed from Original Sources* [Allahabad: Presbyterian Mission Press, 1851], 84–85).

The vein is also mentioned by Carlyle in *On Heroes*: "One hears of Mahomet's beauty; his fine sagacious honest face, brown florid complexion, beaming black eyes;—I somehow like too that vein on the brow which swelled-up black when he was in anger. . . . It was a kind of feature in the Hashem family, this black swelling vein in the brow; Mahomet had it prominent, as would appear" (*Works of Thomas Carlyle* 6.224). Carlyle was presumably EBB's source for the allusion.

Slid heavily on one side and left it dry.
That chances often: many a fervid man
Writes books as cold and flat as grave-yard stones
From which the lichen's scraped; and if Saint Preux
Had written his own letters, as he might,
We had never wept to think of the little mole
'Neath Julie's drooping eyelid.[1] Passion is
But something suffered, after all.
While Art
Sets action on the top of suffering:
The artist's part is both to be and do,
Transfixing with a special, central power
The flat experience of the common man,
And turning outward, with a sudden wrench,
Half agony, half ecstasy, the thing
He feels the inmost, - never felt the less
Because he sings it. Does a torch less burn
For burning next reflectors of blue steel,
That *he* should be the colder for his place
'Twixt two incessant fires, - his personal life's,
And that intense refraction which burns back
Perpetually against him from the round
Of crystal conscience he was born into
If artist-born? O sorrowful great gift
Conferred on poets, of a twofold life,[2]
When one life has been found enough for pain!
We, staggering 'neath our burden as mere men,
Being called to stand up straight as demi-gods,
Support the intolerable strain and stress
Of the universal, and send clearly up
With voices broken by the human sob,
Our poems to find rhymes among the stars!

But soft, - a 'poet' is a word soon said,
A book's a thing soon written. Nay, indeed,
The more the poet shall be questionable,

1. Referring to Jean-Jacques Rousseau's novel *Julie, ou la nouvelle Heloise: Lettres de deux Amans, habitans d'une petite ville au pied des Alpes*. In part 2, letter 25, the lover, Saint Preux, criticizes a portrait of Julie that she has sent to him: "We will pass over the fact that the painter has omitted several of your beauties; but in doing so, he has done nothing but wrong to your face, especially in leaving out some faults. He hasn't included that barely perceptible mark which is under your right eye, nor that which is on the left side of your neck . . . O God, is this man made of bronze? . . . He has forgotten the little scar which is under your lip" (Jean-Jacques Rousseau, *Oeuvres Completes*, ed. B. Gagnebin and M. Raymond [Paris, 1964–69] 2.291; my translation).
2. Cf. RB's *Pauline* (1833), lines 268–77: "I am made up of an intensest life,/Of a most clear idea of consciousness/Of self-distinct from all its qualities,/From all affections, passions, feelings, powers'/And thus far it exists, if tracked in all,/But linked in me to self-supremacy,/ Existing as a centre to all things,/And to a principle of restlessness/Which would be all, have, see, know, taste, feel, all—/This is myself . . ." (*Poetical Works of RB* 1.44).

The more unquestionably comes his book.
And this of mine - well, granting to myself
Some passion in it, - furrowing up the flats,
Mere passion will not prove a volume worth
Its gall and rags even. Bubbles round a keel
Mean nought, excepting that the vessel moves.
There's more than passion goes to make a man
Or book, which is a man too.
                                        I am sad.
I wonder if Pygmalion had these doubts
And, feeling the hard marble first relent,
Grow supple to the straining of his arms,
And tingle through its cold to his burning lip,
Supposed his senses mocked,[3] supposed the toil
Of stretching past the known and seen to reach
The archetypal Beauty out of sight,
Had made his heart beat fast enough for two,
And with his own life dazed and blinded him!
Not so; Pygmalion loved, - and whoso loves
Believes the impossible.
                                    But I am sad:
I cannot thoroughly love a work of mine,
Since none seems worthy of my thought and hope
More highly mated. He has shot them down,
My Phœbus Apollo,[4] soul within my soul,
Who judges, by the attempted, what's attained,
And with the silver arrow from his height
Has struck down all my works before my face
While I said nothing. Is there aught to say?
I called the artist but a greatened man.
He may be childless also, like a man.

I laboured on alone. The wind and dust
And sun of the world beat blistering in my face;
And hope, now for me, now against me, dragged
My spirits onward, as some fallen balloon,
Which, whether caught by blossoming tree or bare,
Is torn alike. I sometimes touched my aim,
Or seemed, - and generous souls cried out, 'Be strong,
Take courage; now you're on our level, - now!
The next step saves you!' I was flushed with praise,

3. Pygmalion, the sculptor of Cyprus, fell in love with the statue he had created, and prayed to Venus that she might animate the lifeless form (Ovid, *Metamorphoses* 10.243–97). Cf. lines 283–88: "The ivory grew soft to his touch and, its hardness vanishing, gave and yielded beneath his fingers. . . . The lover stands amazed, rejoices still in doubt, fears he is mistaken, and tries his hopes again and yet again with his hand" (Loeb translation).

4. While Apollo is the god of music and poetry, he is also, as Phoebus, the avenging god, striking down with his silver arrows those who offend him. See Homer, *Iliad* 1.43–53.

But, pausing just a moment to draw breath,
I could not choose but murmur to myself
'Is this all? all that's done? and all that's gained?
If this then be success, 'tis dismaller
Than any failure.'
O my God, my God,
O supreme Artist, who as sole return
For all the cosmic wonder of Thy work,
Demandest of us just a word . . a name,
'My Father!'[5] thou hast knowledge, only thou,
How dreary 'tis for women to sit still
On winter nights by solitary fires
And hear the nations praising them far off,[6]
Too far! ay, praising our quick sense of love,
Our very heart of passionate womanhood,
Which could not beat so in the verse without
Being present also in the unkissed lips
And eyes undried because there's none to ask
The reason they grew moist.
To sit alone
And think for comfort how, that very night,
Affianced lovers, leaning face to face
With sweet half-listenings for each other's breath,
Are reading haply from a page of ours,
To pause with a thrill (as if their cheeks had touched)
When such a stanza, level to their mood,
Seems floating their own thought out - 'So I feel
For thee,' - 'And I, for thee: this poet knows
What everlasting love is!' - how, that night,
Some father, issuing from the misty roads
Upon the luminous round of lamp and hearth
And happy children, having caught up first
The youngest there until it shrink and shriek
To feel the cold chin prick its dimples through
With winter from the hills, may throw i' the lap
Of the eldest, (who has learnt to drop her lids
To hide some sweetness newer than last year's)
Our book and cry, . . 'Ah you, you care for rhymes;
So here be rhymes to pore on under trees,
When April comes to let you! I've been told
They are not idle as so many are,
But set hearts beating pure as well as fast.
'Tis yours, the book; I'll write your name in it,

5. An allusion to Christ's instruction to the disciples when he taught them what is now called "the Lord's prayer." See Matthew 6.7–13.
6. Elizabeth Gaskell chose these lines from *Aurora Leigh* as epigraph to her *Life of Charlotte Brontë* (1857).

So that you may not lose, however lost
In poet's lore and charming reverie,
The thought of how your father thought of *you*
In riding from the town.'
To have our books
Appraised by love, associated with love,
While *we* sit loveless! is it hard, you think?
At least 'tis mournful. Fame, indeed, 'twas said,
Means simply love. It was a man said that:[7]
And then, there's love and love: the love of all
(To risk in turn a woman's paradox,)
Is but a small thing to the love of one.
You bid a hungry child be satisfied
With a heritage of many corn-fields: nay,
He says he's hungry, - he would rather have
That little barley-cake you keep from him
While reckoning up his harvests. So with us;
(Here, Romney, too, we fail to generalise!)
We're hungry.
Hungry! but it's pitiful
To walk like unweaned babes and suck our thumbs
Because we're hungry. Who, in all this world,
(Wherein we are haply set to pray and fast,
And learn what good is by its opposite)
Has never hungered? Woe to him who has found
The meal enough! if Ugolino's full,
His teeth have crunched some foul unnatural thing:[8]
For here satiety proves penury
More utterly irremediable. And since
We needs must hunger, - better, for man's love,

7. A common theme. See RB *Colombe's Birthday* (1844) 4.412–13: "nothing's what it calls itself!/ Devotion, zeal, faith, loyalty—mere love!" Also see Byron, "Stanzas Written on the Road between Florence and Pisa, November 1821": "O Fame!—if I e'er took delight in thy praises,/ 'Twas less for the sake of thy high-sounding phrases,/Than to see the bright eyes of the dear one discover/She thought that I was not unworthy to love her./There chiefly I sought thee, there only I found thee;/Her glance was the best of the rays that surround thee;/When it sparkled o'er aught that was bright in my story,/I knew it was love, and I felt it was glory." And see S. T. Coleridge, "Love" (1800): "All thoughts, all passions, all delights,/Whatever stirs this mortal frame,/All are but ministers of Love,/And feed his sacred flame." Anna Jameson puts in quotation marks the phrase "fame is love disguised," in "Sketches of Art, Literature, and Character," part I, dialogue III, in her *Visits and Sketches, at Home and Abroad* (London, 1939), 155. I am indebted to Dorothy Mermin for this reference.
8. Count Ugolino della Gherardesca (d. 1289) was leader of the Guelph party at Pisa but intrigued with the rival faction of the Ghibellines. He was betrayed by the Ghibelline Ruggiere degli Ubaldini, archbishop of Pisa, and imprisoned with his sons in the Torre del Fame where they were starved to death. In Dante's *Inferno* (32.121–36) Dante encounters Ugolino situated in Antenora—the area of Hell reserved for those who were traitors to their country—slightly above Ruggieri (who is in Tolomea—the region assigned to those who have betrayed their associates), on whose head Ugolino gnaws. The last line of Ugolino's narrative, "poscia, piu che il dolor, pote il digiuno" ("then fasting had more power than grief") (*Inferno* 33.75), has been interpreted by some as suggesting that Ugolino consumed the bodies of his sons while imprisoned in the tower, an interpretation reinforced by Ugolino's occupation in Hell.

Than God's truth! better, for companions sweet,
Than great convictions! let us bear our weights,
Preferring dreary hearths to desert souls.

Well, well! they say we're envious, we who rhyme;
But I, because I am a woman perhaps
And so rhyme ill, am ill at envying.
I never envied Graham his breadth of style,
Which gives you, with a random smutch or two,
(Near-sighted critics analyse to smutch)
Such delicate perspectives of full life:
Nor Belmore, for the unity of aim
To which he cuts his cedarn poems, fine
As sketchers do their pencils: nor Mark Gage,[9]
For that caressing colour and trancing tone
Whereby you're swept away and melted in
The sensual element, which with a back wave
Restores you to the level of pure souls
And leaves you with Plotinus.[1] None of these,
For native gifts or popular applause,
I've envied; but for this, - that when by chance
Says some one, - 'There goes Belmore, a great man!
He leaves clean work behind him, and requires
No sweeper up of the chips,' . . a girl I know,
Who answers nothing, save with her brown eyes,
Smiles unaware as if a guardian saint
Smiled in her: - for this, too, - that Gage comes home
And lays his last book's prodigal review
Upon his mother's knee, where, years ago,
He laid his childish spelling-book and learned
To chirp and peck the letters from her mouth,
As young birds must. 'Well done,' she murmured then;
She will not say it now more wonderingly:
And yet the last 'Well done' will touch him more,
As catching up to-day and yesterday
In a perfect chord of love:[2] and so, Mark Gage,
I envy you your mother! - and you, Graham,
Because you have a wife who loves you so,
She half forgets, at moments, to be proud

9. Note that all of Aurora's poetic contemporaries and possible rivals here are men.
1. Plotinus (c. 203–62) is the real founder of the Neoplatonic school. His philosophy advocated the purification of the soul by distinguishing it from all that is sensuous or material.
2. EBB bases this story on her own memory of her relationship with her father, who was once the encourager and promoter of her poetic ambition. Cf. the terms of the dedication for her *Poems* (1844) addressed to her father: "When your eyes fall upon this page of dedication . . . your first thought will be of the time far off when I was a child and wrote verses, and when I dedicated them to you who were my public and my critic. . . . Somewhat more faint-hearted than I used to be, it is my fancy thus to seem to return to a visible personal dependence on you, as if indeed I were a child again."

Of being Graham's wife, until a friend observes,
'The boy here, has his father's massive brow,
Done small in wax . . if we push back the curls.'

Who loves me? Dearest father, - mother sweet, -
I speak the names out sometimes by myself,
And make the silence shiver. They sound strange,
As Hindostanee to an Ind-born man[3]
Accustomed many years to English speech;
Or lovely poet-words grown obsolete,
Which will not leave off singing. Up in heaven
I have my father, - with my mother's face
Beside him in a blotch of heavenly light;
No more for earth's familiar, household use,
No more. The best verse written by this hand,
Can never reach them where they sit, to seem
Well-done to *them*. Death quite unfellows us,
Sets dreadful odds betwixt the live and dead,
And makes us part as those at Babel did
Through sudden ignorance of a common tongue.[4]
A living Cæsar would not dare to play
At bowls with such as my dead father is.[5]

And yet this may be less so than appears,
This change and separation. Sparrows five
For just two farthings, and God cares for each.[6]
If God is not too great for little cares,
Is any creature, because gone to God?
I've seen some men, veracious, nowise mad,
Who have thought or dreamed, declared and testified,
They heard the Dead a-ticking like a clock
Which strikes the hours of the eternities,
Beside them, with their natural ears, - and known
That human spirits feel the human way
And hate the unreasoning awe which waves them off
From possible communion.[7] It may be.

3. A man born in India.
4. In Genesis 11.8–9, Babel figures as a city and a tower that the people attempted to build together, but the confusion of languages spoken by the variety of people there meant that everything broke up in disorder and nothing was achieved.
5. A little homily on the brevity of existence, and the vanity of fame. But also a generalized reference to *Hamlet*, 5.1, especially lines 98 ("Did these bones cost no more breeding but to play at loggats with 'em?") and 215–36.
6. Luke 12.6: "Are not five sparrows sold for two farthings, and not one of them is forgotten before God?"
7. During the early 1850s EBB became extremely interested in the practices of spiritualism and attended a number of seances conducted by well-known mediums. Throughout these years RB remained sceptical and declared himself an unbeliever. His well-known poem "Mr. Sludge,

At least, earth separates as well as heaven.
For instance, I have not seen Romney Leigh
Full eighteen months . . add six, you get two years.
They say he's very busy with good works, -
Has parted Leigh Hall into almshouses.[8]
He made one day an almshouse of his heart,
Which ever since is loose upon the latch
For those who pull the string. - I never did.

It always makes me sad to go abroad,
And now I'm sadder that I went to-night
Among the lights and talkers at Lord Howe's.
His wife is gracious, with her glossy braids,
And even voice, and gorgeous eyeballs, calm
As her other jewels. If she's somewhat cold,
Who wonders, when her blood has stood so long
In the ducal reservoir she calls her line
By no means arrogantly? she's not proud;
Not prouder than the swan is of the lake
He has always swum in; - 'tis her element;
And so she takes it with a natural grace,
Ignoring tadpoles. She just knows perhaps
There *are* who travel without outriders,[9]
Which isn't her fault. Ah, to watch her face,
When good Lord Howe expounds his theories
Of social justice and equality!
'Tis curious, what a tender, tolerant bend
Her neck takes: for she loves him, likes his talk,
'Such clever talk - that dear, odd Algernon!'
She listens on, exactly as if he talked
Some Scandinavian myth of Lemures,[1]
Too pretty to dispute, and too absurd.
She's gracious to me as her husband's friend,
And would be gracious, were I not a Leigh,
Being used to smile just so, without her eyes,
On Joseph Strangways, the Leeds mesmerist,
And Delia Dobbs, the lecturer from 'the States'

---

the Medium" is, in part, a response to the events that he witnessed. Aware of general disapprobation, EBB declared that she put only one reference to the spirits into *Aurora Leigh*. This is it. See EBB to Henrietta, July 9, 1856: "No religion, no politics, no spirits!! add 'no bodies'—and you shut out my poor poem from most subjects in heaven and earth. . . . There is one reference to the spirits, but nobody will be offended by it as Robert isn't" (*EBB: Letters to Her Sister*, 250).

8. Split the house up into units to provide accommodation for the poor.
9. A mounted attendant who rides in advance of, or beside, a carriage (OED).
1. The Lemures were Roman spirits, not Scandinavian. They were the specters of the dead come back to torment the living. The point is that Lord Howe's socialist talk is as strange, remote, arcane, and quaint as some foreign folktale.

Upon the 'Woman's question.'[2] Then, for him,
I like him; he's my friend. And all the rooms
Were full of crinkling silks that swept about
The fine dust of most subtle courtesies.
What then? - why then, we come home to be sad.

How lovely One I love not looked to-night!
She's very pretty, Lady Waldemar.
Her maid must use both hands to twist that coil
Of tresses, then be careful lest the rich
Bronze rounds should slip: - she missed, though, a grey hair,
A single one, - I saw it; otherwise
The woman looked immortal. How they told,
Those alabaster shoulders and bare breasts,
On which the pearls, drowned out of sight in milk,
Were lost, excepting for the ruby-clasp!
They split the amaranth[3] velvet-boddice down
To the waist or nearly, with the audacious press
Of full-breathed beauty. If the heart within
Were half as white! - but, if it were, perhaps
The breast were closer covered and the sight
Less aspectable,[4] by half, too.
I heard
The young man with the German student's look -
A sharp face, like a knife in a cleft stick,[5]
Which shot up straight against the parting line
So equally dividing the long hair, -
Say softly to his neighbour, (thirty-five
And mediæval)[6] 'Look that way, Sir Blaise.
She's Lady Waldemar - to the left, - in red -

2. Two fashionable and topical areas for fierce debate in the 1850s. Mesmerism, named for its chief practitioner, F. A. Mesmer (1734–1815), had been much discussed in the 1840s, especially in literary circles when Harriet Martineau was apparently cured of a cancer after mesmeric treatment. EBB knew a great deal about Martineau's case, for the two women had corresponded at that time, and she read her *Letters on Mesmerism* (1845) with much interest. As with all these matters (see note to *Aurora Leigh* 5.563–70), EBB was intrigued by mesmerism and willing to bring an open mind to the evidence.

The "Woman question" had been so called since the 1840s, and EBB had been especially exercised by its issues at the time of the publication of Tennyson's *The Princess* in 1847. Basically the questions at stake were those of employment, education, property rights, the franchise, equality in marriage. EBB, of course, supported a woman's right to all these.

3. A purple color, like that of the foliage of the genus of plants called "amaranthus." The amaranth that Milton mentions (*Lycidas*, 149, and *Paradise Lost* 3.353–56) is an imaginary flower that never fades.
4. Fit to be beheld, fair to look on (OED). The OED adds that the word is rare (it is derived from the Latin adjective *aspectabilis*, from the verb *aspectare*) and that it is "Accented (ae. spektab'l) by Mr. and Mrs. Browning."
5. A generalized description of the dry and ascetic appearance of a typical student of the German universities.
6. Although he is young in years, Sir Blaise is old in terms of his outlook on life, which is influenced by the fashion for things medieval that arose in the 1840s and 1850s and by the reactionary doctrines of the Anglo-Catholic movement led by John Henry Newman and Edward Pusey. See notes to *Aurora Leigh* 1.394 and 5.747.

Whom Romney Leigh, our ablest man just now,
Is soon about to marry.'
Then replied
Sir Blaise Delorme, with quiet, priestlike voice,
Too used to syllable damnations round
To make a natural emphasis worth while:
'Is Leigh your ablest man? the same, I think,
Once jilted by a recreant pretty maid
Adopted from the people? Now, in change,
He seems to have plucked a flower from the other side
Of the social hedge.'
'A flower, a flower,' exclaimed
My German student, - his own eyes full-blown
Bent on her. He was twenty, certainly.

Sir Blaise resumed with gentle arrogance,
As if he had dropped his alms into a hat
And gained the right to counsel, - 'My young friend,
I doubt your ablest man's ability
To get the least good or help meet for him,[7]
For pagan phalanstery or Christian home,
From such a flowery creature.'
'Beautiful!'
My student murmured rapt, - 'Mark how she stirs!
Just waves her head, as if a flower indeed,
Touched far off by the vain breath of our talk.'

At which that bilious Grimwald, (he who writes
For the Renovator) who had seemed absorbed
Upon the table-book of autographs,[8]
(I dare say mentally he crunched the bones
Of all those writers, wishing them alive
To feel his tooth in earnest) turned short round
With low carnivorous laugh[9] - 'A flower, of course!
She neither sews nor spins, - and takes no thought
Of her garments[1] . . falling off.'
The student flinched;

7. A quotation from Genesis 2.18, where God makes Eve as a helpmeet for Adam.
8. Middle- and upper-class houses in the nineteenth century kept albums on display wherein their guests were invited to read and admire the witty sayings and lively drawings of their notable friends and acquaintances and to add their own contributions.
9. "Carnivorous" because Grimwald looks at Lady Waldemar's flesh with lust. Cf. EBB's comments on the voyeuristic admirers of William Etty's nudes in his picture "Ulysses and the Sirens" (exhibited 1837): "I remember it was scarcely to be looked at for hideousness . . . though I heard some carnivorous connoisseurs praising the 'colouring'!!" (*RB/EBB Letters* 2.741).
1. See Matthew 6.28–29: "And why are you anxious about clothing? Consider the lilies of the field, how they grow; they neither toil nor spin; yet I tell you, even Solomon in all his glory was not arrayed like one of these."

Sir Blaise, the same; then both, drawing back their chairs
As if they spied black-beetles on the floor,
Pursued their talk, without a word being thrown
To the critic.
Good Sir Blaise's brow is high
And noticeably narrow: a strong wind,
You fancy, might unroof him suddenly,
And blow that great top attic off his head
So piled with feudal relics. You admire
His nose in profile, though you miss his chin;
But, though you miss his chin, you seldom miss
His ebon cross won innermostly, (carved
For penance by a saintly Styrian monk[2]
Whose flesh was too much with him,) slipping through
Some unaware unbuttoned casualty
Of the under-waistcoat. With an absent air
Sir Blaise sate fingering it and speaking low,
While I, upon the sofa, heard it all.

'My dear young friend, if we could bear our eyes,
Like blessedest Saint Lucy, on a plate,[3]
They would not trick us into choosing wives,
As doublets, by the colour. Otherwise
Our fathers chose, - and therefore, when they had hung
Their household keys about a lady's waist,[4]
The sense of duty gave her dignity;
She kept her bosom holy to her babes,
And, if a moralist reproved her dress,
'Twas, 'Too much starch!' - and not, 'Too little lawn!' '

'Now, pshaw!' returned the other in a heat,
A little fretted by being called 'young friend,'
Or so I took it, - 'for Saint Lucy's sake,
If she's the saint to swear by, let us leave
Our fathers, - plagued enough about our sons!'
(He stroked his beardless chin) 'yes, plagued, sir, plagued:
The future generations lie on us
As heavy as the nightmare of a seer;
Our meat and drink grow painful prophecy:

2. Styria (or Steiermark) was a duchy, and is now a federal state, in southeastern and central Austria. The majority of the population is Catholic.
3. Lucia of Syracuse suffered martyrdom in 303 during the persecution by Diocletian. Jameson gives a version of the legend, which gave rise to the representation depicting the saint carrying her eyes on a plate: a young man so persisted in wooing Lucia, swearing that her beautiful eyes tormented him day and night, that she, who had vowed perpetual chastity, at length removed her own eyes and sent them to him with the message "Here thou hast what thou hast so much desired" (Anna Brownell Jameson, *Sacred and Legendary Art* [London, 1848] 2.236–37).
4. The mistress of the household wore all her keys in a bunch or in a little basket at her waist so that she could dispense them to the servants when appropriate.

I ask you, - have we leisure, if we liked,
To hollow out our weary hands to keep
Your intermittent rushlight[5] of the past
From draughts in lobbies? Prejudice of sex
And marriage-law . . the socket[6] drops them through
While we two speak, - however may protest
Some over-delicate nostrils like your own,
'Gainst odours thence arising.'
'You are young,'
Sir Blaise objected.
'If I am,' he said
With fire, - 'though somewhat less so than I seem,
The young run on before, and see the thing
That's coming. Reverence for the young, I cry.
In that new church for which the world's near ripe,
You'll have the younger in the Elder's chair,
Presiding with his ivory front[7] of hope
O'er foreheads clawed by cruel carrion-birds
Of life's experience.'
'Pray your blessing, sir,'
Sir Blaise replied good-humouredly, - 'I plucked
A silver hair this morning from my beard,
Which left me your inferior. Would I were
Eighteen and worthy to admonish you!
If young men of your order run before
To see such sights as sexual prejudice
And marriage-law dissolved, - in plainer words,
A general concubinage[8] expressed
In a universal pruriency, - the thing
Is scarce worth running fast for, and you'd gain
By loitering with your elders.'
'Ah,' he said,
'Who, getting to the top of Pisgah-hill,[9]
Can talk with one at bottom of the view,
To make it comprehensible? Why, Leigh
Himself, although our ablest man, I said,
Is scarce advanced to see as far as this,

5. A simple light used by the poor, consisting of a rush dipped in wax or oil and ignited.
6. Of the light; the container for the light.
7. Forehead.
8. Most of the socialist reforms of the nineteenth century were plagued by their detractors with accusations that they planned the abolition of marriage and an early version of "free love," which meant that all women would be common sexual property shared by men. This mistaken supposition was a widespread misreading of proposed reforms designed to allow women more individual freedom and certainly not to give men more sexual license. Still it persisted, and the same accusation was made against Robert Owen at the beginning of the century as it was against Fourier and Marx and Engels in the middle. See Marx and Engels, *The Communist Manifesto* (1847), and Barbara Taylor, *Eve and the New Jerusalem* (1983), ch. 6, 183–216.
9. Moses saw the promised land from the summit of Pisgah (Deuteronomy 3.27 and 34.1–4).

Which some are: he takes up imperfectly
The social question - by one handle - leaves
The rest to trail. A Christian socialist[1]
Is Romney Leigh, you understand.'
'Not I.
I disbelieve in Christian-pagans, much
As you in women-fishes. If we mix
Two colours, we lose both, and make a third
Distinct from either. Mark you! to mistake
A colour is the sign of a sick brain,
And mine, I thank the saints, is clear and cool:
A neutral tint is here impossible.
The church - and by the church, I mean of course
The catholic, apostolic, mother-church,[2] -
Draws lines as plain and straight as her own wall;
Inside of which, are Christians, obviously
And outside . . dogs.'[3]
'We thank you. Well I know
The ancient mother-church would fain still bite,
For all her toothless gums, - as Leigh himself
Would fain be a Christian still, for all his wit.
Pass that; you two may settle it, for me.
You're slow in England. In a month I learnt
At Göttingen[4] enough philosophy
To stock your English schools for fifty years;
Pass that, too. Here alone, I stop you short,
- Supposing a true man like Leigh could stand
Unequal in the stature of his life
To the height of his opinions. Choose a wife
Because of a smooth skin? - not he, not he!

1. The leaders of the Christian Socialist movement, F. D. Maurice, Charles Kingsley, Thomas Hughes, and J. M. Ludlow, came together in 1848 in order to propagate their views on social reform. The first *Tract on Christian Socialism* was published in 1849, but it was with the publication of Kingsley's novels *Alton Locke* (1850) and *Yeast* (1851) that the term, and the notion, gained wide currency.
2. Refers to the reactionary ecclesiastical movements of the 1830s and 1840s. Edward Irving (1792–1834), a clergyman of the church of Scotland, established the dissenting "Holy Catholic Apostolic Church" in 1832 when he was forced to leave his post as minister at the church in Regent Square, London.

   Irving's commitment to the apostolic traditions can be interpreted as a premonition of the more significant movement of the 1830s and 1840s, heralded by the publication of *Tracts for the Times* (1833–41). The first tract by John Henry Newman (1801–90) invited the clergy to consider themselves the true successors to the apostles. The "Tractarians" emphasized the debt that the Anglican church owed to the principles and doctrines of the Catholic church.
3. Revelation 22.14–14: "Blessed are they that do his commandments . . . they may enter in through the gates into the city. For without are dogs, and sorcerers, and whoremongers, and murderers, and idolaters, and whosoever loveth and maketh a lie."
4. The university at Göttingen was founded in 1734. RB portrayed his own view of Göttingen's philosophy in *Christmas-Eve and Easter-Day* (1850), "Christmas-Eve," 14–15. See, for instance, "So, he proposed inquiring first/Into the various sources whence/This Myth of Christ is derivable;/Demanding from the evidence,/(Since plainly no such life was liveable)/How these phenomena should class?" (15.857–62).

He'd rail at Venus' self for creaking shoes,
Unless she walked his way of righteousness:
And if he takes a Venus Meretrix,[5]
(No imputation on the lady there)
Be sure that, by some sleight of Christian art,
He has metamorphosed and converted her
To a Blessed Virgin.'
'Soft!' Sir Blaise drew breath
As if it hurt him - 'Soft! no blasphemy,
I pray you!'
'The first Christians did the thing:
Why not the last? asked he of Göttingen,
With just that shade of sneering on the lip,
Compensates for the lagging of the beard, -
'And so the case is. If that fairest fair
Is talked of as the future wife of Leigh,
She's talked of too, at least as certainly,
As Leigh's disciple. You may find her name
On all his missions and commissions, schools,
Asylums, hospitals, - he had her down,
With other ladies whom her starry lead
Persuaded from their spheres, to his country place
In Shropshire, to the famed phalanstery
At Leigh Hall, christianised from Fourier's own,
(In which he has planted out his sapling stocks
Of knowledge into social nurseries)
And there, they say, she tarried half a week,
And milked the cows, and churned, and pressed the curd,
And said 'my sister' to the lowest drab[6]
Of all the assembled castaways; such girls!
Ay, sided with them at the washing-tub -
Conceive, Sir Blaise, those naked perfect arms,
Round glittering arms, plunged elbow-deep in suds,
Like wild swans hid in lilies all a-shake.'

Lord Howe came up. 'What, talking poetry
So near the image of the unfavouring Muse?
That's you, Miss Leigh: I've watched you half an hour,
Precisely as I watched the statue called
A Pallas in the Vatican;[7] - you mind
The face, Sir Blaise? - intensely calm and sad,
As wisdom cut it off from fellowship, -
But *that* spoke louder. Not a word from *you!*

5. *Meretrix* is from the Latin word meaning "a prostitute."
6. Colloquial and archaic word for the working-class girl, or prostitute.
7. This statue, also called Minerva Medica, Minerva Guistiniari, and La Dea Salus, stood in the "Braccio Nuovo" of the Vatican Museum.

And these two gentlemen were bold, I marked,
And unabashed by even your silence.'
'Ah,'
Said I, 'my dear Lord Howe, you shall not speak
To a printing woman who has lost her place,
(The sweet safe corner of the household fire
Behind the heads of children) compliments,
As if she were a woman. We who have clipt
The curls before our eyes, may see at least
As plain as men do. Speak out, man to man;
No compliments, beseech you.'
'Friend to friend,
Let that be. We are sad to-night, I saw,
( - Good night, Sir Blaise! ah, Smith - he has slipped away)
I saw you across the room, and stayed, Miss Leigh,
To keep a crowd of lion-hunters off,[8]
With faces toward your jungle. There were three;
A spacious lady, five feet ten and fat,
Who has the devil in her (and there's room)
For walking to and fro upon the earth,
From Chipewa[9] to China; she requires
Your autograph upon a tinted leaf
'Twixt Queen Pomare's and Emperor Soulouque's.[1]
Pray give it; she has energies, though fat:
For me, I'd rather see a rick on fire
Than such a woman angry. Then a youth
Fresh from the backwoods,[2] green as the underboughs,
Asks modestly, Miss Leigh, to kiss your shoe,
And adds, he has an epic in twelve parts,
Which when you've read, you'll do it for his boot:
All which I saved you, and absorb next week
Both manuscript and man, - because a lord
Is still more potent than a poetess
With any extreme republican. Ah, ah,
You smile, at last, then.'

8. See note to *Aurora Leigh* 3.385–87.
9. More correctly, Chippewa or Chipwyan, a native American tribe. EBB's friend Anna Jameson was the first Englishwoman to travel widely in the backwoods of Canada and to encounter familiarly the native American tribes.
1. Faustin-Elie Soulouque (c. 1782–1867) became president of Haiti in 1847, and later, shaking off the mulatto faction that had brought him power, declared himself Emperor Faustin I of Haiti (1849). As a former slave and a black monarch with a taste for pomp and finery, Soulouque was an irresistible target of ridicule in the European journals. See, for instance, "Appendages of Black Royalty," *Punch* (May 11, 1850), 190; Pomare IV of Tahiti (1813–77) had been at the center of a struggle for supremacy in Tahiti between the British and the French in the 1840s. Engravings of Pomare were widely circulated in Britain at the time and EBB mentioned Queen Pomare in a letter to RB in 1846: ". . . Queen Victoria does not sit upon a mat after the fashion of Queen Pomare, nor should" (*RB/EBB Letters* 1.495).
2. This is clearly an American admirer of Aurora's, given the reference to the backwoods and the fact that in the first draft manuscript his epic "in twelve parts" is called "Bunker Hill."

'Thank you.'
'Leave the smile,
I'll lose the thanks for't, - ay, and throw you in
My transatlantic girl, with golden eyes,
That draw you to her splendid whiteness as
The pistil of a water-lily draws,
Adust with gold. Those girls across the sea
Are tyrannously pretty,[3] - and I swore
(She seemed to me an innocent, frank girl)
To bring her to you for a woman's kiss,
Not now, but on some other day or week:
- We'll call it perjury; I give her up.'
'No, bring her.'
'Now,' said he, 'you make it hard
To touch such goodness with a grimy palm.
I thought to tease you well, and fret you cross,
And steel myself, when rightly vexed with you,
For telling you a thing to tease you more.'

'Of Romney?'
'No, no; nothing worse,' he cried,
'Of Romney Leigh than what is buzzed about, -
That *he* is taken in an eye-trap too,
Like many half as wise. The thing I mean
Refers to you, not him.'
'Refers to me.'

He echoed, - 'Me! You sound it like a stone
Dropped down a dry well very listlessly
By one who never thinks about the toad
Alive at the bottom. Presently perhaps
You'll sound your 'me' more proudly - till I shrink.'

'Lord Howe's the toad, then, in this question?'
'Brief,

We'll take it graver. Give me sofa-room,
And quiet hearing. You know Eglinton,
John Eglinton, of Eglinton in Kent?'[4]

3. EBB may have based this American admirer on "Grace Greenwood" (Sara Jane Clarke), whom she heard of in July 1852 ("Miss Clarke . . . no . . but I am to see her, I understand, & that she is an American Corinna in yellow silk, but pretty") and met in April 1853. See *EBB to MRM*, 3.364, 386.
4. EBB's invention of this character might have owed something to reports of the tournament held at Eglinton castle by the earl of Eglinton and Winton in 1839. Aristocratic young men, dressed in antique armor, jousted according to strict rules of combat for the favors of "The Queen of Beauty" and in the presence of the host's "noble mother." John Killham makes the point, relevant to this incident in *Aurora Leigh*, that even this absurd revival of the chivalric ideal carried serious implications concerning the position of women. See *Tennyson and The Princess: Reflections of an Age* (1958), 272–75.

'Is *he* the toad: - he's rather like the snail,
Known chiefly for the house upon his back:
Divide the man and house - you kill the man;
That's Eglinton of Eglinton, Lord Howe.'
He answered grave. 'A reputable man,
An excellent landlord of the olden stamp
If somewhat slack in new philanthropies,
Who keeps his birthdays with a tenants' dance.[5]
Is hard upon them when they miss the church
Or hold their children back from catechism,
But not ungentle when the aged poor
Pick sticks at hedge-sides:[6] nay, I've heard him say,
'The old dame has a twinge because she stoops;
'That's punishment enough for felony.' '

'O tender-hearted landlord! may I take
My long lease with him, when the time arrives
For gathering winter-faggots!'
'He likes art,
Buys books and pictures . . of a certain kind;
Neglects no patent duty; a good son' . . .

'To a most obedient mother. Born to wear
His father's shoes, he wears her husband's too:
Indeed I've heard it's touching. Dear Lord Howe,
You shall not praise *me* so against your heart,
When I'm at worst for praise and faggots.'
'Be
Less bitter with me, for . . in short,' he said,
'I have a letter, which he urged me so
To bring you . . I could scarcely choose but yield;
Insisting that a new love, passing through
The hand of an old friendship, caught from it
Some reconciling odour.'
'Love, you say?
My lord, I cannot love: I only find
The rhyme for love, - and that's not love, my lord.
Take back your letter.'
'Pause: you'll read it first?'

'I will not read it: it is stereotyped;[7]
The same he wrote to, - anybody's name,

5. It was the custom in old estates to celebrate personal family events with a dance or holiday given to the workers and tenant farmers dependent on the estate owner.
6. Everything on the estate belongs to the landlord, so to pick up sticks for the fire is, strictly speaking, robbery.
7. A printing process in which a solid plate of type metal is made from a mold taken from a forme of type. It was invented toward the end of the eighteenth century and meant that repeat copies

Anne Blythe the actress, when she died so true
A duchess fainted in a private box:
Pauline the dancer, after the great *pas*[8]
In which her little feet winked overhead
Like other fire-flies, and amazed the pit:
Or Baldinacci, when her F in alt[9]
Had touched the silver tops of heaven itself
With such a pungent spirit-dart, the Queen
Laid softly, each to each, her white-gloved palms,
And sighed for joy: or else (I thank your friend)
Aurora Leigh - when some indifferent rhymes,
Like those the boys sang round the holy ox
On Memphis-highway,[1] chance perhaps to set
Our Apis-public lowing. Oh, he wants,
Instead of any worthy wife at home,
A star upon his stage of Eglinton?
Advise him that he is not overshrewd
In being so little modest: a dropped star
Makes bitter waters, says a Book I've read,[2] -
And there's his unread letter.'
'My dear friend,'
Lord Howe began . .
In haste I tore the phrase.
'You mean your friend of Eglinton, or me?'

'I mean you, you,' he answered with some fire.
'A happy life means prudent compromise;
The tare runs through the farmer's garnered sheaves,
And though the gleaner's apron holds pure wheat
We count her poorer.[3] Tare with wheat, we cry,
And good with drawbacks. You, you love your art,
And, certain of vocation, set your soul
On utterance. Only, in this world we have made,
(They say God made it first, but if He did
'Twas so long since, and, since, we have spoiled it so,
He scarce would know it, if He looked this way,
From hells we preach of, with the flames blown out,)
- In this bad, twisted, topsy-turvy world

---

of text could be reprinted cheaply, because the plate was fixed and permanent and did not require the expensive retention of standing type.

8. The great virtuoso set piece in ballet; more usually found in the phrase for two dancers, *pas de deux*.
9. A very high note in the upper register.
1. Apis, or Hap, was the sacred bull of Memphis, worshipped as the incarnation of the god Ptah-Osiris, the offspring of a virgin cow impregnated by lightning.
2. Revelation 8.10–11.
3. After the harvest, the poor are allowed to follow along behind the reapers and pick up what wheat they can. Obviously they pick out the best ears left behind, but they still collect very little in comparison with the whole of the harvest.

Where all the heaviest wrongs get uppermost, -
In this uneven, unfostering England here,
Where ledger-strokes and sword-strokes count indeed,
But soul-strokes merely tell upon the flesh
They strike from, - it is hard to stand for art,
Unless some golden tripod from the sea
Be fished up, by Apollo's divine chance,
To throne such feet as yours, my prophetess,
At Delphi.[4] Think, - the god comes down as fierce
As twenty bloodhounds, shakes you, strangles you,
Until the oracular shriek shall ooze in froth!
At best 'tis not all ease, - at worst too hard:
A place to stand on is a 'vantage gained,
And here's your tripod. To be plain, dear friend,
You're poor, except in what you richly give;
You labour for your own bread painfully,
Or ere you pour our wine. For art's sake, pause.'

I answered slow, - as some wayfaring man,
Who feels himself at night too far from home,
Makes stedfast face against the bitter wind.
'Is art so less a thing than virtue is,
That artists first must cater for their ease
Or ever they make issue past themselves
To generous use? alas, and is it so,
That we, who would be somewhat clean, must sweep
Our ways as well as walk them, and no friend
Confirm us nobly, - 'Leave results to God,
But you, be clean?' What! 'prudent compromise
Makes acceptable life,' you say instead,
You, you, Lord Howe? - in things indifferent, well.
For instance, compromise the wheaten bread
For rye, the meat for lentils, silk for serge,
And sleep on down, if needs, for sleep on straw;
But there, end compromise. I will not bate
One artist-dream on straw or down, my lord,
Nor pinch my liberal soul, though I be poor,
Nor cease to love high, though I live thus low.'

So speaking, with less anger in my voice
Than sorrow, I rose quickly to depart;
While he, thrown back upon the noble shame

4. An ancient shrine to Apollo was situated at Delphi. The priestess of Apollo, the Pythia, seated on a tripod over a fissure in the rock, was inspired by the mephitic vapors that periodically arose therefrom, and the words uttered in her trance were taken as the revelations of Apollo, god of prophecy. Plutarch gives a description of the prophesying priestess, who falls to the ground in a fit and emits the "Pythian shriek" while under the divine influence (*De Defectu Oraculorum*, 51). Cf. *Aurora Leigh* 5.943–45.

Of such high-stumbling natures, murmured words,
The right words after wrong ones. Ah, the man
Is worthy, but so given to entertain
Impossible plans of superhuman life. -
He sets his virtues on so raised a shelf,
To keep them at the grand millennial height,[5]
He has to mount a stool to get at them;
And, meantime, lives on quite the common way,
With everybody's morals.
As we passed,
Lord Howe insisting that his friendly arm
Should oar me across the sparkling brawling stream
Which swept from room to room, - we fell at once
On Lady Waldemar. 'Miss Leigh,' she said,
And gave me such a smile, so cold and bright,
As if she tried it in a 'tiring glass[6]
And liked it; 'all to-night I've strained at you
As babes at baubles held up out of reach
By spiteful nurses, ('Never snatch,' they say,)
And there you sate, most perfectly shut in
By good Sir Blaise and clever Mister Smith
And then our dear Lord Howe! at last indeed
I almost snatched. I have a world to speak
About your cousin's place in Shropshire where
I've been to see his work . . our work, - you heard
I went? . . and of a letter yesterday,
In which if I should read a page or two
You might feel interest, though you're locked of course
In literary toil. - You'll like to hear
Your last book lies at the phalanstery,
As judged innocuous for the elder girls
And younger women who still care for books.
We all must read, you see, before we live,
Till slowly the ineffable light comes up
And, as it deepens, drowns the written word, -
So said your cousin, while we stood and felt
A sunset from his favourite beech-tree seat.
He might have been a poet if he would,
But then he saw the higher thing at once
And climbed to it. I think he looks well now,
Has quite got over that unfortunate . .
Ah, ah . . I know it moved you. Tender-heart!
You took a liking to the wretched girl.
Perhaps you thought the marriage suitable,
Who knows? a poet hankers for romance,

5. The millennium is used here as the time when all ideal values will be achieved.
6. An attiring glass; a mirror.

And so on. As for Romney Leigh, 'tis sure
He never loved her, - never. By the way,
You have not heard of *her* . .? quite out of sight,
And out of saving? lost in every sense?'

She might have gone on talking half an hour
And I stood still, and cold, and pale, I think,
As a garden-statue a child pelts with snow
For pretty pastime. Every now and then
I put in 'yes' or 'no,' I scarce knew why;
The blind man walks wherever the dog pulls,
And so I answered. Till Lord Howe broke in;
'What penance takes the wretch who interrupts
The talk of charming women? I, at last,
Must brave it. Pardon, Lady Waldemar!
The lady on my arm is tired, unwell,
And loyally I've promised she shall say
No harder word this evening, than . . goodnight;
The rest her face speaks for her.' - Then we went.

And I breathe large at home. I drop my cloak
Unclasp my girdle, loose the band that ties
My hair . . now could I but unloose my soul![7]
We are sepulchred alive in this close world,
And want more room.
                                        The charming woman there[8] -
This reckoning up and writing down her talk
Affects me singularly. How she talked
To pain me! woman's spite. - You wear steel-mail;
A woman takes a housewife[9] from her breast
And plucks the delicatest needle out
As 'twere a rose, and pricks you carefully
'Neath nails, 'neath eyelids, in your nostrils, - say,
A beast would roar so tortured, - but a man,
A human creature, must not, shall not flinch,
No, not for shame.
                                    What vexes, after all,
Is just that such as she, with such as I,
Knows how to vex. Sweet heaven, she takes me up

7. Compare the opening to RB's poem *Pauline* (1833): "Pauline, mine own, bend o'er me—thy soft breast/Shall pant to mine—bend o'er me—thy sweet eyes,/And loosened hair and breathing lips and arms/Drawing me to thee—these build up a screen/To shut me in with thee, and from all fear;/So that I might unlock the sleepless brood/Of fancies from my soul."

8. "The Charming Woman" was the title of a popular poem by Helen Selina Sheridan, Lady Dufferin (1807–67), and the phrase became proverbial in the 1830s and 1840s for the kind of woman a man would be ill-advised to marry, "immodest, flirtatious, strong-willed, politically inclined, imprudent with money, or even a bit 'Blue,' " according to Kathleen Hickok, *Representations of Women* (1984), 68, 188.

9. A pocket-case for needles, etc. (OED)

As if she had fingered me and dog-eared me
And spelled me by the fireside half a life!
She knows my turns, my feeble points. - What then?
The knowledge of a thing implies the thing;
Of course, she found *that* in me, she saw *that*,
Her pencil underscored *this* for a fault,
And I, still ignorant. Shut the book up, - close!
And crush that beetle in the leaves.
O heart,
At last we shall grow hard too, like the rest,
And call it self-defence because we are soft.

And after all, now, . . why should I be pained
That Romney Leigh, my cousin, should espouse
This Lady Waldemar? And, say, she held
Her newly-blossomed gladness in my face, . .
'Twas natural surely, if not generous,
Considering how, when winter held her fast,
I helped the frost with mine, and pained her more
Than she pains me. Pains me! - but wherefore pained?
'Tis clear my cousin Romney wants a wife, -
So, good! - The man's need of the woman, here,
Is greater than the woman's of the man,
And easier served; for where the man discerns
A sex, (ah, ah, the man can generalise,
Said he) we see but one, ideally
And really: where we yearn to lose ourselves
And melt like white pearls in another's wine,[1]
He seeks to double himself by what he loves,
And make his drink more costly by our pearls.
At board, at bed, at work and holiday,
It is not good for man to be alone,[2]
And that's his way of thinking, first and last,
And thus my cousin Romney wants a wife.

But then my cousin sets his dignity
On personal virtue. If he understands
By love, like others, self-aggrandisement,
It is that he may verily be great
By doing rightly and kindly. Once he thought,
For charitable ends set duly forth
In Heaven's white judgment-book, to marry . . ah,
We'll call her name Aurora Leigh, although
She's changed since then! - and once, for social ends,

1. Pliny, *Natural History* 9.58. See note to *Aurora Leigh* 3.681–83.
2. Genesis 2.18: "Then the Lord God said, 'It is not good that the man should be alone; I will make him a helpmate fit for him.' "

Poor Marian Erle, my sister Marian Erle,
My woodland sister, sweet maid Marian,
Whose memory moans on in me like the wind
Through ill-shut casements, making me more sad
Than ever I find reasons for. Alas,
Poor pretty plaintive face, embodied ghost!
He finds it easy then, to clap thee off
From pulling at his sleeve and book and pen, -
He locks thee out at night into the cold
Away from butting with thy horny eyes
Against his crystal dreams,[3] that now he's strong
To love anew? that Lady Waldemar
Succeeds my Marian?
After all, why not?
He loved not Marian, more than once he loved
Aurora. If he loves at last that Third,
Albeit she prove as slippery as spilt oil
On marble floors, I will not augur him
Ill-luck for that. Good love, howe'er ill-placed,
Is better for a man's soul in the end,
Than if he loved ill what deserves love well.
A pagan, kissing for a step of Pan
The wild-goat's hoof-print on the loamy down,
Exceeds our modern thinker who turns back
The strata . . granite, limestone, coal, and clay,
Concluding coldly with, 'Here's law! where's God?'[4]

And then at worst, - if Romney loves her not, -
At worst, - if he's incapable of love,
Which may be - then indeed, for such a man
Incapable of love, she's good enough;
For she, at worst too, is a woman still
And loves him . . as the sort of woman can.
My loose long hair began to burn and creep,
Alive to the very ends, about my knees:
I swept it backward as the wind sweeps flame,
With the passion of my hands. Ah, Romney laughed
One day . . (how full the memories come up!)
' - Your Florence fire-flies live on in your hair,'
He said, 'it gleams so.' Well, I wrung them out,
My fire-flies; made a knot as hard as life

3. Possibly a reminiscence of Emily Brontë's *Wuthering Heights* (1847), ch. 3.
4. In pagan times a person might have mistaken an ordinary goat's hoofmark for the footstep of the god Pan, but at least he or she treated the earth with due reverence and believed in the spiritual life, whereas in the nineteenth century and with the introduction of evolutionary theory, people look at the elaborate strata of geological formations and at ancient fossils and say that this is the natural system of evolution, which is all to do with science and has nothing to do with a creative God.

Of those loose, soft, impracticable curls.
And then sate down and thought . . 'She shall not think
Her thought of me,' - and drew my desk and wrote.

'Dear Lady Waldemar, I could not speak
With people round me, nor can sleep to-night
And not speak, after the great news I heard
Of you and of my cousin. May you be
Most happy; and the good he meant the world,
Replenish his own life. Say what I say,
And let my word be sweeter for your mouth,
As you are *you* . . I only Aurora Leigh.'

That's quiet, guarded: though she hold it up
Against the light, she'll not see through it more
Than lies there to be seen. So much for pride;
And now for peace, a little. Let me stop
All writing back . . 'Sweet thanks, my sweetest friend,
'You've made more joyful my great joy itself.'
- No, that's too simple! she would twist it thus,
'My joy would still be as sweet as thyme in drawers,
'However shut up in the dark and dry;
'But violets, aired and dewed by love like yours,
'Out-smell all thyme: we keep that in our clothes,
'But drop the other down our bosoms till
'They smell like' . . ah, I see her writing back
Just so. She'll make a nosegay of her words,
And tie it with blue ribbons at the end
To suit a poet; - pshaw!
                                        And then we'll have
The call to church, the broken, sad, bad dream
Dreamed out at last, the marriage-vow complete
With the marriage-breakfast; praying in white gloves,
Drawn off in haste for drinking pagan toasts
In somewhat stronger wine than any sipped
By gods[5] since Bacchus had his way with grapes.

A postscript stops all that and rescues me.
'You need not write. I have been overworked,
And think of leaving London, England even,
And hastening to get nearer to the sun
Where men sleep better. So, adieu.' - I fold
And seal,—and how I'm out of all the coil;
I breathe now, I spring upward like a branch
The ten-years school-boy with a crooked stick

5. See Homer, *The Iliad*, 5.341–42: "they eat not bread neither drink flaming wine,/wherefore they are bloodless, and are called immortals" (Loeb translation).

May pull down to his level in search of nuts,
But cannot hold a moment.[6] How we twang
Back on the blue sky, and assert our height,
While he stares after! Now, the wonder seems
That I could wrong myself by such a doubt.
We poets always have uneasy hearts,
Because our hearts, large-rounded as the globe,
Can turn but one side to the sun at once.
We are used to dip our artist-hands in gall
And potash, trying potentialities
Of alternated colour, till at last
We get confused, and wonder for our skin
How nature tinged it first. Well - here's the true
Good flesh-colour; I recognise my hand, -
Which Romney Leigh may clasp as just a friend's,
And keep his clean.
                    And now, my Italy.
Alas, if we could ride with naked souls
And make no noise and pay no price at all,
I would have seen thee sooner, Italy,
For still I have heard thee crying through my life,
Thou piercing silence of ecstatic graves,
Men call that name!

                    But even a witch to-day
Must melt down golden pieces in the nard
Wherewith to anoint her broomstick[7] ere she rides;
And poets evermore are scant of gold,
And if they find a piece behind the door
It turns by sunset to a withered leaf.
The Devil himself scarce trusts his patented
Gold-making art to any who make rhymes,
But culls his Faustus from philosophers[8]
And not from poets. 'Leave my Job,' said God;[9]
And so the Devil leaves him without pence,
And poverty proves plainly special grace.
In these new, just, administrative times

6. Compare EBB to RB, February 7, 1846: "When she had gone at half past six, moreover, I grew over-hopeful, & made up my fancy to have a letter at eight!—The branch she had pulled down, sprang upward sky-ward . . . to that high possibility of a letter!" (*RB/EBB Letters* 1.442).
7. Witches were said to prepare for flight by anointing themselves and their broomsticks with a magical ointment.
8. See Marlowe's play *The Tragical History of Doctor Faustus* (1604) and Goethe's drama *Faust* (1808 and 1832). Johann Faust was a wandering conjuror who lived in Germany about 1488–1541. The legend grew up that he was a learned philosopher and alchemist who sold his soul to the devil in return for the secret of alchemy and wealth, power, and sexual indulgence.
9. After Job's many long trials and temptations, God instructed the devil to leave him in peace; see Job 42.10.

Men clamour for an order of merit: why?
Here's black bread on the table and no wine!

At least I am a poet in being poor,
Thank God. I wonder if the manuscript
Of my long poem, if 'twere sold outright,
Would fetch enough to buy me shoes[1] to go
A-foot, (thrown in, the necessary patch
For the other side the Alps)? It cannot be.
I fear that I must sell this residue
Of my father's books, although the Elzevirs[2]
Have fly-leaves over-written by his hand
In faded notes as thick and fine and brown
As cobwebs on a tawny monument
Of the old Greeks - *conferenda hæc cum his -*
*Corruptè citat - lege potiùs,*[3]
And so on, in the scholar's regal way
Of giving judgment on the parts of speech,
As if he sate on all twelve thrones up-piled,
Arraigning Israel.[4] Ay, but books and notes
Must go together. And this Proclus[5] too,
In these dear quaint contracted Grecian types,
Fantastically crumpled[6] like his thoughts
Which would not seem too plain; you go round twice
For one step forward, then you take it back
Because you're somewhat giddy; there's the rule
For Proclus. Ah, I stained this middle leaf
With pressing in't my Florence iris-bell,
Long stalk and all: my father chided me
For that stain of blue blood, - I recollect
The peevish turn his voice took, - 'Silly girls,
Who plant their flowers in our philosophy
To make it fine, and only spoil the book!

1. The nineteenth century's underestimate of the worth of poetry was a critical commonplace familiar to EBB. See, for instance, her remarks on R. H. Horne's epic poem, *Orion* (1843): "As to the author's fantasy of selling it for a farthing. I do not enter into the secret of it—unless, indeed he should intend a sarcasm on the age's generous patronage of poetry, which is possible" (*Letters of EBB* 1.145).
2. The Elzevir family, printing at Amsterdam, Leyden, and the Hague (1592–1680), were famous for their editions of the classics, which were produced in a small, neat form and a specially designed type.
3. "Compare this with that. Corruptly or incorrectly cited." These are Aurora's father's handwritten notes, scribbled in Latin.
4. Matthew 19.28: "[y]e which have followed me, in the regeneration when the Son of man shall sit in the throne of glory, ye also shall sit upon twelve thrones, judging the twelve tribes of Israel."
5. Proclus of Byzantium (c. 411–85), the last significant writer of the Neo-platonic school.
6. Compare RB, "Bishop Blougram's Apology" (1855), lines 110–11: "And little Greek books, with the funny type/They get up well at Leipsic." RB is apparently referring to the small Tauchnitz editions printed in Leipzig.

No more of it, Aurora.' Yes - no more!
Ah, blame of love, that's sweeter than all praise
Of those who love not! 'tis so lost to me,
I cannot, in such beggared life, afford
To lose my Proclus, - not for Florence even.

The kissing Judas, Wolf, shall go instead,
Who builds us such a royal book as this
To honour a chief-poet, folio-built,
And writes above, 'The house of Nobody!'[7]
Who floats in cream, as rich as any sucked
From Juno's breasts,[8] the broad Homeric lines,
And, while with their spondaic prodigious mouths
They lap the lucent margins as babe-gods,
Proclaims them bastards. Wolf's an atheist;
And if the Iliad fell out, as he says,
By mere fortuitous concourse of old songs,
Conclude as much too for the universe.

That Wolf, those Platos:[9] sweep the upper shelves
As clean as this, and so I am almost rich,
Which means, not forced to think of being poor
In sight of ends. To-morrow: no delay.
I'll wait in Paris till good Carrington
Dispose of such and, having chaffered for[1]
My book's price with the publisher, direct
All proceeds to me. Just a line to ask
His help.
            And now I come, my Italy,
My own hills! Are you 'ware of me, my hills,
How I burn toward you? do you feel to-night
The urgency and yearning of my soul,
As sleeping mothers feel the sucking babe
And smile? - Nay, not so much as when in heat
Vain lightnings catch at your inviolate tops

7. Friedrich Augustus Wolf (1759–1824), the editor of *Homeri et Homeridarum Opera et Reliquiae* (1806), an expensive and beautiful edition which Hugh Stuart Boyd gave to EBB in July 1831. "*Twelve books*—and the most splendid paper & type. . . . It is the most magnificent Greek book I have ever looked upon" (*Diary by EBB: The Unpublished Diary of Elizabeth Barrett Barrett* (1831–1832), ed. Philip Kelley and Ronald Hudson [Athens, Ohio, 1969] 57). Wolf's *Prolegomena* to *Homer* (1795) earns him EBB's epithet, for in that influential work he argued that both the *Iliad* and the *Odyssey* were not the works of a single poet but a collection of ballads composed by a number of authors.
8. The origin of the Milky Way was said to derive from Juno's flowing milk, either when she thrust away the infant Mercury whom she was nursing, or when she was suckling the infant Hercules who sucked so greedily that the milk overflowed his mouth and formed the constellation (Hyginus, *Poetica Astronomica* 2.43).
9. EBB possessed the eleven-volume edition of Plato by Immanuel Bekker (London, 1826), and an edition of *Platonic Dialogi V* (Oxford, 1752), which she annotated with her own marginal notes. See *Browning Collections* A1860 and A1861.
1. Bargained for; haggled over.

And tremble while ye are stedfast. Still ye go
Your own determined, calm, indifferent way
Toward sunrise, shade by shade, and light by light,
Of all the grand progression nought left out,
As if God verily made you for yourselves
And would not interrupt your life with ours.

## Sixth Book

The English have a scornful insular way
Of calling the French light. The levity
Is in the judgment only, which yet stands,
For say a foolish thing but oft enough
(And here's the secret of a hundred creeds,
Men get opinions as boys learn to spell,
By re-iteration chiefly,) the same thing
Shall pass at last for absolutely wise,[1]
And not with fools exclusively. And so
We say the French are light, as if we said
The cat mews or the milch-cow[2] gives us milk:
Say rather, cats are milked and milch-cows mew;
For what is lightness but inconseqence,
Vague fluctuation 'twixt effect and cause
Compelled by neither? Is a bullet light,
That dashes from the gun-mouth, while the eye
Winks and the heart beats one, to flatten itself
To a wafer on the white speck on a wall
A hundred paces off? Even so direct,
So sternly undivertible of aim,
Is this French people.

All, idealists
Too absolute and earnest, with them all
The idea of a knife cuts real flesh;
And still, devouring the safe interval
Which nature placed between the thought and act
With those too fiery and impatient souls,
They threaten conflagration to the world,
And rush with most unscrupulous logic on
Impossible practice. Set your orators
To blow upon them with loud windy mouths
Through watchword phrases, jest or sentiment,
Which drive our burly brutal English mobs
Like so much chaff,[3] whichever way they blow, -
This light French people will not thus be driven.
They turn indeed, - but then they turn upon
Some central pivot of their thought and choice,
And veer out by the force of holding fast.
That's hard to understand, for Englishmen
Unused to abstract questions, and untrained

1. Cf. *Aurora Leigh* 1.196–98.
2. A milking or dairy cow.
3. The light husk of the wheat seed after the kernel has been removed.

To trace the involutions, valve by valve,
In each orbed bulb-root of a general truth,
And mark what subtly fine integument[4]
Divides opposed compartments. Freedom's self
Comes concrete to us, to be understood,
Fixed in a feudal form incarnately
To suit our ways of thought and reverence,
The special form, with us, being still the thing.
With us, I say, though I'm of Italy
By mother's birth and grave, by father's grave
And memory; let it be; - a poet's heart
Can swell to a pair of nationalities,
However ill-lodged in a woman's breast.

And so I am strong to love this noble France,
This poet of the nations, who dreams on
And wails on (while the household goes to wreck)
For ever, after some ideal good, -
Some equal poise of sex, some unvowed love
Inviolate, some spontaneous brotherhood,
Some wealth that leaves none poor and finds none tired,[5]
Some freedom of the many that respects
The wisdom of the few. Heroic dreams!
Sublime, to dream so; natural, to wake:
And sad, to use such lofty scaffoldings,
Erected for the building of a church,
To build instead a brothel or a prison -
May God save France!
And if at last she sighs
Her great soul up into a great man's face,
To flush his temples out so gloriously
That few dare carp at Cæsar for being bald,[6]
What then? - this Cæsar represents, not reigns,
And is no despot, though twice absolute:[7]

4. The joining skin or flesh that binds the living element.
5. A fairly accurate summary of the benefits of communal living as perceived by Charles Fourier. Fourier's writings advocated social equality for the sexes, the abolition of the rites of marriage, the feasibility of "industrial attraction" where work was made more attractive than play, a friendly interchange between the rich and the poor, and, most surprisingly, a varied routine of work and play, supplemented by regular and frequent meals, which would lead to "Harmonians" who never feel tired and need very little sleep. See *The Utopian Vision of Charles Fourier: Selected Texts on Work, Love, and Passionate Attraction*, trans. and ed. by Jonathan Beecher and Richard Bienvenu (London, 1972).
6. See Suetonius, *De Vita Caesarum*, "Divus Julius," 45: "his baldness was a disfigurement which troubled him greatly, since he found that it was often the subject of the gibes of his detractors. Because of it he used to comb forward his scanty locks from the crown of his head, and of all the honours voted him by the senate and people there were none which he received or made use of more gladly than the privilege of wearing a laurel wreath at all times" (Loeb translation).
7. A reference to Napoleon III (Charles Louis Napoleon Bonaparte, 1808–73) who was elected president of the republican government of France after the revolution of 1848. In 1851 he

This Head has all the people for a heart;
This purple's lined with the democracy, -
Now let him see to it! for a rent within
Would leave irreparable rags without.

A serious riddle: find such anywhere
Except in France; and when 'tis found in France,
Be sure to read it rightly. So, I mused
Up and down, up and down, the terraced streets,
The glittering boulevards, the white colonnades
Of fair fantastic Paris who wears trees
Like plumes, as if man made them, spire and tower
As if they had grown by nature, tossing up
Her fountains in the sunshine of the squares,
As if in beauty's game she tossed the dice,
Or blew the silver down-balls of her dreams
To sow futurity with seeds of thought
And count the passage of her festive hours.

The city swims in verdure, beautiful
As Venice on the waters,[8] the sea-swan.
What bosky[9] gardens dropped in close-walled courts
Like plums in ladies' laps who start and laugh:
What miles of streets that run on after trees,
Still carrying all the necessary shops,
Those open caskets with the jewels seen!
And trade is art, and art's philosophy,
In Paris. There's a silk for instance, there,
As worth an artist's study for the folds,
As that bronze opposite! nay, the bronze has faults,
Art's here too artful, - conscious as a maid
Who leans to mark her shadow on the wall
Until she lose a 'vantage in her step.
Yet Art walks forward, and knows where to walk;

---

sought reelection to the office, although the constitution forbade the reelection of a past president. When his proposal that the constitution be altered was rejected by the assembly, he staged a successful coup d'état on December 2, 1851. On December 20, a national plebiscite was held, asking the French people to ratify his action, which they did, by 7,439,219 votes to 640,737. The Brownings were living in Paris at the time, and EBB was much interested in the progress of these political events. Her letters describing the coup defend Louis Napoleon's high-handed action: "What has saved him with me from the beginning was his appeal to the people, and what makes his government respectable in my eyes is the answer of the people to that appeal. . . . There never was a more legitimate chief of a State than Louis Napoleon is now—elected by seven millions and a half" (*Letters of EBB* 2.51). In November 1852, a second plebiscite confirmed the restoration of the empire and gave Louis Napoleon the title of Emperor Napoleon III.

8. Compare EBB writing to John Kenyon about Paris, July 7, 1851: "its a splendid city—a city in the country as Venice is a city in the sea. . . . And I admire the bright green trees and gardens everywhere in the heart of the town" (*Letters of EBB* 2.11).
9. Consisting of, or covered with bushes or underwood; full of thickets, bushy (OED).

The artists also are idealists,
Too absolute for nature, logical
To austerity in the application of
The special theory - not a soul content
To paint a crooked pollard[1] and an ass,
As the English will because they find it so
And like it somehow. - There the old Tuileries[2]
Is pulling its high cap down on its eyes,
Confounded, conscience-stricken, and amazed
By the apparition of a new fair face[3]
In those devouring mirrors.[4] Through the grate
Within the gardens, what a heap of babes,[5]
Swept up like leaves beneath the chesnut-trees
From every street and alley of the town,
By ghosts perhaps that blow too bleak this way
A-looking for their heads![6] dear pretty babes,
I wish them luck to have their ball-play out
Before the next change. Here the air is thronged
With statues poised upon their columns fine[7]
As if to stand a moment were a feat,
Against that blue! What squares, - what breathing-room
For a nation that runs fast, - ay, runs against
The dentist's teeth at the corner in pale rows,[8]
Which grin at progress in an epigram.

I walked the day out, listening to the chink
Of the first Napoleon's bones in his second grave
By Victories guarded 'neath the golden dome
That caps all Paris like a bubble.[9] 'Shall

1. A way of pruning trees, lopping off the top and side branches severely so as to confine growth. Pollarding is often part of a domesticated landscape rather than a grand and picturesque one.
2. The palace of the Tuileries had been the official Parisian residence of the French royal family until Louis XIV abandoned it for Versailles. Napoleon made it the Imperial Palace, and Louis-Philippe lived there until 1848. By 1851 much of its former splendor had faded, but Louis Napoleon later restored the palace to imperial magnificence.
3. The empress Eugénie (Maria de Montijo de Guzman, 1825–1920), whom Louis Napoleon married in January 1853.
4. An allusion to the immense mirrors that paneled the western wall of the ballroom called the Gallerie Neuve in the Tuileries.
5. The gardens in front of the Tuileries and enclosed by netted iron railings.
6. During revolutionary rule, the guillotine was erected in the Place de la Concorde, between the gardens of the Tuileries and the Avenue des Champs Elysées.
7. In the nineteenth century there was a good deal of fine sculpture displayed on columns in the gardens of the Tuileries.
8. Sets of false teeth displayed under a glass case announced the surgeon-dentist who manufactured "natural" false teeth. Compare EBB to John Kenyon, July 7, 1851: "Well, now we are in Paris and have to forget the 'belle chiese'; we have beautiful shops instead, false teeth grinning at the corners of the streets, and disreputable prints, and fascinating hats and caps, and brilliant restaurants" (*Letters of EBB* 2.11).
9. In 1840, through the efforts of Louis-Philippe, the body of Napoleon (1769–1821) was returned to Paris from the island of St. Helena where he had died in exile. Napoleon was reinterred in the chapel of St. Louis at the Hôtel des Invalides, his sarcophagus being placed directly underneath the gold-plated dome of the chapel. Work on Napoleon's tomb was still

These dry bones live,' thought Louis Philippe once,
And lived to know.[1] Herein is argument
For kings and politicians, but still more
For poets, who bear buckets to the well
Of ampler draught.[2]
These crowds are very good
For meditation (when we are very strong)
Though love of beauty makes us timorous,
And draws us backward from the coarse town-sights
To count the daisies upon dappled fields
And hear the streams bleat on among the hills
In innocent and indolent repose,
While still with silken elegiac thoughts
We wind out from us the distracting world
And die into the chrysalis of a man,
And leave the best that may, to come of us,
In some brown moth. I would be bold and bear
To look into the swarthiest face of things,
For God's sake who has made them.

Six days' work;
The last day shutting 'twixt its dawn and eve
The whole work bettered of the previous five!
Since God collected and resumed in man
The firmaments, the strata, and the lights,
Fish, fowl, and beast, and insect, - all their trains
Of various life caught back upon His arm,
Reorganised, and constituted MAN,
The microcosm,[3] the adding up of works,[4] -
Within whose fluttering nostrils, then at last
Consummating Himself the Maker sighed,
As some strong winner at the foot-race sighs

being completed in the early 1850s, and it was not officially opened until 1861. The "Victories" that guard Napoleon's grave are twelve statues erected around the crypt. The flags of the armies conquered by Napoleon were displayed between these figures.

1. Ezekiel 37.3: "And he said unto me, Son of man, can these bones live? And I answered, O Lord God, thou knowest." Louis-Philippe (1773–1850), was deposed by the revolution of 1848, to be replaced by a republican government led by Louis Napoleon (see note to lines 6.70–71). Louis Napoleon used his relationship to Napoleon I (to whom he was both nephew and adopted grandson) with good effect during his political career.
2. Apparently an allusion to the saying, "Truth lies at the bottom of a well," which originated with Democritus and was quoted by Cicero, *Academica*, 1.12.44.
3. God created the universe and the earth and all its creatures in five days. On the sixth day he created the first man in Adam, and on the seventh day, he rested. See Genesis 1.1–2.
4. Cf. Robert Browning's expression of this Neoplatonic conception of man as the microcosm of the natural world: "and God renews/His ancient rapture. Thus he dwells in all,/From life's minute beginnings, up at last/To man—the consummation of this scheme/Of being, the completion of this sphere/Of life: whose attributes had here and there/Been scattered o'er the visible world before,/Asking to be combined, dim fragments meant/To be united in some wondrous whole,/Imperfect qualities throughout creation,/Suggesting some one creature yet to make,/Some point where all those scattered rays should meet/Convergent in the faculties of man" (*Paracelsus* [1835] 5.680–92 in *Poetical Works of RB* 1.479, 481).

Touching the goal.
                        Humanity is great;
And, if I would not rather pore upon
An ounce of common, ugly, human dust,
An artisan's palm or a peasant's brow,
Unsmooth, ignoble, save to me and God,
Than track old Nilus to his silver roots,[5]
Or wait on all the changes of the moon
Among the mountain-peaks of Thessaly[6]
(Until her magic crystal round itself
For many a witch to see in)[7] - set it down
As weakness, - strength by no means. How is this
That men of science, osteologists[8]
And surgeons, beat some poets in respect
For nature, - count nought common or unclean,
Spend raptures upon perfect specimens
Of indurated[9] veins, distorted joints,
Or beautiful new cases of curved spine,
While we, we are shocked at nature's falling off,
We dare to shrink back from her warts and blains,[1]
We will not, when she sneezes, look at her,
Not even to say 'God bless her'? That's our wrong;
For that, she will not trust us often with
Her larger sense of beauty and desire,
But tethers us to a lily or a rose
And bids us diet on the dew inside,
Left ignorant that the hungry beggar-boy
(Who stares unseen against our absent eyes,
And wonders at the gods that we must be,
To pass so careless for the oranges!)
Bears yet a breastful of a fellow-world
To this world, undisparaged, undespoiled,
And (while we scorn him for a flower or two,

5. The mystery of the source of the White Nile was the subject of much speculation during the years when EBB composed *Aurora Leigh*. By the early 1850s exploration had extended as far as the rapids and waterfalls of Bahr-el-Ghazel, a fact that might have been known to EBB. Cf. the deleted manuscript reference "Beyond the cataracts" (see textual note). In 1854 an expedition to explore the southern course of the Nile, led by Richard Burton and John Hanning Speke, had to be abandoned. A month after the publication of *Aurora Leigh* in December 1856, Burton and Speke set out again with the support of the Royal Geographical Society, and £1000 donated by the British government. This venture was more successful, but it was not until August 1858 that Speke discovered the lake that he named Victoria and that he rightly supposed to be the source of the White Nile.
6. Thessaly was regarded as the special home of the legendary witches whose peculiar attribute was the ability to draw the moon down from the sky. See Aristophanes, *Clouds*, 746–54; Seneca, *Hippolytus*, 418–22; and Horace, *Epodes* 17.77.
7. EBB encountered the phenomenon of the crystal ball in July 1852, when a ball belonging to Lord Stanhope, and originally acquired from an "Egyptian magician," was displayed at a luncheon given by Mrs. Haworth. See *Letters of EBB* 2.79.
8. Osteology is the science of bones.
9. Hardened.
1. Inflammatory swellings or sores.

As being, Heaven help us, less poetical)
Contains himself both flowers and firmaments
And surging seas and aspectable[2] stars
And all that we would push him out of sight
In order to see nearer. Let us pray
God's grace to keep God's image in repute,
That so, the poet and philanthropist
(Even I and Romney) may stand side by side,
Because we both stand face to face with men,
Contemplating the people in the rough,
Yet each so follow a vocation, his
And mine.
                    I walked on, musing with myself
On life and art, and whether after all
A larger metaphysics might not help
Our physics, a completer poetry
Adjust our daily life and vulgar wants
More fully than the special outside plans,
Phalansteries, material institutes,
The civil conscriptions and lay monasteries
Preferred by modern thinkers,[3] as they thought
The bread of man indeed made all his life,[4]
And washing seven times in the 'People's Baths'
Were sovereign for a people's leprosy,[5]
Still leaving out the essential prophet's word
That comes in power. On which, we thunder down
We prophets, poets,[6] - Virtue's in the *word!*
The maker burnt the darkness up with His,[7]
To inaugurate the use of vocal life;
And, plant a poet's word even, deep enough
In any man's breast, looking presently
For offshoots, you have done more for the man
Than if you dressed him in a broad-cloth coat

2. See note to *Aurora Leigh* 5.627.
3. The communes and phalansteries set up by Robert Owen and Charles Fourier and other socialist philosophers.
4. Deuteronomy 8.3: "And he humbled you and let you hunger and fed you with manna, which you did not know . . . that he might make you know that man does not live by bread alone, but that man lives by everything that proceeds out of the mouth of the Lord."
5. An allusion to the biblical story of Naaman's cure as dictated by Elisha. Naaman, the commander of the Syrian army, was a leper, and his wife's maidservant, who had been carried off from the land of Israel, suggested that he should seek the help of the prophet of Israel then living in Samaria. So the king of Syria sent Naaman to the king of Israel, mistaking him for the prophet so described. But Elisha, hearing of Naaman's request, sent word that he should bathe seven times in the river Jordan and would thus be cured. Although angered by the simplicity of this suggestion, Naaman did as required, and was cured of his leprosy. See 2 Kings 5.1–14. The "People's Baths" were public baths founded on philanthropic principles throughout Europe in many major cities that possessed a large population of the poor.
6. For the association of thunder with the word of the prophet, see Revelation 6.1. Cf. also *Aurora Leigh* 1.859–76.
7. John 1.1–15.

And warmed his Sunday potage[8] at your fire.
Yet Romney leaves me . . .
God! what face is that?
O Romney, O Marian!
Walking on the quays
And pulling thoughts to pieces leisurely,
As if I caught at grasses in a field
And bit them slow between my absent lips
And shred them with my hands . . .
What face is that?
What a face, what a look, what a likeness! Full on mine
The sudden blow of it came down, till all
My blood swam, my eyes dazzled.[9] Then I sprang . . .

It was as if a meditative man
Were dreaming out a summer afternoon
And watching gnats a-prick upon a pond,
When something floats up suddenly, out there,
Turns over . . a dead face, known once alive . .
So old, so new! it would be dreadful now
To lose the sight and keep the doubt of this:
He plunges - ha! he has lost it in the splash.

I plunged - I tore the crowd up, either side,
And rushed on, forward, forward, after her.
Her? whom?
A woman sauntered slow in front,
Munching an apple, - she left off amazed
As if I had snatched it: that's not she, at least.
A man walked arm-linked with a lady veiled,
Both heads dropped closer than the need of talk:
They started; he forgot her with his face,
And she, herself, and clung to him as if
My look were fatal. Such a stream of folk,
And all with cares and business of their own!
I ran the whole quay down against their eyes;
No Marian; nowhere Marian. Almost, now,
I could call Marian, Marian, with the shriek
Of desperate creatures calling for the Dead.
Where is she, was she? was she anywhere?
I stood still, breathless, gazing, straining out
In every uncertain distance, till at last
A gentleman abstracted as myself
Came full against me, then resolved the clash

8. Porridge, but here a generic word for any dish or sustenance.
9. Possibly a reminiscence of John Webster's *The Duchess of Malfi* (ed. Elizabeth Brennan [London, 1964], 6.2.259): "Cover her face. Mine eyes dazzle; she di'd young."

In voluble excuses, - obviously
Some learned member of the Institute[1]
Upon his way there, walking, for his health,
While meditating on the last 'Discourse;'[2]
Pinching the empty air 'twixt finger and thumb,
From which the snuff being ousted by that shock
Defiled his snow-white waistcoat[3] duly pricked
At the button-hole with honourable red;
'Madame, your pardon,' - there he swerved from me
A metre, as confounded as he had heard
That Dumas[4] would be chosen to fill up
The next chair vacant, by his 'men *in us*.'[5]
Since when was genius found respectable?
It passes in its place, indeed, - which means
The seventh floor back, or else the hospital:
Revolving pistols[6] are ingenious things,
But prudent men (Academicians are)
Scarce keep them in the cupboard next the prunes.

And so, abandoned to a bitter mirth,
I loitered to my inn.[7] O world, O world,
O jurists, rhymers, dreamers, what you please,
We play a weary game of hide-and-seek!
We shape a figure of our fantasy,
Call nothing something, and run after it

1. The Institut de France, composed of five learned societies—the Academie Française, the Academie des Inscriptions et Belle-Lettres, the Academie des Sciences, the Academie des Beaux Arts, and the Academie des Sciences Morales et Politiques. Membership of the institute was reserved to those who had distinguished themselves in their discipline, and each member was paid a salary (1,500 francs in 1851) and required to attend regularly.
2. A paper given at the Institut de France was called a *discours*.
3. The costume of academicians, worn on official occasions, consists of a green jacket worn over a white waistcoat.
4. Alexandre Dumas (1802–70), author of *The Count of Monte Cristo* (1844–45), *The Three Musketeers* (1844), and *The Black Tulip* (1850), among many other novels. The establishment in Paris regarded Dumas' profligate private life and extravagant professional success with no small degree of suspicion. The Brownings also appreciated the work of Alexandre Dumas *fils* (1824–95), whose play *La Dame aux Camelias* they saw in April 1852. See *Letters of EBB* 2.66. EBB's allusion is, however, most appropriate to Dumas *père*.
5. Apparently a literal translation of some formal phrase used on the occasion of election to the academy, but I have been unable to discover the original.
6. The revolving pistol was patented by Colt in the 1830s and provided a mechanism that revolved a set of cartridge chambers so as to allow the pistol to be fired rapidly in succession without the need for reloading.
7. Aurora's walk through the center of Paris (lines 61–280) traces a route that must have been familiar to EBB as a result of her extended sojourns in the city (1851–52 and 1855–56). Beginning from the Avenue des Champs Elysées, Aurora passes the gardens around the Place de l'Etoile (88), notes the shops in the Faubourg St. Honoré (93–98), and reaches the Tuileries (109) by way of the Place de la Concorde (117–18). She then makes her way toward the quay where, by looking across the river and to the right, she obtains a view of the dome of the Hôtel des Invalides (129–30). Continuing along the right bank of the Seine, Aurora glimpses Marian and collides with the man whom she takes to be a member of the Institut de France (260–65). This encounter presumably takes place by the Pont des Arts, which is a footbridge over the river leading to the Palais des Arts on the left bank, where the institute is housed.

And lose it, lose ourselves too in the search,
Till clash against us comes a somebody
Who also has lost something and is lost,
Philosopher against philanthropist,
Academician against poet, man
Against woman, against the living the dead, -
Then home, with a bad headache and worse jest!

To change the water for my heliotropes[8]
And yellow roses. Paris has such flowers.
But England, also. 'Twas a yellow rose,
By that south window of the little house,
My cousin Romney gathered with his hand
On all my birthdays for me, save the last;
And then I shook the tree too rough, too rough,
For roses to stay after.
Now, my maps.
I must not linger here from Italy
Till the last nightingale is tired of song,
And the last fire-fly dies off in the maize.
My soul's in haste to leap into the sun
And scorch and seethe itself to a finer mood,
Which here, in this chill north, is apt to stand
Too stiffly in former moulds.
That face persists.
It floats up, it turns over in my mind,
As like to Marian, as one dead is like
The same alive. In very deed a face
And not a fancy, though it vanished so;
The small fair face between the darks of hair,
I used to liken, when I saw her first,
To a point of moonlit water down a well:
The low brow, the frank space between the eyes,
Which always had the brown pathetic look
Of a dumb creature who had been beaten once
And never since was easy with the world.
Ah, ah - now I remember perfectly
Those eyes, to-day, - how overlarge they seemed,
As if some patient passionate despair
(Like a coal dropt and forgot on tapestry,
Which slowly burns a widening circle out)
Had burnt them larger, larger. And those eyes
To-day, I do remember, saw me too,
As I saw them, with conscious lids astrain
In recognition. Now a fantasy,

8. Most commonly Heliotropium Peruvianum, a sunloving plant bearing small, clustered purple flowers and cultivated for its fragrance.

A simple shade or image of the brain,
Is merely passive, does not retro-act,
Is seen, but sees not.
'Twas a real face,
Perhaps a real Marian.
Which being so,
I ought to write to Romney, 'Marian's here;
Be comforted for Marian.'
My pen fell,
My hands struck sharp together, as hands do
Which hold at nothing. Can I write to *him*
A half-truth? can I keep my own soul blind
To the other half, . . the worse? What are our souls,
If still, to run on straight a sober pace
Nor start at every pebble or dead leaf,
They must wear blinkers, ignore facts, suppress
Six tenths of the road? Confront the truth, my soul!
And oh, as truly as that was Marian's face,
The arms of that same Marian clasped a thing
. . Not hid so well beneath the scanty shawl,
I cannot name it now for what it was.
A child. Small business has a cast-away
Like Marian with that crown of prosperous wives
At which the gentlest she grows arrogant
And says, 'my child.' Who finds an emerald ring
On a beggar's middle finger and requires
More testimony to convict a thief?
A child's too costly for so mere a wretch;
She filched it somewhere, and it means, with her,
Instead of honour, blessing, merely shame.

I cannot write to Romney, 'Here she is,
Here's Marian found! I'll set you on her track:
I saw her here, in Paris, . . and her child.
She put away your love two years ago,
But, plainly, not to starve. You suffered then;
And now that you've forgot her utterly
As any last year's annual, in whose place
You've planted a thick flowering evergreen,
I choose, being kind, to write and tell you this
To make you wholly easy - she's not dead,
But only . . damned.'
Stop there: I go too fast;
I'm cruel like the rest, - in haste to take
The first stir in the arras for a rat,[9]

9. A reminiscence of *Hamlet* 3.4.

And set my barking, biting thoughts upon't.
- A child! what then? Suppose a neighbour's sick
And asked her, 'Marian, carry out my child
In this Spring air,' - I punish her for that?
Or say, the child should hold her round the neck
For good child-reasons, that he liked it so
And would not leave her - she had winning ways -
I brand her therefore that she took the child?
Not so.
I will not write to Romney Leigh.
For now he's happy, - and she may indeed
Be guilty, - and the knowledge of her fault
Would draggle his smooth time.[1] But I, whose days
Are not so fine they cannot bear the rain,
And who moreover having seen her face
Must see it again, . . *will* see it, by my hopes
Of one day seeing heaven too. The police
Shall track her, hound her, ferret their own soil;
We'll dig this Paris to its catacombs[2]
But certainly we'll find her, have her out,
And save her, if she will or will not - child
Or no child, - if a child, then one to save!

The long weeks passed on without consequence.
As easy find a footstep on the sand
The morning after spring-tide, as the trace
Of Marian's feet between the incessant surfs
Of this live flood. She may have moved this way, -
But so the star-fish does, and crosses out
The dent of her small shoe. The foiled police
Renounced me. 'Could they find a girl and child,
No other signalment[3] but girl and child?
No data shown but noticeable eyes
And hair in masses, low upon the brow,
As if it were an iron crown and pressed?
Friends heighten, and suppose they specify:
Why, girls with hair and eyes are everywhere
In Paris; they had turned me up in vain

1. The deleted allusion in the first draft manuscript to weaning and aloes (see textual note) was obviously a result of EBB's recent experience of the weaning of her son, Pen Browning (born 1849). In a letter to Eliza Ogilvy, September 22, 1850, EBB describes the process of weaning, which included putting aloes on the breast of Pen's wet-nurse, and explains her anxiety for the child's health during the procedure. She goes on to attempt to persuade Ogilvy not to wean her own daughter too early: "even if we were sure of escaping worse evils than temporary suffering on the part of the child, . . . why, infancy is a part of life, and it is well not to embitter it" (*Elizabeth Barrett Browning's Letters to Mrs David Ogilvy 1849–1861*, ed. Peter N. Heydon and Philip Kelley [London, 1974], 29).
2. The deleted manuscript allusion to "dead man's bones" (see textual note) indicates that EBB was thinking of the catacombs in the Rue de L'Enfer in the Twelfth Arrondisement.
3. Sign; description.

No Marian Erle indeed, but certainly
Mathildes, Justines, Victoires, . . or, if I sought
The English, Betsis, Saras, by the score.
They might as well go out into the fields
To find a speckled bean, that's somehow specked,
And somewhere in the pod.' - They left me so.
Shall *I* leave Marian? have I dreamed a dream?

- I thank God I have found her![4] I must say
'Thank God,' for finding her, although 'tis true
I find the world more sad and wicked for't.
But she -
            I'll write about her, presently.
My hand's a-tremble, as I had just caught up
My heart to write with, in the place of it.
At least you'd take these letters to be writ
At sea, in storm! - wait now . .
                                        A simple chance
Did all. I could not sleep last night, and, tired
Of turning on my pillow and harder thoughts,
Went out at early morning, when the air
Is delicate with some last starry touch,
To wander through the Market-place of Flowers[5]
(The prettiest haunt in Paris), and make sure
At worst that there were roses in the world.
So wandering, musing, with the artist's eye,
That keeps the shade-side of the thing it loves,
Half-absent, whole-observing, while the crowd
Of young vivacious and black-braided heads
Dipped, quick as finches in a blossomed tree,
Among the nosegays, cheapening[6] this and that
In such a cheerful twitter of rapid speech, -
My heart leapt in me, startled by a voice
That slowly, faintly, with long breaths that marked
The interval between the wish and word,
Inquired in stranger's French, 'Would *that* be much,
That branch of flowering mountain-gorse?'[7] - 'So much?
Too much for me, then!' turning the face round
So close upon me that I felt the sigh
It turned with.
                    'Marian, Marian!' - face to face -
'Marian! I find you. Shall I let you go?'

4. This passage marks a break in the chronology of Aurora's narration, which, from the end of book 5 onward, takes the form of a journal with entries written down, as it were, soon after the events described have taken place.
5. The main flower market in Paris took place on the Quai aux Fleurs on the Ile de la Citie.
6. Making cheaper; bargaining for.
7. See *Aurora Leigh* 3.884–91.

I held her two slight wrists with both my hands;
'Ah Marian, Marian, can I let you go?'
- She fluttered from me like a cyclamen,
As white, which taken in a sudden wind
Beats on against the palisade.[8] - 'Let pass,'
She said at last. 'I will not,' I replied;
'I lost my sister Marian many days,
And sought her ever in my walks and prayers,
And, now I find her . . . do we throw away
The bread we worked and prayed for, - crumble it
And drop it, . . to do even so by thee
Whom still I've hungered after more than bread,
My sister Marian? - can I hurt thee, dear?
Then why distrust me? Never tremble so.
Come with me rather where we'll talk and live
And none shall vex us. I've a home for you
And me and no one else' . . .
                                        She shook her head.
'A home for you and me and no one else
Ill-suits one of us: I prefer to such,
A roof of grass on which a flower might spring,
Less costly to me than the cheapest here,
And yet I could not, at this hour, afford
A like home even. That you offer yours,
I thank you. You are good as heaven itself -
As good as one I knew before . . Farewell.'

I loosed her hands, - 'In *his* name, no farewell!'
(She stood as if I held her.) 'For his sake,
For his sake, Romney's! by the good he meant,
Ay, always! by the love he pressed for once, -
And by the grief, reproach, abandonment,
He took in change' . .
                                'He Romney! who grieved *him*?
Who had the heart for't? what reproach touched *him*?
Be merciful, - speak quickly.'
                                        'Therefore come,'
I answered with authority. - 'I think
We dare to speak such things and name such names
In the open squares of Paris!'
                                        Not a word
She said, but in a gentle humbled way
(As one who had forgot herself in grief)
Turned round and followed closely where I went,
As if I led her by a narrow plank

8. Fence; boundary.

Across devouring waters,[9] step by step;
And so in silence we walked on a mile.

And then she stopped: her face was white as wax.
'We go much farther?'
'You are ill,' I asked,
'Or tired?'
She looked the whiter for her smile.
'There's one at home,' she said, 'has need of me
By this time, - and I must not let him wait.'

'Not even,' I asked, 'to hear of Romney Leigh?'

'Not even,' she said, 'to hear of Mister Leigh.'

'In that case,' I resumed, 'I go with you,
And we can talk the same thing there as here.
None waits for me: I have my day to spend.'

Her lips moved in a spasm without a sound, -
But then she spoke. 'It shall be as you please;
And better so - 'tis shorter seen than told:
And though you will not find me worth your pains,
*That*, even, may be worth some pains to know
For one as good as you are.'
Then she led
The way, and I, as by a narrow plank
Across devouring waters, followed her,
Stepping by her footsteps, breathing by her breath,
And holding her with eyes that would not slip;
And so, without a word, we walked a mile,
And so, another mile, without a word.
Until the peopled streets being all dismissed,
House-rows and groups all scattered like a flock,
The market-gardens thickened, and the long
White walls beyond, like spiders' outside threads,
Stretched, feeling blindly toward the country-fields
Through half-built habitations and half-dug
Foundations, - intervals of trenchant chalk
That bit betwixt the grassy uneven turfs
Where goats (vine-tendrils trailing from their mouths)
Stood perched on edges of the cellarage
Which should be, staring as about to leap

9. This passage, and its repetition in lines 500–02, marks the reversal of authority that takes place in terms of Aurora and Marian's relationship. First Aurora leads by virtue of intellect and status; then Marian leads by authority of experience and knowledge.

To find their coming Bacchus.[1] All the place
Seemed less a cultivation than a waste.
Men work here, only, - scarce begin to live:
All's sad, the country struggling with the town,
Like an untamed hawk upon a strong man's fist,
That beats its wings and tries to get away,
And cannot choose be satisfied so soon
To hop through court-yards with his right foot tied,
The vintage plains and pastoral hills in sight.[2]

We stopped beside a house too high and slim
To stand there by itself, but waiting till
Five others, two on this side, three on that,
Should grow up from the sullen second floor
They pause at now, to build it to a row.
The upper windows partly were unglazed
Meantime, - a meagre, unripe house: a line
Of rigid poplars elbowed it behind,
And, just in front, beyond the lime and bricks
That wronged the grass between it and the road,
A great acacia with its slender trunk
And overpoise of multitudinous leaves
(In which a hundred fields might spill their dew
And intense verdure, yet find room enough)
Stood reconciling all the place with green.

I followed up the stair upon her step.
She hurried upward, shot across a face,
A woman's, on the landing, - 'How now, now!
Is no one to have holidays but you?
You said an hour, and stay three hours, I think,
And Julie waiting for your betters here?
Why if he had waked he might have waked, for me.'
- Just murmuring an excusing word she passed
And shut the rest out with the chamber-door,
Myself shut in beside her.
'Twas a room
Scarce larger than a grave, and near as bare;
Two stools, a pallet-bed;[3] I saw the room:
A mouse could find no sort of shelter in't,
Much less a greater secret; curtainless, -

1. The goat was an animal associated with the god Bacchus, who represents the essence of nature. Goats were sacrificed to the god in the ritual of the ecstatic Bacchae; see notes to *Aurora Leigh* 5.319–320.
2. In falconry the hawk is secured on a lead until such time as it has been trained to fly only at the command of its master. The image here is of the suburban sprawl as taming the wildness of the country into the domestication of the city.
3. A narrow and readily portable bed.

The window fixed you with its torturing eye,
Defying you to take a step apart
If peradventure you would hide a thing.
I saw the whole room, I and Marian there
Alone.
        Alone? She threw her bonnet off,
Then, sighing as 'twere sighing the last time,
Approached the bed, and drew a shawl away:
You could not peel a fruit you fear to bruise
More calmly and more carefully than so, -
Nor would you find within, a rosier flushed
Pomegranate -
                There he lay upon his back,
The yearling[4] creature, warm and moist with life
To the bottom of his dimples, - to the ends
Of the lovely tumbled curls about his face;
For since he had been covered over-much
To keep him from the light-glare, both his cheeks
Were hot and scarlet as the first live rose
The shepherd's heart-blood ebbed away into[5]
The faster for his love. And love was here
As instant; in the pretty baby-mouth,
Shut close as if for dreaming that it sucked,
The little naked feet, drawn up the way
Of nested birdlings;[6] everything so soft
And tender, - to the tiny holdfast[7] hands,
Which, closing on a finger into sleep,
Had kept the mould of't.[8]
                        While we stood there dumb,
For oh, that it should take such innocence
To prove just guilt, I thought, and stood there dumb, -
The light upon his eyelids pricked them wide,
And, staring out at us with all their blue,
As half perplexed between the angelhood
He had been away to visit in his sleep,
And our most mortal presence, gradually
He saw his mother's face, accepting it

4. Year-old.
5. The shepherd Adonis, beloved of Aphrodite. He was wounded in the thigh by a boar, and though the goddess flew to his aid, she was unable to save him. As he lay dying, the drops of his blood turned into roses, and Aphrodite's tears into anemones. See Bion, *Idyll* 1, "The Lament for Adonis," lines 64–66: "Ay, ah, Cytherea! Adonis is dead/She wept tear after tear with the blood which was shed,/And both turned into flowers for the earth's garden-close,/Her tears, to the windflower; his blood, to the rose" (EBB's translation from *Poetical Works of EBB* 469–70).
6. Little birds in a nest.
7. A compound word meaning "hold fast."
8. EBB's rapturous description of Marian's child owes a great deal to her pleasure and motherly pride in her own son.

In change for heaven itself with such a smile
As might have well been learnt there, - never moved,
But smiled on, in a drowse of ecstasy,
So happy (half with her and half with heaven)
He could not have the trouble to be stirred,
But smiled and lay there. Like a rose, I said?
As red and still indeed as any rose,
That blows in all the silence of its leaves,
Content in blowing to fulfil its life.

She leaned above him (drinking him as wine)
In that extremity of love, 'twill pass
For agony or rapture, seeing that love
Includes the whole of nature, rounding it
To love . . no more, - since more can never be
Than just love. Self-forgot, cast out of self,
And drowning in the transport of the sight,
Her whole pale passionate face, mouth, forehead, eyes,
One gaze, she stood: then, slowly as he smiled
She smiled too, slowly, smiling unaware,
And drawing from his countenance to hers
A fainter red, as if she watched a flame
And stood in it a-glow. 'How beautiful,'
Said she.
            I answered, trying to be cold.
(Must sin have compensations, was my thought,
As if it were a holy thing like grief?
And is a woman to be fooled aside
From putting vice down, with that woman's toy
A baby?)—'Ay! the child is well enough,'
I answered. 'If his mother's palms are clean
They need be glad of course in clasping such;
But if not, I would rather lay my hand,
Were I she, on God's brazen altar-bars
Red-hot with burning sacrificial lambs,
Than touch the sacred curls of such a child.'

She plunged her fingers in his clustering locks,
As one who would not be afraid of fire;
And then with indrawn steady utterance said,
'My lamb, my lamb! although, through such as thou,
The most unclean got courage and approach
To God, once,[9] - now they cannot, even with men,
Find grace enough for pity and gentle words.'

9. John 1.26: "Behold the Lamb of God, which taketh away the sin of the world."

'My Marian,' I made answer, grave and sad,
'The priest who stole a lamb to offer him,
Was still a thief. And if a woman steals
(Through God's own barrier-hedges of true love,
Which fence out licence in securing love)
A child like this, that smiles so in her face,
She is no mother but a kidnapper,
And he's a dismal orphan, not a son,
Whom all her kisses cannot feed so full
He will not miss hereafter a pure home
To live in, a pure heart to lean against,
A pure good mother's name and memory
To hope by, when the world grows thick and bad
And he feels out for virtue.'
'Oh,' she smiled
With bitter patience, 'the child takes his chance;
Not much worse off in being fatherless
Than I was, fathered. He will say, belike,
His mother was the saddest creature born;
He'll say his mother lived so contrary
To joy, that even the kindest, seeing her,
Grew sometimes almost cruel: he'll not say
She flew contrarious in the face of God
With bat-wings of her vices. Stole my child, -
My flower of earth, my only flower on earth,
My sweet, my beauty!' . . Up she snatched the child,
And, breaking on him in a storm of tears,
Drew out her long sobs from their shivering roots,
Until he took it for a game, and stretched
His feet and flapped his eager arms like wings
And crowed and gurgled through his infant laugh:
'Mine, mine,' she said. 'I have as sure a right
As any glad proud mother in the world,
Who sets her darling down to cut his teeth
Upon her church-ring.[1] If she talks of law,
I talk of law! I claim my mother-dues
By law, - the law which now is paramount, -
The common law, by which the poor and weak
Are trodden underfoot by vicious men,
And loathed for ever after by the good.
Let pass! I did not filch, - I found the child.'
'You found him, Marian?'
'Ay, I found him where
I found my curse, - in the gutter, with my shame!
What have you, any of you, to say to that,

1. Her wedding ring. Marian, unmarried, does not have one.

Who all are happy, and sit safe and high,
And never spoke before to arraign my right
To grief itself? What, what, . . being beaten down
By hoofs of maddened oxen into a ditch,
Half-dead, whole mangled, when a girl at last
Breathes, sees . . and finds there, bedded in her flesh
Because of the extremity of the shock,
Some coin of price! . . and when a good man comes
(That's God! the best men are not quite as good)
And says, 'I dropped the coin there: take it you,
And keep it, - it shall pay you for the loss,' -
You all put up your finger - 'See the thief!
'Observe what precious thing she has come to filch.
'How bad those girls are!' Oh, my flower, my pet,
I dare forget I have you in my arms
And fly off to be angry with the world,
And fright you, hurt you with my tempers, till
You double up your lip? Why, that indeed
Is bad: a naughty mother!'
'You mistake,'
I interrupted; 'if I loved you not,
I should not, Marian, certainly be here.'

'Alas,' she said, 'you are so very good;
And yet I wish indeed you had never come
To make me sob until I vex the child.
It is not wholesome for these pleasure-plats[2]
To be so early watered by our brine.[3]
And then, who knows? he may not like me now
As well, perhaps, as ere he saw me fret, -
One's ugly fretting! he has eyes the same
As angels, but he cannot see as deep,
And so I've kept for ever in his sight
A sort of smile to please him, - as you place
A green thing from the garden in a cup,
To make believe it grows there. Look, my sweet;
My cowslip-ball! we've done with that cross face,
And here's the face come back you used to like.
Ah, ah! he laughs! he likes me. Ah, Miss Leigh,
You're great and pure; but were you purer still, -
As if you had walked, we'll say, no otherwhere
Than up and down the new Jerusalem,
And held your trailing lutestring up yourself
From brushing the twelve stones,[4] for fear of some

2. Pleasure-gardens.
3. Our salt tears.
4. Revelation 21.19–20.

Small speck as little as a needle-prick,
White stitched on white,[5] - the child would keep to *me*,
Would choose his poor lost Marian, like me best,
And, though you stretched your arms, cry back and cling,
As we do when God says it's time to die
And bids us go up higher.[6] Leave us, then;
We two are happy. Does *he* push me off?
He's satisfied with me, as I with him.'

'So soft to one, so hard to others! Nay,'
I cried, more angry that she melted me,
'We make henceforth a cushion of our faults
To sit and practise easy virtues on?
I thought a child was given to sanctify
A woman, - set her in the sight of all
The clear-eyed Heavens, a chosen minister
To do their business and lead spirits up
The difficult blue heights. A woman lives,
Not bettered, quickened toward the truth and good
Through being a mother? . . then she's none! although
She damps her baby's cheeks by kissing them,
As we kill roses.'
'Kill! O Christ,' she said,
And turned her wild sad face from side to side
With most despairing wonder in it, 'What,
What have you in your souls against me then,
All of you? am I wicked, do you think?
God knows me, trusts me with the child; but you,
You think me really wicked?'
'Complaisant,'
I answered softly, 'to a wrong you've done,
Because of certain profits, - which is wrong
Beyond the first wrong, Marian. When you left
The pure place and the noble heart, to take
The hand of a seducer' . .
'Whom? whose hand?
I took the hand of' . .
Springing up erect
And lifting up the child at full arm's length,
As if to bear him like an oriflamme[7]
Unconquerable to armies of reproach, -
'By *him*,' she said, 'my child's head and its curls,

5. Revelation 3.4 and 19.8 passim.
6. Luke 14.10: "But when thou art bidden go and sit down in the lowest room; that when he that bade thee cometh, he may say unto thee, Friend, go up higher."
7. The sacred banner of St. Denis, a banderole of two or three points of red-orange silk. The medieval kings of France received the banner from the hands of the abbot of St. Denis before setting out for war.

By these blue eyes no woman born could dare
A perjury on, I make my mother's oath,
That if I left that Heart, to lighten it,
The blood of mine was still, except for grief!
No cleaner maid than I was, took a step
To a sadder end, - no matron-mother now
Looks backward to her early maidenhood
Through chaster pulses. I speak steadily;
And if I lie so, . . if, being fouled in will
And paltered with[8] in soul by devil's lust,
I dared to bid this angel take my part, . .
Would God sit quiet, let us think, in heaven,
Nor strike me dumb with thunder? Yet I speak:
He clears me therefore. What, 'seduced' 's your word?
Do wolves seduce a wandering fawn in France?
Do eagles, who have pinched a lamb with claws,
Seduce it into carrion? So with me.
I was not ever, as you say, seduced,
But simply, murdered.'
There she paused, and sighed,
With such a sigh as drops from agony
To exhaustion, - sighing while she let the babe
Slide down upon her bosom from her arms,
And all her face's light fell after him
Like a torch quenched in falling. Down she sank,
And sate upon the bedside with the child.

But I, convicted, broken utterly,
With woman's passion clung about her waist
And kissed her hair and eyes, - 'I have been wrong,
Sweet Marian' . . (weeping in a tender rage)
'Sweet holy Marian! And now, Marian, now,
I'll use your oath although my lips are hard,
And by the child, my Marian, by the child,
I swear his mother shall be innocent
Before my conscience, as in the open Book
Of Him who reads for judgment.[9] Innocent,
My sister! let the night be ne'er so dark
The moon is surely somewhere in the sky;
So surely is your whiteness to be found
Through all dark facts. But pardon, pardon me,
And smile a little, Marian, - for the child,
If not for me, my sister.'
The poor lip
Just motioned for the smile and let it go:

8. Palter: to deal crookedly or evasively, to play fast and loose, to use trickery (OED).
9. Revelation 20.12.

And then, with scarce a stirring of the mouth,
As if a statue spoke that could not breathe,
But spoke on calm between its marble lips, -
'I'm glad, I'm very glad you clear me so.
I should be sorry that you set me down
With harlots, or with even a better name
Which misbecomes his mother. For the rest,
I am not on a level with your love,
Nor ever was, you know, - but now am worse,
Because that world of yours has dealt with me
As when the hard sea bites and chews a stone
And changes the first form of it. I've marked
A shore of pebbles bitten to one shape
From all the various life of madrepores;[1]
And so, that little stone, called Marian Erle,
Picked up and dropped by you and another friend,
Was ground and tortured by the incessant sea
And bruised from what she was, - changed! death's a change,
And she, I said, was murdered; Marian's dead.
What can you do with people when they are dead,
But, if you are pious, sing a hymn and go,
Or, if you are tender, heave a sigh and go,
But go by all means, - and permit the grass
To keep its green feud up 'twixt them and you?
Then leave me, - let me rest. I'm dead, I say,
And if, to save the child from death as well,
The mother in me has survived the rest,
Why, that's God's miracle you must not tax,
I'm not less dead for that: I'm nothing more
But just a mother. Only for the child
I'm warm, and cold, and hungry, and afraid,
And smell the flowers a little and see the sun,
And speak still, and am silent, - just for him!
I pray you therefore to mistake me not
And treat me haply as I were alive;
For though you ran a pin into my soul,
I think it would not hurt nor trouble me.
Here's proof, dear lady, - in the market-place
But now, you promised me to say a word

1. Formerly applied loosely to most, or all, of the perforate corals (OED). This choice of metaphor, and the deleted manuscript reference to loss of individuality (see textual note) suggests that the whole of the passage (lines 806–12), concerning the "sea-change" experienced by Marian, was borrowed from the dream sequence in Charles Kingsley's *Alton Locke* (1850): "And I was at the lowest point of created life: a madrepore rooted to the rock, fathoms below the tide-mark; and, worst of all, my individuality was gone. I was not one thing, but many things—a crowd of innumerable polypi; and I grew and grew, and the more I grew the more I divided, and multiplied thousand and then thousandfold. If I could have thought I should have gone mad at it; but I could only feel" (ch. 36).

About . . a friend, who once, long years ago,
Took God's place toward me, when He leans and loves
And does not thunder, . . whom at last I left,
As all of us leave God. You thought perhaps
I seemed to care for hearing of that friend?
Now, judge me! we have sate here half an hour
And talked together of the child and me,
And I not asked as much as, 'What's the thing
'You had to tell me of the friend . . the friend?'
He's sad, I think you said, - he's sick perhaps?
'Tis nought to Marian if he's sad or sick.
Another would have crawled beside your foot
And prayed your words out. Why, a beast, a dog,
A starved cat, if he had fed it once with milk,
Would show less hardness. But I'm dead, you see,
And that explains it.'
Poor, poor thing, she spoke
And shook her head, as white and calm as frost
On days too cold for raining any more,
But still with such a face, so much alive,
I could not choose but take it on my arm
And stroke the placid patience of its cheeks, -
Then told my story out, of Romney Leigh,
How, having lost her, sought her, missed her still,
He, broken-hearted for himself and her,
Had drawn the curtains of the world awhile
As if he had done with morning. There I stopped,
For when she gasped, and pressed me with her eyes,
'And now . . how is it with him? tell me now,'
I felt the shame of compensated grief,[2]
And chose my words with scruple - slowly stepped
Upon the slippery stones set here and there
Across the sliding water. 'Certainly,
As evening empties morning into night,
Another morning takes the evening up
With healthful, providential interchange;
And, though he thought still of her,' -
'Yes, she knew,
She understood: she had supposed indeed
That, as one stops a hole upon a flute,
At which a new note comes and shapes the tune,
Excluding her would bring a worthier in,
And, long ere this, that Lady Waldemar
He loved so' . .
'Loved,' I started, - 'loved her so!

2. Compare *Aurora Leigh* 1.673–79.

Now tell me' . .
'I will tell you,' she replied:
'But, since we're taking oaths, you'll promise first
That he in England, he, shall never learn
In what a dreadful trap his creature here,
Round whose unworthy neck he had meant to tie
The honourable ribbon of his name,
Fell unaware and came to butchery:
Because, - I know him, - as he takes to heart
The grief of every stranger, he's not like
To banish mine as far as I should choose
In wishing him most happy. Now he leaves
To think of me, perverse, who went my way,
Unkind, and left him, - but if once he knew . .
Ah, then, the sharp nail of my cruel wrong
Would fasten me for ever in his sight,
Like some poor curious bird, through each spread wing
Nailed high up over a fierce hunter's fire,[3]
To spoil the dinner of all tenderer folk
Come in by chance. Nay, since your Marian's dead,
You shall not hang her up, but dig a hole
And bury her in silence! ring no bells.'

I answered gaily, though my whole voice wept,
'We'll ring the joy-bells, not the funeral-bells,
Because we have her back, dead or alive.'

She never answered that, but shook her head;
Then low and calm, as one who, safe in heaven,
Shall tell a story of his lower life,
Unmoved by shame or anger, - so she spoke.
She told me she had loved upon her knees,
As others pray, more perfectly absorbed
In the act and aspiration. She felt his
For just his uses, not her own at all,
His stool, to sit on or put up his foot,
His cup, to fill with wine or vinegar,[4]
Whichever drink might please him at the chance
For that should please her always: let him write
His name upon her . . it seemed natural;
It was most precious, standing on his shelf,
To wait until he chose to lift his hand.

3. Possibly a reminiscence of Coleridge's story of the albatross and its mystic significance in his ballad "The Rime of the Ancient Mariner" (1797).

4. Wine represents the good, while sour vinegar represents the bad in life. There is a biblical allusion too, in that wine is used always at celebration (the Last Supper, for instance), while vinegar was given to Christ on a sponge while he suffered on the cross. See Matthew 26.27–29 and 27.48.

Well, well, - I saw her then, and must have seen
How bright her life went floating on her love,
Like wicks the housewives send afloat on oil
Which feeds them to a flame that lasts the night.

To do good seemed so much his business,
That, having done it, she was fain to think,
Must fill up his capacity for joy.
At first she never mooted with herself
If *he* was happy, since he made her so,
Or if he loved her, being so much beloved.
Who thinks of asking if the sun is light,
Observing that it lightens? who's so bold,
To question God of His felicity?
Still less. And thus she took for granted first
What first of all she should have put to proof,
And sinned against him so, but only so.
'What could you hope,' she said, 'of such as she?
You take a kid you like, and turn it out
In some fair garden: though the creature's fond
And gentle, it will leap upon the beds
And break your tulips, bite your tender trees;
The wonder would be if such innocence
Spoiled less: a garden is no place for kids.'

And, by degrees, when he who had chosen her
Brought in his courteous and benignant friends
To spend their goodness on her, which she took
So very gladly, as a part of his, -
By slow degrees it broke on her slow sense
That she too in that Eden of delight[5]
Was out of place, and, like the silly kid,
Still did most mischief where she meant most love,
A thought enough to make a woman mad,
(No beast in this but she may well go mad)
That saying 'I am thine to love and use'
May blow the plague in her protesting breath
To the very man for whom she claims to die, -
That, clinging round his neck, she pulls him down
And drowns him, - and that, lavishing her soul,
She hales perdition on him. 'So, being mad,'
Said Marian . .
'Ah - who stirred such thoughts, you ask?
Whose fault it was, that she should have such thoughts?
None's fault, none's fault. The light comes, and we see:

5. Marian lived in an early innocence, as Adam lived in the Garden of Eden before he knew more, having eaten the fruit of the tree of knowledge. See Genesis 3.1–11.

But if it were not truly for our eyes,
There would be nothing seen, for all the light.
And so with Marian: if she saw at last,
The sense was in her, - Lady Waldemar
Had spoken all in vain else.'
'O my heart,
O prophet in my heart,' I cried aloud,
'Then Lady Waldemar spoke!'
'*Did* she speak,'
Mused Marian softly, 'or did she only sign?
Or did she put a word into her face
And look, and so impress you with the word?
Or leave it in the foldings of her gown,
Like rosemary smells a movement will shake out
When no one's conscious? who shall say, or guess?
One thing alone was certain - from the day
The gracious lady paid a visit first,
She, Marian, saw things different, - felt distrust
Of all that sheltering roof of circumstance
Her hopes were building into with clay nests:
Her heart was restless, pacing up and down
And fluttering, like dumb creatures before storms,
Not knowing wherefore she was ill at ease.'

'And still the lady came,' said Marian Erle,
'Much oftener than *he* knew it, Mister Leigh.
She bade me never tell him she had come,
She liked to love me better than he knew,
So very kind was Lady Waldemar:
And every time she brought with her more light,
And every light made sorrow clearer . . Well,
Ah, well! we cannot give her blame for that;
'Twould be the same thing if an angel came,
Whose right should prove our wrong. And every time
The lady came, she looked more beautiful
And spoke more like a flute among green trees,
Until at last, as one, whose heart being sad
On hearing lovely music, suddenly
Dissolves in weeping, I brake out in tears
Before her, asked her counsel, - 'Had I erred
'In being too happy? would she set me straight?
'For she, being wise and good and born above
'The flats I had never climbed from, could perceive
'If such as I, might grow upon the hills;
'And whether such poor herb sufficed to grow,
'For Romney Leigh to break his fast upon't, -

'Or would he pine on such, or haply starve?'
She wrapt me in her generous arms at once,
And let me dream a moment how it feels
To have a real mother, like some girls:
But when I looked, her face was younger . . ay,
Youth's too bright not to be a little hard,
And beauty keeps itself still uppermost,
That's true! - Though Lady Waldemar was kind
She hurt me, hurt, as if the morning-sun
Should smite us on the eyelids when we sleep,
And wake us up with headache. Ay, and soon
Was light enough to make my heart ache too:
She told me truths I asked for, - 'twas my fault, -
'That Romney could not love me, if he would,
'As men call loving: there are bloods that flow
'Together like some rivers and not mix,
'Through contraries of nature. He indeed
'Was set to wed me, to espouse my class,
'Act out a rash opinion, - and, once wed,
'So just a man and gentle could not choose
'But make my life as smooth as marriage-ring,
'Bespeak me mildly, keep me a cheerful house,
'With servants, brooches, all the flowers I liked,
'And pretty dresses, silk the whole year round' . .
At which I stopped her, - 'This for me. And now
'For *him*.' - She hesitated, - truth grew hard;
She owned, ' 'Twas plain a man like Romney Leigh
'Required a wife more level to himself.
'If day by day he had to bend his height
'To pick up sympathies, opinions, thoughts,
'And interchange the common talk of life
'Which helps a man to live as well as talk,
'His days were heavily taxed. Who buys a staff
'To fit the hand, that reaches but the knee?
'He'd feel it bitter to be forced to miss
'The perfect joy of married suited pairs,
'Who, bursting through the separating hedge
'Of personal dues with that sweet eglantine[6]
'Of equal love, keep saying, 'So *we* think,
"It strikes *us*, - that's *our* fancy." - When I asked
If earnest will, devoted love, employed
In youth like mine, would fail to raise me up
As two strong arms will always raise a child
To a fruit hung overhead, she sighed and sighed . .

6. Honeysuckle.

'That could not be,' she feared. 'You take a pink
'You dig about its roots and water it
'And so improve it to a garden-pink,
'But will not change it to a heliotrope,
'The kind remains. And then, the harder truth -
'This Romney Leigh, so rash to leap a pale,
'So bold for conscience, quick for martyrdom,
'Would suffer steadily and never flinch,
'But suffer surely and keenly, when his class
'Turned shoulder on him for a shameful match,
'And set him up as nine-pin[7] in their talk
'To bowl him down with jestings.' - There, she paused;
And when I used the pause in doubting that
We wronged him after all in what we feared -
'Suppose such things could never touch him more
'In his high conscience (if the things should be,)
'Than, when the queen sits in an upper room,
'The horses in the street can spatter her!' -
A moment, hope came, - but the lady closed
That door and nicked the lock and shut it out,
Observing wisely that, 'the tender heart
'Which made him over-soft to a lower class,
'Would scarcely fail to make him sensitive
'To a higher, - how they thought and what they felt.'

'Alas, alas,' said Marian, rocking slow
The pretty baby who was near asleep,
The eyelids creeping over the blue balls, -
'She made it clear, too clear - I saw the whole!
And yet who knows if I had seen my way
Straight out of it by looking, though 'twas clear,
Unless the generous lady, 'ware of this,
Had set her own house all a-fire for me
To light me forwards? Leaning on my face
Her heavy agate eyes which crushed my will,
She told me tenderly, (as when men come
To a bedside to tell people they must die)
'She knew of knowledge, - ay, of knowledge knew,
'That Romney Leigh had loved *her* formerly.
'And *she* loved *him*, she might say, now the chance
'Was past, - but that, of course, he never guessed, -
'For something came between them, something thin
'As a cobweb, catching every fly of doubt
'To hold it buzzing at the window-pane

7. In the game of nine-pin, the pins or skittles are set up to be knocked down by a ball.

'And help to dim the daylight. Ah, man's pride
'Or woman's - which is greatest? most averse
'To brushing cobwebs? Well, but she and he
'Remained fast friends; it seemed not more than so,
'Because he had bound his hands and could not stir.
'An honourable man, if somewhat rash;
'And she, not even for Romney, would she spill
'A blot . . as little even as a tear . .
'Upon his marriage-contract, - not to gain
'A better joy for two than came by that:
'For though I stood between her heart and heaven,
'She loved me wholly.' '
Did I laugh or curse?
I think I sate there silent, hearing all,
Ay, hearing double, - Marian's tale, at once,
And Romney's marriage-vow, *'I'll keep to* 'THEE,'
Which means that woman-serpent. Is it time
For church now?
'Lady Waldemar spoke more,'
Continued Marian, 'but, as when a soul
Will pass out through the sweetness of a song
Beyond it, voyaging the uphill road,
Even so mine wandered from the things I heard
To those I suffered. It was afterward
I shaped the resolution to the act.
For many hours we talked. What need to talk?
The fate was clear and close; it touched my eyes;
But still the generous lady tried to keep
The case afloat, and would not let it go,
And argued, struggled upon Marian's side,
Which was not Romney's! though she little knew
What ugly monster would take up the end, -
What griping death within the drowning death
Was ready to complete my sum of death.'

I thought, - Perhaps he's sliding now the ring
Upon that woman's finger . .
She went on:
'The lady, failing to prevail her way,
Up-gathered my torn wishes from the ground
And pieced them with her strong benevolence;
And, as I thought I could breathe freer air
Away from England, going without pause
Without farewell, just breaking with a jerk
The blossomed offshoot from my thorny life, -
She promised kindly to provide the means,

With instant passage to the colonies[8]
And full protection, - 'would commit me straight
'To one who once had been her waiting-maid
'And had the customs of the world, intent
'On changing England for Australia
'Herself, to carry out her fortune so.'
For which I thanked the Lady Waldemar,
As men upon their death-beds thank last friends
Who lay the pillow straight: it is not much,
And yet 'tis all of which they are capable,
This lying smoothly in a bed to die.
And so, 'twas fixed; - and so, from day to day,
The woman named came in to visit me.'

Just then the girl stopped speaking, - sate erect,
And stared at me as if I had been a ghost,
(Perhaps I looked as white as any ghost)
With large-eyed horror. 'Does God make,' she said,
'All sorts of creatures really, do you think?
Or is it that the Devil slavers[9] them
So excellently, that we come to doubt
Who's stronger, He who makes, or he who mars?
I never liked the woman's face or voice
Or ways: it made me blush to look at her;
It made me tremble if she touched my hand;
And when she spoke a fondling word I shrank
As if one hated me who had power to hurt;
And, every time she came, my veins ran cold
As somebody were walking on my grave.
At last I spoke to Lady Waldemar:
'Could such an one be good to trust?' I asked.
Whereat the lady stroked my cheek and laughed
Her silver-laugh, (one must be born to laugh,
To put such music in it) - 'Foolish girl,
'Your scattered wits are gathering wool[1] beyond
'The sheep-walk reaches! - leave the thing to me.'
And therefore, half in trust, and half in scorn

8. In the 1850s a great many people emigrated to the British colony of Australia in order to make their fortune. By the middle of the century the male population of Australia was very high, and many impoverished females were encouraged to go to the colony to seek work and, by implication, a husband. Many schemes were set up to promote the emigration of single women, and some of those who took up this offer were especially anxious to go, because it gave them a chance of a new life where their past would not be known. The reformer and philanthropist Caroline Chisholm set up one such emigration scheme, and when Charles Dickens and Angela Burdett Coutts founded their *Urania* cottage plan for the reformation of "fallen" women, they sent many of their girls on to Australia.
9. Figuratively, to fondle, to flatter in a disgusting or sycophantic manner (OED).
1. That is, woolgathering, dreaming or being led astray.

That I had heart still for another fear
In such a safe despair, I left the thing.

'The rest is short. I was obedient:
I wrote my letter which delivered *him*
From Marian to his own prosperities,
And followed that bad guide. The lady? - hush,
I never blame the lady. Ladies who
Sit high, however willing to look down,
Will scarce see lower than their dainty feet;
And Lady Waldemar saw less than I,
With what a Devil's daughter I went forth
Along the swine's road, down the precipice,[2]
In such a curl of hell-foam caught and choked,
No shriek of soul in anguish could pierce through
To fetch some help. They say there's help in heaven
For all such cries. But if one cries from hell . . .
What then? - the heavens are deaf upon that side.

'A woman . . hear me, let me make it plain, . .
A woman . . not a monster . . both her breasts
Made right to suckle babes . . she took me off
A woman also, young and ignorant
And heavy with my grief, my two poor eyes
Near washed away with weeping, till the trees,
The blessed unaccustomed trees and fields
Ran either side the train like stranger dogs
Unworthy of any notice, - took me off
So dull, so blind, so only half alive,
Not seeing by what road, nor by what ship,
Nor toward what place, nor to what end of all.
Men carry a corpse thus, - past the doorway, past
The garden-gate, the children's playground, up
The green lane, - then they leave it in the pit,
To sleep and find corruption, cheek to cheek
With him who stinks since Friday.
'But suppose;
To go down with one's soul into the grave,
To go down half dead, half alive, I say,
And wake up with corruption, . . cheek to cheek
With him who stinks since Friday! There it is,
And that's the horror of't, Miss Leigh.
'You feel?
You understand? - no, do not look at me,

2. An allusion to the fate of the Gaderene swine. See Matthew 8.28–32, Mark 5.1–13, and Luke 8.26–33.

But understand. The blank, blind, weary way,
Which led, where'er it led, away at least;
The shifted ship, to Sydney[3] or to France,
Still bound, wherever else, to another land;
The swooning sickness on the dismal sea,
The foreign shore, the shameful house, the night,
The feeble blood, the heavy-headed grief, . . .
No need to bring their damnable drugged cup,[4]
And yet they brought it. Hell's so prodigal
Of devil's gifts, hunts liberally in packs,
Will kill no poor small creature of the wilds
But fifty red wide throats must smoke at it,
As HIS at me . . when waking up at last . .
I told you that I waked up in the grave.

'Enough so! - it is plain enough so. True,
We wretches cannot tell out all our wrong
Without offence to decent happy folk.
I know that we must scrupulously hint
With half-words, delicate reserves, the thing
Which no one scrupled we should feel in full.
Let pass the rest, then; only leave my oath
Upon this sleeping child, - man's violence,
Not man's seduction, made me what I am,
As lost as . . I told *him* I should be lost.
When mothers fail us, can we help ourselves?
That's fatal! - And you call it being lost,
That down came next day's noon and caught me there
Half gibbering and half raving on the floor,
And wondering what had happened up in heaven,
That suns should dare to shine when God himself
Was certainly abolished.

'I was mad,
How many weeks, I know not, - many weeks.
I think they let me go when I was mad,
They feared my eyes and loosed me, as boys might
A mad dog which they had tortured. Up and down

3. The chief town founded in the Australian colony of Botany Bay.
4. The circumstances of Marian's rape, the brothel, and the drugging, are partly based on EBB's reading of Samuel Richardson's novel *Clarissa* (1747–49). EBB made the comparison between Marian and Clarissa in writing to her sister just before the publication of *Aurora Leigh*: "Something of the kind was done by Richardson in Clarissa—but Clarissa was a sublime creature—more exceptionally attractive than my Marian is—& after all, Clarissa dies—which I don't mean Marian to do. Marian shall have a clear triumph even here." See EBB to Arabel, October 4, 1856; *The Browning's Correspondence: A Checklist*, compiled by Philip Kelley and Ronald Hudson (New York: The Browning Institute, 1978), 56.142. The events of Marian's story are also borrowed from Eugene Sue's sensational novel *Mystères de Paris*, where the innocent Fleur de Marie suffers a similar fate, and based on a number of contemporary scandals, which told extravagant horror stories of abduction and rape through an organized trade in women and young girls.

I went, by road and village, over tracts
Of open foreign country, large and strange,
Crossed everywhere by long thin poplar-lines[5]
Like fingers of some ghastly skeleton Hand
Through sunlight and through moonlight evermore
Pushed out from hell itself to pluck me back,
And resolute to get me, slow and sure;
While every roadside Christ[6] upon his cross
Hung reddening through his gory wounds at me,
And shook his nails in anger, and came down
To follow a mile after, wading up
The low vines and green wheat, crying 'Take the girl!
'She's none of mine from henceforth.' Then I knew
(But this is somewhat dimmer than the rest)
The charitable peasants gave me bread
And leave to sleep in straw: and twice they tied,
At parting, Mary's image[7] round my neck -
How heavy it seemed! as heavy as a stone;
A woman has been strangled with less weight:
I threw it in a ditch to keep it clean
And ease my breath a little, when none looked;
I did not need such safeguards: - brutal men
Stopped short, Miss Leigh, in insult, when they had seen
My face, - I must have had an awful look.
And so I lived: the weeks passed on, - I lived.
'Twas living my old tramp-life o'er again,
But, this time, in a dream, and hunted round
By some prodigious Dream-fear at my back,
Which ended yet: my brain cleared presently;
And there I sate one evening, by the road,
I, Marian Erle, myself, alone, undone,
Facing a sunset low upon the flats
As if it were the finish of all time,
The great red stone upon my sepulchre,
Which angels were too weak to roll away.[8]

5. EBB's description of the French countryside, with its avenues of poplars lining the roads, is as recognizable today as it was in the nineteenth century.
6. Crossroads in France, a Catholic country, are frequently the site of a crucifix, or even, as in Brittany, a whole Calvary scene, whether very elaborate or simple.
7. A medallion depicting the Virgin Mary.
8. Matthew 28.2: "[t]he angel of the Lord descended from heaven, and came and rolled back the stone from the door, and sat upon it." A reference to the burial of Christ, whose tomb was closed by a great stone, which the angel came and rolled away in anticipation of the Resurrection. See Matthew 28.2.

# Seventh Book

'The woman's motive? shall we daub ourselves
With finding roots for nettles? 'tis soft clay
And easily explored. She had the means
The monies, by the lady's liberal grace,
In trust for that Australian scheme and me,
Which so, that she might catch with both her hands
And chink to her naughty uses undisturbed,
She served me (after all it was not strange,
'Twas only what my mother would have done)[1]
A motherly, right damnable good turn.[2]

'Well after. There are nettles everywhere,
But smooth green grasses are more common still;
The blue of heaven is larger than the cloud;
A miller's wife at Clichy[3] took me in
And spent her pity on me, - made me calm
And merely very reasonably sad.
She found me a servant's place in Paris where
I tried to take the cast-off life again,
And stood as quiet as a beaten ass
Who, having fallen through overload, stands up
To let them charge him with another pack.

'A few months, so. My mistress, young and light,
Was easy with me, less for kindness than
Because she led, herself, an easy time
Betwixt her lover and her looking-glass,
Scarce knowing which way she was praised the most.
She felt so pretty and so pleased all day
She could not take the trouble to be cross,
But sometimes, as I stooped to tie her shoe,
Would tap me softly with her slender foot
Still restless with the last night's dancing in't,
And say, 'Fie, pale-face! are you English girls
'All grave and silent? mass-book still, and Lent?
'And first-communion pallor on your cheeks,[4]
'Worn past the time for 't? little fool, be gay!'

1. Sold her body. See *Aurora Leigh* 3.1040–64. The monies, in the form of gold pieces, that result from this sale create a "chinking" noise when Marian's betrayer handles them.
2. EBB wrote this version in her draft manuscript but changed it to "A motherly unmerciful good turn" when she was correcting the proofs for the first edition. Two years later when she revised the poem she decided to go back to the original strongly worded version. See textual note.
3. A town lying to the northwest of Paris on the banks of the Seine.
4. Marian's new mistress, being French, is also a Roman Catholic and uses Catholic terms to characterize Marian's seriousness, which she mistakes for excessive religiosity.

At which she vanished like a fairy, through
A gap of silver laughter.
'Came an hour
When all went otherwise. She did not speak,
But clenched her brows, and clipped me with her eyes
As if a viper with a pair of tongs,
Too far for any touch, yet near enough
To view the writhing creature, - then at last,
'Stand still there, in the holy Virgin's name,
'Thou Marian; thou'rt no reputable girl,
'Although sufficient dull for twenty saints!
'I think thou mock'st me and my house,' she said;
'Confess thou'lt be a mother in a month,
'Thou mask of saintship.'
'Could I answer her?
The light broke in so. It meant *that* then, *that?*
I had not thought of that in all my thoughts,[5]
Through all the cold, numb aching of my brow,
Through all the heaving of impatient life
Which threw me on death at intervals,-through all
The upbreak of the fountains of my heart
The rains had swelled too large: it could mean *that?*
Did God make mothers out of victims, then,
And set such pure amens to hideous deeds?
Why not? he overblows an ugly grave
With violets which blossoms in the spring.
And *I* could be a mother in a month?
I hope it was not wicked to be glad.
I lifted up my voice and wept, and laughed,
To heaven, not her, until it tore my throat.
'Confess, confess!' - what was there to confess,
Except man's cruelty, except my wrong?
Except this anguish, or this ecstasy?
This shame or glory? The light woman there
Was small to take it in: an acorn-cup
Would take the sea in sooner.
' 'Good,' she cried;
'Unmarried and a mother, and she laughs!
'These unchaste girls are always impudent.
'Get out, intriguer! leave my house and trot.
'I wonder you should look me in the face,
'With such a filthy secret.'
'Then I rolled

5. Marian's ignorance seems farfetched from a twentieth-century perspective, but it represents a common nineteenth-century misunderstanding, and EBB herself had a similar experience with her first pregnancy when she refused to believe her maid's diagnosis of her symptoms and suffered a miscarriage at five or six months in March 1847.

My scanty bundle up and went my way,
Washed white with weeping, shuddering head and foot
With blind hysteric passion, staggering forth
Beyond those doors. 'Twas natural of course
She should not ask me where I meant to sleep;
I might sleep well beneath the heavy Seine,
Like others of my sort;[6] the bed was laid
For us. But any woman, womanly,
Had thought of him who should be in a month,
The sinless babe that should be in a month,
And if by chance he might be warmer housed
Than underneath such dreary dripping eaves.'

I broke on Marian there. 'Yet she herself,
A wife, I think, had scandals of her own,
A lover not her husband.'
'Ay,' she said,
'But gold and meal are measured otherwise;
I learnt so much at school,' said Marian Erle.

'O crooked world,' I cried, 'ridiculous
If not so lamentable! 'Tis the way
With these light women of a thrifty vice,
My Marian, - always hard upon the rent
In any sister's virtue![7] while they keep
Their own so darned and patched with perfidy,
That, though a rag itself, it looks as well
Across a street, in balcony or coach,
As any perfect stuff[8] might. For my part,
I'd rather take the wind-side of the stews[9]
Than touch such women with my finger-end!
They top the poor street-walker[1] by their lie
And look the better for being so much worse:

6. Because prostitutes in London and in Paris often worked the streets around the Thames or the Seine hoping for trade among the sailors and other dockworkers, it was very common for desperate women to attempt suicide by throwing themselves into the river.
7. Cf. *King Lear*, 4.6.166–67. Aurora herself was guilty of jumping to conclusions about Marian's apparent loss of virtue when she first met Marian's child. See *Aurora Leigh* 6.631–44.
8. Cloth, material, fabric.
9. Brothels; poor and disreputable houses of resort.
1. The prostitute who solicits for custom on the streets. When *Aurora Leigh* was published in late 1856, EBB was rather amused by what she saw as the outrage aroused by her many references to the unhappy lot of the prostitute. She was also proud of her own unequivocal stand on the issue. "What has given most offence in the book, more than the story of Marian—far more!—has been the reference to the condition of women in our cities, which a woman oughtn't to refer to, by any manner of means, says the conventional tradition. Now I have thought deeply otherwise. If a woman ignores these wrongs, then may women as a sex continue to suffer them; there is no help for any of us—let us be dumb and die. I have spoken therefore, and in speaking have used plain words . . . which, if blurred or softened, would imperil perhaps the force and righteousness of the moral influence" (EBB to Mrs. Martin, February 1857, *Letters of EBB*, 2.254).

The devil's most devilish when respectable.
But you, dear, and your story.'
'All the rest
Is here,' she said, and signed upon the child.
'I found a mistress-sempstress who was kind
And let me sew in peace among her girls.
And what was better than to draw the threads
All day and half the night for him and him?
And so I lived for him, and so he lives,
And so I know, by this time, God lives too.'

She smiled beyond the sun and ended so,
And all my soul rose up to take her part
Against the world's successes, virtues, fames.
'Come with me, sweetest sister,' I returned,
'And sit within my house and do me good
From henceforth, thou and thine! ye are my own
From henceforth. I am lonely in the world,
And thou art lonely, and the child is half
An orphan. Come, - and henceforth thou and I
Being still together will not miss a friend,
Nor he a father, since two mothers shall
Make that up to him. I am journeying south,
And in my Tuscan home I'll find a niche
And set thee there, my saint,[2] the child and thee,
And burn the lights of love before thy face,
And ever at thy sweet look cross myself
From mixing with the world's prosperities;
That so, in gravity and holy calm,
We two may live on toward the truer life.'

She looked me in the face and answered not,
Nor signed she was unworthy, nor gave thanks,
But took the sleeping child and held it out
To meet my kiss, as if requiting me
And trusting me at once. And thus, at once,
I carried him and her to where I live;
She's there now,[3] in the little room, asleep,
I hear the soft child-breathing though the door,
And all three of us, at to-morrow's break,
Pass onward, homeward, to our Italy.
Oh, Romney Leigh, I have your debts to pay,

2. EBB's image, connecting Marian to the Virgin Mary, is designed and political in intention. It continues the allusions set up by the choice of name in "Marian," which is a derivative of Mary.
3. Another example of the way that Aurora's journal narrative moves from the past into the immediate present.

And I'll be just and pay them.
But yourself!
To pay your debts is scarcely difficult,
To buy your life is nearly impossible,
Being sold away to Lamia.[4] My head aches,
I cannot see my road along this dark;
Nor can I creep and grope, as fits the dark,
For these foot-catching robes of womanhood:
A man might walk a little . . but I! - He loves
The Lamia-woman, - and I, write to him
What stops his marriage, and destroys his peace,-
Or what perhaps shall simply trouble him,
Until she only need to touch his sleeve
With just a finger's tremulous white flame,
Saying, 'Ah, - Aurora Leigh! a pretty tale,
'A very pretty poet! I can guess
'The motive'-then, to catch his eyes in hers
And vow she does not wonder, - and they too
To break in laughter as the sea along
A melancholy coast, and float up higher,
In such a laugh, their fatal weeds of love!
Ay, fatal, ay. And who shall answer me
Fate has not hurried tides, - and if to-night
My letter would not be a night too late,
An arrow shot into a man that's dead,
To prove a vain intention? Would I show
The new wife vile, to make the husband mad?[5]
No, Lamia! shut the shutters, bar the doors
From every glimmer on thy serpent-skin!
I will not let thy hideous secret out
To agonise the man I love - I mean
The friend I love . . as friends love.
It is strange,
To-day while Marian told her story like
To absorb most listeners, how I listened chief
To a voice not hers, not yet that enemy's,
Nor God's in wrath, . . but one that mixed with mine
Long years ago among the garden-trees,
And said to *me*, to *me* too, 'Be my wife,
Aurora.'[6] It is strange with what a swell
Of yearning passion, as a snow of ghosts
Might beat against the impervious door of heaven,
I thought, 'Now, if I had been a woman, such
As God made women, to save men by love,-

4. See note to *Aurora Leigh* 1.161–63.
5. See Keats' "Lamia" (1820), lines 239–311.
6. Aurora recalls Romney's proposal of marriage as documented in book 2.

By just my love I might have saved this man,
And made a nobler poem for the world
Than all I have failed in.' But I failed besides
In this; and now he's lost! through me alone!
And, by my only fault, his empty house
Sucks in, at this same hour, a wind from hell
To keep his hearth cold, make his casements creak
For ever to the tune of plague and sin-
O Romney, O my Romney, O my friend,
My cousin and friend! my helper, when I would,
My love, that might be! mine!
Why, how one weeps
When one's too weary! Were a witness by,
He'd say some folly . . that I loved the man,
Who knows? . . and make me laugh again for scorn.
At strongest, women are as weak in flesh,
As men, at weakest, vilest, are in soul:
So, hard for women to keep pace with men!
As well give up at once, sit down at once,
And weep as I do. Tears, tears! *why* we weep?
'Tis worth inquiry? - that we've shamed a life,
Or lost a love, or missed a world, perhaps?
By no means. Simply, that we've walked too far,
Or talked too much, or felt the wind i' the east,-
And so we wept, as if both body and soul
Broke up in water - this way.
Poor mixed rags
Forsooth we're made of, like those other dolls
That lean with pretty faces into fairs.
It seems as if I had a man in me,
Despising such a woman.
Yet indeed,
To see a wrong or suffering moves us all
To undo it though we should undo ourselves;
Ay, all the more, that we undo ourselves,-
That's womanly, past doubt, and not ill-moved.
A natural movement therefore, on my part,
To fill the chair up of my cousin's wife,
And save him from a devil's company!
We're all so, - made so - 'tis our woman's trade
To suffer torment for another's ease.
The world's male chivalry has perished out,
But women are knights-errant to the last;
And if Cervantes had been Shakspeare too,
He had made his Don a Donna.[7]

7. In *Don Quixote* (1605; 2nd vol., 1615), Miguel de Cervantes Saavedra (1547–1616) ridiculed the exaggerated chivalric romance. His hero was an aging knight with bad eyesight who

So it clears,
And so we rain our skies blue.
Put away
This weakness. If, as I have just now said,
A man's within me, - let him act himself,
Ignoring the poor conscious trouble of blood
That's called the woman merely. I will write
Plain words to England, - if too late, too late,
If ill-accounted, then accounted ill;
We'll trust the heavens with something.
'Dear Lord Howe,
You'll find a story on another leaf
Of Marian Erle, - what noble friend of yours
She trusted once, through what flagitious[8] means,
To what disastrous end; - the story's true.
I found her wandering on the Paris quays,
A babe upon her breast, - unnatural
Unseasonable outcast on such snow
Unthawed to this time. I will tax in this
Your friendship, friend, if that convicted She
Be not his wife yet, to denounce the facts
To himself,-but, otherwise, to let them pass
On tip-toe like escaping murderers,
And tell my cousin merely - Marian lives,
Is found, and finds her home with such a friend,
Myself, Aurora. Which good news, 'She's found,'
Will help to make him merry in his love:
I sent it, tell him, for my marriage-gift,
As good as orange-water for the nerves,
Or perfumed gloves for headache, - though aware
That he, except of love, is scarcely sick:
I mean the new love this time, . . since last year.
Such quick forgetting on the part of men!
Is any shrewder trick upon the cards
To enrich them? pray instruct me how 'tis done:
First, clubs, - and while you look at clubs, 'tis spades;
That's prodigy. The lightning strikes a man,
And when we think to find him dead and charred . .
Why, there he is on a sudden, playing pipes

wandered the world looking for the perfect woman and for deeds of heroism that he might perform. Aurora argues that women are now the true heirs and exponents of chivalry, because contemporary stereotypes and values insist on their caring concern for others. In fact, of course, Aurora's distress over what she supposes to be Romney's unfortunate marriage to Lady Waldemar is dictated not by a general concern for the unhappiness of others, but by a very personal and specific distress arising out of the fact of her own (so far denied) love for Romney.

8. Wicked, villainous, criminal.

Beneath the splintered elm-tree![9] Crime and shame
And all their hoggery trample your smooth world,
Nor leave more foot-marks than Apollo's kine
Whose hoofs were muffled by the thieving god
In tamarisk-leaves and myrtle.[1] I'm so sad,
So weary and sad to-night, I'm somewhat sour, -
Forgive me. To be blue[2] and shrew at once,
Exceeds all toleration except yours,
But yours, I know, is infinite. Farewell.
To-morrow we take train for Italy.
Speak gently of me to your gracious wife,
As one, however far, shall yet be near
In loving wishes to your house.'
I sign.
And now I loose my heart upon a page,
This -
'Lady Waldemar, I'm very glad
I never liked you; which you knew so well
You spared me, in your turn, to like me much:
Your liking surely had done worse for me
Than has your loathing, though the last appears
Sufficiently unscrupulous to hurt,
And not afraid of judgment. Now, there's space
Between our faces, - I stand off, as if
I judged a stranger's portrait and pronounced.
Indifferently the type was good or bad.
What matter to me that the lines are false,
I ask you? did I ever ink my lips
By drawing your name through them as a friend's,
Or touch your hands as lovers do? Thank God
I never did: and since you're proved so vile,

9. RB used this metaphor, borrowed from *Aurora Leigh*, in 1866 when commenting on Frederic Chapman's surprisingly swift resignation to the death of his wife: "last Wednesday, going to dinner given by the Proprietors of the Fortnightly Review . . . —there was the man 'under his thunder-split tree, playing Pan's pipes' " (*Dearest Isa: Robert Browning's Letters to Isabella Blagden*, ed. Edward C. McAleer [Austin, 1951], 232).

1. Homer, *Hymns* 3, "To Hermes," 73–86. As soon as he was born, Hermes sprang up and went in search of the sacred oxen of the gods, which were kept on the Pierian heights and guarded by Apollo. His exploits made him the special patron of thieves.

EBB makes an error about whose footprints were masked with the tamarisk and myrtle: "From their herd did the Son of Maia, Far-gazing Argeiphontes, sunder off fifty lowing kine. From side to side he drave them, over the sandy ground, inverting their trail. Forgetting not the art of his cunning, he reversed their hoof-prints—the front behind, the hinder in front—and himself fared again down the mountain. When he had cast his shoon into the sand of the sea, he plaited wondrous work beyond imagining and thought, weaving together tamarisk and myrtle twigs. Then roping together a sheaf of this sprouting wood, which he had plucked on Pieria, he tied it as light sandals under his unshod feet, leaves and all, to disguise his footmarks, and turned himself from side to side like one hurrying on a secret errand" (*The Homeric Hymns Translated into English Prose*, trans. John Edgar [Edinburgh, 1891], 53).

2. To be sad and gloomy.

Ay, vile, I say, - we'll show it presently, -
I'm not obliged to nurse my friend in you,
Or wash out my own blots, in counting yours,
Or even excuse myself to honest souls
Who seek to press my lip or clasp my palm, -
'Alas, but Lady Waldemar came first!'

' 'Tis true, by this time you may near me so
That you're my cousin's wife. You've gambled deep
As Lucifer, and won the morning-star[3]
In that case, - and the noble house of Leigh
Must henceforth with its good roof shelter you:
I cannot speak and burn you up between
Those rafters, I who am born a Leigh, - nor speak
And pierce your breast through Romney's, I who live
His friend and cousin, - so, you're safe. You two
Must grow together like the tares and wheat
Till God's great fire.[4] - But make the best of time.

'And hide this letter: let it speak no more
Than I shall, how you tricked poor Marian Erle,
And set her own love digging its own grave
Within her green hope's pretty garden-ground, -
Ay, sent her forth with someone of your sort
To a wicked house in France, from which she fled
With curses in her eyes and ears and throat,
Her whole soul choked with curses, - mad in short,
And madly scouring up and down for weeks
The foreign hedgeless country,[5] lone and lost, -
So innocent, male-fiends might slink within
Remote hell-corners,[6] seeing her so defiled.

'But you, - you are a woman and more bold.
To do you justice, you'd not shrink to face . .

3. Lucifer, or the morning-star, was the brightest of the angels before his fall from heaven: "How art thou fallen from heaven, O Lucifer, son of the morning!" (Isaiah 14.12). Christ redeemed mankind, saving them from the temptations of Lucifer and succeeding to the title of morning star. "I am the root and offspring of David, and the bright and morning star" (Revelation 22.16).
4. Reference to the parable told by Jesus comparing the kingdom of heaven to a man who sowed good seed in his field. Then an enemy came along and sowed weeds, but when the servants asked if they should go and gather them, the master said no, for fear that they should pull up the good plants with the weeds: "Let both grow together until the harvest; and at harvest time I will tell the reapers, Gather the weeds first and bind them in bundles to be burned, but gather the wheat into my barn" (Matthew 13.30).
5. The hedgerows of England were a distinctive feature of the landscape in the nineteenth century and appeared much less frequently in other European countries.
6. Possibly a reminiscence of the description of Lovelace in his distraction after the news of Clarissa's death: "And *now* he is but very middling; sits grinning like a man in straw; curses and swears, and is confounded gloomy; and creeps into holes and corners, like an old hedgehog hunted for his grease" (Samuel Richardson, *Clarissa* [1747–48], vol. 4, letter 69).

We'll say, the unfledged life in the other room,
Which, treading down God's corn, you trod in sight
Of all the dogs, in reach of all the guns, -
Ay, Marian's babe, her poor unfathered child,
Her yearling babe! - you'd face him when he wakes
And opens up his wonderful blue eyes:
You'd meet them and not wink perhaps, nor fear
God's triumph in them and supreme revenge
When righting His creation's balance-scale
(You pulled as low as Tophet)[7] to the top
Of most celestial innocence. For me
Who am not as bold, I own those infant eyes
Have set me praying.
'While they look at heaven,
No need of protestation in my words
Against the place you've made them! let them look.
They'll do your business with the heavens, be sure:
I spare you common curses.
Ponder this,
If haply you're the wife of Romney Leigh,
(For which inheritance beyond your birth
You sold that poisonous porridge called your soul)[8]
I charge you, be his faithful and true wife!
Keep warm his hearth and clean his board, and, when
He speaks, be quick with your obedience;
Still grind your paltry wants and low desires
To dust beneath his heel; though, even thus,
The ground must hurt him, - it was writ of old,
'Ye shall not yoke together ox and ass,'[9]
The nobler and ignobler. Ay, but you
Shall do your part as well as such ill things
Can do aught good. You shall not vex him, - mark,
You shall not vex him, jar him when he's sad,
Or cross him when he's eager. Understand
To trick him with apparent sympathies,
Nor let him see thee in the face too near
And unlearn thy sweet seeming. Pay the price
Of lies, by being constrained to lie on still:
'Tis easy for thy sort: a million more
Will scarcely damn thee deeper.
'Doing which
You are very safe from Marian and myself;
We'll breathe as softly as the infant here,

7. See note to *Aurora Leigh* 1.420.
8. Genesis 25.29–34. A reference to the story of Esau, the first-born son of Isaac, who sold his birthright to his younger brother, Jacob, for a "mess of pottage," when he came home hungry from the hunt.
9. Deuteronomy 22.10: "Thou shalt not plow with an ox and an ass together."

And stir no dangerous embers. Fail a point,
And show our Romney wounded, ill-content,
Tormented in his home, we open mouth,
And such a noise will follow, the last trump's[1]
Will scarcely seem more dreadful, even to you;
You'll have no pipers after:[2] Romney will
(I know him) push you forth as none of his,
All other men declaring it well done,
While women, even the worst, your like, will draw
Their skirts back, not to brush you in the street,
And so I warn you. I'm . . . Aurora Leigh.'

The letter written I felt satisfied.
The ashes, smouldering in me, were thrown out
By handfuls from me: I had writ my heart
And wept my tears, and now was cool and calm;
And, going straightway to the neighbouring room,
I lifted up the curtains of the bed
Where Marian Erle, the babe upon her arm,
Both faces leaned together like a pair
Of folded innocences self-complete,
Each smiling from the other, smiled and slept.
There seemed no sin, no shame, no wrath, no grief.
I felt she too had spoken words that night,
But softer certainly, and said to God,
Who laughs in heaven perhaps that such as I
Should make ado for such as she. 'Defiled'
I wrote? 'defiled' I thought her? Stoop,
Stoop lower, Aurora! get the angels' leave
To creep in somewhere, humbly, on your knees,
Within this round of sequestration[3] white
In which they have wrapt earth's foundlings, heaven's elect.[4]

The next day we took train to Italy[5]
And fled on southward in the roar of steam.
The marriage-bells of Romney must be loud,
To sound so clear through all: I was not well,
And truly, though the truth is like a jest,
I could not choose but fancy, half the way,

1. 1 Corinthians 15.52.
2. Revelation 18.21–22: "Thus with violence shall that great Babylon be thrown down, and shall be found no more at all. And the voice of harpers, and musicians, and of pipers, and trumpeters, shall be heard no more at all in thee."
3. Being cloistered, shut off from the world.
4. See Matthew 5.3: "Blessed are the poor in spirit, for theirs is the kingdom of heaven."
5. The route that Aurora describes—by way of Dijon, Lyons, along the banks of the Rhône to Avignon, and thence to Marseilles—was possible only after 1854, when the section of railway between Valence and Avignon was opened (*Murray's Handbook for Travellers in France*, 432). The journey from Paris to Marseilles took about eighteen-and-a-half hours (xx).

I stood alone i' the belfry, fifty bells
Of naked iron, mad with merriment,
(As one who laughs and cannot stop himself)
All clanking at me, in me, over me,
Until I shrieked a shriek I could not hear,
And swooned with noise, - but still, along my swoon,
Was 'ware the baffled changes backward rang,
Prepared, at each emerging sense, to beat
And crash it out with clangour. I was weak;
I struggled for the posture of my soul
In upright consciousness of place and time,
But evermore, 'twixt waking and asleep,
Slipped somehow, staggered, caught at Marian's eyes
A moment, (it is very good for strength
To know that some one needs you to be strong)
And so recovered what I called myself,
For that time.
I just knew it when we swept
Above the old roofs of Dijon: Lyons dropped
A spark into the night, half trodden out
Unseen. But presently the winding Rhone
Washed out the moonlight large along his banks
Which strained their yielding curves out clear and clean
To hold it, - shadow of town and castle just blurred
Upon the hurrying river. Such an air
Blew thence upon the forehead, - half an air
And half a water, - that I leaned and looked,
Then, turning back to Marian, smiled to mark
That she looked only on her child, who slept,
His face toward the moon too.
So we passed
The liberal open country and the close,
And shot through tunnels,[6] like a lightning-wedge
By great Thor-hammers[7] driven through the rock,
Which, quivering through the intestine blackness, splits,
And lets it in at once: the train swept in
Athrob with effort, trembling with resolve,
The fierce denouncing whistle wailing on
And dying off smothered in the shuddering dark,
While we, self-awed, drew troubled breath, oppressed
As other Titans, underneath the pile
And nightmare of the mountains.[8] Out, at last,

6. Presumably the series of tunnels that cut through the mountains to the north of Marseilles. One of these tunnels, under the Montagne de la Nerth, was some two-and-three-quarter miles long (*Murray's Handbook for Travellers in France*, 466).
7. According to Teutonic legend, Thor possessed the attribute of a magic hammer, Miölnir.
8. In ancient mythology, the twelve gigantic children of Uranus and Gaea were vanquished by Jupiter, who imprisoned them in the abyss below Tartarus.

To catch the dawn afloat upon the land!
- Hills, slung forth broadly and gauntly everywhere,
Not crampt in their foundations, pushing wide
Rich outspreads of the vineyards and the corn,
(As if they entertained i' the name of France)
While, down their straining sides, streamed manifest
A soil as red as Charlemagne's[9] knightly blood,
To consecrate the verdure. Some one said,
'Marseilles!' And lo, the city of Marseilles,
With all her ships behind her, and beyond,
The scimitar of ever-shining sea
For right-hand use, bared blue against the sky!

That night we spent between the purple heaven
And purple water:[1] I think Marian slept;
But I, as a dog a-watch for his master's foot,
Who cannot sleep or eat before he hears,
I sate upon the deck and watched the night
And listened through the stars for Italy.
Those marriage-bells I spoke of, sounded far,
As some child's go-cart in the street beneath
To a dying man who will not pass the day,
And knows it, holding by a hand he loves.
I too sate quiet, satisfied with death,
Sate silent: I could hear my own soul speak,
And had my friend - for Nature comes sometimes
And says, 'I am ambassador for God.'
I felt the wind soft from the land of souls;
The old miraculous mountains heaved in sight,[2]
One straining past another along the shore,
The way of grand dull Odyssean ghosts,
Athirst to drink the cool blue wine of seas
And stare on voyagers.[3] Peak pushing peak
They stood: I watched beyond that Tyrian[4] belt
Of intense sea betwixt them and the ship,

9. See note to *Aurora Leigh* 1.771.
1. French government contract steamers of the Messageries Imperiales Company sailed from Marseilles every Monday at 11 a.m. to reach Genoa on Tuesday at 6 a.m. (*Murray's Handbook for Travellers in France*, xxi, 471). Cf. *Aurora Leigh* 7.485: "Genoa broke with day."
2. Cf. EBB's description of her 1846 journey to Italy: "I sate upon deck, too, in our passage from Marseilles to Genoa, and had a vision of mountains, six or seven deep, one behind the other" (*Letters of EBB* 1.324).
3. Homer, *Odyssey* 11.1–50. Odysseus, directed by Circe, visited the underworld to seek the advice of Teiresias. When he came to the banks of Oceanus, which bounds the earth, Odysseus dug a trench and poured into it a libation to all the dead—first milk, then honey and wine, and finally the blood of sacrificial animals. "Then there gathered from out of Erebus the spirits of those that are dead. . . . These came thronging in crowds about the pit from every side, with a wondrous cry" (11.35–36, 42–43; Loeb translation).
4. Purple dye made at the Phoenician city of Tyre.

Down all their sides the misty olive-woods
Dissolving in the weak congenial moon
And still disclosing some brown convent-tower
That seems as if it grew from some brown rock,
Or many a little lighted village, dropt
Like a fallen star upon so high a point,
You wonder what can keep it in its place
From sliding headlong with the waterfalls
Which powder all the myrtle and orange groves
With spray of silver. Thus my Italy
Was stealing on us. Genoa broke with day,
The Doria's long pale palace[5] striking out,
From green hills in advance of the white town,
A marble finger dominant to ships,
Seen glimmering through the uncertain grey of dawn.

And then I did not think, 'my Italy,'
I thought, 'my father!' O my father's house,
Without his presence! - Places are too much
Or else too little, for immortal man, -
Too little, when love's May o'ergrows the ground,
Too much, when that luxuriant robe of green
Is rustling to our ankles in dead leaves.
'Tis only good to be or here or there,
Because we had a dream on such a stone,[6]
Or this or that, - but, once being wholly waked
And come back to the stone without the dream,
We trip upon 't, - alas, and hurt ourselves;
Or else it falls on us and grinds us flat,
The heaviest grave-stone on this burying earth.
- But while I stood and mused, a quiet touch
Fell light upon my arm, and turning round,
A pair of moistened eyes convicted[7] mine.
'What, Marian! is the babe astir so soon?'
'He sleeps,' she answered; 'I have crept up thrice,
And seen you sitting, standing, still at watch.
I thought it did you good till now, but now' . . .
'But now,' I said, 'you leave the child alone.'
'And you're alone,' she answered, - and she looked
As if I too were something. Sweet the help
Of one we have helped! Thanks, Marian, for such help.

5. The Palazzo Doria Pamphilii, situated in gardens that extend to the seashore: "These gardens, with the palace in their centre, form a noble feature in the panorama of the port of Genoa" (*Murray's Handbook for Travellers in Northern Italy* [1854], 1.92). The Brownings visited the palace while at Genoa in 1852. See *Letters of EBB* 2.94, 95.
6. An allusion to Jacob's dream (Genesis 28.11–16).
7. Convinced or challenged.

I found a house at Florence on the hill
Of Bellosguardo.[8] 'Tis a tower which keeps
A post of double-observation o'er
That valley of Arno[9] (holding as a hand
The outspread city,) straight toward Fiesole[1]
And Mount Morello[2] and the setting sun,
The Vallombrosan mountains opposite,[3]
Which sunrise fills as full as crystal cups
Turned red to the brim because their wine is red.
No sun could die nor yet be born unseen
By dwellers at my villa: morn and eve
Were magnified before us in the pure
Illimitable space and pause of sky,
Intense as angels' garments blanched with God,
Less blue than radiant. From the outer wall
Of the garden, drops the mystic floating grey
Of olive-trees, (with interruptions green
From maize and vine) until 'tis caught and torn
Upon the abrupt black line of cypresses
Which signs the way to Florence.[4] Beautiful
The city lies along the ample vale,
Cathedral, tower and palace, piazza and street,
The river trailing like a silver cord
Through all,[5] and curling loosely, both before
And after, over the whole stretch of land
Sown whitely up and down its opposite slopes
With farms and villas.

8. The original of Aurora's house is generally assumed to be the Villa Bricchieri (now called Bricchieri-Colombi), where a marble plaque inscribed with *Aurora Leigh* 7.515–29 can be seen on the front of the villa. The house, which dates at least to the early part of the fifteenth century, stands on the hill of Bellosguardo, just beyond the village piazza. A small terrace affords a fine view overlooking Florence. Isa Blagden, a close friend of the Brownings, lived here from 1856 to 1861. Evidence suggests, however, that EBB was not thinking of this particular house. Isa Blagden took a five-year lease on the Villa Bricchieri in 1856 (see *Dearest Isa*, xxiii) while the Brownings were away from Florence, living in Paris and London (June 1855–October 1856). The Villa Bricchieri would not have become really familiar to EBB until after October 1856, when *Aurora Leigh* was already in the hands of the publishers. Furthermore, compare EBB to Anna Jameson, April 9, 1857: "On April 6 we had tea out of doors, on the terrace of our friend Miss Blagden in her villa up [at] Bellosguardo (not exactly Aurora Leigh's, mind). You seem to be lifted up above the world in a divine ecstasy. Oh, what a vision!" (*Letters of EBB* 2.259). Another friend of the poets, Robert Bulwer Lytton, rented a villa at Bellosguardo during 1853. The Brownings attended an evening party held at his villa: "Such a view! Florence dissolving in the purple of the hills; and the stars looking on" (*Letters of EBB* 2.125).
9. The Arno is the river that runs through Florence.
1. A hill and town to the northeast of Florence, renowned for its gardens and views of the valley of the Arno.
2. One of the hills surrounding Florence.
3. See note to *Aurora Leigh* 1.616. The mountains and forests of Vallombrosa lie to the east of Florence. From Bellosguardo, the Vallombrosan mountains are seen strictly "opposite," though also somewhat "to the right" (see textual note).
4. The road back to Florence from Bellosguardo is lined with cypress trees.
5. The Arno.

Many weeks had passed,
No word was granted. - Last, a letter came
From Vincent Carrington:-'My dear Miss Leigh,
You've been as silent as a poet should,
When any other man is sure to speak.
If sick, if vexed, if dumb, a silver piece
Will split a man's tongue, - straight he speaks and says,
'Received that cheque.' But you! . . I send you funds
To Paris, and you make no sign at all.
Remember I'm responsible and wait
A sign of you, Miss Leigh.
'Meantime your book
Is eloquent as if you were not dumb;
And common critics, ordinarily deaf
To such fine meanings, and, like deaf men, loth
To seem deaf, answering chance-wise, yes or no,
'It must be' or 'it must not,' (most pronounced
When least convinced) pronounce for once aright:
You'd think they really heard, - and so they do . .
The burr of three or four who really hear
And praise your book aright: Fame's smallest trump
Is a great ear-trumpet for the deaf as posts,
No other being effective. Fear not, friend;
We think here you have written a good book,
And you, a woman! It was in you - yes,
I felt 'twas in you: yet I doubted half
If that od-force of German Reichenbach,
Which still from female finger-tips burns blue,
Could strike out as our masculine white heats[6]

6. Carl von Reichenbach (1788–1869), industrialist and scientist. Having made a fortune, and attained the rank of baron, Reichenbach retired to his castle in Reisenberg to conduct research into magnetism and electricity. The result of his work was the discovery of the "od," an all-pervading force present in nature and manifesting itself as heat or light emanating from certain objects, particularly crystals. This "od-force" could be perceived only by those who were innately sensitive or whose perceptions were heightened by illness. Reichenbach explained the properties of the "od" or "odyle" in a series of papers published in March and May 1845 as a supplement to Leibig and Wohler's *Annalen der Chemie und Pharmacie*, a leading periodical in chemistry studies.

EBB was apparently first introduced to Reichenbach's theory by Harriet Martineau (herself a firm believer in mesmerism), who mentioned Reichenbach's work in a letter to EBB in February 1846. See *RB/EBB Letters* 2.461. Shortly after this date, EBB seems to have acquired a fairly precise knowledge of Reichenbach's theory, for she writes to RB on April 21, 1846, using a metaphor derived from Reichenbach's findings: "*Love*, I have learnt to believe in. I see the new light which Reichenbach shows pouring forth visibly from these crystals tossed out. But when you say that the blue, I see, is red, and that the [. . .] little crystals are the fixed stars of the Heavens, how am I to think of you but that you are deluded . . mistaken? . . ." (*RB/EBB Letters* 2.640). EBB's metaphor corresponds closely to Reichenbach's theory. The od-force was supposed to issue from all parts of the body, but was especially visible to the sensitive as a light streaming from the fingertips. In healthy men this phenomenon was supposed to be marked, while it was weaker and rarer in females. Hence Vincent Carrington's remarks about the pale "blue" light discernable in women as opposed to "our masculine white heats." RB also refers to Reichenbach's od-force in "'A Lover's Quarrel" (1855), stanza 7: "The yearning slips/Thro' the finger-tips/In a fire which a few discern,/And a very few feel burn."

To quicken a man. Forgive me. All my heart
Is quick with yours since, just a fortnight since,
I read your book and loved it.
'Will you love
My wife, too? Here's my secret I might keep
A month more from you! but I yield it up
Because I know you'll write the sooner for't
Most women (of your height even) counting love
Life's only serious business.[7] Who's my wife
That shall be in a month, you ask? nor guess?
Remember what a pair of topaz eyes
You once detected, turned against the wall,
That morning in my London painting-room;
The face half-sketched, and slurred; the eyes alone!
But you . . you caught them up with yours, and said
'Kate Ward's eyes, surely.' - Now I own the truth:
I had thrown them there to keep them safe from Jove,
They would so naughtily find out their way
To both the heads of both my Danaës[8]
Where just it made me mad to look at them.
Such eyes! I could not paint or think of eyes
But those, - and so I flung them into paint
And turned them to the wall's care. Ay, but now
I've let them out, my Kate's: I've painted her,
(I change my style and leave mythologies)
The whole sweet face; it looks upon my soul
Like a face on water, to beget itself,[9]
A half-length portrait, in a hanging cloak
Like one you wore once; 'tis a little frayed, -
I pressed too for the nude harmonious arm -
But she, she'd have her way, and have her cloak;
She said she could be like you only so,
And would not miss the fortune. Ah, my friend,
You'll write and say she shall not miss your love
Through meeting mine? in faith, she would not change.
She has your books by heart more than my words,
And quotes you up against me till I'm pushed
Where, three months since, her eyes were: nay, in fact,
Nought satisfied her but to make me paint
Your last book folded in her dimpled hands
Instead of my brown palette as I wished,
And, grant me, the presentment had been newer;
She'd grant me nothing: I compounded for

7. A common platitude, but compare Byron's *Don Juan*, (1819–24), canto 1, stanza 194, "Man's love is of man's life a thing apart,/'Tis woman's whole existence."
8. See *Aurora Leigh* 3.121–35.
9. Proverbs 27.19: "As in water face answereth to face, so the heart of man to man."

The naming of the wedding-day next month,
And gladly too. 'Tis pretty, to remark
How women can love women of your sort,
And tie their hearts with love-knots to your feet,
Grow insolent about you against men
And put us down by putting up the lip,
As if a man, - there *are* such, let us own,
Who write not ill, - remains a man, poor wretch,
While you—! Write weaker than Aurora Leigh,
And there'll be women who believe of you
(Besides my Kate) that if you walked on sand
You would not leave a foot-print.[1]
'Are you put
To wonder by my marriage, like poor Leigh?
'Kate Ward!' he said. 'Kate Ward!' he said anew.
'I thought . . .' he said, and stopped, - 'I did not think . . .'
And then he dropped to silence.
'Ah, he's changed.
I had not seen him, you're aware, for long,
But went of course. I have not touched on this
Through all this letter, - conscious of your heart,
And writing lightlier for the heavy fact,
As clocks are voluble with lead.
'How poor,
To say I'm sorry! dear Leigh, dearest Leigh.
In those old days of Shropshire, - pardon me, -
When he and you fought many a field of gold
On what you should do,[2] or you should not do,
Make bread or verses, (it just came to that)
I though you'd one day draw a silken peace
Through a golden ring. I thought so: foolishly,
The event proved, - for you went more opposite
To each other, month by month, and year by year,
Until this happened. God knows best, we say,
But hoarsely. When the fever took him first,
Just after I had writ to you in France,
They tell me Lady Waldemar mixed drinks
And counted grains,[3] like any salaried nurse,

1. The first draft manuscript reference (see textual note) to "Abram's guest" alludes to the occasion when a mysterious visitor told the elderly Abraham and Sarah that they would yet have a child. See Genesis 18. The other manuscript reference to "Endor" is to the visit Samuel paid to the witch of Endor; see 1 Samuel 28.
2. "The Field of the Cloth of Gold" was the name given to the famous occasion when Henry VIII met François I at a field near Guisnes in France. The meeting was to cement their allegiance, and the event was so called because of the magnificence and splendor of each day's entertainment.
3. Measured out doses of opium, a common pallative used by many, including EBB, in the nineteenth century.

Excepting that she wept too. Then Lord Howe,
You're right about Lord Howe, Lord Howe's a trump,
And yet, with such in his hand,[4] a man like Leigh
May lose as *he* does. There's an end to all,
Yes, even this letter, though this second sheet
May find you doubtful. Write a word for Kate:
She reads my letters always, like a wife,
And if she sees her name I'll see her smile
And share the luck. So, bless you, friend of two!
I will not ask you what your feeling is
At Florence with my pictures;[5] I can hear
Your heart a-flutter over the snow-hills:
And, just to pace the Pitti[6] with you once,
I'd give a half-hour of to-morrow's walk
With Kate . . I think so. Vincent Carrington.'

The noon was hot; the air scorched like the sun
And was shut out. The closed persiani[7] threw
Their long-scored shadows on my villa-floor,
And interlined the golden atmosphere
Straight, still, - across the pictures on the wall,
The statuette on the console, (of young Love
And Psyche made one marble by a kiss)[8]
The low couch where I leaned, the table near,[9]
The vase of lilies Marian pulled last night
(Each green leaf and each white leaf ruled in black
As if for writing some new text of fate)
And the open letter, rested on my knee,
But there the lines swerved, trembled, though I sate
Untroubled, plainly, reading it again
And three times. Well, he's married; that is clear.
No wonder that he's married, nor much more
That Vincent's therefore 'sorry'. Why, of course
The lady nursed him when he was not well,
Mixed drinks, - unless nepenthe[1] was the drink

4. A cardgame reference. A trump is a winning card that one holds in a "hand" of cards.
5. There are many well known collections and examples of the work of the old masters in Florence, especially at the Uffizi galleries and in the Pitti Palace.
6. See note to *Aurora Leigh* 1.132. The palace houses one of Florence's finest art collections.
7. Blinds and shutters.
8. Probably a reproduction of the group called Cupid and Psyche, which is in the Capitoline Museum in Rome. Many small-scale versions in bronze, earthenware, and porcelain were made of this statue during the eighteenth century. A similar group, representing Cupid and Psyche with wings was in the Uffizi gallery in Florence, and this figure was also a popular subject for reproduction.
9. This and the deleted manuscript description at line 7.668 (see textual note) suggest that EBB is using a description of her own drawing room at Casa Guidi in Florence. See the painting of the room by George Mignaty that is now held at Mills College, Oakland, California, and that is reproduced in *The Browning Collections* (1984), plate 1.
1. An Egyptian drug, which brings forgetfulness of pain and sorrow, mentioned in Homer, *Odyssey* 6.219–32.

'Twas scarce worth telling. But a man in love
Will see the whole sex in his mistress' hood,
The prettier for its lining of fair rose,
Although he catches back and says at last,
'I'm sorry.' Sorry. Lady Waldemar
At prettiest, under the said hood, preserved
From such a light as I could hold to her face
To flare its ugly wrinkles out to shame,
Is scarce a wife for Romney, as friends judge,
Aurora Leigh or Vincent Carrington,
That's plain. And if he's 'conscious of my heart' . .
It may be natural, though the phrase is strong;
(One's apt to use strong phrases, being in love)
And even that stuff of 'fields of gold,' 'gold rings,'
And what he 'thought,' poor Vincent, what he 'thought,'
May never mean enough to ruffle me.
- Why, this room stifles. Better burn than choke;
Best have air, air, although it comes with fire, -
Throw open blinds and windows to the noon
And take a blister on my brow instead
Of this dead weight! best, perfectly be stunned
By those insufferable cicale, sick
And hoarse with rapture of the summer-heat,
That sing, like poets, till their hearts break, - sing
Till men say, 'It's too tedious.'
Books succeed,
And lives fail. Do I feel it so, at last?
Kate loves a worn-out cloak for being like mine,
While I live self-despised for being myself,
And yearn toward some one else, who yearns away
From what he is, in his turn. Strain a step
For ever, yet gain no step? Are we such,
We cannot, with our admirations even,
Our tip-toe aspirations, touch a thing
That's higher than we? is all a dismal flat,
And God alone above each, as the sun
O'er level lagunes, to make them shine and stink, -
Laying stress upon us with immediate flame,
While we respond with our miasmal[2] fog
And call it mounting higher because we grow
More highly fatal?
Tush, Aurora Leigh!
You wear your sackcloth looped in Cæsar's way[3]
And brag your failings as mankind's. Be still.

2. Shadowy, obscuring.
3. A reference to Suetonius's account of Caesar's dress: "They say, too, that he was fantastic in his dress; that he wore a senator's tunic with fringed sleeves reaching to the wrist, and always

There *is* what's higher, in this very world,
Than you can live, or catch at. Stand aside,
And look at others - instance little Kate!
She'll make a perfect wife for Carrington.
She always has been looking round the earth
For something good and green to alight upon
And nestle into, with those soft-winged eyes,
Subsiding now beneath his manly hand
'Twixt trembling lids of inexpressive[4] joy.
I will not scorn her, after all, too much,
That so much she should love me: a wise man
Can pluck a leaf, and find a lecture in't;
And I, too, . . God has made me, - I've a heart
That's capable of worship, love, and loss;
We say the same of Shakspeare's. I'll be meek
And learn to reverence, even this poor myself.

The book, too - pass it. 'A good book,' says he,
'And you a woman.' I had laughed at that,
But long since. I'm a woman, - it is true;
Alas, and woe to us, when we feel it most!
Then, least care have we for the crowns and goals
And compliments on writing our good books.
The book has some truth in it, I believe,
And truth outlives pain, as the soul does life.
I know we talk our Phaedons to the end,[5]
Through all the dismal faces that we make,
O'er-wrinkled with dishonouring agony
From decomposing drugs. I have written truth,
And I a woman, - feebly, partially,
Inaptly in presentation, Romney'll add,
Because a woman. For the truth itself,
That's neither man's nor woman's, but just God's;
None else has reason to be proud of truth:
Himself will see it sifted, disenthralled,
And kept upon the height and in the light,
As far as and no farther than 'tis truth;
For, now He has left off calling firmaments
And strata, flowers and creatures, very good,[6]
He says it still of truth, which is His own.

had a girdle over it, though a rather loose one; and this, they say, was the occasion of Sulla's *mot*, when he often warned the nobles to keep an eye on the ill-girt boy" (*De Vita Caesarum*, 1, "Divus Julius," 45 [Loeb translation]).

4. Not capable of being expressed.
5. One of the *Dialogues* of Plato (427–347 BC). The *Meno* argues the preexistence and immortality of the soul, and the *Phaedo* substantiates this argument by relating the events of the last hours of Socrates' life, before he took the fatal poison. Socrates is represented as proposing the desirability of death, arguing that the physical body hinders the soul's perception of truth.
6. Genesis 1.31.

Truth, so far, in my book; - the truth which draws
Through all things upwards, - that a twofold world
Must go to a perfect cosmos.[7] Natural things
And spiritual, - who separates those two
In art, in morals, or the social drift,
Tears up the bond of nature and brings death,
Paints futile pictures, writes unreal verse,
Leads vulgar days, deals ignorantly with men,
Is wrong, in short, at all points. We divide
This apple of life, and cut it through the pips, -
The perfect round which fitted Venus' hand[8]
Has perished as utterly as if we ate
Both halves. Without the spiritual, observe,
The natural's impossible, - no form,
No motion: without sensuous, spiritual
Is inappreciable, - no beauty or power:
And in this twofold sphere the twofold man
(For still the artist is intensely a man)
Holds firmly by the natural, to reach
The spiritual beyond it, - fixes still
The type with mortal vision, to pierce through,
With eyes immortal, to the antetype
Some call the ideal, - better called the real,[9]
And certain to be called so presently
When things shall have their names.[1] Look long enough
On any peasant's face here, coarse and lined,
You'll catch Antinous[2] somewhere in that clay,
As perfect featured as he yearns at Rome
From marble pale with beauty; then persist,
And, if your apprehension's competent,
You'll find some fairer angel at his back,
As much exceeding him as he the boor,

7. An idea derived from Swedenborg and referring to his concept that the material life on earth is but the shadow and counterpart to the spiritual life, which goes on elsewhere. See note to *Aurora Leigh* 5.120–24.

8. Hermes, the messenger of the gods, brought Aphrodite, Athena, and Hera to Paris, then living as a cowherd, although his true identity was son of Priam, king of Troy. Paris was to judge which of the three goddesses was "the fairest" and to award the golden apple to the winner. He gave the apple to Aphrodite (Venus in Roman terms), who promised him the most beautiful woman in the world as a wife. See Hyginus, *Fabula* 81 and Ovid *Heroides* 17.104.

9. The "ideal" here means the spiritual existence, but Aurora's point is that the spiritual is the true life as opposed to the insignificance of the transitory material world.

1. Apparently, on the Day of Judgment; see Revelation 21.12–14: the names of the tribes of Israel and the names of the twelve apostles will be written on the gates and the foundations of the new Jerusalem.

2. The statue called the Belvedere Antinous, also known as Mercury or Admirandus. From 1800 to 1815, the statue was displayed in the Musée Central des Arts in Paris, where it was described in the catalogue as "one of the most perfect statues that has come down to us from antiquity" (*Notice* 9 (1800): 57–59; quoted in Francis Haskell and Nicholas Penny, *Taste and the Antique: The Lure of Classical Sculpture 1500–1900* [New Haven, CT, and London, 1981], 142). Since 1816, when the statue was returned to Rome, it has stood in the Belvedere Courtyard of the Vatican Museum.

And pushing him with empyreal[3] disdain
For ever out of sight. Ay, Carrington
Is glad of such a creed: an artist must,
Who paints a tree, a leaf, a common stone
With just his hand, and finds it suddenly
A-piece with and conterminous to his soul.
Why else do these things move him, leaf, or stone?
The bird's not moved, that pecks at a spring-shoot;
Nor yet the horse, before a quarry a-graze:
But man, the two-fold creature, apprehends
The two-fold manner, in and outwardly,
And nothing in the world comes single to him,
A mere itself, - cup, column, or candlestick,
All patterns of what shall be in the Mount;[4]
The whole temporal show related royally,
And built up to eterne significance
Through the open arms of God. 'There's nothing great
Nor small,' has said a poet of our day,[5]
Whose voice will ring beyond the curfew of eve[6]
And not be thrown out by the matin's bell:[7]
And truly, I reiterate, nothing's small!
No lily-muffled hum of a summer-bee,
But finds some coupling with the spinning stars;
No pebble at your foot, but proves a sphere;
No chaffinch, but implies the cherubim;
And, (glancing on my own thin, veinéd wrist,)
In such a little tremour of the blood
The whole strong clamour of a vehement soul
Doth utter itself distinct. Earth's crammed with heaven,
And every common bush afire with God;[8]
But only he who sees, takes off his shoes,
The rest sit round it and pluck blackberries,
And daub their natural faces unaware
More and more from the first similitude.[9]

Truth, so far, in my book! a truth which draws
From all things upward. I, Aurora, still

3. Heavenly.
4. Alluding to the instructions that God gave to Moses while he was on Mount Sinai for the building of the lamp of the tabernacle (Exodus 25.31–40).
5. RB, who wrote, "All service ranks the same with God:/If now, as formerly he trod/Paradise, his presence fills/Our earth, each only as God wills/Can work—God's puppets, best and worst,/ Are we; there is no last nor first.//Say not 'a small event!' Why 'small'?/Costs it more pain that this, ye call/A 'great event,' should come to pass,/Than that? Untwine me from the mass/Of deeds which make up life, one deed/Power shall fall short in or exceed!" (Introduction to *Pippa Passes* [1841], 190–201).
6. The signal that night falls.
7. The bell rung for morning prayers or *matins*.
8. Exodus 3.2–5.
9. Genesis 1.27. The first similitude is Adam's likeness to God, in whose image he was made.

Have felt it hound me through the wastes of life
As Jove did Io; and, until that Hand
Shall overtake me wholly and on my head
Lay down its large unfluctuating peace,
The feverish gad-fly pricks me up and down.[1]
It must be. Art's the witness of what Is
Behind this show. If this world's show were all,
Then imitation would be all in Art;
There, Jove's hand grips us! - For we stand here, we,
If genuine artists, witnessing for God's
Complete, consummate, undivided work;
- That every natural flower which grows on earth
Implies a flower upon the spiritual side,
Substantial, archetypal,[2] all a-glow
With blossoming causes, - not so far away,
But we, whose spirit-sense is somewhat cleared,
May catch at something of the bloom and breath, -
Too vaguely apprehended, though indeed
Still apprehended, consciously nor not,
And still transferred to picture, music, verse,
For thrilling audient and beholding souls
By signs and touches which are known to souls.
How known, they know not, - why, they cannot find,
So straight call out on genius, say, 'A man
Produced this,' when much rather they should say,
' 'Tis insight and he saw this.'
Thus is Art
Self-magnified in magnifying a truth
Which, fully recognised, would change the world
And shift its morals. If a man could feel,
Not one day, in the artist's ecstasy,
But every day, feast, fast, or working-day,
The spiritual significance burn through
The hieroglyphic of material shows,
Henceforward he would paint the globe with wings,
And reverence fish and fowl, the bull, the tree,
And even his very body as a man, -
Which now he counts so vile, that all the towns

1. According to Aeschylus's version of the myth, Zeus (or Jove) transformed Io into a heifer and condemned her to wander through the world, goaded by a gnat, or gadfly: "The god desirous of this mortal's love/Hath cursed her with these wanderings./Ah, fair child,/Thou hast met a bitter groom for bridal troth" (*Prometheus Bound*, 860–65). Prometheus foretold that Io would at length be released by Zeus on the banks of the Nile: "Io, there,/Shall Zeus give back to thee thy perfect mind/And only by the pressure and the touch/Of a hand not terrible" (991–94). See EBB's translation (*Poetical Works of EBB*, 462, 464).

Ovid's more familiar version of the tale relates how Zeus changed Io into a heifer to conceal her from his jealous wife, Hera, who, knowing the true identity of the animal, sent a Fury to pursue her (Ovid, *Metamorphoses* 1.568–746).

2. Another reference to the doctrines of Emmanuel Swedenborg. See note to *Aurora Leigh* 5.120–24.

Make offal of their daughters[3] for its use,
On summer-nights, when God is sad in heaven
To think what goes on in his recreant world
He made quite other; while that moon He made
To shine there, at the first love's covenant,[4]
Shines still, convictive as a marriage-ring
Before adulterous eyes.
How sure it is,
That, if we say a true word, instantly
We feel 'tis God's, not ours, and pass it on
Like bread at sacrament we taste and pass
Nor handle for a moment,[5] as indeed
We dared to set up any claim to such!
And I - my poem, - let my readers talk.
I'm closer to it - I can speak as well:
I'll say with Romney, that the book is weak,
The range uneven, the points of sight obscure,
The music interrupted.
Let us go.
The end of woman (or of man, I think)
Is not a book. Alas, the best of books
Is but a word in Art, which soon grows cramped,
Stiff, dubious-statured with the weight of years,
And drops an accent or digamma down
Some cranny of unfathomable time,[6]
Beyond the critic's reaching. Art itself,
We've called the larger life, must feel the soul
Live past it. For more's felt than is perceived,
And more's perceived than can be interpreted,
And Love strikes higher with his lambent[7] flame
Than Art can pile the faggots.
Is it so?
When Jove's hand meets us with composing touch,
And when at last we are hushed and satisfied,
Then Io does not call it truth, but love?

Well, well! my father was an Englishman:
My mother's blood in me is not so strong
That I should bear this stress of Tuscan noon
And keep my wits. The town, there, seems to seethe

3. Another explicit reference to, and condemnation of, the prevalence of prostitution.
4. The marriage of Adam and Eve.
5. Colossians 2.21.
6. The digamma was the sixth letter of the Greek alphabet—probably a consonant similar to W—which was lost when the sound expressed by it was no longer used in literary language.
7. Powerful.

In this Medæan boil-pot[8] of the sun,
And all the patient hills are bubbling round
As if a prick would leave them flat. Does heaven
Keep far off, not to set us in a blaze?
Not so, - let drag your fiery fringes, heaven,
And burn us up to quiet. Ah, we know
Too much here, not to know what's best for peace;
We have too much light here, not to want more fire
To purify and end us. We talk, talk,
Conclude upon divine philosophies,
And get the thanks of men for hopeful books,
Whereat we take our own life up, and . . pshaw!
Unless we piece it with another's life
(A yard of silk to carry out our lawn)[9]
As well suppose my little handkerchief
Would cover Samminiato,[1] church and all,
If out I threw it past the cypresses,
As, in this ragged, narrow life of mine,
Contain my own conclusions.
But at least
We'll shut up the persiani and sit down,
And when my head's done aching, in the cool,
Write just a word to Kate and Carrington.
May joy be with them! she has chosen well,
And he not ill.
I should be glad, I think,
Except for Romney. Had *he* married Kate,
I surely, surely, should be very glad.
This Florence sits upon me easily,
With native air and tongue. My graves are calm,
And do not too much hurt me. Marian's good
Gentle and loving, - lets me hold the child,
Or drags him up the hills to find me flowers
And fill these vases ere I'm quite awake, -
My grandiose red tulips, which grow wild,
Or Dante's purple lilies,[2] which he blew
To a larger bubble with his prophet breath,

8. Medea, the wife of Jason, restored the health of his father Aeson by boiling up magic herbs and other ingredients in a bronze pot, draining Aeson's blood, and filling his veins with the liquor (Ovid, *Metamorphoses* 7.262–93).
9. Cf. Matthew 9.16: "No man putteth a piece of a new cloth unto an old garment, for that which is put in to fill it up taketh from the garment, and the rent is made worse."
1. The church and convent of San Miniato al Monte stand on a hill to the southeast of Florence. The striking facade of the church is clearly visible on the right of the view from Bellosguardo.
2. Apparently an allusion to Dante's *Divina Commedia*, "Purgatorio," canto 22, lines 57–59. Beatrice, in mystical procession, leads Dante through a wood to a tree that bursts into flower, "[s]o showing colour less than of the rose and more than of the violet, the tree was renewed which before had its branches so bare" (*The Divine Comedy*, trans. John D. Sinclair [Oxford, 1971], 2.421).

Or one of those tall flowering reeds that stand
In Arno, like a sheaf of sceptres left
By some remote dynasty of dead gods[3]
To suck the stream for ages and get green,
And blossom wheresoe'er a hand divine
Had warmed the place with ichor.[4] Such I find
At early morning laid across my bed,
And wake up pelted with a childish laugh
Which even Marian's low precipitous 'hush'
Has vainly interposed to put away, -
While I, with shut eyes, smile and motion for
The dewy kiss that's very sure to come
From mouth and cheeks, the whole child's face at once
Dissolved on mine, - as if a nosegay burst
Its string with the weight of roses overblown,
And dropt upon me. Surely I should be glad.
The little creature almost loves me now.
And calls my name, 'Alola,' stripping off
The *rs* like thorns, to make it smooth enough
To take between his dainty, milk-fed lips,
God love him! I should certainly be glad,
Except, God help me, that I'm sorrowful
Because of Romney.
Romney, Romney! Well
This grows absurd! - too like a tune that runs
I' the head, and forces all things in the world,
Wind, rain, the creaking gnat, or stuttering fly,[5]
To sing itself and vex you, - yet perhaps
A paltry tune you never fairly liked,
Some 'I'd be a butterfly,' or 'C'est l'amour:'[6]
We're made so, - not such tyrants to ourselves
But still we are slaves to nature. Some of us

3. An allusion to the myth of the god Pan, who was once all-powerful. When he pursued the nymph Syrinx, she was turned into a reed in order to escape his attentions. He then made a set of pipes out of the reeds, and these became his symbolic instrument. EBB often used the myths of Pan in her poetry; see particularly "The Dead Pan" (1844) and "A Musical Instrument" (1860).
4. The juice that, in place of blood, flows in the veins of the gods (Homer, *Iliad* 5.340).
5. Possibly a reminiscence of Alfred Tennyson's "Mariana" from his *Poems, Chiefly Lyrical* (1830): "All day within the dreamy house,/The doors upon their hinges creak'd:/The blue fly sung in the pane . . . The sparrow's chirrup on the roof,/The slow clock ticking, and the sound/Which to the wooing wind aloof/The poplar made, did all confound/Her sense . . ."
6. "C'est l'amour l'amour l'amour,/qui fait le monde a la ronde,/et chaque jour a son tour,/le monde fait l'amour" (a popular tune, performed in Paris in *La Marchande de Goujons* around 1821–22). A reviewer of "C'est l'amour," as arranged by W. H. Cutler, remarks, "C'est l'amour is an animated, pretty air let it appear in what form it may" (*The Harmonicon: A Journal of Music* 2, part 1 (1824): 69. Like "I'd be a butterfly," it remained a favorite for many years; "I'd be a butterfly born in a bower,/Where roses and lilies and violets meet" (a popular ballad by Thomas Haynes Bayly [1797–1839]).

Are turned, too, overmuch like some poor verse
With a trick of ritournelle:[7] the same thing goes
And comes back ever.
                    Vincent Carrington
Is 'sorry,' and I'm sorry; but *he*'s strong
To mount from sorrow to his heaven of love,
And when he says at moments, 'Poor, poor Leigh,
Who'll never call his own so true a heart,
So fair a face even,' - he must quickly lose
The pain of pity, in the blush he makes
By his very pitying eyes. The snow, for him,
Has fallen in May and finds the whole earth warm,
And melts at the first touch of the green grass.

But Romney, - he has chosen, after all.
I think he had as excellent a sun
To see by, as most others, and perhaps
Has scarce seen really worse than some of us
When all's said. Let him pass. I'm not too much
A woman, not to be a man for once
And bury all my Dead like Alaric,[8]
Depositing the treasures of my soul
In this drained water-course, then letting flow
The river of life again with commerce-ships
And pleasure-barges full of silks and songs.
Blow, winds, and help us.
                    Ah, we mock ourselves
With talking of the winds; perhaps as much
With other resolutions. How it weighs,
This hot, sick air! and how I covet here
The Dead's provision on the river-couch,
With silver curtains drawn on tinkling rings!
Or else their rest in quiet crypts, - laid by
From heat and noise; - from those cicale, say,
And this more vexing heart-beat.
                    So it is:
We covet for the soul, the body's part,

7. A technical musical term for the "little return" of a tune that is repeated.
8. Alaric (c. 370–410), leader of the tribes of the Goths and conqueror of Rome, died after leaving Rome and was buried in the riverbed of the Busento, near Cosenza: "His people mourned for him with the utmost affection. Then turning from its course the river Busentus near the city of Cosentia . . . they led out a band of captives into the midst of its bed to dig out a place for his grave. In the depths of this pit they buried Alaric, together with many treasures, and they turned the waters back into their channel. And that none might ever know the place, they put to death all the diggers" (Jordanes [AD 552], *Getica* 3.158, in *The Gothic History of Jordanes*, trans. Charles Christopher Mierow [Princeton, 1915], 95). The incident is related in Edward Gibbons' *Decline and Fall of the Roman Empire* (1776–88), ch. 31. Felicia Hemans described Alaric's tomb in her poem "Alaric in Italy."

To die and rot. Even so, Aurora, ends
Our aspiration who bespoke our place
So far in the east.[9] The occidental[1] flats
Had fed us fatter, therefore? we have climbed
Where herbage[2] ends? we want the beast's part now,
And tire of the angel's? - Men define a man,
The creature who stands front-ward to the stars,
The creature who looks inward to himself,
The tool-wright, laughing creature.[3] 'Tis enough:
We'll say instead, the inconsequent creature, man,
For that's his specialty. What creature else
Conceives the circle, and then walks the square?
Loves things proved bad, and leaves a thing proved good?
You think the bee makes honey half a year,
To loathe the comb in winter and desire
The little ant's food rather? But a man -
Note men! - they are but women after all,
As women are but Auroras! - there are men
Born tender, apt to pale at a trodden worm,
Who paint for pastime, in their favourite dream,
Spruce auto-vestments flowered with crocus-flames:[4]
There are, too, who believe in hell, and lie;
There are, too, who believe in heaven, and fear:
There are, who waste their souls in working out
Life's problem on these sands betwixt two tides,
Concluding, - 'Give us the oyster's part, in death.'[5]

Alas, long-suffering and most patient God,
Thou needst be surelier God to bear with us
Than even to have made us! thou aspire, aspire
From henceforth for me! thou who hast thyself
Endured this fleshhood, knowing how as a soaked
And sucking vesture it can drag us down
And choke us in the melancholy Deep,

9. The east, or the place where the sun rises, is often invoked in biblical terms as the place of the abode of God; see for instance Ezekiel 43.2: "And behold, the glory of the God of Israel came from the east."
1. Western.
2. Grass, or greenery.
3. Cf. Thomas Carlyle, *Sartor Resartus* (1833), bk. 1, ch. 5: "this Definition of the Tool-making Animal, appears to us, of all that Animal-sort, considerably the precisest and best? Man is called the Laughing Animal; but do not the apes laugh, or attempt to do it? . . ." (*Works of Thomas Carlyle*, 6.24–25).
4. The tunic in which heretics were clothed at an auto-da-fé, called the auto-vestment, or "sanbenito," was a garment displaying a red cross back and front and, if the heretic was unrepentant, grotesquely embroidered with figures of flames and devils.
5. Compare the 1856 reading (see textual note). In medieval natural history, the oyster represented the lowest order of animal life.

Sustain me, that with thee I walk these waves,[6]
Resisting! - breathe me upward, thou in me
Aspiring who art the way, the truth, the life,[7]
That no truth henceforth seem indifferent,
No way to truth laborious, and no life,
Not even this life I live, intolerable!

The days went by. I took up the old days,
With all their Tuscan pleasures worn and spoiled,
Like some lost book we dropt in the long grass
On such a happy summer-afternoon
When last we read it with a loving friend,
And find in autumn when the friend is gone,
The grass cut short, the weather changed, too late,
And stare at, as at something wonderful
For sorrow, - thinking how two hands before
Had held up what is left to only one,
And how we smiled when such a vehement nail
Impressed the tiny dint here which presents
This verse in fire for ever. Tenderly
And mournfully I lived. I knew the birds
And insects, - which look fathered by the flowers
And emulous[8] of their hues: I recognised
The moths, with the great overpoise of wings
Which makes a mystery of them how at all
They can stop flying: butterflies, that bear
Upon their blue wings such red embers round,
They seem to scorch the blue air into holes
Each flight they take: and fire-flies, that suspire[9]
In short soft lapses of transported flame
Across the tingling Dark, while overhead
The constant and inviolable stars
Outburn those light-of-love: melodious owls,
(If music had but one note and was sad,
'Twould sound just so); and all the silent swirl
Of bats that seem to follow in the air
Some grand circumference of a shadowy dome
To which we are blind: and then the nightingales,
Which pluck our heart across a garden-wall

6. When the disciples and Jesus put out to sea, a great storm arose and they were afraid. In the fourth watch of the night they saw Jesus walking toward them on the water and wondered if he were a ghost. Peter asked that he should also be made capable of walking on the water to show that it was Christ himself. Jesus answered, "Come," and he did so, but began to sink when he lost heart, so that Jesus rebuked him for his lack of faith (Matthew 14.24–31).
7. John 14.6.
8. Copying, imitating.
9. Sigh.

(When walking in the town) and carry it
So high into the bowery almond-trees)
We tremble and are afraid, and feel as if
The golden flood of moonlight unaware
Dissolved the pillars of the steady earth
And made it less substantial. And I knew
The harmless opal snakes, the large-mouthed frogs
(Those noisy vaunters of their shallow streams);
And lizards, the green lightnings of the wall,
Which, if you sit down quiet, nor sigh loud,
Will flatter you and take you for a stone,
And flash familiarly about your feet
With such prodigious eyes in such small heads! -
I knew them, (though they had somewhat dwindled from
My childish imagery,) and kept in mind
How last I sate among them equally,
In fellowship and mateship, as a child
Feels equal still toward insect, beast, and bird,
Before the Adam in him has foregone
All privilege of Eden,[1] - making friends
And talk with such a bird or such a goat,
And buying many a two-inch-wide rush-cage
To let out the caged cricket on a tree,[2]
Saying, 'Oh, my dear grillino,[3] were you cramped?
And are you happy with the ilex-leaves?[4]
And do you love me who have let you go?
Say *yes* in singing, and I'll understand.'

But now the creatures all seemed farther off,
No longer mine, not like me, only *there*,
A gulph between us. I could yearn indeed,
Like other rich men, for a drop of dew
To cool this heat, - a drop of the early dew,
The irrecoverable child-innocence
(Before the heart took fire and withered life)
When childhood might pair equally with birds;
But now . . the birds were grown too proud for us!
Alas, the very sun forbids the dew.

1. A reference to the time when Adam lived in the Garden of Eden in equality with the other newly created animals.
2. On Ascension Day, crickets were sold in tiny cages on the streets of Florence. The practice is described by Isa Blagden in her story *A Tuscan Wedding*: "Beside the flowergirls are mischievous urchins . . . offering in every direction to the unsuspecting 'forestieri' little cages about three inches square, containing a 'grillo cantate' " (*The Woman I Loved . . . and A Tuscan Wedding* [London, 1865], 238). The people released the crickets in their houses as an emblem and harbinger of life and happiness.
3. Little cricket.
4. The leaves of the laurel bushes.

And I, I had come back to an empty nest,
Which every bird's too wise for. How I heard
My father's step on that deserted ground,
His voice along that silence, as he told
The names of bird and insect, tree and flower,
And all the presentations of the stars
Across Valdarno, interposing still
'My child,' 'my child.' When fathers say 'my child,'
'Tis easier to conceive the universe,
And life's transitions down the steps of law.

I rode once to the little mountain-house
As fast as if to find my father there,
But, when in sight of't, within fifty yards,
I dropped my horse's bridle on his neck
And paused upon his flank. The house's front
Was cased with lingots of ripe Indian corn
In tesselated order and device
Of golden patterns, not a stone of wall
Uncovered, - not an inch of room to grow
A vine-leaf. The old porch had disappeared;
And right in the open doorway sate a girl
At plaiting straws, her black hair strained away
To a scarlet kerchief caught beneath her chin
In Tuscan fashion, - her full ebon[5] eyes,
Which looked too heavy to be lifted so,
Still dropt and lifted toward the mulberry-tree[6]
On which the lads were busy with their staves
In shout and laughter, stripping every bough
As bare as winter, of those summer leaves
My father had not changed for all the silk
In which the ugly silkworms hide themselves.
Enough. My horse recoiled before my heart;
I turned the rein abruptly. Back we went
As fast, to Florence.
                                        That was trial enough
Of graves. I would not visit, if I could,
My father's, or my mother's any more,
To see if stone-cutter or lichen beat
So early in the race, or throw my flowers,
Which could not out-smell heaven or sweeten earth.
They live too far above, that I should look

5. Ebony, black.
6. The leaves of the mulberry tree are stripped to provide food for silkworms, who then spin the cocoons from which the silk industry produces the thread for marketing.

So far below to find them: let me think
That rather they are visiting my grave,
Called life here, (undeveloped yet to life)
And that they drop upon me, now and then,
For token or for solace, some small weed
Least odorous of the growths of paradise,
To spare such pungent scents as kill with joy.

My old Assunta, too, was dead, was dead -
O land of all men's past![7] for me alone,
It would not mix its tenses. I was past,
It seemed, like others, - only not in heaven.
And many a Tuscan eve I wandered down
The cypress alley like a restless ghost
That tries its feeble ineffectual breath
Upon its own charred funeral-brands put out
Too soon, where black and stiff stood up the trees
Against the broad vermilion of the skies.
Such skies! - all clouds abolished in a sweep
Of God's skirt, with a dazzle to ghosts and men,
As down I went, saluting on the bridge
The hem of such before 'twas caught away
Beyond the peaks of Lucca.[8] Underneath,
The river, just escaping from the weight
Of that intolerable glory, ran
In acquiescent shadow murmurously;
While, up beside it, streamed the festa-folk
With fellow-murmurs from their feet and fans,
And *issimo* and *ino* and sweet poise
Of vowels[9] in their pleasant scandalous talk;
Returning from the grand-duke's dairy-farm[1]
Before the trees grew dangerous at eight,
(For, 'trust no tree by moonlight,' Tuscans say)[2]
To eat their ice at Donay's[3] tenderly, -
Each lovely lady close to a cavalier
Who holds her dear fan while she feeds her smile
On meditative spoonfuls of vanille

7. In that Italy was the scene of much important artistic and political innovation, especially in the Roman, late medieval, and Renaissance periods, representing the "past" of all of civilized Europe.
8. As Lucca, to the west of Florence, lies on a plain bounded by hills, EBB is presumably referring to the mountains that rise up around the resort of Bagni di Lucca.
9. An attempt to render a musical impression of the sounds of the Italian language.
1. The Cascine or Cascina (literally, "dairyfarm"), a park on the banks of the Arno, a short distance to the west of the city.
2. Unidentified. Apparently a local proverb but not included in G. Guisti's collection *Raccolta di Proverbi Toscani* (Florence, 1853).
3. The café Doney or Donay, which was situated in the Piazza Sta. Trinita. "We go about, sit on the bridge and see people pass, or take an ice inside Doney's after the vulgarest fashion—We know next to nobody" (*New Letters of RB*, 43).

And listens to his hot-breathed vows of love
Enough to thaw her cream and scorch his beard.

'Twas little matter. I could pass them by
Indifferently, not fearing to be known.
No danger of being wrecked upon a friend,
And forced to take an iceberg for an isle!
The very English, here, must wait and learn
To hang the cobweb of their gossip out
To catch a fly. I'm happy. It's sublime,
This perfect solitude of foreign lands!
To be, as if you had not been till then,
And were then, simply that you chose to be:
To spring up, not be brought forth from the ground,
Like grasshoppers at Athens,[4] and skip thrice
Before a woman makes a pounce on you
And plants you in her hair! - possess, yourself,
A new world all alive with creatures new,
New sun, new moon, new flowers, new people - ah,
And be possessed by none of them! no right
In one, to call your name, inquire your where,
Or what you think of Mister Some-one's book,
Or Mister Other's marriage or decease,
Or how's the headache which you had last week,
Or why you look so pale still, since it's gone?
- Such most surprising riddance of one's life
Comes next one's death; 'tis disembodiment
Without the pang. I marvel, people choose
To stand stock-still like fakirs,[5] till the moss
Grows on them[6] and they cry out, self-admired,
'How verdant and how virtuous!' Well, I'm glad:
Or should be, if grown foreign to myself
As surely as to others.
Musing so,
I walked the narrow unrecognising streets,
Where many a palace-front peers gloomily
Through stony vizors iron-barred,[7] (prepared
Alike, should foe or lover pass that way,

4. Referring to the ancient tradition that the Athenians were descended from a race of grasshoppers.
5. Some Hindu ascetics, or *sadhus*, attempted to subjugate the flesh by standing still continuously for days or weeks on end, sometimes leaning on a support. Some *thasasri*, as they were called, stood in this way, on only one leg. See J. C. Oman, *The Mystics, Ascetics, and Saints of India* (London, 1903), 46.
6. Derived from the proverb, "A rolling stone gathers no moss."
7. "[T]he streets are, with few exceptions, narrow. The older buildings are grand from their massive character: the basement story being often of great solidity, sometimes of rustic work . . . A profusion of iron-work adds to their prison-like appearance, which is increased by the comparative scarcity of windows and the smallness of the apertures" (*Murray's Handbook for Travellers in Northern Italy* [1854], 448).

For guest or victim) and came wandering out
Upon the churches with mild open doors
And plaintive wail of vespers,[8] where a few,
Those chiefly women, sprinkled round in blots
Upon the dusky pavement, knelt and prayed
Toward the altar's silver glory. Oft a ray
(I liked to sit and watch) would tremble out,
Just touch some face more lifted, more in need,
(Of course a woman's) - while I dreamed a tale
To fit its fortunes. There was one who looked
As if the earth had suddenly grown too large
For such a little humpbacked thing as she;
The pitiful black kerchief round her neck
Sole proof she had had a mother. One, again,
Looked sick for love, - seemed praying some soft saint
To put more virtue in the new fine scarf
She spent a fortnight's meals on, yesterday,
That cruel Gigi might return his eyes
From Giuliana. There was one, so old,
So old, to kneel grew easier than to stand, -
So solitary, she accepts at last
Our Lady for her gossip, and frets on
Against the sinful world which goes its rounds
In marrying and being married,[9] just the same
As when 'twas almost good and had the right,
(Her Gian alive, and she herself eighteen).
'And yet, now even, if Madonna willed,
She'd win a tern in Thursday's lottery[1]
And better all things. Did she dream for nought,
That, boiling cabbage for the fast-day's soup,
It smelt like blessed entrails?[2] such a dream
For nought? would sweetest Mary cheat her so,
And lose that certain candle, straight and white
As any fair grand-duchess in her teens,

8. Evening prayers.
9. An allusion to Matthew's account of how people in the days of Noah carried on with the business of their earthly lives without realizing that a catastrophe was at hand. See Matthew 24.38–39: "For as in those days before the flood they were eating and drinking, marrying and giving marriage, until the day when Noah entered the ark, and they did not know until the flood came and swept them all away, so will be the coming of the Son of man."
1. In a lottery, a tern is three winning numbers drawn together (OED). During the 1840s, it was the practice of the Tuscan government to raise funds by holding lotteries. In *A Visit to Italy* (London, 1842), 1.260–63, Frances Trollope described the occasion of a lottery draw in the Piazza del Gran'Duca in Florence. Frances Trollope condemned the effects of the stimulus of the lottery on the populace, declaring, "These lotteries are the greatest blot upon the Buon'Governo . . . and the offices where the tickets are sold are to Florence and to Tuscany generally, what our gin-palaces are to London and to England."
2. Numerous legends of saints include as evidence of the sanctity of the holy life the fact that, after death, their entrails smelled deliciously and did not rot, as is the way with normal people.

Which otherwise should flare here in a week?
*Benigna sis,*[3] thou beauteous Queen of heaven!'

I sate there musing, and imagining
Such utterance from such faces: poor blind souls
That writhe toward heaven along the devil's trail, -
Who knows, I thought, but He may stretch his hand
And pick them up? 'tis written in the Book
He heareth the young ravens when they cry,[4]
And yet they cry for carrion. - O my God,
And we, who make excuses for the rest,
We do it in our measure. Then I knelt,
And dropped my head upon the pavement too,
And prayed, since I was foolish in desire
Like other creatures, craving offal-food,
That He would stop his ears to what I said,
And only listen to the run and beat
Of this poor, passionate, helpless blood -
And then
I lay, and spoke not: but He heard in heaven.

So many Tuscan evenings passed the same.
I could not lose a sunset on the bridge,
And would not miss a vigil in the church,
And liked to mingle with the out-door crowd
So strange and gay and ignorant of my face,
For men you know not are as good as trees.
And only once, at the Santissima,[5]
I almost chanced upon a man I knew,
Sir Blaise Delorme. He saw me certainly,
And somewhat hurried, as he crossed himself,
The smoothness of the action, - then half bowed,
But only half, and merely to my shade,
I slipped so quick behind the porphyry plinth
And left him dubious if 'twas really I
Or peradventure Satan's usual trick
To keep a mounting saint uncanonised.
But he was safe for that time, and I too;
The argent angels in the altar-flare[6]
Absorbed his soul next moment. The good man!
In England we were scarce acquaintances,

3. Blessed be thou.
4. Psalms 147.9: "He giveth to the beast his food, and to the young ravens which cry." See also Job 38.41 and Luke 12.24.
5. The church of Santissima Annunziata. See note to *Aurora Leigh* 1.77.
6. In the chapel of the Annunziata, built in honor of the miraculous fresco of the Annunciation, in which the face of the Virgin was believed to have been painted by angels, is an extravagant seventeenth-century altar made of silver. See *Murray's Handbook for Travellers in Northern Italy* (1854), 484.

That here in Florence he should keep my thought
Beyond the image on his eye, which came
And went: and yet his thought disturbed my life:
For, after that, I oftener sate at home
On evenings, watching how they fined themselves
With gradual conscience to a perfect night,
Until the moon, diminished to a curve,
Lay out there like a sickle for His hand
Who cometh down at last to reap the earth.[7]
At such times, ended seemed my trade of verse;
I feared to jingle bells upon my robe[8]
Before the four-faced silent cherubim:[9]
With God so near me, could I sing of God?
I did not write, nor read, nor even think,
But sate absorbed amid the quickening glooms,
Most like some passive broken lump of salt
Dropt in by chance to a bowl of œnomel,[1]
To spoil the drink a little and lose itself,
Dissolving slowly, slowly, until lost.

7. Revelation 14.14–16.
8. From the description of Aaron's priestly robes in Exodus 39.24–25: "And they made upon the hems of the robe pomegranates of blue, and purple, and scarlet, and twined linen. And they made bells of pure gold, and put the bells between the pomegranates upon the hem of the robe, round about between the pomegranates."
RB had called his series of pamphlets *Bells and Pomegranates* (1841–46), and he gave EBB the following explanation of the title: "The Rabbis make Bells & Pomegranates symbolical of Pleasure and Profit, the Gay and the Grave, the Poetry & the Prose, Singing and Sermonizing" (*RB/EBB Letters* 1.241).
9. Ezekiel 1.6: "And every one had four faces, and every one had four wings."
1. A mixture of wine and honey, used as a beverage by the ancient Greeks (OED).

# Eighth Book

One eve it happened, when I sate alone,
Alone, upon the terrace of my tower,[1]
A book upon my knees to counterfeit
The reading that I never read at all,
While Marian, in the garden down below,
Knelt by the fountain I could just hear thrill
The drowsy silence of the exhausted day,
And peeled a new fig from that purple heap
In the grass beside her, turning out the red
To feed her eager child (who sucked at it
With vehement lips across a gap of air
As he stood opposite, face and curls a-flame
With that last sun-ray, crying, 'give me, give,'
And stamping with imperious baby-feet,
We're all born princes) - something startled me, -
The laugh of sad and innocent souls,that breaks
Abruptly, as if frightened at itself.
'Twas Marian laughed. I saw her glance above
In sudden shame that I should hear her laugh,
And straightway dropped my eyes upon my book,
And knew, the first time, 'twas Boccaccio's tale,
The Falcon's, of the lover who for love
Destroyed the best that loved him.[2] Some of us
Do it still, and then we sit and laugh no more.
Laugh *you*, sweet Marian, - you've the right to laugh,
Since God himself is for you, and a child!
For me there's somewhat less, - and so I sigh.

The heavens were making room to hold the night,
The sevenfold heavens unfolding all their gates[3]
To let the stars out slowly (prophesied

1. See note to *Aurora Leigh* 7.515–16.
2. In Boccaccio's *Decameron*, the fifth day, ninth story, Federigo Alberighi loved Monna Giovanna, a widow whom he had long since wooed unsuccessfully. Surprised by her visit, and having no food in the house, he sacrificed his beloved pet falcon and dressed it for her dinner. Unfortunately, when Monna Giovanna revealed the reason for her call, she explained that her young son was desperately ill and pined with wishing for Federigo's falcon, so she had come to ask the favor of the gift of the bird for her son. Of course, Federigo no longer had that gift in his power. The boy died, but Giovanna remembered her former lover's caring attention and subsequently married him. It is typical of EBB's interpretive handling of her literary allusions that she slightly changes (or misremembers) the terms of the story in order to make it more apposite to Aurora's own situation with regard to Romney, so that it is in effect Aurora who destroys "the best that loved" her.
3. Seven is a mystic number as expressed in the common phrase "seventh heaven" and in the numerology of the Bible; see the seven golden candlesticks in Revelation 1.12 and the seven seals opened on Judgment Day in Revelation 8.1. The allusion here suggests the imminence of Aurora's personal "revelation."

In close-approaching advent, not discerned),
While still the cue-owls[4] from the cypresses
Of the Poggio[5] called and counted every pulse
Of the skyey palpitation. Gradually
The purple and transparent shadows slow
Had filled up the whole valley to the brim,
And flooded all the city, which you saw
As some drowned city in some enchanted sea,
Cut off from nature, - drawing you who gaze,
With passionate desire, to leap and plunge
And find a sea-king with a voice of waves,[6]
And treacherous soft eyes, and slippery locks
You cannot kiss but you shall bring away
Their salt upon your lips.[7] The duomo-bell[8]
Strikes ten, as if it struck ten fathoms down,
So deep; and twenty churches[9] answer it
The same, with twenty various instances,
Some gaslights tremble along squares and streets;
The Pitti's palace-front[1] is drawn in fire;
And, past the quays,[2] Maria Novella Place,
In which the mystic obelisks stand up
Triangular, pyramidal, each based
Upon its four-square brazen tortoises,[3]
To guard that fair church, Buonarroti's Bride,[4]

4. The Scops-owl, which in Italy is called *chiu* or *ciu* in imitation of its call. Cf. RB's "Andrea del Sarto" (1855), line 210: "The cue-owls speak the name we call them by."
5. The Poggio Imperiale was a palace belonging to the grand duke of Tuscany situated outside the walls of Florence through the Porta Romana, which is also the way toward Bellosguardo. The road is lined with an avenue of cypresses. The Pratolino, which is also mentioned in the fair copy manuscript, is another grand villa nearby.
6. Cf. Ezekiel 43.2, Revelation 14.2, 19.6, and particularly 1.15: "[a]nd his voice as the sound of many waters."
7. Cf. this vivid sea-king image with the image of the god in EBB's *Sonnets from the Portuguese* (1850), 37: "As if a shipwrecked Pagan, safe in port, His guardian sea-god to commemorate,/ Should set a sculptured porpoise, gills a-snort/And vibrant tail, within the temple-gate." This disturbing and sexy image of the sea-god or sea-king is a common EBB "drowning" metaphor for desire.
8. The bell of the Cathedral Santa Maria del Fiore in Florence.
9. Twenty is a more plausible number for Florentine churches than the "fifty" (see textual note) of the first edition.
1. See note to *Aurora Leigh* 1.312. The facade of the Pitti palace is easily distinguished from the hill of Bellosguardo.
2. Of the Arno.
3. Two obelisks supported by tortoises, cast by Giovanni di Bologna, are situated in the Piazza of Santa Maria Novella. Four tortoises support each pyramid, not three as in the first edition (see textual note).
4. The design of the church of Santa Maria Novella (erected 1279–1357) was said to have been praised by Michelangelo, who called it "La Sposa." This anecdote is not in Vasari's *Lives*. EBB may have found the story in Samuel Roger's *Italy* (1822): "From that small spire, just caught/By the bright ray, that church among the rest/By One of Old distinguished as The Bride." Francis Palgrave also commented on the legend in *Murray's Handbook for Travellers in Northern Italy* (1842): "It must be considered as a forcible reproof to the more recent contemners of Gothic architecture, that Michel Angelo should have given to this church the title of his bride, or sweetheart, for upon epithet the authorities are not agreed; but yet some portion of this endearment must be ascribed to Michel Angelo's tact, of putting his patrons in good

That stares out from her large blind dial-eyes,
(Her quadrant and armillary dials, black
With rhythms of many suns and moons)[5] in vain
Inquiry for so rich a soul as his.
Methinks I have plunged, I see it all so clear . . .
And, O my heart, . . . the sea-king!

In my ears
The sound of waters.[6] There he stood, my king!

I felt him, rather than beheld him. Up
I rose, as if he were my king indeed,
And then sate down, in trouble at myself,
And struggling for my woman's empery.[7]
'Tis pitiful; but women are so made:
We'll die for you perhaps, - 'tis probable;
But we'll not spare you an inch of our full height:
We'll have our whole just stature, - five feet four,
Though laid out in our coffins: pitiful.
- 'You, Romney![8]—Lady Waldemar is here?'

He answered in a voice which was not his.
'I have her letter; you shall read it soon:
But first, I must be heard a little, I,
Who have waited long and travelled far for that.
Although you thought to have shut a tedious book
And farewell. Ah, you dog-eared such a page,[9]
And here you find me.'
Did he touch my hand,
Or but my sleeve? I trembled, hand and foot, -
He must have touched me. - 'Will you sit?' I asked,
And motioned to a chair; but down he sate,
A little slowly, as a man in doubt,
Upon the couch beside me, - couch and chair
Being wheeled upon the terrace.
'You are come,

humour by bestowing laudatory remarks upon what they already possessed" (517). EBB owned a copy of the 1842 edition of *Murray's Handbook* (see *RB/EBB Letters* 2.1080). The paragraph quoted above was cut in subsequent editions.

5. "Inserted in the front of the facade of Santa Maria Novella are two curious astronomical instruments, placed there by the Padre Ignazio Dante, astronomer of Cosmo I-a quadrant dial (1572) and an armilliary dial (1574). The use of the first is expressed in an inscription on the E. side of it" (*Murray's Handbook for Travellers in Northern Italy* [1854], pt. 2, 469).
6. See note to line 8.41.
7. Power.
8. "Percy Vane" throughout this passage in the first draft manuscript.
9. Reading metaphors appear frequently in *Aurora Leigh*, especially in describing the way that Aurora and Romney relate to each other or fail to understand each other. Cf. *Aurora Leigh* 2.836–37, 5.39–41, and see Margaret Reynolds, "Aurora Leigh: 'Writing Her Story for Her Better Self,' " in *Browning Society Notes* 17, nos. 1–3 (1987–88): 5–11.

My cousin Romney? - this is wonderful.
But all is wonder on such summer-nights;
And nothing should surprise us any more,
Who see that miracle of stars. Behold.'

I signed above, where all the stars were out,
As if an urgent heat had started there
A secret writing from a sombre page,
A blank, last moment, crowded suddenly
With hurrying splendours.
'Then you do not know' -
He murmured.
'Yes, I know,' I said, 'I know.
I had the news from Vincent Carrington.[1]
And yet I did not think you'd leave the work
In England, for so much even, - though of course
You'll make a work-day of your holiday
And turn it to our Tuscan people's use, -
Who much need helping since the Austrian boar
(So bold to cross the Alp to Lombardy[2]
And dash his brute front unabashed against
The steep snow-bosses of that shield of God[3]
Who soon shall rise in wrath and shake it clear,)
Came hither also, raking up our grape
And olive-gardens with his tyrannous tusk,
And rolling on our maize with all his swine.'

'You had the news from Vincent Carrington,'
He echoed, - picking up the phrase beyond,
As if he knew the rest was merely talk
To fill a gap and keep out a strong wind;
'You had, then, Vincent's personal news?'

1. "Wilbraham" in the first draft manuscript.
2. Referring to the Austro-Sardinian War of 1848–49. In 1848 several movements attempting to realize the goal of a united Italy were initiated. In Milan, the people rose up against the Austrian army of occupation, which had been in Lombardy and Venetia in Northern Italy since 1815. The Austrian army, under Johann Joseph Radetsky (1766–1858), retired to await reinforcements, while armies and insurgents from the Italian states rallied around Charles Albert of Sardinia (1798–1858). The campaign began in April 1848, at first bringing a degree of success to the Italian cause. But at length the superior forces of Austria brought the war to an end by defeating the Italian contingent at Novara in March 1849. Charles Albert abdicated and died shortly afterward in exile in Portugal.
   In Florence, EBB saw Leopold II, who, frightened by the growing demands for reform, had fled in February 1848 only to return to Tuscany supported by an Austrian army of occupation: " 'Signora-signora-ecco i Tedeschi!' The Austrians had arrived. We ran out on the terrace together—and up from the end of the street and close under our windows came the artillery, and luggage—waggons—the soldiers sitting upon the cannons motionless, like dusty statues. Slowly the hateful procession filed under our windows. The people shrank back to let them pass, in the deepest silence—not a word spoken, scarcely a breath drawn" (May 2–5, 1849, *EBB: Letters to Her Sister*, 107). EBB describes her experience of, and reaction to, the events of 1849 in *Casa Guidi Windows* (1851), pt. 2.
3. The Alps.

'His own,'
I answered. 'All that ruined world of yours
Seems crumbling into marriage. Carrington
Has chosen wisely.'
'Do you take it so?'[4]
He cried, 'and is it possible at last' . .
He paused there, - and then, inward to himself,
'Too much at last, too late! - yet certainly' . .
(And there his voice swayed as an Alpine plank
That feels a passionate torrent underneath)
'The knowledge, had I known it first or last,
Could scarce have changed the actual case for *me*.
And best for *her* at this time.'
Nay, I thought,
He loves Kate Ward, it seems, now, like a man,
Because he has married Lady Waldemar!
Ah, Vincent's letter said how Leigh was moved
To hear that Vincent was betrothed to Kate.
With what cracked pitchers go we to deep wells
In this world![5] Then I spoke, - 'I did not think,
My cousin, you had ever known Kate Ward.'

'In fact I never knew her. 'Tis enough
That Vincent did, and therefore chose his wife
For other reasons than those topaz eyes
We've heard of. Not to undervalue them,
For all that. One takes up the world with eyes.'

- Including Romney Leigh, I thought again,
Albeit he knows them only by repute.
How vile must all men be, since *he's* a man.

His deep pathetic voice, as if he guessed
I did not surely love him, took the word;
'You never got a letter from Lord Howe
A month back, dear Aurora?'
'None,' I said.

'I felt it was so,' he replied: 'yet, strange!
Sir Blaise Delorme has passed through Florence?'
'Ay,
By chance I saw him in Our Lady's church,[6]
(I saw him, mark you, but he saw not me)

4. Romney apparently imagines that Aurora and Vincent Carrington might have had some understanding.
5. See note to *Aurora Leigh* 6.135–36.
6. The church of Santissima Annunziata. See *Aurora Leigh* 7.1279.

Clean-washed in holy water from the count
Of things terrestrial, - letters, and the rest;
He had crossed us out together with his sins.[7]
Ay, strange; but only strange that good Lord Howe
Preferred him to the post because of pauls.[8]
For me I'm sworn to never trust a man -
At least with letters.'

'There were facts to tell,
To smooth with eye and accent. Howe supposed . . .
Well, well, no matter! there was dubious need;
You heard the news from Vincent Carrington.
And yet perhaps you had been startled less
To see me, dear Aurora, if you had read
That letter.'

- Now he sets me down as vexed.
I think I've draped myself in woman's pride
To a perfect purpose. Oh, I'm vexed, it seems!
My friend Lord Howe deputes his friend Sir Blaise
To break as softly as a sparrow's egg
That lets a bird out tenderly, the news
Of Romney's marriage to a certain saint;
*To smooth with eye and accent*, - indicate
His possible presence. Excellently well
You've played your part, my Lady Waldemar, -
As I've played mine.

'Dear Romney,' I began,
'You did not use, of old, to be so like
A Greek king coming from a taken Troy
'Twas needful that precursors spread your path
With three-piled carpets, to receive your foot[9]
And dull the sound of't. For myself, be sure,
Although it frankly grinds the gravel here,
I still can bear it. Yet I'm sorry too
To lose this famous letter, which Sir Blaise
Has twisted to a lighter absently
To fire some holy taper: dear Lord Howe
Writes letters good for all things but to lose;
And many a flower of London gossipry[1]

7. A conflated image, which plays on the idea of deleting as in "crossing out" and the idea of Sir Blaise crossing himself after absolution.
8. The value of a paul in the mid-nineteenth century was equal to fivepence-halfpenny English.
9. See Aeschylus's *Agamemnon*, 905–49. When Agamemnon returns from Troy, Clytemnestra, his faithless wife, feigning reverence for the king, insists that he enter the palace treading on a path of costly tapestries. Agamemnon refuses—"Fame needs no carpetings and broideries to make her loud proclaim" (926–27). Eventually, however, Agamemnon succumbs, and enters the palace, where Clytemnestra murders him.
1. Gossiping. Cf. EBB to John Kenyon, May 16, 1853: "Think kindly of us in the midst of your brilliant London gossipry" (*Letters of EBB* 2.115).

Has dropt wherever such a stem broke off.
Of course I feel that, lonely among my vines,
Where nothing's talked of, save the blight again,
And no more Chianti![2] Still the letter's use
As preparation. . . . . Did I start indeed?
Last night I started at a cockchafer,
And shook a half-hour after.[3] Have you learnt
No more of women, 'spite of privilege,
Than still to take account too seriously
Of such weak flutterings? Why, we like it, sir,
We get our powers and our effects that way:
The trees stand stiff and still at time of frost,
If no wind tears them; but, let summer come,
When trees are happy, - and a breath avails
To set them trembling through a million leaves
In luxury of emotion. Something less
It takes to move a woman: let her start
And shake at pleasure, - nor conclude at yours,
The winter's bitter, - but the summer's green.'

He answered, 'Be the summer ever green
With you, Aurora! - though you sweep your sex
With somewhat bitter gusts from where you live
Above them, - whirling downward from your heights
Your very own pine-cones, in a grand disdain
Of the lowland burrs with which you scatter them.
So high and cold to others and yourself,
A little less to Romney were unjust,
And thus, I would not have you. Let it pass:
I feel content so. You can bear indeed
My sudden step beside you: but for me,
'Twould move me sore to hear your softened voice, -
Aurora's voice, - if softened unaware
In pity of what I am.'
Ah friend, I thought,
As husband of the Lady Waldemar
You're granted very sorely pitiable!
And yet Aurora Leigh must guard her voice
From softening in the pity of your case,
As if from lie or licence. Certainly

2. The local wine produced throughout Tuscany.
3. Cf. EBB's reaction to the noise of the deathwatch beetle in 1831: "As on our return, I was sitting by myself in our bedroom, I heard what I used to hear in the summer of 1828 [just before the death of her mother in October 1828], & only *then*—the *deathwatch*. I grew sick & pale, & dizzy—& slept miserably all night—solely I believe from the strong unaccountable impression produced on me, by this circumstance. I have mentioned it to nobody, & don't much like mentioning it here. There never was a more foolishly weakly superstitious being than I am" (*Diary of EBB*, 54).

We'll soak up all the slush and soil of life
With softened voices, ere we come to *you*.

At which I interrupted my own thought
And spoke out calmly. 'Let us ponder, friend:
What'er our state we must have made it first;
And though the thing displease us, ay, perhaps
Displease us warrantably,[4] never doubt
That other states, thought possible once, and then
Rejected by the instinct of our lives,
If then adopted had displeased us more
Than this on which the choice, the will, the love,
Has stamped the honour of a patent act
From henceforth. What we choose may not be good,
But, that we choose it, proves it good for *us*
Potentially, fantastically, now
Or last year, rather than a thing we saw,
And saw no need for choosing. Moths will burn
Their wings, - which proves that light is good for moths,
Who else had flown not where they agonise.'

'Ay, light is good,' he echoed, and there paused;
And then abruptly, . . 'Marian. Marian's well?'

I bowed my head but found no word. 'Twas hard
To speak of *her* to Lady Waldemar's
New husband. How much did he know, at last?
How much? how little?—He would take no sign,
But straight repeated, - 'Marian. Is she well?'

'She's well,' I answered.

She was there in sight
An hour back, but the night had drawn her home,
Where still I heard her in an upper room,
Her low voice singing to the child in bed,
Who restless with the summer-heat and play
And slumber snatched at noon, was long sometimes
In falling off, and took a score of songs
And mother-hushes ere she saw him sound.

'She's well,' I answered.

'Here?' he asked.

'Yes, here.'

4. Rightly, with reason.

He stopped and sighed. 'That shall be presently,
But now this must be. I have words to say,
And would be alone to say them, I with you,
And no third troubling.'

'Speak then,' I returned,
'She will not vex you.'

At which, suddenly
He turned his face upon me with its smile
As if to crush me. 'I have read your book,
Aurora.'
'You have read it,' I replied.
'And I have writ it, - we have done with it.
And now the rest?'
'The rest is like the first,'
He answered, - 'for the book is in my heart,
Lives in me, wakes in me, and dreams in me:
My daily bread tastes of it, - and my wine[5]
Which has no smack of it, I pour it out,
It seems unnatural drinking.'
Bitterly
I took the word up; 'Never waste your wine.
The book lived in me ere it lived in you;
I know it closer than another does,
And how it's foolish, feeble, and afraid,
And all unworthy so much compliment.
Beseech you, keep your wine, - and, when you drink,
Still wish some happier fortune to a friend,
Than even to have written a far better book.'

He answered gently, 'That is consequent:
The poet looks beyond the book he has made,
Or else he had not made it.[6] If a man
Could make a man, he'd henceforth be a god
In feeling what a little thing is man:
It is not my case. And this special book,
I did not make it, to make light of it:
It stands above my knowledge, draws me up;
'Tis high to me. It may be that the book
Is not so high, but I so low, instead;
Still high to me. I mean no compliment:
I will not say there are not, young or old,

5. A reference to the sacrament of the communion, which includes the taking of bread and wine.
6. Cf. EBB to RB, January 15, 1845: "What no mere critic sees, but what you, an artist, know, is the difference between the thing desired & the thing attained, between the idea in the writer's mind & the eidolon [image] cast off in his work" (*RB/EBB Letters* 1.9).

Male writers, ay, or female, let it pass,
Who'll write us richer and completer books.
A man may love a woman perfectly,
And yet by no means ignorantly maintain
A thousand women have not larger eyes:
Enough that she alone has looked at him
With eyes that, large or small, have won his soul.
And so, this book, Aurora, - so, your book.'

'Alas,' I answered, 'is it so, indeed?'
And then was silent.

'Is it so, indeed,'
He echoed, 'that *alas* is all your word?'

I said, - 'I'm thinking of a far-off June,
When you and I, upon my birthday once,
Discoursed of life and art,[7] with both untried.
I'm thinking, Romney, how 'twas morning then,
And now 'tis night.'

'And now,' he said, ' 'tis night.'

'I'm thinking,' I resumed, ' 'tis somewhat sad,
That if I had known, that morning in the dew,
My cousin Romney would have said such words
On such a night at close of many years,
In speaking of a future book of mine,
It would have pleased me better as a hope,
Than as an actual grace it can at all:
That's sad, I'm thinking,'
'Ay,' he said, ' 'tis night.'

'And there,' I added lightly, 'are the stars!
And here, we'll talk of stars and not of books.'

'You have the stars,' he murmured, - 'it is well:
Be like them! shine, Aurora, on my dark,
Though high and cold and only like a star,
And for this short night only, - you, who keep
The same Aurora of the bright June day
That withered up the flowers before my face,
And turned me from the garden evermore[8]

7. This is the conversation reported in book 2 of *Aurora Leigh*. The terms of the argument there are revised and repeated in book 8.
8. Romney describes his fallen state in relation to the banishment of Adam and Eve from the Garden of Eden.

Because I was not worthy. Oh, deserved,
Deserved! that I, who verily had not learnt
God's lesson half, attaining as a dunce
To obliterate good words with fractious thumbs
And cheat myself of the context, - *I* should push
Aside, with male ferocious impudence,
The world's Aurora who had conned[9] her part
On the other side the leaf! ignore her so,
Because she was a woman and a queen,
And had no beard to bristle through her song,
My teacher, who has taught me with a book,
My Miriam, whose sweet mouth, when nearly drowned
I still heard singing on the shore![1] Deserved,
That here I should look up unto the stars
And miss the glory' . .
'Can I understand?'
I broke in. 'You speak wildly, Romney Leigh,
Or I hear wildly. In that morning-time
We recollect, the roses were too red,
The trees too green, reproach too natural
If one should see not what the other saw:
And now, it's night, remember; we have shades
In place of colours; we are now grown cold,
And old, my cousin Romney. Pardon me, -
I'm very happy that you like my book,
And very sorry that I quoted back
A ten years' birthday. 'Twas so mad a thing
In any woman, I scarce marvel much
You took it for a venturous piece of spite,
Provoking such excuses as indeed
I cannot call you slack in.'
'Understand,'
He answered sadly, 'something, if but so.
This night is softer than an English day,
And men may well come hither when they're sick,[2]
To draw in easier breath from larger air.
'Tis thus with me; I come to you, - to you,

9. Learned, memorized by heart.
1. After the drowning of the Egyptians in the Red Sea, the Israelites rejoiced: "And Miriam, the prophetess, the sister of Aaron, took a timbrel in her hand; and all the women went out after her with timbrels and with dances" (Exodus 15.20). See also *Aurora Leigh* 2.171.
2. During the nineteenth century a warm climate was often recommended to invalids in Britain and especially to those suffering from lung complaints. The most famous convalescent trip in literature is John Keats' journey to Rome in 1819 when he was trying to conquer tuberculosis. He died in Rome before he could receive any real benefit. EBB herself had for many years been advised to travel to Italy by her doctors, but it remained a fantasy until her elopement because of her father's prohibition. The warmer climate did benefit her.

My Italy of women,[3] just to breathe
My soul out once before you, ere I go,
As humble as God makes me at the last
(I thank Him), quite out of the way of men
And yours, Aurora, - like a punished child,
His cheeks all blurred with tears and naughtiness,
To silence in a corner. I am come
To speak, beloved' . .
'Wisely, cousin Leigh
And worthily of us both!'
'Yes, worthily;
For this time I must speak out and confess
That I, so truculent in assumption once,
So absolute in dogma, proud in aim,
And fierce in expectation, - I, who felt
The whole world tugging at my skirts for help,
As if no other man than I, could pull,
Nor woman, but I led her by the hand,
Nor cloth hold, but I had it in my coat,
Do know myself to-night for what I was
On that June-day, Aurora. Poor bright day,
Which meant the best . . a woman and a rose,
And which I smote upon the cheek with words
Until it turned and rent me! Young you were,
That birthday, poet, but you talked the right:
While I, . . I built up follies like a wall
To intercept the sunshine and your face.
Your face! that's worse.'
'Speak wisely, cousin Leigh.'

'Yes, wisely, dear Aurora, though too late:
But then, not wisely. I was heavy then,
And stupid, and distracted with the cries
Of tortured prisoners in the polished brass
Of that Phalarian bull, society,[4]
Which seems to bellow bravely like ten bulls,

3. The identification of Aurora with Italy—conceived of here as epitomizing the restorative and nourishing feminine principle—might well owe something to Germaine de Stael's *Corinne; or Italy* (1807).

4. Phalaris (c. 570–54 BC), the tyrant of Agrientum in Sicily, was said to have devised a brazen bull in which prisoners were incarcerated while fires were lit under their cage. See Pindar, *Pythian Odes* 1.96–97. The shrieks of the victims were whimsically supposed to represent the bellowing of the bull.

Carlyle also described social evils in terms of the Phalarian bull in *Past and Present*, bk. 3, ch. 13: "I will venture to believe that in no time, since the beginnings of Society, was the lot of those same dumb millions of toilers so entirely unbearable as it is in the days now passing over us. It is not to die, or even to die of hunger, that makes a man wretched; . . . it is to die slowly all our life long, imprisoned in a deaf, dead, Infinite Injustice, as in the accursed iron belly of a 'Phalaris' Bull! This is and remains forever intolerable to all men whom God has made" (*Works of Thomas Carlyle* 9.234).

But, if you listen, moans and cries instead
Despairingly, like victims tossed and gored
And trampled by their hoofs. I heard the cries
Too close: I could not hear the angels lift
A fold of rustling air, nor what they said
To help my pity. I beheld the world
As one great famishing carnivorous mouth, -
A huge, deserted, callow, blind bird Thing,
With piteous open beak that hurt my heart,
Till down upon the filthy ground I dropped,
And tore the violets up to get the worms.
Worms, worms, was all my cry: an open mouth,
A gross want, bread to fill it to the lips,
No more. That poor men narrowed their demands
To such an end, was virtue, I supposed,
Adjudicating that to see it so
Was reason. Oh, I did not push the case
Up higher, and ponder how it answers when
The rich take up the same cry for themselves,
Professing equally, - 'An open mouth
A gross need, food to fill us, and no more.'
Why that's so far from virtue, only vice
Can find excuse for't![5] that makes libertines,
And slurs our cruel streets from end to end
With eighty thousand women in one smile,
Who only smile at night beneath the gas.[6]
The body's satisfaction and no more,
Is used for argument against the soul's,
Here too; the want, here too, implies the right..
- How dark I stood that morning in the sun,
My best Aurora, (though I saw your eyes)
When first you told me . . oh, I recollect
The sound, and how you lifted your small hand,
And how your white dress and your burnished curls
Went greatening round you in the still blue air,

5. In finding a suitable location for contemporary "vice," EBB tried using Crockford's, a famous London gambling house. See textual note.

6. The figure of eighty thousand prostitutes for London alone was frequently cited in the mid-nineteenth century. See, for instance, Michael Ryan, *Prostitution in London* (London, 1839), 89. William Acton, writing in 1857, noted, "The number of prostitutes in London has been variously estimated, according to the opportunities, credulity, or religious fervour of observers" (*Prostitution, Considered in Its Moral, Social, and Sanitary Aspects* [London, 1857], 15). Acton attributes the figure of eighty thousand to the bishop of Exeter and "Mr. Talbot, secretary for the society for the protection of young females." Police figures cited by Acton suggests that the number was fewer than eighty thousand. In 1855 EBB quoted a figure of forty thousand: "What of the forty thousand wretched women in this city? The silent writhing of them is to me more appalling than the roar of cannons" (*Letters of EBB* 2.213).

During the 1850s the problem of prostitution and the need for active reform and legislation was being drawn to the attention of the public, notably by influential articles in the *Westminster Review* and the *Morning Chronicle*. Nevertheless, *Aurora Leigh* was condemned for its reference to prostitution. See note to *Aurora Leigh* 7.103.

As if an inspiration from within
Had blown them all out when you spoke the words,
Even these, - 'You will not compass your poor ends
'Of barley-feeding and material ease,
'Without the poet's individualism
'To work your universal. It takes a soul,
'To move a body, - it takes a high-souled man,
'To move the masses, even to a cleaner stye:
'It takes the ideal, to blow an inch inside
'The dust of the actual: and your Fouriers[7] failed,
'Because not poets enough to understand
'That life develops from within.' I say
Your words, - I could say other words of yours,
For none of all your words will let me go;
Like sweet verbena[8] which, being brushed against,
Will hold us three hours after by the smell
In spite of long walks upon windy hills.
But these words dealt in sharper perfume, - these
Were ever on me, stinging through my dreams,
And saying themselves for ever o'er my acts
Like some unhappy verdict. That I failed,
Is certain. Stye or no stye, to contrive
The swine's propulsion toward the precipice,[9]
Proved easy and plain. I subtly organised
And ordered, built the cards up high and higher,
Till, some one breathing, all fell flat again;
In setting right society's wide wrong,
Mere life's so fatal. So I failed indeed
Once, twice, and oftener, - hearing through the rents
Of obstinate purpose, still those words of yours,
'*You will not compass your poor ends, not you!*'
But harder than you said them; every time
Still farther from your voice, until they came
To overcrow me with triumphant scorn
Which vexed me to resistance. Set down this
For condemnation, - I was guilty here;
I stood upon my deed and fought my doubt,
As men will, - for I doubted, - till at last
My deed gave way beneath me suddenly
And left me what I am: - the curtain dropped,
My part quite ended, all the footlights quenched,
My own soul hissing at me through the dark,

7. See note to *Aurora Leigh* 2.483.
8. The plant vervain and others of the genus verbena produce a perfume, sometimes called "oil of verbena," from the leaves.
9. Matthew 8.28–32, Mark 15.1–13, Luke 8.26–33. A reference to the story of the Gadarene swine. Jesus cured a man who had been possessed by devils for many years. The devils passed into a flock of swine who promptly threw themselves over a precipice into the sea.

I ready for confession, - I was wrong,
I've sorely failed, I've slipped the ends of life,
I yield, you have conquered.'
'Stay,' I answered him;
I've something for your hearing, also. I
Have failed too.'
'You!' he said, 'you're very great;
The sadness of your greatness fits you well:
As if the plume upon a hero's casque
Should nod a shadow upon his victor face.'[1]

I took him up austerely, - 'You have read
My book, but not my heart; for recollect,
'Tis writ in Sanscrit[2] which you bungle at.
I've surely failed, I know, if failure means
To look back sadly on work gladly done, -
To wander on my mountains of Delight,
So called, (I can remember a friend's words
As well as you, sir), weary and in want
Of even a sheep-path, thinking bitterly . .
Well, well! no matter. I but say so much,
To keep you, Romney Leigh, from saying more
And let you feel I am not so high indeed,
That I can bear to have you at my foot, -
Or safe, that I can help you. That June-day,
Too deeply sunk in craterous sunsets now
For you or me to dig it up alive, -
To pluck it out all bleeding with spent flame
At the roots, before those moralising stars
We have got instead, - that poor lost day, you said
Some words as truthful as the thing of mine
You cared to keep in memory; and I hold
If I, that day, and, being the girl I was,
Had shown a gentler spirit, less arrogance,
It had not hurt me. You will scarce mistake
The point here: I but only think, you see,
More justly, that's more humbly, of myself,
Than when I tried a crown on and supposed . . .
Nay, laugh, sir, - I'll laugh with you! - pray you, laugh.

1. An imaginative extension of the story told in the *Iliad* of the occasion when the hero Hector said farewell to his wife and child and the child wept to see the plume on his helmet "nodding horror down." See EBB's translation of the *Iliad* 5. The story is referred to in *Aurora Leigh* 5.149.
2. EBB constantly used an array of foreign and exotic untranslatable languages to explain the impossibility of reading another's heart. Among the languages she used in this way are Sanskrit, Egyptian, hieroglyphics, Hebrew, Attic, Bosnian, and Chaldee. These images appear often in the courtship letters to RB as well as in her *Sonnets from the Portuguese*. See Angela Leighton, "Stirring a Dust of Figures: Elizabeth Barrett Browning and Love" in *Browning Society Notes* 17, nos. 1–3 (1987–88): 11–24.

I've had so many birthdays since that day
I've learnt to prize mirth's opportunities,
Which come too seldom. Was it you who said
I was not changed? the same Aurora? Ah,
We could laugh there, too! Why, Ulysses' dog
Knew *him*,[3] and wagged his tail and died: but if
I had owned a dog, I too, before my Troy,
And if you brought him here, . . I warrant you
He'd look into my face, bark lustily,
And live on stoutly, as the creatures will
Whose spirits are not troubled by long loves.
A dog would never know me, I'm so changed,
Much less a friend . . except that you're misled
By the colour of the hair, the trick of the voice,
Like that Aurora Leigh's.'
'Sweet trick of voice!
I would be a dog for this, to know it at last,
And die upon the falls of it. O love,
O best Aurora! are you then so sad
You scarcely had been sadder as my wife?'

'Your wife, sir! I must certainly be changed,
If I, Aurora, can have said a thing
So light, it catches at the knightly spurs
Of a noble gentleman like Romney Leigh
And trips him from his honourable sense
Of what befits' . .
'You wholly misconceive,'
He answered.
I returned, - 'I'm glad of it.
But keep from misconception, too, yourself:
I am not humbled to so low a point,
Nor so far saddened. If I am sad at all,
Ten layers of birthdays on a woman's head
Are apt to fossilise her girlish mirth,
Though ne'er so merry: I'm perforce more wise,
And that, in truth, means sadder. For the rest,
Look here, sir: I was right upon the whole
That birthday morning. 'Tis impossible
To get at men excepting through their souls,
However open their carnivorous jaws;
And poets get directlier at the soul,
Than any of your œconomists: - for which

3. When Ulysses returned to Ithaca after ten years at Troy and ten years wandering, he arrived in disguise, because he wished to spy out the state of things concerning his wife, Penelope, who was being wooed by a number of suitors supposing Ulysses to be dead. Still Ulysses' old dog knew him in spite of his disguise and rushed to greet him, but died at the moment of reunion from the excess of joy. See Homer, *Odyssey* 7.290–327.

You must not overlook the poet's work
When scheming for the world's necessities.
The soul's the way. Not even Christ Himself
Can save man else than as He holds man's soul;
And therefore did he come into our flesh,
As some wise hunter creeping on this knees
With a torch, into the blackness of a cave,
To face and quell the beast there, - take the soul,
And so possess the whole man, body and soul.
I said, so far, right, yes; not farther, though:
We both were wrong that June-day, - both as wrong
As an east wind had been. I who talked of art,
And you who grieved for all men's griefs . . what then?
We surely made too small a part for God
In these things. What we are, imports us more
Than what we eat;[4] and life, you've granted me,
Develops from within. But innermost
Of the inmost, more interior of the interne,
God claims his own, Divine humanity
Renewing nature, - or the piercingest verse,
Prest in by subtlest poet, still must keep
As much upon the outside of a man
As the very bowl in which he dips his beard.
- And then, . . the rest; I cannot surely speak:
Perhaps I doubt more than you doubted then,
If I, the poet's veritable charge,
Have borne upon my forehead.[5] If I have,
It might feel somewhat liker to a crown,
The foolish green one even. - Ah, I think,
And chiefly when the sun shines, that I've failed.
But what then, Romney? Though we fail indeed,
You . . I . . a score of such weak workers, . . He
Fails never. If He cannot work by us,
He will work over us. Does He want a man,
Much less a woman, think you? Every time
The star winks there, so many souls are born,
Who all shall work too. Let our own be calm:
We should be ashamed to sit beneath those stars,
Impatient that we're nothing.'
'Could we sit
Just so for ever, sweetest friend,' he said,

4. An allusion to the aphorism of Anthelme Brillat-Savarin (1755–1826): "Dis-moi ce que tu manges, je tu dirai ce que tu es" ("Tell me what you eat, and I will tell you what you are") (*Physiologie de Gout* [1825]).
5. One of the priestly insignia that God decreed Aaron should wear. See Exodus 28.36–38: "And thou shalt make a plate of pure gold, and grave upon it, like the engravings of a signet, HOLINESS TO THE LORD. And thou shalt put it on a blue lace; upon the forefront of the mitre it shall be. And it shall be upon Aaron's forehead. . . ."

'My failure would seem better than success.
And yet indeed your book has dealt with me
More gently, cousin, than you ever will!
Your book brought down entire the bright June-day,
And set me wandering in the garden walks,
And let me watch the garland in a place
You blushed so . . nay, forgive me, do not stir, -
I only thank the book for what it taught,
And what, permitted. Poet, doubt yourself,
But never doubt that you're a poet to me
From henceforth. You have written poems, sweet,
Which moved me in secret, as the sap is moved
In still March-branches, signless as a stone:
But this last book o'ercame me like soft rain
Which falls at midnight, when the tightened bark
Breaks out into unhesitating buds
And sudden protestations of the spring.
In all your other books, I saw but *you:*
A man may see the moon so, in a pond,
And not be nearer therefore to the moon,
Nor use the sight . . except to drown himself:
And so I forced my heart back from the sight,
For what had *I*, I thought, to do with *her*,
Aurora . . Romney? But, in this last book,
You showed me something separate from yourself,
Beyond you, and I bore to take it in
And let it draw me. You have shown me truths,
O June-day friend, that help me now at night
When June is over! truths not yours, indeed,
But set within my reach by means of you,
Presented by your voice and verse the way
To take them clearest. Verily I was wrong;
And verily many thinkers of this age,
Ay, many Christian teachers, half in heaven,
Are wrong in just my sense who understood
Our natural world too insularly, as if
No spiritual counterpart completed it
Consummating its meaning, rounding all
To justice and perfection, line by line,
Form by form, nothing single nor alone,
The great below clenched by the great above,
Shade here authenticating substance there,[6]
The body proving spirit, as the effect
The cause: we meantime being too grossly apt

6. Romney eventually understands and repeats back to Aurora the Swedenborgian notions of the parallel spiritual and natural words that she has been preaching. See notes to *Aurora Leigh* 5.120–24 and 7.840–43.

To hold the natural, as dogs a bone,
(Though reason and nature beat us in the face)
So obstinately, that we'll break our teeth
Or ever we let go. For everywhere
We're too materialistic, - eating clay
(Like men of the west)[7] instead of Adam's corn
And Noah's wine,[8] clay by handfuls, clay by lumps,
Until we're filled up to the throat with clay,
And grow the grimy colour of the ground
On which we are feeding. Ay, materialist
The age's name is.[9] God himself, with some,
Is apprehended as the bare result
Of what his hand materially has made,
Expressed in such an algebraic sign
Called God; - that is, to put it otherwise,
They add up nature to a nought of God
And cross the quotient.[1] There are many even,
Whose names are written in the Christian church[2]
To no dishonour, diet still on mud
And splash the altars with it. You might think
The clay, Christ laid upon their eyelids[3] when,
Still blind, he called them to the use of sight,
Remained there to retard its exercise
With clogging incrustations. Close to heaven,
They see for mysteries, through the open doors,
Vague puffs of smoke from pots of earthenware;
And fain would enter, when their time shall come,
With quite another body than Saint Paul
Has promised,[4] - husk and chaff, the whole barley-corn,
Or where's the resurrection?'
'Thus it is,'

7. The Philistines, enemies of the children of Israel, lived in the west; see Isaiah 11.14. The serpent who tempted Eve was also condemned to eat dust; see Genesis 3.14.
8. Genesis 3.17–18 and 9.20. Adam's corn and Noah's wine obviously are used here as God-given and therefore good things.
9. Cf. Thomas Carlyle, "Signs of the Times" (1829): "This is not a Religious age. Only the material, the immediately practical, not the divine and spiritual, is important to us" (*Works of Thomas Carlyle* 3.111).
1. The result obtained by dividing one arithmetical or algebraic quantity by another (OED).
2. A glancing reference to Luke 10.20 (". . . rejoice that your names are written in heaven") and 2 Philippians 4.3 (". . .and the rest of my fellow workers whose names are written in the book of life").
3. See John 9.1–17. When Jesus and his disciples passed by a man who had been blind from birth, they asked who had sinned that the man was so punished; was it he, or his parents? Jesus answered, "It was not that this man has sinned, or his parents, but that the works of God might be made manifest in him." Then he took clay and mixed it with his spittle and anointed the man's eyes with it and told him to go and bathe his eyes in the Pool of Siloam. When the man did this, he was cured.
4. Paul promises the resurrection of the spiritual body, not the natural body. See 1 Corinthians 15.35–44. See also EBB to Mary Russell Mitford, October 19, 1854: "I believe that the body of flesh is a mere husk which drops off at death, while the spiritual body (see St Paul) emerges in glorious resurrection at once" (EBB to MRM 3.420).

I sighed. And he resumed with mournful face.
'Beginning so, and filling up with clay
The wards[5] of this great key, the natural world,
And fumbling vainly therefore at the lock
Of the spiritual, we feel ourselves shut in
With all the wild-beast roar of struggling life,
The terrors and compunctions of our souls,
As saints with lions,[6] - we who are not saints,
And have no heavenly lordship in our stare
To awe them backward. Ay, we are forced, so pent,
To judge the whole too partially, . . confound
Conclusions. Is there any common phrase
Significant, with the adverb heard alone,
The verb being absent, and the pronoun out?
But we, distracted in the roar of life,
Still insolently at God's adverb snatch,
And bruit[7] against Him that his thought is void,
His meaning hopeless, - cry, that everywhere
The government is slipping from his hand,
Unless some other Christ (say Romney Leigh)
Come up and toil and moil and change the world,
Because the First has proved inadequate,
However we talk bigly of His work
And piously of His person. We blaspheme
At last, to finish our doxology,[8]
Despairing on the earth for which He died.'

'So now,' I asked, 'you have more hope of men?'

'I hope,' he answered. 'I am come to think
That God will have his work done, as you said,
And that we need not be disturbed too much
For Romney Leigh or others having failed
With this or that quack nostrum,[9] - recipes
For keeping summits by annulling depths,
For wrestling with luxurious lounging sleeves,
And acting heroism without a scratch.
We fail, - what then? Aurora, if I smiled
To see you, in your lovely morning-pride,
Try on the poet's wreath which suits the noon,

5. The ridges projecting from the inside plate of a lock and the incisions in the key that correspond to the wards of the lock.
6. See Daniel 6.16–24. Because the prophet Daniel insisted on praying to his own God against the decree of the king of Babylon, he was cast into a den of lions. But in the morning he had escaped unscathed, because the Lord sent his angel and closed the mouths of the lions.
7. To noise, or report abroad.
8. The utterance of praise to God, particularly in a short formula.
9. Fake cure; a useless salve offered by a con-man.

(Sweet cousin, walls must get the weather-stain
Before they grow the ivy!) certainly
I stood myself there worthier of contempt,
Self-rated, in disastrous arrogance,
As competent to sorrow for mankind
And even their odds. A man may well despair,
Who counts himself so needful to success.
I failed: I throw the remedy back on God,
And sit down here beside you, in good hope.'

'And yet take heed,' I answered, 'lest we lean
Too dangerously on the other side,
And so fail twice. Be sure, no earnest work
Of any honest creature, howbeit weak,
Imperfect, ill-adapted, fails so much,
It is not gathered as a grain of sand
To enlarge the sum of human action used
For carrying out God's end. No creature works
So ill, observe, that therefore he's cashiered.[1]
The honest earnest man must stand and work,
The woman also, - otherwise she drops
At once below the dignity of man,
Accepting serfdom. Free men freely work.
Whoever fears God, fears to sit at ease.'

He cried, 'True. After Adam, work was curse;[2]
The natural creature labours, sweats, and frets.
But, after Christ, work turns to privilege,
And henceforth, one with our humanity,
The Six-day Worker[3] working still in us
Has called us freely to work on with Him
In high companionship. So, happiest!
I count that Heaven itself is only work
To a surer issue. Let us work, indeed,
But no more work as Adam, - nor as Leigh
Erewhile, as if the only man on earth,
Responsible for all the thistles blown
And tigers couchant, struggling in amaze
Against disease and winter, snarling on
For ever, that the world's not paradise,
Oh cousin, let us be content, in work,
To do the thing we can, and not presume

1. Released, fired.
2. See Genesis 3.17–19: ". . . cursed is the ground because of you; in toil you shall eat of it all the days of your life; thorns and thistles it shall bring forth to you; and you shall eat the plants of the field. In the sweat of your face you shall eat bread till you return to the ground. . . ."
3. God, who made the earth in six days and rested on the seventh.

To fret because it's little. 'Twill employ
Seven men, they say, to make a perfect pin;[4]
Who makes the head, content to miss the point,
Who makes the point, agreed to leave the join:
And if a man should cry, 'I want a pin,
'And I just make it straightway, head and point,'
His wisdom is not worth the pin he wants.
Seven men to a pin, - and not a man too much!
Seven generations, haply to this world,
To right it visibly a finger's breadth,
And mend its rents a little. Oh, to storm
And say, 'This world here is intolerable;
'I will not eat this corn, nor drink this wine,
'Nor love this woman, flinging her my soul
'Without a bond for't as a lover should,
'Nor use the generous leave of happiness
'As not too good for using generously' -
(Since virtue kindles at the touch of joy
Like a man's cheek laid on a woman's hand,
And God, who knows it, looks for quick returns
From joys) - to stand and claim to have a life
Beyond the bounds of the individual man,
And raze all personal cloisters of the soul
To build up public stores and magazines,
As if God's creatures otherwise were lost,
The builder surely saved by any means!
To think, - I have a pattern on my nail,
And I will carve the world new after it
And solve so these hard social questions, - nay,
Impossible social questions, since their roots
Strike deep in Evil's own existence here
Which God permits because the question's hard
To abolish evil nor attaint free-will.[5]
Ay, hard to God, but not to Romney Leigh!
For Romney has a pattern on his nail,
(Whatever may be lacking on the Mount)[6]
And, not being overnice to separate
What's element from what's convention, hastes
By line on line to draw you out a world,
Without your help indeed, unless you take

4. Unidentified.
5. Cf. EBB to B. R. Haydon in 1842; "Of the permission of evil, I have sometimes thought painfully, as others have: and my idea, my fancy is, that it was *necessary* in order to the communication to a finite nature of the consciousness of good. An infinite Being like the Creator sees the essential & the abstract object; but we who are finite understand nothing except by comparison & contrast" (*Invisible Friends: The Correspondence of Elizabeth Barrett and Benjamin Robert Haydon, 1842–1845*, ed. Willard B. Pope [Cambridge, MA, 1972], 13).
6. Mount Sinai, where Moses received directions for the construction of the tabernacle. See Exodus 25–31.

His yoke upon you and will learn of him,
So much he has to teach! so good a world!
The same, the whole creation's groaning for!
No rich nor poor, no gain nor loss nor stint;
No potage in it able to exclude
A brother's birthright,[7] and no right of birth,
The potage, - both secured to every man,
And perfect virtue dealt out like the rest
Gratuitously, with the soup at six,
To whoso does not seek it.'
'Softly, sir,'
I interrupted, - 'I had a cousin once
I held in reverence. If he strained too wide,
It was not to take honour but give help;
The gesture was heroic. If his hand
Accomplished nothing . . . (well, it is not proved)
That empty hand thrown impotently out
Were sooner caught, I think, by One in heaven,
Than many a hand that reaped a harvest in
And keeps the scythe's glow on it. Pray you, then,
For my sake merely, use less bitterness
In speaking of my cousin.'
'Ah,' he said,
'Aurora! when the prophet beats the ass,
The angel intercedes.'[8] He shook his head -
'And yet to mean so well and fail so foul,
Expresses ne'er another beast than man;
The antithesis is human. Harken, dear;
There's too much abstract willing, purposing,
In this poor world. We talk by aggregates,
And think by systems, and, being used to face
Our evils in statistics, are inclined
To cap them with unreal remedies
Drawn out in haste on the other side the slate.'

'That's true,' I answered, fain to throw up thought
And make a game of't, - 'Yes, we generalise
Enough to please you. If we pray at all,
We pray no longer for our daily bread
But next centenary's harvests. If we give,
Our cup of water is not tendered till
We lay down pipes and found a Company
With Branches. Ass or angel, 'tis the same:
A woman cannot do the thing she ought,

7. Genesis 25.29–34. The reference is to the story of Esau, Isaac's elder son, who sold his birthright to the younger Jacob for a mess of pottage.
8. Numbers 22.21–34.

Which means whatever perfect thing she can,
In life, in art, in science, but she fears
To let the perfect action take her part,
And rest there: she must prove what she can do
Before she does it, prate of women's rights,
Of woman's mission, woman's function, till
The men (who are prating too on their side) cry,
'A woman's function plainly is . . to talk.'
Poor souls, they are very reasonably vexed;
They cannot hear each other talk.'
'And you,
An artist, judge so?'
'I, an artist, - yes:
Because, precisely, I'm an artist, sir,
And woman, if another sate in sight,
I'd whisper, - Soft, my sister! not a word!
By speaking we prove only we can speak,
Which he, the man here, never doubted. What
He doubts is, whether we can *do* the thing
With decent grace we've not yet done at all.
Now, do it; bring your statue, - you have room!
He'll see it even by the starlight here;
And if 'tis e'er so little like the god
Who looks out from the marble silently
Along the track of his own shining dart
Through the dusk of ages, there's no need to speak;[9]
The universe shall henceforth speak for you,
And witness, 'She who did this thing, was born
To do it, - claims her license in her work.'
And so with more works. Whoso cures the plague,
Though twice a woman, shall be called a leech:[1]
Who rights a land's finances, is excused
For touching coppers, though her hands be white, -
But we, we talk!'
'It is the age's mood,'
He said; 'we boast, and do not. We put up
Hostelry signs where'er we lodge a day,
Some red colossal cow with mighty paps

9. Aurora's account of the work of a woman sculptor might owe something to EBB's friendship with the American artist Harriet Hosmer, whom she met in 1854 and who portrayed many classical gods and other figures in her sculpture. Cf. EBB on Hosmer: "I should mention, too, Miss Hosmer (but she is better than a talker), the young American sculptress, who is a great pet of mine and of Robert's, and who emancipates the eccentric life of a perfectly 'emancipated female' from all shadow of blame by the purity of hers. She lives here all alone (at twenty-two). . . ; dines and breakfasts at the cafes precisely as a young man would; works from six o'clock in the morning till night, as a great artist must, and this with an absence of pretension and simplicity of manners which accord rather with the childish dimples in her rosy cheeks than with her broad forehead and high aims" (May 10, 1854, *EBB to MRM* 3.409).
1. A doctor.

A Cyclops' fingers could not strain to milk,[2] -
Then bring out presently our saucer-full
Of curds. We want more quiet in our works,
More knowledge of the bounds in which we work;
More knowledge that each individual man
Remains an Adam to the general race,
Constrained to see, like Adam, that he keep
His personal state's condition honestly,
Or vain all thoughts of his to help the world,
Which still must be developed from its *one*
If bettered in its many. We indeed,
Who think to lay it out new like a park,
We take a work on us which is not man's,
For God alone sits far enough above
To speculate so largely. None of us
(Not Romney Leigh) is mad enough to say,
We'll have a grove of oaks upon that slope
And sink the need of acorns. Government,
If veritable and lawful, is not given
By imposition of the foreign hand,
Nor chosen from a pretty pattern-book
Of some domestic idealogue[3] who sits
And coldly chooses empire, where as well
He might republic. Genuine government
Is but the expression of a nation, good
Or less good, - even as all society,
Howe'er unequal, monstrous, crazed and cursed,
Is but the expression of men's single lives,
The loud sum of the silent units. What,
We'd change the aggregate and yet retain
Each separate figure? whom do we cheat by that?
Now, not even Romney.'
'Cousin, you are sad,
Did all your social labour at Leigh Hall,
And elsewhere, come to nought then?'
'It *was* nought,'
He answered mildly. 'There is room indeed
For statues still, in this large world of God's,
But not for vacuums, - so I am not sad;
Not sadder than is good for what I am.
My vain phalanstery dissolved itself;

2. Alluding to Ulysses's encounter with Polyphemus, the Cyclops: "Thereafter he sat down and milked the ewes and bleating goats all in turn. . . . Then presently he curdled half the white milk, and gathered it in wicker baskets and laid it away, and the other half he set in vessels that he might have it to take and drink, and that it might serve him supper" (*Odyssey* 9.244–49; Loeb translation).

3. Apparently an error for *ideologue*—a person occupied with an idea or ideas, especially with such as are regarded as impractical (OED).

My men and women of disordered lives,
I brought in orderly to dine and sleep,
Broke up those waxen masks I made them wear,
With fierce contortions of the natural face, -
And cursed me for my tyrannous constraint
In forcing crooked creatures to live straight;
And set the country hounds upon my back
To bite and tear me for my wicked deed
Of trying to do good without the church
Or even the squires, Aurora. Do you mind
Your ancient neighbours? The great book-club teems
With 'sketches,' 'summaries,' and 'last tracts' but twelve,
On socialistic troublers of close bonds
Betwixt the generous rich and grateful poor.
The vicar preached from 'Revelations' (till
The doctor woke), and found me with 'the frogs'[4]
On three successive Sundays; ay, and stopped
To weep a little (for he's getting old)
That such perdition should o'ertake a man
Of such fair acres, - in the parish, too!
He printed his discourses 'by request,'
And if your book shall sell as his did, then
Your verses are less good than I suppose.
The women of the neighbourhood subscribed,
And sent me a copy bound in scarlet silk,
Tooled edges, blazoned with the arms of Leigh:
I own that touched me.'
'What, the pretty ones?
Poor Romney!'
'Otherwise the effect was small:
I had my windows broken once or twice
By liberal peasants naturally incensed
At such a vexer of Arcadian peace,[5]
Who would not let men call their wives their own
To kick like Britons, and made obstacles
When things went smoothly as a baby drugged,
Toward freedom and starvation, - bringing down
The wicked London tavern-thieves and drabs
To affront the blessed hillside drabs and thieves
With mended morals, quotha,[6] - fine new lives! -
My windows paid for't. I was shot at, once,
By an active poacher who had hit a hare

4. Revelation 16.13: "And I saw three unclean spirits like frogs come out of the mouth of the dragon, and out of the mouth of the beast, and out of the mouth of the false prophet."
5. In ancient Greece Arcadia was a country in the middle of the Peloponnese that was famous for its wooded mountains and fertile pastures. It was where the god Pan lived and has become a poetic synonym for rural peace.
6. An archaism for "they said."

From the other barrel, (tired of springeing game
So long upon my acres, undisturbed,
And restless for the country's virtue, - yet
He missed me) ay, and pelted very oft
In riding through the village. 'There he goes
'Who'd drive away our Christian gentlefolks,
'To catch us undefended in the trap
'He baits with poisonous cheese, and lock us up
'In that pernicious prison of Leigh Hall
'With all his murderers! Give another name
'And say Leigh Hell, and burn it up with fire.'
And so they did, at last, Aurora.'
'Did?'

'You never heard it, cousin? Vincent's news
Came stinted, then.'
'They did? they burnt Leigh Hall?'
'You're sorry, dear Aurora? Yes indeed,
They did it perfectly: a thorough work,
And not a failure, this time. Let us grant
'Tis somewhat easier, though, to burn a house
Than build a system; - yet that's easy, too,
In a dream. Books, pictures, - ay, the pictures! what,
You think your dear Vandykes[7] would give them pause?
Our proud ancestral Leighs, with those peaked beards,
Or bosoms white as foam thrown up on rocks
From the old-spent wave. Such calm defiant looks
They flared up with! now nevermore to twit
The bones in the family-vault with ugly death.
Not one was rescued, save the Lady Maud,
Who threw you down, that morning you were born,
The undeniable lineal mouth and chin
To wear for ever for her gracious sake,
For which good deed I saved her; the rest went:
And you, you're sorry, cousin. Well, for me,
With all my phalansterians safely out,
(Poor hearts, they helped the burners, it was said,
And certainly a few clapped hands and yelled)
The ruin did not hurt me as it might, -
As when for instance I was hurt one day
A certain letter being destroyed.[8] In fact,
To see the great house flare so . . oaken floors,
Our fathers made so fine with rushes once
Before our mothers furbished them with trains,

7. See note to *Aurora Leigh* 4.309.
8. That is, the letter that Romney wrote to Aurora's aunt in order to endow her with money and that Aurora tore up. See book 2.

Carved wainscoats, panelled walls, the favourite slide
For draining off a martyr, (or a rogue)
The echoing galleries, half a half-mile long,
And all the various stairs that took you up
And took you down, and took you round about
Upon their slippery darkness, recollect,
All helping to keep up one blazing jest!
The flames through all the casements pushing forth
Like red-hot devils crinkled into snakes,
All signifying, - 'Look you, Romney Leigh,
'We save the people from your saving, here,
'Yet so as by fire! we make a pretty show
'Besides, - and that's the best you've ever done.'
- To see this, almost moved myself to clap!
The 'vale et plaude'[9] came too with effect
When, in the roof fell, and the fire that paused,
Stunned momently beneath the stroke of slates
And tumbling rafters, rose at once and roared,
And wrapping the whole house (which disappeared
In a mounting whirlwind of dilated flame,)
Blew upward, straight, its drift of fiery chaff
In the face of Heaven, which blenched, and ran up higher.'

'Poor Romney!'
'Sometimes when I dream,' he said,
'I hear the silence after, 'twas so still.
For all those wild beasts, yelling, cursing round,
Were suddenly silent, while you counted five,
So silent, that you heard a young bird fall
From the top-nest in the neighbouring rookery,
Through edging over-rashly toward the light.
The old rooks had already fled too far,
To hear the screech they fled with, though you saw
Some flying still, like scatterings of dead leaves
In autumn-gusts, seen dark against the sky, -
All flying, - ousted, like the House of Leigh.'

'Dear Romney!'
'Evidently 'twould have been
A fine sight for a poet, sweet, like you,
To make the verse blaze after. I myself,
Even I, felt something in the grand old trees,
Which stood that moment like brute Druid gods
Amazed upon the rim of ruin, where,
As into a blackened socket, the great fire

9. Farewell with praise.

Had dropped, - still throwing up splinters now and then
To show them grey with all their centuries,
Left there to witness that on such a day
The House went out.'
'Ah!'
'While you counted five,
I seemed to feel a little like a Leigh, -
But then it passed, Aurora. A child cried,
And I had enough to think of what to do
With all those houseless wretches in the dark,
And ponder where they'd dance the next time, they
Who had burnt the viol.'[1]
'Did you think of that?
Who burns his viol will not dance, I know,
To cymbals, Romney.'
'O my sweet sad voice,'
He cried, - 'O voice that speaks and overcomes!
The sun is silent, but Aurora speaks.'

'Alas,' I said, 'I speak I know not what:
I'm back in childhood, thinking as a child,
A foolish fancy - will it make you smile?
I shall not from the window of my room
Catch sight of those old chimneys any more.'[2]

'No more,' he answered. 'If you pushed one day
Through all the green hills to our fathers' house,
You'd come upon a great charred circle, where
The patient earth was singed an acre round;
With one stone-stair, symbolic of my life,
Ascending, winding, leading up to nought!
'Tis worth a poet's seeing. Will you go?'

I made no answer. Had I any right
To weep with this man, that I dared to speak?
A woman stood between his soul and mine,
And waved us off from touching evermore,
With those unclean white hands of hers. Enough.
We had burnt our viols and were silent.
So,
The silence lengthened till it pressed. I spoke,
To breathe: 'I think you were ill afterward.'

1. Possibly an allusion to Amos 6.5, where destruction by burning is threatened to the unrighteous who "chant to the sound of the viol."
2. The description of the furnishing and character of Leigh Hall here might be based on EBB's memories of Eastnor Castle near Ledbury. While she lived at Hope End, she was a visitor at the castle on several occasions, and the chimneys and towers of Eastnor were clearly visible from the house at Hope End.

'More ill,' he answered, 'had been scarcely ill.
I hoped this feeble fumbling at life's knot
Might end concisely, - but I failed to die,
As formerly I failed to live, - and thus
Grew willing, having tried all other ways,
To try just God's. Humility's so good,
When pride's impossible. Mark us, how we make
Our virtues, cousin, from our worn-out sins,
Which smack of them from henceforth. Is it right,
For instance, to wed here while you love there?
And yet because a man sins once, the sin
Cleaves to him, in necessity to sin,
That if he sin not *so*, to damn himself,
He sins *so*, to damn others with himself:
And thus, to wed here, loving there, becomes
A duty. Virtue buds a dubious leaf
Round mortal brows; your ivy's better, dear.
- Yet she, 'tis certain, is my very wife,
The very lamb left mangled by the wolves
Through my own bad shepherding:[3] and could I choose
But take her on my shoulder past this stretch
Of rough, uneasy wilderness, poor lamb,
Poor child, poor child? - Aurora, my beloved
I will not vex you any more to-night,
But, having spoken what I came to say,
The rest shall please you. What she can, in me, -
Protection, tender liking, freedom, ease,
She shall have surely, liberally, for her
And hers, Aurora. Small amends they'll make
For hideous evils which she had not known
Except by me, and for this imminent loss,
This forfeit presence of a gracious friend,
Which also she must forfeit for my sake,
Since, . . . . drop your hand in mine a moment, sweet,
We're parting!—ah, my snowdrop, what a touch,
As if the wind had swept it off! you grudge
Your gelid[4] sweetness on my palm but so,
A moment? angry, that I could not bear
*You* . . speaking, breathing, living, side by side
With some one called my wife . . and live, myself?
Nay, be not cruel - you must understand!
Your lightest footfall on a floor of mine
Would shake the house, my lintel being uncrossed

3. John 10.11–16.
4. Cold.

'Gainst angels:[5] henceforth it is night with me,
And so, henceforth, I put the shutters up:
Auroras must not come to spoil my dark.'

He smiled so feebly, with an empty hand
Stretched sideway from me, - as indeed he looked
To any one but me to give him help;
And, while the moon came suddenly out full,
The double-rose of our Italian moons,
Sufficient plainly for the heaven and earth,
(The stars struck dumb and washed away in dews
Of golden glory, and the mountains steeped
In divine languor) he, the man, appeared
So pale and patient, like the marble man
A sculptor puts his personal sadness in
To join his grandeur of ideal thought, -
As if his mallet struck me from my height
Of passionate indignation, I who had risen
Pale, doubting paused, . . . . Was Romney mad indeed?
Had all this wrong of heart made sick the brain?

Then quiet, with a sort of tremulous pride,
'Go, cousin,' I said coldly; 'a farewell
Was sooner spoken 'twixt a pair of friends
In those old days, than seems to suit you now.
Howbeit, since then, I've writ a book or two,
I'm somewhat dull still in the manly art
Of phrase and metaphrase. Why, any man
Can carve a score of white Loves out of snow,
As Buonarroti in my Florence there,[6]
And set them on the wall in some safe shade,
As safe, sir, as your marriage! very good;
Though if a woman took one from the ledge
To put it on the table by her flowers
And let it mind her of a certain friend,
'Twould drop at once (so better), would not bear
Her nail-mark even, where she took it up

5. Refers to the final plague that God sent to Egypt when the first-born of every household was struck down in the night. The Israelites were instructed to mark their own doors with the blood of sacrifice to indicate the houses that the angel should pass over. See Exodus 12.22–23.

6. Refers to an anecdote from Vasari's *Lives:* "It is said that Piero de' Medici, the heir of Lorenzo, who had long been intimate with Michelagnolo, often sent for him . . . and that, one winter, when much snow fell in Florence, he caused Michelagnolo to make in his court a Statue of Snow, which was exceedingly beautiful" (*Lives of the Most Eminent Painters* 5.235). Commentators disagree as to the nature of Piero's request, some seeing it as a youthful frolic, others as a profound insult to Michelangelo's genius. In *Casa Guidi Windows* (1851), EBB saw the incident in the light of the latter interpretation (1.98–144).

A little tenderly, - so best, I say:
For me, I would not touch the fragile thing
And risk to spoil it half an hour before
The sun shall shine to melt it: leave it there.
I'm plain at speech, direct in purpose: when
I speak, you'll take the meaning as it is,
And not allow for puckerings in the silk
By clever stitches: - I'm a woman, sir,
I use the woman's figures naturally,
As you the male license. So, I wish you well.
I'm simply sorry for the griefs you've had,
And not for your sake only, but mankind's.
This race is never grateful: from the first,
One fills their cup at supper with pure wine,
Which back they give at cross-time on a spunge,
In vinegar and gall.'[7]
'If gratefuller,'
He murmured, 'by so much less pitiable!
God's self would never have come down to die,
Could man have thanked him for it.'
'Happily
'Tis patent that, whatever,' I resumed,
'You suffered from this thanklessness of men,
You sink no more than Moses' bulrush-boat[8]
When once relieved of Moses, - for you're light,
You're light, my cousin! which is well for you,
And manly. For myself, - now mark me, sir,
They burnt Leigh Hall; but if, consummated
To devils, heightened beyond Lucifers,
They had burnt instead, a star or two of those
We saw above there just a moment back,
Before the moon abolished them, - destroyed
And riddled them in ashes through a sieve
On the head of the foundering universe, - what then?
If you and I remained still you and I,
It could not shift our places as mere friends,
Nor render decent you should toss a phrase
Beyond the point of actual feeling! - nay,
You shall not interrupt me: as you said,
We're parting. Certainly, not once nor twice
To-night you've mocked me somewhat, or yourself,

7. Alluding to the Last Supper (Matthew 26.27–29 passim) and the crucifixion (Matthew 27.48 and John 19.29).
8. Exodus 2.3–10. While the Israelites were enslaved in Egypt, the Pharaoh decreed that all boy babies born to them should be thrown into the Nile. When Moses was born, his mother hid him for some time and then made a basket of bulrushes and set his sister to watch over him. When Pharaoh's daughter came down to the river to bathe, she took pity on the child and he was saved.

And I, at least, have not deserved it so
That I should meet it unsurprised. But now,
Enough: we're parting . . parting. Cousin Leigh,
I wish you well through all the acts of life
And life's relations, wedlock not the least,
And it shall 'please me,' in your words, to know
You yield your wife, protection, freedom, ease,
And very tender liking. May you live
So happy with her, Romney, that your friends
Shall praise her for it. Meantime some of us
Are wholly dull in keeping ignorant
Of what she has suffered by you, and what debt
Of sorrow your rich love sits down to pay:
But if 'tis sweet for love to pay its debt,
'Tis sweeter still for love to give its gift,
And you, be liberal in the sweeter way,
You can, I think. At least, as touches me,
You owe her, cousin Romney, no amends.
She is not used to hold my gown so fast,
You need entreat her now to let it go;
The lady never was a friend of mine,
Nor capable, - I thought you knew as much, -
Of losing for your sake so poor a prize
As such a worthless friendship. Be content,
Good cousin, therefore, both for her and you!
I'll never spoil your dark, nor dull your noon,
Nor vex you when you're merry, or at rest:
You shall not need to put a shutter up
To keep out this Aurora, - though your north
Can make Auroras which vex nobody,
Scarce known from night,[9] I fancied! let me add,
My larks fly higher than some windows. Well,
You've read your Leighs. Indeed 'twould shake a house,
If such as I came in with outstretched hand
Still warm and thrilling from the clasp of one . .
Of one we know, . . to acknowledge, palm to palm,
As mistress there, the Lady Waldemar.'

'Now God be with us' . . with a sudden clash
Of voice he interrupted - 'what name's that?
You spoke a name, Aurora.'
'Pardon me;
I would that, Romney, I could name your wife
Nor wound you, yet be worthy.'
'Are we mad?'

9. A play on Aurora's name. Referring to the aurora borealis or northern lights, which can illuminate the sky so brightly that the night seems like day.

He echoed - 'wife! mine! Lady Waldemar!
I think you said my wife.' He sprang to his feet,
And threw his noble head back toward the moon
As one who swims against a stormy sea,
Then laughed with such a helpless, hopeless scorn,
I stood and trembled.
'May God judge me so,'
He said at last, - 'I came convicted here,
And humbled sorely if not enough. I came,
Because this woman from her crystal soul
Had shown me something which a man calls light:
Because too, formerly, I sinned by her
As then and ever since I have, by God,
Through arrogance of nature, - though I loved . .
Whom best, I need not say, since that is writ
Too plainly in the book of my misdeeds:
And thus I came here to abase myself,
And fasten, kneeling, on her regent brows
A garland which I startled thence one day
Of her beautiful June-youth. But here again
I'm baffled, - fail in my abasement as
My aggrandisement: there's no room left for me
At any woman's foot who misconceives
My nature, purpose, possible actions. What!
Are you the Aurora who made large my dreams
To frame your greatness? you conceive so small?
You stand so less than woman, through being more,
And lose your natural instinct (like a beast)
Through intellectual culture? since indeed
I do not think that any common she
Would dare adopt such monstrous forgeries
For the legible life-signature of such
As I, with all my blots, - with all my blots!
At last then, peerless cousin, we are peers,
At last we're even. Ah, you've left your height,
And here upon my level we take hands,
And here I reach you to forgive you, sweet,
And that's a fall, Aurora. Long ago
You seldom understood me, - but before,
I could not blame you. Then, you only seemed
So high above, you could not see below;
But now I breathe, - but now I pardon! - nay,
We're parting. Dearest, men have burnt my house,
Maligned my motives, - but not one, I swear,
Has wronged my soul as this Aurora has,
Who called the Lady Waldemar my wife.'

'Not married to her! yet you said' . .
                                        'Again?
'Nay, read the lines' (he held a letter out)
'She sent you through me.'
                                By the moonlight there,
I tore the meaning out with passionate haste
Much rather than I read it. Thus it ran.

# Ninth Book

Even thus, I pause to write it out at length,
The letter of the Lady Waldemar.

'I prayed your cousin Leigh to take you this,
He says he'll do it. After years of love,
Or what is called so, when a women frets
And fools upon one string[1] of a man's name,
And fingers it for-ever till it breaks, -
He may perhaps do for her such a thing,
And she accept it without detriment
Although she should not love him any more.
And I, who do not love him, nor love you,
Nor you, Aurora, - choose you shall repent
Your most ungracious letter and confess,
Constrained by his convictions, (he's convinced,)
You've wronged me foully. Are you made so ill,
You woman - to impute such ill to *me?*
We both had mothers, - lay in their bosom once.
And after all, I thank you, Aurora Leigh,
For proving to myself that there are things
I would not do, - not for my life, nor him,
Though something I have somewhat overdone, -
For instance, when I went to see the gods
One morning on Olympus, with a step
That shook the thunder from a certain cloud,[2]
Committing myself vilely. Could I think,
The Muse[3] I pulled my heart out from my breast
To soften, had herself a sort of heart,
And loved my mortal?[4] He at least loved her,
I heard him say so, - 'twas my recompense,
When, watching at his bedside fourteen days,
He broke out ever like a flame at whiles
Between the heats of fever, - 'Is it thou?
'Breathe closer, sweetest mouth!' and when at last
The fever gone, the wasted face extinct,
As if it irked him much to know me there,
He said, ' 'Twas kind, 'twas good, 'twas womanly,'
(And fifty praises to excuse no love)

1. The metaphor is drawn from a musical analogy and refers to the string of an instrument.
2. Refers to Lady Waldemar's visit to Aurora, which took place in book 3, and to her compliments at that time. Mount Olympus was traditionally the home of the Greek gods and especially of Zeus, or Jupiter, who controls the thunder.
3. Aurora.
4. Romney. Lady Waldemar continues the metaphor.

'But was the picture safe he had ventured for?'
And then, half wandering, - 'I have loved her well,
'Although she could not love me.' - 'Say instead,'
I answered, 'she does love you.' - 'Twas my turn
To rave: I would have married him so changed,
Although the world had jeered me properly
For taking up with Cupid at his worst,
The silver quiver worn off on his hair.[5]
'No, no', he murmured, 'no, she loves me not;
'Aurora Leigh does better: bring her book
'And read it softly, Lady Waldemar,
'Until I thank your friendship more for that
'Than even for harder service.' So I read
Your book, Aurora, for an hour that day:
I kept its pauses, marked its emphasis;
My voice, empaled upon its hooks of rhyme,
Not once would writhe, nor quiver, nor revolt;
I read on calmly, - calmly shut it up,
Observing, 'There's some merit in the book;
'And yet the merit in't is thrown away,
'As chances still with women if we write
'Or write not: we want string to tie our flowers,
'So drop them as we walk, which serves to show
'The way we went. Good morning, Mister Leigh;
'You'll find another reader the next time.
'A woman who does better than to love,
'I hate; she will do nothing very well:
'Male poets are preferable, straining less
'And teaching more.'[6] I triumphed o'er you both,
And left him.
'When I saw him afterward
I had read your shameful letter, and my heart.
He came with health recovered, strong though pale,
Lord Howe and he, a courteous pair of friends,
To say what men dare say to women, when
Their debtors. But I stopped them with a word,
And proved I had never trodden such a road
To carry so much dirt upon my shoe.
Then, putting into it something of disdain,
I asked forsooth his pardon, and my own,
For having done no better than to love,
And that not wisely, - though 'twas long ago,

5. Cupid is the Roman god of love. He carries a bow and a quiver of arrows whose darts inflict love on those they wound. The "silver quiver" has worn off on his hair because it has gone grey.
6. A common opinion concerning the relative merits of male and female poets as expressed by many writers on contemporary poetic theory. Men were deemed to offer the authoritative and prophetic strain of poetry, while women could manage only a domestic and sentimental style.

And had been mended radically since.
I told him, as I tell you now, Miss Leigh,
And proved, I took some trouble for his sake
(Because I knew he did not love the girl)
To spoil my hands with working in the stream
Of that poor bubbling nature, - till she went,
Consigned to one I trusted, my own maid
Who once had lived full five months in my house,
(Dressed hair superbly) with a lavish purse
To carry to Australia where she had left
A husband, said she. If the creature lied,
The mission failed, we all do fail and lie
More or less - and I'm sorry - which is all
Expected from us when we fail the most
And go to church to own it. What I meant,
Was just the best for him, and me, and her . .
Best even for Marian! - I am sorry for't,
And very sorry. Yet my creature said
She saw her stop to speak in Oxford Street
To one . . no matter! I had sooner cut
My hand off (though 'twere kissed the hour before,
And promised a duke's troth-ring[7] for the next)
Than crush her silly head with so much wrong.
Poor child! I would have mended it with gold,
Until it gleamed like St. Sophia's dome[8]
When all the faithful troop to morning prayer:
But he, he nipped the bud of such a thought
With that cold Leigh look which I fancied once,
And broke in, 'Henceforth she was called his wife:
'His wife required no succour: he was bound
'To Florence, to resume this broken bond;
'Enough so. Both were happy, he and Howe,
'To acquit me of the heaviest charge of all - '
- At which I shot my tongue against my fly
And struck him;[9] 'Would he carry, - he was just,
'A letter from me to Aurora Leigh,
'And ratify from his authentic mouth
'My answer to her accusation?' - 'Yes,
'If such a letter were prepared in time.'
- He's just, your cousin, ay, abhorrently:
He'd wash his hands in blood, to keep them clean.
And so, cold, courteous, a mere gentleman,

7. Betrothal ring.
8. The dome of the cathedral of Hagia Sophia (Holy Wisdom) at Constantinople, built by Justinian I, was decorated with gold.
9. Cf. Lady Waldemar's image with the figure (later deleted) that appeared in the first draft manuscript at 7.312. See textual note. Also, cf. "Bianca Among the Nightingales" (1862), stanza 11: "She had not reached him at my heart/With her fine tongue, as snakes indeed/Kill flies."

He bowed, we parted.
'Parted. Face no more,
Voice no more, love no more! wiped wholly out
Like some ill scholar's scrawl from heart and slate,[1] -
Ay, spit on and so wiped out utterly
By some coarse scholar! I have been too coarse,
Too human. Have we business, in our rank,
With blood i' the veins? I will have henceforth none,
Not even to keep the colour at my lip:
A rose is pink and pretty without blood,
Why not a woman? When we've played in vain
The game, to adore, - we have resources still,
And can play on at leisure, being adored:
Here's Smith already swearing at my feet
That I'm the typic[2] She. Away with Smith! -
Smith smacks of Leigh, - and henceforth I'll admit
No socialist within three crinolines,[3]
To live and have his being.[4] But for you,
Though insolent your letter and absurd,
And though I hate you frankly, - take my Smith!
For when you have seen this famous marriage tied,
A most unspotted Erle to a noble Leigh
(His love astray on one he should not love),
Howbeit you may not want his love, beware,
You'll want some comfort. So I leave you Smith,
Take Smith! - he talks Leigh's subjects, somewhat worse;
Adopts a thought of Leigh's, and dwindles it;
Goes leagues beyond, to be no inch behind;
Will mind you of him, as a shoe-string may
Of a man: and women, when they are made like you,
Grow tender to a shoe-string, footprint even,
Adore averted shoulders in a glass,
And memories of what, present once, was loathed.
And yet, you loathed not Romney, - though you played
At 'fox and goose'[5] about him with your soul;

1. Slate boards were used in schools as writing surfaces for exercises. Chalk was used and wiped off to make a "clean slate."
2. Typical, in the old sense; that is, the very type of womanhood.
3. Refers not to the cage crinoline, which was introduced in Paris only in the summer of 1856, but to the wide skirts worn before that date, which were supported with petticoats of crinoline, a stiff fabric made of horsehair and cotton thread. EBB herself did not adopt the cage crinoline until late in 1857. See *EBB: Letters to her Sister*, 287.
4. See Acts 17.27–28: ". . . they should seek God, in the hope that they might feel after him and find him. Yet he is not far from each one of us, for 'in him we live and move and have our being.' "
5. The board game of "fox and geese," played with seventeen pieces called geese and one fox. The business of the game is to surround the fox with geese so that he cannot move. But the fox can, under certain circumstances, take the geese, depleting the numbers so as to make it impossible to block the fox. See Joseph Strutt, *The Sports and Pastimes of the People of England*, a new edition much enlarged and corrected by J. Charles Cox (London, 1903), 258–59. The point of Lady Waldemar's remarks at lines 155–56 is that, according to the rules of

Pass over fox, you rub out fox, - ignore
A feeling, you eradicate it, - the act's
Identical.
'I wish you joy, Miss Leigh,
You've made a happy marriage for your friend,
And all the honour, well-assorted love,
Derives from you who love him, whom he loves!
You need not wish *me* joy to think of it;
I have so much. Observe, Aurora Leigh
Your droop of eyelid is the same as his,
And, but for you, I might have won his love,
And, to you, I have shown my naked heart;
For which three things, I hate, hate, hate you. Hush
Suppose a fourth! - I cannot choose but think
That, with him, I were virtuouser than you
Without him: so I hate you from this gulf
And hollow of my soul, which opens out
To what, except for you, had been my heaven,
And is, instead, a place to curse by! LOVE.'

An active kind of curse. I stood there cursed,
Confounded. I had seized and caught the sense
Of the letter, with its twenty stinging snakes,
In a moment's sweep of eyesight, and I stood
Dazed. - 'Ah! not married.'
'You mistake,' he said,
'I'm married. Is not Marian Erle my wife?
As God sees things, I have a wife and child;
And I, as I'm a man who honours God,
Am here to claim them as my child and wife.'

I felt it hard to breathe, much less to speak.
Nor word of mine was needed. Some one else
Was there for answering. 'Romney,' she began,
'My great good angel, Romney.'
Then at first,
I knew that Marian Erle was beautiful.
She stood there, still and pallid as a saint,
Dilated, like a saint in ecstasy,
As if the floating moonshine interposed
Betwixt her foot and the earth, and raised her up
To float upon it. 'I had left my child,
Who sleeps,' she said, 'and having drawn this way
I heard you speaking, . . friend! - Confirm me now.

the game, while it is permissible to "rub out" or take a goose, it is never possible to take the fox and remove him from the board. EBB quotes "the old game of fox and goose" several times in her letters. See *Letters of EBB* 1.230 and *RB/EBB Letters* 1.487, 584.

You take this Marian, such as wicked men
Have made her, for your honourable wife?'

The thrilling, solemn, proud, pathetic voice.
He stretched his arms out toward the thrilling voice,
As if to draw it on to his embrace.
- 'I take her as God made her, and as men
Must fail to unmake her, for my honoured wife.'

She never raised her eyes, nor took a step,
But stood there in her place, and spoke again.
- 'You take this Marian's child, which is her shame
In sight of men and women, for your child,
Of whom you will not ever feel ashamed?'

The thrilling, tender, proud, pathetic voice.
He stepped on toward it, still with outstretched arms,
As if to quench upon his breast that voice.
- 'May God so father me, as I do him,
And so forsake me, as I let him feel
He's orphaned haply. Here I take the child
To share my cup, to slumber on my knee,
To play his loudest gambol at my foot,
To hold my finger in the public ways,
Till none shall need inquire, 'Whose child is this,'
The gesture saying so tenderly, 'My own.' '

She stood a moment silent in her place;
Then turning toward me very slow and cold,
- 'And you, - what say you? - will you blame me much,
If, careful for that outcast child of mine,
I catch this hand that's stretched to me and him,
Nor dare to leave him friendless in the world
Where men have stoned me?[6] Have I not the right
To take so mere an aftermath[7] from life,
Else found so wholly bare? Or is it wrong
To let your cousin, for a generous bent,
Put out his ungloved fingers among briars
To set a tumbling bird's nest somewhat straight?
You will not tell him, though we're innocent,
We are not harmless, . . and that both our harms
Will stick to his good smooth noble life like burrs,
Never to drop off though he shakes the cloak?

6. Possibly a reference to the story of the woman taken in adultery who was condemned to die for sexual sin until saved by Jesus, who challenged the crowd, saying, "Let he who is without sin, cast the first stone." See John 8.3–11.
7. A second or later mowing (OED).

You've been my friend: you will not now be his?
You've known him that he's worthy of a friend,
And you're his cousin, lady, after all,
And therefore more than free to take his part,
Explaining, since the nest is surely spoilt
And Marian what you know her, - though a wife,
The world would hardly understand her case
Of being just hurt and honest; while for him,
'Twould ever twit him with his bastard child
And married harlot. Speak, while yet there's time:
You would not stand and let a good man's dog
Turn round and rend him, because his, and reared
Of a generous breed, - and will you let his act,
Because it's generous? Speak. I'm bound to you,
And I'll be bound by only you, in this.'

The thrilling solemn voice, so passionless,
Sustained, yet low, without a rise or fall,
As one who had authority to speak,
And not as Marian.
I looked up to feel
If God stood near me, and beheld his heaven
As blue as Aaron's priestly robe appeared
To Aaron when he took it off to die.[8]
And then I spoke - 'Accept the gift, I say,
My sister Marian, and be satisfied.
The hand that gives, has still a soul behind
Which will not let it quail for having given,
Though foolish worldlings talk they know not what
Of what they know not. Romney's strong enough
For this: do you be strong to know he's strong:
He stands on Right's side; never flinch for him,
As if he stood on the other. You'll be bound
By me? I am a woman of repute;
No fly-blow gossip ever specked my life;
My name is clean and open as this hand,
Whose glove there's not a man dares blab about
As if he had touched it freely. Here's my hand
To clasp your hand, my Marian, owned as pure!
As pure, - as I'm a woman and a Leigh! -
And, as I'm both, I'll witness to the world
That Romney Leigh is honoured in his choice
Who chooses Marian for his honoured wife.'

8. Exodus 28.31: "And thou shalt make the robe of the ephod all of blue." Numbers 20.26: "And strip Aaron of his garments, and put them upon Eleazar his son: and Aaron shall be gathered unto his people, and shall die there." Aaron's implied regret is EBB's invention.

Her broad wild woodland eyes shot out a light,
Her smile was wonderful for rapture. 'Thanks,
My great Aurora.' Forward then she sprang,
And dropping her impassioned spaniel head
With all its brown abandonment of curls[9]
On Romney's feet, we heard the kisses drawn
Through sobs upon the foot, upon the ground -
'O Romney! O my angel! O unchanged,
Though since we've parted I have past the grave!
But Death itself could only better *thee*,
Not change thee! - *Thee* I do not thank at all:
I but thank God who made thee what thou art,
So wholly godlike.'
When he tried in vain
To raise her to his embrace, escaping thence
As any leaping fawn from a huntsman's grasp,
She bounded off and 'lighted beyond reach,
Before him, with a staglike majesty
Of soft, serene defiance, - as she knew
He could not touch her, so was tolerant
He had cared to try. She stood there with her great
Drowned eyes, and dripping cheeks, and strange sweet smile
That lived through all, as if one held a light
Across a waste of waters, - shook her head
To keep some thoughts down deeper in her soul, -
Then, white and tranquil like a summer-cloud
Which, having rained itself to a tardy peace,
Stands still in heaven as if it ruled the day,
Spoke out again - 'Although, my generous friend,
Since last we met and parted you're unchanged,
And, having promised faith to Marian Erle,
Maintain it, as she were not changed at all;
And though that's worthy, though that's full of balm
To any conscious spirit of a girl
Who once has loved you as I loved you once, -
Yet still it will not make her . . if she's dead,
And gone away where none can give or take
In marriage,[1] - able to revive, return
And wed you, - will it, Romney? Here's the point;
My friend, we'll see it plainer: you and I
Must never, never, never join hands so.
Nay, let me say it, - for I said it first
To God, and placed it, rounded to an oath,

9. This is another clear of example of how Marian's appearance is based on EBB's own. See notes to *Aurora Leigh* 3.810–23, and see also EBB's two poems on her spaniel, Flush, "To Flush, My Dog" (1843) and "Flush or Faunus" (1850).
1. Matthew 22.30, Mark 12.35, and Luke 20.35.

Far, far above the moon there, at His feet,
As surely as I wept just now at yours, -
We never, never, never join hands so.
And now, be patient with me; do not think
I'm speaking from a false humility.
The truth is, I am grown so proud with grief,
And He has said so often through his nights
And through his mornings, 'Weep a little still,
'Thou foolish Marian, because women must,
'But do not blush at all except for sin,' -
That I, who felt myself unworthy once
Of virtuous Romney and his high-born race,
Have come to learn, - a woman, poor or rich,
Despised or honoured, is a human soul,
And what her soul is, that, she is herself,[2]
Although she should be spit upon of men,
As is the pavement of the churches here,[3]
Still good enough to pray in. And being chaste
And honest, and inclined to do the right,
And love the truth, and live my life out green
And smooth beneath his steps, I should not fear
To make him thus a less uneasy time
Than many a happier woman. Very proud
You see me. Pardon, that I set a trap
To hear a confirmation in your voice,
Both yours and yours. It is so good to know
'Twas really God who said the same before;
And thus it is in heaven, that first God speaks,
And then his angels. Oh, it does me good,
It wipes me clean and sweet from devil's dirt,
That Romney Leigh should think me worthy still
Of being his true and honourable wife!
Henceforth I need not say, on leaving earth,
I had no glory in it. For the rest,
The reason's ready (master, angel, friend,
Be patient with me) wherefore you and I
Can never, never, never join hands so.
I know you'll not be angry like a man
(For *you* are none) when I shall tell the truth,
Which is, I do not love you, Romney Leigh,
I do not love you. Ah well! catch my hands,
Miss Leigh, and burn into my eyes with yours, -
I swear I do not love him. Did I once?

2. Cf. EBB to Sarianna Browning, November 1856: "Marian had to be dragged through the uttermost debasement of circumstances to arrive at the sentiment of personal dignity" (*Letters of EBB* 2.242).

3. As far as the British were concerned, spitting was regarded as a nasty Continental (and American) habit.

'Tis said that women have been bruised to death
And yet, if once they loved, that love of theirs
Could never be drained out with all their blood:
I've heard such things and pondered. Did I indeed
Love once; or did I only worship? Yes,
Perhaps, O friend, I set you up so high
Above all actual good or hope of good
Or fear of evil, all that could be mine,
I haply set you above love itself,
And out of reach of these poor woman's arms,
Angelic Romney. What was in my thought?
To be your slave, your help, your toy, your tool.
To be your love . . I never thought of that:
To give you love . . still less. I gave you love?
I think I did not give you anything;
I was but only yours, - upon my knees,
All yours, in soul and body, in head and heart,
A creature you had taken from the ground
Still crumbling through your fingers to your feet
To join the dust she came from. Did I love,
Or did I worship? judge, Aurora Leigh!
But, if indeed I loved, 'twas long ago, -
So long! before the sun and moon were made,
Before the hells were open, - ah, before
I heard my child cry in the desert night,
And knew he had no father. It may be
I'm not as strong as other women are,
Who, torn and crushed, are not undone from love.
It may be I am colder than the dead,
Who, being dead, love always. But for me,
Once killed, this ghost of Marian loves no more,
No more . . except the child! . . no more at all.
I told your cousin, sir, that I was dead;
And now, she thinks I'll get up from my grave,
And wear my chin-cloth[4] for a wedding-veil,
And glide along the churchyard like a bride
While all the dead keep whispering through the withes,[5]
'You would be better in your place with us,
'You pitiful corruption!' At the thought,
The damps break out on me like leprosy
Although I'm clean. Ay, clean as Marian Erle!
As Marian Leigh, I know, I were not clean:
Nor have I so much life that I should love,
Except the child. Ah God! I could not bear
To see my darling on a good man's knees,

4. Winding sheet, or shroud.
5. Dialect word meaning "willow." See OED.

And know, by such a look, or such a sigh,
Or such a silence, that he thought sometimes,
'This child was fathered by some cursed wretch' . .
For, Romney, - angels are less tender-wise
Than God and mothers: even *you* would think
What *we* think never. He is ours, the child;
And we would sooner vex a soul in heaven
By coupling with it the dead body's thought,
It left behind it in a last month's grave,
Than, in my child, see other than . . my child.
We only, never call him fatherless
Who has God and his mother. O my babe,
My pretty, pretty blossom, an ill-wind
Once blew upon my breast! can any think
I'd have another, - one called happier,
A fathered child, with father's love and race
That's worn as bold and open as a smile,
To vex my darling when he's asked his name
And has no answer? What! a happier child
Than mine, my best, - who laughed so loud to-night
He could not sleep for pastime? Nay, I swear
By life and love, that, if I lived like some,
And loved like . . *some*, ay, loved you, Romney Leigh,
As some love, (eyes that have wept so much, see clear,)
I've room for no more children in my arms,
My kisses are all melted on one mouth,
I would not push my darling to a stool
To dandle babies. Here's a hand shall keep
For ever clean without a marriage-ring,
To tend my boy until he cease to need
One steadying finger of it, and desert
(Not miss) his mother's lap, to sit with men.
And when I miss him (not he me) I'll come
And say, 'Now give me some of Romney's work,
To help your outcast orphans of the world
And comfort grief with grief.' For you, meantime,
Most noble Romney, wed a noble wife,
And open on each other your great souls, -
I need not farther bless you. If I dared
But strain and touch her in her upper sphere
And say, 'Come down to Romney - pay my debt!'
I should be joyful with the stream of joy
Sent through me. But the moon is in my face . .
I dare not, - though I guess the name he loves,
I'm learned with my studies of old days,
Remembering how he crushed his under-lip
When some one came and spoke, or did not come:

Aurora, I could touch her with my hand,
And fly because I dare not.'
She was gone.
He smiled so sternly that I spoke in haste.
'Forgive her - she sees clearly for herself:
Her instinct's holy.'
'*I* forgive!' he said,
'I only marvel how she sees so sure,
While others' . . there he paused, - then hoarse, abrupt, -
'Aurora! you forgive us, her and me!
For her, the thing she sees, poor loyal child,
If once corrected by the thing I know,
Had been unspoken, since she loves you well,
Has leave to love you: - while for me, alas,
If once or twice I let my heart escape
This night, . . remember, where hearts slip and fall
They break beside: we're parting, - parting, - ah,
You do not love, that you should surely know
What that word means. Forgive, be tolerant;
It had not been, but that I felt myself
So safe in impuissance[6] and despair,
I could not hurt you though I tossed my arms
And sighed my soul out. The most utter wretch
Will choose his postures when he comes to die,
However in the presence of a queen;
And you'll forgive me some unseemly spasms
Which meant no more than dying. Do you think
I had ever come here in my perfect mind,
Unless I had come here in my settled mind
Bound Marian's, bound to keep the bond and give
My name, my house, my hand, the things I could,
To Marian? For even *I* could give as much:
Even I, affronting her exalted soul
By a supposition that she wanted these,
Could act the husband's coat and hat set up
To creak i' the wind and drive the world-crows off
From pecking in her garden. Straw can fill
A hole to keep out vermin. Now, at last,
I own heaven's angels round her life suffice
To fight the rats of our society,
Without this Romney: I can see it at last;
And here is ended my pretension which
The most pretended. Over-proud of course,
Even so! - but not so stupid . . blind . . that I,

6. Impotence, powerlessness, the OED notes, "[b]y the Brownings stressed impu'i•ssance." This instance is the only example of EBB's use of the word in her poetry. See *An Elizabeth Barrett Browning Concordance*, comp. Gladys W. Hudson (Detroit, 1973).

Whom thus the great Taskmaster of the world
Has set to meditate mistaken work,
My dreary face against a dim blank wall
Throughout man's natural lifetime, - could pretend
Or wish . . O love, I have loved you! O my soul,
I have lost you! - but I swear by all yourself,
And all you might have been to me these years
If that June-morning had not failed my hope, -
I'm not so bestial, to regret that day
This night, - this night, which still to you is fair!
Nay, not so blind, Aurora. I attest
Those stars above us which I cannot see . . .'

'You cannot' . .
'That if Heaven itself should stoop,
Remix the lots, and give me another chance,
I'd say, 'No other!' - I'd record my blank.
Aurora never should be wife of mine.'

'Not see the stars!'
' 'Tis worse still, not to see
To find your hand, although we're parting, dear.
A moment let me hold it ere we part;
And understand my last words - these, at last!
I would not have you thinking when I'm gone
That Romney dared to hanker for your love
In thought or vision, if attainable,
(Which certainly for me it never was)
And wished to use it for a dog to-day
To help the blind man stumbling. God forbid!
And now I know He held you in his palm,
And kept you open-eyed to all my faults,
To save you at last from such a dreary end.
Believe me, dear, that, if I had known like Him
What loss was coming on me, I had done
As well in this as He has. - Farewell you
Who are still my light, - farewell! How late it is:
I know that, now. You've been too patient, sweet.
I will but blow my whistle toward the lane,
And some one comes, - the same who brought me here.
Get in - Good-night.'
'A moment. Heavenly Christ!
A moment. Speak once, Romney. 'Tis not true.
I hold your hands, I look into your face -
You see me?'
'No more than the blessed stars.
Be blessed too, Aurora. Nay, my sweet,

You tremble. Tender-hearted! Do you mind
Of yore, dear, how you used to cheat old John,
And let the mice out slily from his traps,
Until he marvelled at the soul in mice
Which took the cheese and left the snare? The same
Dear soft heart always! 'Twas for this I grieved
Howe's letter never reached you. Ah, you had heard
Of illness, - not the issue, not the extent:
My life long sick with tossings up and down,
The sudden revulsion in the blazing house,
The strain and struggle both of body and soul,
Which left fire running in my veins for blood:
Scarce lacked that thunderbolt of the falling beam
Which nicked me on the forehead as I passed
The gallery-door with a burden. Say heaven's bolt,
Not William Erle's, not Marian's father's, - tramp
And poacher, whom I found for what he was,
And eager for her sake to rescue him,
Forth swept from the open highway of the world,
Road-dust and all, - till, like a woodland boar
Most naturally unwilling to be tamed,
He notched me with his tooth.[7] But not a word
To Marian! and I do not think, besides,
He turned the tilting of the beam my way, -
And if he laughed, as many swear, poor wretch,
Nor he nor I supposed the hurt so deep.
We'll hope his next laugh may be merrier,
In a better cause.'

'Blind, Romney?'[8]

'Ah, my friend,

You'll learn to say it in a cheerful voice.

7. An allusion to Aeschylus' *Agamemnon*, 717–36: "a man reared in his house a lion's whelp, robbed of its mother's milk yet still desiring the breast. Gentle it was in the prelude of its life, kindly to children, and a delight to the old. . . . But brought to full growth by time it showed forth the nature it had drawn from its parents. Unbidden, in requital for its fostering, it prepared a feast with ruinous slaughter of the flocks. . . ." (Loeb translation).

The same story, with its emphasis on the reemergence of the natural character of the beast, occurs in Samuel Richardson's *Clarissa* (1747–48): "A lady took a great fancy to a young lion, or a bear, I forget which—but a bear, or a tiger I believe it was. It was made her a present of when a whelp. She fed it with her own hand: she nursed up the wicked cub with great tenderness . . . at last, somehow, neglecting to satisfy its hungry maw, or having otherwise disobliged it on some occasion, it resumed its nature; and on a sudden fell upon her, and tore her in pieces . . ." ([London, 1978], 3.206).

8. Soon after the first publication of *Aurora Leigh*, EBB's friend Anna Jameson remarked on the similarity of the circumstances of Romney's blinding to the denouement of Charlotte Bronte's *Jane Eyre* (1847); see EBB to Anna Jameson December 26, 1856, *Letters of EBB* 2.245–46. EBB said that she had forgotten the events of *Jane Eyre*, but the resemblance was noticed by other contemporaries. See William Bell Scott to William Michael Rossetti, December 22, 1856, *Ruskin: Rossetti: Pre-Raphaelitism: Papers, 1854–1862*, ed. William Michael Rossetti (London 1899), 147. At least one contemporary reviewer (quite probably George Eliot), regretted the current fashion for mutilating heroes; see *The Westminster Review* (January 1857): 306–10.

I, too, at first desponded. To be blind,
Turned out of nature, mulcted[9] as a man,
Refused the daily largesse of the sun
To humble creatures! When the fever's heat
Dropped from me, as the flame did from my house,
And left me ruined like it, stripped of all
The hues and shapes of aspectable[1] life,
A mere bare blind stone in the blaze of day,
A man, upon the outside of the earth,
As dark as ten feet under, in the grave, -
Why that seemed hard.'
'No hope?'
'A tear! you weep,
Divine Aurora? tears upon my hand!
I've seen you weeping for a mouse, a bird, -
But, weep for me, Aurora? Yes, there's hope.
Not hope of sight, - I could be learned, dear,
And tell you in what Greek and Latin name
The visual nerve is withered to the root,
Though the outer eyes appear indifferent,
Unspotted in their crystals.[2] But there's hope.
The spirit, from behind this dethroned sense,
Sees, waits in patience till the walls break up
From which the bas-relief and fresco[3] have dropt:
There's hope. The man here, once so arrogant
And restless, so ambitious, for his part,
Of dealing with statistically packed
Disorders (from a pattern on his nail),
And packing such things quite another way, -
Is now contented. From his personal loss
He has come to hope for others when they lose,
And wear a gladder faith in what we gain . .
Through bitter experience, compensation sweet,

9. Deprived, punished by having something taken away, made less.
1. See note to *Aurora Leigh* 5.627.
2. EBB's account of Romney's blindness: "the only injury received by Romney in the fire was from a blow and from the emotion produced by the *circumstances* of the fire. Not only did he *not* lose his eyes in the fire, but he describes the ruin of his house as no blind man could. He was standing there, a spectator. Afterwards he had a fever, and the eyes, the visual nerve, perished, showing no external strain—perished as Milton's did. I believe that a great shock on the nerves might produce such an effect in certain constitutions. . . . For it was necessary, I thought, to the bringing-out of my thought, that Romney should be mulcted in his natural sight . . ." (EBB to Anna Jameson, December 26, 1856, *Letters of EBB* 2.246. See also John Milton, "To Mr. Cyriack Skinner upon His Blindness" (1694), lines 1–3: "Cyriack, this three years day these eys, though clear/To outward view, of blemish or of spot;/Bereft of light thir seeing have forgot."
3. A bas-relief is a raised frieze that has a three-dimensional texturelike sculpture. A fresco is another kind of wall decoration, where the paint is applied directly and "fresh" to the plaster of the walls. The metaphor that Romney uses here takes the idea of the body as the walls of a house that encompasses the spirit, and the sense of seeing as the visual art that decorates and enhances the physical life.

Like that tear, sweetest. I am quiet now,
As tender surely for the suffering world,
But quiet, - sitting at the wall to learn,[4]
Content henceforth to do the thing I can:
For, though as powerless, said I, as a stone,
A stone can still give shelter to a worm,
And it is worth while being a stone for that:
There's hope, Aurora.'
'Is there hope for me?
For me? - and is there room beneath the stone
For such a worm? - And if I came and said . .
What all this weeping scarce will let me say,
And yet what women cannot say at all
But weeping bitterly . . (the pride keeps up,
Until the heart breaks under it) . . I love, -
I love you, Romney' . . .
'Silence!' he exclaimed.
'A woman's pity sometimes makes her mad.
A man's distraction must not cheat his soul
To take advantage of it. Yet, 'tis hard -
Farewell, Aurora.'
'But I love you, sir;
And when a woman says she loves a man,
The man must hear her, though he love her not,
Which . . hush! . . he has leave to answer in his turn;
She will not surely blame him. As for me,
You call it pity, - think I'm generous?
'Twere somewhat easier, for a woman proud
As I am, and I'm very vilely proud,
To let it pass as such, and press on you
Love born of pity, - seeing that excellent loves
Are born so, often, nor the quicklier die, -
And this would set me higher by the head
Than now I stand. No matter: let the truth
Stand high; Aurora must be humble: no,
My love's not pity merely. Obviously
I'm not a generous woman, never was,
Or else, of old, I had not looked so near
To weights and measures, grudging you the power
To give, as first I scorned your power to judge
For me, Aurora. I would have no gifts
Forsooth, but God's, - and I would use *them* too
According to my pleasure and my choice,

4. Possibly a reminiscence of 2 Kings 20.1–2: "In those days Hezekiah became sick and was at the point of death. And Isaiah the Prophet the son of Amoz came to him, and said to him, 'Thus says the Lord, "Set your house in order; for you shall die, you shall die, you shall not recover." ' Then Hezekiah turned his face to the wall. . . ."

As He and I were equals, you below,
Excluded from that level of interchange
Admitting benefaction. You were wrong
In much? you said so. I was wrong in most.
Oh, most! You only thought to rescue men
By half-means, half-way, seeing half their wants,
While thinking nothing of your personal gain.
But I who saw the human nature broad
At both sides, comprehending too the soul's,
And all the high necessities of Art,
Betrayed the thing I saw, and wronged my own life
For which I pleaded. Passioned to exalt
The artist's instinct in me at the cost
Of putting down the woman's, I forgot
No perfect artist is developed here
From any imperfect woman. Flower from root,
And spiritual from natural, grade by grade
In all our life. A handful of the earth
To make God's image![5] the despised poor earth,
The healthy odorous earth, - I missed with it
The divine Breath that blows the nostrils out
To ineffable inflatus,[6] - ay, the breath
Which love is. Art is much, but love is more.
O Art, my Art, thou'rt much, but Love is more!
Art symbolises heaven, but Love is God
And makes heaven. I, Aurora, fell from mine.
I would not be a woman like the rest,
A simple woman who believes in love
And owns the right of love because she loves,
And, hearing she's beloved, is satisfied
With what contents God: I must analyse,
Confront, and question; just as if a fly
Refused to warm itself in any sun
Till such was *in leone:*[7] I must fret
Forsooth because the month was only May
Be faithless of the kind of proffered love,
And captious,[8] lest it miss my dignity,
And scornful, that my lover sought a wife
To use . . to use! O Romney, O my love,
I am changed since then, changed wholly, - for indeed
If now you'd stoop so low to take my love
And use it roughly, without stint or spare,
As men use common things with more behind,
(And, in this, ever would be more behind)

5. See Genesis 1.26–27 and 2.7.
6. Breathing out, but with the same sense as "inspiration."
7. The zodiacal constellation entered by the sun toward the end of July.
8. Fault-finding, quibbling.

To any mean and ordinary end, -
The joy would set me like a star in heaven,
So high up, I should shine because of height
And not of virtue. Yet in one respect,
Just one, beloved, I am in no wise changed:
I love you, loved you . . loved you first and last,
And love you on for ever. Now I know
I loved you always, Romney. She who died[9]
Knew that, and said so; Lady Waldemar
Knows that; . . and Marian. I had known the same,
Except that I was prouder than I knew,
And not so honest. Ay, and, as I live,
I should have died so, crushing in my hand
This rose of love, the wasp inside and all,
Ignoring ever to my soul and you
Both rose and pain, except for this great loss,
This great despair, - to stand before your face
And know you do not see me where I stand.
You think, perhaps, I am not changed from pride,
And that I chiefly bear to say such words,
Because you cannot shame me with your eyes?
O calm, grand eyes, extinguished in a storm,
Blown out like lights o'er melancholy seas,
Though shrieked for by the shipwrecked, - O my Dark,
My Cloud, - to go before me every day[1]
While I go ever toward the wilderness, -
I would that you could see me bare to the soul!
If this be pity, 'tis so for myself,
And not for Romney! *he* can stand alone;
A man like *him* is never overcome:
No woman like me, counts him pitiable
While saints applaud him. He mistook the world;
But I mistook my own heart, and that slip
Was fatal. Romney, - will you leave me here?
So wrong, so proud, so weak, so unconsoled,
So mere a woman! - and I love you so,
I love you, Romney -'
Could I see his face,
I wept so? Did I drop against his breast,
Or did his arms constrain me? were my cheeks
Hot, overflooded, with my tears, or his?
And which of our two large explosive hearts
So shook me? That, I know not. There were words

9. Aurora's aunt.
1. Exodus 13.21: "And the Lord went before them by day in a pillar of cloud, to lead them the way." Refers to the wandering of the Israelites in the wilderness while God led them to the Promised Land.

That broke in utterance . . melted, in the fire, -
Embrace, that was convulsion, . . then a kiss
As long and silent as the ecstatic night,
And deep, deep, shuddering breaths, which meant beyond
Whatever could be told by word or kiss.

But what he said . . I have written day by day,
With somewhat even writing.[2] Did I think
That such a passionate rain would intercept
And dash this last page? What he said, indeed,
I fain would write it down here like the rest,
To keep it in my eyes, as in my ears,
The heart's sweet scripture, to be read at night
When weary, or at morning when afraid,
And lean my heaviest oath on when I swear
That, when all's done, all tried, all counted here,
All great arts, and all good philosophies,
This love just puts its hand out in a dream
And straight outreaches all things.
What he said,
I fain would write. But if an angel spoke
In thunder,[3] should we haply know much more
Than that it thundered? If a cloud came down
And wrapt us wholly,[4] could we draw its shape,
As if on the outside and not overcome?
And so he spake. His breath against my face
Confused his words, yet made them more intense.
(As when the sudden finger of the wind
Will wipe a row of single city-lamps
To a pure white line of flame, more luminous
Because of obliteration) more intense,
The intimate presence carrying in itself
Complete communication, as with souls
Who, having put the body off, perceive
Through simply being. Thus, 'twas granted me
To know he loved me to the depth and height
Of such large natures,[5] ever competent,
With grand horizons by the sea or land,
To love's grand sunrise. Small spheres hold small fires
But he loved largely, as a man can love
Who, baffled in his love, dares live his life,

2. Another explanation of the narrative method employed in *Aurora Leigh* from book 5 onward, when Aurora writes her experiences soon after the event in a journal form.
3. Revelation 10.3.
4. Revelation 10.1: "And I saw another mighty angel came down from heaven, clothed with a cloud."
5. Cf. EBB's *Sonnets from the Portuguese* 43 (1850), 1–3: "How do I love thee? Let me count the ways./I love thee to the depth and breadth and height/My soul can reach, when feeling out of sight/For the ends of Being and ideal Grace" (*Poetical Works of EBB*, 223).

Accept the ends which God loves, for his own,
And lift a constant aspect.
From the day
I brought to England my poor searching face,
(An orphan even of my father's grave)
He had loved me, watched me, watched his soul in mine,
Which in me grew and heightened into love.
For he, a boy still, had been told the tale
Of how a fairy bride from Italy
With smells of oleanders[6] in her hair,
Was coming through the vines to touch his hand;[7]
Whereat the blood of boyhood on the palm
Made sudden heats. And when at last I came,
And lived before him, lived, and rarely smiled,
He smiled and loved me for the thing I was,
As every child will love the year's first flower
(Not certainly the fairest of the year,
But, in which, the complete year seems to blow)
The poor sad snowdrop, - growing between drifts,
Mysterious medium 'twixt the plant and frost,
So faint with winter while so quick with spring,
And doubtful if to thaw itself away
With that snow near it. Not that Romney Leigh
Had loved me coldly. If I thought so once,
It was as if I had held my hand in fire
And shook for cold.[8] But now I understood
For ever, that the very fire and heat
Of troubling passion in him burned him clear,
And shaped, to dubious order, word and act:
That, just because he loved me over all,
All wealth, all lands, all social privilege,
To which chance made him unexpected heir,
And, just because on all these lesser gifts,
Constrained by conscience and the sense of wrong
He had stamped with steady hand God's arrow-mark
Of dedication to the human need,
He thought it should be so too, with his love.
He, passionately loving, would bring down
His love, his life, his best, (because the best)
His bride of dreams, who walked so still and high

6. An evergreen plant with thin olive-colored leaves and gaudy strong-smelling flowers that is a native of Italy and flourishes there in wild and cultivated situations.
7. Romney's romance of fateful destiny governing the lives of Aurora and Romney might owe something to the similar fateful union in Tennyson's *Maud* (1855). See *Maud* 1.17. See also note to *Aurora Leigh* 2.626. EBB heard Tennyson read Maud aloud while she was staying in London in October 1855. At that time she had not written this last section of *Aurora Leigh* but had only worked on her first draft, which ends at 9.608.
8. Cf. Shakespeare's *Richard II*, 1.3.294–95: "O! who can hold a fire in his hand/By thinking on the frosty Caucasus?"

Through flowery poems as through meadow-grass,
The dust of golden lilies on her feet,
That *she* should walk beside him on the rocks
In all that clang and hewing out of men,
And help the work of help which was his life,
And prove he kept back nothing, - not his soul.
And when I failed him, - for I failed him, I, -
And when it seemed he had missed my love, he thought
'Aurora makes room for a working-noon,'
And so, self-girded with torn strips of hope,
Took up his life as if it were for death
(Just capable of one heroic aim,)
And threw it in the thickest of the world, -
At which men laughed as if he had drowned a dog.
No wonder, - since Aurora failed him first!
The morning and the evening made his day.

But oh, the night! oh, bitter-sweet! oh, sweet!
O dark, O moon and stars, O ecstasy
Of darkness! O great mystery of love,
In which absorbed, loss, anguish, treason's self
Enlarges rapture, - as a pebble dropt
In some full wine-cup over-brims the wine!
While we two sate together, leaned that night
So close my very garments crept and thrilled
With strange electric life, and both my cheeks
Grew red, then pale, with touches from my hair
In which his breath was, - while the golden moon
Was hung before our faces as the badge
Of some sublime inherited despair,
Since ever to be seen by only one, -
A voice said, low and rapid as a sigh,
Yet breaking, I felt conscious, from a smile,
'Thank God, who made me blind, to make me see!
Shine on, Aurora, dearest light of souls,
Which rul'st for evermore both day and night!
I am happy.'
I flung closer to his breast,
As sword that, after battle, flings to sheath;
And, in that hurtle of united souls,
The mystic motions which in common moods
Are shut beyond our sense, broke in on us,
And, as we sate, we felt the old earth spin,
And all the starry turbulence of worlds
Swing round us in their audient[9] circles, till,

9. Listening.

If that same golden moon were overhead
Or if beneath our feet, we did not know.

And then calm, equal, smooth with weights of joy,
His voice rose, as some chief musician's song
Amid the old Jewish temple's Selah-pause,[1]
And bade me mark how we two met at last
Upon this moon-bathed promontory of earth,
To give up much on each side, then take all.
'Beloved,' it sang, 'we must be here to work;
And men who work can only work for men,
And, not to work in vain, must comprehend
Humanity and so work humanly,
And raise men's bodies still by raising souls,
As God did first.'
'But stand upon the earth,'
I said, 'to raise them, (this is human too,
There's nothing high which has not first been low,
My humbleness, said One, has made me great!)[2]
As God did last.'
'And work all silently
And simply,' he returned, 'as God does all;
Distort our nature never for our work,
Nor count our right hands stronger for being hoofs.
The man most man, with tenderest human hands,
Works best for men, - as God in Nazareth.'[3]

He paused upon the word, and then resumed;
'Fewer programmes, we who have no prescience.
Fewer systems, we who are held and do not hold.
Less mapping out of masses to be saved,
By nations or by sexes. Fourier's void,
And Comte absurd, - and Cabet,[4] puerile.

1. See EBB's *Essay on Mind* (1826), line 1229: "Then comes the *Selah!* and the voice is hushed." EBB added a note to the *Essay on Mind* in which she quotes Augustin Calmet (1672–1757): "one conjecture is, that it means the end or a pause, and that the ancient musicians put it occasionally in the margin of their psalters, to shew where a musical pause was to be made, and where the tune ended." EBB's information came from Calmet's *Dictionaire historique, critique . . . de la Bible* (Paris, 1722–28). See *Calmet's Dictionary of the Holy Bible* . . . (C. Taylor: London, 1823), vol. 2, under "Selah."
2. Matthew 18.4: "Whosoever therefore shall humble himself as this little child, the same is greatest in the kingdom of heaven."
3. Although born in Bethlehem, Jesus grew up in Nazareth and lived there till the age of thirty.
4. Etienne Cabet (1788–1856), French socialist and republican. Cabet took part in the revolution of 1830 and held public office under Louis-Philippe until he published his *Histoire populaire de la révolution Française de 1789 à 1830* (1830–49), which criticized the conservatism of the government. As an exile in England, he became an ardent disciple of Robert Owen (1771–1858) and published *Voyage en Icarie* (1840), a socialist romance that found favor with French radicals. Supported by Owen, Cabet purchased some land in America on the Red River in Texas and, in 1848, some fifteen hundred "Icarians" set out to put Cabet's theories into practice. In 1849 Cabet joined the settlement and moved it to Nauvoo in Illinois. His dictatorial

Subsist no rules of life outside of life,
No perfect manners, without Christian souls:
The Christ himself had been no Lawgiver
Unless He had given the life, too, with the law.'[5]

I echoed thoughtfully - 'The man, most man,
Works best for men, and, if most man indeed,
He gets his manhood plainest from his soul:
While obviously this stringent[6] soul itself
Obeys the old law of development,
The Spirit ever witnessing in ours,
And Love, the soul of soul, within the soul,
Evolving it sublimely. First, God's love.'

'And next,' he smiled, 'the love of wedded souls,[7]
Which still presents that mystery's counterpart.
Sweet shadow-rose, upon the water of life,
Of such a mystic substance, Sharon gave
A name to![8] human, vital, fructuous rose,
Whose calyx holds the multitude of leaves,
Loves filial, loves fraternal, neighbour-loves
And civic - all fair petals, all good scents,
All reddened, sweetened from one central Heart!'

'Alas,' I cried, 'it was not long ago,
You swore this very social rose smelt ill.'

'Alas,' he answered, 'is it a rose at all?
The filial's thankless, the fraternal's hard,
The rest is lost. I do but stand and think,

---

methods led eventually to his expulsion from the colony in 1856. As might be expected, EBB was not sympathetic to Cabet's political views and particularly condemned the control of the press that he advocated: "the suppression of all journals except one in the right sense, being, according to Cabet, a condition of a perfectly 'free state,' " (*EBB to Mrs. Ogilvy*, 73); Isidore August Marie François Xavier Comte (1798–1857), positivist philosopher, whose major works were the *Course of Positive Philosophy* (1830–42) and the *System of Positive Polity* (1851–54). See EBB to Fanny Haworth, February 12, 1854: "As to Comte and his translations, a thinker who will not receive the notion of God as a probability, throws me off at once—I have no sympathy with him or his." See *Checklist* 54.32, quote from Kenyon Typescript. In the autumn of 1858, EBB met Richard Congreve, a disciple of Comte's and his executor, who explained Comte's philosophy to her and remonstrated with her on Aurora Leigh's "disrespect" for the philosopher. EBB, however, remained unimpressed, finding humanism insufficient excuse for atheism (EBB to Anna Jameson, October 5, 1858; see *Checklist* 58.115). Congreve seems to have done more harm than good, for in revising *Aurora Leigh* for the fourth edition, a task begun in November 1858, EBB altered her first edition description of Comte as "dwarfed," to "absurd" (see textual note).

5. Isaiah 33.22: "For the Lord is our judge, the Lord is our lawgiver, the Lord is our king; he will save us." See also Matthew 22.36–40 and John 15.12–13.
6. Rigorous, strict, convincing.
7. Cf. Milton, *Paradise Lost*, 4.750–53: "Hail, wedded love, mysterious law, true source/Of human offspring, sole propriety/In Paradise of all things common else."
8. Song of Solomon 2.1.

Across the waters of a troubled life
This Flower of Heaven so vainly overhangs,
What perfect counterpart would be in sight
If tanks were clearer. Let us clean the tubes,
And wait for rains.[9] O poet, O my love,
Since *I* was too ambitious in my deed
And thought to distance all men in success,
(Till God came on me, marked the place and said,
'Ill-doer, henceforth keep within this line,
Attempting less than others,' - and I stand
And work among Christ's little ones, content,)
Come thou, my compensation, my dear sight,
My morning-star, my morning,[1] - rise and shine,
And touch my hills with radiance not their own.
Shine out for two, Aurora, and fulfil
My falling-short that must be! work for two,
As I, though thus restrained, for two, shall love![2]
Gaze on, with inscient[3] vision toward the sun,
And, from his visceral heat, pluck out the roots
Of light beyond him. Art's a service - mark:
A silver key is given to thy clasp,
And thou shalt stand unwearied, night and day,
And fix it in the hard, slow-turning wards,[4]
To open, so, that intermediate door
Betwixt the different planes of sensuous form
And form insensuous, that inferior men
May learn to feel on still through these to those,
And bless thy ministration. The world waits
For help. Beloved, let us love so well,
Our work shall still be better for our love,
And still our love be sweeter for our work,
And both commended, for the sake of each,
By all true workers and true lovers born.
Now press the clarion on thy woman's lip
(Love's holy kiss shall still keep consecrate)
And breathe thy fine keen breath along the brass,
And blow all class-walls level as Jericho's

9. Compare *Casa Guidi Windows* (1851) 2.761–64: "And be God's witness that the elemental/ New springs of life are gushing everywhere/To cleanse the water-courses, and prevent all/ Concrete obstructions which infest the air."
1. A play on Aurora's name, which means the dawn.
2. Romney here reverses the nineteenth-century conventions of activities associated with the constructions of gender; the woman will work rather than love, and the man will love instead of work. Another example of the bold way in which *Aurora Leigh* challenged contemporary expectations.
3. Having inward knowledge or insight. According to the OED this sense of the word is rare, and the only quotation cited is *Aurora Leigh*. The more usual meaning of the word is "ignorant."
4. The ridges projecting from the inside plate of a lock and the incisions in the key that correspond to the wards to lock.

Past Jordan,[5] - crying from the top of souls,
To souls, that, here assembled on earth's flats,
They get them to some purer eminence
Than any hitherto beheld for clouds!
What height we know not, - but the way we know,
And how by mounting ever, we attain,
And so climb on. It is the hour for souls,
That bodies, leavened by the will and love,
Be lightened to redemption. The world's old,
But the old world waits the time to be renewed,
Toward which, new hearts in individual growth
Must quicken, and increase to multitude
In new dynasties of the race of men;[6]
Developed whence, shall grow spontaneously
New churches, new œconomies, new laws
Admitting freedom, new societies
Excluding falsehood: HE shall make all new.'

My Romney! - Lifting up my hand in his,
As wheeled by Seeing spirits toward the east,
He turned instinctively, where, faint and far,
Along the tingling desert of the sky,
Beyond the circle of the conscious hills,
Were laid in jasper-stone as clear as glass
The first foundations of that new, near Day
Which should be builded out of heaven to God.
He stood a moment with erected brows
In silence, as a creature might who gazed, -
Stood calm, and fed his blind, majestic eyes
Upon the thought of perfect noon: and when
I saw his soul saw, - 'Jasper first,' I said,
'And second, sapphire; third, chalcedony;
The rest in order, - last, an amethyst.'[7]

THE END.

5. Joshua 6.1–20.
6. The adoption of an evolutionary narrative, which EBB uses here and elsewhere in *Aurora Leigh*, was a feature of many contemporary Victorian writings. See Gillian Beer, *Darwin's Plots: Evolutionary Narrative in Darwin, George Eliot, and Nineteenth-Century Fiction* (New York: Routledge, 1982).
7. The foundations of the New Jerusalem. See Revelation 21.19–20: "And the foundations of the wall of the city were garnished with all manner of precious stones. The first foundation was jasper; the second sapphire; the third, a chalcedony; the fourth, an emerald; the fifth, sardonyx; the sixth, sardius; the seventh, chrysolyte; the eighth, beryl; the ninth, a topaz; the tenth, a chrysoprasus; the eleventh, a jacinth, the twelfth, an amethyst."

# A Note on the Text

The text for this Norton Critical Edition is that published in my edition of *Aurora Leigh* (Ohio University Press, 1992). I am grateful to Ohio University Press for their permission to use this text.

The copy-text is the revised "fourth" edition of *Aurora Leigh*, which was published in June 1859. This text was collated with the first edition of 1856 (postdated 1857) and with all the extant manuscripts and corrected proofs. A complete list of these manuscripts and proofs can be found in the list of signs and abbreviations for the explanatory and textual notes (below). There is a full description of this material in my edition published by Ohio University Press.

The wording of the 1859 copy-text has been emended where any of the following circumstances apply:

1. Where Elizabeth Barrett Browning corrected the revised edition after its publication in 1859.
2. Where the printer has not followed the wishes of the author as discovered in the manuscript or printed text being used as printer's copy.
3. Where the author plainly wished an alteration to be made but inadvertantly failed to direct the correction.
4. Where an obvious error has occurred in the printed text, but was never corrected by the author.

The same principles have been applied to the emending of the punctuation and formal details of the text, but only where the author had a clear preference, and not in cases where a printer's version has been tacitly accepted by the author, having been passed in proof.

The spelling of *gray* is emended to *grey* throughout to conform with Barrett Browning's own practice, which was honored in the first edition, but altered in the revised. For the sake of consistency, *enquire* has been emended to *inquire* (the dominant spelling in the revised edition), *Shakespeare* to *Shakspeare*, and *sat* to *sate*. A complete list of emendations to the copy-text can be found in my edition of *Aurora Leigh* (Ohio University Press, 1992), pp. 126–34.

# Selected Textual Notes

*Signs and Abbreviations*

| | |
|---|---|
| EBB | Elizabeth Barrett Browning |
| RB | Robert Browning |
| { } | editorial comment |
| < > | deletion |
| [ ] | addition or substitution |
| > | overwritten, to produce a revised reading |
| (i.w.) | illegible word or words |
| ( ?) | tentative reading |
| // | paragraph division |
| / | line division |
| corr | corrected to copy text reading in EBB's (or RB's) hand |
| N.P. | new paragraph |
| MS1 | first draft manuscript at Wellesley College. |
| MS1a | 4 pages (1 leaf) representing draft of 5.1160–274 at McGill University. |
| MS2a<br>MS2b | two fragments of manuscript, drafted later than MS1 and earlier than MS2; at Baylor University and Dartmouth College respectively. |
| MS2 | complete autograph manuscript sent to printers, at Harvard. |
| MS2c | one page in EBB's hand representing a draft of lines 8.38–61, later than MS1 but earlier than the version of the same lines appearing on the proximate pages of MS2; with MS2 at Harvard. |
| 56B proof | incomplete set of page proofs for the first English edition in the Bodleian Library. |
| 56B proof a | pages 151–54 (lines 4.434–545) of 56B proof, at Baylor University. |
| 56C proof | complete set of page proofs for the first English edition later sent to the United States for use as copy for the first American edition; in the Robert H. Taylor Collection, Princeton University. |
| 1856 | first English edition. |
| 1856 Am | first American edition. |

1856 corr — copy of the first English edition, which EBB annotated with revisions and corrections for the revised edition; at the Bibliotheca Bodmeriana, Cologny-Genéve.

59 proof — complete set of proofs for the revised edition; at the Lilly Library, Indiana University.

59 proof list corr — list of corrections and revisions in EBB's hand based on 59 proof and sent to printers; at Pierpont Morgan Library.

1859 — the revised ("fourth") edition.

1859 list corr — manuscript list of corrections headed "Aurora Leigh—4th edition"; facsimile in British Museum.

1859 Isa — copy of the revised edition presented to Isa Blagden; at Yale University.

## FIRST BOOK

AURORA LEIGH] {There is no title in MS1}, Aurora Vane>Leigh/ [Aurora Leigh -/ First Book]/ <An autobiography> MS2.

FIRST BOOK] {MS1 was written straight through without book divisions or headings. In MS2, books 1–6 were originally given the subheading "An autobiography."}

1.1–8. {These lines first appear in MS2. MS1 begins with a long passage that eventually yielded draft passages for books 1 and 3, but that was obviously intended as one coherent scene.}

1.9.] God help me, I am <young> still - <twenty six> [what men call] young. MS1; <God help me, I>I, writing here, am still what men call young; MS2.

1.12. outer Infinite] [outer] Infinite <wonder = sea> MS1.

1.20–25.] My father's slow hand <as it> stroked my hair/(I sitting at his feet-) & <hear> [catch] the laugh/With which my uncle captain, fresh from Spain/Enquired>Enquires<what money> [how many] moidores<were used> [melted down]/ <To> [Had] make those glittering curls - MS1.

1.30. rare blue] great black MS1, MS2, 56B proof corr.

1.50. Of<making the young life most sweet to itself>MS1. {Following line 50 in MS1} And sewing broidery upon pinafores.

1.117.] [For men who grieve much are fantastical] MS1.

1.156.] Was Psyche losing sight at <(first of dawn?) [Cupid]/<Deserted> [The first time] MS1.

1.235–50.] Which (little?)>suppliants cling to. So passed Italy {in pencil} [my country passed]. -/And then the little ship in the great seas!/And then the lonely heart in the great world MS1. {The rest of this passage, dealing with the sea voyage, has no equivalent in MS1.}

1.256.] {In MS1 this line is followed by a pastoral description partly deleted and eventually used at lines 1123–28, 1081–87, and 1121–45. Lines 260–69 also appear, much worked over, vertically in the left margin.}

1.306–7.] Accounting that to leap from perch to perch/ And peck the sweet white sugar through the wires/ Was act & joy enough for any bird MS1.

1.402–3.] Of liberal education; (tongues not books . . .)/ <Excerpts, beauties, "classic bits">/ I learnt a little algebra little MS1.

1.409.] Of the Burmese empire -<all the names of course/ Of the Abyssinian rivers> by how many feet MS1.

1.410. Teneriffe] Himmeleh MS1, MS2-1856, 1856 corr.

1.413. Klagenfurt] {In MS1 another name, possibly beginning "Gor," was tried and deleted before EBB settled on "Klagenfurt."}

1.431.] {In MS1, the following line written vertically in the margin seems to have been intended to follow line 431} Her aims in education were set high. MS1.

1.492.] {No equivalent line in MS1.} Was civil to her <nephew Percy Vane> MS1 corr.

1.499–559. {This passage, introducing Romney, does not appear in MS1.}

1.674.] In some new voice some <sweet> new beguiling <[new enchanted]> [wanton winning] voice MS1; In some transformed, apocryphal, new voice MS2–1856, 59 proof corr, 59 proof list corr. {In 59 proof list corr, EBB writes "I have omitted a mistake of importance on page 25 line 3, for 'apocryphal, new voice,' read 'apocalyptic voice,' EBB.'}

1.832.] {In MS1, two deleted lines follow line 832 that do not seem to relate to the proximate lines} <(I?) washed my garments clean & smoothed them calm/ And stood

aside from where the bulls had fought> MS1.
1.857.] <Those spyglass shufflers of the heaven & earth> MS1.
1.870. Lay telegraphs] Build pyramids MS2-1856, 1856 corr.
1.872. president] senators MS2-1856, 59 proof corr, 59 proof list corr.
1.875.] {Following line 875 in MS1} <This breath upon your cheeks is from the mouth/Of holy spirits who cry amen to God..> MS1.
1.905.] {Following line 905 in MS1 are these deleted lines} <Like some chief-angel spreading out his wings/To catch the (jasper?) glory . . opens up/Heavens windows wide & (draws?) you from the earth/With (contents?) of the (infinite?)> MS1.
1.1064. blue] <grey> [blue] MS2.
1.1095. Carrington] <Wilbraham> MS2 corr.
1.1120–21.] {Between lines 1120 and 1121 appear the following readings} With <thorn &> <briar> hazle for the undergrowth MS1; The woods, the hazles of their undergrowth; MS2-56B proof. {This line was omitted from its proper place in the sequence in 56B proof and appears, in that proof, at the base of page 41 after line 1145. There it was marked for deletion by EBB.}

## SECOND BOOK

2.59.]My public! - <There I stood> Arthur Duncomb - with a mouth/<Much> [Twice] graver than his eyes/{Added in the margin of MS1} [The public on the benches/ Harry Vaughan/With mouth twice graver] MS1; cousin <Percy> MS2 corr.
2.96–101.] The best of the Auroras -//What's the use/Of keeping well & white & being the best/Of useless things, I <wonder> [ask you]?. <if the best> Let me [I would] go MS1.
2.107–9.] <If heads that think> [That hold a thought] to <help> [touch] the world, must ache/<God grant me then the> headaches! -//<With a touch [of saucy scorn]/Of scorn the prouder for that look of his> MS1.
2.237.] {In MS1 a deleted draft for lines 236–38 includes a line following line 237} <Your inferiority being understood> MS1.
2.242. 'The country that] Our England who MS1.
2.254–55.] On tightropes at a fair for gingerbread/Than <dancing> <dancing> on an> the authors stage [&<write> [please] the babies lifted up at> to arms> see <length> MS1; At fairs on tightrope, <(i.w.)> [till the babies dropped]/<(make peasant babes?)> [Their gingerbread for joy - than shift the <author's> types] MS2.
2.271.] <Masters make slaves & rich men make the poor> MS1 corr.
2.298.] [I think] it Could not much/[Console] <Affect the mammoth or the> [Encourage the race] mastodons to know MS1.
2.330.] {Several deleted and largely illegible lines occur here in MS1, among them} At equal years <because like the finches/They keep us in the dark to make us sing> MS1.
2.413. Do I look a Hagar, think you?'] <Polygamy scarce suits me> MS1 corr.
2.437–38.] That every creature male or female (i.w.)>has/<Has so much insight, so much>/<A conscience in the use of faculty/Responsible for so much>[Stands single <before God at least> in responsible act & thought] MS1.
2.439.] As also in birth & death. <You cannot put/Your kind of insight in the place of ours> MS1.
2.624. Vane Leigh] Ralph Duncombe MS1; Ralph Vane>Leigh MS2. Romney] Arthur MS1, Percy> Romney MS2 corr.
2.699.] <Of that unmanning ignominious blush> MS1.
2.812.] Of his dead love - <And the meekest saint> [his Inez - <Why> I preserve>keep] MS1.
2.813–14.] <Who saw me do it, from Heavens high vantage post/Forgave the pride through pity of the pain -> MS1.
2.873 Susannah] Why Mabel MS1; And Mabel MS2 corr.
2.882.] < Like beasts before an earthquake> MS1.
2.892–93.] <But looking back I have no (wish?) to say/The thing was cruel> MS1.
2.896.] {Preceding line 896 in MS1 is the deleted line} <I wish I had watched my father's sister's eyes>
2.934–38.] {In MS1, these lines are added vertically in the left margin.}
2.976. weighing half a ton] weighing half a ton <[freighted with (tent-floors?)]> MS1.
2.1070.] Which < brought a freight back of the (rugged?)> [came back heaped with elemental] gold/<From India by the last weeks (full?) north wind> MS1. {This line appears to have been added late in MS2; signs of erasure suggest that it was revised there.}
2.1073.] [At] Which some <Rhine castle & princedom turn (i.w.) And princedom in conjunction, into her lap> <And old> Rhine castle & principality <& estates conjoined> MS1.
2.1176.] He broke the silence = <Child, he said, poor child/Who>Why fight against the mother=breast & milk/And choose> take the stranger's gall - God change the world/For you[r] <sake Aurora>[sake dear] & make it mild to you/And juster than I have found you> MS1.
2.1177.] Although Arthur>Walter Vane . . because a stranger might> [no stranger - <& (i.w.)>only Walter Vane] MS1.

## THIRD BOOK

3.1–5.] {All MS1 variants for lines 3.1–101 are drawn from pages 1–5 of MS1.}

3.12.] Death, death, it is not in our death indeed/That we die most - <Ideas used for death> [It is from life we get]/<The negatives of>Of will &>of power &> of delight>/[The Ideas we use for death - <the negatives> It is in life]/{In pencil, written vertically in the left margin in EBB's hand} [Death death - we die not most in death indeed/We get from life the ideas we use for death/Life's negatives complete death for us] MS1.

3.54–57.] <Receive it fair Elisha <a fair cloak> [though<indeed>I think]>/[The printer wants more copy for my book] Elijah's effluence you will miss in it -/[My cousin here> Sharpe wants money for his debts . .]/<It never fell from Heaven - >/ My brother Mark wants money for his hands/My lover Craig wants money for all needs/And <therefore> [so] a rich wife - <which unhappily>/<I am not, being a poor artist. With> MS1.

3.58–60.] Art's burning chariot [of thick fire] which we ride in <burning.> [we]/[Is apt to singe the]/<The gloss off> purple <garments> into <holes> rags -/Although <I drop my cloak to you> fair> [you ask me for my cloak] Kate Ward/My fair Elisha [Because it] <because> for <it has wear> [the quaint cut]/<Some> [And] pretty Spanish buttons; <if no effluence> [fit for the back.] MS1.

3.61–65.] My lover Craig wants money for all needs/And <therefore> [so] a rich wife - <which unhappily>/{Added in the left margin} [he is forced alas/To marry where his heart is not, because/<He finds his purse still empty though his heart>/He finds no purse there where he lost his heart/The more's the pity for my lover Craig -/I'm only a poor artist certainly./Adieu] MS1.

3.66.68.] My critic Hammond wants another book/To please my gracious public which demands/A cheerful genius & no subtle>abstract truths./My critic Hammond wants another book/My critic Belfield wants a different book - MS1.

3.86.] And <all great poets ought to laugh aloud> [true poets shd. laugh inextinguishably]/{Added in pencil in the margin} [unquenchably] MS1.

3.87–90.] Like <Shakespeare and the> <Homer's]>gods - <Put ichor in the veins> [That's very hard]/<And [Ambrosia in] drug the cup with moly & we will laugh>/The gods may laugh & Shakespeare - Dante smiled/<So bitterly we all cry, rather weep> MS1.

3.92–95.] At any housedoor . . Here I know last week/A mother died, had> and here <must die next week> [a child is dead <today>]/While all the other children sit surprised/At the new silence . . <yet> now smile as if on merriment MS1.

3.99.] The apocalypse of life is getting on MS1.

3.101.] I want good counsel - Will you let me in/Tomorrow morning at eleven o clock/ Before you have a public at your door/The public strikes the knocker - Yes?/& MS1.

3.102–50.] {This passage does not appear in MS1.}

3.157.] {This line does not appear in MS1. It was clearly introduced into MS2 at a late stage. There is no indication of any variant reading for the name "Romney Leigh."}

3.207.] <And when I had reached <to something> [a step beyond] at once/The public cried <aloud> [out] at the falling off/ Regretting the "first manner" - > MS1.

3.215–21.] <And emblems> <Some tokens too of <pensive> [some male> young] bachelors/Who <sealed> [wrote] from college with a <broken> [stringless] lyre/And [broken] (columns?) < split through to show> [showing they had lived/Too long at twenty though the muse had helped>/ <The tedious> [A <broken lyre against>] [flower upon] a tomb . . <to show> [a broken lyre]/[For proof] The writers at eighteen [or so] <had lived too long/With all the Muses helping or sometimes> MS1.

3.233. Romney] Walter MS1; Percy MS2.

3.234–35.] I felt <his strong disdain <lean all its weight> [touch silently]/With all the weight of his invisible soul> MS1 corr.

3.240. made thrusts with a toy-sword] . . <and as I tossed the ball> [danced tightrope at the fair] MS1.

3.327–28.] For soul & (i.w.) <I say, I did my true> [the hounds of famine just thrown off the scent] I could stand up [straight] & work/ < Peculiar personal work> unless I cross/ The thing God set me to <with the strength he gave> MS1.

3.333.] <The foliage <out like> [into] flame - so life with man/<Then roughens all that> [Until the] manhood pure of brow [stands complete]/With fire, passion & tempestuous thoughts> MS1.

3.371.] {Following line 371 in MS1 is the deleted line} <For all your learning & distinction - > MS1.

3.460. Lyons' velvet] silk & Mechlin MS1; Lyons <moire silks> MS2 corr.

3.500.] {This line does not appear in MS2-1856 but was added during revision for the fourth edition} 1856 corr.

3.517. Dancing] <dancing> [drunken] MS1; Drunken MS2-1856, 1856 corr.

3.546.] <With college (i.w.) wine & Greek & debt/With (i.w.) hate of Greek & wine . . & lived apart/(from?) gownsmen for he scorned both such & was/(i.w.)/With equal scorn

of (women?) & of Greek & wine <[And mathematics]>/[Learned . . yes!] A reading man who <read> [shunned] the Greek [& took (i.w.)] (i.w.)/modern prison's paper instead of Homer's ships/(i.w.) read never (writ?) on wax - who threw aside/The <cause of> [Caesar's] toga <(i.w.) & took up the> [For that workman's blouse> MS1.

3.549. Melbourne's] {No equivalent in MS1}; <Cartwright's &> [Cartwrights] MS2.

3.596. with a place for Sue] . . <Michelet &> Sue MS1 corr.

3.600. . . such as wearing gowns] . . [such as] wearing <bonnets made> [hats] MS1; hats>gowns MS2 corr.

3.637.] {In MS1 a discarded line precedes line 637} From<top of those high towers of ancestry> [the <broad summit of> [crinelled] top of your ancestral towers] MS1.

3.650. fantasy] appetite MS1, MS2-1856, 1856 corr.

3.659. drover's] <milk-man's> [poulterer's] MS1.

3.738. Oppressed in my deliverance] Hardly as in a <bad> [sick] dream MS1; As hard as in a sick dream MS2; As hard as in a sick room 56B proof-1856, 1856 corr.

3.840.] <But man was forced to cheat to find her room/To lie in <when> [yet] unswaddled> MS1.

3.850–57.] {The indentation and inverted commas that indicate reported speech did not appear in MS2 or the first edition (1856). They were introduced by EBB (in 1856 corr.) as a correction for the revised edition (1859).}

3.909.] Rose <Tylney> [Bell] a <small> [seven years] [gentle] child/<So quick so clever> [& past her stature] <with> such <cheeks & lips> [a pretty thing] [child] MS1.

3.926.] {Following line 926 in MS1 is an added line not used in the later draft} [Her light heart brought her into heavy grief (life?)>sin] MS1.

3.948.] {Following line 948 in MS1 is a deleted, and largely illegible, draft of lines 946–58 that includes the following fragments} <In such a blood red soil it made the may/Flower whiter and the verdure>/ <Which run down by the sea betwixt green [high] banks/And overarching <hedges> [elms] like caverns green>/ <To pull <you> [us] from the flats - Or else perhaps/ They came back only as the rabbits do/To find the place they [<once> had] burrowed in> MS1.

3.981–82. {These lines are much worked over in MS1, but the phrases "From Milton," and "And Lycidas," and "paradise" can be discerned.}

3.982. Selkirk] <Christian> MS1.

3.1005–9.] <A word>, Some fragmentary <& melodious> phrases here & there/Of <some> [that] articulate music which had pierced/[To] Her soul <with sweetness & (possessed?) her> [& reproduced itself afresh]/In <all her gentle looks & graceful ways> [the lifting of her eyelids & motions - in the way]/<She moved her lips to speech> [In finer motions of the lips & eyes]/<She did not own the wheatfield verily/[This Ruth,] But still she had walked <like Ruth> among the corn/And <gleaned> [held] the wheat ears faster in her hand/Because she had <gleaned so few> - She said/Than women of this> the<order have to throw> [people use If flowers] MS1.

3.1063.] {Following line 1063, on page 104 of the first draft manuscript MS1, is a draft of an unpublished poem that begins "Twas the feast day of St. John."}

3.1070–88.] {The account of Marian's flight is much corrected and worked over in MS1.}

3.1078.] <Till trees & fields & roads revived like ghosts>/And turned upon her & ran after her MS1.

3.1243.] {Added in MS2 after line 1243 in RB's hand, and signed, with initials, "*(Read Feb. 5. Shrove Tuesday, Paris, 1856.)// RB.*"}

## FOURTH BOOK

4.36–37.]But pity <too> <also> had <needs> <necessities She cd not leave/A sister-soul to drown out in the dark> MS1.

4.52.] <Who used to think her best good fortune meant/That others <simply> [(i.w.)] sh$^{d}$ be kind to her?/And now God made her into a sort of queen> MS1.

4.79–81.] <As bees to flowers as flies to rotten fruit/As <men> [ministering] spirits <of ministration> to the sick & sad/Came Walter Vane to miserable rooms> MS1.

4.82.] As sunbeams to <dark (prisons?)><[to dark dungeons]>/As ministering spirits to lost men<(i.w.)> MS1.

4.101.] <Which overcame her as the rising sun/The palpitating hills> {Added vertically in the margin}<While (he?)> she stood thrilled & flushed - as <morning> [orient] lands/In tremulous expectation of the sun]> MS1 corr.

4.159.] < . . almost dignified> [as<savage> [wild] creatures <stir> now] MS1; as wild creatures . . now MS2.

4.223–26.] Perhaps I am bold- yet you do not scorn/The soldier when he treads against the flame/[Though] He's bold too <& you praise me> [and <(i.w.)> lady (i.w.) boldly say]/That <notwithstanding I am> [since I know myself for] low & vile MS1.

4.321.] And (words?) so came sadder like the

bell/That tolls into the midnight (among?) us MS1.

4.341. the Trenton] <upon Biscay> MS1.

4.343. loud transition-time] <crisis of the times> MS1.

4.372.] From Catherine's court <to Belgrave at once> MS1.

4.382.] <Play out Orestes part to cheat ourselves> MS1.

4.399.] <the bear would fight/And Isabella <reign beyond next year> If Isabella could keep seat in Spain> MS1.

4.401.] <And would the corn league take the question up/Of general trade> MS1.

4.404.] <To help the proletarians [Upon the fingers of the <upper class> rich] - Is it true> MS1.

4.405.] <Potatoe plants are dying from the world [earth]> MS1.

4.406.] Like moly <on a sudden> & will the League not die out too MS1.

4.408.] {Written vertically in the margin of MS1} Voices hard & fast/As if we sharpened knives MS1.

4.419.] To spill saltpetre where had been no fire MS1.

4.423–24.] {Two pages were cut out of MS1 here, the stubs only remaining. But as the draft order of the lines in this passage still makes sense, it would seem that the pages, which probably bore rough drafts of the proximate passages, were removed by EBB during the process of composition.}

4.438.] <A month from thence they married in the church/Eccentric marriage!> Half St. Giles in frieze MS1. {In MS1 the original sequence of the passage, which became lines 438–791 of the published version, is as follows: 438; 538–95; 438–538; 596–601; 770–91; 602–767. Evidence in MS1 suggests that EBB rearranged the order of the lines during the early stages of composition.}

4.494.] And good good mothers <pluck the first grown flower> [on their husbands arm]/[Stoop down to <(i.w.)> pluck the < poor (dust row?)> flower]/Upon their <(i.w.)> [own] childs [solitary] grave <to adorn their hair> MS1, MS2 corr.

4.533.] Who got her>When [wanting] tickets for the queen's mask-ball MS1, Who wanted tickets for the birthnight-ball; MS2-56B proof a {Corrected in EBB's hand in 56B proof a to read} When wanting tickets for the birthnight-ball 56C proof-1856, 1856 corr.

4.547.] In hideous populations - Empty dens/And [the wild beasts] <[at large] [out of doors foraging] In the streets some policemen out of doors> MS1.

4.595.] On Raffael's pure Madonna of the bird [Virgin of the golden finch]//<I went to Walter's wedding - I was faint/And ill that morning &> I'll set it down at once I have been wrong - {See textual notes to line 4.438.} MS1.

4.627.] You stayed for the Division - <Lost by God>one> [Knight Allinger] MS1.

4.630. Liverpool] Manchester MS1.

4.635.] <The Duke of (Aran's?) eldest daughter/Miss Bell . . just out . . They'd thank you Dear/For taking <her for that bride> [your bride among them] - She$^{d}$. thank still more/If he had <done it> [taken her] Mister Walter Vane - /No names - he's at your elbow> MS1.

4.674. poor Damiens'] Ravaillac's MS1, MS2.

4.770.] {In MS1 the lines now following 770 were originally conceived of as following line 601. See textual notes to line 4.438 above. The rhetorical description of the people, in lines 770–73, is much written over and revised and largely illegible.} The terrible people <in apocalypse>/Their eyes (dull?)> eat out with plague & poverty] <Grave-pale . . plague-eaten come to see & hear/Led forwards like King Œdipus at noon/And (witness?) with the common Mayfair world? Among the well-dressed olive-grounds to fair/(i.w.)> Athenian (i.w.) ladies & smooth gentlemen/<Reflecting in as vexed disquieted/The apparition>> {Added in the margin} <[The terrible people weak & old & poor/Their eyes eat out with plague & poverty/Led out like King (Ægisthus?) in the sun]> MS1.

4.779.] {In MS1 line 779 is followed by these deleted lines} <With fear-dashed faces, & faint fluttering souls/Abashed by the position! Could these meet/And not clash? <Make no thunder> [Could these touch, these contraries]/And make no thunder?> MS1.

4.786.] Except to <think of burning vinegar>/<Yet> Some <strange fire> [wondrous trick] of nature worked in them/[And] <Till> unaware they stood disquieted/With fear-dashed faces & faint fluttering souls/Abashed by the position . . <Could these meet/These two & not clash> [And make no thunder] MS1.

4.792.] {Following line 792 in MS1} <And Walter Vane with <(i.w.)> his calm [luminous <pale> face]/Stood up among his fifty noble friends/<And speaking softly from> [(Shouted?) (i.w.)] the altar-stair & said/<My brothers> [So stood] - upon his right hand - Brothers mine> {Written vertically in pencil in the margin} <I was not well that morning - the hot (touch?)/With all that heaving, steaming of crammed life/Rocked round me like the sea & then broke up/Like the earth in earthquake> MS1.

4.959.] <Until I shall have seen the face of Christ> MS1.

4.976.] At hoping I could help you <at your work> MS1. {Evidence of erasure in MS2 suggests that EBB wrote the present version of this line at a late stage in composition.}

4.977.] {This line does not appear in MS1 and was plainly added at a late stage in MS2, where it is interlined.}

4.996.] [she was worked upon to/<By some perfidious intermeddling> tongue] MS1.
4.997. {This line does not appear in MS1 and was added late in MS2.}
4.1023–29.] {The lines dealing with Lady Waldemar were inserted vertically in the margin of MS1 as a late addition. The name "Waldemar" is used in the margin while the earlier variant "Waldegrave" appears in the body of the text.}
4.1049. Rosel] Maud MS1.
4.1059.] <&< And simply that> the veriest <[plague-struck]> slave who drops [in Joppa's street]/<In the street at Joppa with the blotch on him> MS1.
4.1062.] <Their sisters & breathe death into their face> MS1.
4.1129.] {The following passage, much worked over and ringed (for deletion?) appears in MS1.} <A most> [The] incessant <labour of the heart & brain>/Upon the fiery anvils of the time/<The (ceaseless?) days work three hours speeches> (i.w.)>Without success <(as yet?)> (i.w.) shaping (anything?)/[To a horseshoe] <(i.w.) [work] practical success [result] with all>/And <that?> (i.w.) <blazing of sparks>/<Those fiery beads thrown up> With all that red jactation of (brute?) fire MS1.
4.1222.] {Added after line 1222, at the base of page 193 in MS2, is the following note in RB's hand, *"(Read Feb. 14 '56 Thursday Morning.)//RB."*}

## FIFTH BOOK

5.1.] Bow your head/Aurora Vane - Be humble <Never> [Shall we] hope MS1.
5.2.] To <sow with seeds of fire this furrowed earth> MS1.
5.56. Romney] Walter MS1.
5.84.] {Preceding line 84 in MS1 is a deleted line} <The forms of poems are the life that moves> MS1.
5.103–12.] {In MS1 a deleted draft for the lines that eventually became lines 120–24 appears in the main body of the manuscript. In the margin are the following deleted lines} <All the earth laid out/By Adam like a silent (rose?) (i.w.) [(corse?)]/Since Christ in anguish stretched [upon] [crowned] [Himself]/And breathed his God-breath upon mouth & eyes/Now lives remembers throbs in every limb/With mystical relations> MS1.
5.116–17.] <Earth's alive>/<It lives a healthy> [And not be <any> [a] magic-trick [or Pagan play]/The great material nature <(is?)> skin of our skin]/That body of our body MS1.
5.150–52.] <Like (tired)? as Shandy's> - Every age MS1.
5.169.] Mount Athos had been carved as Xerxes dreamed MS1.
5.169. as Alexander schemed] as Persian Xerxes dreamed MS2; as Persian Xerxes schemed 56B proof 1856, 1856 corr.
5.213. As Fleet Street to our] As Regent Street to MS1, MS2-1856, 1856 corr.
5.216.] The full [veined] <free> heaving <bosom of the time> [double-breasted] MS1.
5.235.] All time & place - <We call the (rite?) the (i.w.)/And <cannot pray unless the Gothic mode> MS1.
5.242.] {Following line 242 in MS1} <What then - some fifty years ago the stage/Required a wig for Pyrrhus> MS1.
5.253. London or for Edinburgh] Edinburgh or Manchester [Liverpool] MS1.
5.257.] {Following line 257 in MS1} In deference to <anothers <sight> [vision]> [a school or scholar] MS1.
5.286.] <At <Covent Garden> [Drury Lane] <though> [because] their grosser <wits> [brains]> MS1.
5.292–99.] {This passage concerning Aeschylus was added at a late stage in MS1, the verses being written in the left margin of page 164 and crosswise over the main body of the text in manuscript.}
5.316–17.] <to brothers [kindred] - Sweet Beatrice [Imogen Viola] to kin>/<[To Imogen] My sister> To Hamlet, <brother> [Imogen & that sweetest kin] - Dear/<My brother kin Upon the soul's> side MS1.
5.321–23.] His <dull> [filmed] eyes fluttered by the <flying cloud> [blinding whirl]. Of choral vestures - his faint life sucked out/<By mystical white> [In the white devouring] vortices - what time/The [(Rose?)] tragic voices clear & keen [clanging clear] as swords MS1.
5.325.] <And made the blue air wink for ecstasy> MS1.
5.326. Themis' son] <Theseus stern & still> MS1; Jove or Mars MS2, 56B proof corr, 56C proof corr {This correction, in both sets of proofs, is made in RB's hand.}
5.516.] As if <Augustine helped> [Plotinus ruled] you <to the wish/That the world were over> MS1.
5.552.] <Or seem> well [done] to them - <They shake their heads/As soon might think to play at cowslip-ball/With some dead father> MS1.
5.606.] At <(Starfe?> <[Julia Monk]> <[Celia> Delia Cobb]> [Or Delia Dobbs] the <Chartist> lecturer great [something] from Leeds> the States MS1.
5.612–13.] How <pretty> [lovely] Lady Waldegrave looked [tonight] MS1.
5.622. amaranth] <green> MS1.
5.633. Blaise] Ralph MS1, MS2.
5.635. Romney Leigh] Walter Vere MS1.
5.675–80.] {In MS1 this passage is drafted and

deleted twice on pages 175 and 177 before it appears in a fairly clear version on page 178.}

5.677. saintly Styrian] holy [(Lystrian?] monk < at (Rome?)> MS1; holy Lystrian MS2.

5.756. Göttingen] Gottenberg MS2.

5.775.] {Following line 775 in MS1} [A woman is no worse for being fair] MS1.

5.796.] <And> [So] near <the marble> statue of a muse - Calliope [statue of a breathless] [the bust of an unfavouring] MS1. {Following line 796 in MS1} <I wonder at your bravery gentlemen> MS1.

5.821.] <From California to the Caffreland> MS1.

5.823. Emperor Soulouque's] a spinning Dervishes [Soulouques the Emperor (Ismail's?)] MS1; the emperor Soulouque's MS2.

5.829.] {Following line 829 in MS1} <Called Bunker Hill> MS1.

5.829. epic in twelve parts] epic <written> in twelve books> parts MS1.

5.899. - anybody's name] <Baldi> . . leave the name a blank MS1.

5.900. Anne Blythe] <(Monicca?) Lennox> MS1 corr.

5.902. Pauline] Lindore MS1, MS2.

5.987. Waldemar] Waldegrave MS1. Leigh] Vane MS1.

5.994. Blaise] Ralph MS2.

5.1015.] {Following line 1015 in MS1} <you are soft/All poets are romantic> MS1.

5.1018. hankers for romance] <has eccentric views> MS1 corr.

5.1060.] {In MS1 a deleted version of the passage 1051–61 includes a line following 1060} <The book is spoiled for noble studies> MS1.

5.1066. Waldemar] Waldegrave MS1.

5.1205.] <[And not] the [poets]//So - I sell/ My new great poem in the morning> MS1a.

5.1262. Carrington] <Wilbraham> MS2 corr.

## SIXTH BOOK

6.51–52.] However ill-lodged in a woman's breast,/Can <(tame?)> [swell to] a pair of nationalities,/And brave the judgement of a hundred> thousand heads. MS2.

6.81.] {The passage characterizing Paris is much revised in MS1; one version is added in a clear hand in the margin} [Of fair fantastic Paris who still plays/At beauty as a game & fairly wins/While round <the anxious> [about the] world holds heavy bets/On every turn of the hand! she wears her trees] MS1.

6.126.] At every turn<ing under a glass> [beneath a chrystal] case/What dentist's teeth in ghastly even rows MS1.

6.167. Or wait on all] < Beyond the cataracts> MS1.

6.184–85.] But shuts us up in <close clipped periods>/To <such traditions as we're left with [with sunsets & the stars]> MS1.

6.211.] The new Conscriptions <with a civil end & use> MS1 corr.

6.233–34.] On <mine> my [face fell] the blow of it - I reeled> [mine the sudden blow of it came down full]/<Like a sword stroke - My a >eyes <moment> dazzled/I reeled. My eyes were dark - Next moment I sprang on> MS1.

6.268.] <His pinch of snuff suspended <like a sword> [in mid air]/As if in deprecation of the choice/Of <Dumas or another man of genius . . perhaps [a simple man of genius who wrote deathless books]/To a place in the academy> MS1.

6.278–80.] <Who keeps his gunpowder <with groceries> [upon the shelf]/With his sugar & prunes?> MS1.

6.303.] <With so much dross to burn out in the sun> MS1.

6.306.] <To burn away myself [be burnt cleaner] -/They clean asbestos so by burning it> MS1.

6.310.] <Why what an apparition of a soul> MS1.

6.310. Marian] Mabel MS1.

6.323.] <Like a hot coal dropped on parchment> MS1; Like a dropt coal forgot on tapestry, MS2.

6.345.] Not hid so well <indeed> beneath the <end/Of scanty shawl dragged painfully across> MS1 corr.

6.350.] <You find a diamond in a pauper's hand> MS1.

6.360.] <But understand me [take some comfort] that was not to starve/For certain reasons which we could not guess> MS1.

6.380.] <To trouble his joy as babes are weaned/The aloes (i.w.)> MS1.

6.386.] <Of> & [dead men's bones] (i.w.) the catacombs> MS1 corr.

6.405.] {No equivalent in MS1. The line is interlined, having been added late, in MS2.}

6.406. Mathildes, Justines, Victoires] <And Janes & Amelias> [Victoires Mathildes, Reginas] MS1.

6.459.] And me and no one else <& we will talk>/[At that she <first> [stopped]/ <Stopped> [From] trembling <like> [as] <a shivering> sick dove's shivering stops/ <That's (so?)> (i.w.) calmed by> [In sudden] death - but she looked up resolved] MS1.

6.482.] <As if I led her by a thread of hair/ <She feared to break by a single step> [Which short & frail if she sh$^{d}$ drop or break]> MS1.

6.547. Julie] Jerome MS1 corr.

6.567. yearling] two-years MS2.

6.718.] <Would choose me <rather stink-

ing> [this poor Mabel] from the ditch> MS1.

6.736. As we kill roses] <With harlot's kisses> MS1 corr.

6.771–77.] <There she let the child/Slide down upon her bosom from her arms/And all her face's light dropped after him/With such a sigh as follows ecstasy/In absolute exhaustion-Then> down she sank/And sate upon the bed & did not weep/As still [<white> &] as frost . . when its too cold/ For raining any more.> MS1.

6.772. agony] ecstasy MS2.

6.777.] <And sate upon the bed & did not weep/As [white &] still as frost . . when it's too cold/For raining any more.> MS1.

6.778.] But I convicted, <mastered at my heart> MS1.

6.808.] <Away from> the <[happy] individual> life <they had> MS1 corr.

6.897–900.] {These lines do not appear in this place in MS1 (p. 233) but are drafted in the left margin of page 230 beside the draft of lines 5.814–19.}

6.961–63.] {Aurora's exclamation does not appear in MS1.}

6.1006.] {In MS1 following line 1006} [Which mothers [love will never>not] <do not - So it was that she>] MS1.

6.1033.] {Following line 1033 in MS1} Of what use . . So I would fill his soul with cramps.

6.1098–103. {In MS1 these lines are added vertically in the margin: The handwriting is much neater than that on the rest of the page and the name "Marian" appears. The passage was probably added at the time when EBB was transcribing the poem into fair copy, MS2.} She (i.w.)> loved me truly/Did I <speak> [laugh] or curse -/I think I sate there silent hearing all/<And seeing> [Nor] hearing double -<while I sate> [Marian's tale at once]/<Poor Marian's story & the marriage>/And Percy's vow I'll keep alone to thee/Which means that woman Was it time/To ring the marriage bells yet - MS1.

6.1116.] The>What ugly monster waiting>ed in the deep MS1.

6.1118.] Was ready to <accomplish Mabel's>sum of death MS1.

6.1119–20.] {No equivalent in MS1.}

6.1152.] <I could not bear her hand upon> my hand MS1.

6.1154.] <And thought, I pray you rather hate me/Whom surely I can never take to love/ Who had power to break my body with such (pain?)> MS1.

6.1198.] {Following line 1198 in MS1} <<But >[Being only] half-<dead> [alive] - I woke up <within> [in the] <my> grave/[I caught the caterpillar on my cheek]/<I knew all afterward> In its damp horror -//Hush - you understand>MS1.

6.1204–18.] {In MS1 this passage appears in three draft versions.}

6.1216.] {In MS1 following line 1216} <Against it agonising death with fear> MS1.

6.1226–27.] <Upon this sleeping child in sight of heaven/That man's most hideous violence & not man's/Seduction left me <gibbering on the floor> [the lost wretch I was]> MS1.

6.1244.] {Following line 1244 in MS1} Combing the low brown vineyards & green wheat/ [Meanwhile] In horrible languor [do-nothing-ness] <I was mad> MS1.

6.1247–52.] {This passage is added in a firm hand in the margin of MS1.}

6.1255–60.] {A version of these lines appears in the margin of MS1.}

6.1266–67.] <But tracked through all the ins & outs of it/With some dream=wolf to chafe & frighten me> MS1.

6.1271.] Alone - <& with> [undone] a sunset facing me/<Like God's angel upon the hideous (i.w.)>(tomb?)> MS1.

## SEVENTH BOOK

7.7. naughty] filthy MS1.

7.10. right damnable] {Reading as copy-text in MS2; corrected in 56B proof to read} unmerciful 56B proof-1856, 1856 corr.

7.51.–55.] <And all the dull uneasy doubtful pain> <For all the numb dull pain across my brows/That <rippling> [heaving] of some <secondary> [strange<mystic> substantial] life/Within me which had made my side heave/These five months back as if it were a sign/Of some up-breaking of the fountain - life> MS1.

7.60.] And I shall be a mother in a month/My soul cleared up at once as <if the> [some keen] wind/[Had sunk a keen shaft in the cloud-crammed sky/And drawn the <bubbling> [meek] blue up [to well up round the moon]]MS1.

7.64–65.] <What was there for me to confess/ Confess the wickedness of hell & pain/Confess <my agonies> [the anguish] of such a one betrayed [mortal soul]> MS1.

7.114.] She<put such knowledge in> [smiled towards the sun] & ended then/<As one who has seen something beyond death> MS1.

126 {Following line 126 in MS1} <To (fall?)> [Wherein] to sit for ever with the child/As that painted fair Madonna <to thy feet> [The Italians set their (i.w.) around]> MS1.

7.170.] O Lamia - <keep alone thy serpent watch> MS1.

7.172. hideous] filthy MS1.

7.266–68.] {In MS1, a draft version of these lines appears on the final page of the notebook with a marginal note in EBB's hand, "Homer's Hymn."}

7.294.] {Written in the margin of MS1.} <I took the wind-side of your leprosy/And drew my garments round me - I'm not bound/ To nurse you or be smooth with such as you> MS1.

7.312.] <Worked subtly on her tender simple heart/[Struck out] With long fine [subtle arrowy] serpent tongue=dart/And ended her the little simple fly> MS1.

7.328. yearling] two-year MS2.

7.456.] {Following line 456 in MS2} <I listened through the stars for Italy> MS2.

7.462.] And knows it holding by some <tender [faithful]> hand/<Of one last brother> MS1.

7.483.] [Which break off from the pines & tumble down/<And> [To] powder all the myrtle groves below] MS1; <Which break off from the pines & tumble down>/Which drop and powder all the myrtle-groves MS2-1856, 1856 corr.

7.516.] Of [By] Bellosguardo - <tis a [a brown square]> tower that holds MS1.

7.520. Mount Morello] San Marino MS1.

7.521. opposite] to the right MS2-1856, 1856 corr.

7.541.] {In MS1 line 541 is followed by a draft of the passage that appears in MS2 and all published versions as 8.1–61.}

7.562.] No other being effective - [<Never fear for the rest>/I will> did not think to paint you as Daphne /<And all> Asprout with laurel - [(yet?)] you have run too fast/ For gods & critics <some (trying?)> [to keep up with you]/And>You won't be popular tis just (a word?)/<If so it should please heaven - I fear for you> An it please heaven - Courage then I give you joy] MS1.

7.622.] You<'d> leave <no [deeper]> footprint <than was left/By Abram's tent [Abram's guest] [Samuel's host] at Endor> MS1.

7.623.] <Your cousin Percy met me> - <Why Miss Vane>/Who stared as <if he heard me with his eyes> [men do at <melancholy> [amazing] news]/As if to hear <it over with ears and> eyes as well MS1.

7.645. grains, like] drops as MS2.

7.647.] {Following line 647 in MS1} <In spite of childish scrawls on t'other side> MS1.

7.668.] The heaped up <the> cushions falling off the couch/<And table by it heaped with> open [scattered] books MS1. {Following line 668 in MS2} <The heaped up cushions and the open books> MS2.

7.679.] <And so the thing was scarcely worth a word> [Mixed drinks . . unless the drink was hippocras] MS1.

7.679. nepenthe was the drink] the drink was moly, quite MS2.

7.747–48.] Through < gasps & spasms dishonoring faces made>[all the pale <unconscious> faces that we make]/<[Distorted in] Because of that dishonoring poison> MS1.

7.749. decomposing drugs] most mortal drug MS2; any mortal drug 56B proof-1856, 1856 corr.

7.917. Samminiato] <Mount Marino> MS1 corr.

7.1026. oyster's] beast's MS1, MS2-1856, 1856 corr.

7.1107.] {Following line 1107 in MS1} <The voice for me/That named them all & chronicled the nests> MS1.

7.1179.] <Before the ill air caught them (through the night?)> [On foot or carriage, - ere the evil wind]/Should take them & the trees grow dangerous MS1.

7.1191.] The very English had not <learnt my name> MS1.

7.1281. Blaise] Ralph MS1; <Ralph> MS2 corr.

7.1309. a bowl of oenomel] a <cup> [bowl] of hypecras MS1.

7.1311.] {Following line 1311 in MS1} For ever - MS1.

## EIGHTH BOOK

8.1–61.] {In MS1 this passage (on pages 269–71 of MS1) was first conceived as following line 7.541, though indications in the manuscript suggest that the decision to use the passage as the introduction to book 8 was made soon after its composition.}

8.17.] {In MS1, following line 17} <Yet proving it might be lured [tamed] to stay> MS1.

8.28–29.] <[The moon had dwindled to one golden round]>/The sevenfold heavens seemed pressing down at once /<With all their starry gods> MS1.

8.33. the Poggio called and]<Pratolino> MS2 corr.

8.36–61.] {These lines appear in sequence on pages numbered 347 and 348 of MS2. They also appear in a draft, chronologically later than MS1 but earlier than the MS2 version on the promixate pages, on one other page, also numbered 347. This page (MS2c) was obviously retained for the sake of the inscription in RB's hand that appears at the bottom of the sheet, "(Read this Book, this divine Book, Wednesday Night July 9th '56. RB. 39 Devonshire Place.)"}

8.46. twenty] fifty MS1, MS2c, MS2-1856, 1856 corr.

8.47. twenty] fifty MS1, MS2c, MS2-1856, 1856 corr.

8.53. Upon its four-square] <Each on a > [Both based on single] trines of MS1; On a single trine of MS2c, MS2-1856, 1856 corr.

8.61.] {In MS1, on page 297 to follow line 61 as written on page 271} <The lamp was lighted in the room & flared/And burnt the dark>MS1.

8.101.] {A deleted passage in MS1 includes the line} <Beasts will rush [leap] on blindly & undismayed against MS1.

8.144. Blaise] Ralph MS1.

8.170–71.] <[Indeed] You were not [did not] use<d> to be so like <conquering>/A son of Atreus fresh from a taken <Troy> [town]> MS1.

8.273–74.] [And that its <poor &> naked & afraid/And no wise worthy so much compliment] MS1.

8.280.] <Or could not> make it - like just > & so a plastic man/Who having made man is a god> henceforth MS1.

8.283.] <But I who have not writ this special book/(i.w.)> (Cogent?) act in male & female> MS1.

8.313.] {A deleted passage follows line 313 in MS1} <How keen we were that morning in reproach/How fierce in aspiration> expectation! how we tugged/At each side as to tear the world in twain/With that great [all that] help we'd bring it> MS1.

8.317.] Be like them <come into my dark to shine/Be gentle when I say how dark it is/I've come to you for that <my Italy> for only that/My Holy land of women/(To have?) your star shine on me> MS1.

8.366.] And worthily of both <of us -// To:>No speak indeed/Of that same June-day, when you cut <my> [your] life/Just free from mine to sail a bluer sea/Because <I was not worthy> [my pilot only knew the shore]/And kept the shallow - To speak out & say> MS1.

8.401.] {Following line 401 in MS1} <A level road for each> all men breast to breast/ <And> (That?) walk along> [all may] walk like brothers> MS1.

8.412.] To call it reason - <on such (rates?) we build [that has <(dimmed?)> darked our streets]/Our Crockford's (raucous?)> MS1, Suppose it reason! That has <darked> [slurred] our streets MS2.

8.415–16.] <And many pangs> [Who only smile] at night beneath the gas/And one way only . . thrown to ravenous beasts/For meat & satisfaction - body's want MS1.

8.522.] <Your wife, sir - Dogs may bark - but gentleman/(i.w.)> But gentleman are used to guard their speech> MS1.

8.551.] {Drafted in the left margin on page 315 in MS1} <[Did] [Truly] <Yes> so far right not farther tho' <I was wrong> / <also - putting poets in God's place/I made God's (i.w.) word so small a place>/Ignoring mankind's needs as you never did/I made so small a place> MS1.

8.688.] <For turning rounds to squares & squares to rounds> MS1.

8.689.] For learning wrestling with long lounging sleeves MS2-1856, 1856 corr.

8.785.] <I held in reverence - I revere him now/He lifted & loved (i.w.)/This globe of God's, <he did it not in pride> [upon a single palm] /<Renouncing> [Despising (aids?)] renouncing personal aims/To do the thing he could not [And overthrew some sweetness] in the attempt/To set the pots right - [if too much indeed]/He fretted]> MS1.

8.823.] {Added in the margin of MS1} <In statue, picture, book,/And reasonably angered are these men - > MS1.

8.850.] Queen Juno's <hand might strain at> MS1; <(i.w.) Juno's> fingers could not strain to milk, - MS2 corr.

8.867.] <And never plant the acorns> [& take no thought of acorns or of time/Plant one at least] <And [then] scorn to wait> a century/ And hope in [pious] patience MS1.

8.898–99.] Or even the squires, Aurora - Do you mind/Your ancient neighbours? Oh, the vicar preached/From Revelations found me with the frogs/[He] And (founded?) a fast day by special (request?) MS1.

8.955. Maud] <Jacynth> MS1 corr.

8.980.] [We are making a love knot for you] MS1.

8.1011–12.] <Had dropped & sent up faint & sudden gleams/By fits, that stood amazed & turned to stone/And grey with their discovered centuries> MS1.

8.1012.] {Following line 1012 in MS1} Discovered, turned to monumental stone; {and MS2} <Aghast and turned to monumental stone> MS2 corr.

8.1022.] {Following line 1022 in MS1} <I heard it rather with my soul than ears /> {Added in the margin} [<He said> So deep [his accents (i.w.)I]<you> heard the[ir] <accent> touch/The waters of the soul - but I broke in/In haste to take a higher level - Nay] MS1.

8.1042. We had burnt our viols] <I had given away my Percy> MS1.

8.1056.] {Deleted in MS1 and following line 1056} <For sinning past like at St James church> MS1.

8.1110.] {Following line 1110 in MS1} <And that [I like] directness, simpleness & truth> MS1.

8.1196.] Still warm with Marian's clinging clasp/Of <victim Marian> MS1.

8.1206.] {Following line 1206 in MS1} And laughed <my blood cold> MS1.

8.1216. arrogance of nature] a manly arrogance MS1.

8.1232.] {Deleted in MS2, is a line following 1232} <Who wears a thimble and plays carpet stitch> MS2 corr.

8.1245. {Following line 1245 in MS1} <And vexed my heart which sought them foolishly> MS1.

8.1251–53.] {No equivalent lines in MS1.}

## NINTH BOOK

9.1–177.] {No equivalent passage in MS1.}

9.17.] {Following line 17 in MS2} <The same as you did & I too have long hair> MS2 corr.

9.136.] {Following line 136 in MS2} <But you Miss Vane although you've written this > MS2 corr.

9.182.] I did not answer - <As the earth was drunk/With moonshine round <& round> [it <reeled> swung] beneath my feet> MS1.

9.184. Romney] Percy MS1.

9.185. Romney] Percy MS1.

9.186. Erle] Gray MS1.

9.226.] {Following line 226 in MS1} Bring down his houses honour <for this (deed?)> MS1.

9.230–31.] <Our lives are> will <such> burrs/As touch me leave a stain upon his life> MS1.

9.232.] {Following line 232 in MS1} <While men shall twit him with his natural son/And married mistress> MS1.

9.242. while yet there's time] <& take his part/Who's worthy of a saviour> MS1.

9.260–63.] {Added in the margin of MS1} <Percy's strong enough/For this, and you must struggle to be strong/To suffer him to bear it Shall we only stand/On God's side and yet <act as> [tremble] and recede/As if <we stood on the other> [God was not]> MS1.

9.305.] {Following line 305} <And Marian's grateful, happy, lifted up to Heaven/Who had been so sunken to the pit of hell/In conscious> MS1.

9.306. girl] <bruised bride> MS1 corr.

9.345.] {Following line 345 in MS1} <This wretched ruin with her bastard child> MS1.

9.370.] <This thing thy chattel - but thy love> MS1.

9.371.] {Following line 371} <No more than> finding strawberries from fern <[on my mountain gorse]>/To <mingle with> [sweeten] your milk MS1; <Than if I had looked for strawberries on gorse/For sweetening, sir, your milk> I gave you love? MS2 corr.

9.416.] This is the blossom of the evil wind <my rootless flower>/We'll round him with a sunbeam into joy/<And not a> MS1.

9.441.] {In MS1 following line 441} In love & benediction <There is one [She I know]> MS1.

9.470.] <And could not touch you with the highest spurt/Of all my poor salt spume [And shelved so high in death & nevermore]> MS1 corr.

9.512.] {Following line 512 in MS1} <I would not have you think/Although I am written in a crabbed (hand?)>/[I know] <My last words> I <am> m writ in such [poor crabbed] <crampt lines>/You always find me hard to understand/But this at least remember - this at last MS1.

9.523.] What loss was coming I had done <like him/And saved you from my wooing> MS1 corr.

9.586.] {Following line 586 in MS1} <Statistically packed to pack anew/With other labels written [neatly] by my hand [pen] MS1.

9.608.] {The draft MS1 ends here.}

9.704.] I would <(bare?) naked soul before the (thy eyes?)> MS2 corr.

9.869. absurd] is dwarfed MS2-1856, 1856 corr.

# BACKGROUNDS AND CONTEXTS

# Letters of Elizabeth Barrett Browning and Robert Browning on *Aurora Leigh*

## To Mary Russell Mitford, December 30, 1844†

* * *

No—I am afraid of Napoleon for a subject: & also it w$^{d}$ not I fancy, suit me. If I had a story of my own I might be as wild as I liked, & I sh$^{d}$ have a chance besides of interesting other people by it in a way I could not do with a known story. And I dont want to have to do with masses of men,—I sh$^{d}$ make dull work of it so. A few characters—a simple story—& plenty of room for passion & thought—*that* is what I want . . & am not likely to find easily . . without your inspiration. Oh yes, my dearest friend,—I wrote 'Lady Geraldine' on your principles, I admit: but still you shall grant to me that Lady Geraldine's Courtship[1] has more mysticism (or what is called mysticism) in it,—hid in the story . . than all the other ballad-poems of the two volumes. I hold *that*. But people care for a story—there's the truth! And I who care so much for stories, am not to find fault with them. And now tell me,—where is the obstacle to making as interesting a story of a poem as of a prose work—Echo answers *where*. Conversations & events, why may they not be given as rapidly & passionately & lucidly in verse as in prose—echo answers *why*. You see nobody is offended by my approach to the conventions of vulgar life in 'Lady Geraldine'—and it gives me courage to go on, & touch this real everyday life of our age, & hold it with my two hands. I want to write a poem of a new class, in a measure—a Don Juan, without the mockery & impurity, . . under one aspect,—& having unity, as a work of art,—& admitting of as much philosophical dreaming & digression (which is in fact a characteristic of the age) as I like to use. Might it not be done, even if I could not do it? & I think of trying at any rate.

* * *

† From *The Letters of Elizabeth Barrett Browning to Mary Russell Mitford, 1836–1854*, ed. Meredith B. Raymond and Mary Rose Sullivan (Winfield, Kansas: Wedgestone, 1983), III, 49. Reprinted by permission.

Mary Russell Mitford (1787–1855) was a writer and editor. She met EBB in May 1836, and they maintained a close friendship both in person and by letter for twenty years. Flush, EBB's dog, was a gift from MRM.

1. A long narrative poem written by EBB in July 1844 when her publisher wanted some additional material to fill up the first volume of her *Poems* (1844). The setting is a contemporary nineteeth-century one and concerns the love of a poet for the daughter of an earl. It includes a reference to Robert Browning that was partly instrumental in bringing RB to first write to EBB.

## To Robert Browning, February 27, 1845†

* * *

But my chief *intention* just now is the writing of a sort of novel-poem—a poem as completely modern as 'Geraldine's Courtship,' running into the midst of our conventions, and rushing into drawing-rooms and the like, 'where angels fear to tread'; and so, meeting face to face and without mask the Humanity of the age, and speaking the truth as I conceive of it out plainly. That is my intention. It is not mature enough yet to be called a plan. I am waiting for a story, and I won't take one, because I want to make one, and I like to make my own stories, because then I can take liberties with them in the treatment.

* * *

## To Robert Browning, February 26, 1846†

* * *

As for the writing, I will write . . I have written . . I am writing. You do not fancy that I have given up writing?—No. Only I have certainly been more loitering and distracted than usual in what I have done, which is not my fault—nor your directly—and I feel an indisposition to setting about the romance,[2] the hand of the soul shakes. I am too happy and not calm enough, I suppose, to have the right inclination. Well—it will come. But all in blots and fragments there are verses enough, to fill a volume done in the last year.

* * *

## To John Kenyon, [March 1855]†

* * *

Between five & six thousand lines written, & more still to write—Blank verse—. Why not?—An autobiography of a poetess—(not me) . .

† From *The Letters of Robert Browning and Elizabeth Barrett Browning*, ed. R. B. Browning (London, 1899), I, 32.

Robert Browning (1812–89) was an English poet. Prompted by his admiration for her poetry, RB first wrote to EBB in January 1845. They met in May 1845 and conducted a love affair by letter and with occasional brief and secret meetings, because EBB's father disapproved of anyone who wanted to marry any of his children. They married secretly in September 1846 and later eloped to Italy, where they lived, apart from short visits to England, until EBB's death in 1861. With their one son, Pen, RB returned to live in England.

In this letter of February 1845, EBB replies to RB's question about her work in progress.

† From *The Letters of Robert Browning and Elizabeth Barrett Browning*, I, 514.

2. Refers back to the idea for *Aurora Leigh* mentioned in EBB's letter of February 1845 to RB. The "volume . . . all in blots and fragments" that EBB speaks of in this letter may be an early initial sketch for *Aurora Leigh*, but she could also be thinking of the *Sonnets from the Portuguese* (1850), which EBB wrote during 1845–46 and presented as a love-gift to RB in 1849.

† By permission of the Houghton Library, Harvard University. See Philip Kelley and Ronald Hudson, *The Brownings' Correspondence: A Checklist* (New York: The Browning Institute,

opposing the practical & the ideal lifes, & showing how the practical & real (so called) is but the external evolution of the ideal & spiritual—that it is *from inner to outer*, . . whether in life, morals, or art—A good deal, in this relation, upon the social question, & against the socialists—A good deal, in fact, about everything in the world & beyond . . . taken from the times, "hot and hot." I rather took fright at "Hard Times,"[3] as Robert told me from a review (we neither of us have seen the book) that it treated of an opposition of the Real & Ideal—But upon consideration I took breath & courage—because it's *impossible* that Dickens & I could walk precisely the same ground—If we did, there would be still, "badger's foot" and "ourangoutang's,"—distinct enough. "The Devil," you say. *Dont*—I believe my book will be clear enough,—alive enough, even if the story may be wanting in "rapidity"—There are characters—talks.

* * *

## To Anna Jameson, January [26?], 1856†

* * *

You see I was thrown behind terribly with the Rue de Grenelle misfortunes,[4] and when I came to face the heap of dishevelled m = s.—with still the heap unwritten . . it seemed scarcely possible to draw a poem out of it all. I was desperate . . what with the real thing & the despondency superinduced by not feeling strong, . . England & the preface to Paris having nearly done for me. So then I had to try to be reasonable, (which involved a struggle) and decided on the most reasonable process of transcribing the finished books of the poem . . in order to enable me

1978), 55:30. All hitherto unpublished material quoted by kind permission of Philip Kelley and John Murray,

John Kenyon (1784–1856) was a distant relative of EBB's and a schoolmate of RB's father. He was a close friend of both EBB and RB and stood, as it were, in the place of a father to EBB after her father disowned her in 1846. He settled money on the couple after the birth of their son, Pen, and left them a legacy that meant they were financially secure after 1856. *Aurora Leigh* was dedicated to John Kenyon, and just before he died he sent out numerous gift copies of the book to his friends.

3. A novel by Charles Dickens (1812–70), published in 1855. From the 1840s until his death Dickens was the most popular novelist of the time. *Hard Times*, however, was not one of his most successful books, as it set out a rather diagrammatic opposition between "Fact," represented by the moralist Gradgrind, and "Fancy," represented by the circus ringmaster Sleary.

† Reprinted by permission of the Henry W. and Albert A. Berg Collection, The New York Public Library, Astor, Lenox, and Tilden Foundations.

Anna Jameson (1794–1860) was an art critic. She met RB in 1840 and EBB in 1842, but knew nothing of their secret courtship, so was astonished in September 1846 when RB sought her out in Paris and asked for her aid in looking after his new wife, who was worn out with emotion and travel. Anna Jameson traveled on to Italy with the couple and remained a close friend to both.

4. The Brownings had left their home in Florence for an extended visit to France and England in June 1855. They spent that summer in London and returned to Paris in October to stay for the winter in apartments in the Rue de Grenelle, which had been rented for them. But the apartment was unsatisfactory and they had to remove to rooms in the Rue du Colysee in December 1855.

to see what was done, & judge what remained to do—Very busy I have been, & the first book is finished, about which Robert has given me a little courage—(I showed it to him in mere faintness of spirit—but he has done me great good by his good word.)

* * *

## To Arabella Barrett, January [29–30], 1856†

* * *

* * *So busy I am—worked out of breath, to get on with the poem. I finished the second book, & gave it to Robert to read, & he lifted me up as high as his dear arms could go, with encouraging sayings of it. He thinks it exceeds anything I have done yet. Oh—I do hope & trust it's a true judgement. I begin to be braver. Yes—I was horribly desponding about it, (& almost most things besides, at one time)—but we get into light again, (in spite of Hume's disgracing me,[5] Arabel)—and I go on fagging, fagging. See what I do everyday. We breakfast at nine—& before I am out of bed I hear Peni[6] say his two french verbs, (which he says beautifully)—& Robert, before I am drest, hears him say his spelling. After breakfast I hear him the rest of his lessons till the hour and a half are out. He never has more than an hour & a half, unless he is very naughty & keeps me a quarter of an hour longer. Afterwards, from a little after eleven I write sedulously, till half past three or four & we dine.* * *

## To Arabella Barrett, [February 27, 1856]†

* * *I get on with the poem, & have finished the fifth book—altogether more than six thousand lines written & transcribed. Still I hope to have it contained in one thick volume. There will be two or three more books. Robert praises it magnificently —thinks it "out & out" the best thing I ever did—which certainly it ought to be—& says it is interesting as a story. Its quite unlike anything of mine—&, I hope, of any-

† See *Checklist* 56:24.

Arabella Barrett (1813–68) was the sixth child and fourth daughter of Edward and Mary Moulton-Barrett. She was very close to her sister EBB and they maintained a voluminous correspondence after EBB's departure for Italy. Arabella never married but remained at home looking after her father until his death, unreconciled to EBB, in 1857. When EBB died, RB settled near to Arabella, and she devoted herself to caring for RB and Pen.

5. Daniel Dunglas Hume (he later changed his name to Home) was a fashionable medium, whom EBB believed in. RB was sceptical, and Hume is said to be the original of a scathing portrait in "Mr Sludge the Medium." Early in 1856, while she was staying in Paris, EBB heard from her friends in Florence that Hume had been "thrown over" by one of his patrons there because of "some failure in his moral character." EBB admitted that this was quite likely, but still claimed that he was a true medium.

6. EBB's son, Pen. His name comes from his childish inability to pronounce Wiedemann, his middle name and RB's mother's maiden name.

† See *Checklist* 56:38.

body's else. As to Swedenborgianism, spiritualism & c.[7] the advantage for me is that though I write myself out with a good deal of frankness, neither you nor Robert will find much, if anything in me objectionable—the poetry will wrap me up & make me acceptable. Why? just because I express myself better, more intensely, in poetry—& then you *see* the truth of me—understand me—which you dont, in poor conversational prose. It's so with Robert, at any rate. And as for *you*, I dont feel the least afraid that you will excommunicate me, or be vexed, after reading what is written. Think of that darling Robert being moved really to tears when he told me his opinion of the poem. Twice he broke into tears. Dont mention it when you write—but I must tell you, for his sake.* * *

## To Arabella Barrett, [March 13, 1856]†

* * *I have finished my sixth book, & am now in the composition-part. I was anxious about the sixth book & Robert,—as the situation is rather *hazarde*[8]—"What next?" will you say, Arabel? But he was delighted with it & didn't set it down as *too* indecent. He keeps saying—"Out & out superior to anything you have done." I myself (now I am out of my panic) am inclined to think so too. There is more power & variety than in my previous things. At the same time there is much provocation to attacks—I am perfectly aware of that also* * *

## To Arabella Barrett, [September 21, 1856]†

* * *We go tomorrow,—and having been worked nearly to death today (to say nothing of the cold which is mortal) I have a moment to thank you in, for your two dear disappointing letters . . . I am so glad you like that revise. As to "burly brutal"—my dearest George,[9] my dearest Arabel, you are both wrong. 'Burly' is rather complimentary than other wise. When anybody shall call *me* 'burly'—(in the spiritual world perhaps) I shall consider it satisfactory. 'Brutal', is the specific

7. Emanuel Swedenborg (1688–1772), Swedish philosopher and mystic. According to his system the universe consists of two worlds—one of spirit and one of nature—that are reflected in the duality of a spiritual ideal world and a physical real world. EBB was a passionate adherent of Swedenborg's work, though he was often deemed something of a crank by her contemporaries, and she refers directly to his philosophy in *Aurora Leigh* at 5.116–25 and 7.840–50. EBB believed in spiritualism, table-turning, automatic writing, and so on, and saw these manifestations as natural phenomena resulting from a correspondence between the spirit world and the natural world. But she was conscious that spiritualism was regarded with suspicion by her contemporaries and sought to keep her references to it in *Aurora Leigh* to a minimum.

† See *Checklist* 56:47.

8. French; "hazardous." EBB is worried about decency in the story of Marian's rape and impregnation.

† See *Checklist* 56:133.

9. EBB's brother George Goodin Barrett Moulton-Barrett (1816–95). He was a lawyer and though, like her other brothers, George broke with EBB after her marriage, he was reconciled in 1851 and made himself useful to the Brownings in worldly matters.

word for English mobs. They are not frantic & cruel, as a French mob, when hard pressed, can be, (see French revolution) but 'brutal' they are, & must be—& nobody ever denied them to be, as far as I have heard. Really I scarcely know what I am writing. Only—I'm so glad I'm not at Ventnor[1] to see George's face, after a proof I shall send you presently. Tell me if he thinks it "unfit writing for a lady"—that I may put my head under the table-cloth. The volume is wearing to an end, and we are in the last 'Book' but one. Here we are at the end of September! Its time to end, indeed. * * *

### To Arabella Barrett, [October 4, 1856] †

* * *I can't miss today's post—and yet I'm driven to the wall, & there's scarcely time to write. Five proofs remain for printing—the presses being all engaged with the previous part of the book—so that I must begin at the beginning & finish the review of all, before you have any more proofs. . . . Now the poem. No, George, not "worse than Don Juan"[2] by any manner of means,—because the intention is *not* licentious. There's a great difference. I admit, it's a horrible situation—but I wanted a horrible situation to prove a beautiful verity. The intention of the poem *everywhere* is to raise the spiritual above the natural; this is carried out in everything. Marian, subjected to the most hideous of trials, in fact though with an unconsenting will, is made to emerge with a glory of purity & even of moral dignity, (increased by her very misfortune) to which, at the end, no reader shall be insensible. You shall feel the virtue of chastity, in her, more even than in Aurora. Something of the kind was done by Richardson in Clarissa[3]—but Clarissa was a sublime creature—more exceptionally attractive than my Marian is—& after all, Clarissa dies—which I dont mean Marian to do. Marian shall have a clear triumph even here. Oh—I think it very likely that the poem will be shoved away from the reading of young girls—but if it stoops low on certain dunghills, *that is,* in order that it may leap high to the most skyey significances. * * *

1. A holiday resort, on the Isle of Wight, where the Barrett family spent the summer of 1856. EBB visited them there in August and traveled on to West Cowes, also on the Isle of Wight, to visit John Kenyon.

† See *Checklist* 56:142.

2. An epic satire by George Gordon Byron, published in 1819–24. Because the work deals with the various love affairs of the young Juan, this book seems to have been a bugbear to all the Barretts. As a child EBB herself was forbidden to read it by her father. Obviously she managed to read it later.

3. *Clarissa: of the History of a Young Lady,* a novel in letters by Samuel Richardson, published in 1747–49. Lovelace is an adventuring rake who persuades the beleaguered Clarissa to put herself under his protection, even though she knows that he is planning to seduce her. She resists him through some eight volumes, but in the end he rapes her, and Clarissa, disgraced, allows herself to die.

## To Isa Blagden, [October 20, 1856]†

* * *

Bessie Parkes[4] is writing very vigorous articles on the woman question,[5] in opposition to Mr Patmore,[6] poet & husband, who expounds infamous doctrines on the same subject—see 'National Review'—& send [thus] them 'with the author's regards' to Mrs Browning—Also if you heard Bessie Parkes—she & the rest of us militant, foam with rage—But he'll have the best of it as far as I am concerned: inasmuch as I hear he is to Review in the North British my poor 'Aurora Leigh', who has the unfeminine impropriety to express her opinion on various "abstract subjects",—which Mr. Patmore can't abide, he says.

So glad I am that you like my name 'Aurora Leigh'. I thought you wouldn't object much on that ground. My brother George, who has seen the proof sheets, says, that it is by far the best & strongest of my works,—but for the rest, "more indecent than Don Juan"—to a degree which must exclude it "from the boudoir-table of any lady" . . (his own words) & prevent all girls from touching it with the end of their finger—How you will laugh! how I did laugh!—

* * *

## To Henrietta Surtees Cook, October 22, 1856†

One word of goodbye. We go to-morrow—and couldn't before, being so put upon, and pressed upon, and trampled on by affairs of all kinds.

† By permission of the Syndics of the Fitzwilliam Museum.
Isa Blagden (1816–73) was a prominent member of the expatriate community in Florence, and especially close to the Brownings. After EBB's death it was to Isa that RB turned for help, and she traveled with him and Pen to England and remained a firm friend until her death.

4. Bessie Rayner Parkes (1829–1925) was a feminist and an activist in the cause for women's rights. She did not know EBB well, but they were acquainted, and EBB approved of her efforts to obtain better education and improved opportunities and equalities for women. In the 1850s Bessie Parkes was instrumental in presenting a petition to parliament concerning married women's property (a married woman could not then own any—it belonged to her husband) and EBB was one of the signatories.
5. From the 1840s on, many women (and men) had been arguing over both the legal status of women and their lack of educational and employment opportunity, as well as over the "nature" of the feminine and the relation of the sexes. These debates were popularly known as "the women question," and the term continued in use until about the 1880s.
6. Coventry Patmore (1823–96), English poet. Patmore had begun to publish his famous poem *The Angel in the House* in 1854. His reactionary views on the nature of women and their place in the home were expressed in this work and made EBB realize that her own forward thinking in *Aurora Leigh* was not likely to be welcomed by him.

† From *Elizabeth Barrett Browning: Letters to her Sister 1846–1859*, ed. Leonard Huxley (London, 1929), 260.
Henrietta Surtees Cook (1809–60) was EBB's sister Henrietta Barrett Moulton-Barrett. In 1850 Henrietta married William Surtees Cook and, like EBB, was disowned by her father. She moved to Somerset in England and bore two sons and a daughter. Her early death from breast cancer was a source of great suffering to EBB.

After this, I have only *fifty autographs* to write; and then my work is all but done, in the way of writing. * * *

"Aurora Leigh" shall be sent to you. I dare say it will shock you; but you will like a few things, perhaps—*rather!*

* * *

## To Sarianna Browning, [November 1856]†

* * *Dearest Sarianna, I am very much pleased that you like the poem, having feared a little that you might not. M. Milsand[7] will *not*, I prophesy; 'seeing as from a tower the end of all.' The 'Athenæum' is right in supposing that it will be much liked *and* much disliked by people in general, although the press is so far astonishing in its goodwill, and although the extravagance of private letters might well surprise the warmest of my friends. But, patience! In a little while we shall have the other side of the question, and the whips will fall fast after the nosegays. Still, I am surprised, I own, at the amount of success; and that golden-hearted Robert is in ecstasies about it—far more than if it all related to a book of his own. The form of the story, and also something in the philosophy, seem to have caught the crowd. As to the poetry by itself, anything good in *that* repels rather. I am not as blind as Romney, not to perceive this. He had to be blinded, observe, to be made to see; just as Marian had to be dragged through the uttermost debasement of circumstances to arrive at the sentiment of personal dignity. I am sorry, but indeed it seemed necessary. * * *

## Robert Browning to Edward Chapman, December 2, 1856†

* * *

I receive by today's post *Aurora Leigh*—from you or yours, I conjecture—but no word of comment. There is always such a thing to fear in these parts as a letter's miscarrying—has that been so? If not, it's a shame of you, black and burning, not to have been at that trouble. But a letter

† From *The Letters of Elizabeth Barrett Browning*, ed. Frederic G. Kenyon (London, 1897), II, 242.

Sarianna Browning (1814–1903) was Robert Browning's only sister. Sarianna never married, but lived with her father until his death in 1866. She then lived with RB and with Pen in Italy and died at his estate at Casalino near Florence,

7. A prominent French critic (1817–86). He met RB in October 1851 and was a frequent visitor. He formed a particular friendship with Robert Browning senior and with Sarianna Browning when they visited RB and EBB in Paris. Milsand's review of *Aurora Leigh* in the *Revue des Deux Mondes* was highly complimentary.

† From *New Letters of Robert Browning*, ed. DeVane and Knickerbocker (London: John Murray, 1951), 96–97.

Edward Chapmen was RB's publisher. RB left his previous publisher, Edward Moxon, in 1848 and took his work thereafter to Chapman and Hall. EBB did the same, because they agreed that Moxon had not been an efficient publisher of their works.

from Mr. Procter[8] comes too, and speaks of your needing to go to press very soon with another edition, and the book we receive *may* be sent for presumable corrections. In this case, print tomorrow, if you please. There is nothing whatever to correct, that we are able to see at present, the book having been *settled* for some time to come while we were in London for that purpose. My wife made up her mind to it as it *is*, and for the present, as I say, cannot reconsider the subject. All the "modern" passages, illustrations, are vitally necessary, she thinks,—and I think quite as strongly,—and could not be detached without capital injury to the rest of the poem. And for the rest, there would seem to be no verbal errors to signify; however we will look to that, and let you know or not, as it may seem worth while. But the principal thing is to pray you not to keep people waiting a moment in waiting for further notice from us (*Us*—I am the church-organ-bellows' blower that talked about *our* playing, but you know what I do in the looking after commas and dots to i's).

I saw the *Athenaeum*, *Globe*, and *Daily News*, that's all, hearing of eulogy from the *Lit. Gaz.* and blackguardism from the "Press"; all like those night-men who are always emptying their cart at my door, and welcome when I remember that after all they don't touch our bread with their beastly hands, as they used to do. Don't you mind them, and leave me to rub their noses in their own filth some fine day.

* * *

## To Arabella Barrett, [December 10–18, 1856]†

* * *As for papa,[9] I am a little comforted about him just for the present—but the thought of him has been hanging like a stone about my heart for ever so long; now when I ought to be elated & delighted, I suppose, at the success of my poem. Well—I am glad, of course,-but it's wonderful how little happy, this reaching, in a degree, what has been with me an object in life, has made me. If there was nobody to be uneasy about, how different it would *feel*, I say to myself. Robert, at least, is happy in the success of the poem. When people write & talk of the "jealousy" of authors & husbands, let them look at him! Only that he has the most exceptional heart of gold, to be found, perhaps, in this

8. Bryan Waller Procter (1787–1874), the poet who wrote under the pseudonym "Barry Cornwall." The Procter household was the center of a wide artistic circle, and he was the early encourager of RB and Charles Dickens, among others.

† See *Checklist* 56:189.

9. Arabella, EEB's younger sister, still lived with their father at Wimpole Street in 1856, and she gave EBB news of him in her letters. EBB herself, of couse, had never heard from him since he wrote her an "unsparing" letter disowning her as a consequence of her marriage to RB. During their visit to England in 1852 the Brownings attempted a reconciliation. But Edward Moulton-Barrett replied with another harsh letter to RB and by sending back to them, unopened, every single one of the many letters EBB had written to him since her elopement in 1846. As her father had always been her most ardent supporter in her early writing career, EBB still thought sadly of this loss with each new publication.

world, or nearly so—in the bosom of men. Yes, Arabel, I have come after ten years to that conclusion. He has a quite wonderful great-heartedness. To go back to the poem, its success has been extraordinary-rendering it necessary to go to press with the second edition, a fortnight after publication. What surprises me most is, that there have been no violent attacks, except from the 'Press'—only, of course, these *must* come with the monthly & quarterly reviews. Meantime, it is taken up into favour with certain persons, to the amount of a mania—with some, perhaps, on account of the story, & with others probably, on account of the philosophy which is—not originated-but *presented* for the first time poetically. It strikes me that men like Ruskin[1] for instance, are excited by this chiefly. Otherwise I dont account for the state of things at all. I take no credit to myself for it, for the best poets are inevitably most neglected—nobody can be surer of that, than I. For the rest, I am very pleased that I should have pleased you in this, -not displease you, as I feared some things might. I would not send a copy to Mr. Stratten.[2] It seemed to me unbecoming for obvious reasons; (tell me what he says) but that I should have allowed him to buy a copy, seems wrong too. Arabel-I want Mary Hunter[3] to have a copy-but she must wait for the second edition now—& I should advise her to wait for the third, which will be in two volumes, Chapman says, & of the smaller form . . . Some days have passed since I wrote the above; for just then I was interrupted by Robert's coming in with his letter containing the sorrowful, sorrowful news from Cowes.[4] . . . We should have wanted much, except for him. His last act with regard to that book of mine, was to buy & distribute among his friends forty seven copies-which was important to me chiefly, of course, as being expressive of the tender feeling with which he accepted my dedication . . . the success of 'Aurora' is a great thing—will be as to money-results. The extravagant things said about that poem, would make you smile (as they make me)-and there's one sort of compliment which would please you particularly—people are

1. John Ruskin (1819–1900), art critic and philosopher. From his early work in *Modern Painters* (1834, 1846, 1856) Ruskin obtained great popularity and was an important influence on at least two generations of writers and thinkers, most notably the pre-Raphaelite school around Dante Gabriel Rossetti and the decadent school around Oscar Wilde. Ruskin met the Brownings in the 1850s. He was skeptical about the quality of RB's work but in no doubt about EBB's and was especially enthusiastic in his reading of *Aurora Leigh*.
2. The Reverend James Stratten, who was a clergyman at the Paddington Chapel, which the Barretts attended when they moved to London in 1836. EBB admired him as a clergyman but chose not to confide in him when she was planning to run away with RB, because she knew that if word of Stratten's knowledge came out, her father would forbid Arabella, much the most religious of the sisters, to attend his chapel. Presumably it would have been "unbecoming" for EBB to send Stratten a copy of *Aurora Leigh* because it contained some things a clergyman might not have wished to read, especially in the case of EBB's spiritual and Swedenborgian philosophy, which was by no means conventional Christian thinking.
3. The daughter (1826–?) of George Barrett Hunter (no relation), who was minister at the Marsh Independent Chapel at Sidmouth while the Barretts lived there in 1832. Mary's mother was in an asylum for the insane, and EBB regarded Mary with motherly affection, writing little poems for her when Mary was a child and letters of advice when she reached adulthood.
4. That is, of the death of John Kenyon, which took place in December 1856.

fond of calling it "a gospel". That's happy-is'nt it? You suppose perhaps that one unlucky individual calls it so? Not in the least: it's the favorite phrase, in letters from England—in gossip at Florence—And even from America the other day, the publisher writes—"we have received Mrs. Browning's *gospel*". I said to Robert,—"Now this grows too much. I really must gratify Arabel by telling her at once." So I tell you. Is it entirely prophane[sic], or simply ridiculous? I leave you to choose. Still, that there *is* an amount of spiritual truth in the book to which the public is unaccustomed, I know very well—only, I was helped to it—did not originate it—& was tempted much (by a natural feeling of honesty) to say so in the poem, & was withheld by nothing except a conviction that the naming of the name of Swedenborg,[5] that great Seer into the two worlds, would have utterly destroyed any hope of general acceptance & consequent utility. Instead of Mrs. Browning's 'gospel', it wd. have been Mrs. Browning's rhodomantade![6] "What! that imposter, Swedenborg! that madman, Swedenborg." But that imposter & madman, such as he is, holds sublime truths in his right hand, & most humbly I have used them as I could. My desire is, that the weakness in *me*, may not hinder the influence. Mind you tell me what Mr. Stratten says. (Not that you need repeat to him what I have written above.) Mind you thank dearest George for the newspapers, he sent to me. Did you see the Daily News? The Tablet turns on me like a tiger, & calls "Aurora" a "brazen-faced woman"—& the whole poem "like a novel by Frederic Soulie"[7]—which means, something highly improper. But I agree with you in wondering at the manner in which, generally speaking, I have escaped the charge of impropriety; it's quite beyond my own expectation. Oh yes, Arabel, dearest,—seeing a book by bite, as you & George read mine, was just the way to throw out the doubtful things in a sort of artificial relief. The whole keeps down the parts, & makes them seem decenter, of course. Any way, I am *very* much pleased that you should like the book as you say—it's a great pleasure to me. Such a letter has come from Mr. Ruskin![8] unqualified in its praise.* * *

## To Isa Blagden, [December 1856] †

* * *

I am rather glad you have not seen the 'Athenæum'; the analysis it gives of my poem is so very unfair and partial. You would say the conception was really *null*. It does not console me at all that I should be

5. See note 7 to letter from EBB to Arabella Barrett, February 27, 1856, p. 333.
6. A vain and extravagant boast.
7. Frédéric Soulié (1800–47), French dramatist and author of sensationalist novels.
8. See note 1 above. The letter from Ruskin to which EBB refers is John Ruskin to RB, November 27, 1856, in *The Works of John Ruskin*, ed. E. T. Cook and Alexander Wedderburn (London, 1903–1912), 36, 247.

† From *The Letters of Elizabeth Barrett Browning*, II, 243.

praised and over-praised, the idea given of the poem remaining so absolutely futile. Even the outside shell of the plan is but half given, and the double action of the metaphysical intention entirely ignored. I protest against it. Still, Robert thinks the article not likely to do harm. Perhaps not. Only one hates to be misrepresented.

* * *

## To Anna Jameson, December 26, 1856†

* * *

Yet your letter, my dearest Mona Nina, arrived in time to give me great, great pleasure—true pleasure indeed, and most tenderly do I thank you for it. I have had many of such letters from persons loved less, and whose opinions had less weight; and you will like to hear that in a fortnight after publication Chapman had to go to press with the second edition. In fact, the kind of reception given to the book has much surprised me, as I was prepared for an outcry of quite another kind, and extravagances in a quite opposite sense. This has been left, however, to the 'Press,' the 'Post,' and the 'Tablet,' who calls 'Aurora' 'a brazen-faced woman,' and brands the story as a romance in the manner of Frederic Soulié—in reference, of course, to its gross indecency.

I can't leave this subject without noticing (by the way) what you say of the likeness to the catastrophe of 'Jane Eyre.'[9] I have sent to the library here for 'Jane Eyre' (but haven't got it yet) in order to refresh my memory on this point; but, as far as I do recall the facts, the hero was monstrously disfigured and blinded in a fire the particulars of which escape me, and the circumstance of his being hideously scarred is the thing impressed chiefly on the reader's mind; certainly it remains innermost in mine. Now if you read over again those pages of my poem, you will find that the only injury received by Romney in the fire was from a blow and from the emotion produced by the *circumstances* of the fire. Not only did he *not* lose his eyes in the fire, but he describes the ruin of his house as no blind man could. He was standing there, a spectator. Afterwards he had a fever, and the eyes, the visual nerve, perished, showing no external stain—perished as Milton's did.[1] I believe that a great shock on the nerves might produce such an effect in certain constitutions, and the reader on referring as far back as Marian's letter (when she avoided the marriage) may observe that his eyes had never been strong, that her desire had been to read his notes at night, and save

† From *The Letters of Elizabeth Barrett Browning*, II, 245.

9. The novel by Charlotte Brontë (1816–55), published in 1847.

1. John Milton (1608–74), English poet, who went blind in 1651. In his poem "To Mr Cyriack Skinner upon his Blindness," Milton describes how, though his sight was gone, his eyes outwardly appeared as clear and bright as ever.

them. For it was necessary, I thought, to the bringing-out of my thought, that Romney should be mulcted[2] in his natural sight. The 'Examiner' saw that. Tell me if, on looking into the book again, you modify your feeling at all.

* * *

## To Anna Jameson, January 9, [1857]†

* * *I have very extravagent letters about 'Aurora', which really I could laugh or cry over . . with more reason for crying, perhaps—It surprises me that the book shouldn't have given more offence in various quarters—but, I dare say, Blackwood[3] will make amends for any short-comings in this respect—You tell me that the 'form' is objected to—meaning, probably, the modern effects &c, of which dear Mr Procter[4] has spoken to me—But "the form", in this sense is my experiment, & I dont "give it up" yet, having considered the subject much & long.

* * *

## To Henrietta Surtees Cook, January 10, 1857†

* * *

Dearest Henrietta, thank you and dear Surtees[5] for your sympathy and kindness about the book. The second edition should have been out by this time; but Chapman's name begins with a C like a crab's, and there's a likeness otherwise.

In America it is published. We can barely hear of it, and of the reception which is said to be very favourable. I can scarcely understand how more offence has not been given and taken in certain quarters. Only, there's a review in Blackwood, and Blackwood will grind me to powder, I don't doubt, as far as Blackwood can.

Oh yes—we heard of the Press. And the Guardian—tell me, Henrietta, if your Guardian did not bark like a mastiff and tear me. Robert says I am longing to be abused a little—mind, *I* don't say so.

Mr. Jarves[6] came to enquire very seriously the other day, whether

2. To be deprived of, or punished with the loss of something.
† Reprinted by permission of the Henry W. and Albert A. Berg Collection, The New York Public Library, Astor, Lenox, and Tilden Foundations.
3. That is, *Blackwood's Edinburgh Magazine*, a prominent critical journal.
4. See note 8 to letter from RB to Edward Chapman, December 2, 1856, p. 337.
† From *Elizabeth Barrett Browning: Letters to her Sister 1846–1859*, 265.
5. Henrietta's husband.
6. James Jackson Jarves, an American who visited Florence in 1854 and became acquainted with the Brownings. He maintained a correspondence with EBB on their mutual interest in spiritualism. Jarves wrote an account of his Italian journey in *Italian Rambles: Studies of Life and Manners in New and Old Italy* (London, 1883).

there was any truth in the story going about Florence that "Aurora" was written by the "spirits," and that I disavowed any share in it except the mere mechanical holding of the pen!!! Think of that.

* * *

## To Arabella Barrett, January 25, [1857]†

* * *Tell me if Papa[7] has made any observation about the second edition of "Aurora". I think so much of these things in reference to him—but I daresay he is absolutely indifferent to me & my writings.

* * *You see, the story is attractive, & then there's a certain boldness in the sentiments,—for as to the poetry I never will believe that the muses are moveable by mere poetry. On the other side, I do hear that there's a party in England, holding up their hands at the scandal of a woman's writing [having written] such a book. And Mrs. Ogilvy[8] tells me that the mamas "wont allow their daughters to read it"—Well the daughters must be very young—& my comfort is that they will grow older—Certainly some of the most enthusiastic voices which have reached me have been voices of noble women. Dreadfully obstinate I am, & selfwilled, Arabel—

* * *

## To Anna Jameson, February 2, 1857†

* * *

And as for the critics—yes, indeed, I agree with you that I have no reason to complain. More than that, I confess to you that I am entirely astonished at the amount of reception I have met with—I who expected to be put in the stocks and pelted with the eggs of the last twenty years' 'singing birds' as a disorderly woman and freethinking poet! People have been so kind that, in the first place, I really come to modify my opinions somewhat upon their conventionality, to see the progress made in freedom of thought. Think of quite decent women taking the part of the book in a sort of *effervescence* which I hear of with astonishment. In fact, there has been an enormous quantity of extravagance talked and written on the subject, and I *know it*—oh, I know it. I wish I deserved some

† Reprinted by permission of the Henry W. and Albert A. Berg Collection, The New York Public Library, Astor, Lenox, and Tilden Foundations.

7. Edward Barrett Moulton-Barrett. See note 9 to letter to Arabella Barrett, December 10–18, 1856, p. 337.

8. Eliza Ogilvy (1822–1912). Mr. and Mrs. David Ogilvy met the Brownings when they were in Rome in 1847. Later they settled in Florence and took rooms in Casa Guidi just below the Brownings' apartment. As EBB's son, Pen, and Eliza's daughter, Marcia, were both born at Casa Guidi their friendship, and later their correspondence, was largely baby-based.

† From *The Letters of Elizabeth Barrett Browning*, II, 252–53.

things—some things; I wish it were all true. But I see too distinctly what I *ought* to have written. Still, it is nearer the mark than my former efforts—fuller, stronger, more sustained—and one may be encouraged to push on to something worthier, for I don't feel as if I had done yet—no indeed. I have had from Leigh Hunt[9] a very pleasant letter of twenty pages, and I think I told you of the two from John Ruskin.[1] In America, also, there's great success, and the publisher is said to have shed tears over the proofs (perhaps in reference to the hundred pounds he had to pay for them), and the critics congratulate me on having worked myself clear of all my affectations, mannerisms, and other morbidities.

Even 'Blackwood' is not to be complained of, seeing that the writer evidently belongs to an elder school, and judges from his own point of view. He is wrong, though, even in classical matters, as it seems to *me*.

* * *

## To Julia Martin, February [1857]†

My dearest Mrs. Martin,—I needn't say how much, how very much, pleasure your letter gave me. That the poem should really have touched you, reached you, with whatever drawbacks, is a joy. And then that Mr. Martin should have read it with any sort of interest! It was more than I counted on, as you know. Thank you, dearest Mrs. Martin—thank both of you for so much sympathy.

In respect to certain objections, I am quite sure you do me the justice to believe that I do not willingly give cause for offence. Without going as far as Robert, who holds that I 'couldn't be coarse if I tried,' (only that!) you will grant that I don't habitually dabble in the dirt; it's not the way of my mind or life. If, therefore, I move certain subjects in this work, it is because my conscience was first moved in me not to ignore them. What has given most offence in the book, more than the story of Marian—far more!—has been the reference to the condition of women in our cities, which a woman oughtn't to refer to, by any manner of means, says the conventional tradition. Now I have thought deeply otherwise. If a woman ignores these wrongs, then may women as a sex

9. James Henry Leigh Hunt (1784–1859), English poet and journalist. A friend of the Byron and Shelley circle, RB sought out Leigh Hunt because of this connection. The letter from Leigh Hunt to which EBB refers is Leigh Hunt to RB, January 1, 1857, in "*Aurora Leigh*: An Unpublished Letter from Leigh Hunt," *The Cornhill Magazine*, new series 3 (December 1897), 76.

1. See note 1 to letter from EBB to Arabella Barrett, December 10–18, 1856, p. 338.

† From *The Letters of Elizabeth Browning*, II, 256–57.

Julia Martin (1793–1867?) was a friend of EBB's from the days of her youth at Hope End, Edward Barrett's estate in Herefordshire. The estate of James and Julia Martin was at Old Colwall and adjoined the Hope End estate. When EBB visited England in 1855 Julia Martin invited her to stay at Old Colwall, but EBB replied that she could never bear to return to her beloved Hope End. Julia Martin tried to intervene with Edward Barrett and persuade him to forgive the three children who had married, but she failed.

continue to suffer them; there is no help for any of us—let us be dumb and die. I have spoken therefore, and in speaking have used plain words—words which look like blots, and which you yourself would put away—words which, if blurred or softened, would imperil perhaps the force and righteousness of the moral influence. Still, I certainly will, when the time comes, go over the poem carefully, and see where an offence can be got rid of without loss otherwise. The second edition was issued so early that Robert would not let me alter even a comma, would not let me look between the pages in order to the least alteration. He said (the truth) that my head was dizzy-blind with the book, and that, if I changed anything, it would be probably for the worse; like arranging a room in the dark. Oh no. Indeed he is not vexed that you should say what you do. On the contrary, he was *pleased* because of the much more that you said. As to your friend with the susceptible 'morals'—well, I could not help smiling indeed. I am assured too, by a friend of my own, that the 'mamas of England' in a body refuse to let their daughters read it. Still, the daughters emancipate themselves and *do*, that is certain; for the number of *young* women, not merely 'the strong-minded' as a sect, but pretty, affluent, happy women, surrounded by all the temptations of English respectability, that cover it with the most extravagant praises is surprising to me, who was not prepared for that particular kind of welcome. It's true that there's a quantity of hate to balance the love, only I think it chiefly seems to come from the less advanced part of society. (See how modest that sounds! But you will know what I mean.) I mean, from persons whose opinions are not in a state of growth, and who do not like to be disturbed from a settled position. Oh, that there are faults in the book, no human being knows so well as I; defects, weaknesses, great gaps of intelligence. Don't let me stop to recount them.

The review in 'Blackwood' proves to be by Mr. Aytoun;[2] and coming from the camp of the enemy (artistically and socially) cannot be considered other than generous. It is not quite so by the 'North British,' where another poet (Patmore),[3] who knows more, is somewhat depreciatory, I can't help feeling.

Now will you be sick of my literature; but you liked to hear, you said. If you would see, besides, I would show you what George sent me the other day, a number of the 'National Magazine,' with the most hideous engraving, from a medallion, you could imagine—the head of a 'strong-minded' giantess on the neck of a bull, and my name underneath! Penini said, 'It's not a bit like: it's too old, and *not half so pretty*'—which was comforting under the trying circumstance, if anything could comfort one in despair. * * *

2. William Edmondstone Aytoun (1813–65), Scottish poet and critic. Aytoun was conservative in politics and outlook, while the Brownings were liberal.
3. See note 6 to letter from EBB to Isa Blagden, October 20, 1856, p. 335.

## To Jane Wills-Sandford, March 2, [1857]†

* * *let me say now, how deep a pleasure it gave me that you should like my poor Aurora so much. The pleasure was deep both to me and to the second me called Robert, and we read your notes together & agreed that you had fixed on the best passages with an unfailing instinct. We have had letters from such critics as Ruskin & Leigh Hunt;[4] & you & they, for the most part, point to the same things. There was two letters from Ruskin, and one of twenty pages from Leigh Hunt. From Alfred Tennyson[5] I have not heard, but I hear that he read the poem to his wife—which pleases me. The reviews have been numerous, & generally most favorable—and we had to go to press for the second edition a fortnight after publication as such was the sale. I wish I could give you the dates of reviews, but really I can't. Some were lent to me & I returned them; & some I only heard of. There was one in the Daily News, in the Globe, in the Leader, in the Literary Gazette,—oh, I forget. The Westminster Review, &c, &c. In Blackwood, there's a review not ungenerous considering that it comes from the camp of the enemy. (Mr. Aytoun)[6] from a different school on art, politics & social questions. I think the writer perfectly wrong, but certainly I dont complain of him. In the North British it is otherwise. The criticism here is depreciatory* * *

## To Julia Martin, March 10, [1857]†

* * *While I am away, I dont care to excess that the Dublin University magazine, for instance, should in the number just out, compare me to '*Afra Behn*'![7] and talk of my book as "sealed to my own sex," though I should *hate* to hear the charges on it from a quantity of friendly persons sure to come to condole with one on that head. I should like to wait till all this dust has past a little—though dust is beareable after all. There are worse things than dust. . . . How kindly you write and think: Yes—the attacks produce discussion, and provoke contradiction of course.

† By permission of the Houghton Library, Harvard University.
Jane Wills-Sanford was a friend of the Brownings in Florence. She wrote a manuscript memoir of EBB that gives an account of her last illness and death, June 20 to July 1, 1861 (now in the Armstrong Browning Library at Waco, Texas).

4. See note 9 to letter from EBB to Anna Jameson, February 2, 1857, p. 343; see note 1 to letter from EBB to Arabella Barrett, December 10–18, 1856, p. 338.
5. English poet (1809–92). Tennyson had been made Poet Laureate in 1850, and the Brownings were on familiar terms with the family during their visits to England in 1852 and 1855. In 1855 Tennyson kept a party, which included EBB and RB and Dante Gabriel Rossetti, up half the night while he read aloud to them from his new poem, *Maud*.
6. See note 2 to letter from EBB to Julia Martin, February 1857, p. 344.

† By permission of the Wellesley College Library.

7. Aphra Behn (1640–89), English dramatist and novelist. Partly because of the liberated style of her own life, partly because of a popular prejudice against women writers that called into question their sexual morals, and partly because the hero of her play *The Rover* (1677–81) was a libertine, Aphra Behn acquired a reputation as a woman of easy virtue.

"Afra Behn" on one side, and "the Bible of the Age" on another.! But there are pretty pleasant letters from women—young, I should think—who write to thank me for "help"—for new views of "love, truth, and purity;" That's very comforting. And the second edition is said to be nearly out, and the third is in course of preparation. Only the elections may mar a little this sale.* * *

## To Arabella Barrett, March [20–] 21, [1857]†

* * *Do you see in the press that Jessy White[8] is lecturing all over the United Kingdom & Ireland on the Italian question,—& upon very misconceived opinions I grieve to say. She's a noble creature on a wrong track—frightfully wrong, in my mind, which I have not kept from her, as you may suppose—but, though she loves me, I have not prevailed. I had a letter from her from Scotland the other day—from Glasgow—& she seems to be received well at the houses of the different professors both there & in Edinburgh. She says that 'Aurora' is "the rage" in Scotland, & that it will do more good for women, than a hundred petitions to parliament—Certainly I had not expected acceptance with 'the Scotch,—but the times are ripening towards certain questions, everywhere.

* * *

## To Arabella Barrett, April 3, [1857]†

* * *I saw an American paper yesterday—so funny . . about Aurora Leigh. The editor selects from a pile of letters about "that marvellous poem" . . . seeing that there has been a controversy on the exact meaning of the concluding lines.! The letters are said to be "very creditable to the Biblical knowledge of the community"—How absurd, to be sure.! I hear also that certain persons in England who cried loudest against the 'indecencies', are changing their tone altogether. In America the reception seems to be great. But we shant make a fortune by it after all—We should have starved a little this year if the money were not to be paid-

* * *

† Reprinted by permission of the Henry W. and Albert A. Berg Collection, The New York Public Library, Astor, Lenox, and Tilden Foundations.

8. Jessie White Mario (1832–1906), journalist, biographer, field nurse, and spy. Jessie White was English, but met Garibaldi in 1854 and committed herself to the cause of Italian unification, working for him in practical and political ways. During 1856 and 1857 she toured the north of England trying to raise funds. She had met EBB in Florence, and they were friendly for some time but later quarreled over politics. In Italy Jessie White was known as "Miss Hurricane."

† Reprinted by permission of the Henry W. and Albert A. Berg Collection, The New York Public Library, Astor, Lenox, and Tilden Foundations.

## To Julia Martin, May 14, [1858]†

* * *Oh—I never told you better than flattered I was that you should have taken Aurora Leigh with you. Did you see in the list of Lectures to be delivered by Gerald Massey,[9] (advertised in the Athenaeum) one on "Aurora Leigh, and the womans question?"[1]. . . . I did not fancy that this poem would be so identified as it has been, with that question, which was only a collateral object with my intentions in writing.

* * *

## Robert Browning to Edward Chapman, July 13, 1858†

Here are we arrived, for further progress to some French Bathing place, as enjoined by the doctor. My wife was very poorly and there was no such evident remedy as this,—so we did as we were bid. We don't go to England (obeying the same medicine-man) but return as soon as sufficiently salted—I suppose at the end of September.[2]

So you won't see me. Now, pray lighten my share of that affliction by sending in our account *at once (spoken insinuatingly)*; not that I mean to help myself to the money immediately, but that I want uncommonly to know what is what and how is how about all our books; and if you want any fresh doing up of *Aurora Leigh*, now is your time, when we are and shall be within a day's reach. Do kindly send me this directly if you can, and in process of time who knows but we shall (*voice dies off mysteriously: Mr. Chapman communicates to Mr. Frederick*[3] *earnestly; Mr. Frederick turns over ledger energetically, and scene closes* with the warm applause, not to say "encore" of)* * *

## To Anna Jameson, [October 5, 1858]†

* * *Mdme. du Quair[4] brought a Mr. Congreve[5] to us the other evening,—late a pupil of Mr. Arnold[6] & clergyman of the church of

† Reprinted by permission of the British Library.
9. A London critic and journalist.
1. See note 5 to letter from EBB to Isa Blagden, October 20, 1856, p. 335.
† From *New Letters of Robert Browning*, 107. See note to letter from RB to Edward Chapman, December 2, 1856, p. 336.
2. After the traveling and work associated with *Aurora Leigh* and the grief occasioned by the deaths of John Kenyon (December 1856) and her estranged father (April 1857) EBB was ill and depressed. Doctors advised RB that a stay at the French Atlantic coast and a program of sea-bathing might be beneficial to her health. In 1858 the Brownings set out for Paris and settled at Le Havre by the sea for the summer.
3. Frederick Chapman, Edward's cousin and partner in the business of Chapman and Hall.
† Reproduced by permission of The Huntington Library, San Marino, California.
4. An acquaintance in Paris.
5. Richard Congreve, English philosopher and follower of Auguste Comte.
6. Thomas Arnold (1795–1842), headmaster at Rugby School from 1828 until 1842.

England, now disciple & executor of Comte,[7] to remonstrate with me on Aurora Leigh's disrespect to his philosopher & to expound the philosophy. I was not moved, otherwise than to moralize much on the want of logic & reason in thinking men. Its "religion of Atheism", and the "communion" on one side only, remain to me enormous contradictions—the Athaenacian creed[8] perfectly easy & self evident in comparison. As long as men (& such men as Comte was) enunciate such mad inconsistencies, I shall not be inclined to accept his dogma & fall down & worship Humanity *per se.* * * *

## To Isa Blagden, [c. April 7, 1861]†

* * *All reviews (except the exceptions) are so much gained———
. . . except, I mean, when the reviewer says that you intend to curse your country & pollute the divine purity of English women—

By the bye, I heard the other day of seven young English unmarried ladies, (belonging to the highest class of society) in the "way" which ladies *dont* love being in, when they have no lords.! But I dont myself think that its the result of 'Aurora Leigh' for all that!—* * *

* * *

## [Fragmentary Notes on the Plot]†

* * *

A small sheet (no watermark, 12.9 cm by 13.2 cm) torn (from a notebook?) in the left margin and across the bottom, with notes on one side in Elizabeth Barrett Browning's hand. This manuscript may be one of the many used by the author in making notes before beginning to write in her first draft notebook, or it may have been written during composition to check the working out of the oppositions in the plot. The manuscript was in the possession of Robert Wiedemann Barrett Browning at his death in 1912 and was sold to a consortium which included Wilfrid and Alice Meynell as part of Lot 124 at the Browning sale of 1913. In 1947 it was sold (with three other scraps) by Arthur Rogers of Newcastle-upon-Tyne to Harold G. Rugg of Hanover, New Hampshire.

7. Auguste Comte (1798–1857), French positivist philosopher. EBB had certainly read the work of Comte by the 1850s, but was not convinced by his arguments because he did not allow for the presence of God in the universe. Richard Congreve came to remonstrate about the unflattering allusion to Comte's work that appeared in *Aurora Leigh*, but his efforts were to no avail. See note to *Aurora Leigh* 9.869, p. 309.
8. That is, the Athanasian creed. See note to *Aurora Leigh* 1.393, p. 16.

† By permission of the Syndics of the Fitzwilliam Museum.

† Reprinted by permission of the Dartmouth College Library.

[Italy & [against] England]
<Aurora born in Italy—>
1 Education against development
System against instinct
Love & philanthropy

---

2 The Ideal against the practical—

---

3 The Ideal works itself out

# SARAH STICKNEY ELLIS

## [The Declining Character of the Women of England and How It Might Be Rectified]†

### *Characteristics of the Women of England*

Every country has its peculiar characteristics, not only of climate and scenery, of public institutions, government, and laws; but every country has also its *moral characteristics*, upon which is founded its true title to a station, either high or low, in the scale of nations.

The national characteristics of England are the perpetual boast of her patriotic sons; and there is one especially, which it behoves all British subjects not only to exult in, but to cherish and maintain. Leaving the justice of her laws, the extent of her commerce, and the amount of her resources, to the orator, the statesman, and the political economist, there yet remains one of the noblest features in her national character, which may not improperly be regarded as within the compass of a woman's understanding, and the province of a woman's pen. It is the domestic character of England—the home comforts, and fireside virtues for which she is so justly celebrated. These I hope to be able to speak of without presumption, as intimately associated with, and dependent upon, the moral feelings and habits of the women of this favoured country.

It is therefore in reference of these alone that I shall endeavour to treat the subject of England's nationality; and in order to do this with more precision, it is necessary to draw the line of observation within a narrower circle, and to describe what are the characteristics of the women of England. I ought, perhaps, in strict propriety, to say what *were* their characteristics; because I would justify the obtrusiveness of a

† From *The Women of England* (London, 1838), 9–13, 16–17, 21–25, 44, 45, 53–54, 63–65, 67–68, 73–77. See note to *Aurora Leigh* 1.427–42, p. 18.

work like this, by first premising that the women of England are deteriorating in their moral character, and that false notions of refinement are rendering them less influential, less useful, and less happy than they were.

In speaking of what English women were, I would not be understood to refer to what they were a century ago. Facilities in the way of mental improvement have greatly increased during this period. In connexion with moral discipline, these facilities are invaluable; but I consider the two excellencies as having been combined in the greatest perfection in the general average of women who have now attained to middle, or rather advanced age. When the cultivation of the mental faculties had so far advanced as to take precedence of the moral, by leaving no time for domestic usefulness, and the practice of personal exertion in the way of promoting general happiness, the character of the women of England assumed a different aspect, which is now beginning to tell upon society in the sickly sensibilities, the feeble frames, and the useless habits of the rising generation.

In stating this humiliating fact, I must be blind indeed to the most cheering aspect of modern society, not to perceive that there are signal instances of women who carry about with them into every sphere of domestic duty, even the most humble and obscure, the accomplishments and refinements of modern education; and who deem it rather an honour than a degradation to be permitted to add to the sum of human happiness, by diffusing the embellishments of mind and manners over the homely and familiar aspect of every-day existence.

Such, however, do not constitute the majority of the female population of Great Britain. By far the greater portion of the young ladies (for they are no longer *women*) of the present day, are distinguished by a morbid listlessness of mind and body, except when under the influence of stimulus, a constant pining for excitement, and an eagerness to escape from every thing like practical and individual duty. Of course, I speak of those whose minds are not under the influence of religious principle. Would that the exception could extend to all who *profess* to be governed by this principle!

Gentle, inoffensive, delicate, and passively amiable as many young ladies are, it seems an ungracious task to attempt to rouse them from their summer dream; and were it not that wintry days will come, and the surface of life be ruffled, and the mariner, even she who steers the smallest bark, be put upon the inquiry for what port she is really bound—were it not that the cry of utter helplessness is of no avail in rescuing from the waters of affliction, and the plea of ignorance unheard upon the far-extending and deep ocean of experience, and the question of accountability perpetually sounding, like the voice of a warning spirit, above the storms and the billows of this lower world—I would be one of the very last to call the dreamer back to a consciousness of present things. But this state of listless indifference, my sisters, must not be. You have deep responsibilities, you have urgent claims; a nation's moral wealth is in your keeping. Let us inquire then in what way it may be best preserved. Let us consider what you are, and have been, and by what peculiarities of feeling and habit you have been able to throw so much additional weight into the scale of your country's worth.

* * *

There is a principle in woman's love, that renders it impossible for her to be satisfied without actually *doing* something for the object of her regard. I speak only of woman in her refined and elevated character. Vanity can satiate itself with admiration, and selfishness can feed upon services received; but woman's love is an everflowing and inexhaustible fountain, that must be perpetually imparting from the source of its own blessedness. It needs but slight experience to know, that the mere act of loving our fellow-creatures does little towards the promotion of their happiness. The human heart is not so credulous as to continue to believe in affection without practical proof. Thus the interchange of mutual kind offices begets a confidence which cannot be made to grow out of any other foundation; and while gratitude is added to the connecting link, the character on each side is strengthened by the personal energy required for the performance of every duty.

There may exist great sympathy, kindness, and benevolence of feeling, without the power of bringing any of these emotions into exercise for the benefit of others. They exist as emotions only. And thus the means, which appear to us as the most gracious and benignant of any that could have been adopted by our heavenly Father, for rousing us into necessary exertion, are permitted to die away, fruitless and unproductive, in the breast where they ought to have operated as a blessing and a means of happiness to others.

* * *

It is perhaps the nearest approach we can make towards any thing like a definition of what is most striking in the characteristics of the women of England, to say, that the nature of their domestic circumstances is such as to invest their characters with the threefold recommendation of *promptitude in action, energy of thought, and benevolence of feeling.* With all the responsibilities of family comfort and social enjoyment resting upon them, and unaided by those troops of menials who throng the halls of the affluent and the great, they are kept alive to the necessity of making their own personal exertions conducive to the great end of promoting the happiness of those around them. They cannot sink into supineness, or suffer any of their daily duties to be neglected, but some beloved member of the household is made to feel the consequences, by enduring inconveniences which it is alike their pride and their pleasure to remove. The frequently recurring avocations of domestic life admit of no delay. When the performance of any kindly office has to be asked for, solicited, and re-solicited, it loses more than half its charm. It is therefore strictly in keeping with the fine tone of an elevated character, to be beforehand with expectation, and thus to show, by the most delicate yet most effectual of all human means, that the object of attention, even when unheard and unseen, has been the subject of kind and affectionate solicitude.

By experience in these apparently minute affairs, a woman of kindly feeling and properly disciplined mind, soon learns to regulate her actions also according to the principles of true wisdom, and hence arises that energy of thought for which the women of England are so peculiarly distinguished. Every passing event, however insignificant to the eye of the world, has its crisis, every occurrence its emergency, every cause its effect; and upon these she has to calculate with precision, or the machinery of household comfort is arrested in its movements, and thrown into disorder.

Woman, however, would but ill supply the place appointed her by providence, were she endowed with no other faculties than those of promptitude in action, and energy of thought. Valuable as these may be, they would render her but a cold and cheerless companion, without the kindly affections and tender offices that sweeten human life. It is a high privilege, then, which the women of England enjoy, to be necessarily, and by the force of circumstances, thrown upon their affections, for the rule of their conduct in daily life. "What shall I do to gratify myself—to be admired—or to vary the tenor of my existence?" are not the questions which a woman of right feeling asks on first awaking to the avocations of the day. Much more congenial to the highest attributes of woman's character, are inquiries such as these: "How shall I endeavour through this day to turn the time, the health, and the means permitted me to enjoy, to the best account? Is any one sick, I must visit their chamber without delay, and try to give their apartment an air of comfort, by arranging such things as the wearied nurse may not have thought of. Is any one about to set off on a journey, I must see that the early meal is spread, or prepare it with my own hands, in order that the servant, who was working late last night, may profit by unbroken rest. Did I fail in what was kind or considerate to any of the family yesterday; I will meet them this morning with a cordial welcome, and show, in the most delicate way I can, that I am anxious to atone for the past. Was any one exhausted by the last day's exertion, I will be an hour before them this morning, and let them see that their labour is so much in advance. Or, if nothing extraordinary occurs to claim my attention, I will meet the family with a consciousness that, being the least engaged of any member of it, I am consequently the most at liberty to devote myself to the general good of the whole, by cultivating cheerful conversation, adapting myself to the prevailing tone of feeling, and leading those who are least happy, to think and speak of what will make them more so."

Who can believe that days, months, and years spent in a continual course of thought and action similar to this, will not produce a powerful effect upon the character; and not upon the individual who thinks, and acts, alone, but upon all to whom her influence extends? In short, the customs of English society have so constituted women the guardians of the comfort of their homes, that, like the Vestals of old, they cannot allow the lamp they cherish to be extinguished, or to fail for want of oil, without an equal share of degradation attaching to their names.

* * *

It would be an easy and a grateful task, thus, by metaphor and illustration, to prove the various excellencies and amiable peculiarities of woman, did not the utility of the present work demand a more minute and homely detail of that which constitutes her practical and individual duty. It is too much the custom with writers, to speak in these general terms of the *loveliness* of the female character; as if woman were some fragrant flower, created only to bloom, and exhale in sweets; when perhaps these very writers are themselves most strict in requiring that the domestic drudgery of their own households should each day be faithfully filled up. How much more generous, just, and noble it would be to deal fairly by woman in these matters, and to tell her that to be *individually*, what she is praised for being *in general*, it is necessary for her to lay aside all her natural caprice, her love of self-indulgence, her vanity, her indolence—in short, her very *self*—and assuming a new nature, which nothing less than watchfulness and prayer can enable her constantly to maintain, to spend her mental and moral capabilities in devising means for promoting the happiness of others, while her own derives a remote and secondary existence from theirs.

* * *

How often has man returned to his home with a mind confused by the many voices, which in the mart, the exchange, or the public assembly, have addressed themselves to his inborn selfishness, or his worldly pride; and while his integrity was shaken, and his resolution gave way beneath the pressure of apparent necessity, or the insidious pretences of expediency, he has stood corrected before the clear eye of woman, as it looked directly to the naked truth, and detected the lurking evil of the specious act he was about to commit. Nay, so potent may have become this secret influence, that he may have borne it about with him like a kind of second conscience, for mental reference, and spiritual counsel, in moments of trial; and when the snares of the world were around him, and temptations from within and without have bribed over the witness in his own bosom, he has thought of the humble monitress who sat alone, guarding the fireside comforts of his distant home; and the remembrance of her character, clothed in moral beauty, has scattered the clouds before his mental vision, and sent him back to that beloved home, a wiser and a better man.

The women of England, possessing the grand privilege of being better instructed than those of any other country, in the minutiæ of domestic comfort, have obtained a degree of importance in society far beyond what their unobtrusive virtues would appear to claim. The long-established customs of their country have placed in their hands the high and holy duty of cherishing and protecting the minor morals of life, from whence springs all that is elevated in purpose, and glorious in action. The sphere of their direct personal influence is central, and consequently small; but its extreme operations are as widely extended as the range of human feeling. They may be less striking in society than some of the women of other countries, and may feel themselves, on brilliant and stirring occasions, as simple, rude, and unsophisticated in the popular science of excitement; but as far as the noble daring of Britain has sent forth her adventurous sons, and that is to every point of danger on the habitable globe, they have borne along with them a generosity, a disinterestedness, and a moral courage, derived in so small measure from the female influence of their native country.

* * *

In order to ascertain what kind of education is most effective in making woman what she ought to be, the best method is to inquire into the character, station, and peculiar duties of woman throughout the largest portion of her earthly career; and then ask, for what she is most valued, admired, and beloved?

In answer to this, I have little hesitation in saying,—For her disinterested kindness. Look at all the heroines, whether of romance or reality—at all the female characters that are held up to universal admiration—at all who have gone down to honoured graves, amongst the tears and the lamentations of their survivors. Have these been the learned, the accomplished women; the women who could speak many languages, who could solve problems, and elucidate systems of philosophy? No: or if they have, they have also been women who were dignified with the majesty of moral greatness—women who regarded not themselves, their own feebleness, or their own susceptibility of pain, but who, endued with an almost super-human energy, could trample under-foot every impediment that intervened between them and the accomplishment of some great object upon which their hopes were fixed, while that object was wholly unconnected with their own personal exaltation or enjoyment, and related only to some beloved object, whose suffering was their sorrow, whose good their gain.

Woman, with all her accumulation of minute disquietudes, her weakness, and her sensibility, is but a meagre item in the catalogue of humanity; but, roused by a sufficient motive to forget all these, or, rather, continually forgetting them because she has other and nobler thoughts to occupy her mind, woman is truly and majestically great.

Never yet, however, was woman great, because she had great acquirements; nor can she ever be great in herself—personally, and without instrumentality—as an object, not an agent.

From the beginning to the end of school education, the improvement of *self*, so far as relates to intellectual attainments, is made the rule and the motive of all that is done. Rewards are appointed and portioned out for what has been learned, not what has been imparted. To gain, is the universal order of the establishment; and those who have heaped together the greatest sum of knowledge are usually regarded as the most meritorious. Excellent discourses may be delivered by the preceptress upon the christian duties of benevolence and disinterested love; but the whole system is one of pure selfishness, fed by accumulation, and rewarded by applause. To be at the head of the class, to gain the ticket or the prize, are the points of universal ambition; and few individuals, amongst the community of aspirants, are taught to look forward with a rational presentiment to that future, when their merit will be to give the place of honour to others, and their happiness to give it to those who are more worthy than themselves.

We will not assert that no one entertains such thoughts; for there is a voice in woman's heart too strong for education—a principle which the march of intellect is unable to overthrow.

* * *

In making these and similar remarks, I am aware that I may bring upon myself the charge of wishing to exclude from our schools all intellectual attainments whatever; for how, it will be asked, can learning be acquired without emulation, and without rewards for the diligent, and punishments for the idle?

So far, however, from wishing to cast a shade of disrespect over such attainments, I am decidedly of opinion that no human being can know too much, so long as the sphere of knowledge does not extend to what is positively evil. I am also of opinion that there is scarcely any department of art or science, still less of mental application, which is not calculated to strengthen and improve the mind; but at the same time I regard the improvement of the *heart* of so much greater consequence, that if time and opportunity should fail for both, I would strenuously recommend that women should be sent home from school with fewer accomplishments, and more of the will and the power to perform the various duties necessarily devolving upon them.

* * *

With regard of the women of England, I have already ventured to assert that the quality for which, above all others, they are esteemed and valued, is their disinterested kindness. A selfish woman may not improperly be regarded as a monster, especially in that sphere of life, where there is a constant demand made upon her services. But how are women taught at school to forget themselves, and to cultivate that high tone of generous feeling to which the world is so much indebted for the hope and the joy, the peace and the consolation, which the influence and companionship of woman is able to diffuse throughout its very deserts, visiting, as with blessed sunshine, the abodes of the wretched and the poor, and sharing cheerfully the lot of the afflicted.

In what school, or under what system of modern education, can it be said that the chief aim of the teachers, the object to which their laborious exertions are mainly directed, is to correct the evil of selfishness in the hearts of their pupils? Improved methods of charging and surcharging the memory are eagerly sought out, and pursued, at any cost of time and patience, if not of health itself; but who ever thinks of establishing a *selfish* class amongst the girls of her establishment, or of awarding the honours and distinctions of the school to such as have exhibited the most meritorious instances of self-denial for the benefit of others.

It may be objected to this plan, that virtue ought to be its own reward, and that honours and rewards adjudged to the most meritorious in a moral point of view, would be likely to induce a degree of self-complacency wholly inconsistent with christian meekness. I am aware that, in our imperfect state, no plan can be laid down for the promotion of good, with which evil will not be liable to mix. All I contend for is, that the same system of discipline, with the same end in view, should be begun and carried on at school, as that to which the scholar will necessarily be subjected in after life; and that throughout the training of her early years, the same standard of merit should be adopted, as she will find herself compelled to look up to, when released from that training, and sent forth into the world to think and act for herself.

At school it has been the business of every day to raise herself above her companions by attainments greater than theirs; in after life it will be the business of every day to give place to others, to think of their happiness, and to make sacrifices of her own to promote it. If such acts of self-denial, when practised at school, should endanger the equanimity of her mind by the approbation they obtain, what will they do in the world she is about to enter, where the unanimous opinion of mankind, both in this, and in past ages, is in their favour, and where she must perpetually hear woman spoken of in terms of the highest commendation, not for her learning, but for her disinterested kindness, her earnest zeal in promoting the happiness of her fellow-creatures, and the patience and forbearance with which she studies to mitigate affliction and relieve distress?

Would it not be safer, then, to begin at a very early age to make the practice of these virtues the chief object of their lives, guarding at the same time against any self-complacency that might attach to the performance of them, by keeping always before their view, higher and nobler instances of virtue in others; and especially by a strict and constant reference to the utter worthlessness of all human merit, in comparison with the mercy and forgiveness that must ever impose a debt of gratitude upon our own souls?

Taking into consideration the various excellencies and peculiarities of woman, I am inclined to think that the sphere which of all others admits of the highest development of her character, is the chamber of sickness; and how frequently and mournfully familiar are the scenes in which she is thus called to act and feel, let the private history of every family declare.

There is but a very small proportion of the daughters of farmers, manufacturers, and trades-people, in England, who are ever called upon for their Latin, their Italian, or even for their French; but all women in this sphere of life are liable to be called upon to visit and care for the sick; and if in the hour of weakness and of suffering, they prove to be unacquainted with any probable means of alleviation, and wholly ignorant of the most judicious and suitable mode of offering relief and consolation, they are indeed deficient in one of the highest attainments in the way of usefulness, to which a woman can aspire.

* * *

# CATHERINE NAPIER

## [Women's Rights and Duties] †

* * *

Nature, then, having placed the stronger mind where she gave the stronger body, and accompanied it with a more enterprising ambitious spirit, the custom that consigns to the male sex the chief command in society, and all the offices which require the greatest strength and abil-

† From *Woman's Rights and Duties, Considered with Relation to Their Influence on Society and on Her Own Condition,* By a Woman (London, 1838), 211–15, 276–79, and 390. *Woman's Rights and Duties, Considered with Relation to Their Influence on Society and on Her Own Condition* was published anonymously in 1838, its author (Catherine Napier [dates unknown]) declaring herself and her qualifications only by claiming the work as "By a Woman." Although conduct books produced especially for women had been enormously popular since the middle of the eighteenth century, there was a considerable upsurge in the number published during the 1830s and 1840s, when the "woman question" about the character of the feminine and the role of women in society was being widely argued. See note to *Aurora Leigh* 1.427–42, p. 18. Mrs. Napier's other works were *A Month at Oostcamp* (miscellaneous pieces in prose and verse published in 1844) and two volumes of poetry, *The City of the World* (1845) and *The Lay of the Palace* (1852).

ity, has a better foundation than force, or the prejudices that result from it. The hard, laborious, stern, and coarse duties of the warrior, lawyer, legislator, or physician, require all tender emotions to be frequently repressed. The firmest texture of nerve is required to stand the severity of mental labour, and the greatest abilities are wanted where the duties of society are most difficult. It would be as little in agreement with the nature of things to see the exclusive possession of these taken from the abler sex, to be divided with the weaker, as it is, in the savage condition, to behold severe bodily toil inflicted on the feeble frame of the woman, and the softness of feeling, which nature has provided her with for the tenderest of her offices, that of nurturing the young, outraged by contempt, menaces, and blows.

It is therefore an impartial decree, which consigns all the offices that require the greatest ability to men. For, is it less the interest of woman than of man, that property, life, and liberty, should be secured—that aggression should be quickly and easily repressed—that contentment and order should prevail instead of tumult? that industry should be well paid—provisions cheap and plentiful—that trade should cover their tables and their persons with the comforts, conveniences, and luxuries which habit has rendered necessary, or an innocent sensibility pleasurable? Is it less momentous to them that religious opinions should be free from persecution—that a wise foreign policy should maintain those blessings in peace, and preserve us from the tribulation of foreign dominion? In objects of less selfish interest, are women less anxious than men, or more so, to see the practice of slavery expelled from the face of the earth? or our colonial government redeemed in every remaining instance, from the stain that has too often attended it, of being numbered with the most oppressive of European?

In the dangerous and difficult sciences of medicine and surgery, is it less important to women than to men, that the life which hangs by a thread, should be trusted to those whose nerves and abilities ensure the greatest skill? or in law, that the decision of rights, the vindication of innocence, should be in the hands of those who can most patiently endure the driest studies, and most boldly follow human nature, through all its various forms and all its foul pursuits?

Ills enough, Heaven knows! ensue from the weaknesses and incapacity of men, but to confer the offices, which demand all the skills and energy that can be had, on those who are weaker still, would be injurious alike to both. The commanding and influential stations in society belong, therefore, naturally and properly to the male sex: this of necessity entails the chief rule in private life also. But it is here that the rights of women come in, and that the danger of unjust encroachment upon them commences.[1]

1. A question has occasionally been raised, and I believe by more than one writer, whether the right of voting be not unjustly withheld from women. But it seems an almost conclusive

Everything that tends to lessen the comparative purity and refinement of women, is most pointedly adverse to their real interests; these are the qualities that enable them to be the guardians and sustainers of national morals: and their rights must be founded on their natural attributes and their moral dignity. To these respect and consideration cannot be denied, and every step mankind advances in civilisation gives strength to those sentiments. Women have neither the physical strength nor the mental power, to compete with men in the departments which depend on those qualifications; and however little we were to suppose their inferiority, in the long run they would always be defeated and discredited, in their competition for employment with the abler sex. Were so unnatural a state of society to arise, as that they should become the competitors instead of the assistants of man, they would lose their hold on his protection and tenderness, without being able to shield themselves from his harshness. The business of life would be far worse conducted, when the division of labour so clearly pointed out by nature was done away: and the just influence which women ought to have, would be destroyed by breaking down the barrier of opinion, which consigns them to the duties of a domestic and private station, and preserves them from the contamination of gross and contentious scenes.

But the same arguments that establish the right of the male sex to the sole possession of public authority, must leave the *chief* control of domestic life in their hands also. All the most laborious, the greater and more lucrative social offices, being filled by them, it follows, that generally speaking it is they who produce the wealth and property of society, and the property they create they have assuredly the best right to control; within the rules of virtue and law they may spend it as they will. The children whom the husband supports, the wife who accepts him, engaging to follow his fortunes, must be content to live as he pleases, or as his business requires. This is the law of nature and of reason. If his tastes or his profession be unpleasant to her, she must see to it beforehand; for ever after their interests must be one. In every important decision that is taken, one counsel must prevail: if it cannot be mutual, it must be assigned as a legal right to the owner of the property and the abler sex. Hence he is the head of the family; he must be responsible to law and

objection to giving them the franchise, that by the very principle upon which it is bestowed, women are unfit for it, being always under influence. There are no doubt some cases of exception to that rule, but so there are to every other rule, by which persons are excluded from the right. Perhaps no other rule is so extensively true, as that women are under influence. But farther, women have no *political* interests apart from those of men. The public measures that are taken, the restrictions or taxes imposed on the community do not affect them more than male subjects. In all such respects, the interests of the two sexes are identified. As citizens, therefore, they are sufficiently represented already. To give them the franchise would just double the number of voters, without introducing any new interest, and far from improving society, few things would tend more to dissever and corrupt it.

* * *

opinion for the decorum of his house, and must have the power of restraining what he holds to be discreditable or wrong. Happy if he could be made equally responsible, even to his own conscience, for unjustly encroaching on rights which should never be taken from a woman, except for positive vice or incapacity! Her right to all the self-government that can be left to her, without deranging *his* purposes or *his* enjoyment, is as real as his own; and his purposes and enjoyments are not to be measured by mere pride or fancy, but by reason and justice; even then he remains judge in his own cause. As the right of man to the chief power, public and domestic, has been deduced from his greater ability, so the aptitude of the female mind and character for the details of domestic life, and the improvement of society in manners and morals, establish her rights also to a share of control; otherwise her utility must be greatly impaired, and her enjoyment cruelly and needlessly sacrificed.

* * *

Politics are a very extensive and very various science. It is evidently unfit for all men to be deeply versed in it, since the majority could not be so, except at the expense of their own special duties. It is more for the advantage of society that each man should be properly instructed in his own business, than that all should be politicians. It is still less needful that women, who have no active political duties to perform, should enter into the depths and subtilties of that science; but there is a certain degree of knowledge on the subject, without which a person can scarcely be deemed a citizen. With far greater justice might it be said, people who have not to calculate almanacks need know nothing of the solar system, than that they who have not to vote or to legislate need know nothing of the social system in which they all move.

There are certain general principles which form the basis of all government, and on which the prosperity, nay, the very existence, of society depends; such as that life and property shall be secured, and that everybody must forego some share of their natural freedom, for the greater security and advantage of all; and there are particular principles which constitute the different forms of government of different nations, such as the monarchical, the democratic, and others. These in a great measure form the national spirit and character. Peace and security depend mainly upon the agreement of the spirit and character of the people with their institutions, and on the unanimity with which they assent to their maintenance. It is surely essential to propriety of social conduct, that people should not be ignorant, either of the knowledge which justifies all government, or of that which serves to cement the society in which we live, and wherein lie all our duties. In a free government, the diffusion of it seems the only security there is against the crude and extravagant notions of men without knowledge, and full of passion. Can it be for the interest of society, that anybody should be totally destitute of elementary instruction on the subject; though many perhaps must remain so from necessity, either through extreme poverty, meanness of intellect, or that unconquerable aversion to all efforts of thought, by which nature has stamped some people for triflers?

Let us turn our eyes to the condition of a country agitated by faction, and say whether it can be doubted that better instruction would restrain a great deal of its turbulence. On one side we discern passionate resistance to the most obvious improvements; old confuted maxims of misrule defended pertinaciously by men who ought to take the lead in the progress of the times; illiberal designs maintained through dishonest intrigues, which kindle an unnatural and reluctant hatred against a class, which it is the disposition of the people to look up to. On the other side we find furious declamation, regardless of truth or reason, abounding with absurd flattery towards a people brutalized by intemperance and ignorance, and who need not be made more turbulent and conceited than they are: crude theories, generated in the brains of those who mistake their own intolerance of subordination for the spirit of liberty; boasting contempt for moral and religious restraint, by way of philosophy; and vehement advocacy of particular measures, the most complicated and doubtful imaginable, through means, of the mischief and misery of which there is unhappily no doubt at all.

Let any one but contemplate the results of the conflict between such parties, how in the countries most favoured by fortune, the whole fabric maybe made to shake with their violence; and let him say, in candour, whether, since the multitude cannot be forced back to the condition of sheep, the wide dissemination of well-grounded elementary knowledge be not urgently wanted; and if so, whether women who have so much control over education and so much influence in society, ought not to be rendered instrumental to that purpose.

# DINAH MULOCK

## A Woman's Thoughts About Women†

I premise that these thoughts do not concern married women, for whom there are always plenty to think, and who have generally quite

† From *A Woman's Thoughts About Women* (London, 1858), 1–16. Dinah Mulock, later Craik (1826–87), an English novelist, was best known for *John Halifax: Gentleman* (1858), though she published over twenty novels, books of poetry, short stories, and tales for children. Her early commitment to the cause of women's rights grew out of her early experience, when her feckless father was consigned to a lunatic asylum and she was left to fend for her mother and two younger brothers. She succeeded in this by writing and continued to maintain her independent career throughout her life. She herself made a happy marriage, but *A Woman's Thoughts*

enough to think of for themselves and those belonging to them. They have cast their lot for good or ill, have realised in greater or less degree the natural destiny of our sex. They must find out its comforts, cares, and responsibilities, and make the best of all. It is the single women, belonging to those supernumerary ranks, which, political economists tell us, are yearly increasing, who most need thinking about.

First, in their early estate, when they have so much in their possession—youth, bloom, and health giving them that temporary influence over the other sex which may result, and is meant to result, in a permanent one. Secondly, when this sovereignty is passing away, the chance of marriage lessening, or wholly ended, or voluntarily set aside, and the individual making up her mind to that which, respect for Grandfather Adam and Grandmother Eve must compel us to admit, is an unnatural condition of being.

Why this undue proportion of single women should almost always result from over-civilisation, and whether, since society's advance is usually indicated by the advance, morally and intellectually, of its women—this progress, by raising women's ideal standard of the "holy estate," will not necessarily cause a decline in the very *un*holy estate which it is most frequently made—are questions too wide to be entered upon here. We have only to deal with facts—with a certain acknowledged state of things, perhaps incapable of remedy, but by no means incapable of amelioration.

But, granted these facts, and leaving to wiser heads the explanation of them—if indeed there be any—it seems advisable, or at least allowable, that any woman who has thought of a good deal about the matter, should not fear to express in word—or deed, which is better,—any conclusions, which out of her own observation and experience she may have arrived at. And looking around upon the middle classes, which form the staple stock of the community, it appears to me that the chief canker at the root of women's lives is the want of something to do.

Herein I refer, as this chapter must be understood especially to refer, not to those whom ill or good fortune—*query*, is it not often the latter?—has forced to earn their bread; but "to young ladies," who have never been brought up to do anything. Tom, Dick, and Harry, their brothers, has each had it knocked into him from schooldays that he is to do something, to be somebody. Counting-house, shop, or college, afford him a clear future on which to concentrate all his energies and aims. He has got the grand *pabulum* of the human soul—occupation. If any inherent want in his character, any unlucky combination of circumstances, nullifies this, what a poor creature the man becomes!—what a dawdling,

*About Women* (1858) as well as a number of her novels—notably *A Life for a Life* (1859) and *Christian's Mistake* (1865)—show that she protested a society in which marriage was the only career available to middle-class women and that she questioned the stereotyping of gender roles.

moping, sitting-over-the-fire, thumb-twiddling, lazy, ill-tempered animal! And why? "Oh, poor fellow! 'tis because he has got nothing to do!"

Yet this is precisely the condition of women for a third, a half, often the whole of their existence.

That Providence ordained it so—made men to work, and women to be idle—is a doctrine that few will be bold enough to assert openly. Tacitly they do, when they preach up lovely uselessness, fascinating frivolity, delicious helplessness—all those polite impertinences and poetical degradations to which the foolish, lazy, or selfish of our sex are prone to incline an ear, but which any woman of common sense must repudiate as insulting not only her womanhood but her Creator.

Equally blasphemous, and perhaps even more harmful, is the outcry about "the equality of the sexes;" the frantic attempt to force women, many of whom are either ignorant of or unequal for their own duties—into the position and duties of men. A pretty state of matters would ensue! Who that ever listened for two hours to the verbose confused inanities of a ladies' committee, would immediately go and give his vote for a female House of Commons? or who, on the receipt of a lady's letter of business—I speak of the average—would henceforth desire to have our courts of justice stocked with matronly lawyers, and our colleges thronged by

"Sweet girl-graduates with their golden hair?"

As for finance, in its various branches—if you pause to consider the extreme difficulty there always is in balancing Mrs. Smith's housekeeping-book, or Miss Smith's quarterly allowance, I think, my dear Paternal Smith, you need not be much afraid lest this loud acclaim for "women's rights" should ever end in pushing you from your stools, in counting-house, college, or elsewhere.

No; equality of the sexes is not in the nature of things. Man and woman were made for, and not like one another. One only "right" we have to assert in common with mankind—and that is as much in our own hands as theirs—the right of having something to do.

That both sexes were meant to labour, one "by the sweat of his brow," the other "in sorrow to bring forth"—and bring up—"children"—cannot, I fancy, be questioned. Nor, when the gradual changes of the civilised world, or some special destiny, chosen or compelled, have prevented that first, highest, and in earlier times almost universal lot, does this accidental fate in any way abrogate the necessity, moral, physical, and mental, for a woman to have occupation in other forms.

But how few parents ever consider this? Tom, Dick, and Harry, aforesaid, leave school and plunge into life; "the girls" likewise finish their education, come home, and stay at home. That is enough. Nobody thinks it needful to waste a care upon them. Bless them, pretty dears, how sweet they are! papa's nosegay of beauty to adorn his drawing-room.

He delights to give them all they can desire—clothes, amusements, society; he and mamma together take every domestic care off their hands; they have abundance of time and nothing to occupy it; plenty of money, and little use for it; pleasure without end, but not one definite object of interest or employment; flattery and flummery enough, but no solid food whatever to satisfy mind or heart—if they happen to possess either—at the very emptiest and most craving season of both. They have literally nothing whatever to do, except to fall in love; which they accordingly do, the most of them, as fast as ever they can.

"Many think they are in love, when in fact they are only idle"—is one of the truest sayings of that great wise bore, Imlac, in *Rasselas*,[1] and it has been proved by many a shipwrecked life, of girls especially. This "falling in love" being usually a mere delusion of the fancy, and not the real thing at all, the object is generally unattainable or unworthy. Papa is displeased, mamma somewhat shocked and scandalised; it is a "foolish affair," and no matrimonial results ensue. There only ensues—what?

A long, dreary season, of pain, real or imaginary, yet not the less real because it is imaginary; of anger and mortification, of impotent struggle—against unjust parents, the girl believes, or, is romantically inclined, against cruel destiny. Gradually this mood wears out; she learns to regard "love" as folly, and turns her whole hope and aim to—matrimony! Matrimony in the abstract; not *the* man, but any man—any person who will snatch her out of the dulness of her life, and give her something really to live for, something to fill up the hopeless blank of idleness into which her days are gradually sinking.

Well, the man may come, or he may not. If the latter melancholy result occurs, the poor girl passes into her third stage of young-ladyhood, fritters or mopes away her existence, sullenly bears it, or dashes herself blindfold against its restrictions; is unhappy, and makes her family unhappy; perhaps herself cruelly conscious of all this, yet unable to find the true root of bitterness in her heart: not knowing exactly what she wants, yet aware of a morbid, perpetual want of something. What is it?

Alas! the boys only have had the benefit of that well-known juvenile apophthegm, that

"Satan finds some mischief still
For idle hands to do:"

it has never crossed the parents' minds that the rhyme could apply to the delicate digital extremities of the daughters.

And so their whole energies are devoted to the massacre of old Time. They prick him to death with crochet and embroidery needles; strum

1. *The History of Rasselas, Prince of Abyssinia*, a romance by Dr. Samuel Johnson, published in 1759. The book is not a novel in any conventional sense, though it does offer a series of fantastic adventures and exotic scenes. It is rather a didactic essay on "the choice of life," which question is pursued by Rasselas himself; his sister, Nekayah; and her maid, Pekuah; under the guidance of the wise, much traveled philosopher, Imlac [*Editor*].

him deaf with piano and harp playing—*not* music; cut him up with morning-visitors, or leave his carcass in ten-minute parcels at every "friend's" house they can think of. Finally, they dance him defunct at all sort of unnatural hours; and then, rejoicing in the excellent excuse, smother him in sleep for a third of the following day. Thus he dies, a slow, inoffensive, perfectly natural death; and they will never recognise his murder till, on the confines of this world, or from the unknown shores of the next, the question meets them: "What have you done with Time?"—Time, the only mortal gift bestowed equally on every living soul, and, excepting the soul, the only mortal loss which is totally irretrievable.

Yet this great sin, this irredeemable loss, in many women arises from pure ignorance. Men are taught as a matter of business to recognise the value of time, to apportion and employ it: women rarely or never. The most of them have no definite appreciation of the article as a tangible divisible commodity at all. They would laugh at a mantua-maker who cut up a dress-length into trimmings, and then expected to make out of two yards of silk a full skirt. Yet that the same laws of proportion should apply to time and its measurements—that you cannot dawdle away a whole forenoon, and then attempt to cram into the afternoon the entire business of the day—that every minute's unpunctuality constitutes a debt or a theft (lucky, indeed, if you yourself are the only party robbed or made creditor thereof!): these slight facts rarely seem to cross the feminine imagination.

It is not their fault; they have never been "accustomed to business." They hear that with men "time is money;" but it never strikes them that the same commodity, equally theirs, is to them not money, perhaps, but *life*—life in its highest form and noblest uses—life bestowed upon every human being, distinctly and individually, without reference to any other being, and for which every one of us, married or unmarried, woman as well as man, will assuredly be held accountable before God.

My young-lady friends, of from seventeen upwards, your time, and the use of it, is as essential to you as to any father or brother of you all. You are accountable for it just as much as he is. If you waste it, you waste not only your substance, but your very souls—not that which is your own, but your Maker's.

Ay, there the core of the matter lies. From the hour that honest Adam and Eve were put into the garden, not—as I once heard some sensible preacher observe—"not to be idle in it, but to dress it and to keep it," the Father of all has never put one man or one woman into this world without giving each something to do there, in it and for it: some visible tangible work, to be left behind them when they die.

Young ladies, 'tis worth a grave thought—what, if called away at eighteen, twenty, or thirty, the most of you would leave behind you when you die? Much embroidery, doubtless; various pleasant, kindly, illegible letters; a moderate store of good deeds; and a cart-load of good intentions. Nothing else—save your name on a tombstone, or lingering for a few more years in family or friendly memory. "Poor dear——! what a nice lively girl she was!" For any benefit accruing through you to your generation, you might as well never have lived at all.

But "what am I to do with my life?" as once asked me one girl out of the numbers who begin to feel aware that, whether marrying or not, each possesses an individual life, to spend, to use, or to lose. And herein lies the momentous question.

The difference between man's vocation and woman's seems naturally to be this—one is abroad, the other at home: one external, the other internal: one active, the other passive. He has to go and seek out his path; hers usually lies close under her feet. Yet each is as distinct, as honourable, as difficult; and whatever custom may urge to the contrary—if the life is meant to be a worthy or a happy one—each must resolutely and unshrinkingly be trod. But—*how?*

A definite answer to this question is simply impossible. So diverse are characters, tastes, capabilities, and circumstances, that to lay down a distinct line of occupation for any six women of one's own acquaintance, would be the merest absurdity.

"Herein the patient must minister to herself."

To few is the choice so easy, the field of duty so wide, that she need puzzle very long over what she ought to do. Generally—and this is the best and safest guide—she will find her work lying very near at hand: some desultory tastes to condense into regular studies, some faulty household quietly to remodel, some child to teach, or parent to watch over. All these being needless or unattainable, she may extend her service out of the home into the world, which perhaps never at any time so much needed the help of us women. And hardly one of its charities and duties can be done so thoroughly as by a wise and tender woman's hand.

Here occurs another of those plain rules which are the only guidance possible in the matter—a Bible rule, too—"*Whatsoever thy hand findeth to do, do it with thy might.*" Question it not, philosophise not over it—do it!—only *do it!* Thoroughly and completely, never satisfied with less than perfectness. Be it ever so great or so small, from the founding of a village-school to the making of a collar—do it "with thy might;" and never lay it aside till it is done.

* * *

# CHARLES FOURIER

## [A Trial Phalanx]†

### *The Establishment of a Trial Phalanx*

We will suppose that the trial is made by a monarch, or by a wealthy individual like one of the Devonshires, Northumberlands, Bedforts, the Sheremetevs, Labanovs, Czartoryskis, the Esterhazys, Belmontes, Medina-Celis, the Barings, Lafittes, Hopes, etc.,[1] or finally by a powerful company which desires to avoid all tentative measures and proceed directly to the organization of Full Harmony, the eighth period in its plenitude. I am going to indicate the procedure to follow in this case.

An association of 1500 or 1600 people requires a site comprising at least one square league of land, that is to say a surface area of six million square *toises*.[2] (Let us not forget that one-third as much would suffice for the simple mode.)

A good stream of water should be available; the land should be hilly and suitable for a variety of crops; there should be a forest nearby; and the site should be fairly near a large city but far enough away to avoid unwelcome visitors.

The trial Phalanx will stand alone and it will get no help from neighboring Phalanxes. As a result of this isolation, there will be so many gaps in attraction, so many passional[3] calms to fear in its maneuvers, that is will be particularly important to provide it with the help of a good site fit for a variety of functions. Flat country, like that surrounding Anvers, Leipzig or Orleans[4] would be quite inappropriate and would

† From "Theorie de l'unitie universelle" (1841–1843) and *Le nouveau monde industrial et societaire* (1848) in Jonathan Beecher and Richard Bienvenu, trans. and ed., *The Utopian Vision of Charles Fourier* (London, 1972), 235–40 and 275–78. 

The early years of the nineteenth century saw many thinkers attempting to formulate new methods of social reform, most of them along communal lines. Generally these theorists got no further than thinking about reform, but a few of them did actually establish communities on the basis of their ideals, with varying degrees of success. Charles Fourier (1772–1837), a French philosopher and social reformer, proposed cooperation and harmony among humankind, suggesting that these goals could be achieved by reordering society into communities—or phalanges—each of about 1,600 people. Within each phalanx each individual was given a rigorous but varied timetable of tasks commensurate with his or her status and ability. This happy disposition of talents and goods would allow for everyone to be provided with their practical needs as well as promoting a contented community that allowed for individual development and some measure of sexual freedom. In *The New Industrial and Social World* (1848) Fourier sets out both his reasoning and a number of detailed plans for the establishment of a trial phalanx [*Editor*].

1. Family names of the wealthy and aristocratic lines in various European countries, including England, Russia, Austria, Italy, France [*Editor*].
2. The *toise* was equal to about two yards.
3. "Passional" is Fourier's phrase for "intense commitment." Thus a "passional calm" is a bad thing, a period during which the Harmonians' commitment is less enthusiastic (e.g., during the winter, when there is little to do) [*Editor*].
4. Anvers and Orleans are large towns in France. Leipzig is in Germany [*Editor*].

cause the breakdown of many series, owing to the uniformity of the land surface. It will therefore be necessary to select a diversified region, like that near Lausanne, or at the very least a fine valley provided with a stream and a forest, like the valley from Brussels to Halle. A fine location near Paris would be the stretch of land between Poissy and Conflans, Poissy and Meulan.

The 1500 or 1600 people brought together will be in a state of graduated inequality as to wealth, age, personality, and theoretical and practical knowledge. The group should be as varied as possible; for the greater the variety in the passions and faculties of the members, the easier it will be to harmonize them in a limited amount of time.

All possible types of agricultural work should be represented in this trial community, including that involving hot-houses and conservatories. There should also be at least three types of manufacturing work for winter and for rainy days, as well as diverse types of work in the applied sciences and arts, apart from what is taught in the schools. A passional series will be assigned to each type of work, and it will divide up its members into subdivisions and groups according to the instructions given earlier.

At the very outset an evaluation should be made of the capital deposited as shares in the enterprise: land, material, flocks, tools, etc. This matter is one of the first to be dealt with; and I shall discuss it in detail further on. Let us now confine ourselves to saying that all these deposits of material will be represented by transferable shares in the association. Let us leave these minute reckonings and turn our attention to the workings of attraction.

A great difficulty to be overcome in the trial Phalanx will be the formation of transcendent ties or collective bonds among the series before the end of the warm season. Before winter comes a passionate union must be established between the members; they must be made to feel a sense of collective and individual devotion to the Phalanx; and above all a perfect harmony must be established concerning the division of profits among the three elements: *Capital*, *Labor* and *Talent*.

The difficulty will be greater in northern countries than in those of the south, given the fact that the growing season lasts eight months in the south and just five months in the north.

Since a trial Phalanx must begin with agricultural labor, it will not be in full operation until the month of May (in a climate of 50 degrees latitude, like the region around London or Paris); and since the general bonds, the harmonic ties of the series, must be established before the end of the farming season in October, there will scarcely be five months of full activity in regions of fifty degrees latitude. Everything will have to be done in that short time.

Thus it would be much easier to make the trial in a region where the climate is temperate, for instance near Florence, Naples, Valencia or

Lisbon where the growing season lasts eight or nine months. In such an area it would be particularly easy to consolidate the bonds of union since there would only be three or four months of passional calm between the end of the first season and the beginning of the second. By the second spring, with the renewal of its agricultural labors, the Phalanx would form its ties and cabals anew with much greater zeal and with more intensity than in the first year. The Phalanx would thenceforth be in a state of complete consolidation, and strong enough to avoid passional calms during the second winter.

If, instead of being surrounded by civilized populations, the trial Phalanx had neighbors who had been brought up in the seventh period, or merely in the sixth, it could count on moral support which would lend strength to its intrigues and help it in getting organized. But in fact it will be surrounded only by those social vipers who are called civilized—*Progenies viperarum,* as the Gospel puts it—people whose deceitful proximity will be a spiritual menace to the first Phalanx just as a horde of plague-bearers would be a material menace to a healthy city. This city would be obliged to drive them away and to level its cannons against those who approached its walls.

The experimental Phalanx will be obliged to take similar actions, *in a moral sense,* against the contagion of civilized customs. It will be forced to withdraw itself from all passional or spiritual relations with its perfidious neighbors. (It should be recalled that the two terms "passional" and "spiritual" are synonymous by contrast to "material.")

The civilized are so accustomed to falsity that they practice it even in those circumstances when they would like to practice truthfulness. Propriety and morality make liars out of civilized men. With such habits, the civilized would destroy the mechanism of Harmony if they were permitted to interfere.

This mistrust will not prevent the first Harmonians from admitting a few civilized people as spectators consigned to a "moral quarantine," and this conditional admission will be the object of a highly lucrative speculation which will yield a profit of some twenty millions to the trial Phalanx if it handles the matter skillfully. (The figures will be given farther on.)

Let us discuss the composition of the trial Phalanx. At least seven-eighths of its members should be people involved in farming or industry. The remainder will consist of capitalists, savants and artists. . . . The Phalanx would be poorly graduated and difficult to balance if, among its capitalists, there were several worth 100,000 francs and several worth 50,000 francs without any of intermediate wealth. In such circumstances, one should try to find men with fortunes of 60, 70, 80, and 90,000 francs. The most precisely graduated Phalanx yields the highest degree of social harmony and the greatest profits.

In readying the gardens and workshops of the trial Phalanx one should try to predict and estimate the approximate quantity of attraction which each branch of industry is likely to excite. For example, we know that the plum-tree has less attraction than the pear-tree; and so we will plant fewer plum-trees than pear-trees. The quantity of attraction will be the sole rule to follow in each branch of agricultural and manufacturing work.

Economists would follow a different line of reasoning. They would insist that it is necessary to cultivate whatever produces the greatest yield and to produce a large quantity of the most productive objects. The trial Phalanx should avoid this error; its methods should be different from those of the Phalanxes that will follow it. When all regions have embraced Harmony and when they are all organized in combination with each other, then it will no doubt be necessary to adapt farming to the dictates of interest and attraction. But the goal of the experimental community is quite different: it is to get a group of 1500 or 1600 people working out of pure attraction. If one could predict that they would be more actively attracted to work by thistles and thorns than by orchards and flowers, then it would be necessary to give up orchards and flowers and replace them with thistles and thorns in the experimental community.

In point of fact, as soon as it has attained its two goals, industrial attraction and passional equilibrium, the trial Phalanx will have the means to widen the scope of its labors so as to include any useful tasks which may have been neglected at the outset. Moreover, its strength will be doubled when neighboring communities organize their own Phalanxes and when the whole region is able to intervene in the mechanism of attraction. Thus in the initial experiment it is necessary to concentrate on the creation of industrial attraction without being particular about the type of work involved.

I have had to insist on this point because the critics may wonder at the fact that I require for the first community a great many flowers, orchards and small animals but very little in the way of large-scale agriculture. The reason for this is that some of the stimuli which make large-scale farming attractive will only emerge after the establishment of a network of Phalanxes capable of aiding each other. The first community, which will be deprived of such resources, should adopt appropriate tactics and resolve the problem of industrial attraction by the means at its disposal.

The most appealing species of animals and vegetables are fairly well known, and it will be easy to estimate the proportions to be respected in the industrial preparations for the experimental Phalanx. Of course there will necessarily be some errors at the outset, and it will take several years before a Phalanx can make an exact reckoning of the proportions to be established among all types of work.

Yet since the capital invested in the establishment of the trial Phalanx will be reimbursed at a rate of twelve to one, the shareholders will scarcely be inclined to worry about the fact that a few errors in the distribution of labor will reduce profits during the first years. The main point will be to attain the goal of industrial attraction and passional equilibrium. This will be the sign of victory; and the shareholders or founders should keep in mind that when they have obtained this victory, when they have provided a practical demonstration of the equilibrium of the passions and shown the way to a happy future, their fellow men will find all the world's treasures inadequate to reward them for having provided an escape from the labyrinth of civilization, barbarism, and savagery.

* * *

### *Work and the Distributive Passions*

The physical organization of the series will pose no problems. . . . The obstacle to fear will involve the action of certain passions that the moralists would like to repress. For the best formed series would lose all its qualities of industrial attraction, of direct harmony of inequalities, of indirect harmony of antithetical elements, etc., if one neglected to develop the three basic drives which I have called the distributive or mechanizing passions. To thwart any one of the three would be to spoil a series and to deprive it of industrial attraction. . . .

By working in very short sessions of an hour and a half, two hours at most, every member of Harmony can perform seven or eight different kinds of attractive work in a single day. On the next day he can vary his activities by taking part in different groups. This method is dictated by the eleventh passion, the *Butterfly*, which impels men and women to flit from pleasure to pleasure, to avoid the excesses that ceaselessly plague the people of civilization who prolong a job for six hours, a festival six hours, a ball six hours (and that during the night) at the expense of their sleep and their health.

Civilized pleasures are always associated with unproductive activities, but in the societary state varied work will become a source of varied pleasures. Let me illustrate this point by outlining the daily activities of two Harmonians, one rich and the other poor.

### *LUCAS' DAY IN JUNE*

*Time*

3:30 Rising, preparations.
4:00 Session with a group assigned to the stables.
5:00 Session with a group of gardeners.
7:00 Breakfast.
7:30 Session with the reapers' group.

9:30 Session with the vegetable-growers' group, under a tent.
11:00 Session with the barnyard series.
1:00 DINNER.
2:00 Session with the forestry series.
4:00 Session with a manufacturing group.
6:00 Session with the irrigation series.
8:00 Session at the Exchange.
8:30 Supper.
9:00 Entertainment.
10:00 Bed.

*Nota.* An Exchange is maintained in each Phalanx, not for speculation on interest rates and commodities but for arranging work and pleasure gatherings.

I have described here a day with but three meals, a day in the first phases of Harmony. But when Harmony is in full operation, its active life and the practice of short and varied work sessions will make people prodigiously hungry. Men born and reared in Harmony will be obliged to eat five meals a day, and even these will scarcely be enough to consume the immense quantity of food produced by this new order, an order in which the rich—with their varied activities—will be stronger and hungrier than the poor. This is just the opposite of the civilized system.

I am now going to describe the five-meal day of a rich man in Harmony. His activities are much more varied than those of Lucas, who was one of the villagers enrolled at the outset.

## *MONDOR'S DAY IN THE SUMMER*

*Time*

Sleep from 10:30 at night to 3:00 in the morning.
3:30 Rising, preparations.
4:00 Morning court, review of the night's adventures.
4:30 Breakfast, followed by the industrial parade.
5:30 Session with the group of hunters.
7:00 Session with the group of fishermen.
8:00 Lunch, newspapers.
9:00 Session with a group of horticulturalists, under a tent.
10:00 Mass.
10:30 Session with the group of pheasant-breeders.
11:30 Session at the library.
1:00 DINNER.
2:30 Session with the green-house group.
4:00 Session with the group of exotic plant growers.
5:00 Session with the fish-tank group.
6:00 Snack, in the fields.

| | |
|---|---|
| 6:30 | Session with the sheep-raising group. |
| 8:00 | Session at the Exchange. |
| 9:00 | Supper, fifth meal. |
| 9:30 | Art exhibition, concert, dance, theater, receptions. |
| 10:30 | Bed. |

It is obvious from this description that only a few moments are left for sleep. Harmonians sleep very little. Advanced hygiene along with varied work sessions will inure them against work fatigue. They will not wear themselves out during the day and they will need only a very small amount of sleep. They will become accustomed to this from childhood thanks to an abundance of pleasures more numerous than the day is long.

* * *

# WILLIAM RATHBONE GREG

## Prostitution †

[This review article on the subject of prostitution contributed to a widespread debate on the subject in the 1850s. Many philanthropists and reformers in cities were worried at the time about the numbers of women earning their living through prostitution, the numbers destitute on the streets, and, especially, the possibility of the spread of disease. Popular opinion viewed the problem as a moral one, in which woman's "natural" inclination to virtue had failed and led to vicious habits. Greg, like Elizabeth Barrett Browning in *Aurora Leigh*, saw the problem rather as one caused by men's lack of sexual responsibility and society's irrational scapegoating of the "fallen woman."

The books that Greg reviewed in this article were *De la prostitution dans la ville de Paris* (Paris, 1837) by Alexis-Jean-Baptiste Parent-Duchatelet; *The Miseries of Prostitution* (London, 1844) by James Beard Talbot; *Prostitution in London* (London, 1839) by Michael Ryan; and a series of letters on the state of the London poor that had been published in the newspaper called the *Morning Chronicle*.]

There are some questions so painful and perplexing, that statesmen, moralists, and philanthropists shrink from them by common consent. The subject to which the following pages are devoted, is one of these.

† From *The Westminster Review* 53 (1850), 448–63 and 474–79. All notes are by the editor of this Norton Critical Edition.

William Rathbone Greg (1809–81) was a mill owner and manager who later took up a career writing essays on political and economic subjects. During the 1850s he contributed regularly to all four of the leading quarterly magazines. His essays were collected in 1882 and 1884.

Of all the social problems which philosophy has to deal with, this is, we believe, the darkest, the knottiest, and the saddest. From whatever point of view it is regarded, it presents considerations so difficult and so grievous, that in this country no ruler or writer has yet been found with nerve to face the sadness, or resolution to encounter the difficulties. Statesmen see the mighty evil lying on the main pathway of the world, and, with a groan of pity and despair, "pass by on the other side." They act like the timid patient, who, fearing and feeling the existence of a terrible disease, dares not examine its symptoms or probe its depth, lest he should realise it too clearly, and possibly aggravate its intensity by the mere investigation. Or, like a more foolish animal still, they hide their head at the mention of the danger, as if they hoped, by ignoring, to annihilate it.

It is from a strong conviction that this is not worthy behaviour on the part of those who aspire to guide either the actions or the opinions of others, that, after much hesitation and many misgivings, we have undertaken to speak of so dismal and delicate a matter. We are aware that mischief is risked by bringing the subject prominently before the public eye, and that the benefit to be derived from the discussion should be so clear and certain, as unquestionably to overbalance this risk. We are aware that it is a matter on which it is not easy to speak openly—not always possible to speak with confidence as to facts, causes, or consequences; we are aware that we shall expose ourselves to much scoffing from the vulgar and light-minded; much dishonest misrepresentation from those who recklessly echo any popular cry; much unmerited anger from those who deem that refinement forbids them to speak of things which it does not forbid them to do; much serious blame on the part of those who think that no object can justify us in compelling attention to so revolting a moral sore. We have weighed all these obstacles; and we have concluded that the end we have in view, and the chance of the good we may effect and the suffering we may mitigate, warrant us in disregarding them. We think that such considerations have already too long withheld serious and benevolent men from facing one of the sorest evils that the English sun now shines upon. Our divines, our philanthropists, our missionaries, nay, even our *soeurs de la charité*,[1] do not shrink from entering, in person, the most loathsome abodes of sin and misery,—or from penetrating into the lowest dens of filth and pollution, where human despair and degradation ever dragged itself to die,—when led thither by the impulse of compassion and the hope of good. Why, then, should we allow indolence, disgust, or the fear of misconstruction, to deter us from entering upon an inquiry as to the possibility of mitigating the very worst form which human wretchedness and degradation can assume? The best and purest of our race do not feel them-

1. French; "sisters of charity." That is, nuns in a Catholic order dedicated to healing and assisting the poor.

selves repelled from, or tarnished by, the darkest haunts of actual guilt and horror, where pain is to be assuaged, or where souls are to be saved. Let us act by *subjects*, as they act by *scenes*.

Feeling, then, that it is a false and mischievous delicacy, and a culpable moral cowardice, which shrinks from the consideration of the great social vice of Prostitution, because the subject is a loathsome one;—feeling, also, that no good can be hoped unless we are at liberty to treat the subject, and all its collaterals, with perfect freedom, both of thought and speech;—convinced that the evil must be probed with a courageous and unshrinking hand before a cure can be suggested, or palliatives can safely be applied;—we have deliberately resolved to call public attention to it, though we do so with pain, reluctance, and diffidence.

And, first—to preclude misrepresentation, as far as this is possible—we must show our colours by expressing our own feelings as to fornication. Our morality will be considered by the divine as strangely lax and inconsistent, and by the man of the world, the ordinary thinker, and mass who follow current ideas without thinking at all—as savage and absurd; nevertheless, we conceive it to harmonise with the ethics of nature and the dictates of unsophisticated sense. We look upon fornication, then (by which we always mean promiscuous intercourse with women who prostitute themselves for pay), as the worst and lowest form of sexual irregularity, the most revolting to the unpolluted feelings, the most indicative of a *low* nature, the most degrading and sapping to the loftier life,—

"The sin, of all, most sure to blight,—
The sin, of all, that the soul's light
Is soonest lost, extinguish'd in."

Sexual indulgence, however guilty in its circumstances, however tragic in its results, is, when accompanied by love, a sin *according to nature*; fornication is a sin *against nature*; its peculiarity and heinousness consist in its divorcing from all feeling of love that which was meant by nature as the last and intensest expression of passionate love; in its putting asunder that which God has joined; in its reducing the deepest gratification of unreserved affection to a mere momentary and brutal indulgence; in its making that only one of our appetites, which is redeemed from mere *animality* by the hallowing influence of the better and tenderer feelings with which nature has connected it, *as* animal as all the rest. It is a voluntary exchange of the passionate love of a spiritual and intellectual being, for the mere hunger and thirst of the beast. It is a profanation of that which the higher organization of man enables him to elevate and refine. It is the introduction of filth into the pure sanctuary of the affections.

We have said that fornication reduces the most fervent expression of deep and devoted human love to a mere animal gratification. But it does more than this: it not only brings man down to a level with the brutes, but it has one feature which places him far, far below them. Sexual connexion, with them, is the simple indulgence of a natural desire *mutually felt*: in the case of human prostitution, it is in many, probably in most instances, a brutal desire on the one side only, and a reluctant and loathing submission, purchased by money, on the other. Among cattle, the sexes meet by common instinct and a common wish;—it is reserved for the human animal to treat the female as a mere victim for his lust. The peculiar guilt of prostitution, then, consists, in our view of the matter, in its being *unnatural*; a violation of our truer instincts—not a mere frailty in yielding to them. On this matter, therefore, we feel at least as strongly as any divine can do.

In the second place, we feel called upon to protest against the manner in which prostitutes are almost universally regarded, spoken of, and treated in this country, as dishonouring alike to our religion and our manhood. This iniquity pervades all classes, and both sexes. No language is too savage for these wretched women. They are outcasts, Pariahs, lepers. Their touch, even in the extremity of suffering, is shaken off as if it were pollution and disease. It is discreditable to a woman even to be supposed to know of their existence. They are kicked, cuffed, trampled on with impunity by every one. Their oaths are seldom regarded in a court of justice, scarcely ever in a police court. They seem to be considered far more out of the pale of humanity than negroes on a slave plantation, or fellahs in a pasha's dungeon.

* * *

If the *extremity* of human wretchedness—if a condition which combines within itself every element of suffering, mental and physical, circumstantial and intrinsic—is a passport to our compassion, every heart should bleed for the position of an English prostitute, as it never bled at any form of woe before. We wish it were in our power to give a picture, simple, faithful, uncoloured, but "too severely true," of the horrors which constitute the daily life of a woman of the town. The world—the unknowing world—is apt to fancy her revelling in he *enjoyment* of licentious pleasures; lost and dead to all sense of remorse and shame; wallowing in mire because she loves it. Alas! there is no truth in *this* conception, or only in the most exceptional cases. Passing over all the agonies of grief and terror she must have endured before she reached her present degradation; the vain struggles to retrieve the first false, fatal step; the feeling of her inevitable future pressing her down with all the hopeless weight of destiny; the dreams of a happy past that haunt her in the night-watches, and keep her ever trembling on the verge of madness;—passing over all this, what is her position when she has reached the last step of her downward progress, and has become a common prostitute? Every calamity that can afflict human nature seems to have gathered round her,—cold, hunger, disease, often absolute starvation. Insufficiently fed, insufficiently clad, she is driven out alike by necessity and by the dread of solitude, to wander through the streets by night, for the chance of earning a meal by the most loathsome labour that imagination can picture, or a penal justice could inflict. For, be it remembered, desire has, by this time, long ceased; the mere momentary excitement of sexual indulgence is no longer attainable; repetition has changed pleasure into absolute repugnance; and these miserable women ply their wretched trade with a loathing and abhorrence which only perpetual semi-intoxication can deaden or endure. The curses, the blows, the nameless brutalities they have to submit to from their ruffianly associates of the brothel and saloon, are as nothing to the hideous punishment inherent in the daily practice of their sin. Their evidence, and the evidence of all who have come in contact with them, is unanimous on this point—that gin alone enables them to live or act; that without its constant stimulus and stupefaction, they would long since have died from mere physical exhaustion, or gone mad from mental horrors. The reaction from the nightly excitement is too terrible to be borne, and gin is again resorted to as a morning draught. Even this wretched stimulus often fails; and there can be few of our readers who have not seen some of these unhappy creatures, after a winter's night spent in walking wearily to and fro for hours, amid snow, frost, or piercing winds, in dress too flimsy even for the hottest season, sink down upon a door-step, fainting and worn out; too feeble to be able, and too miserable to desire to rise. All this time, too, disease of many kinds is busy with its victim; and positive pain is added to severe privation and distracting thought. Do not let it be supposed that they are insensible to the horrors of their situation; we believe this is rarely the case altogether; where it is so, they owe it to the spirits in which they invariably indulge.

* * *

The career of these women is a brief one; their downward path a marked and inevitable one; and they know this well. They are almost never rescued; escape themselves they cannot. *Vestigia nulla retrorsum.*[2] The swindler may repent, the drunkard may reform; society aids and encourages them in their thorny path of repentance and atonement, and welcomes back with joy and generous forgetfulness the lost sheep and the prodigal son.[3] But the prostitute may *not* pause—*may* NOT *recover:* at the very first halting, timid step she may make to the right or to the left, with a view to flight from her appalling doom, the whole resistless influences of the surrounding world, the good as well as the bad, close around her to hunt her back into perdition.

2. Latin; "footsteps can never be retraced." That is, the "fallen" woman, once her virginity and chastity are lost, can never be redeemed, but will always be marked as an outcast and reprobate.
3. Biblical references. See Luke 15.

Then comes the last sad scene of all, when drink, disease, and starvation have laid her on her death-bed. On a wretched pallet in a filthy garret, with no companions but the ruffians, drunkards, and harlots with whom she had cast in her lot; amid brutal curses, ribald language, and drunken laughter; with a past—which, even were there no future, would be dreadful to contemplate—laying its weight of despair upon her soul; with a prospective beyond the grave which the little she retains of her early religion lights up for her with the lurid light of hell,—this poor daughter of humanity terminates a life, of which, if the sin has been grievous and the weakness lamentable, the expiation has been fearfully tremendous.

We have seen that even in their lowest degradation these poor creatures never wholly lose the sense of shame or sensitiveness to the opinions of the world. It is pleasing also to find that another of the chief virtues which belong to the female character, seems never to become extinct with them or even to be materially impaired. Their kindness to each other, when sick or destitute, and indeed to all who are in suffering or distress, has attracted the attention and called forth the admiration of all who have been thrown much into contact with them. "The English Opium Eater"[4] bears eloquent testimony to the unquenchable tenderness of their nature, and the ready generosity with which they lavish aid to the needy out of their scanty and precarious means. Duchatelet[5] states that their affection for children, whether their own or not, is carried to a point surpassing that common to women, and that, in consequence, they make the most careful and valuable of nurses.

* * *

A very touching instance of these amiable feelings was related to us a short time ago. A poor girl who, after a few years spent in infamy and wretchedness, was rapidly sinking into a decline, had still no means of livelihood but in the continued practice of her calling. But, with a mixture of kindness and of conscience which may well surprise us under such circumstances, her companions in degradation resolved among themselves that, as they said, "at least she should not be compelled to die in sin," and contributed out of their own poor and sad earnings a

4. *Confessions of an English Opium Eater* by Thomas De Quincey, published in 1822. It tells the story of De Quincey's own addiction to opium, from the strange reveries of his early experience to the appalling nightmares of the later states. A long central section describes his destitution on the streets of London and how he was befriended and supported by a fifteen-year-old prostitute named Ann.

5. Alexis-Jean-Baptiste Parent-Duchatelet (1790–1836) became a doctor at the age of twenty-five and was deeply interested in the state of medicine and hygiene in Paris during the beginning of the nineteenth century. He was a member of a special commission charged with monitoring and preventing the spread of cholera in the city. He became a doctor at the Hospice de la Pitie in Paris and died of exhaustion brought on by overwork. His many publications contrived to bring both medical, social, and ethical questions to the public notice. *Prostitution in the City of Paris*, published posthumously, was a huge popular success and helped to bring about more tolerant attitudes toward working women.

sufficient sum to enable her to pass her few remaining weeks in comfort and repentance. This is not a trait of the wholly lost.

But if sympathy be due to these unhappy women on the mere ground of the sufferings they undergo, it will perhaps be even more readily rendered when we examine a little into the antecedents which have led them to their fate. There is, we think, a very general misapprehension, especially among the fair sex, as to the original causes which reduce this unfortunate class of girls to their state of degradation—the primary circumstances of their fall from chastity. On this matter, those who know the most will assuredly judge the most leniently. Those who think of this class of sinners as severely as closet moralists, and voluptuaries with filthy fancies and soiled souls, and—alas! as most women are apt to do—fancy the original occasion of their lapse from virtue to have been either lust, immodest and unruly desires, silly vanity, or the deliberate exchange of innocence for luxury and show. We believe they are quite mistaken: it is the first *never*, or so rarely, that in treating of the subject we may be entitled to ignore the exceptions; it is the latter only in a small portion of the cases that occur. It is very important to a true view and a sound feeling on these matters, to set this error right. Women's *desires* scarcely ever lead to their fall; for (save in a class of whom we shall speak presently) the desire scarcely exists in a definite and conscious form, till they *have* fallen. In this point there is a radical and essential difference between the sexes: the arrangements of nature and the customs of society would be even more unequal than they are, were it not so. In men, in general, the sexual desire is inherent and spontaneous, and belongs to the condition of puberty. In the other sex, the desire is dormant, if not non-existent, till excited; always till excited by undue familiarities; almost always till excited by actual intercourse. Those feelings which coarse and licentious minds are so ready to attribute to girls, are almost invariably *consequences*. Women whose position and education have protected them from exciting causes, constantly pass through life without ever being cognizant of the promptings of the senses. Happy for them that it is so! We do not mean to say that uneasiness may not be felt—that health may not sometimes suffer; but there is no consciousness of the cause. Among all the higher and middle classes, and, to a greater extent than would commonly be believed, among the lower classes also, where they either come of virtuous parents, or have been carefully brought up, this may be affirmed as a general fact. Were it not for this kind decision of nature, which, in England, has been assisted by that correctness of feeling which pervades our education, the consequences would, we believe, be frightful. If the passions of women were ready, strong, and spontaneous, in a degree even remotely approaching the form they assume in the coarser sex, there can be little doubt that sexual irregularities would reach a height, of which, at present, we have happily no conception. Imagine for a moment, the sufferings and struggles the virtuous among them would, on that supposition, have to undergo, in a country where, to hundreds of thousands marriage is impossible, and to hundreds of thousands more, is postponed till the period of youth is passed: and where modesty, decency, and honour, alike preclude them from that indulgence which men practise without restraint or shame. No! Nature has laid many heavy burdens on the delicate shoulders of the weaker sex: let us rejoice that this at least is spared them.

The causes which lead to the fall of women are various; but all of them are of a nature to move grief and compassion rather than indignation and contempt, in all minds cognizant of the strange composition of humanity—the follies of the wise, the weakness of the strong, the lapses of the good; cognizant, also, of those surprising and deplorable inconsistencies "by which faults may sometimes be found to have grown out of virtues, and very many of our heaviest offences to have been grafted by human imperfection upon the best and kindest of our affections."

The first and perhaps the largest class of prostitutes are those who may fairly be said to have had no choice in the matter—who were born and bred in sin; whose parents were thieves and prostitutes before them; whose dwelling has always been in an atmosphere of squalid misery and sordid guilt; who have never had a glimpse or a hearing of a better life; whom fate has marked from their cradle for a course of degradation; for whom there is no *fall*, for they stood already on the lowest level of existence; in whom there is no crime, for they had, and could have, neither an aspiration, a struggle, nor a choice. Such abound in London, in Dublin, in Glasgow; and, though to a less extent, in almost all large towns. Their families form the *classes dangereuses*[6] of French statisticians; and it is from these that is recruited the population of the gaols, the lowest brothels, the hulks, and latterly, to some extent, the ragged schools. How this class is to be checked, controlled, diminished, and finally extirpated, presents one of the most difficult practical problems for English statesmen, and one, to the solution of which they must address themselves without delay; but it is one with which, at present, we have not to do. All that we wish to urge is, that the prostitutes who spring from this class, are clearly the victims of circumstances; and therefore must on all hands be allowed to be objects of the most unalloyed compassion.

Others, unquestionably, and alas! too many, fall from the snares of vanity. They are flattered by the attentions of those above them in station, and gratified by a language more refined and courteous than they hear from those of their own sphere. They enjoy the present pleasure, think they can secure themselves against being led on too far, and, like

6. French; literally, "dangerous classes." In the nineteenth century this would have included such people as beggars, thieves, and prostitutes; that is, all those who appeared to threaten society. Today these are people who would be deemed "at risk."

foolish moths, flutter round the flame which is to dazzle and consume them. For these we have no justification, and little apology to offer. Silly parents, and a defective or injudicious education, form their most frequent excuse. Still, even these are not worthy of the treatment they meet with, even from those of their own sex, who cannot be unconscious of the same foibles—still less from men. Let those who are without sin among us, cast the first stone at them.

Some, too, there are for whom no plea can be offered—who voluntarily and deliberately sell themselves to shame, and barter, in a cold spirit of bargain, chastity and reputation for carriages, jewels, and a luxurious table. All that can here be urged is the simple fact—too notorious to be denied, too disgraceful for the announcement of it to be listened to with patience—that in this respect the unfortunate women who ultimately come upon the town, are far from being the chief or the most numerous delinquents. For one woman who thus, of deliberate choice, sells herself to a lover, ten sell themselves to a husband. Let not the world cry shame upon us for the juxtaposition. The barter is as naked and as cold in the one case as in the other; the thing bartered is the same; the difference between the two transactions lies in the price that is paid down.

Many—and these are commonly the most innocent and the most wronged of all—are deceived by unreal marriages; and in these cases their culpability consists in the folly which confided in their lover to the extent of concealing their intention from their friends—in all cases a weak and in most cases a blameable concealment; but surely not one worthy of the fearful punishment which overtakes it. Many—far more than would generally be believed—fall from pure unknowingness. Their affections are engaged, their confidence secured; thinking no evil themselves, they permit caresses which in themselves, and to them, indicate no wrong, and are led on ignorantly and thoughtlessly from one familiarity to another, not conscious where those familiarities must inevitably end till ultimate resistance becomes almost impossible; and they learn, when it is too late—what women can never learn too early or impress too strongly on their minds—that a lover's encroachments, to be repelled successfully, must be repelled and negatived at the very outset.

We believe we shall be borne out by the observation of all who have inquired much into the antecedents of this unfortunate class of women—those, at least, who have not sprung from the *very* low, or the actually vicious sections of the community—in stating that a vast proportion of those who, after passing through the career of kept mistresses, ultimately come upon the town, fall in the first instance from a mere exaggeration and perversion of one of the best qualities of a woman's heart. They yield to desires in which they do not share, from a weak generosity which cannot refuse anything to the passionate entreaties of the man they love. There is in the warm fond heart of woman a strange and sublime unselfishness, which men too commonly discover only to profit by,—a positive love of self-sacrifice,—an active, so to speak, an *aggressive* desire to show their affection, by giving up to those who have won it something they hold very dear. It is an unreasoning and dangerous yearning of the spirit, precisely analogous to that which prompts the surrenders and self-tortures of the religious devotee. Both seek to prove their devotion to the idol they have enshrined, by casting down before his altar their richest and most cherished treasures. This is no romantic or over-coloured picture; those who deem it so have not known the better portion of the sex, or do not deserve to have known them. We refer confidently to all whose memory unhappily may furnish an answer to the question, whether an appeal to this perverted generosity is not almost always the final resistless argument to which female virtue succumbs. When we consider these things, and remember also, as we must now proceed to show, how many thousands trace their ruin to actual want—*the want of those dependent on them*—we believe, upon our honour, that nine out of ten originally modest women who fall from virtue, fall from motives or feelings in which sensuality and self have no share; nay, under circumstances in which selfishness, had they not been of too generous a nature to listen to its dictates, would have saved them.

We now come to speak of that hard necessity—that grinding poverty approaching to actual want—which, by unanimous testimony, is declared to be the most prolific source of prostitution, in this and in all other countries. In Paris the elaborate researches of Duchatelet[7] have established this point in the clearest manner. After speaking of the prostitutes supplied by those families who live in vice and hopeless abandonment, he proceeds thus:—

> "Of all causes of prostitution in Paris, and probably in all great towns, there are none more influential than the want of work, and indigence resulting from insufficient earnings. What are the earnings of our laundresses, our sempstresses, our milliners? Compare the wages of the most skilful with those of the more ordinary and moderately able, and we shall see if it be possible for these latter to procure even the strict necessaries of life; and if we further compare the price of their work with that of their dishonour, we shall cease to be surprised that so great a number should fall into irregularities thus made almost inevitable. This state of things has naturally a tendency to increase, in the actual state of our society, in consequence of the usurpation by men of a large class of occupations, which it would be fitter and more honourable in our sex to resign to the other. Is it not shameful, for example, to see in Paris thousands of men in the prime of their age, in *cafés*, shops, and warehouses, leading the sedentary and effeminate life which is only suitable for women?"—Vol. i. p. 96.

7. See note 5 on p. 378.

M. Duchatelet adds some other facts, which fully confirm the testimony we shall have to bring respecting an unfortunate class in our own country, viz.: that filial and maternal affection drive many to at least occasional prostitution, as a means, and the only means left to them, of earning bread for those dependent on them for support.

> "It is difficult to believe the trade of prostitution should have been embraced by certain women as a means of fulfilling their maternal or filial duties—nothing, however, is more true. It is by no means rare to see married women, widowed, or deserted by their husbands, and in consequence deprived of all support, become prostitutes with the sole object of saving their family from dying of hunger. It is still more common to find young girls, unable to procure from their honest occupations an adequate provision for their aged and infirm parents, reduced to prostitute themselves in order to eke out their livelihood. I have found too many particulars regarding these two classes, not to be convinced that they are much more numerous in Paris than is generally imagined."—Vol. i. p. 98.

He afterwards sums up the results of his investigations into the cases of 5,183 Parisian prostitutes, as follows:—

"2,696 driven to the profession by parental abandonment, excessive want, and actual destitution.
89 to earn food for the support of their parents or children.
280 driven by shame to fly from their homes.
2,118 abandoned by their seducers, and having nothing to turn to.
5,183"

We shall not take much pains in proving that poverty is the chief determining cause which drives women into prostitution in England, as in France; partly because we have no adequate statistics, and we are not disposed to present our readers with mere fallacious estimates, but mainly because no one doubts the proposition. Granting all that is or can be said of the idleness, extravagance, and love of dress of these poor women, the number of those who would adopt such a life, were any other means of obtaining an adequate maintenance open to them, will be allowed on all hands to be small indeed.

* * *

Let us now cast a short glance at the *extent* of this hideous gangrene of English society. We have given a sketch of the life of one prostitute: we have to multiply this by thousands for every large town, by tens of thousands for the metropolis. We shall not pretend to give any definite numbers; little is known with certainty; and the estimates, even among those likely to be best informed, vary enormously. Colquhoun,[8] at the end of the last century, gave the numbers residing in London alone at 50,000. This is now admitted on all hands to have been a monstrous exaggeration. Mr. Mayne, one of the Commissioners of Police, states the number of regular prostitutes who might be traced, at from 8,000 to 10,000 in the metropolis, *exclusive of the city*; but he adds, "There is no means of ascertaining the number of female servants, milliners, and women in the upper and middle ranks of society, who might properly be classed with prostitutes, or the women who frequent theatres exclusively, barracks, ships, prisons, &c., &c." Mr. Talbot[9] states, as the result of the most careful inquiries that have been made, that the number in Edinburgh is about 800; in Glasgow, 1,800; in Liverpool, 2,900; in Leeds, 700; in Bristol, 1,300; in Manchester, about 700; and in Norwich, between 500 and 700. If to these we add the number furnished by other towns, and the numbers who everywhere escape the knowledge of the police, the impression among the best informed is, that the number who live by prostitution, whose sole profession it may be said to be, cannot be under 50,000 in Great Britain. This of course does not include those women of loose character who follow also some ostensible and honest occupation.

We are desirous of avoiding all needless details which would deter readers from following us to our conclusions. We shall therefore pass over many facts, which it might otherwise have been desirable to publish, and will refer those who wish for further information, to the works of Dr. Ryan,[1] and more especially to that of Mr. Talbot. We shall here content ourselves with three or four brief statements.

1. Most of the higher class of brothels are supplied by means of regularly-employed and highly-paid procuresses, whose occupation it is to entice to their houses female servants and governesses applying in answer to advertisements, and young women—frequently young ladies—who come up to London for employment, and do not know where to fix their lodgings. Sometimes by cajolery, sometimes by force, sometimes by drugs, they are kept close prisoners till their ruin is effected; when they are handed over to the brothel-keepers, and their place supplied by fresh victims.

8. Patrick Colquhoun (1745–1820), metropolitan police magistrate. Originally from Scotland, Colquhoun came to London in 1789, and as police magistrate he instituted many reforms. In 1795 he published a *Treatise on the Police of the Metropolis, explaining the various Crimes and Misdemeanours which are at present felt as a pressure upon the Community, and suggesting Remedies for their Prevention, by a Magistrate.* His work included an analysis of prostitution in the city. It went into several editions, being reprinted well into the nineteenth century, and was often cited as a primary authority on crime and the city.

9. James Beard Talbot (1800 or 1801–81), philanthropist and founder, in 1835, of the London Society for the Protection of Young Females.

1. Michael Ryan (1800–41), physician to the Metropolitan Free Hospital in London. Ryan gave a course of lectures on population, marriage, and divorce called "A Question of State Medicine," which he published in 1831. He also wrote two books. Ryan was an influential doctor, but his interests and anxieties lay rather with the diseases of sexual contact than with other social issues. Most notably his writings in the 1830s included an explicit attack on the use of birth control practices.

2. One of the most painful facts connected with the whole subject, is the tender age at which thousands of these poor creatures are seduced. On no point is the evidence more clear than this. Not only is a vast proportion of existing prostitutes under twenty, but the number who become prostitutes at the age of fifteen, twelve, and even ten years, is such as almost to exceed credibility. This is known from the testimony of the hospitals into which they are brought to be treated for syphilitic diseases. Mr. Laing (Talbot, p. 29) tells us of one child who died of a worn-out constitution at the age of thirteen! It is for the old and withered *débauché* that these youngest victims are ordinarily selected.

3. The extent to which the frequentation of brothels is carried among all classes and professions, and even among the married of both sexes, is little suspected by the public at large. On this topic some frightful disclosures have, from time to time, had to be hushed up; though not soon enough to prevent an astounding glimpse of the hideous iniquity within.

* * *

4. It is notorious that nearly all prostitutes except the highest class are either thieves themselves, or are connected with and supporters of professional thieves. It is calculated, by those most conversant with police courts, that more than one half of those convicted of larceny are prostitutes or their associates.

5. One of the most important practical points connected with this painful subject, is the deplorable extent and virulence of disease which prostitution is the means of spreading throughout the community. Sanitary matters occupy so large a share of public attention at the present moment, that so important a branch of them cannot be wholly overlooked. The amount of social evil arising from syphilitic maladies, statistics cannot measure, even if trustworthy statistics on the subject were within our reach, which they are not. All that we know with certainty is, that the Lock Hospitals (those devoted to syphilitic patients) throughout the country are always full, and generally insufficient. One witness affirms that not one man in ten goes through life without being diseased at one period or another of his career. We do not believe this statement: but we do know that the disease prevails to an extent that is perfectly appalling; and that where there are 50,000 prostitutes scattered over the country (a vast majority of whom are, or have been diseased), spreading infection on every side of them, quarantines against the plague, and costly precautions against cholera, seem very like straining at gnats and swallowing camels. It must not be imagined that the mischief of syphilis can be measured by the number of those who are ostensibly its victims, even could we ascertain this datum. We must take into account the sufferings of those innocent individuals in private life who are infected through the sins of others; we must take into account the happiness of many families thus irretrievably destroyed; the thousands of children

who are in consequence born into the world with a constitution incurably unsound; the certain, but incalculable deterioration of public health and of the vigour of the race, which must ensue in the course of a generation or two more. None but medical men can have an adequate insight into the degree or the ramifications of this great social mischief; and medical men will tell us that it is not easy to overrate either. Surely this is a point which must soon command the most anxious attention of the state authorities.

* * *

Such being the evil we have to deal with, we now come to the practical and most painful questions—Can it be eradicated?—and if not, what can and ought to be done to mitigate its mischief and diminish its amount? And is the *quasi*-sanction[2] given to the practice, by such a recognition of it as is involved in the attempt to control it by certain administrative regulations, a greater or less evil than the consequences which at present flow from its unchecked prevalence?

Can Prostitution be eradicated?—At present, *per saltum* and *ab extra*,[3] certainly not. In a state of society like that which now prevails in England,—with livelihood so difficult, and marriage so impeded by scantiness of means,—with so many thousands constantly on the verge, and sometimes beyond the verge, of starvation, and whose urgent poverty will therefore overrule their reluctant wills,—with idleness so prevalent among the rich, and education so defective among the poor,—with the vice so sanctioned by the custom of centuries as to have become a thing of course,—with the hundreds of female devils who prowl about day and night seeking for their prey,—with the countless temptations which beset the path of the innocent, and the countless obstacles which are cast in the backward steps of the repentant,—we fear that the extinction of the practice, or even its reduction from a rule to an exception, must be a most slow, gradual, and incalculably difficult process. That it may, in time, and by bringing to bear upon it all the sound, moral, social, and economic influences in our power, be more and more discarded by the respectable, as a low and disreputable habit, and confined to the vulgar and the vicious, we are not without strong hopes; but at present we must be content, however reluctantly, to regard it as one of those admitted and established evils which the statist has to accept and to deal with as he best may.

* * *

2. *Quasi* is a Latin word meaning "as if." Here the meaning is "as if a sanction," or a form of permission or ignoring that functions "like a sanction."
3. Latin; "from the outside." Latin; "at a bound," "with a leap," and so, in effect, "all at once." The meaning of Greg's phrase is something like "At present, all at once, and from the outside, certainly not."

# M. A. STODART

## [Poetry and the Poetess]†

The domain of poetry is wide; her power over the human heart immense. It is hers to describe, with truth and force, those objects which are too vast, and those which are too minute for ordinary ken; the former escaping common observation, from the inability of an ordinary eye to take the range of the whole at one view; and the latter, from the delicacy of observation required for their survey. It is hers to express in vigorous and powerful language the workings of the stronger passions of the human heart, when the whole man is convulsed, and when thought and feeling spurn the common words of calm, quiet, every-day life. And it is hers too to embody and give permanence to those delicate, evanescent emotions which pass over the mind like the blush over a maiden's brow, and which can no more be distinguished by the powers of an ordinary mind, than the blending and intermingling of the rainbow units. It is the province of poetry to arouse by her trumpet-call to vigorous action, and to melt by her plaintive warblings to gentle and tender emotion. Sometimes she is found amid scenes of horror and sublimity, hanging over the beetling precipice and listening to the roar of the torrent far, far beneath; at other times she delights to rove amid scenes of rural beauty, watching the sun-beams flickering on the fields, listening to the warbling of the birds, or rejoicing in even the simple little flowerets which spring up beneath her feet; but whether she is amid scenes of sublimity or scenes of beauty, still true to herself, she inspires feelings and sentiments and gives expressions to them. The 'thoughts that voluntary move harmonious numbers' are her gift. When religion takes poetry into her service, the province of the handmaid is yet farther extended, her power amazingly increased. Linked to eternal, immutable truth, how wide is her range, how sweet, how potent is her song! Secret springs of the human heart before untouched, because unknown, are now subject to her thrilling sway. And her sphere of vision is no longer bounded by an earthly horizon. Far, far away, 'beyond this dim spot which men

† From *Female Writers: Thoughts on Their Proper Sphere and on Their Powers of Usefulness* (London, 1842). All notes are by the editor of this Norton Critical Edition.

Miss Mary Ann Stodart (dates unknown) was an educational writer who published a number of books for girls during the 1830s and '40s. These included *Hints on Reading addressed to a Young Lady* (London, 1839), *Every-day Duties, in Letters to a Young Lady* (London, 1840), and *Principles of Education practically considered; with an especial reference to the present state of female education in England* (London, 1844). The full title of Mary Ann Stodart's *Female Writers: Thoughts on Their Proper Sphere and on Their Powers of Usefulness* (London, 1842) gives a clear indication of the tone of its contents. Stodart writes on many areas in her little book, and her title has become something of a catch phrase for women and writing in the nineteenth century. A well-known book of criticism on the Brontës, written by Inga-Stina Ewbank, is called *Their Proper Sphere* (1966). Stodart's chapter on women and poetry speaks generally (the extract here) before going on to consider the merits of particular poets.

call earth', she soars on the wings of faith and hope, till the harmonies of heaven fall upon her delighted ear, and the splendours of heaven beam upon her raptured eye.

The power of poetry is not confined to those who take rank and precedence as the poets of the land. That would be a cold and an inglorious doctrine.

> Many are poets, who have never penned
> Their inspiration, and perchance the best

Many unconsciously are poets; thoughts and feelings struggle within, and sometimes flash out in glowing, burning words, marking their path in a line of living light. Poetry is the forcible expression of truth. Far from us and ours to be debasing doctrine that its proper region is fiction. Poetry rejoices in the truth; there it can spread its wings with ease and freedom, unfettered and unimpeded. In the words of a living poet of great and heart-stirring power,

> Song is but the eloquence of truth.

And a mighty, glorious eloquence it is. The monarch seated on his throne bends beneath its power, and the savage, roaming in his wild woods, acknowledges its sway.

Is the hand of poor weak women ever permitted to sweep the living lyre, and to elicit its thrilling tones? The notes are varied; it is a lyre of many strings, an instrument of wider range than any constructed by mortal hand; what tones, what notes vibrate most in unison with woman's heart, and will be most likely, when struck by her hand, to speak to the heart of others?

We cannot doubt the answer. All that is beautiful in form, delicate in sentiment, graceful in action, will form the peculiar province of the gentle powers of woman. O scorn us not! We may not, we cannot 'murmur tales of iron wars', follow the currents of a heady flight; portray with the vivid power of Homeric song,[1] the horrid din of war, the rush of contending warriors, the prancing of the noble steed, the clang, the tumult, the stirring interests of the battle-field—no—but we can do what mightier man would perhaps disdain—we can follow one solitary soldier as he drags his wounded limbs beneath the sheltering hedge; and while we mark his glazing eye, we can read with woman's keenness, the thoughts of wife, children, and home, which are playing around his heart. We may not be able to sustain a strain of high and equal majesty like the bard of Martha,[2] but we can follow out the sorrows of the for-

1. Homer, ancient Greek poet, and apparent author of the two famous epic poems *The Iliad* and *The Odyssey*. Homer is considered the father of Western poetry.
2. This may be a reference to Goethe's *Faust* (1798), in which a character named Martha appears.

saken Dido,[3] weep over the untimely fate of the warrior-friends, and sympathize with the feminine eagerness of Camilla,[4] as, womanly even in her power, she forgets self-defence and a warrior's duties, in order to seize on the splendid ornaments of an officer in the opposing army [*Aeneid* 11.5.731]. We cannot range through heaven and hell with the fiery wing of our glorious poet Milton;[5] we cannot ascend to the height of great argument, and justify the ways of God to man. No woman could have delineated the character of Satan, so evidently 'not less archangel ruined'; no woman could have tracked the flight of Satan across Chaos;[6] or depicted that mysterious assemblage when the rebel angel stood before 'the anarch old'; but we can imagine that some wonderfully endowed woman *might* have pencilled out some of the light and graceful traits of that beautiful garden of Eden, and the happiness of our first parents, a picture which partakes so eminently of the beautiful as to afford a contrast to the sublimity of the other parts of our wonderful national poem. It is not within our province to dive into the deep recesses of the human heart with that myriad-minded man, our own Shakespeare, and to drag into the open day-light the hidden secrets of the soul. No! but there are light and delicate moments which a woman's pen may express, and which Shakespeare, though unrivalled amid poets for his knowledge of woman's heart, has not even guessed. We have struck on the point where lies the true poetic power of woman, it is in the heart—over the heart—and especially in the peculiarities of her own heart. We have but few remains of the earliest and best Greek poetesses; or her who earned the high title of the Lesbian muse; but those remains, 'more golden than gold' [the words of Sappho herself, preserved by Demetrius Phalereus],[7] are all breathings from the dearest affections of the heart. The exquisite fragment preserved by Longi-

3. According to legend, Dido was queen of Carthage. She founded this city on the coast of Africa and defended it against all comers, so that it became prosperous and mighty. In Virgil's *Aeneid* she is represented bewailing the loss of Aeneas after he abandoned her to go on to found Rome, and she was said to have committed suicide after his departure.
4. Queen of the Volsci, Camilla was early dedicated to the service of Diana, the virgin goddess of the moon. Accompanied by three warrior women Camilla led her own army against Aeneas in support of Turnus. In the *Aeneid*, she killed many men in battle but was then fatally wounded by a blow to the breast.
5. John Milton (1608–74), English poet. Milton wrote many books both poetic and political, but his most famous work, and the one alluded to here, is *Paradise Lost* (1667), which deals with the fall of Lucifer and the banishment of Adam and Eve from the garden of Eden.
6. Referring to a scene in Milton's *Paradise Lost* in which Lucifer, or Satan as he becomes after his fall from grace, flies through the universe.
7. The Greek poet Sappho stands at the head of the form of lyric poetry as Homer stands at the head of epic poetry. Sappho lived about 600 BC on the island of Lesbos. She was said to have composed nine books of poetry, but only one complete poem and a number of fragments survive. "More golden than gold" is a quotation from Sappho given by Demetrius Phalereus (3rd century BC) in his book *On Style*. Talking about the use of exaggeration and hyperbole, he provides this example: "far more sweet-sounding than a lyre . . . more golden than gold . . ." (Loeb translation).

nus,[8] and known to the English reader, through the translation of Phillips,[9] so praised in the Spectator, is of this class, and describes the strong but silent emotions of the heart, with delicate correctness of touch. A man could no more have written that ode, than he could touch the wing of a butterfly without striking off its plumage. And in the tender and affectionate hymn to Venus,[1] how exquisitely beautiful is every touch! how graceful every line, every word! In perusing it, we cannot feel surprised that critics should hold up Sappho as an example of the beautiful in writing. And this thus illustrates another principle; if it is the part of every woman of cultivated life to admire what is beautiful, it is the part of the woman of genius to express it.

The domain of beauty is indeed peculiarly the sphere of the female poet. We can see the man of high poetic genius delighting in the wide-rolling ocean, as it leaves its yeasty waves, in dark restless might beneath a frowning sky; his soul is strengthened to hold high converse with the elements, and with the spirits which his magician-wand calls forth from the vasty deep. But the poetic power of woman will demand a greater scene; she will have to track the little streamlet, as like a thread of silver it winds along the peaceful vale; or she will watch the light smoke of the peaceful cottage as it gracefully curls above the surrounding trees, and her heart will ponder on what a true-hearted woman ever loves to portray, the kindly charities of home. We can see the poet watching with high exultation the bold and fearless eagle, as in steady grandeur, it rises from the earth and gazes unappalled on the splendours of the noon-tide sun; but woman, gentle woman, will sooner bend over the turtle-dove, admire its beautiful form, its delicate plumage, read the quick glances of its eye, and with responsive readiness give meaning to its tender cooing. The man of poetic genius will gaze perhaps on the old majestic oak, which has for ages, withstood the wintry winds as they careered wildly around; the woman in the meanwhile will stoop to gather the little 'Forget-me-not' that grows in the neighbouring hedge, and as she gazes on the blue-eyed flower, thoughts of meeting and parting, a theme of such potent influence over every human heart, and it may be, of especial interest to the female heart, will crowd over her mind, and perhaps fill her speaking with tears of deep feeling, of fond affection.

The words of one of our own poets are true;

8. Longinus Dionysius Cassius (d. 273) wrote a famous treatise, *On Sublimity*, in which he speaks about Sappho's poetry and quotes a fragment that has since become very well-known: "He seems as fortunate as the gods to me, the man who sits opposite you and listens nearby to your sweet voice and lovely laughter. Truly that sets my heart trembling in my breast. For when I look at you for a moment, then it is no longer possible for me to speak; my tongue has snapped, at once a subtle fire has stolen beneath my flesh, I see nothing with my eyes, my ears hum, sweat pours from me, a trembling seizes me all over, I am greener than grass, and seems to me that I am little short of dying. But all can be endured, since . . . even a poor man . . ." (Loeb translation).

9. Ambrose Phillips published the first English translation of Sappho in 1711.

1. The only complete extant poem by Sappho. More usually called "Hymn to Aphrodite," the Greek goddess of love.

Different minds
Incline to different objects; one pursues
The vast alone, the wonderful, the wild
AKENSIDE[2]

Place two persons in precisely the same scene; how different will be the objects that will engage their attention; how widely different the mode of expressing their feelings! What different associations will the same object summon up, according to the training and the resource of the mind!

It is not only with regard to literature that these remarks are made. The love of the beautiful, is a most important ingredient in the mind of woman. It is not only a source of high and pure enjoyment, but it is so healthy, so invigorating to be able heartily to admire what is deserving of admiration. In connexion with this subject, we refer with pride and pleasure to a female poet of our own country; one who was pre-eminently devoted to what was beautiful in nature, art, and action; it is hardly necessary to name Felicia Hemans.[3] * * *

# ELIZABETH BARRETT AND RICHARD HENGIST HORNE

## [Elizabeth Barrett on Thomas Carlyle and the "Prophet-Poet"]†

According to the view of the *microcosmus*, what is said of the world itself, may be said of every individual in it; and what is said of the individual, may be predicated of the world. Now, the individual mind has been compared to a prisoner in a dark room, or in a room which would be dark but for the windows of the same, meaning the senses, in a figure; nothing being in the mind without the mediation of the senses, as

2. Mark Akenside (1721–70), poet, physician, and the author of *Pleasures of Imagination* (1744).
3. (1793–1835); the first of the many professional women poets who worked in the nineteenth century. Her verse was published in numerous annuals and magazines and had huge popularity, which lasted throughout the century. Her best-known poem today is "Casabianca," which begins "The boy stood on the burning deck," but her work deserves to be better known.

† From *A New Spirit of the Age* (London, 1844), 253–80. All notes are by the editor of this Norton Critical Edition.

Richard Hengist Horne (1802–84), writer, editor, and adventurer, was one of Elizabeth Barrett's correspondents from about 1839. In 1843 Horne began to plan a volume of essays called *A New Spirit of the Age*, in which the notable names of the day were to be considered. EBB became involved in this work and, as she said, contributed "a writing of notes . . . of slips of paper . . . now on one subject, & now on another . . . which were thrown into the great cauldron & boiled up with other matter." But EBB's manuscript notes still exist and from these it is clear that the greater part of the essays on Carlyle, Landor, and Tennyson were composed by EBB.

Locke[1] held,—"except," as Leibnitz[2] acutely added in modification, "the mind itself." Thus is it with the individual, and thus with the general humanity. Were it not for the Something from without, and the Something within, which are both Revelations, we should sit on the floor of our dark dungeon, between its close stifling walls, gnawing vainly with the teeth of the mind, at the chains we wear. But conclusions which genius has leapt successfully, and science proved, have come to aid us. It is well to talk of the progress of the public mind. The public mind,—that is, the average intelligence of the many,—never does make progress, except by imbibing great principles from great men, which, after long and frequent reiteration, become part of the moral sense of a people. The educators are the true and only movers. Progress implies the most active of energies, such as genius is, such as science is; and general progress implies, and indeed essentially consists of, individual progresses, men of genius, and other good teachers, working. A Ulysses[3] must pass with the first goat,—call him Nobody, or by his right name. And to return to our first figure,—what the senses are to the individual mind, men of genius are to the general mind. Scantily assigned by Providence for necessary ends, one original thinker strikes a window out here, and another there; wielding the mallet sharply, and leaving it to others to fashion grooves and frames, and complete advantage into convenience.

That Mr. Carlyle is one of the men of genius thus referred to, and that he has knocked out his window from the blind wall of his century, we may add without any fear of contradiction. We may say, too, that it is a window to the east; and that some men complain of a certain bleakness in the wind which enters at it, when they should rather congratulate themselves and him on the aspect of the new sun beheld through it, the orient hope of which he has so discovered to their eyes. And let us take occasion to observe here, and to bear in memory through every subsequent remark we may be called upon to make, that it has not been

1. John Locke (1632–1704), English physician and philosopher. His principal work, *Essay Concerning Human Understanding* (1690), makes his claim to be the founder of analytic philosophy of the mind.
2. Gottfried Wilhelm Leibniz (1646–1716), German philosopher and mathematician. One of the most important figures in the German Enlightenment, Leibniz argued against an idea of the universe as mechanically organized, and proposed that the mysterious harmony of matter and spirit had to be ordered by an all-powerful spirit. His principal works were his *Theodociee* (1710) and *Monadologie* (1714).
3. The Greek hero for the island of Ithaca who fought with Menelaus and Agamemnon at the seige of Troy. The story of his long wanderings after the fall of Troy is told in Homer's *Odyssey*. One of the tales there relates how Ulysses and his men were taken captive by the one-eyed giant Cyclops called Polyphemus and imprisoned in his cave along with the giant's goats. In order to escape, the wily Ulysses waited until the giant was drunk and sleepy, then heated an iron bar and put out the Cyclops' only eye. Blind, and in a terrible rage, Polyphemus shut up the entrance to the cave and threatened to eat the frightened sailors. But Ulysses had a plan even for this. In the morning he tied his men to the underbellies of the giant goats, and so as Polyphemus released his goats to the pasture, carefully feeling each one to make sure that it carried no passenger, he also unwittingly released Ulysses and his men so that they were able to flee to their ship and escape the island.

his object to discover to us any specific prospect—not the mountain to the right, nor the oakwood to the left, nor the river which runs down between,—but the SUN, which renders all these visible.

When "the most thinking people" had, at the sound of all sorts of steam-engines, sufficiently worshipped that idol of utilitarianism which Jeremy Bentham,[4] the king, had set up, and which Thomas Carlyle, the transcendentalist, and many others, who never read a page of Bentham's works, have resolved to narrow to their own misconceptions of this philosopher,—the voice of a prophet was heard praying three times a day, with magnanimous reiteration, towards Jerusalem,—towards old Jerusalem, be it observed; and also towards the place of sun-rising for ultimate generations. And the voice spoke a strange language,—nearly as strange as Bentham's own, and as susceptible of translation into English. Not English by any means, the critics said it spoke; nor even German, nor Greek; although partaking considerably more of the two last than of English; but more of Saxon than either, we humbly beg to add. Yet if the grammarians and public teachers could not measure it out to pass as classic English, after the measure of Swift or Addison, or even of Bacon and Milton,[5] if new words sprang gauntly in it from savage derivatives, and rushed together in outlandish combinations,—if the collocation was distortion, wandering wildly up and down,—if the comments were everywhere in a heap, like the "pots and pans" of Bassano, classic or not, English or not; it was certainly a true language,—a language "*μεφοπων ανθφωπων*;"[6] the significant articulation of a living soul: God's breath was in the vowels of it. And the clashing of these harsh compounds at last drew the bees into assembly, each murmuring his honey-dream. And the hearers who stood longest to listen, became sensible of a still grave music issuing like smoke from the clefts of the rock. If it was not "style" and "classicism," it was something better; it was soul-language. There was a divinity at the shaping of these rough-hewn periods.

We dwell the longer upon the construction of Mr. Carlyle's sentences, because of him it is preeminently true, that the speech is the man. All powerful writers will leave, more or less, the pressure of their individual-

4. (1748–1832); Utilitarian philosopher. In his numerous pamphlets, and especially in his famous work *Introduction to Principles of Morals and Legislation* (1789), Bentham proposed his system of Utility, an ethical doctrine best remembered for the statement "It is the greatest happiness of the greatest number that is the measure of right and wrong." Bentham's theories have been much abused and ridiculed and were often the butt of satire in the nineteenth century; the usual stance being that Bentham represented all that was in opposition to the imagination and the power of mystery. Bentham is a famous corpse, because, true to his Utilitarian principles, he left his body to be dissected for science, and so it sits to this day, embalmed, at University College, London.
5. John Milton (1608–74), English poet; Jonathan Swift (1667–1745), Irish poet and satirist, best known as the author of *Gulliver's Travels* (1726); Joseph Addison (1672–1719), English writer of poetry, plays, and essays, many of which were published in *The Spectator*. Addison's prose style was particularly admired (most notably by Samuel Johnson) and his literary taste and influence lasted a long time. He had many admirers in the Victorian period. Francis Bacon (1561–1626), English politician, scientist, and writer.
6. Greek; "a language shared by men," or "a language known to men."

ity on the medium of their communication with the public. Even the idiomatic writers, who trust their thoughts to a customary or conventional phraseology, and thus attain to a recognized level perfection in the medium, at the expense of being less instantly incisive and expressive (according to an obvious social analogy) have each an individual aspect. But the individuality of this writer is strongly pronounced. It is graven—like the Queen's arrow on the poker and tongs of her national prisons—upon the meanest word of his utterance. He uses no moulds in his modelling, as you may see by the impression of his thumb-nail upon the clay. He throws his truth with so much vehemence, that the print of the palm of his hand is left on it. Let no man scoff at the language of Carlyle—for if it forms part of his idiosyncracy, his idiosyncracy forms part of his truth;—and let no man say that we recommend Carlylisms—for it is obvious, from our very argument, that, in the mouth of an imitator, they would unlearn their uses, and be conventional as Addison, or a mere chaos of capitals, and compounds, and *broken* language.

We have named Carlyle in connection with Bentham, and we believe that you will find in "your philosophy,"[7] no better antithesis for one, than is the other. There is as much resemblance between them as is necessary for antithetic unlikeness. Each headed a great movement among thinking men; and each made a language for himself to speak with; and neither of them originated what they taught. Bentham's work was done by systematizing; Carlyle's, by reviving and reiterating. And as from the beginning of the world, the two great principles of matter and spirit have combated,—whether in man's personality, between the flesh and the soul; or in his speculativeness, between the practical and the ideal; or in his mental expression, between science and poetry,—Bentham and Carlyle assumed to lead the double van on opposite sides. Bentham gave an impulse to the material energies of his age, of the stuff of which he was himself made,—while Carlyle threw himself before the crushing chariots, not in sacrifice, but deprecation; "Go aside—*there is a spirit even in the wheels!*" In brief, and to take up that classification of virtues made by Proclus and the later Platonists,[8]—Bentham headed such as were *πολιτικάι*, Carlyle exalts that which is *τελεστική*,[9] venerant and religious virtue.

Every reader may not be acquainted, as every thinker should, with the Essays of R. W. Emerson,[1] of Concord, Massachusetts. He is a

7. A quotation from Shakespeare's *Hamlet:* "There are more things in heaven and earth, Horatio,/Than are dreamt of in your philosophy," *Hamlet*, 1.5.166.
8. Proclus (c. 411–85) was a philosopher who represented and reinterpreted the writings of the great Greek philosopher Plato (c. 428–348 BC).
9. Greek; "everlasting, eternal." Greek; "of or for the people"; in this sense, "political" or "expedient."
1. Ralph Waldo Emerson (1803–82), American philosopher and poet. Emerson met Thomas Carlyle on a visit to England in 1833 and was an admirer of the older writer's work. His career was watched with interest by Elizabeth Barrett Browning, who maintained a cordial friendship with him.

follower of Mr. Carlyle, and in the true spirit; that is, no imitator, but a worker out of his own thoughts. To one of the English editions of this volume, Mr. Carlyle has written a short Preface, in which the following gaunt and ghastly, grotesque and graphic passage occurs; and which, moreover, is characteristic and to our immediate point.

> "In a word, while so many Benthamisms, Socialisms, Fourrierisms,[2] *professing* to have no soul, go staggering and lowing like monstrous moon-calves, the product of a heavy-laden moon-struck age;[3] and in this same baleful 'twelfth hour of the night' even galvanic Puseyisms,[4] as we say, are visible, and dancings of the sheeted dead,—shall not any voice of a living man be welcome to us, even because it is alive."

That the disciples of Bentham, and Robert Owen[5] and Fourrier should be accused of professing to have no soul, because their main object has been to ameliorate the bodily condition of mankind; or that an indifference to poetry and the fine arts, except as light amusements, to be taken alternately with gymnastics and foot-ball, should be construed into a denial of the existence of such things, we do not consider fair dealing. True, they all think of first providing for the body; and looking around at the enormous amount of human suffering from physical causes, it is no great wonder that they chiefly devote their efforts to that amelioration. A man who is starving is not in a fit state for poetry, nor even for prayer. Neither is a man fit for prayer, who is diseased, or ragged, or unclean—except the *one* prayer for that very amelioration which the abused philosophers of the body seek to obtain for him. With respect, however, to the disciples of Bentham, Owen, and Fourrier, it is no wonder that he should be at utter variance. No great amount of love "is lost between them." Not that Carlyle reads or knows much of their systems; and not that they read or know anything of his writings. In these natural antipathies all philosophers are in an equal state of unreasonableness. Or shall we rather call it wisdom, to follow the strong instincts of nature, without any prevaricating reasonings upon the in-felt fact. Carlyle could make little good out of their systems, if he read them; and they could make nothing at all of his writings. The opposite parties might force themselves to meet gravely, with hard lines of the

2. A noun derived by Carlyle from the name of the French social theorist Charles François-Marie Fourier (1772–1837), whose work was despised by Barrett Browning and much disparaged in *Aurora Leigh* (see note to 2.483, p. 52). Typically, Carlyle gets the spelling wrong.
3. A description derived from one of the insulting names given to Caliban in Shakespeare's *The Tempest;* see 2.2.114–20.
4. Another popular movement at which Carlyle was swiping. Edward Bouverie Pusey (1800–82) was one of the chief voices in the so-called "Oxford movement" of the 1830s and 1840s, a movement that proposed, in some degree, a return to the doctrinal positions of the Roman Catholic Church as opposed to the staunchly Protestant Anglican position.
5. (1771–1858); British socialist and philanthropist. Owen set up a model village in Scotland and another in America in an attempt to put his theories about the possibilities of communal living into practice.

efforts of understanding in their faces, and all manner of professions of dispassionate investigation and mutual love of truth—and they would clash foreheads at the first step, and part in fury! "The Body is the first thing to be helped!" cry the Benthamites, Owenites, Fourrierites,—loudly echoed by Lord Ellenborough and the Bishop of London—"Get more Soul!" cries Carlyle, "and help yourselves!"[6]

But the wants of the body will win the day—the movements of the present age show that plainly. The immortal soul can well afford to wait till its case is repaired. The death-groans of humanity must first be humanely silenced. More Soul, do we crave for the world? The world has long had a sphere-full of unused Soul in it, before Christ, and since. If Plato and Socrates, and Michael Angelo and Raphael, and Shakspere and Milton, and Handel and Haydn, and all the great poets, philosophers, and music-magicians, that have left their Souls among us, have still rendered us no protection against starvation, or the disease and damage of the senses and brain by reason of want of food, in GOD's name let us now think a little of the Body—the mortal case and medium of his Image. What should we think of a philosopher who went to one of our manufacturing towns where the operatives work from sixteen to eighteen hours a-day, and are nevertheless badly clothed, dirty, and without sufficient food,—and to whom the philosopher, as a remedial measure, suggested that they should get more soul? Many at this hour are slowly, or rapidly, dying from want. Can we tell them to think of their souls? No—give the fire some more fuel, and *then* expect more light, and the warmth of an aspiring flame. That these two extremes of body and soul philosophy, may, as Emerson declares, involve one and the same principle, viz., the welfare and progress of mankind, may be true; but at present the poor principle is "between two stools"—or between the horns of a dilemma not inaptly represented by Mr. Carlyle's misapplied figure of the staggering moon-calf.

We have observed that Carlyle is not an originator; and although he is a man of genius and original mind, and although he has knocked out his window in the wall of his century—and we know it,—we must repeat that, in a strict sense, he is not an originator. Perhaps our figure of the window might have been more correctly stated as the re-opening of an old window, long bricked up or encrusted over,—and probably this man of a strong mallet, and sufficient right hand, thought the recovery of the old window, a better and more glorious achievement, than the making of many new windows. His office certainly is not to "exchange new lamps for old ones." His quality of a "gold-reviver" is the nearest to a novel acquirement. He tells us what we knew, but had forgotten, or refused to remember; and his reiterations startle and astonish us like informations. We "have souls," he tells us. Who doubted it in the nine-

6. A paraphrase of Carlyle's often repeated sentiments, much quoted in *Aurora Leigh*. See 2.479–85.

teenth century; yet who thought of it in the roar of the steam-engine? He tells us that work is every man's duty. Who doubted *that* among the factory-masters?—or among the charity-children, when spelling from the catechism of the national church, that they will "do their duty in the state of life to which it shall please God to call them?" Yet how deep and like a new sound, do the words "soul," "work," "duty," strike down upon the flashing anvils of the age, till the whole age vibrates! And again he tells us, "Have faith." Why, did we not know that we must have "faith?" Is there a religious teacher in the land who does not repeat from God's revelation, year by year, day by day—Have faith? or is there a quack in the land who does not call to his assistance the energy of "faith?" And again—"Truth is a good thing." Is *that* new? Is it not written in the theories of the moralist, and of the child?—yes, and in the moral code of Parliament men, and other honourable gentlemen, side by side with bribery and corruption, and the "melancholy necessity" of the duelist's pistol and twelve places? Yet we thrill at the words, as if some new thunder of divine instruction ruffled the starry air,—as if an angel's foot sounded down it, step by step, coming with a message.

Thus it is obvious that Mr. Carlyle is not an originator, but a renewer, although his medium is highly original; and it remains to us to recognise that he is none the less important teacher on that account, and that there was none the less necessity for his teaching. "The great fire-heart," as he calls it, of human nature may burn too long without stirring; burn inwardly, cake outwardly, and sink deeply into its own ashes: and, to emancipate the flame clearly and brightly, it is necessary to stir it up strongly from the lowest bar. To do this, by whatever form of creation and illustration, is the aim and end of all poetry of a high order,—this,—to resume human nature from its beginning, and return to first principles of thought and first elements of feeling; this,—to dissolve from eye and ear the film of habit and convention, and open a free passage for beauty and truth, to gush in upon unencrusted perceptive faculties: for poetry like religion should make a man a child again in purity and unadulterated perceptivity.

No poet yearns more earnestly to make the inner life shine out, than does Carlyle. No poet regrets more sorrowfully, with a look across the crowded and crushing intellects of the world,—that the dust rising up from men's energies, should have blinded them to the brightness of their instincts,—and that understanding (according to the German view) should take precedence of a yet more spiritualized faculty. He is reproached with not being practical. "Mr. Carlyle," they say, "is not practical." But he is practical for many intents of the inner life, and teaches well the Doing of Being. "What would he make of us?" say the complainers. "He reproaches us with the necessities of the age, he taunts us with the very progress of time, his requirements are so impossible that they make us despair of the republic." And this is true. If we were to give him a sceptre, and cry, "Rule over us," nothing could exceed the dumb, motionless, confounded figure he would stand: his first words, on recovering himself, would be, "Ye have souls! work—believe." He would not know what else to think, or say for us, and not at all what to do with us. He would pluck, absently, at the sceptre, for the wool of the fillet to which his hands were accustomed; for he is no king, except in his own peculiar sense of a prophet and priest-king,—and a vague prophet, be it understood. His recurrence to first principles and elements of action, is in fact, so constant and passionate, that his attention is not free for the development of actions. The hand is the gnomon by which he judges of the soul; and little cares he for the hand otherwise than as a spirit-index. He will not wash your hands for you, be sure, however he may moralise on their blackness. Whether he writes history, or philosophy, or criticism, his perpetual appeal is to those common elements of humanity which it is his object to cast into relief and light. His work on the French Revolution is a great poem with this same object;—a return upon the life of humanity, and an eliciting of the pure material and initial element of life, out of the fire and torment of it. The work has fitly been called graphical and picturesque; but it is so *by force of being* philosophical and poetical. For instance, where the writer says that "Marat[7] was in a cradle like the rest of us," it is no touch of rhetoric, though it may seem so, but a resumption of the philosophy of the whole work. Life suggests to him the cradle, the grave, and eternity, with scarce a step between. In that brief interval he sometimes exhorts that you should work; and sometimes it would appear as if he exhorted you not to work at all, but to sit still and think. He is dazzled by the continual contemplation of a soul beating its tiny wings amidst the pale vapours of Infinity. Why, such a man (not speaking it irreverently) is not fit to live. He is only fit to be where his soul most aims at. He sinks our corporal condition, with all its wants, and says, "Be a man!" A dead-man with a promoted spirit seems our only chance in this philosophy.

Carlyle has a great power of re-production, and can bring back his man from the grave of years, not like a ghost, but with all his vital flesh as well as his thoughts about him. The reproduced man thinks, feels, and acts like himself at his most characteristic climax—and the next instant the Magician pitches him into Eternity, saying, "It all comes to that." But his power over the man, while he lasts, is entire, and the individual is almost always dealt with as in time-present. His scenes of by-gone years, are all acted now, before your eyes. By contrast Carlyle often displays truth; from the assimilations in the world, he wrings the product of the differences; and by that masterly method of individualising persons, which is remarkable in his historical writing, the reader

7. Jean-Paul Marat (1743–93), French politician, writer, and physician, practiced medicine in London and Paris; took active part in prerevolutionary agitation.

sometimes attains what Carlyle himself seems to abhor, viz., a broad generalisation of principles. His great forte and chief practice is individualisation. And when he casts his living heart into an old monk's diary, and, with the full warm gradual throbs of genius and power, throws out the cowled head into a glory; the reason is not, as some disquieted readers have hinted, that Mr. Carlyle regrets the cloisteral ages and defunct superstitions,—the reason is not, that Mr. Carlyle is *too* poetical to be philosophical, but that he is *so* poetical as to be philosophical in essence when treating of things. The reason is, that Mr. Carlyle recognizes, in a manner that no mere historian ever does, but as the true poet always will do,—the same human nature through every cycle of individual and social existence. He is a poet also, by his insight into the activity of moral causes working through the intellectual agencies of the mind. He is also a poet in the mode. He conducts his argument with no philosophical arrangements and marshalling of "for and against;" his paragraphs come and go as they please. He proceeds, like a poet, rather by analogy and subtle association than by uses of logic. His illustrations not only illustrate, but bear a part in the reasoning;—the images standing out, like grand and beautiful caryatides,[8] to sustain the heights of the argument. Of his language we have spoken. Somewhat too slow, broken up, and involved for eloquence, and too individual to be classical, it is yet the language of a gifted painter and poet, the colour of whose soul eats itself into the words. * * *

8. Stone figures, usually depicting women, that were used in classical architecture and generally shown bearing a roof or portico on their heads or up-raised arms.

# CRITICISM

# Contemporary Critical Reception

## H. F. CHORLEY

### From *The Athenaeum* (November 22, 1856)†

Our best living English poetess—our greatest English poetess of any time—has essayed in 'Aurora Leigh' to blend the epic with the didactic novel. The medium in which the story floats is that impassioned language—spotted and flowered with the imagery suggested by fancy or stored up by learning,—which has given the verse of Mrs. Browning a more fiery acceptance from the young and spiritual, and her name a higher renown than any woman has heretofore gained.

We dwell on the sex of the author of 'Aurora Leigh' in no disrespectful spirit of comparison, but simply because to overlook it is rendered impossible by the poetess herself. 'Aurora Leigh,' into which she says "have entered her highest convictions upon Life and Art," is her contribution to the chorus of protest and mutual exhortation, which Woman is now raising, in hope of gaining the due place and sympathy which, it is held, have been denied to her since the days when Man was created, the first of the pair in Eden. Who can quarrel with the intent? Who would silence any struggle made by those who fancy themselves desolate, oppressed, undervalued,—to unlock the prison-doors,—to melt the heart of injustice? Mrs. Browning is never unwomanly in her passionate pleadings for women: unwomanly she could not be, after having wrought out that beautiful and tender conception of Eve, which gives such peculiar grace to her 'Drama of Exile.' Her Confession (for like all works of its class, 'Aurora Leigh' has in it a tone of confession,) amounts to an admission of failure: its conclusion is that indicated from another point of view by Mrs. Hemans,[1] in her 'Properzia Rossi.' The moral is

† Henry Fothergill Chorley (1808–72), English writer, dramatist, and journalist. Chorley reviewed much of EBB's work from *The Seraphim* (1838) onward and he was a great admirer of her poetry. In 1850, when Wordsworth died, *The Athenaeum* suggested that EBB should be made Poet Laureate, and the idea probably came from Chorley. EBB corresponded with Chorley from the 1840s, but did not actually meet him until after her marriage [*Editor*].

1. Felicia Hemans (1793–1835), English poet [*Editor*].

the insufficiency of Fame and Ambition, be either ever so generous, to make up for the absence of Love:—a class-vindication wound up by an appeal against class-separation. Thus, as in all the works of its kind, which women have so freely poured out from their full hearts during late years, we see the agony more clearly than the remedy. We are shown, at first, restlessness disdaining quiet; till, fevered and forlorn, as time and grief do their work, the restless heart ends in courting the very repose it so scorned when first tendered. But while Truth closes the tale, in its progress Imagination has been strained beyond permissible freedom. In brief, we regret to declare that Mrs. Browning's longest and most matured effort, jewelled though it be with rich thought and rare fancies, is in its argument unnatural, and in its form infelicitous.

Aurora Leigh is a born poetess, the child of an English father and an Italian mother,—on the father's side connected with wealth and old name. She is sent over to England, when an orphan, to be cared for and educated by a maiden aunt,—that well-worn spectral apparition of convention in buckram, without which no tale of woman's aspirings, it seems, can be told. Such persons, whose narrow capacities bring on limited views of duty, have been long abused; but their time, it appears, has not yet come. Meanwhile, they serve their turn with those who make fantastic panoramas of life. Without such aunts (grim substitute for the stepmother of ancient romance!) no woman of genius could be cradled into poetry through wrong; and Mrs. Browning only adopts a convention in denouncing convention. Aurora is wooed by her cousin, Romney Leigh, a rich, high-hearted philanthropist, to whom her heart is not disinclined. But he is too big in the consciousness of his own philanthropy; and waywardly she conceives the idea that she is asked to become his wife in a strain of persuasion unworthy the ear of a great and gifted woman,— that she is sought from low motives, (as, indeed, are most wives,) and that her career, as an unassisted and independent woman of genius, will be brighter if she retains her heart in her own keeping. Accordingly Aurora rejects Romney as a husband,—spurns his generous attempts to smooth the path of life for her by tendering a share of the family fortune. Putting on poverty as a singing robe, she adopts authorship in London, becomes famous and admired, and dwells like a star apart. Foiled of his object, Romney Leigh embraces his plans of social reforms with an earnestness, in which there is the intoxication of a wounded spirit as much as the conviction of one called to the priest's office. He opens a phalanstery, affects only the society of the sick, sorrowful, or guilty, and, willing to attest his superiority to class prejudice by the most solemn act a man can do, prepares to marry one Marian Erle, a milliner's apprentice,—who is humble, ignorant, but as devoted and as noble in her way as either Romney or Aurora. The latter (in spite of her having begun to discover that she had made a mistake in rejecting her cousin, and in fancying that fame could supply the place of love) seeks out Marian. The girls' story is powerfully told, but is unreal in the poetry and holiness of nature it reveals in one nurtured, tortured, and beset as she has been. Such resistance as hers must have hardened the victim in the struggle,—whereas Marian is soft as a briar-rose, besides being pure as the dew-bead on it. Aurora welcomes and embraces her with enthusiastic devotion. Not so other of Romney's female friends. A wicked influence is at work against the poor sempstress:—a woman of fashion, one Lady Waldemar, who has fallen in love with Romney Leigh, (and for his sake, with Christian socialism) so practises upon Marian, that on the appointed wedding-day, when St. Giles and St. James are bidden to church to see the Socialist gentleman married (a parade somewhat insolent in its condescension), the bride is not forthcoming, but in her place a mysterious letter. Instead of the bridal revel, where Rank and Rags were to sit at the same board, there is a brawl in the church:—Marian is gone—no one knows whither.

As years roll on, Aurora's authorship prospers. She is praised in the reviews—she is a lion in London *soirées;* and from not any of the most common-place and frivolous of these transactions, with all their train of prosaic and poverty-stricken adjuncts, does *our* artist shrink as a subject for art. Nevertheless, Aurora finds out that she is alone in spirit after all; and more stung than she cares to own, by a rumour in the *coteries* that Cousin Romney is about to marry this evil Lady Waldemar, she resolves to give up England for a time, and go home to Italy. On her way—in Paris—she lights on Marian, now the unwedded mother of a beautiful boy, and learns from her the sequel to her story: how Lady Waldemar had not only detached her from the noble gentleman who would have married her; had not only, as we have seen, prevailed on her to give up Cousin Romney; but, under pretext of sending her out to the Colonies, had allowed her to fall into the hands of an infamous woman, by whom Marian—herself innocent—was forced into ruin. In this hideous page of the romance Mrs. Browning puts forth all her power. Aurora at once takes the outraged Marian to her heart, carries her off with her child to Italy, and writes home her disclosure of Lady Waldemar's machinations—in order that it may reach Romney. After them, in due course of time, he arrives. By the old trick, well worn in novels and plays, Aurora receives him, under the misapprehension that he is Lady Waldemar's husband; but he presently assures her that, so far from being so, he has come to Italy still to marry Marian, and to adopt the child of violence and misery as his own. Once more, however, and this time unprompted by all except her own nature, Marian refuses to marry Romney—assuring him that she does not love him now; that indeed she never did love him as he deserved to be loved; that she will live for her child, and no creature else: and it is in this crisis that Aurora and Romney at last come to an understanding. The artist has found the hollowness of Art to fill and to satisfy; and the philanthropist's experiences are drearier still. He has been rewarded for his care for the vile and the humble by having his father's house burnt over his head—in the catastrophe having lost his sight, it is hinted, owing to the vengeance of Marian's reprobate father.

Such is a brief sketch of the argument of 'Aurora Leigh'; and not a few who read it will be tempted to say, This looks not like a poem, but a novel, belonging to the period which has produced 'Ruth,' and 'Villette,' and 'The Blithedale Romance.' We will not stop to ask how far the invention be true to life and to art; since the form of its presentment may be pleaded in excuse for anything unreal in character, false in sentiment, or exaggerated in incident, which exists in the plot and the persons working it out. But what are we to say if we waive purpose—if we do not discuss the wisdom of the form selected (large concessions these, yet due to one so gifted and so passionately in earnest as Mrs. Browning)—if we treat 'Aurora Leigh' as a poetical romance? Simply, that we have no experience of such a mingling of what is precious with what is mean—of the voice of clarion and the lyric cadence of harp with the cracked school-room spinet—of tears and small-talk—of eloquent apostrophe and adust speculation—of the grandeur of passion and the pettiness of modes and manners—as we find in these nine books of blank verse. Milton's organ is put by Mrs. Browning to play polkas in May-Fair drawing-rooms, and fitted out by her with its *Æsthetic Review* stop, which drones out lengths and strains of a strange quality. But it yields, too, beneath her fingers those glorious chords and melodies, which (musicians have fancied) are the real occupation and utterance of that instrument. Is this severe? Let any one that thinks so take the following commencement of the scene in the church at Romney's interrupted wedding as a passage from a poem. * * *

'Aurora Leigh' contains too many pages as perversely trivial, too many passages as carelessly dry, as the above. We cannot forgive either the flippancy or the dreary disquisition from one like Mrs. Browning, when her theme, too, is of art and artists. Such are affectations, not discoveries. There is humanity even in May-Fair babble; there may be thought in criticism, be it ever so clear; but to bring *Mr. Yellowplush*, with his powder and calves, into a serious poem of grief and aspiration;—and when we would see *Corinna* to come upon a Gifford or Conder nibbling his pen for a succinct paragraph,—these things, we repeat, are novelties to which no diffusion of the new light will reconcile serious readers.

Why these fopperies and mistakes grieve us in Mrs. Browning we will show forthwith; for not one of her former works is richer in passages of power and beauty, in noble lines and lofty thoughts than 'Aurora Leigh.' * * *

Here we must hand over 'Aurora Leigh' to those who will wonder at, or decry, or enthusiastically commend, or pass over the differences and discords of the tale; for it will have readers of all the four classes. To some it will be so much rank foolishness,—to others almost a scriptural revelation. The huge mistake of its plan, the disdain of selectness in its details, could not be exhausted were we to write for column and column,—nor would page on page suffice to contain the high thoughts, the deep feelings, the fantastic images showered over the tale with the authority of a prophetess, the grace of a muse, the prodigality of a queen. Such a poem, we dare aver, has never before been written by woman; and if our apprehension of its discords and discrepancies has been keen and expressed without measure, it is because our admiration of its writer's genius, and our sympathy with the nobility of her purpose, are also keen and without measure.

# GEORGE ELIOT

## From *Westminster Review* (January 1857) †

Foster, the essayist, has somewhere said that the person who interests us most is the one that most gives us the idea of *ample being*. Applying this remark to books, which are but persons in a transmigrated form, we discern one grand source of the profound impression produced in us by "Aurora Leigh." Other poems of our own day may have higher finish, or a higher degree of certain poetic qualities; but no poem embraces so wide a range of thought and emotion, or takes such complete possession of our nature. Mrs. Browning is, perhaps, the first woman who has produced a work which exhibits all the peculiar powers without the negations of her sex; which superadds to masculine vigour, breadth, and culture, feminine subtlety of perception, feminine quickness of sensibility, and feminine tenderness. It is difficult to point to a woman of genius who is not either too little feminine, or too exclusively so. But in this, her longest and greatest poem, Mrs. Browning has shown herself all the greater poet because she is intensely a poetess.

The *story* of "Aurora Leigh" has no other merit than that of offering certain elements of life, and certain situations which are peculiarly fitted to call forth the writer's rich thought and experience. It has nothing either fresh or felicitous in structure or incident; and we are especially sorry that Mrs. Browning has added one more to the imitations of the catastrophe in "Jane Eyre," by smiting her hero with blindness before he

† From *The Westminster Review* (January 1857), 306–10. George Eliot (1819–80) was editor of *The Westminster Review* from 1852 until 1854, but is better known as a novelist, which career she began in 1856.

is made happy in the love of Aurora. Life has sadness and bitterness enough for a disappointed philanthropist like Romney Leigh, short of maiming or blindness; and the outflow of love and compassion towards physical ills is less rare in woman than complete sympathy with mental sorrows. Hence we think the lavish mutilation of heroes' bodies, which has become the habit of novelists, while it happily does not represent probabilities in the present state of things, weakens instead of strengthening tragic effect; and, as we said, we regret that Mrs. Browning has given this habit her strong sanction. Other criticisms might be passed on "Aurora Leigh," considered as a representation of incident and dialogue, but we are little inclined to spend our small space in pointing out faults which will be very slightly felt by any one who has heart and mind enough to respond to all the beautiful feeling, the large thought, and the rich melodious song of this rare poem. "Quel grand homme est le seigneur Pococurante! rien ne peut lui plaire!"[1] is a kind of praise to which we do not in the least aspire. We would rather be suspected of obtuseness to many faults than fail in giving the due tribute of reverence and admiration to a single great merit.

The most striking characteristic of "Aurora Leigh," distinguishing it from the larger proportion of that contemporary poetry which wins the applause of reviewers, is, that its melody, fancy, and imagination—what we may call its poetical *body*—is everywhere informed by a *soul*, namely, by genuine thought and feeling. There is no petty striving after special effects, no heaping up of images for their own sake, no trivial play of fancy run quite astray from the control of deeper sensibility; there is simply a full mind pouring itself out in song as its natural and easiest medium. This mind has its far-stretching thoughts, its abundant treasure of well-digested learning, its acute observation of life, its yearning sympathy with multiform human sorrow, its store of personal domestic love and joy; and these are given out in a delightful alternation of pathos, reflection, satire playful or pungent, and picturesque description, which carries us with swifter pulses than usual through four hundred pages, and makes us sorry to find ourselves at the end. Our extracts will necessarily be very limited; and we must urge the reader to bear in mind that "Aurora Leigh" is a poem which even large extracts cannot fairly represent. It has the calm, even flow of a broad river, not the spray and rainbows of a mountain torrent.

1. French; "the lord Pococurante is such a grand man . . . nothing is able to please him! [*Editor*].

# W. E. AYTOUN

## From *Blackwood's Edinburgh Magazine* (January 1857)†

* * *

All authors, after they have once gained possession of the public ear, are liable for the future to be tried by their own standard. This is, to a certain extent, a disadvantage; for it by no means rarely happens that the first work of an author is also his best, either because his earlier impulses have been stronger than his later ones; because, through flattery, he has been led to suppose that his measure of power is greater than it is in reality; or because he has adopted false theories of art, and so has gone astray. It may be an uncomfortable thing for a poet to shiver under the shade of his own laurels; still there is consolation in knowing that he was the planter of the tree. There is no escape from this kind of criticism, which proceeds upon a strictly natural and correct principle, and is moreover calculated to check that intellectual drowsiness which is often the result of success. No author is the worse for being shaken rather roughly by the shoulder when he exhibits symptoms of somnolence. Nay, though he may be a little peevish at first, he will ultimately, if he is a fellow of any sense, be grateful to his monitor for having roused him from a lethargy which might be fatal to his fame.

For the application of his gifts, every author is responsible. He may exercise them well and usefully, or he may apply them to ignoble purposes. He may, by the aid of art, exhibit them in the most attractive form, or his execution may be mean and slovenly. In the one case he is deserving of praise; in the other he is liable to censure. Keeping this principle in view, we shall proceed to the consideration of this new volume from the pen of Mrs Browning,—a lady whose rare genius has already won for her an exalted place among the poets of the age. Endowed with a powerful intellect, she at least has no reason to anticipate the treatment prophesied for her literary heroine, Aurora. * * *

Mrs Browning takes the field like Britomart or Joan of Arc, and declares that she will not accept courtesy or forbearance from the critics on account of her sex. She challenges a truthful opinion, and that opinion she shall have.

*Aurora Leigh* is a story of the present time in nine books. When we say a story, it must not be understood in the sense of a continuous narrative or rather poem of action, for a great portion of the work is reflective. Still, there is a story which we shall trace for the information of the

† William Edmondstone Aytoun (1813–65), Scottish poet and critic, was conservative in outlook and, as far as EBB was concerned, therefore belonged to "the camp of the enemy." See her letter, EBB to Julia Martin, February [1857], pp. 343–44 [*Editor*].

reader, abstaining in the mean time from comment, and not making more quotations than are necessary for its elucidation. The poem is a monologue, and the opening scene is laid in Tuscany.

The father of Aurora Leigh, an Englishman of fortune and a scholar, fell in love with a young Florentine girl, whom he first saw bearing a taper in a religious procession. They were married; but the wife died shortly after she had given birth to her sole daughter, Aurora. The widower, in a frenzy of grief, withdrew to a cottage among the mountains, and there occupied his time in the education of his child, who soon became a proficient in the classics. * * *

This mode of tuition—the same, by the way, which Dominie Sampson proposed for the mental culture of Lucy Bertram—had a strong effect upon the character of Aurora, who throughout the poem discourses in a most learned manner. When she was only thirteen her father died, and she was brought away, most reluctantly, from her pleasant Italy, to dwell in foggy England with a virgin aunt, who is thus described. * * *

This prim old lady was not exactly to Miss Aurora's mind; indeed, there was not much love lost between them, for Aunt Marjory had been sorely incensed, and with good reason, as will presently appear, at her brother's marriage with a foreigner, and never thoroughly forgave the daughter. However, she did her duty by her in her own fashion, supplementing her education by giving her instruction in such things as are usually taught to English girls, an intellectual regimen which excited the profoundest disgust in Aurora. However, she had strength enough to stand the trial, though occasionally threatening to die; and her patience was at length rewarded by finding her father's books in a garret. These she devoured furtively, and lighting upon the poets, at once perceived her vocation. * * *

So Aurora began to make verses, and found herself all the better for the exercise. But there were more Leighs in the world than Aurora. She had a cousin, Romney Leigh, the proprietor of Leigh Hall, who, even as a youth, exhibited queer tendencies. * * *

This young gentleman, after his own odd fashion, has conceived an attachment for Aurora; nor is he an object of total indifference to her, though her mind is more occupied with versification than with love. The two characters, male and female, are meant to stand in strong contrast to each other. Romney is a Socialist, bent on devoting himself to the regeneration of mankind, and the improvement of the condition of the working classes, by carrying into effect the schemes of Fourier and Owen—the aim of Aurora is, through Art, to raise the aspirations of the people. The man is physical, the woman metaphysical. The one is for increasing bodily comfort, the other for stimulating the mind. Both are enthusiasts, and both are intolerably dogmatic. Now it so happens that, on the morning of the twentieth anniversary of her birthday, Miss

Aurora sallies forth early, with the laudable purpose of crowning herself after the manner of Corinna, and is surprised by Romney in the act of placing an ivy wreath upon her brows. Romney has picked up a volume of her manuscript poems, which he returns, not, however, with any complimentary phrase, but rather sneeringly, and forthwith begins to read her a lecture, in a high puritanical strain, upon the vanity of her pursuits. This, of course, rouses the ire of Aurora, who retorts with great spirit on his materialistic tendencies. In the midst of this discussion he has the bad taste to propose, not so much, as he puts it, through love, but because he wants a helpmate to assist him in the erection of public washing-houses, soup-kitchens, and hospitals; whereupon our high-souled poetess flies off at a tangent. * * *

Aunt Marjory, when she hears of this refusal, is frantic, and rates Aurora soundly for rejecting a fortune laid at her feet. She explains that, by a special clause in the Leigh entail, offspring by a foreign wife were cut off from succession—that no sooner was Aurora born than the next heir, Romney Leigh's father, proposed that a marriage should be arranged between his son and the child, so that the penalties of disinherison might be avoided—and that Romney, by asking her to marry him, was in fact carrying out that intention. Otherwise Aurora is a beggar, for her aunt has no fortune to leave her. Such suggestions as these, when they occur in romance and poetry, always prove arguments in favour of obstinacy; and Aurora, even though she likes Romney, fixes upon them as insuperable obstacles to the marriage. * * *

In short, she will be her own mistress, and work out her own independence. Her aunt dies, leaving Aurora about three hundred pounds. She peremptorily rejects a large sum of money which Romney, with delicate generosity, had attempted to place at her disposal, without allowing her to incur the sense of obligation, and starts for the metropolis. * * *

Locating herself at Kensington, she begins her literary career, and achieves distinction. One day she is waited on by a certain Lady Waldemar, who gives her the astounding information that her cousin Romney, whom she had not seen for three years, is on the eve of marriage. * * *

This Lady WAldemar is personally in love with Romney Leigh, and come to ask the aid of Aurora in breaking off the ill-assorted marriage. Aurora, however, having conceived a disgust to her visitor (which is not surprising, seeing that her conversation is so flavoured with allusions to garlic, that even the Lady of Shallot would have recoiled from her whispers), refuses to have any participation in the matter, but resolves immediately to see this girl, Marian Erle, who resides in a garret somewhere in the purlieus of St Giles. After passing through the abominations of that quarter, and receiving the maledictions of thief and prostitute, the poetess discovers the object of her search, and hears her story. Marian

Erle, the selected bride of Romney Leigh, was the daughter of a tramp and squatter on the Malvern Hills, and her education was essentially a hedge one. Her father drank and beat his wife, and the wife in turn beat her child. When Marian arrived at the age of puberty, her unnatural mother was about to sell her as a victim to the lusts of "a squire," when the girl, in horror, ran away, burst a blood-vessel in her flight, was found senseless on the road by a waggoner, and conveyed to an hospital in a neighbouring town, where Romney Leigh was a visitor. Finding that she was friendless and homeless, he procured her a place in a sewing establishment in London, which she quitted to attend the deathbed of a poor consumptive companion, who had sunk under the pressure of over-work. Here Romney Leigh again appeared, and, after the death of her friend, proposed to marry her. * * *

While Marian is telling her story to Aurora, Romney comes in, looks certainly a little surprised at finding his cousin there, but is by no means disconcerted. Naturally enough, Aurora supposes that he must be influenced by a very strong passion for the girl whom he is about to make his wife, and congratulates him, with what sincerity we need not inquire, on having made choice of so fair and gentle a creature. Romney, however, utterly denies the soft impeachment, in so far as it implies that his affections were any way engaged. Ordinary men contract marriages from love—*he* is influenced by a far higher principle. * * *

In short, the man has not an atom of love for the girl, whom he proposes to wed entirely from motives of general philanthropy! At this Aurora is somewhat disgusted; but, wishing to show kindness to her cousin—perhaps to testify her own indifference, which, however, is rather feigned than real—she suggests that the marriage should take place at her house. But Master Romney will not hear of such an arrangement, as it might weaken the effect of the grand moral lesson which he intends to convey to society. * * *

The following sketch of the company assembled to witness the marriage ceremony is too racy and rich to be omitted here. As the union was to be typical of the impending abolition of all class distinctions, Romney determined that it should be celebrated in the presence of high and low, and issued cards accordingly. * * *

So there they wait—that strangely assorted company—the denizens of St Giles thronging on the inhabitants of St James—both parties curious to behold the marriage which is to inaugurate the future revolution and fusion of society. Romney Leigh appears to do the honours; but time rolls on, and still the bride comes not. The fashionables stare and talk gossip; the vulgar murmur, and desires a smoke—until a rumour to the effect that something is amiss, permeates the throng. * * *

At this St Giles rises in insurrection, cursing Romney as a seducer, and accusing him of having made away with the girl. There is a superb row, with threats of violence and arson, until the police enter and clear the church.

Beyond an enigmatical letter of leave-taking, which gives no explanation of her avoiding the marriage ceremony, we hear nothing of Marian for a long time. Romney retires to Leigh Hall, which he has turned into a "phalanstery," by which term, we presume, is meant an Owenite community. Miss Aurora continues her devotion to the muses, and becomes more notable day by day; but a horrid suspicion crosses her that Lady Waldemar has found the weak side of her wealthy cousin. For, at a conversazione at the house of a certain Lord Howe, she learns that the fair and intriguing Waldemar is commonly considered as Romney's pet disciple—nay, that she is considered as his bride intended. In the words of Mrs Browning, which we give without the metrical divisions,—

> "You may find her name on all his missions and commissions, schools, asylums, hospitals. He has had her down with other ladies, whom her starry lead persuaded form other spheres, to his country-place in Shropshire, in the famed phalanstery at Leigh Hall, christianised from Fourier's own, in which he has planted out his sapling stocks of knowledge into social bursaries; and there, they say, she has tarried half a week, and milked the cows, and churned, and pressed the curd, and said 'my sister' to the lowest drab of all the assembled castaways. Such girls! Ay, sided with them at the washing-tub."

Lady Waldemar, in a very spiteful speech, confirms this impression; and Miss Aurora, who all this time has had a secret hankering for her cousin, determines to square her balances with her publisher, and to depart for Italy.

In Paris she encounters Marian, and finds her a mother. The explanation is, that Lady Waldemar had tampered with the girl; and by representing to her that her marriage with Romney would be his social ruin, induced her to take flight on the day preceding that which had been arranged for the nuptials. The place of her future destiny was Australia, but her ladyship had confided her to the charge of an unprincipled *soubrette*, who, whether or not by design of her mistress, took Marian over to France, conveyed her to an infamous house, and sold her, while under the influence of drugs, to violation. On awakening to a sense of her situation and wrongs, the unfortunate girl became mad, and was allowed to make her escape, underwent various adventures and vicissitudes, and finally brought into the world a male child, in whom her whole existence was wrapt up, and for whom alone she lived, when she was recognised and challenged by Aurora in the streets of Paris. The sequel may be easily imagined. Miss Leigh, convinced of Marian's innocence, insists that she, with her child, shall accompany her to Florence; and there are some letters and cross purposes, into which, for the mere sake of the story, it is not necessary to enter. In fine, Aurora, in the full belief that Lady Waldemar, to whom she has sent a most insulting letter, is now the wife of her cousin, becomes melancholy and heart-sick, and time drags wearily on, until one night, watching the stars form her terrace, she is startled by the sudden apparition of Romney by her side. Gentler than in his early youth, and far more humble, Romney first pays homage to her genius, and then confesses that his social schemes have proved an utter failure. * * *

The worst of it was, that the garrotters, ticket-of-leave men, and street-walkers, with whom he had filled his house, thought the proceeding rare fun, and joined in the incendiarism; and Will Erle, Marian's father, "tramp and poacher," whom he had attempted to reclaim, struck Romney on the head with a burning brand as he was leaving the house, inflicting an injury which brought him nearly to the verge of the grave. In the course of conversation Romney undeceives Aurora as to his connection with Lady Waldemar, but declares that he considers himself bound, notwithstanding her misfortune, to wed Marian, and to adopt her child. Marian, who was overheard this, comes forward, and after a passionate scene of great beauty, rejects the offer. Here we cannot resist a quotation. * * *

And so Marian departs. But now comes an awful disclosure—Romney is blind. The blow struck by the poacher had destroyed the visual nerves; and for that unfortunate Lord of Leigh, the glory of the sun, moon, and stars, was but a remembrance. So Aurora, who had always loved him, even though she would not allow it to herself—and whom he had never ceased to love amidst his perverted dreams of duty—gives her whole woman's heart of the helpless; and the poem closes with the interchange of vows and aspirations.

Such is the story, which no admirer of Mrs Browning's genius ought in prudence to defend. In our opinion it is fantastic, unnatural, exaggerated; and all the worse, because it professes to be a tale of our own times. No one who understands of how much value probability is to a tale, can read the foregoing sketch, or indeed peruse the poem, without a painful feeling that Mrs Browning has been perpetrating, in essentials, an extravaganza or caricature, instead of giving to the public a real lifelike picture; for who can accept, as truthful representation, Romney's proposal of marriage to an ignorant uneducated girl whom he does not love; or that scene in the church, which is absolutely of Rabelaisian conception? We must not be seduced by beauty and power of execution from entering our protest against this radical error, which appears more glaring as we pass form the story to the next point, which is the dilineation of character. Aurora Leigh is not an attractive character. After making the most liberal allowance for pride, and fanaticism for art, an inflexible independence, she is incongruous and contradictory both in her sentiments and in her actions. She is not a genuine woman; one half of her heart seems bounding with the beat of humanity, while the other half is ossified. What we miss in her is instinctiveness, which is the greatest charm of women. No doubt she displays it now and then, and sometimes very conspicuously, but it is not made the general attribute of her nature; and in her dealings with Romney Leigh, instinct disappears altogether. For we hold it absolutely impossible that a woman, gifted as she is represented to be, would have countenanced a kinsman, whom she respected only, in the desperate folly of wedding an uneducated girl form the lowest grade of society, whom he did not love, simply for the sake of a theory; thereby making himself a public laughingstock, without the least chance of advancing the progress of his own preposterous opinions. There is nothing reconcilable with duty. The part which Aurora takes in the transaction, degrades rather than raises her in our eyes; nor is she otherwise thoroughly amiable; for, with all deference to Mrs Browning, and with ideas of our own perhaps more chivalric than are commonly promulgated, we must maintain that woman was created to be dependent on the man, and not in the primary sense his lady and his mistress. The extreme independence of Aurora detracts from the feminine charm, and mars the interest which we otherwise might have felt in so intellectual a heroine. In fact, she is made to resemble too closely some of the female portraits of George Sand, which never were to our liking. In Romney we fail to take any kind of interest. Though honourable and generous, he is such a very decided noodle that we grudge him his prominence in the poem, do not feel much sympathy for his misfortunes, and cannot help wondering that Aurora should have entertained one spark of affection for so deplorable a milksop. Excess of enthusiasm we can allow; and folly, affecting to talk the words of wisdom, meets us at every turning: but Romney is a walking hyperbole. The character of Marian is very beautifully drawn and well sustained, but her thoughts and language are not those of a girl reared in the midst of sordid poverty, vice, and ignorance. This is an error in art which we are sure Mrs Browning, upon mature consideration, will acknowledge; and it might easily have been avoided by the simple expedient of making Marian's origin and antecedents a few shades more respectable, which still would have left enough disparity between her and Romney to produce the effect which Mrs Browning desires. Lady Waldemar is a disgusting character. Mrs Browning intended her to appear as despicable; but it was not therefore necessary to make her talk coarse and revolting. * * *

* * *

In poetry, passages such as that which we have quoted are intolerable, because, by juxtaposition with others, exquisite in themselves, they impair our capacity for enjoyment. Anything very hideous or revolting taints the air around it, and produces a sensation of loathing, from which we do not immediately recover. Hence poets, even when their situations are of the most tragic nature—even when they are dealing with subjects questionable in morality—do, for the most part, sedulously avoid anything like coarseness of expression, and frame their language so as to convey the general idea without presenting special images which are calculated to disgust. Indeed, whilst reading this poem, which abounds in references to art, we have been impressed with a doubt whether, with all her genius, accomplishment, and experience, Mrs Browning has ever thought seriously of the principles upon which art is founded. For genius, as we all know, or ought to know, is not of itself sufficient for the construction of a great poem. Artists, like architects, must work by rule—not slavishly indeed, but ever keeping in mind that there are certain principles which experience has tested and approved, and that to deviate form these is literally to court defeat. Not that we should implicitly receive the doctrines laid down by critics, scholiasts, or commentators, or pin our faith to the formula of Longinus; but we should regard the works of the great masters, both ancient and modern as profitable for instruction as well as for delight, and be cautious how we innovate. We may consider it almost as a certainty that every leading principle of art has been weighed and sifted by our predecessors; and that most of the theories, which are paraded as discoveries, were deliberately examined by them, and rejected because they were false or impracticable. In the fifth book of this poem there is a dissertation upon poetry, in which Mrs Browning very plainly indicates her opinion that the chief aim of a poet should be to illustrate the age in which he lives. * * *

This, in our apprehension, would lead to a total sacrifice of the ideal. It is not the province of the poet to depict things as they are, but so to refine and purify as to purge out the grosser matter; and this he cannot do if he attempts to give a faithful picture of his own times. for in order to be faithful, he must necessarily include much which is abhorrent to art, and revolting to the taste, for which no exactness of delineation will be accepted as a proper excuse. All poetical characters, all poetical situations, must be idealised. The language is not that of common life, which belongs essentially to the domain of prose. Therein lies the distinction between a novel and a poem. In the first, we expect that the language employed by the characters shall be strictly natural, not excluding even imperfections, and that their sentiments shall not be too elevated or extravagant for the occasion. In the second, we expect idealisation—language more refined, more adorned, and more forcible than that which is ordinarily employed; and sentiments purer and loftier than find utterance in our daily speech. Whilst dealing with a remote subject the poet can easily effect this, but not so when he brings forward characters of his own age. We have been told that both the late John

Kemble and his sister Mrs Siddons had become so accustomed to the flow of blank verse that they carried the trick of it into private life, and used sorely to try the risible faculties of the company by demanding beef or beer in tragic tones and rhythm. That which would have sounded magnificently on the stage was ludicrous at a modern table. Mrs Browning has evidently felt the difficulty, but she cannot conquer it. In this poem she has willfully alternated passages of sorry prose with bursts of splendid poetry; and her prose is all the worse because she has been compelled to dislocate its joints in order to make it read like blank verse. Let us again revert to the experiment of exhibiting one or two of these passages printed in the usual form.—

> "We are sad to-night. I saw—(goodnight, Sir Blaise! ah Smith—he has slipped away) I saw you across the room, and stayed, Miss Leigh, to keep a crowd of lion-hunters off, with faces toward your jungle. There were three; a spacious lady five feet ten, and fat; who has the devil in her (and there's room) for walking to and fro upon the earth from Chippewa to China; she requires your autograph upon a tinted leaf 'twixt Queen Pomare's and Emperor Soulouque's; pray give it; she has energies, though fat; for me, I'd rather see a rick on fire than such a woman angry. Then a youth fresh from the backwoods, green as the underboughs, asks modestly, Miss Leigh, to kiss your shoe, and adds, he has an epic in twelve parts, which when you've read, you'll do it for his boot,—all which I saved you, and absorb next week both manuscript and man."

Is that poetry? Assuredly not. Is it prose? If so, it is as poor and faulty a specimen as ever was presented to our notice. It would not pass muster even in a third-rate novel, where sense is an element of minor consideration, and style is habitually disregarded. Here is an extract from an epistle by Lady Waldemar:—

> "Parted. Face no more, voice no more, love no more! wiped wholly out like some ill scholar's scrawl from heart and slate—ay, spit on, and so wiped out utterly by some coarse scholar. I have been too coarse, too human. Have we business in our rank with blood in the veins? I will have henceforth none; not even to keep the colour at my lip. A rose is pink and pretty without blood,—why not a woman? When we've played in vain the game, to adore,—who have resources still, and can play on at leisure, being adored: here's Smith already swearing at my feet that I'm the typic She. Away with Smith?—Smith smacks of Leigh, and, henceforth, I'll admit no Socialist within three crinolines, to live and have his being. But for you, though insolent your letter and absurd, and though I hate you frankly, take my Smith! For when you have seen this famous marriage tied, a most unspotted Erle to a noble Leigh (his love astray on one he should not love), howbeit you should not

want his love, beware, you'll want some comfort. So I leave you Smith; take Smith!"

What a rare specimen of a rhythmical fashionable letter! Still more singular is the effect when the mob becomes articulate:—

"Then spoke a man, 'Now look to it, coves, that all the beef and drink be not filched from us like the other fun; for beer's split easier than a woman is. This gentry is not honest with the poor; they bring us up to trick us.' 'Go it, Jim,' a woman screamed back, 'I'm a tender soul; I never banged a child at two years old, and drew blood from him, but I sobbed for it next moment—and I've had a plague of seven. I'm tender; I've no stomach even for beef, until I know about the girl that's lost—that's killed, mayhap. I did misdoubt, at first, the fine lord meant no good by her or us. He maybe got the upper hand of her by holding up a wedding-ring, and then . . a choking finger on her throat last night, and just a clever take to keep us still, as she is, poor lost innocent!' "

Reading such passages as these—so flat, distorted, and unworthy—shall we not exclaim with Mrs Browning herself,

"Weep, my Æschylus,
But low and far, upon Sicilian shores?"

It is not the part of critics to strain their vision so as to detect spots on the disc of the sun; but it is their duty to mark the appearance of even a partial eclipse. It is far easier, as it is more pleasant, to praise than to condemn; but praise, injudiciously or indiscriminately bestowed, cannot be commended, since it leads to the perpetuation of error. In dealing with the works of authors of high name and established repute, it is of the utmost importance that the judgment should be clear and calm; for we know by experience that the aberrations or eccentricities of a distinguished artist are immediately copied by a crew of imitators, who, unable to vie with their original in beauties, can at least rival him, in his faults. We doubt not that, before a year is over, many poems on the model of *Aurora Leigh* will be written and published; and that conversations in the pot-house, casino, and even worse places, will be reduced to blank verse, and exhibited as specimens of high art. To dignify the mean, is not the province of poetry—let us rather say that there are atmospheres so tainted that in them poetry cannot live. Its course is in the empyrean or in the fresh wholesome air, but if it attempts to descend to pits and charnel-vaults, it is stifled by the noxious exhalations. We by no means confound the humble with the mean. The most sanctified affections, the purest thoughts, the holiest aspirations, are as likely to be found in the cottage as in the castle. Wherever there is a flower, however lowly, beauty may be seen; the prayer of a monarch is not more heeded in heaven than the supplication of an outcast; the cry of a mother is as plaintive from the dungeon as though it sounded from the halls of a palace. This very poem which we are reviewing affords a remarkable illustration of the æsthetical point which we are anxious to enforce. We have already said that the character of Marian Erle is beautifully drawn and well sustained, and yet it is the humblest of them all. But in depicting her, Mrs Browning has abstained from all meanness. If she errs at all, it is by making the girl appear more refined in thought and expression than is justified by her previous history, but that is an error on the safe side, and one which may be readily excused. Marian, little better than a pariah-girl, does undoubtedly attract our sympathies more than the polished and high-minded Aurora, the daughter of a noble race—not certainly as the bride of Romney, but as the mother of a hapless child. There, indeed, Mrs Browning has achieved a triumph; for never yet—no, not in her "Cry of the Children," one of the most pathetic and tear-stirring poems in the English language—has she written anything comparable to the passages which refer to Marian and her babe.* * *

Now contrast that with the stuff which we have put into the form of prose, and then tell us, good reader, if we are not justified in feeling annoyed, and even incensed, that a lady capable of producing so exquisite a picture, should condescend to fashion into verse what is essentially mean, gross, and puerile? We must have no evasions here, for this is an important question of art. We may be told that Shakespeare, in his highest tragedies, has introduced the comic element; and his example, so distinguished as almost to amount to an unimpeachable authority, may be cited in defence of Mrs Browning. But, on examination, we shall find that there is no analogy. In the first place, whenever Shakespeare descends to low comedy, he makes his characters discourse in prose, thereby marking broadly the elevation of sentiment and dignity which belongs to verse, and he does so even when low comedy is excluded. When Hamlet is familiar, as with the players, Polonius, the gravediggers, or Osric, he speaks in prose; and the rhythmical periods are reserved for the higher and more impassioned situations. So in *Othello*, in the scenes between Iago, Cassio, and Roderigo. So in *Julius Cæsar* (in which, being a classical play, the temptation lay towards stateliness), whenever the citizens or the cynical Casca are introduced and in *Henry V.*, in the night-scene before Agincourt, there is even a more remarkable instance of this. It was evidently the view of Shakespeare that verse is the proper vehicle for poetry alone: he would not dignify ignoble thoughts or common sentiments by admitting them to that lofty chariot. Mrs Browning follows the march of modern improvement. She makes no distinction between her first and her third class passengers, but rattles them along at the same speed upon her rhythmical railway.

There is no instance of a poem of considerable length which is free from faults and blemishes; and whatever may be said to the contrary, the detection of existing faults is the real business of the critic. He either is, or is supposed to be, the holder of the touchstone, by means of which true metal is distinguished from that which is base, and he is bound in duty to declare the result of his investigation. In the present instance, while dealing with *Aurora Leigh*, we have been at some pains to arrive at the metal. Our task has been rather that of an Australian or Californian gold-seeker, who puts into his cradle or his pan a spadeful of doubtful material. From the first shaking there emerges mud—from the second, pebbles—but, after clearance, the pure gold is found at the bottom, and in no inconsiderable quantities.

If we have not been able conscientiously to praise the story, either as regards conception or execution, no such restriction is laid upon us while dealing with isolated passages. Mrs Browning possesses in a very high degree the faculty of description, presenting us often with the most brilliantly coloured pictures. In this respect, if we may be allowed to institute such a comparison, she resembles Turner, being sometimes even extravagant in the vividness of her tints. By this we mean that she has a decided tendency, not only to multiply, but to intensify images, and occasionally carries this so far as to bewilder the reader. * * *

* * *

The reader will find in the volume itself descriptions almost as vivid and charming as the above of English scenery; for Mrs Browning, when her palette is not overcharged with carmine, can paint such things as perfectly as Morland, Gainsborough, or Constable. * * *

Nor is the great genius of Mrs Browning less conspicuous in other portions of the poem which relate to the natural affections. Once and again, whilst perusing this volume, have we experienced a sensation of regret that one so admirably gifted should have wasted much of her power upon what are, after all, mere artistic experiments, when, by adhering throughout to natural sentiment and natural expression, she might have produced a work so noble as to leave no room for cavilling or reproach. The tendency to experiment, which is simply a token of a morbid craving for originality, has been the bane of many poets. Their first victory being won, they think it incumbent on them to shift their campaigning-ground, and later their strategy, forgetful that the method which has brought them success, and which they intuitively adopted because it was most suited to their powers, is precisely that most likely to insure them a future triumph. For ourselves, we are free to confess that we have not much faith in new theories of art; we are rather inclined to class them in the same category with schemes for the regeneration of society. Mrs Browning, beyond all modern poets, has no need of resorting to fantasias for the sake of attracting an audience. For whenever she deserts her theories, and touches a natural chord, we acknowledge her as a mistress of song.* * *

* * *

It has been well remarked that the chief defect of modern British poems consists in the carelessness of their construction. Plot, arrangement, and even probability, are regarded as things of minor moment; and the whole attention of the artist is lavished upon expression. This, if we are to judge from antecedents, is a symptom of literary decadence. The same tendency is observable in the later literature of Greece and Rome; nay, it may be remarked within a narrower sphere—as, for example, in the writings of Euripides—the last of the great Hellenic triumvirate. æschylus excelled in energy and masculine strength; Sophocles in his development of the passions; Euripides in expression—but, with Euripides, Athenian tragedy declined. It is ever an evil sign when mere talk is considered by a nation as something preferable to action, for it shows that sound and pretension are becoming more esteemed than sense and deliberate purpose. We might, upon this text, say something the reverse of complimentary to a large body of politicians; but we refrain from mingling the political with the poetical element. It is, however, impossible to deny the fact that, by many, brilliant writing, or writing which seems brilliant, is esteemed as of the highest kind, without regard to congruity or design. This is a grievous error, which cannot be exposed too broadly; and to it we trace the almost total extinction, in our own day, of the British drama. Our great dramatists, with Shakespeare at their head, succeeded in gaining the attention of the public by the interests of their plots, far more than by the felicity of their diction; and until that truth is again recognised and acted on, we need not expect a resuscitation of the drama. Also be it remembered, that a plot—that is, a theme—well-considered, developed, and divided, must, to make it effective, be adequately and naturally expressed. Adequate expression is no more than the proper language of emotion; and emotion must be traceable to some evident and intelligible cause. All this is disregarded by our "new poets," as they love to style themselves, who come upon their imaginary stage, tearing their hair, proclaiming their inward wretchedness, and spouting sorry metaphysics in still sorrier verse, for no imaginable reason whatever. One of them has the curse of genius upon him, and seems to think that delirium is the normal state of the human mind. Another rails at Providence because he has not been placed in a situation which he supposes commensurate to his merits. A third, when he sets his characters in motion, pulls the strings so violently as to make them leap like fantoccini. A fourth is a mere crowder, and spins merciless rigmaroles about the "heart of the coming age." Now, with the exception of the crowder, each of these men has some intellect and power; but they do not know how to apply it. They think that the public will be content to receive their crude thoughts as genuine notes of issue from the Bank of Genius, if so be that they are dressed up in a gaudy, glittering, and hyperbolical form; and they ransack, not only earth and sea, but heaven itself for ornaments. All this while they forget that there is no meaning in their talk; that people who are desirous to hear a story, do not call the minstrel in for the purpose of listening to his disappointed aspirations, or the bleatings of his individual woes, but because they require of him, as a professed member of the greatest craft since the prophets disappeared, a tale of energy or emotion that shall stir the heart, or open one of the many fountains of our common sympathy.

We could wish—though wishes avail not for the past—that Mrs Browning had selected a more natural and intelligible theme which would have given full scope for the display of her extraordinary powers; and we trust that she will yet reconsider her opinion as to the abstract fitness for poetical use of a subject illustrative of the times in which we live. It may be that there is no difficulty which genius cannot conquer; at the same time, we cannot commend the wisdom of those who go out of their way on purpose to search for difficulties. It is curious to observe that poets in all ages have shrunk from the task of chronicling contemporaneous deeds. These are first consigned to the tutelage of the muse of history; nor is it until time has done its consecrating office, that poetry ventures to approach them. The bards of old touched their harps, not for the glorification of their compatriots, but in memory of the deeds of their ancestors. No one supposes that the time has yet arrived when the Peninsular War or the sea-victories of Britain can be taken up as proper epical themes, though Nelson and Wellington have both entered into the famous mansions of the dead. This universal repugnance to the adoption of immediate subjects for poetical treatment, seems to us a very strong argument against its propriety; and certainly Mrs Browning has not succeeded, by practice, in establishing her theory. There is sound truth in the observation that no man ever yet was a hero in the eyes of his valet, and the remark is equally just if we extend it from individuals to the masses. We select our demigods from the dead, not from the living. We cannot allow fancy to be trammelled in its work by perpetual reference to realities.

Still, with all its faults, this is a remarkable poem; strong in energy, rich in thought, abundant in beauty; and it more than sustains that high reputation which, by her previous efforts, Mrs Browning has so honourably won.

# COVENTRY PATMORE

## From *North British Review* (February 1857)†

The poetical reputation of Mrs. Browning, late Miss Barrett, has been growing slowly, until it has reached a height which has never before been attained by any modern poetess, though several others have had wider circles of readers. An intellect of a very unusual order has been ripened by an education scarcely less unusual for a woman; and Mrs. Browning now honourably enjoys the title of poetess in her own right, and not merely by courtesy.

The poems before us are divisible into three tolerably distinct classes; first, the imaginative compositions, which form the bulk of *Miss Barrett's* poems, and several of which *Mrs. Browning* tells us she "would willingly have withdrawn, if it were not almost impossible to extricate what has once been caught and involved in the machinery of the press." Secondly, the poems which have immediately arisen from personal feeling and personal observation. Of these the chief are the so-called "Sonnets from the Portuguese," and "Casa Guidi Windows." Thirdly, the novel-in-verse, or present-day epic, called "Aurora Leigh." Besides the poems belonging to these three classes, there are several "occasional pieces" of more or less significance.

Pieces which the authoress confesses that she "would willingly have withdrawn," are, by that confession, almost withdrawn from criticism. We imagine that the two dramas, "a Drama of Exile," and "the Seraphim," are among the number of those which Mrs. Browning, in her last edition, introduces with "a request to the generous reader that he may use their weakness, which no subsequent revision has succeeded in strengthening, less as a reproach to the writer, than as a means of marking some progress in her other attempts." We will only say concerning these and some other youthful essays, that we think the authoress mistaken in supposing that the "machinery of the press" will give them the deprecated perpetuity, unless she herself continues to reprint them; and that their value "as a means of marking some progress in her other attempts," is of a kind which her personal friends will appreciate much better than the world, for whom, we presume, she writes and publishes.

* * *

"Aurora Leigh" is the latest, and Mrs. Browning tells us, in the dedication, "the most mature" of her works; the one into which her "highest

† Coventry Patmore (1823–96) was an English poet and the author of *The Angel in the House* (1854–63). EBB knew that her views on women's education and women's position were not likely to find favor with Patmore. See her letter, EBB to Isa Blagden, October 20, 1856, p. 335 [*Editor*].

convictions upon Life and Art have entered." It was not well judged to prejudice the reader, at the very outset, with the inevitable doubt, "Is a poem the right place for 'highest convictions upon Life and Art?' " This poem is two thousand lines longer than "Paradise Lost." We do not know how to describe it better than by saying that it is a novel in verse,—a novel of the modern didactic species, written chiefly for the advocacy of distinct "convictions upon Life and Art." If poetry ought to consist only of "thoughts that voluntary move harmonious numbers," a very large portion of this work ought unquestionably to have been in prose. But the question seems open to discussion, and we give Mrs. Browning the benefit of the doubt. Perhaps the chief misfortune for the poem is, that there may always be two opinions on all "convictions upon Life and Art." For example, we ourselves dissent altogether from certain of the views advocated. We think that "conventions," which are society's unwritten laws, are condemned in too sweeping and unexamining a style; that the importance of an ordinary education in the formation of character is too emphatically denied by the example of Marian Erle, whom we regard as an impossible person, under her circumstances; that Art is not the highest power in the world; and so forth. "Aurora Leigh" would assuredly have been a more *poetical* work if it had made the question, "Do you agree with it?" an absurd one, and had only allowed of the question, "Do you or do you not understand it?" The safest way of speaking of this poem, which, expressly or by implication, has so considerable a polemic element in it, is to place a simple analysis of it before our readers.

* * *

The command of imagery shown by Mrs. Browning, in this poem, is really surprising, even in this day when every poetaster seems to be endowed with a more or less startling amount of that power; but Mrs. Browning seldom goes out of her way for an image, as nearly all our other versifiers are in the habit of doing continually. There is a vital continuity, through the whole of this immensely long work, which is thus remarkably, and most favourably distinguished from the sand-weaving of so many of her contemporaries. The earnestness of the authoress is, also, plainly without affectation, and her enthusiasm for truth and beauty, as she apprehends them, unbounded. A work upon such a scale, and with such a scope, had it been faultless, would have been the greatest work of the age; but unhappily there are faults, and very serious ones, over and above those which we have already hinted. The poem has evidently been written in a very small proportion of the time which a work so very ambitiously conceived ought to have taken. The language which in passionate scenes is simple and real, in other parts becomes very turgid and unpoetical; for example:—

"What if even God
Were chiefly God by working out himself
To an individualism of the Infinite,
Eterne, intense, profuse,—still throwing up
The golden spray of multitudinous worlds
In measure to the proclive weight and rush
Of his inner nature,—the spontaneous love
Still proof and outflow of spontaneous life?"

Or, in a different style, the style, unfortunately, of hundreds of lines:—

"In those days, though, I never analyzed
Myself even: all analysis comes late."

Or again:—

"Those faces! 'twas as if you had stirred up hell
To heave its lowest dreg-fiends uppermost
In fiery swirls of slime,—such strangled fronts,
Such obdurate jaws were thrown up constantly."

These, and other artistic defects, detract somewhat from the general effect of the poem; but no one who reads it, with true poetic sympathy, can withhold his tribute of admiration from a work possessing so many of the highest excellencies.

# JOHN NICHOL

## From *Westminster Review* 68 (October 1857)†

Mrs. Barrett Browning has won for herself the first place among our female poets. Falling short of the exquisite grace characterizing the masterpieces of Felicia Hemans,[1] without the simplicity of L. E. L.[2] or the variety of dramatic power which distinguishes Joanna Baillie,[3] her earlier volumes contain poems evincing a depth of thought and subtlety of expression peculiarly her own. The "Graves of a Household" is not more delicately beautiful than those verses of "Caterina to Camoens," or more passionately tender than "Isobel's Child." "The Romaunt of the Page," "The Swan's Nest among the Reeds," "Lady Geraldine's Courtship,"

† John Nichol (1833–94), scholar and critic, was the first professor of English literature at the newly established Glasgow University in Scotland from 1861 until 1889 [*Editor*].

1. (1793–1835); English poet [*Editor*].
2. Letitia Elizabeth Landon (1802–38), English poet [*Editor*].
3. (1762–1851); Scottish dramatist and poet [*Editor*].

"The Rhyme of the Duchess May," "The Rhapsody of Life," with some of the best sonnets and the most stirring lyrics in the language, give proof of poetic genius no less various than powerful, and would of themselves vindicate for the Authoress the position we have assigned her. No one could fail therefore to regard "Aurora Leigh"—the most mature, as well as the longest of her works—that into which she says her "highest convictions upon Life and Art have entered"—with profoundest interest and sanguine expectations.

The attempt to write a *novel*,—which shall be also a *poem*,—is a daring one. We have abandoned the absurdity of setting limits to the sphere of poetry, but there is a certain incongruity between the natural variety and expansion of the one, and the concentration required in the other. The general success of this effort is remarkable. Few volumes of verse have such intense interest. It has been found by an ingenious critic to contain more lines than "Paradise Lost" or the "Odyssey,"—yet there are few people who do not try to read it at a sitting. Once into the vortex of the story, we are whirled on, forgetful of criticism, of the Authoress, and of ourselves. This is a high recommendation, and has contributed largely towards the enthusiastic reception of the work; but when one has leisure to be censorious, he is met by defects equally striking. The difficulties of the design have not been entirely surmounted. The Authoress is given to a diffusive style: she drags us through many pages in "Aurora Leigh" which are unnecessary, trifling, and wearisome. That it may become a story, it sometimes ceases to be a poem. Blank verse is the most flexible and accommodating of all measures: it can sound, as in "The Brook," like graceful conversation, or with the Æolian pulsation of the "Morte d'Arthur," preserving its harmonious fulness; but in "Aurora Leigh" there are cases in which Mrs. Browning has broken loose altogether from the meshes of versification, and run riot in prose cut up into lines of ten syllables. Is there any sign of verse, for example, in the following:—"When he came from college to the country, very often he crossed the hills on visits to my aunt, with gifts of blue grapes from the hothouses, a book in one hand,—mere statistics, (if I chanced to lift the cover) count of all the goats whose beards are sprouting." Yet, with the simple change of *often* into *oft*, Mrs. Browning has made six lines out of it, as good as about one-third of those in the volume. There are so many minor faults throughout the poem, that they cease to be *minor* faults, and are a serious hindrance to our enjoyment of its beauties. Those are not mere deviations from conventional practice. At the present day such deviations, in Art at least, are not apt to be harshly judged. The age is past when critics presumed to lay down rules for poetry, strict as the dogmas of heraldry, and more meaningless. The reaction against classicism has reached its climax. Even the Unities have died out. We favour an artist who has ventured on a new method, or sought to evolve a new design; let him but keep within the bounds of reason, he obtains the praise of originality.

It would be fortunate if, in revolting against restraint, we were never led to transgress those laws of rhythm and construction which, fixed by Nature herself, are never forgotten but with offence to harmony, taste, and sense. The affectation of Originality is the next fault to the want of it. Irregular lines, extravagant metaphors, jarring combinations, are the occasional *defects*, never the *signs* of genius. An ostentation of strength is the most infallible proof of weakness. A profusion of words is no voucher for richness of thought. Those are not the best scholars who make the most numerous quotations from the Greek. We know no poem so good as this, with so many glaring offences against those first principles. Mrs. Browning's greatest failure is in her metaphors: some of them are excellent, but when they are bad—and they are often bad,—they are very bad. By a single ugly phrase, a single hideous word, dragged in, one would think, from the furthest ends of the earth, she every now and then mars the harmony of a whole page of beauty. She sadly wants simplicity, and the calm strength that flows from it. She writes in a high fever. She is constantly introducing geographical, geological, and antiquarian references, almost always out of place, and often incorrect.[4] Here are three wise lines of her own, which ought to have preserved her from many errors:

"We strain our natures at doing something great,
Far less because it's something great to do,
Than, haply, that we, so, commend ourselves
As being not small." (5.45–48)

Mrs. Browning seems at once proud and ashamed of her womanhood. She protests, not unjustly, against the practice of judging artists by their sex; but she takes the wrong means to prove her manhood. In recoil from mincing fastidiousness, she now and then becomes coarse. She will not be taxed with squeamishness, and introduces words unnecessarily, which are eschewed in the most familiar conversation. To escape the imputation of over-refinement she swears without provocation. Those are grave accusations: but the Authoress would be the first to disclaim the shield of that spurious gallantry which accords her sex an exemption from the full severity of legitimate censure. A few examples, taken almost at random from among many, will vindicate the justice of our remarks.

4. Is it hypercritical to advert to the fact that the main incident in "Aurora Leigh" is, as Mrs. Browning represents the circumstances, *physiologically impossible*? Mrs. Browning ought to have known that a reversal of any great law of nature is beyond poetic licence. [Nichol may be referring to the contemporary medical belief that a child could not be conceived without a woman's consent, that is, without orgasm, and that therefore for Marian to conceive as a result of a rape was impossible.—*Editor*.]

The description of a face that haunted Aurora's early years, gives scope for a perfect shoal of mangled and pompous similes. It was, she says, "by turns

"Ghost, fiend, and angel, fairy, witch, and sprite,—
A dauntless Muse, who eyes a dreadful Fate,
A loving Psyche who loses sight of Love,
A still Medusa, with mild milky brows
All curdled and all clothed upon with snakes
Whose slime falls fast as sweat will; or anon
Our Lady of the Passion, stabbed with swords
Where the Babe sucked; or Lamia in her first
Moonlighted pallor, ere she shrunk and blinked,
And shuddering, wriggled down to the unclean."
(1.154–63)

What a confusion of violence is the account given of London streets and the wretched beings who dwell there:—

"Faces! phew,
We'll call them vices festering to despairs,
Or sorrows petrifying to vices: not
A finger-touch of God left whole in them;
All ruined—lost—the countenance worn out
As the garments, the will dissolute as the acts,
The passions loose and draggling in the dirt
To trip the foot up at the first free step!
Those faces! 'twas as if you had stirred up hell
To heave its lowest dreg-fiends uppermost
In fiery swirls of slime," &c. (4.579–89)

How much more full of meaning, to one who has seen such sights, is the simple phrase of our Laureate's, in "Maud:"—

"And I loathe the squares and streets,
*And the faces that one meets.*"

In another passage Mrs. Browning designates the hard heart of society as—

"This social Sphinx,
"Who sits between the sepulchres and stews,
Makes mock and mow against the crystal heavens,
And bullies God,"— (4.1184–87)

Payne Knight is compared to a "mythic mountaineer"

"Who travelled higher than he was born to live,
And showed sometimes the goitre in his throat
Discoursing of an image seen through fog."
(5.143–45)

To illustrate the way in which individual words are often misused, we may take the following. "My life," Romney says

> "Scarce lacked that thunderbolt of the falling beam,
> Which *nicked* me on the forehead as I passed."
> (9.546–47)

Of Florence she says—

> "The town, there, seems to seethe
> In this Medæan *boil-pot* of the sun,
> And all the patient hills are bubbling round
> As if a prick would leave them flat."
> (7.901–04)

Of Romney Leigh excited

> "Was that his face I saw? . . . . . .
> Which tossed a sudden horror like a *sponge*[5]
> Into all eyes,"
> (4.797–99)

Of an angel face, that it shone in Heaven in "a *blotch*" of light!

To Lady Waldemar, Aurora writes with a strange confusion of biblical reference—

> "For which inheritance beyond your birth
> You sold that *poisonous porridge*[6] called your soul."
> (7.342–43)

Those pieces of bad taste mainly arise from that straining after strength which mars some of the Authoress's best writings; but there are others which, in their rough treatment of themes we are accustomed to see handled with reverence, are still more repulsive. Witness the comparison of Christ to a hunter of wild beasts (8.544–49).

In the picture of London (3.169–86), she has so overlaid her colours, as quite to destroy the effect of what might have been a most impressive sketch. Sometimes the mixture of metaphors is such as to make the passage utterly unintelligible; as for instance, in the invective against the German scholar, Wolf,[7] who, good unsuspecting man, when he first ventured to criticise Homer in his study at Halle, never dreamt of being called such names by an English poetess (5.1246–57).

A considerable portion of the book is devoted to a minute and not very profitable analysis of the process of making verses. There is surely some "playing at art" here, and science too:—

5. See note to *Aurora Leigh* 4.798, p. 130 [*Editor*].
6. See note to *Aurora Leigh* 7.342–43, p. 225 [*Editor*].
7. See note to *Aurora Leigh* 5.1249, p. 180 [*Editor*].

"I *ripped* my verses up,
And found no blood upon the rapier's point;
The heart in them was just an embryo's heart,
Which never yet had beat that it should die;
Just gasps of make-believe galvanic life;
Mere tones inorganized to any tune."—(3.245–50)

This "ripping up" does not seem to have been sufficiently savage; but Mrs. Browning has her excuse for the jolting of her Pegasus—

"But I felt
My heart's life throbbing in my verse to show
It lived, it also—certes incomplete—
Disordered with all Adam in the blood,
But even its very tumours, warts, and wens
Still organized by and implying life."—(3.338–43)

Yet it is those very warts and wens that we complain of as degrading her best poetry from the first to the second rank. It is that exaggerated mysticism and confusion of phrases that has given men, who pride themselves on their common sense, a distaste to metaphorical or even imaginative writing,and has done more than anything else to lower the esteem in which works of Art are held.

* * *

We do not blame Mrs. Browning for not doing what she does not profess to do,—she has, indeed, professed too much,—but for doing wrongly part of what she does. The work—full of beauty, large-heartedness, and valour, though it be,—has artistic defects sufficient to render it unworthy the place assigned to it by a great critic, as the greatest poem of the century:—it would have had a more prominent position in the first rank had it taught a truer and a nobler lesson.

Perhaps the worst effect of exaggeration is that it excites the opposite extreme. When Art is advocated by the depreciation of the other influences for the elevation of mankind, it receives the deepest injury. They who ignore its real glory and grandeur retaliate by a corresponding depreciation. the great agencies for harmonizing and adorning life should go hand in hand. The world prospers then, when "the poet and the philanthropist stand side by side" in grand equality; and its rough labour is most ennobled when music and poetry accompany and complement the worker's toil.

# Essays in Criticism

## LILIAN WHITING

### [The Lyrical Philosophy of *Aurora Leigh*] †

* * *

The inevitable seclusion of Mrs. Browning's life resulting from her invalid state doubtless contributed to render her spiritual vision more intense, although had not her higher nature so completely dominated her, this would hardly have been the result. A world that would have been a circumscribed imprisonment to the ordinary invalid was to her the opening into all the infinite realms of diviner life. This spirituality of her genius, combined, as it was, with the largest philosophic thought and high intellectual culture, gives her claim to rank among the nobler poets of all time. There is no need of invidious distinction in estimating Mrs. Browning, nor of saying that she stands supreme among women poets. For whether the poet be man or woman is not of itself of importance; and if Mrs. Browning in her philosophic grasp surpasses all others, she has also in pure lyric art been surpassed. All true poets, whether men or women, have each some individual claim which it is a part of the higher criticism to appreciate; and one who should fail in this individual appreciation of the many would thereby invalidate his title to any attempt to interpret adequately Elizabeth Barrett Browning. "The first to see merit, she was the last to censure faults," said Kate Field of her, and "she gave the praise that she felt with a generous hand. No one so heartily rejoiced in the success of others; no one was so modest in her own triumphs." Were she now here, she would be the first to recognize the mystic beauty of Christina Rossetti, the subtile philosophy of Julia Ward Howe, the lyric loveliness of Louise Chandler Moulton, the high heroic thought of Helen Hunt Jackson, the exquisite insight and delicate art of Edith Thomas. No true appreciation of one singer is gained by depreciation of others. Like a bouquet of flowers the perfection of each is the perfection of all, and it is not for an American writing of this noble

† From Lilian Whiting, A *Study of Elizabeth Barrett Browning* (London: Gay and Bird, 1899), 130–34.

English poet, to fail in recognition of the women poets of her own country, or of that great English lyrist, Christina Rossetti.

Yet with the completest recognition one joyfully offers to other poets who have charmed the hours it must be conceded that Mrs. Browning's power to kindle thought and to illuminate spiritual problems is unsurpassed by any English-speaking poet since Shakespeare. She is not only the most philosophical poet, seeing the questions of the times in their large relations, but she has given in her work a complete gospel of applied Christianity, and she sees all poetry as a divine instrument through which to radiate influence.

> "Art's a service,—mark:
> A silver key is given to thy clasp.
> And thou shalt stand unwearied, night and day,
> And fix it in the hard, slow-turning wards."

She believed that life "develops from within;" that

> "It takes a soul
> To move a body."

The pernicious doctrine of "Art for art's sake" so often entwined in æsthetic fervors never clouded her clear, honest vision. She saw in Art the most potent factor for high service, and she held that it existed for Love's sake, for the sake of human co-operation with the purposes of God.

There are passages in "Aurora Leigh" which may not unjustly be held to rival Shakespeare. To the profundity of thought resulting from the union of great natural powers and classic culture, she united the intuitive gift of spiritual divination. Often defective in poetic expression, she was almost supreme in poetic grasp and vision. * * *

## MARJORY A. BALD

### [The Negative Approach]†

It is difficult to write of Mrs Browning with justice or temperance. She has been so foolishly and so extravagantly praised that it is easy from sheer contra-suggestion to descend to folly and extravagance of blame. At the very outset it must be confessed that Mrs Browning's poetry was feeble. This was inevitable in the case of a woman feeble in spirit as well as body. It is a paltry thing to stand staring at weakness; and there is no

† From Marjory A. Bald, *Women Writers of the Nineteenth Century* (Cambridge: Cambridge University Press, 1923), 209–16.

justification for writing at length of faults now generally recognised, unless it be with the sincere intention to discover in the process some elements of worth. In spite of her defects Elizabeth Browning enjoyed an extraordinary popularity. All the world knows now what Robert Browning thought of her—and all the world acknowledges that he was "no fool." Although to us her failures are obtrusive, somewhere in this woman there must have been something which commanded respect; and it is our task to look for it. Whether we shall find it is another matter; but at least we can try; and we shall search honestly without any pretence at finding anything, good or bad, which is actually non-existent.

The only possible method is to proceed "from the known to the unknown"—from the recognised weakness to the undiscovered power. It may be that Mrs Browning was not one of those who "out of weakness are made strong"; still she was at times made convalescent, and even for this we should be thankful.

We can take the facts of her life for granted—the years of study, retirement, and bodily weakness, broken on the one hand by the death of her favourite brother, and on the other by the entrance of Robert Browning; then the secret marriage and flight, followed by fifteen years of almost perfect happiness. All these matters have become hackneyed. What will never become hackneyed is any trace of artistic vitality.

We begin then, in somewhat ungracious fashion, with Mrs Browning's faults; of which almost the most striking is her acute self-consciousness. If this feeling is analysed, it will be found to contain three distinct elements. She was conscious of her sufferings, of her sex, and of her vocation as artist.

"I am morbid, I know," she wrote. "Like the lady who lay in the grave, and was ever after of the colour of a shroud, so I am white-souled, and the past has left its mark with me for ever." References of the same nature are to be found everywhere in her poetry, and leave on it the desolating taint of all self-depreciation, so closely related to self-pity. Even the *Sonnets from the Portuguese* have this flaw, this limpness of introspection:

For frequent tears have run
The colours from my life, and left so dead
And pale a stuff, it were not fitly done
To give the same as pillow to thy head.
Go further! Let it serve to trample on.

In the second place she could not forget her sex—and for the simple reason that she was, or tried to be, an artist. Occasionally she may speak in general terms of the negative position of women, who are only praised—

As long as they keep quiet by the fire,
And never say "no" when the world says "ay."

Nevertheless when she speaks of "the woman's movement," it is nearly always the literary woman of whom she is thinking. The high-spirited Brontes sprang to the adventure of literature. Whereas they felt the zest of pioneering, Mrs Browning was cast down by its loneliness and difficulty. Not born to lead, she searched in vain for predecessors.—"I look everywhere," she wrote, "for grandmothers, and see none. It is not in the filial spirit I am deficient, I do assure you—witness my reverent love of the grandfathers!" At all points she seemed baffled by ignorance of the way. On the one side we hear her speaking through Aurora—

> No perfect artist is developed here
> From any imperfect woman.

On the other side, we find her constantly struggling against the current opinion that the artistic vocation robs a woman of her completeness, till she becomes

> A printing woman who has lost her place
> (The sweet safe corner of the household fire
> Behind the heads of children).

Whereas a woman more sure of her own position would have been content to live down popular prejudices, Mrs Browning weakened her energy by voluble protests. We feel this in Aurora's retort to Romney:

> I perceive!
> The headache is too noble for my sex.
> You think the heartache would sound decenter,
> Since that's the woman's special, proper ache,
> And altogether tolerable, except
> To a woman.

She could not admire even Florence Nightingale without an aftertaste of personal bitterness. The noble work done by women in the Crimea she declared to be no solution of the woman's question—in other words, of the literary woman's question.—"Every man," she cried, "is on his knees before ladies carrying lint, calling them 'angelic she's,' whereas, if they stir an inch as thinkers or artists from the beaten line (involving more good to general humanity than is involved in lint), the very same men would curse the impudence of the very same women, and stop there."—The singularity and detachment of the woman artist seemed to lie upon her spirit even when she herself had escaped from solitude into a perfect fellowship. In the comfort of her own home, kindled by the praise of her own husband, she could yet exclaim:

> How dreary 'tis for women to sit still
> On winter nights by solitary fires,
> And hear the nations praising them far off,
> Too far!

In spite of all her protest Mrs Browning listened too attentively for the world's estimates—and particularly for it estimates of censure. She seemed unable to clear her mind of misgivings as to the possibility of artistic supremacy for women. She was deeply hurt by the popular conception, so bitterly voiced by Aurora, that women are

> Poor to think,
> Yet rich enough to sympathise with thought.

In Romney Leigh's criticism of Aurora she seems to be declaring her own experience of the world's depreciation. Women, says Romney, are too personal to become great artists:

> All's yours and you,—
> All, coloured with your blood, or otherwise
> Just nothing to you......
> ...............This same world,
> Uncomprehended by you, must remain
> Uninfluenced by you.—Women as you are,
> Mere women, personal and passionate,
> You give us doating mothers, and chaste wives,
> Sublime Madonnas, and enduring saints!
> We get no Christ from you,—and verily
> We shall not get a poet in my mind.

This alternative—the choice between apprehension of the multitude and love of the individual—seems to have been definitely placed before both Charlotte Bronte and George Eliot. St John, for instance, with his devotion to a great cause, is in some ways a parallel to Romney Leigh. But Jane Eyre, battling for the privacies and liberties of the individual soul, finds no fitting counterpart in Aurora, whose many words carry less conviction than Jane's decisive actions. The whole distinction is this:—while Charlotte Bronte—and George Eliot also—made up their minds about their attitude to large impersonal matters, Mrs Browning hesitated and faltered.

Some years before the creation of Aurora she had written to Robert Browning in words of great significance.—"I am, in a manner, as a *blind poet*. Certainly there is compensation to a degree. I have had much of the inner life, and from the habit of self-consciousness and self-analysis, I make great guesses at Human nature in the main." Herein lies the clue to much of her weakness. If she had been as sincere as Christina Rossetti, she would not have made guesses; she would have accepted her narrow restricted life as the one reality of which she could speak with conviction. By an unswerving fidelity to the truths which she knew and experienced, she would have extracted from meagre resources some treasure of beauty. But this is precisely what she did not do. It is not at all astonishing that she became tired of her uninspiriting self.

There are not many people, who, when forced upon themselves, can, like Christina Rossetti, probe bravely to the very core of their unrest,—to find in the intense reality of the inner life both solace and revival. Many people, afraid to face their own inadequacy, run away from themselves, and seek shelter in impersonal things. This is a form of self-forgettal based, not on denial and sacrifice, but on timidity.—It is impossible to close one's eyes to the working of this tendency in Mrs Browning. "My only idea of happiness," she wrote, ". . . lies deep in poetry and its associations. . . . You throw off *yourself*." Instead of developing the poetry latent in her own soul, she often contented herself with a species of metrical journalism. Like Tennyson, she allowed herself to be caught in the web of current events. She declaimed and argued about Italian freedom, the slave-trade, or social abuses; but nearly always there is something lacking. Too often disregarding what Matthew Arnold called "the buried river" of the inner life, she spoke on the surface of experience; and her words failed of power—

'Tis eloquent, 'tis just, but 'tis not true.

While reading *Casa Guidi Windows* or the *Poems of Progress*, we constantly hear ringing in our ears Hamlet's outcry against the Player's simulated emotions—

What's Hecuba to him, or he to Hecuba?

What, we exclaim, was Italy to Mrs Browning?—Is there not something artificial, something almost of pose, in this wordy devotion to what was, after all, a foreign cause?—It was good that she should be interested in Italy; but had she no other interest, more vital and intimate?—She very rarely attains to the

Words that breathe, and words that burn.

Indeed the prevailing characteristic of her utterance is that it pants and flickers. As we read, we fall back upon King Lear's wistful appeal to Cordelia—

But goes thy heart with this?

Unlike Lear, we cannot obtain an affirmative answer. Mrs Browning often seems to have written with only part of her heart; and we cannot be expected to make a wholehearted response.

So far we have been dealing with her artistic consciousness in its relation to sex. But Mrs Browning had other theories of art which, though personal, were not necessarily feminine. In common with her husband, she felt keenly the detachment of the literary creator, and expressed this sentiment most strongly in Aurora's bitter outcry to Lord Howe:

> Love, you say?
> My lord, I cannot love. I only find
> The rhymes for love,—and that's not love, my lord.

In another place she hints at the possibilities of inarticulate art—the tragedy of the "mute, inglorious Milton";

> I called the artist but a greatened man,
> He may be childless also, like a man.

Notwithstanding, it is her general custom, when writing of the personal life of the artist, to deal with its compensations—its privacies and high communions.—"Most of my events," she wrote, "and nearly all of my intense pleasures, have passed in my *thoughts*. . . . The Greeks were my demi-gods, and haunted me out of Pope's Homer, until I dreamt more of Agammemnon than of Moses the black pony."—A few years later we find her writing—"Men and women of letters are the first in the whole world to me, and I would rather be the least among them than dwell in the courts of princes."—It is not always easy or desirable to feel sympathy for this attitude of detachment.—"I am one," she said, "who could have forgotten the plague, listening to Boccaccio's stories."—It is doubtful whether any genuine artist could have found power in neglecting the dreadful reality for the pleasing fiction; it is certain that Robert Browning would have looked the plague, as all other evils, full in the face. His wife failed to recognise that it is the great courage which produces the great art.—Some of her other declarations as to the absorption of the artist do not tally with her own practice. Writing to the *Athenaeum*, she remarked:

> When Milton said that a poet's life should be a poem, he spoke a high moral truth; if he had added a reversion of the saying, that a poet's poetry should be his life,—he would have spoken a critical truth, not low. . . . "Art," it was said long ago, "requires the whole man," and "Nobody," it was said later, "can be a poet who is anything else"; but the present idea of Art requires the segment of a man, and everybody who is anything at all is a poet in a parenthesis.

She did not apply her theories or carry them to their logical conclusions. She had before her the chance of being like Christina Rossetti, a poet and nothing else—living and writing out of her inner resources; but she tried to be something else as well—a political and social theorist. The real difficulty was that she could not make up her mind between two ideals—poetry of the inner life, and poetry, like her husband's, of a penetrating and general humanity. She could not decide which ideal was best in accord with her own temperament, and reaped the inevitable harvest of halting between two opinions. She did not devote herself wholly to either ideal, and quite against her own intentions, only the "segment" of herself made itself felt in her writings.

These are theories of the artistic life. Mrs Browning also had her opinions on the artistic function. She most indignantly cast back the challenge made by such "practical" men as Romney, that Art is not of much use in a workaday world:

> When Egypt's slain, I say, let Miriam sing!
> Before..............Where's Moses?

In the teeth of such taunts Mrs Browning maintained that Art could be of the highest efficiency, and this by virtue of its spiritual testimony. It affords an explanation of material symbols—

> Earth's crammed with heaven,
> And every common bush afire with God;
> But only he who sees, takes off his shoes;
> The rest sit round it, and pluck blackberries.

The artist teaches men to see the mystic fires of God—

> Art's the witness of what Is
> Behind this show.

This witness must be most thorough and painstaking. It must describe the show as well as interpret its meaning.—It appeared to Mrs Browning that the "show" must be a matter of common experience; and for this reason she usually chose themes of current, modern life. For these themes she claimed an utter freedom of speech.—

> If a woman ignores these wrongs, then may women as a sex continue to suffer them; there is no help for any of us—let us be decent and die. I have spoken therefore, and in speaking have used plain words—words which look like blots—. . . words which, if blurred or softened, would imperil perhaps the force and righteousness of the moral influence.

Thackeray, as is well known, reluctantly refused one of her poems for the *Cornhill*, on the grounds that it was too outspoken.—"There are things," he wrote, "which *my* squeamish public will not bear on Mondays, though on Sundays they will listen to them without scruple."—From Mrs Browning's answer we quote one significant line: "I am deeply convinced that the corruption of our society requires, not shut doors and windows, but light and air." The modern reader objects to Mrs Browning's frankness, but not from the Victorian standpoint. He objects, not to the attack, but to the method of attack. It may be a writer's duty to deal with unpleasant subjects; but it is also his duty to curb and select his phrases. He should aim, not at "words which look like blots," but at speech which burns like flames. No doubt he should be merciless; but the fiercest utterance has an element of terseness; and Mrs Browning never learnt that secret.

# VIRGINIA WOOLF

## "Aurora Leigh"†

By one of those ironies of fashion that might have amused the Brownings themselves, it seems likely that they are now far better known in the flesh than they have ever been in the spirit. Passionate lovers, in curls and side whiskers, oppressed, defiant, eloping—in this guise thousands of people must know and love the Brownings who have never read a line of their poetry. They have become two of the most conspicuous figures in that bright and animated company of authors who, thanks to our modern habit of writing memoirs and printing letters and sitting to be photographed, live in the flesh, not merely as of old in the word; are known by their hats, not merely by their poems. What damage the art of photography has inflicted upon the art of literature has yet to be reckoned. How far we are going to read a poet when we can read about a poet is a problem to lay before biographers. Meanwhile, nobody can deny the power of the Brownings to excite our sympathy and rouse our interest. "Lady Geraldine's Courtship" is glanced at perhaps by two professors in American universities once a year; but we all know how Miss Barrett lay on her sofa; how she escaped from the dark house in Wimpole Street one September morning; how she met health and happiness, freedom, and Robert Browning in the church round the corner.

But fate has not been kind to Mrs. Browning as a writer. Nobody reads her, nobody discusses her, nobody troubles to put her in her place. One has only to compare her reputation with Christina Rossetti's to trace her decline. Christina Rossetti mounts irresistibly to the first place among English women poets. Elizabeth, so much more loudly applauded during her lifetime, falls farther and farther behind. The primers dismiss her with contumely. Her importance, they say, "has now become merely historical. Neither education nor association with her husband ever succeeded in teaching her the value of words and a sense of form." In short, the only place in the mansion of literature that is assigned her is downstairs in the servants' quarters, where, in company with Mrs. Hemans, Eliza Cook, Jean Ingelow, Alexander Smith, Edwin Arnold, and Robert Montgomery, she bangs the crockery about and eats vast handfuls of peas on the point of her knife.

† "Aurora Leigh" from THE SECOND COMMON READER by Virginia Woolf, copyright 1932 by Harcourt Brace & Company and renewed 1960 by Leonard Woolf, reprinted by permission of the publisher.

If, therefore, we take *Aurora Leigh* from the shelf it is not so much in order to read it as to muse with kindly condescension over this token of bygone fashion, as we toy with the fringes of our grandmother's mantles and muse over the alabaster models of the Taj Mahal which once adorned their drawing-room tables. But to the Victorians, undoubtedly, the book was very dear. Thirteen editions of *Aurora Leigh* had been demanded by the year 1873. And, to judge from the dedication, Mrs. Browning herself was not afraid to say that she set great store by it—"the most mature of my works," she calls it, "and the one into which my highest convictions upon Life and Art have entered". Her letters show that she had had the book in mind for many years. She was brooding over it when she first met Browning, and her intention with regard to it forms almost the first of those confidences about their work which the lovers delighted to share.

> . . . my chief *intention* [she wrote] just now is the writing of a sort of novel-poem . . . running into the midst of our conventions, and rushing into drawing-rooms and the like, "where angels fear to tread"; and so, meeting face to face and without mask the Humanity of the age, and speaking the truth of it out plainly. That is my intention.

But for reasons which later become clear, she hoarded her intention throughout the ten astonishing years of escape and happiness; and when at last the book appeared in 1856 she might well feel that she had poured into it the best that she had to give. Perhaps the hoarding and the saturation which resulted have something to do with the surprise that awaits us. At any rate we cannot read the first twenty pages of *Aurora Leigh* without becoming aware that the Ancient Mariner who lingers, for unknown reasons, at the porch of one book and not of another has us by the hand, and makes us listen like a three years' child while Mrs. Browning pours out in nine volume of blank verse the story of Aurora Leigh. Speed and energy, forthrightness and complete self-confidence—these are the qualities that hold us enthralled. Floated off our feet by them, we learn how Aurora was the child of an Italian mother "whose rare blue eyes were shut from seeing her when she was scarcely four years old." Her father was "an austere Englishman, Who, after a dry life-time spent at home In college-learning, law and parish talk, Was flooded with a passion unaware", but died too, and the child was sent back to England to be brought up by an aunt. The aunt, of the well-known family of the Leighs, stood upon the hall step of her country house dressed in black to welcome her. Her somewhat narrow forehead was braided tight with brown hair pricked with grey; she had a close, mild mouth; eyes of no colour; and cheeks like roses pressed in books, "Kept more for ruth than pleasure,—if past bloom, Past fading also". The lady had lived a quiet life, exercising her Christian gifts upon knitting stockings and stitching petticoats "because we are of one flesh, after all, and need one flannel". At her hand Aurora suffered the education that was thought proper for women. She learnt a little French, a little algebra; the internal laws of the Burmese empire; what navigable river joins itself to Lara; what census of the year five was taken at Klagenfurt; also how to draw nereids neatly draped, to spin glass, to stuff birds, and model flowers in wax. For the Aunt liked a woman to be womanly. Of an evening she did cross-stitch and, owing to some mistake in her choice of silk, once embroidered a shepherdess with pink eyes. Under this torture of women's education, the passionate Aurora exclaimed, certain women have died; others pine; a few who have, as Aurora had, "relations with the unseen", survive, and walk demurely, and are civil to their cousins and listen to the vicar and pour out tea. Aurora herself was blessed with a little room. It was green papered, had a green carpet and there were green curtains to the bed, as if to match the insipid greenery of the English country-side. There she retired; there she read. "I had found the secret of a garret room Piled high with cases in my father's name, Piled high, packed large, where, creeping in and out . . . like some small nimble mouse between the ribs of a mastodon" she read and read. The mouse indeed (it is the way with Mrs. Browning's mice) took wings and soared, for "It is rather when We gloriously forget ourselves and plunge Soul-forward, headlong, into a book's profound, Impassioned for its beauty and salt of truth—'Tis then we get the right good from a book". And so she read and read, until her cousin Romney called to walk with her, or the painter Vincent Carrington, "whom men judge hardly as bee-bonneted Because he holds that paint a body well you paint a soul by implication", tapped on the window.

This hasty abstract of the first volume of *Aurora Leigh* does it of course no sort of justice; but having gulped down the original much as Aurora herself advises, soul-forward, headlong, we find ourselves in a state where some attempt at the ordering of our multitudinous impressions becomes imperative. The first of these impressions and the most pervasive is the sense of the writer's presence. Through the voice of Aurora the character, the circumstances, the idiosyncrasies of Elizabeth Barrett Browning ring in our ears. Mrs. Browning could no more conceal herself than she could control herself, a sign no doubt of imperfection in an artist, but a sign also that life has impinged upon art more than life should. Again and again in the pages we have read, Aurora the fictitious seems to be throwing light upon Elizabeth the actual. The idea of the poem, we must remember, came to her in the early forties when the connexion between a woman's art and a woman's life was unnaturally close, so that it is impossible for the most austere of critics not sometimes to touch the flesh when his eyes should be fixed upon the page. And as everybody knows, the life of Elizabeth Barrett was of a nature to affect the most authentic and individual of gifts. Her mother had died when she was a child; she had read profusely and privately; her favourite brother was drowned; her health broke down; she had been immured by the tyranny of her father in almost conventual seclusion in a bedroom in Wimpole Street. But instead of rehearsing the well-known facts, it is better to read in her own words her own account of the effect they had upon her.

> I have lived only inwardly [she wrote] or with *sorrow*, for a strong emotion. Before this seclusion of my illness, I was secluded still, and there are few of the youngest women in the world who have not seen more, heard more, known more, of society, than I, who am scarcely to be called young now. I grew up in the country—I had no social opportunities, had my heart in books and poetry, and my experience in reveries. And so time passed and passed—and afterwards, when my illness came . . . and no prospect (as appeared at one time) of ever passing the threshold of one room again; why then, I turned to thinking with some bitterness . . . that I had stood blind in this temple I was about to leave—that I had seen no Human nature, that my brothers and sisters of the earth were *names* to me, that I had beheld no great mountain or river, nothing in fact. . . . And do you also know what a disadvantage this ignorance is to my art? Why, if I live on and yet do not escape from this seclusion, do you not perceive that I labour under signal disadvantages—that I am, in a manner as a *blind poet?* Certainly, there is compensation to a degree. I have had much of the inner life, and from the habit of self-consciousness and self-analysis, I make great guesses at Human nature in the main. But how willingly I would as a poet exchange some of this lumbering, ponderous, helpless knowledge of books, for some experience of life and man, for some. . . .

She breaks off, with three little dots, and we may take advantage of her pause to turn once more to *Aurora Leigh*.

What damage had her life done her as a poet? A great one, we cannot deny. For it is clear, as we turn the pages of *Aurora Leigh* or of the *Letters*—one often echoes the other—that the mind which found its natural expression in this swift and chaotic poem about real men and women was not the mind to profit by solitude. A lyrical, a scholarly, a fastidious mind might have used seclusion and solitude to perfect its powers. Tennyson asked no better than to live with books in the heart of the country. But the mind of Elizabeth Barrett was lively and secular and satirical. She was no scholar. Books were to her not an end in themselves but a substitute for living. She raced through folios because she was forbidden to scamper on the grass. She wrestled with Aeschylus and Plato because it was out of the question that she should argue about politics with live men and women. Her favourite reading as an invalid was Balzac and George Sand and other "immortal improprieties" because "they kept the colour in my life to some degree." Nothing is more striking when at last she broke the prison bars than the fervour with which she flung herself into the life of the moment. She loved to sit in a café and watch people passing; she loved the arguments, the politics, and the strife of the modern world. The past and its ruins, even the past of Italy and Italian ruins, interested her much less than the theories of Mr. Hume the medium, or the politics of Napoleon, Emperor of the French. Italian pictures, Greek poetry, roused in her a clumsy and conventional enthusiasm in strange contrast with the original independence of her mind when it applied itself to actual facts.

Such being her natural bent, it is not surprising that even in the depths of her sick-room her mind turned to modern life as a subject for poetry. She waited, wisely, until her escape had given her some measure of knowledge and proportion. But it cannot be doubted that the long years of seclusion had done her irreparable damage as an artist. She had lived shut off, guessing at what was outside, and inevitably magnifying what was within. The loss of Flush, the spaniel, affected her as the loss of a child might have affected another woman. The tap of ivy on the pane became the thrash of trees in a gale. Every sound was enlarged, every incident exaggerated, for the silence of the sick-room was profound and the monotony of Wimpole Street was intense. When at last she was able to "rush into drawing-rooms and the like and meet face to face without mask the Humanity of the age and speak the truth of it out plainly", she was too weak to stand the shock. Ordinary daylight, current gossip, the usual traffic of human beings left her exhausted, ecstatic, and dazzled into a state where she saw so much and felt so much that she did not altogether know what she felt or what she saw.

*Aurora Leigh*, the novel-poem, is not, therefore, the masterpiece that it might have been. Rather it is a masterpiece in embryo; a work whose genius floats diffused and fluctuating in some pre-natal stage waiting the final stroke of creative power to bring it into being. Stimulating and boring, ungainly and eloquent, monstrous and exquisite, all by turns, it overwhelms and bewilders; but, nevertheless, it still commands our interest and inspires our respect. For it becomes clear as we read that, whatever Mrs. Browning's faults, she was one of those rare writers who risk themselves adventurously and disinterestedly in an imaginative life which is independent of their private lives and demands to be considered apart from personalities. Her "intention" survives; the interest of her theory redeems much that is faulty in her practice. Abridged and simplified from Aurora's argument in the fifth book, that theory runs something like this. The true work of poets, she said, is to present their own age, not Charlemagne's. More passion takes place in drawing-rooms than at Roncesvalles with Roland and his knights. "To flinch from modern varnish, coat or flounce, Cry out for togas and the picturesque, Is fatal—foolish too." For living art presents and records real life, and the only life we can truly know is our own. But what form, she asks, can a poem on modern life take? The drama is impossible, for only servile and docile plays have any chance of success. Moreover, what we (in 1846) have to say about life is not fit for "boards, actors, prompters, gaslight, and costume; our stage is now the soul itself". What then can she do? The problem is difficult, performance is bound to fall short of endeavour; but she has at least wrung her life-blood on to every page of her book, and, for the rest "Let me think of forms less, and the external. Trust the spirit . . . Keep up the fire and leave the generous flames to shape themselves." And so the fire blazed and the flames leapt high.

The desire to deal with modern life in poetry was not confined to Miss Barrett. Robert Browning said that he had had the same ambition all his life. Coventry Patmore's "Angel in the House" and Clough's "Bothie" were both attempts of the same kind and preceded *Aurora Leigh* by some years. It was natural enough. The novelists were dealing triumphantly with modern life in prose. *Jane Eyre, Vanity Fair, David Copperfield, Richard Feveral* all trod fast on each other's heels between the years 1847 and 1860. The poets may well have felt, with Aurora Leigh, that modern life had an intensity and a meaning of its own. Why should these spoils fall solely into the laps of the prose writers? Why should the poet be forced back to the remoteness of Charlemagne and Roland, to the toga and the picturesque, when the humours and tragedies of village life, drawing-room life, club life, and street life all cried aloud for celebration? It was true that the old form in which poetry had dealt with life—the drama—was obsolete; but was there none other that could take its place? Mrs. Browning, convinced of the divinity of poetry, pondered, seized as much as she could of actual experience, and then at last threw down her challenge to the Brontës and the Thackerays in nine books of blank verse. It was in blank verse that she sang of Shoreditch and Kensington; of my aunt and the vicar; of Romney Leigh and Vincent Carrington; of Marian Erle and Lord Howe; of fashionable weddings and drab suburban streets, and bonnets and whiskers and four-wheeled cabs, and railway trains. The poets can treat of these things, she exclaimed, as well as of knights and dames, moats and drawbridges and castle courts. But can they? Let us see what happens to a poet when he poaches upon a novelist's preserves and gives us not an epic or a lyric but the story of many lives that move and change and are inspired by the interests and passions that are ours in the middle of the reign of Queen Victoria.

In the first place there is the story; a tale has to be told; the poet must somehow convey to us the necessary information that his hero has been asked out to dinner. This is a statement that a novelist would convey as quietly and prosaically as possible; for example, "While I was kissing her glove, sadly enough, a note was brought saying that her father sent his regards and asked me to dine with them next day". That is harmless. But the poet has to write:

While thus I grieved, and kissed her glove,
  My man brought in her note to say,
Papa had bid her send his love,
  And would I dine with them next day!

Which is absurd. The simple words have been made to strut and posture and take on an emphasis which makes them ridiculous. Then again, what will the poet do with dialogue? In modern life, as Mrs. Browning indicated when she said that our stage is now the soul, the tongue has superseded the sword. It is in talk that the high moments of life, the shock of character upon character, are defined. But poetry when it tries to follow the words on people's lips is terribly impeded. Listen to Romney in a moment of high emotion talking to his old love Marian about the baby she has borne to another man:

May God so father me, as I do him,
And so forsake me, as I let him feel
He's orphaned haply. Here I take the child
To share my cup, to slumber on my knee,
To play his loudest gambol at my foot,
To hold my finger in the public ways . . .

and so on. Romney, in short, rants and reels like any of those Elizabethan heroes whom Mrs. Browning had warned so imperiously out of her modern living-room. Blank verse has proved itself the most remorseless enemy of living speech. Talk tossed up on the surge and swing of the verse becomes high, rhetorical, impassioned; and as talk, since action is ruled out, must go on and on, the reader's mind stiffens and glazes under the monotony of the rhythm. Following the lift of her rhythm rather than the emotions of her characters, Mrs. Browning is swept on into generalisation and declamation. Forced by the nature of her medium, she ignores the slighter, the subtler, the more hidden shades of emotion by which a novelist builds up touch by touch a character in prose. Change and development, the effect of one character upon another—all this is abandoned. The poem becomes one long soliloquy, and the only character that is known to us and the only story that is told us are the character and story of Aurora Leigh herself.

Thus, if Mrs. Browning meant by a novel-poem a book in which character is closely and subtly revealed, the relations of many hearts laid bare, and a story unfalteringly unfolded, she failed completely. But if she meant rather to give us a sense of life in general, of people who are unmistakably Victorian, wrestling with the problems of their own time, all brightened, intensified, and compacted by the fire of poetry, she succeeded. Aurora Leigh, with her passionate interest in social questions, her conflict as artist and woman, her longing for knowledge and freedom, is the true daughter of her age. Romney, too, is no less certainly a mid-Victorian gentleman of high ideals who has thought deeply about the social question, and has founded, unfortunately, a phalanstery in Shropshire. The aunt, the antimacassars, and the country house from which Aurora escapes are real enough to fetch high prices in the Tottenham Court Road at this moment. The broader aspects of what it felt like to be a Victorian are seized as surely and stamped as vividly upon us as in any novel by Trollope or Mrs. Gaskell.

And indeed if we compare the prose novel and the novel-poem the triumphs are by no means all to the credit of prose. As we rush through page after page of narrative in which a dozen scenes that the novelist would smooth out separately are pressed into one, in which pages of deliberate description are fused into a single line, we cannot help feeling that the poet has outpaced the prose writer. Her page is packed twice as full as his. Characters, too, if they are not shown in conflict but snipped off and summed up with something of the exaggeration of a caricaturist, have a heightened and symbolical significance which prose with its gradual approach cannot rival. The general aspect of things—market, sunset, church—have a brilliance and a continuity, owing to the compressions and elisions of poetry, which mock the prose writer and his slow accumulations of careful detail. For these reasons *Aurora Leigh* remains, with all its imperfections, a book that still lives and breathes and has its being. And when we think how still and cold the plays of Beddoes or of Sir Henry Taylor lie, in spite of all their beauty, and how seldom in our own day we disturb the repose of the classical dramas of Robert Bridges, we may suspect that Elizabeth Barrett was inspired by a flash of true genius when she rushed into the drawing-room and said that here, where we live and work, is the true place for the poet. At any rate, her courage was justified in her own case. Her bad taste, her tortured ingenuity, her floundering, scrambling, and confused impetuosity have space to spend themselves here without inflicting a deadly wound, while her ardour and abundance, her brilliant descriptive powers, her shrewd and caustic humour, infect us with her own enthusiasm. We laugh, we protest, we complain—it is absurd, it is impossible, we cannot tolerate this exaggeration a moment longer—but, nevertheless, we read to the end enthralled. What more can an author ask? But the best compliment that we can pay *Aurora Leigh* is that it makes us wonder why it has left no successors. Surely the street, the drawing-room, are promising subjects; modern life is worthy of the muse. But the rapid sketch that Elizabeth Barrett Browning threw off when she leapt from her couch and dashed into the drawing-room remains unfinished. The conservatism or the timidity of poets still leaves the chief spoils of modern life to the novelist. We have no novel-poem of the age of George the Fifth.

# J. M. S. TOMPKINS

## [Aurora's Mistakes]†

* * *We are not, however, justified in taking all Aurora's remarks as the considered opinions of her creator. Aurora is a dramatic character. The relation in which Mrs Browning stands to her is very much like that in which Charlotte Brontë stands to Jane Eyre, which Professor Kathleen Tillotson has defined.[1] She gives her heroine her mind and temperament and a little of her experience, especially in the childhood scenes and the stages by which her poetry develops; but beyond that Aurora is a dramatic creation and the structure of the poem is dramatic. During much of it, Aurora speaks under pressure. On her twentieth birthday she has rejected the hand of her cousin Romney to pursue the vocation of poet in which he does not believe. She begins her narrative seven years later, and it is continued, at diminishing intervals, for some three years more. She has established her claim to be a poet, and has had time to realize her loneliness:

> How dreary 'tis for women to sit still
> On winter nights by solitary fires,
> And hear the nations praising them far off.

She is by now, however, committed to a continually renewed defence of her choice, and this for her involves not only the conviction that she did not love him but that he did not love her. Since she is haunted by the thought of him, since her reflections on men and women, on poets and critics, on art and society, continually shrink from an initially wide compass down to the two points of "Romney and me," this is a conviction which can be maintained only by pride and will and at times they distort her judgment. This is often overlooked; but I have no doubt that we are meant to take it into consideration. It is part of the analysis, and is sometimes pressed on us with more than a touch of comedy. The fifth book of the poem begins with thirty lines of depressed self-communing by Aurora about her art; then she expresses her conviction that she is bound to fail in her ambition, since she fails to hold one man, her cousin,

> And he born tender, made intelligent,

but "obtuse to *me*, of *me* incurious." The pronoun is in italics. Reacting at once, she chides the "vile woman's way" of letting the "personal thought"—the judgment of one friend—stand between her and "Art's

† *The Fawcett Lecture 1961–62* (London: 1961), 12–14. Reprinted by permission of Royal Holloway, University of London.
1. Cf. *Novels of the Eighteen-Forties* (London, 1954), p. 292.

pure temple". Then, twenty pages further on, it comes to light that she has heard a rumour of Romney's coming marriage to Lady Waldemar. This is a sufficiently clear pointer, but it does not seem that it has been much noticed. For instance, we are told that there are no credible characters in the poem, except Aurora, and that Lady Waldemar, in particular, is a melodramatic villainess. It is the easier to pass this assertion unexamined because Mrs Browning does, for the most part, put her own language, which is Aurora's, into the mouths of the other characters, if not on their first appearance then later on. Not that this language is consistently high-flown; far from it, it will run along for a page or more in an easy, well-bred, spoken English, with sudden, convincing, informal cadences, but when her poetic imagination presents her with the rich image, the unexpected, learned analogy, the strong choice word, the artful order, she cannot gainsay it. She paraphrases Marian Erle's long narrative—

> She told the tale with simple, rustic turns—
> . . . . . . I have rather writ
> The thing I understood so, than the thing
> I heard so—

with the result that the features of this earlier Tess[2] show through an embroidered veil. This does not so much matter with Marian Erle, who is an idealized character, springing out of the most unlikely circumstances; but it does matter with Aurora's aunt and Lady Waldemar. Both are clearly presented on their first appearance—the narrow, virtuous woman, whose one indulged passion is the hatred of her brother's Italian wife, and the clever, graceful, selfish society woman—but in both cases the impact is blurred when they begin to talk with Aurora's tongue. Aurora's account of Lady Waldemar's visit to her to get her help in breaking the proposed marriage between Romney Leigh and the sempstress Marian is in Mrs Browning's best vein of pungent sobriety.

> She had the low voice of your English dames,
> Unused, it seems, to need rise half a note
> To get attention . . .
> So wary and afraid of hurting you,
> By no means that you are not really vile,
> But that they would not touch you with their foot
> To push you to your place; so self-possessed
> Yet gracious and conciliating, it takes
> An effort in their presence to speak truth:
> You know the sort of woman,—brilliant stuff,
> And out of nature.

2. The title character in Thomas Hardy's novel *Tess of the d'Urbervilles* (1891).

Lady Waldemar confides to the literary woman, whom she believes less than a woman—"your hearts being starved to make your heads"—that she loves Romney Leigh and would marry him, and we can hear her pretty, petulant voice:

For me, I've done
What women may, we're somewhat limited,
We modest women, but I've done my best.

What follows on this spirited sketch, we are told, is Lady Waldemar's decline into the conventional villainess, the incredible bad woman. No. What happens is much more interesting. Aurora's unacknowledged love for Romney and unacknowledged jealousy of her rival get to work on Lady Waldemar. The snake-image appears. She becomes Lamia, the unhallowed bride, the demonic creature, in Aurora's heated fancy, an infinitely sinister, brilliantly-enamelled figure. But, in fact, Lady Waldemar never qualifies for such a classification. She is unscrupulous and fundamentally irresponsible about anyone outside her own class; when she prises Marian Erle loose from Romney, she takes no care to ensure that her former maid, who has agreed to take the girl to Australia, really does so; but when Aurora accuses her of consigning Marian knowingly to a French brothel, she can turn on her censor with a credible mixture of indignation, feminine malice, and genuine wonder. "Are you made so ill, You woman—to impute such ill to *me*?" It is a justified return-stroke. Aurora has put herself badly in the wrong. Indeed, Aurora the poet and austere witness of truth and Aurora the mere woman are locked in struggle through the poem, and her salvation is not all her own work.

* * *

# ELLEN MOERS

## [The Myth of Corinne] †

* * *

Book 2, the most important of the novel, is called "Corinne au Capitole."[1] It establishes the ultimate fantasy of the performing heroine with a brio, a luster, and a folly beyond the possibility of future novelists to exceed. All this takes place in the Capitol of the capital of the world. Oswald awakens to the brilliant sun of Rome, and to the ringing of bells

† Excerpted from *Literary Women* (London: W. H. Allen Co., 1977), 179–83.  All notes are by the editor of this Norton Critical Edition.

1. French; "Corinne at the Capitol." *Corinne, or Italy* (1807) by Madame de Staël.

and booming of cannons which announce that, that very day, there will be carried in triumph to the Capitoline Hill, there to be crowned with the laurel wreath of genius, as Petrarch and Tasso were before her, the most famous woman of Italy: "Corinne, poëte, écrivain, improvisatrice, et l'une des plus belles personnes de Rome."[2]

All of Rome seems to have turned into the streets for the occasion. The babble of the populace arouses Oswald's curiosity about a woman whose nationality, past, and even real name are unknown (but not her age: she is twenty-six, a year older than he)—and predisposes him to admire Corinne before he sees her. "In England he would have judged such a woman very severely, but in Italy he could ignore social conventions and take an interest in the crowning of Corinne similar to that of an adventure in Ariosto." This love affair begins with a clashing of cultures as well as a clanging of bells.

Music sounds. A parade of Roman and foreign dignitaries marches by. Then come the four white horses which draw the chariot mounted with an antique throne, on which, in a noble attitude, sits Corinne. Young girls dressed in white walk by her side, but Corinne herself is no maiden: she is a mature woman of what we would call solid build. Mme de Staël insists on her beautiful arms and asks us to think of Greek statuary, just as George Eliot does with the "large round arm" of Maggie Tulliver at the time of that heroine's apotheosis:

> . . . the dimpled elbow . . . the varied gently-lessening curves down to the delicate wrist . . . the firm softness. A woman's arm touched the soul of a great sculptor two thousand years ago, so that he wrought an image of it for the Parthenon which moves us still. . . . Maggie's was such an arm as that. . . .

Corinne is robed in white like the Domenichino sibyl, with a blue drapery flowing from her shoulder and an Indian shawl wound round her head and through her beautiful black hair. It is an "extremely picturesque" costume, Mme de Staël points out, "but not so far out of fashion as to be liable to the charge of affectation." For an idea of the style, do not look at the Gérard portrait of Mme de Staël in the garb of Corinne, which is simply too depressing, but instead look at Dorothea Brooke in *Middlemarch* as posed by George Eliot in a museum in Rome—

> standing against a pedestal near the reclining marble; a breathing blooming girl, whose worm, not shamed by the Ariadne, was clad in Quakerish grey drapery; her long cloak, fastened at the neck, was thrown backward from her arms, and one beautiful ungloved hand pillowed her cheek, pushing somewhat backward the white beaver bonnet which made a sort of halo to her face around the simply braided dark-brown hair.

2. French; "Corinne, poet, writer, improvisatrice, and one of the most beautiful persons in Rome."

"Vive Corinne! vive le génie! vive la beauté!"[3] cheers the marvelously responsive Italian crowd: long live genius, long live beauty, long live Corinne. And Oswald loves. Or, to be more precise, he suddenly experiences a transforming shock that runs like a thrill of electrical energy (the image is Mme de Staël's) from this moment to the end of the novel, a shock to his soul and to his cultural prejudices. All Oswald's British respectability, dignity, impassivity, and taciturnity; all his essential religious deference to the sacred idols of *the home*—privacy, discretion, solitude, patriotism, paternal ancestry—are shaken by a threefold experience: Italy, its climate and culture; applause by the masses of spiritual rather than military genius; and the woman of genius. As Mme de Staël puts it, "The admiration of the populace grew ever greater the closer she came to the Capitol, that place so rich in memories. This beautiful sky, these enthusiastic Romans, and above all Corinne herself electrified the imagination of Oswald."

For what Oswald is made to love in Corinne is not the woman in the genius but, if the expression is pardonable, the whole package: the woman of genius at the moment and in the place of her greatest public triumph. It isn't easy, and in fact does not work out very well, but at least it must be said that what Mme de Staël puts at issue is no simple *amour*, but the total transformation of cultural attitudes (and perhaps civilization itself) by the romance of the woman of genius.

At last the procession reaches the Capitol. Senators, cardinal, academicians are seated, as well as a spill-over crowd. Corinne touches her knee to the ground before taking her seat and listening to the speeches and odes recited in her praise. Then she rises to improvise on the theme of "The Glory and the Happiness of Italy"—almost a chapter-length of throbbing prose. It is the first of many such improvisations which are dotted through the novel, and which were rendered into English verse, in the most widely read translation of *Corinne*, by Letitia E. Landon, herself one of Corinne's disciples, known as "L.E.L." and as the author of a poem called "The Improvisatrice."

The final chapter of Book 2 deals with the actual crowning. A senator rises with the laurel wreath. Corinne detaches her turban, letting her ebony curls flow free, and advances her bare head with a smile of undissimulated pleasure on her face: no longer a modest woman, for she has just spoken very well indeed; no longer a fearful woman, but an inspired priestess dedicated to the cult of genius. Music sounds, the crown descends, Corinne's eyes fill with tears—and my own emotions are at this point too strong to permit me to continue with what is almost a literal translation of the passage. I have been following Mme de Staël's scenario very precisely, for the steps in Corinne's triumph were very precisely observed not only by Oswald but by writers after her: first the gossip over-

3. French; "long live Corinne! Long live genius! Long live beauty!"

heard by a skeptical stranger, than the fanfare, then the procession, then the distant view—oh so lovely, so unusual—of the heroine, then the formal praises; only then the actual performance (very difficult for a novelist to make convincing); and at last the crown. Reading this material with a woman's eye makes it hard to keep a straight face; but I am bound to say that *Corinne* is one of very few works by women which is trivialized rather than honored by being read as a woman's work.

What contemporary readers saw in the triumph of Corinne was not the adolescence of Maggie Tullivers to come, but a remarkably courageous celebration of the rights of spiritual genius and intellectual freedom, in defiance of the spreading imperial rule of a military genius named Napoleon. "Corinne is the sovereign independence of genius even at the time of the most absolute oppression," wrote Sainte-Beuve, "Corinne who has herself crowned in Rome, in the Capitol of the eternal city, where the conqueror who exiles her will not set foot." That Napoleon was a man and Mme de Staël a woman was a matter of historical accident, and did not affect the Emperor's decision to exile the author of *Corinne*. That the claim for art over force, for mind over might was made—in somewhat original and Romantic terms—by a woman, and in a woman's novel, was an historical accident with major literary repercussions. But the politicizing of genius, that is, the demonstration of genius by means of public acclamation, by an actual crowning, was Mme de Staël's principal attention, before self-aggrandizement, before feminism, when she wrote Book 2 of *Corinne*.

Literary women, however, dearly wanted that crown: some formal, palpable, public tribute to female genius. The most charming of all Victorian crowning scenes, because the one which most consciously records a young woman's reactions to *Corinne*, is in *Aurora Leigh*. Mrs. Browning's heroine, an aspiring poet, playfully makes herself a poet's crown for her twentieth birthday: not of bay leaves, the classical laurel ("The fates deny us if we are overbold") but of "that headlong ivy! not a leaf will grow/But thinking of a wreath." In the midst of her solitary play-acting, Aurora finds that she is being observed by "My public!—cousin Romney—with a mouth/Twice graver than his eyes."

The very name of poet, for Aurora Leigh, "Is royal, and to sign it like a queen" is what she yearns to but dares not do, for " 't is too easy to go mad/And ape a Bourbon in a crown of straws." These images of crowns, and queens, and even Bourbons traveled across the ocean to the poetry of Emily Dickinson, who revered Mrs. Browning herself as "the Head too High to Crown" and wrote wistfully, in the accents of the girl poet Aurora Leigh,

I'm saying every day
"If I should be a Queen, tomorrow"—
If it be, I wake a Bourbon
None on me, bend supercilious—

George Eliot is always trying to put a golden halo on Dorothea Brooke's head, and, in a different mood, she pins a gold star on Gwendolen Harleth's archery dress in *Daniel Deronda*. She also has a "star of brilliants" descend from the royal box on the brow of Armgart, the prima donna in George Eliot's verse play of that title. When accused of enjoying the "ecstasy" of satisfied ambition, "Why not?" Armgart asks,

> Am I a sage whose word must fall like seed
> Silently buried toward a far-off spring?
> I sing to living men. . . .
>
> . . . If the world brings me gifts,
> Gold, incense, myrrh—'twill be the needful sign
> That I have stirred it as the high year stirs
> Before I sink to winter.

I think it must be said that women writers who have attempted the literary portrait of genius have insisted more than men on showing it off at the moment of public acclaim; and that the literary result is more often raw fantasy than finished art. But the compulsion to write public triumphs, in the nineteenth century, surely resulted from the impossibility of ever having them in real life. The sort of experience that only moderately distinguished women today consider routine—making speeches, chairing meetings, lecturing, arguing in court—was absolutely closed to a Jane Austen, a Brontë, indeed to a Mme de Staël, and was only beginning to be conceivable at the time of a George Eliot or a George Sand. It should not surprise us that women's literature reveals their craving for the *forms* of public recognition, starved for centuries. "Give Thyme or Parsley wreath," Anne Bradstreet had written in her 1960 Prologue; "I ask no Bayes"—but she certainly wanted some kind of wreath.

* * *

# CORA KAPLAN

## [The Right to Write] †

* * *

In the opening of Book 5 of *Aurora Leigh* there is a long discursive section on the poet's vocation where the author dismisses the lyric mode—ballad, pastoral and Barrett Browning's own favourite, the son-

† From *Aurora Leigh and Other Poems* by Elizabeth Barrett Browning, ed. Cora Kaplan (London: The Women's Press, 1978), 8–12. Reprinted by permission of The Women's Press, 34 Great Sutton Street, London EC1V 0DX.

net—as static forms: the poet 'can stand/Like Atlas in the sonnet and support/His own heavens pregnant with dynastic stars;/But then he must stand still, nor take a step.' The move into epic poetry chipped at her reputation in establishment circles, but enhanced her popularity. It was a venture into a male stronghold; epic and dramatic verse are associated with the Classicists and with Shakespeare, Milton, Shelley and Tennyson, and later, Browning. In 1893 the influential critic Edmund Gosse wrote that women have achieved nothing 'in the great solid branches of poetry in epic, in tragedy, in didactic and philosophical verse. . . . The reason is apparently that the artistic nature is not strongly developed in her.' This typical retrospective judgment may be a clue to *Aurora Leigh*'s modern oblivion, and one reason why such an important and diverse poet as Barrett Browning is now known almost exclusively as the author of *Sonnets from the Portuguese* (1850), her brilliant series of love lyrics to her husband. Twentieth-century male poet-critics echo Gosse's belief that women's voice in poetry, as in life, should be confined to the lyric. How can one account then for a sustained narrative poem that is both didactic and philosophical as well as passionate and female, an unmannerly intervention in the 'high' patriarchal discourse of bourgeois culture? *Aurora Leigh* makes few apologies for this rude eruption into the after-dinner subjects that go with the port and cigars. Barrett Browning knew less about 'this live throbbing age,/That brawls, cheats, maddens, calculates, aspires,' than Mrs Gaskell. But it is the latter, in *Mary Barton*, who intervenes with the authorial voice to offer a timid sop to male expertise: 'I am not sure if I can express myself in the technical terms of either masters or workmen. . . .'

The taboo, it is stronger than prejudice, against women's entry into public discourse as speakers or writers, was in grave danger of being definitively broken in the mid-nineteenth century as more and more educated, literate women entered the arena as imaginative writers, social critics and reformers. The oppression of women within the dominant class was in no way as materially brutal as the oppression of women of the working class, but it had its own rationale and articulation. The mid-century saw the development of a liberal 'separate but equal' argument which sometimes tangled with, sometimes included the definition of women's sphere and the development of the cult of true womanhood. The publicity given on the woman question hardly dented the continued elaboration of mores and manners which ensured that daughters were marriageable, i.e. virgins. Patriarchal dominance involved the suppression of women's speech outside the home and a rigorous censorship of what she could read or write. All the major women writers were both vulnerable to and sensitive about charges of 'coarseness'. The Brontë sisters, Sand and Barrett Browning were labelled coarse by their critics, and, occasionally, by other women. Sexual impurity, even in thought, was *the* unforgivable sin, the social lever through which Victorian culture controlled its females, and kept them from an alliance with their looser lived working-class sisters.

The debates on the woman question which took up so many pages of leading British periodicals between 1803 and 1860 should not be seen as marginal to a male-dominated ruling class, increasingly threatened from below by an organising proletariat. Caught between this and the need to accommodate a limited demand for equity from informed women of their own class, they were equally committed to the absolute necessity of maintaining social control over females, and its corollary, the sexual division of labour. To get a sense of the space and importance given to the issue, one only has to leaf through the major quarterlies for a given year. The winter 1857 issue of the *North British Review* had both a substantial review of *Aurora Leigh* and a long review article dealing with eight books, titled 'The Employment of Women', which ranges from an abrupt dismissal of Margaret Fuller's *Woman in the Nineteenth Century* for its romantic obscurity, to a serious discussion of Anna Jameson's *The Communion of Labour*, a work which argued that middle-class women should be 'employed' in ameliorating the condition of the female poor. In support of Mrs Jameson the article quotes both Tennyson's *The Princess* and *Aurora Leigh*.

The right to write was closely connected with every wider choice that women might wish to make. In an age characterised by the importance of the popular press as the place of ideological production and the spread of female literacy, it was of prime importance to warn women off questioning traditional sexual morality. Public writing and public speech, closely allied were both real and symbolic acts of self-determination for women. Barrett Browning uses the phrase 'I write' four times in the first two stanzas of Book I, emphasising the connection between the first person narrative and the 'act' of women's speech; between the expression of woman's feelings and thoughts and the legitimate professional exercise of that expression. Barrett Browning makes the link between women's intervention into political debate and her role as imaginative writer quite clear in her defence of Harriet Beecher Stowe's *Uncle Tom's Cabin*. She rejoices in Stowe's success as 'a woman and a human being' and pushes the message home to her timid female correspondent:

> Oh, and is it possible that you think a woman has no business with questions like the question of slavery? Then she had better use a pen no more. She had better subside into slavery and concubinage herself I think as in the times of old, shut herself up with the Penelopes in the 'women's apartment', and take no rank among thinkers and speakers.

Writing is a skilled task learnt at the expense of 'Long green days/Worn bare of grass and sunshine, - long calm nights/From which the silken sleeps were fretted out . . . with no amateur's/Irreverent haste and busy idleness/I set myself to art!" *Aurora Leigh* enters, however tentatively, into debates on *all* the forbidden subjects. In the first person epic voice of a major poet, it breaks a very specific silence, almost a gentlemen's agreement between women authors and the arbiters of high culture in Victorian England, that allowed women to write if only they would shut up about it.

Barrett Browning makes the condition of the poem's very existence the fact that its protagonist is a woman and a poet. Aurora's biography is a detailed account both of the socialisation of women and the making of a poet. Her rejection of her cousin's proposal is directly related to her sense of her own vocation. Books 3 and 4 are full of the trivia of a young writer's daily life. Book 5, the poem's centrepiece, begins as a long digression on the poet's task. Having established Aurora as artist so firmly in the first half of the poem, she can afford to let Books 6 to 9 take up the narrative line and extend the discussion of female autonomy to her working-class character, Marian Erle, and Marian's scheming opposite, Lady Waldemar. Aurora has a vocation and a recognised status and can be identified by more than her sexual or emotional relationships within the poem. The female voice, simultaneously the author's and Aurora's, speaks with authority on just those questions about politics and high culture from which women were generally excluded. *Aurora Leigh*'s other subject, the relationship between art and political change, is reformulated by the fact that, in the poem, the poet is female and the political reformer male. The poetic and all it stands for in *Aurora Leigh*—inspiration, Christian love, individual expression—becomes feminised as a consequence. The mechanical dogmas of utopian socialism, Romney's 'formulas', are straw theories with little chance against this warm wind. Abstract political discourse yields, at the end of the work, to poetry.

So much we can find in *Aurora Leigh* without situating the poem too precisely in the historical moment of its production. Read in the 1970s, it does at first seem to be, as Ellen Moers has said, '*the* feminist poem', radical in its celebration of the centrality of female experience. In spite of its conventional happy ending it is possible to see it as contributing to a feminist theory of art which argues that women's language, precisely because it has been suppressed by patriarchal societies, re-enters discourse with a shattering revolutionary force, speaking all that is repressed and forbidden in human experience. Certainly Elizabeth Barrett Browning saw herself as part of a submerged literary tradition of female writers. Physically she compared herself to Sappho, 'little and black'; Mme de Staël was her romantic precursor, George Sand her contemporary idol. No woman poet in English after Emily Dickinson and before Sylvia Plath rang such extreme changes on the 'woman's figure', but women's writing, both prose and poetry, is now a rich cultural resource. Its relation to political change in the situation of women is no less problematic for us than it was for Barrett Browning and her contemporaries. We have only to look at the sections of the poem which are crude and alienating, the vicious picture of the rural and urban poor, to see that there are painful contradictions in a liberal feminist position on art or politics.

Both liberal and radical feminism insist that patriarchal domination is *the* problem of human cultures. It tends to ignore or diminish the importance of class conflict, race and the operations of capital, and to make small distinction between the oppressions of middle-class women and working-class or Third World women. The strains in *Aurora Leigh* which prefigure modern radical feminism are not only the heroine's relation to art, but also the way in which Barrett Browning manipulates her working-class figure, Marian Erle. Marian is given the most brutal early history of any figure in the poem—drunken ignorant parents, a mother who 'sells' her to the first male buyer—but she enters the world of our genteel protagonists literate and unsullied. Taken up by Romney as a symbolic cause—his marriage to her is intended as a sort of virtuous miscegenation between the classes—she is betrayed, raped and abandoned in a series of villanies which suggest that sisterhood is a frail concept at best. When Aurora finds and rescues her in Book 7, a genuine alliance of female sympathy is formed between women of different classes who have the added complication of loving the same man.

But this sisterhood is bought in the narrative at the expense of a representation of the poor as a lumpen motley of thieves, drunkards, rapists and childbeaters, except for Marian, whose embourgeoisement in terms of language and understanding occurs at embarrassing speed. Only children (innocents) and prostitutes (exploited by men) escape with full sympathy. What is really missing is any adequate attempt at analysis of the intersecting oppressions of capitalism and patriarchy. Elizabeth Barrett Browning has as her particular political target in the poem the Christian Socialism adapted from Fourier and Owen and practised by F. D. Maurice, Charles Kingsley and others, but since she has no answer to the misery of the poor except her own brand of Christian love—and poetry—her solutions to class conflict are even less adequate than theirs. Inevitably a theory which identifies the radical practice of art with the achievement of radical social change, or asserts the unity of female experience without examining the forms taken by that experience in different social groups, will emerge with a theory of art and politics unconnected with material reality and deeply élitist. This is true of the book read in her time and ours.

*Aurora Leigh* is more than a single text. It is different as it is read and understood at each separate point in history, as it is inserted into historically particular ideological structures. There is a danger in either blaming the poem for its political incoherence by relegating those debates to history or in praising it only for the euphoria with which it ruptures and transforms female language. Works of art should not be attacked because they do not conform to notions of political correctness, but they must be understood in relation to the seductive ideologies and political possibilities both of the times in which they were written and the times in which they are read. Otherwise Barrett Browning's belief that the 'artist's part is both to do and to be' stands in place of, not on behalf of, political transformation.

* * *

# SANDRA GILBERT AND SUSAN GUBAR

## [Reconciling Love and Work] †

* * *Elizabeth Barrett Browning * * * made most of her finest poetry out of her reconciliation to that graceful or passionate self-abnegation which, for a nineteenth-century woman, was necessity's highest virtue. But because she had little natural taste for the drastic asceticism Rossetti's temperament and background seem to have fostered, Barrett Browning ultimately substituted a more familiar Victorian aesthetic of service for the younger woman's somewhat idiosyncratic aesthetic of pain. Her masterpiece, *Aurora Leigh* (1856), develops this aesthetic most fully, though it is also in part an epic of feminist self-affirmation. *Aurora Leigh* is too long to analyze here in the kind of detail we have devoted to "Goblin Market," but it certainly deserves some comment, not only because (as Virginia Woolf reports having discovered to her delight)[1] it is so much better than most of its nonreaders realize, but also because it embodies what may well have been the most reasonable compromise between assertion and submission that a sane and worldly woman poet could achieve in the nineteenth century. Indeed, as we shall see, Emily Dickinson's implicit rejection of Barrett Browning's compromise no doubt indicates just how "made" and unworldly the "myth" of Amherst was.

Briefly, *Aurora Leigh* is a *Künstlerroman* in blank verse about the growth of a woman poet and the education of her heart through pride, sympathy, love, and suffering. Born in Florence to an Englishman and the Italian bride he has been disinherited for marrying, its heroine comes to England as a thirteen-year-old orphan, to be initiated into the torments of feminine gentility by her censorious maiden aunt, an

† From *The Madwoman in the Attic: The Woman Writer and the Nineteenth-Century Literary Imagination* by Sandra Gilbert and Susan Gubar (New Haven: Yale UP, 1979), 575–80. Reprinted by permission of Yale University Press.

1. See Woolf, "Aurora Leigh," in *The Common Reader*. [See pp. 439–46 in this edition—*Editor.*]

ungentle spinster who acts (like so many women in novels by women) as patriarchy's agent in "breeding" young ladies for decorous domesticity. Partly perhaps because of her un-English and therefore unconventional childhood, Aurora refuses to submit to her aunt's strictures; early, studying her dead father's books, she decides to become a poet. When her highminded, politically ambitious cousin Romney Leigh—a sort of reincarnated St. John Rivers—asks her to become his wife and helpmate, she proudly declines his offer, explaining that she has her vocation, too: art, which is at least as necessary as social service.[2]

Here, although the specific polarities of self-developing art and self-abnegating "work" recall the prototypical Victorian polarities Tennyson described in, say, "The Palace of Art," Barrett Browning gives the girl's self-justifying speech a feminist dimension that sets her rejection of Romney into precisely the tradition of rebellious self-affirmation that Jane Eyre so notoriously pioneered when she rejected St. John's marriage proposal. Repudiating Romney's patronizing insinuation that women "play at art as children play at swords,/To show a pretty spirit, chiefly admired/Because true action is impossible," she refuses also his invitation to "love and work with me," to work "for uses, not/For such sleek fringes (do you call them ends,/Still less God's glory?) as we sew ourselves/Upon the velvet of those baldoquins/Held 'twixt us and the sun." As passionately assertive as Jane, she insists that "every creature, female as the male,/Stands single in responsible act and thought . . . [and] I, too, have my vocation,—work to do, . . . Most serious work, most necessary work."[3] At this point in the book, she is "all glittering with the dawn,-dew, all erect" and, in a metaphor Dickinson was later to convert to her own uses, "famished for the noon." For this reason, it seems to her, as with masculine aggressiveness she seeks "empire and much tribute," that it is both contemptible and contemptuous for someone to say "I have some worthy work for thee below./Come, sweep my barns, and keep my hospitals,/And I will pay thee with a current coin/ Which men give women."

Significantly, however, *Aurora Leigh* begins where *Jane Eyre* leaves off. Jane rejects St. John's invitation to a life of self-denying work, and enters instead a self-gratifying earthly paradise about which Brontë is unable to give us many details; but Aurora has a whole career ahead of her, and a career—poetry—whose perils are precisely those dangers of hyperbolic self-aggrandizement associated with the prideful "it" that she revealingly calls "the devil of my youth." Thus where Jane's assertion was the product of a long struggle for identity, Aurora's is the postulate

2. The hint of incest in the courtship of the lovers, together with the striking parallelism of Aurora Leigh's name with the name of Byron's half-sister Augusta Leigh, suggests that Barrett Browning may be simultaneously retelling and "purifying" the legendary story of Byron's shocking romance with Augusta. It has also been suggested that Mrs. Gaskell's *Ruth* was the source for the Marian Erle story.
3. *Aurora Leigh*, pp. 22–27. [See 2.437–38 and 2.455–59 in this edition—*Editor.*]

with which a long renunciation (or repression) or identity must begin. Jane had to learn to be herself. Aurora has to learn not to be herself.

The particular agent of Aurora's education is Marian Erle, a "woman of the people" who functions as a sisterly double, showing her the way to act and suffer, first by loving and serving Romney, and then by (not quite intentionally) sacrificing her virginity for him. Romney is about to marry Marian Erle as a political gesture toward social equality but Marian is persuaded to renounce him by Lady Waldemar, a self-indulgent and "bitchy" aristocrat who is in love with him herself. Packed off to France under the care of one of this "lady's" servants, Marian—in properly Richardsonian fashion—is trapped in a whorehouse, drugged, raped, impregnated, and driven temporarily mad. What Aurora has to learn from all this is, first, sympathy, and then service. Tormented by her belief that Romney (whom she really loves) plans to marry lady Waldemar, Aurora goes to Paris, where she encounters the abused Marian and her illegitimate child. By this time Aurora Leigh is a famous and quite formidable poet. But she quickly decides to make a home in her "motherland" of Florence for Marian and the child, a decision that does seem to strike a happy feminist balance between service and "selfishness." Aurora will continue to write her ambitious poems, yet Marian and her child will be secure.

Watching Marian tend the baby, however, the proud poet has learned more than the pleasures of humility. She has learned to envy that "extremity of love" in which a woman is "self-forgot, cast out of self." At this point, Romney appears in Florence and reveals that he has no intention of marrying Lady Waldemar, and moreover that he has been blinded while attempting to rescue Marian's drunken father from a conflagration that destroyed the Leighs' ancestral mansion. On the surface, therefore, he seems to have metamorphosed from a stonily righteous St. John Rivers to a seductively vulnerable Rochester. Softened by her affection for Marian and chastened by this news,Aurora finally concedes to her Victorian audience that "Art is much; but love is more," especially for a woman.

> Art symbolizes heaven; but love is God
> And makes heaven. I, Aurora, fell from mine,
> I would not be a woman like the rest,
> A simple woman who believes in love,
> And owns the right of love because she loves,
> And, hearing she's beloved, is satisfied
> With what contents God: I must analyze,
> Confront, and question, just as if a fly
> Refused to warm itself in any sun
> Till such was *in leone*. . . .[4]

4. Ibid., p. 173. [See 9.658–67 in this edition—*Editor.*]

The imagery of her confession is significant, suggesting that in her love Aurora is as unlike Jane Eyre as Romney, despite his blindness, is unlike Rochester. For a woman not to love is to "fall" from heaven like Satan or Eve; to love, on the other hand, is to be like a contented fly, basking in the noontide sun without rivalrously seeking to displace it.

Married to blind Romney, Aurora will be both as wife and as artist her husband's helpmeet. She will not so much desire the sun (the way she did when younger) as she will study it, harvest it, benefit from it. "Gaze on, with inscient vision, toward the sun," Romney admonishes her, "And from his visceral heat pluck out the roots of light beyond him," for "Art's a service, mark?/A silver key is given to thy clasp,/And thou shalt stand unwearied, night and day,/And fix it in the hard, slow-turning wards."[5] In other words, the artist, and specifically the woman poet, is neither a glittering and inspired figure nor a passionately self-assertive Jane Eyre. Rather, she is a modest bride of Apollo who labors for her glorious blind master—and for humanity too—in an "unwearied" trance of self-abnegation almost as intense as the silent agony Rossetti's dream queen endured in "From House to Home."

As her name indicates, therefore, Aurora becomes the dawn goddess who ministers to the god Dickinson was to call "the man of noon" by laying "the first foundations" of *his* reconstructed house. As Romney feeds his "blind majestic eyes/Upon the thought of perfect noon," his artist-wife describes the biblical stones of light she sees in the east—jasper, sapphire, chalcedony, amethyst—from which the visionary walls are being built. Like Dorothea ministering to Casaubon, she enacts Milton's daughter's idealized role: the role of dutiful handmaiden to a blind but powerful master. And just as sightless but still severely patriarchal Romney now seems to be half Rochester and half St. John Rivers, she and her author appear to have achieved a perfect compromise between the docility required by Victorian marriage and the energy demanded by poetry. They have redefined the relationship between the poet's "inspiration" and the poet herself so that it reflects the relationship of a Victorian sage and his submissive helpmeet.

At the same time, however, just as George Eliot's allusion to Milton's daughters hints at secret fantasies of rebellion even while ostensibly articulating a patriarchal doctrine of female servitude, Barrett Browning's compromise aesthetic of service conceals (but does not obliterate) Aurora Leigh's revolutionary impulses. For though the chastened Aurora vows to work *for* Romney, the work Barrett Browning imagines her doing is violent and visionary. As if to mute the shock value of her imaginings, Barrett Browning has Romney rather than Aurora describe Aurora's task. Part of this poet's compromise consists in her diplomatic recognition that Victorian readers might be more likely to accept mille-

5. Ibid., p. 177. [See 9.915–18 in this edition—*Editor.*]

narian utterances from a male character. But the millenarian program Romney outlines is not, of course,his own; it is the revolutionary fantasy of his author—and of her heroine, his wife-to-be—discreetly transferred from female to male lips. He himself concedes this point, though he also elaborates upon the tactful notion that a loving Victorian marriage will sanctify even revolution.

> Now press the clarion on thy woman's lip,
> (Love's holy kiss shall still keep consecrate)
> And breathe thy fine keen breath along the brass,
> And blow all class-walls level as Jericho's . . .

he cries, adding, so there should be no mistake about the sweeping nature of his program, that

> . . . the old world waits the time to be renewed,
> Toward which new hearts in individual growth
> Must quicken, and increase to multitude
> In new dynasties of the race of men,
> Developed whence shall grow spontaneously
> New churches, new economies, new laws
> Admitting freedom, new societies
> Excluding falsehood: HE shall make all new.[6]

The fact that a divine patriarch, aided by a human patriarch and his helpmeet, shall "make all new" does not, finally, conceal the more startling fact that all must and shall, in Barrett Browning's scheme, be *made new*.

Emily Dickinson, who wrote that she experienced a "Conversion of the Mind" when she first read "that Foreign Lady" Elizabeth Barrett Browning, must have perceived the Romantic rage for social transformation concealed behind the veil of self-abnegating servitude with which *Aurora Leigh* concludes.[7] She must have noticed, too, that the celestial city Aurora sees in the sunrise at the end of the poem is, after all, Aurora's and not blind Romney's to see, perhaps because it is that shining capital, the *new* Jerusalem. If the "heat and violence" of Aurora Leigh's heart have been tamed, then, at least her dawn-fires have not been entirely extinguished. It is for this reason, no doubt, that Barrett Browning, while looking everywhere for "grandmothers," became herself the grand mother of all modern women poets in England and America. Certainly she was the spiritual mother of Emily Dickinson who, as we shall see, rejected her compromises but was perpetually inspired by the "inscient vision" with which she solved the vexing "problem" of poetry by women.

6. Ibid., p. 178. [See 9.929–32 and 942–49 in this edition—*Editor*.]
7. See *The Poems of Emily Dickinson*, ed. Thomas Johnson (Cambridge, Mass.: The Belknap Press of Harvard University Press, 1955), p. 593, "I think I was enchanted/When first a sombre Girl—/I read that Foreign Lady—/The Dark—felt beautiful—"

# RACHEL BLAU DUPLESSIS

## To "bear my mother's name": *Künstlerromane* by Women Writers†

> No song or poem will bear my mother's name. . . . Perhaps she was herself a poet—though only her daughter's name is signed to the poems that we know.
>
> Alice Walker, "In Search of Our Mothers' Gardens" (1974)

The love plot and *Bildungs* plot are fused in a particular fictional strategy, a figure emerging in a range of narratives from Elizabeth Barrett Browning's *Aurora Leigh* to Margaret Atwood's *Surfacing*. And the central struggle between designated role and meaningful vocation is negotiated by different narrative tactics in nineteenth- and twentieth-century texts. The figure of a female artist encodes the conflict between any empowered woman and the barriers to her achievement.[1] Using the female artist as a literary motif dramatizes and heightens the already-present contradiction in bourgeois ideology between the ideals of striving, improvement, and visible public works, and the feminine version of that formula: passivity, "accomplishments," and invisible private acts.

For bourgeois women, torn between their class values and the subset of values historically affirmed for their gender caste, the figure of the female artist expressed the doubled experience of a dominant ideology that was supposed to be muted in them and that therefore became oppositional for their gender. Making a female character be a "woman of genius" sets in motion not only conventional notions of womanhood but also conventional romantic notions of the genius, the person apart, who, because unique and gifted, could be released from social ties and expectations.[2] Genius theory is a particular exaggeration of bourgeois individualism, and its evocation increases the tension between middle-class women as a special group and the dominant assumptions of their class. Because it is precisely expression and the desire to refuse silence that are at issue in artistic creation, the contradiction between dominant and muted areas can also be played out in the motif of the imbedded artwork, another narrative marker of these *Künstlerromane*.

† From *Writing Beyond the Ending: Narrative Strategies of Twentieth-Century Women Writers* by Rachel Blau DuPlessis (Bloomington: Indiana University Press, 1985), 84–87.  Line references to this Norton Critical Edition of *Aurora Leigh* have been added in brackets.

1. A note on terminology. "Female artist" will refer only to the fictional figure; the person who invented the narrative is a woman writer. "Art work" will mean the imaginary text, painting, or performance described, the production of the female artist.
2. Janet Wolff, *The Social Production of Art* (London: Macmillan Press, Ltd., 1981), p. 27.

*Aurora Leigh* (1856) by Elizabeth Barrett Browning is the mid-century text of an emergent ideological formation, as, *Ruth Hall* (1855), a sweet American book, is that of dominant sentiments. *Aurora Leigh* is a booklength narrative poem about the fusing of artist and woman, and the testing of values surrounding class and spiritual vision.[3] In the final moments of this work, the artist Aurora accepts her suitor in marriage, having discovered that all her notable successes are compromised without affection.

> Passioned to exalt
> The artist's instinct in me at the cost
> Of putting down the woman's, I forgot
> No perfect artist is developed here
> From any imperfect woman.
> (*AL* 380) [9.645–59]

Aurora's expostulation of Love's primacy at the end of the work ("Art is much, but love is more./O Art, my Art, thou'rt much, but Love is more!" *AL*, 381) [9.656–57] is well separated from the even more powerful statements of her allegiance to art and her meditations on craft, in Books 2 and 5, which describe the upsurge of her passionate inspiration as the "lava-lymph" (*AL*, 195) [5.3].

> Never flinch,
> But still, unscrupulously epic, catch
> Upon the burning lava of a song
> The full-veined, heaving, double-breasted Age:
> That, when the next shall come, the men of that
> May touch the impress with reverent hand, and say
> "Behold,—behold the paps we all have sucked!"
> (*AL*, 201–202) [5.213–19]

*Aurora Leigh* is irrepressibly rich in imagery of volcanoes and breasts, of maternal power to nourish; and by evoking the physical female, the poem claims both biological and cultural authority to speak.

Heterosexual love may have moral and ideological primacy in *Aurora Leigh*, as articulated at the end, but vocation, itself bound with maternal bliss and the power of love/hate relations among women, has textual primacy. Vocation, asserted early and often, is, moreover, stated in the critical context of a beady-eyed analysis of female education for domesticity, acquiesence, and superficiality. Aurora's choice of vocation is made against the will of her closest relatives, including Romney. She asserts female right to a profession not because of financial exigency or family crisis, but out of sheer desire and for the sake of sheer power. Her

3. Elizabeth Barrett Browning, *Aurora Leigh and Other Poems*, introduced by Cora Kaplan (London: The Woman's Press, Ltd., 1978; hence forth *AL*).

ecstatic commitment to the vocation of poet and her achievement tend to make valid the ideology of striving and success that she embodies, joining that set of values to female possibility.

Between the beginning and the end, Romney and Aurora have exchanged roles, in a chaistic move that tends to make their marriage somewhat credible, despite the plot mechanism that has him involved with three women, representing three social classes and three female types. Aurora has seen the centrality of love, he the vitality of her art. While he had, in Book 2, been the fountainhead of smugly discouraging statements about women as artists ("We get no Christ from you,—and verily/We shall not get a poet, in my mind," *AL*, 81) [2.224–25], at the end he comes to recognize that her achievement was more vital than his in inducing the conversion experiences that are the real boot of any social change. This readjustment takes shape in a distinct and punitive shock to his views. For Romney, like an escapee from *Jane Eyre*, is first rejected, like St. John Rivers, and then, like Rochester, blinded. This wounding of male heroes is, according to Elaine Showalter, a symbolic way of making them experience the passivity, dependency, and powerlessness associated with women's experiences of gender.[4] And, as in Brontë's *Shirley*, the rebellious lower orders express, in unacceptable form, the rancor and hostility of all the powerless, women included. For Romney's blindness is direct punishment for his political theories. A mean-spirited, animalistic rebellion causes the accident that blinds him. The poor have been so brutalized that their souls are nasty, unawakened, unspiritual; their true awakening will be brought about only by poetry and God, not by politics.

Because he can no longer continue these handicapped reformist activities, the private sphere of love and the cosmic sphere of religion become the world in which all his needs can—must—be satisfied. So the man is made to live in the "separate sphere," in the feminine culture of love and God. The creation of Romney's short-fall, his "castration" by the malicious verve of the unwashed masses, creates a power vacuum where the upper-class or upper-middle-class hero used to be. Aurora is then available to claim both masculine and feminine rewards—the hero's reward of success and the heroine's reward of marriage—in a rescripting of nineteenth-century motifs that joins romantic love to the public sphere of vocation.

> Shine out for two, Aurora, and fulfil
> My falling-short that must be! work for two,
> As I, though thus restrained, for two, shall love!
> (*Al*, 389) [9.910–12]

4. Elaine Showalter, *A Literature of Their Own: British Women Novelists from Brontë to Lessing* (Princeton, N.J.: Princeton University Press, 1977), p. 152.

Since Aurora had offered to sacrifice and to be used (*AL*, 381) [9.674–79], what more aggrandizing way to fulfill her desire for abasement than to demand that she do twice as often and twice as intensely what she has already proven she can do very well. Being an artist is, at the end, reinterpreted as self-sacrifice for the woman, and thus is aligned with feminine ideology. This work, then, created a powerful reference point, but it did not change the nineteenth-century convention of representation that saw the price of artistic ambition as the loss of femininity.

Most of the nineteenth-century works with female artists as heroes observe the pieties, putting their final emphasis on the woman, not the genius; the narratives are lacerated with conflicts between femininity and ambition. There are works in which the only reason for an artistic vocation is the utterly desperate and melodramatic destitution of the main character—say a widow with young children, cast out from her sanctimonious, petty family. Such is the case with Fanny Fern's *Ruth Hall: A Domestic Tale of the Present Time*, published (in America) a year before *Aurora Leigh*. In this work, when a child asks, "When I get to be a woman shall I write books, Momma?" the proper answer is clearly Ruth's "God forbid . . . no happy woman ever writes. From Harry's grave sprang Floy [her pen name]."[5] This statement may be taken as the mid-century base line of attitudes, in which a woman's entry into public discourse elicits a shudder of self-disgust and is allowable only if it is undertaken in mourning and domesticity.

* * *

# SUSAN STANFORD FRIEDMAN

## Gender and Genre Anxiety: Elizabeth Barrett Browning and H. D. as Epic Poets †

* * *

The underlying parallels that exist beneath surface difference in the processes by which Barrett Browning and H. D. feminized epic convention exist as well in the deep structures of *Aurora Leigh* and *Helen in Egypt*. On the surface, the two epic narratives are radically different—in ways that often reflect the contrasts between Victorian and modernist fiction. *Aurora Leigh* charts the development of a woman artist in the

5. Fanny Fern [Mrs. Sarah Payson (Willis) Parton], *Ruth Hall: A Domestic Tale of the Present Time* (New York: Mason Brothers, 1985), p. 333.

† Reprinted by permission from *Tulsa Studies in Women's Literature* 5, no. 2 (Fall 1986): 217–23. The author's notes have been deleted. Page and line references to this Norton Critical Edition of *Aurora Leigh* have been added in brackets.

particularities of Victorian social, economic, and political construction. Set in historical time and place, the narrative is chronologically sequential and linear. Aurora's story begins with her childhood in Florence and moves logically through the stages of her growth as a woman and artist. As in the conventional *Bildungsroman*, each point in her development is an initiation that poses a solution to the problem of the moment, only to become a dilemma itself in the next book. This dialectical process stops in the final celebration of a marriage based in work and love. In contrast, *Helen in Egypt* presents mythic tableaux of woman's confinement and transcendence in the generalities of culture itself. As a visionary saga, *Helen in Egypt* is set in mythic time. Space and time, reality and causality, are never established definitively. Helen and Achilles may be dead or alive, in time or out of time. Greece, Egypt, Leuké and Troy are places, but they identify a state of mind, not a locale in history. The stages of self-discovery follow not a pattern of events, but rather the associational patterns of the mind—from the conscious to the unconscious, from the analytic to the synthetic, from the present to the past and future, from the intellectual to the visionary. Modeled on the interpretive patterns of psychoanalysis, *Helen in Egypt* centers not on events, but in reflections on events. Its narrative is layered, timeless, and circular as Helen's consciousness weaves a meditative web of memories and reflections.

At a deeper level of narrative structure, however, *Aurora Leigh* and *Helen in Egypt* share major elements that demonstrate the impact of genre feminization. First, both Barrett Browning and H. D. reversed the conventions of the epic by moving woman from the symbolic margins of the epic to its very center of action. This centrality of women was commonplace in the novel, but the transformation of woman from Being to Doing, from object to subject was a radical re-vision of epic convention. As a consequence of having a woman serve as the center of consciousness, the heroic was redefined in female terms, while the personal was made public. This change is particularly evident in H. D.'s text because her epic rewrites Homer's *Iliad*. Her choice of Helen as hero directly confronts the denial of power and speech to women, not only in the conventional epic, but also in patriarchal culture in general. Helen has been man's creation, the image he worshipped as the epitome of beauty and condemned as the source of evil. No longer the projection of man's fantasy, H. D.'s Helen names her own identity and explores the meaning of her destiny.

Barrett Browning's and H. D.'s re-visions of the heroic highlight the second structural parallel in their epics. The scene of action and the fundamental conflict that impels the narrative is not the public domain of the conventional epic, but the private domain of both the lyric and the women's novel of development. Both Aurora and Helen face a dilemma of desire against a backdrop of differently delineated patriarchal cultures: the simultaneous need for both relationship and independence in a world that makes these mutually exclusive for women—a conflict central in *Sonnets from the Portuguese* and H. D.'s own novels. Aurora confronts the nineteenth-century division of woman into man's helpmeet and man's whore, as well as the prescriptions of feminine dependence in the economic, political, social, and artistic spheres. Helen learns that women in the Mycenaean world exist as man's booty, man's possession, man's symbol of desire or disgust. Both Aurora's and Helen's quest for autonomous identity and love involves their denial or patriarchal representations and their search for a heterosexual relationship within which they can function as whole human beings—linguistically, emotionally, spiritually and sexually.

Rebellion fundamentally fuels the narrative of both epics as the necessary precondition for love and autonomy. The symbolic scene of defiance for Aurora and Helen is an interaction with a man who simultaneously epitomizes patriarchy and desire. The *Kunstler* narrative of *Aurora Leigh* centers on the conflict between Aurora's artistic ambitions and her love for Romney, a love so threatening to her desire for autonomy that she remains unaware of it until the Seventh Book of the epic (224) [see p. 216]. Romney's first proposal of marriage in the Second Book collapses multiple dimensions of nineteenth-century patriarchy. He attacks her poetry as irrelevant and feminine, by nature without genius or serious purpose. He offers marriage as woman's only route to fulfillment; absorbed in his work and being, her life will achieve significance (41–51) [see pp. 40–51]. Breaking the conventional marriage plot of the novel, Aurora summarily refuses, declaring " 'You misconceive the question like a man,/Who sees a woman as the complement/Of his sex merely. You forget too much/That every creature, female as the male,/Stands single in responsible act and thought/. . . . /I, too, have my vocation,—work to do' " (51–52) [*Aurora Leigh* 2.434–55].

Aurora's resounding feminist refusal makes possible her success as an artist, but the development of her aesthetics is at odds with the choice between life and art that she was forced to make. At the pinnacle of success and loneliness in the Fifth Book, Aurora realizes that being a poet has cut her off from love, indeed from the very feeling that she has determined to be the lifeblood of living art. To be a poet who expresses the "burning lava of a song," she must be in touch with "true life," love and feeling. But to be a poet, she must renounce her womanhood, a denial of the female body symbolized by her choice of an ivy crown in place of flowers and by the disappearance of the "rose" from her cheeks (38–39, 86) [see pp. 39–40, 81].

Helen's conflict with patriarchy is embodied in her hieroglyphic meeting with Achilles on the shores of Egypt where she believes Zeus has placed her for the duration of the Trojan War. Having repressed all memory of her love for Paris and her presence at Troy, Helen is shocked by Achilles' hatred and terrified by his violence as he turns to attack her. But when she calls out his mother's name, his hate becomes love, his violence becomes worship (1–16).[1] As the repressed memories come flooding back, Helen realizes that she is indeed innocent of evil, but innocent in a different sense from the patriarchal defenses of Steisischorus and Euripides, who told of how Zeus sent a phantom Helen to Troy and kept the chaste wife in Egypt. She builds her "pallinode," her song against culture, on the archetypal confrontation between matriarchal and patriarchal values. She incarnates the power of Eros, while Achilles embodies the force of Thanatos. Helen's search for identity involves her meditations on how that archetypal meeting serves as paradigm for her life, the history of war, and "all myth, the one reality" (155). But like Aurora, Helen discovers that her initial solution to the impositions of patriarchy leads her into a loveless trap. Her vision of polarized patriarchal and matriarchal worlds does not explain how Achilles' hate became love, how her own powerlessness and fear became potency and love. Helen's quest cannot end with the discovery of and rebellion against patriarchy. Rather, this discovery is the precondition for quest.

The patriarchal dualisms of *Helen in Egypt* and *Aurora Leigh* are different, but both epics pose dichotomies tied to the intersections of heterosexual love and patriarchy, divisions that the hero seeks to transcend. As a third structural parallel, the major male character in both epics undergoes a transformation that is essential to the resolution of heterosexual conflict. Achilles and Romney do not occupy center stage in the narrative. But unlike most women in male epics, these men are not peripheral and state temptors, rewards, or symbols. Instead, Achilles and Romney develop along lines that parallel Helen and Aurora. Both men face the same patriarchal dualisms that constrict Aurora and Helen, though they face these dualisms from a position of male privilege. Their growing awareness of how these divisions destroy their humanity takes place offstage, by implication, but their abandonment of the traditional masculine ethos is essential to the narrative. Romney's first loveless proposal of marriage to Aurora represents the primacy of work over love as well as his belief that woman's place is at her husband's side, doing his work and will. His offer to marry the impoverished Marian Earle repeats his oppressive stance toward women, and she, like Aurora, refuses to be so used. Only when Romney learns to love Aurora for herself, which includes her poetry, can he approach her again. But even this change is insufficient until his blinding in the Ninth Book dissolves his masculine privilege by forcing him to become dependent on Aurora. Echoing Rochester's blinding in *Jane Eyre,* Romney's blindness represents a symbolic castration of his former patriarchal authority

1. Page references for H. D. are from *Helen in Egypt* (1961; reprinted New York: New Directions, 1974) [*Editor*].

and signals his transformation into a human being capable of love and work in an equitable relationship.

Achilles too must undergo fundamental change before he is ready for his marriage to Helen on Leuké. As the world leader of the masculine iron-ring of war, Achilles the victimizer must become the victim. "Love's arrow" pierces his vulnerable ankle, which he forgot to protect as he stared entranced at Helen upon the ramparts. This moment of "La Mort, L'Amour" brings about his symbolic "castration" and transformation. When the limping shade of Achilles meets Helen on the sands of Egypt, he becomes "the new Mortal/shedding his glory" (10). In reliving the past with Helen, he says, " 'I can see you still, a mist/or a fountain of water/in that desert; we died of thirst' " (48). His recognition of masculine inadequacy and Helen's incarnation of Isis initiates his own quest. He goes off to Leuké by himself to search for the Thetis within, the mother or feminine self that he repressed when he became a warrior. With the eidolon of Thetis restored to consciousness, he is ready to wed Helen and father their androgynous child Euphorion in the final books of the epic. Like Romney, Achilles ultimately renounced his male privilege and reabsorbed into his conscious self the capacity for love traditionally projected onto woman.

Although the abandonment of masculine privilege is essential and the resolution of heterosexual conflict is symbolized by a marriage, the narrative focus in both epics remains on the development of the women. As the fourth structural parallel, this development unfolds within the context of women's relationships with other women. While Helen and Aurora stimulate the offstage transformation of Achilles and Romney, sister and mother figures provide the occasion for the growth in Helen and Aurora. Aurora's despair at resolving the double bind of the woman writer leads her at the end of the Fifth Book to sell her books (her father's legacy of words) and head for the hills of her mother's Florence, "my Italy/My own hills" (197–98) [*Aurora Leigh* 5.1266–67]. The abandonment of her father's England for her mother's Italy signals Aurora's readiness to confront the meaning of her womanhood, which she has associated with her mother, wordlessness, and the lush green body of nature. As an aspiring writer, Aurora had to disobey the only words she remembers her mother saying: " 'Hush, hush—here's too much noise!' " (1) [*Aurora Leigh* 1.17]. Barbara Gelpi has shown how the child's ambivalence toward her dead mother's portrait—she sees her mother as both angel and witch, Muse and Medusa—prefigures the adult poet's ambivalence toward her sex. Not until that ambivalence is resolved can Aurora become the poet of living art or the woman whose life balances love and work. As Gelpi points out, the agent of Aurora's transformation is Marian, the "fallen woman" raped into unwedded motherhood, the woman whose entrapment serves as a paradigm of women's oppression, the woman whose presence in the epic most deeply offended Barrett Browning's contemporary readers.[2] On her way to Florence, Aurora discovers Marian in the Parisian "Market-place of Flowers," from which she silently leads the lonely poet back to her baby:

> Then she led
> The way, and I, as by a narrow plank
> Across devouring waters, followed her,
> Stepping by her footsteps, breathing by her breath,
> And holding her with eyes that would not slip;
> And so, without a word, we walked a mile,
> And so, another mile, without a word.
> (214) [*Aurora Leigh* 6.500–506]

Bonded wordlessly and scopically together, Aurora and Marian symbolically cross the treacherous waters to the meaning of motherhood itself. Their journey ends in Marian's tiny hovel where the stunned Aurora watches Marian fuse in love with her infant who is "hot and scarlet as the first live rose" (216) [*Aurora Leigh* 6.572]. The communion between mother and child is silent, wordless, a "reading" of eyes, which contrasts with Aurora's own poetic mastery of words. Lyrical imagery of flowers, birds, and the natural world beyond culture tie Marian to Aurora's mother, a symbolism especially evident in Aurora's suggestion that they go live in Florence, "two mothers" to the babe. Aurora's enchantment with Marian does not have to be read as her capitulation to conventional Victorian motherhood. Instead, her bond with mother and child signifies her own journey back to the maternal body, the female body symbolized by the rose. The restoration of a regenerative bond with her own mother awakens the feeling, sexual self she had renounced in her attempt to escape patriarchal definition. Her love for Marian, with its acceptance of motherhood itself, represents her acceptance of her own womanhood. Restored to what she had feared, she could work to combine the worldless with the word, nature and culture, feeling and intellect, selflessness and self. Her interaction with Marion allows her to realize that she has all along deeply loved Romney, an awareness that sets in motion the *dénouement* of the epic.

The significance of the mother as symbol of love, sexuality; and the female body in the narrative structure of the epic is evident in the fact that Barrett Browning's otherwise linear narrative ends where it began: in Florence, the geographic representation of the maternal body. This structural circularity centered in the mother as the site (sight, cite) of desire anticipates some contemporary feminist writers who see the text of feminine writing as the inscription of pre-oedipal desire for the maternal body.

Like Aurora, Helen must return to the mother as the embodiment of

2. Barbara Charlesworth Gelpi, "*Aurora Leigh*: The Vocation of a Woman Poet," *Victorian Poetry* 19 (Spring 1981): 36–39 and 44–45 [*Editor*].

desire. Although the mythological setting is utterly different, Helen's transformation similarly requires that she come to terms with the womanhood so denigrated by patriarchy. Hated as the Greek Eve, Helen must redefine Eros as the source of life instead of death. The women "characters" who exist in Helen's reflections and visions are the agents of change that lead her to abandon the guilt-ridden image of "hated Helen" and accept herself as the incarnation of the matriarchal Goddess. Her memories of her twin Clytaemnestra begin the revisionary process. Instead of seeing the murder of Agamemnon as proof of female treachery, Helen understands that her sister had "the wings of an angry swan," attacking the war-lords who had taken her daughter Iphigenia for sacrifice on the pretext of a marriage so the ships could sail to Troy (76). Clytaemnestra's act was a rebellion against the prior wrongs of the patriarchal "High Command." Clytaemnestra served for Helen as sister, mother figure, and alter ego, as did Marian for Aurora, although Clytaemnestra's violence contrasts with Marian's selfless devotion.

Standing behind both women is the mother-symbol, the power and powerlessness of the procreative woman to which both Helen and Aurora had to return without ambivalence. For Helen, this confrontation with the Mother comes in the form of her gradual identification with the three phases of the Mother Goddess—the white, the red, and the black, or Aphrodite, Isis, and Koré. Adapting Robert Graves's *The White Goddess*, H. D. has Helen learn to see her various selves not as evil fragments, but as embodiments of different aspects of the matriarchal Goddess: Helen in springtime love with Paris in Troy was Aphrodite; Helen in summer passion with Achilles in Egypt was Thetis and Isis, the mothers of Achilles and Horus; Helen in Leuké with Achilles was Koré, the goddess of death and divination. This healing identification with the Goddess in her sexual, procreative, and priestly forms allows Helen finally to approach Achilles without shame, her womanhood redefined. Like Aurora, Helen accomplishes a re-vision of her own womanhood through her relationships with women, a form of female bonding that readies her for a heterosexual relationship in which she will not be destroyed.

In conclusion, the significant differences between *Aurora Leigh* and *Helen in Egypt* do not invalidate the concept of a distinct woman's epic, tied more closely to the forms and themes of a female literary tradition than to the male epic tradition. These differences reflect the importance of contemporary literary conventions for each author, but far more significant are the parallels in the genesis and structure of the two epics. Both Barrett Browning and H. D. recognized the implicit maleness of the epic tradition, shared a resulting gender-related anxiety of genre, and formulated a concept of the epic that relied heavily on the tradition of the novel and the lyric. Both epics consequently encoded their authors' rejection of male epic models and promoted a hybrid form that fused the epic, the novel, and the lyric. Additionally, the narratives of both epics are profoundly different from the male epic tradition, most fundamentally because their common structure poses an essential critique of patriarchy. Rather than create epics that reify patriarchal culture, Barrett Browning and H. D. wrote epics that explored their conflict with that culture and evidenced their poetic attempt to transform it. *Aurora Leigh* and *Helen in Egypt* represent a deconstruction of the binary gender system underlying poetic genres, norms personified by Homer as the father of the epic and Sappho as the mother of the lyric. Replacing the father with the mother, Barrett Browning and H. D. brought the discourse of the personal and the marginal into the genre of the public and the patriarch.

## ANGELA LEIGHTON

## ' "Come with me, sweetest sister" ': The Poet's Last Quest †

> Nay, if there's room for poets in this world
> A little overgrown (I think there is),
> Their sole work is to represent the age,
> Their age, not Charlemagne's,—this live, throbbing age,
> That brawls, cheats, maddens, calculates, aspires,
> And spends more passion, more heroic heat,
> Betwixt the mirrors of its drawing-rooms,
> Than Roland with his knights at Roncesvalles.
>
> (5.200–7)

In *Aurora Leigh* Barrett Browning superimposes on the imagination's private quest and elegy for the dead, a public manifesto for poetry. Poets, she declares, must reject the past, and embrace instead the unglamorous domestic realities of the age. This message of commitment to the contemporary world is one which she promulgates with enthusiasm, but which is not fulfilled in practice until Aurora rejects her own personal past, and embraces the loneliness of her 'orphaned' state. Thus the theory of imaginative contemporaneity, which is Barrett Browning's distinctive and powerful poetic creed, is linked to Aurora's eventual rejection of the quest for her dead father. The woman's poetic theory is tested on the pulses of the daughter. It is only by being dispossessed of the imagination's sense of 'the Dead' that this woman poet finally succeeds in realising her own poetics of contemporary commitment. The landscapes of *Aurora Leigh* are those which were feared and predicted

† Reprinted by permission from *Elizabeth Barrett Browning* by Angela Leighton (Brighton: Harvester, 1986), 140–57.

in *Casa Guidi Windows*. They are the bare and ordinary 'plains' of the present, from where it is no longer possible to 'look back to the hills behind'.

In *Aurora Leigh*, Barrett Browning thus rejects the temptation to retreat into a more heroic past, and repeatedly declares her intention to search the spirit of the age at its most secular and urbane. Perhaps the very seclusion of her adult life before marriage made her appreciate the age and the world outside all the more vividly. 'Denial of access to the Real made it fascinating to women,'[1] writes Ellen Moers. Once free in the real world of travel and political conflict, Barrett Browning's imagination had to make up for long years of deprivation. Yet, as early as 1845 she had stated her poetic principles to Robert, with touching optimism, from her invalid's seclusion: 'Let us all aspire rather to *Life* . . . For there is poetry *everywhere*'. *Aurora Leigh* is the witness of how far that '*everywhere*' was to be enlarged for her during the next ten years.

*Aurora Leigh* does not succeed in being a consistently great poem, but it does succeed in being a new kind of poem, and of communicating the message of its newness. The passionate, garrulous, hectoring, inspired Aurora discourses on the world before her with the conviction of an imaginative discovery. It is this sense of mission towards the times which probably inspired the enthusiasm with which the work was received, particularly by other writers and poets. George Eliot read it at least three times, and wrote of her strong 'sense of communion'[2] with the author. Swinburne, Leigh Hunt, Landor, Ruskin, Robert Lytton and Dante Gabriel Rossetti all praised it generously, and stinted no comparison with the works of the greatest poets.[3] It seems that *Aurora Leigh* offered a theory and practice of imaginative contemporariness which precisely answered the needs of the age.

However, the poem confronts the contemporary world, 'this live, throbbing age', from the express point of view of a woman. This bias is overt and stressed. As a result, the work is one of the most outspoken pieces of 'feminist' imaginative writing in the mid-nineteenth century. Barrett Browning was delighted to hear of the small scandals it provoked: that a lady of sixty, for instance, felt morally corrupted by it, and that the 'mammas of England'[4] had forbidden their daughters to read it. In fact, she exaggerates the public outcry which greeted the work's publication; but her pleasure in stirring up a scandal is evident. In one of her letters she assesses the reasons for this public disapprobation:

> What has given most offence in the book, more than the story of Marian—far more!—has been the reference to the condition of

1. Ellen Moers, *Literary Women* (London, The Women's Press, 1978), p. 83.
2. *The George Eliot Letters*, 2.342.
3. See Gardner B. Taplin, *The Life of Elizabeth Barrett Browning* (London, John Murray, 1957), pp. 310–11.
4. Ibid., p. 312.

> women in our cities, which a woman oughtn't to refer to, by any manner of means, says the conventional tradition. Now I have thought deeply otherwise. If a woman ignores these wrongs, then may woman as a sex continue to suffer them; there is no help for any of us—let us be dumb and die.

In fact, there are few outspoken references to 'the condition of women in our cities' in *Aurora Leigh*, and those few *are* connected with 'the story of Marian', who is tricked into a brothel where she is drugged and raped. It is she who provides the link with the other 'women in our cities', and who justifies the author's intention to refer to them.

However, the real 'feminist' provocation of *Aurora Leigh* is not the fact of an occasional chance reference to prostitution, but the attitude of the speaker towards the subject. In Book 6, Marian Erle's description of her experience in the brothel ends by exactly paralleling the point in the letter. She declares:

> 'Enough so!—it is plain enough so. True,
> We wretches cannot tell out all our wrong
> Without offence to decent happy folk.
> I know that we must scrupulously hint
> With half-words, delicate reserves, the thing
> Which no one scrupled we should feel in full.'
> (6.1219–24)

Instead of apologising for what she must say, Marian turns the accusation against those who forbid a woman to mention these things. She forcefully refuses to court either sympathy or forgiveness, and instead lays the blame at the feet of 'decent happy folk' who are nice with words, but are unaffronted by the facts. It is this declared intention to break the verbal taboos of the age which characterises Barrett Browning's references to prostitution, and which probably gave offence to the Victorian public. The triple female speaker of this poem—Barrett Browning, Aurora and Marian—is a sure and unsubtle ruse by which to break 'the conventional tradition' that 'a woman oughtn't to refer to' these things.

Barrett Browning's portrayal of Marian Erle is to some extent indebted to Mrs Gaskell's *Ruth*, which she read in 1853, and of which she wrote enthusiastically and complicitously to its author: 'I am grateful to you as a woman for having so treated such a subject'.[5] But Barrett Browning's own treatment of the 'subject' of the fallen woman differs significantly from her predecessor's. Unlike Mrs Gaskell, she is not concerned to gain a Christian forgiveness for her heroine, but rather to expose the absurdity of a culture in which virtue is an affair of words, not deeds. It is the conspiracy of silence among the 'decent happy folk', especially among the women, which she would break by writing. Such silence permits the

5. *Letters Addressed to Mrs Gaskell by Celebrated Contemporaries*, ed. Ross D. Waller (Manchester, Manchester University Press, 1935), p. 42.

very evils which it will not name, and thus is ultimately responsible, as Lady Waldemar is believed responsible in the story, for the sexual exploitation of other women. 'If a woman ignores these wrongs, then may women as a sex continue to suffer them,' Barrett Browning declared. Her responsibility as a poet is towards those other women whom silence has victimised. Marian's experience of being drugged and raped is one which the age refuses to hear, and especially refuses to hear from the lips of a woman. Not only, therefore, does Barrett Browning provocatively assume the moral and political right to speak, but she also accuses the guardians of decency and delicacy of being themselves corrupt. To be 'dumb', she claims, is to assent to suffering. If women in particular are 'dumb', as men would have them, they assent to their own suffering as a sex. The political motive of simply speaking out, of refusing to 'be dumb and die', is one which, in *Aurora Leigh*, Barrett Browning outrageously flaunts.

This subversive attitude to the codes of verbal propriety enforced on women is evident in much of Barrett Browning's work. In 1861, the year of her death, she submitted a poem, 'Lord Walter's Wife', to the *Cornhill Magazine*, which was then edited by Thackeray. To her surprise—but also to her glee—it was rejected for being morally unsuitable. 'Thackeray has turned me out of the "Cornhill" for indecency', she reported, with barely disguised pride. The poem criticises that attitude of men which claims the prerogative to flirt, even with a married woman, but is quick to condemn the very same woman if she responds. It is not only the double standard which is under attack, but also the insulting assumption that the woman's role is to listen in passive and unreciprocating silence to the man's amorous declarations. ' "You take us for harlots, I tell you, and not for the women we are",'[6] Lord Walters's wife responds indignantly.

To Thackeray himself, Barrett Browning wrote a forceful vindication of her intentions in the poem:

> I don't like coarse subjects, or the coarse treatment of any subject. But I am deeply convinced that the corruption of our society requires not shut doors and windows, but light and air: and that it is exactly because pure and prosperous women choose to *ignore* vice, that miserable women suffer wrong by it everywhere. Has paterfamilias, with his Oriental traditions and veiled female faces, very successfully dealt with a certain class of evil? What if materfamilias, with her quick sure instincts and honest innocent eyes, do more towards their expulsion by simply looking at them and calling them by their names?

The passage reveals how quickly the Victorian mind moves from the idea of a mildly adulterous flirtation to the idea of the fallen woman.

6. Elizabeth Barrett Browning, 'Lord Walter's Wife,' in *Complete Works*, 6.9–14.

Barrett Browning has written a poem about flirtation, but she defends it as if it were about prostitution. Her language then seems to tread a very fine line between moral condemnation and political justification. The 'pure', her language tells, are likely to be also the 'prosperous', while 'vice' is something by which 'miserable women suffer wrong'. She keeps a strong moral perspective while subtly implying not only that 'vice' is an oppression laid upon the poor, but that it is also the direct result of the chosen ignorance of the 'pure and prosperous'. The blame returns to the door of sheltered, wealthy women.

But it also returns against men. The simile of the harem is a powerful and wrathful one. The fathers' way of dealing with these things is to keep the women hushed and veiled, and thus, from enforced sexual modesty, impotent to change the system in which they too are trapped. The modesty of the wives of 'paterfamilias' is a blindfold which forbids them to see their own situation as well. It is time, Barrett Browning claims, that women took off their veils and used their eyes. By 'simply looking at them and calling them by their names', women might rid society of the vices of which they are all victims. This statement is characteristic in that it does not range Madonnas against Magdalens, pure women against fallen women; it ranges them all against men, against 'paterfamilias'. Whether veiled or unveiled, women's lot is that of the harem. Both the exaggerated modesty of the 'pure and prosperous' and the exploited immodesty of the 'miserable' serve to perpetuate the sexual rule of men.

It is this radical liaison between women, who are united in the purpose of speaking out, which characterises *Aurora Leigh*. It is true, as Cora Kaplan writes, that Marian Erle's 'embourgeoisement in terms of language and understanding occurs at embarrassing speed.'[7] The characterisation of *Aurora Leigh* is, indeed, often extremist and unconvincing. However, in some ways the figure of Marian represents a significant advance in the literature of the fallen woman. While Hester Prynne, Hetty Sorrel and Ruth are all to some extent made an exception, and 'pardoned for sexual activity' because they 'love',[8] Marian is simply raped in a brothel. She is thus linked with the other unmentionable women who, for whatever reason, have also been tricked into a brothel. The fact of the rape makes Marian, not an individual exception to the rule of vice, but an example for a general cause. She is only one of the 'miserable women' who 'suffer wrong . . . everywhere'. Barrett Browning then contests the whole Victorian myth of contamination by bringing Marian out of the brothel to live with her unsullied heroine,[9] not because Aurora must learn Christian charity, but because, as a woman,

7. Cora Kaplan, Introduction to *Aurora Leigh* (London, The Women's Press, 1983), p. 12.
8. Kate Millett, *Sexual Politics* (1969; London, Virago, 1977), p. 37.
9. Nina Auerbach, *Woman and the Demon: The Life of a Victorian Myth* (Cambridge, Mass., Harvard University Press, 1982), p. 151.

she must write about such things. The relation between Aurora and Marian constitutes an ideological league of women defying, both in practice and in word, the divisions of their society.

Marian's description of her rape may be in one sense an improbably articulate account. But in another sense that very confidence of speech makes a powerful political point. Instead of retiring into a self-effacing and thus conventionally innocent silence, she accuses the world around her, which is so vociferous to condemn but not to cure. When asked by Aurora how she came by her child, Marian answers impatiently:

> 'I found him where
> I found my curse,—in the gutter, with my shame!
> What have you, any of you, to say to that,
> Who all are happy, and sit safe and high,
> And never spoke before to arraign my right
> To grief itself? What, what, . . . being beaten down
> By hoofs of maddened oxen into a ditch,
> Half-dead, whole mangled, when a girl at last
> Breathes, sees . . . and finds there, bedded in her flesh
> Because of the extremity of the shock,
> Some coin of price!
>
> . . .
>
> You all put up your finger—"See the thief!
> "Observe what precious thing she has come to filch.
> "How bad those girls are!" '
>
> (6.671–81, 685–7)

The issue here is not whether the fallen woman is guilty, but whether those who ' "never spoke before" ' are guilty. Marian attacks the hypocritical readiness of society to condemn what it is too modest to speak about.

The link between sexual innocence and silence is one which Barrett Browning is keen to break in every way, and Marian's otherwise unconvincing rise to the middle class is one of the tactics she uses. While Hester Prynne weaves a strange half-guilty, half-liberating meaning round the letter 'A', and Hetty Sorrel remains helpless and inarticulate, and Ruth keeps to an unassertive and saintly quietude, Marian speaks strongly in her own defence. She thus breaks the intriguing enigma that surrounds the figure of the fallen woman, and breaks the ideological association, so often used to justify her in Victorian literature, between innocence and silence. Such silence, Barrett Browning claims, is merely an excuse for the system of 'paterfamilias' to continue. It is an excuse to keep women confined in the condition either of the harem or the brothel.

The principle of speaking, then, which Barrett Browning asserts so confidently and magnanimously in the *Sonnets from the Portuguese*, becomes, in *Aurora Leigh*, a principle of political and sexual defiance. It has as its starting point the fact that women are supposed to ' "sit safe and high" '. She defies this convention, not by any very clear-sighted or informed depiction of prostitution, but simply by her declared intention to write about it. Silence, for this poet, is not a sign of innocence but a sign of guilt. Thus, although she has no very strong understanding of her working-class heroine as a character, she has a very strong sense of how, being the subject of speech is itself a subversion of the rules. Even Marian is not just a mute and helpless object. The notorious and defiant characteristic of this poem—'one of the longest poems in the world'[1] according to Swinburne—is that its three female speakers—Barrett Browning, Aurora and Marian—will *not* 'be dumb and die'.

Just how much the Victorian myth of contamination was a verbal myth is shown by the critics' reaction to *Ruth*. ' "An unfit subject for fiction" is *the* thing to say about it,'[2] Mrs Gaskell wrote ruefully. The unfitness was of course not literary, but moral. The subject of the fallen woman was one that might sully the author. As shown by that critic who deplored Mrs Gaskell's 'loss of reputation',[3] the sexual slur falls on the woman who dares to speak or write. All Mrs Gaskell's protestations about Ruth's heavenly purity could not appease this moral censoriousness. In fact, Barrett Browning reproached Mrs Gaskell for having Ruth die at the end,[4] and in her own variant of the story rejects any hint of expiation. Marian not only condemns the hypocrisy of the world; she also refuses to accept the world's version of respectability. Romney's offer of marriage and legalised paternity has no attraction for her. She rejects the social authority of the father's name with indignation: 'We only never call him fatherless/Who has God and his mother' (9.414–15). This narrative tactic to free Romney for Aurora, however emotionally unconvincing, makes an ideological point which is in keeping with Barrett Browning's purpose. Not only is Marian innocent, but she proves that innocence by having the confidence to live and speak in her own right. That confidence is the real ideological victory of *Aurora Leigh*.

However, the role of Marian is not only that of the vindicated fallen woman. Although Marian tells her own story, with challenging moral assurance, it is Aurora who writes it. The relationship between them thus reflects on Aurora's purpose as a poet. Not only does she take up with the other woman, and without the man for whom they should be rivals; she also takes up Marian's story as her own. That the story is a forbidden one throws into relief Aurora's consciousness of being a woman poet whose purpose is to break the rule of silence. In Marian

1. See Taplin, op. cit., p. 310.
2. *The Letters of Mrs Gaskell,* Letter 148, p. 220.
3. See Winifred Gérin, *Elizabeth Gaskell: A Biography* (Oxford, Oxford University Press, 1980), p. 139.
4. *Letters Addressed to Mrs Gaskell*, p. 42.

she finds a subject which the world denies and which convention prohibits her from telling. She tells it, therefore, with crusading energy:

> all my soul rose up to take her part
> Against the world's successes, virtues, fames.
> 'Come with me, sweetest sister,' I returned . . .
> (7.115–17)

Aurora's imagination finds in Marian the unpermitted story of the age, and she embraces it with zeal. As Dolores Rosenblum writes: 'The finding of Marian confirms Aurora's previous discovery of a living poetics',[5] and thus justifies her new mission to express 'this live, throbbing age' in art. Marian is the object of Aurora's quest to tell.

This quest is described in Book 6. Aurora has a glimpse of Marian's face in the Paris streets and immediately sets out to fine her. But the urgency with which she pursues her object suggests a need which goes beyond the requirements of the plot. It is not only concern for her lost sister which drives Aurora; it is an obsession to find at least one face that is not, like all the others, absent or dead. The pursuit through the Paris streets parallels another journey in Aurora's consciousness that takes her back through her old guilty intimations of mortality. It is as if her imagination cannot, at first, trust this quest to be different.

Aurora's first sight of Marian's face occurs just after she has made one of her declarations of poetic principle. She disparages those poets who stay tethered to the worn poeticisms of 'lily' and 'rose' (6.184), and declares that there is more real poetry in 'the hungry beggar-boy' (6.186) who has been foolishly scorned 'for a flower or two' (6.192). Barrett Browning advocates not only that poetry should be contemporary, but also that it should be humanised. It is at this point is the poem that she glimpses Marian's face among the crowds. Marian appears like the muse of Aurora's new, different, contemporary poetics. She is not exactly the 'beggar-boy', but his female equivalent.

However, the poet's imagination is not yet educated in the contemporaneity she advocates in theory. Immediately, Marian's living face blurs with the memory of others. Above all it is confused, as Alethea Hayter[6] points out, with the memory of Bro's. Aurora imagines it surfacing like the face of the dead:

> When something floats up suddenly, out there,
> Turns over . . . a dead face, known once alive . . .
> So old, so new!
> (6.238–40)

This confusion of the 'old' and the 'new' suggests how far back Barrett Browning's imagination has travelled. Marian brings to the surface of

5. Dolores Rosenblum, 'Face to Face: Elizabeth Barrett Browning's *Aurora Leigh* and Nineteenth-Century Poetry', *Victorian Studies*, 26 (1983), 321–38, p. 327.
6. Alethea Hayter, *Mrs Browning: A Poet's Work and its Setting* (London, Faber, 1962), p. 99.

consciousness the idea of a face which the poet never dared imagine before. She writes:

> That face persists,
> It floats up, it turns over in my mind,
> As like to Marian as one dead is like
> The same alive.
>
> (6.308–11)

This confusion between the dead and the living—between, as it were, the dead brother and the living sister—shows how far the figure of Marian is still only a substitute for the old forsaking muses. Her face appears like all the faces that the June sky or the bitter sea have separated from the surviving woman poet.

This association is stressed by Aurora's strange, panicky and pessimistic reaction to Marian's disappearance among the crowds:

> No Marian; nowhere Marian. Almost, now,
> I could call Marian, Marian, with the shriek
> Of desperate creatures calling for the Dead.
>
> (6.255–7)

There is no narrative logic to this sudden and persistent association of Marian with 'the Dead'. It is entirely a product of Barrett Browning's own experiences and imaginative needs. Once again, *Aurora Leigh* conveys two parallel stories. There is the story of the narrative, which is one of literal economic and emotional survival for the woman poet. But there is also the story of her imaginative quests, which shows her much less certain of that independence which really means disinheritance from her past. Marian's tantalising evasion of Aurora in Paris finds its meaning in the sub-text of Aurora's repeatedly 'orphaned' consciousness.

However, the quest for Marian is ultimately different. Unable to sleep, Aurora goes one day at dawn to the flower market, and there finds the object of her search. Once found, Marian is grasped with violent possessiveness:

> 'Marian, Marian!'—face to face—
> 'Marian! I find you. Shall I let you go?'
> I held her two slight wrists with both my hands;
> 'Ah Marian, Marian, can I let you go?'
> —She fluttered from me like a cyclamen,
> As white, which taken in a sudden wind
> Beats on against the palisade.—'Let pass',
> She said at last. 'I will not,' I replied;
> 'I lost my sister Marian many days,
> And sought her ever in my walks and prayers,
> And, now I find her . . .
>
> (6.411–51)

Whereas the old quests for father and mother had to fail, because the daughter lives and writes only by being 'orphaned' of the father's law and of the mother's womanliness, the quest for a sister succeeds. She is the muse of this woman poet's contemporaneity and commitment. This is the end of Aurora's many days' search, but it is also the end of Barrett Browning's many years' search for the object that will serve for a new, vitally contemporary woman's poetry. ' "I lost my sister Marian many days . . . And, now I find her." '

Critics have described the figure of Marian as, for instance, that of a 'mother-muse',[7] which Aurora must reject, as 'a symbol for the birth of [Aurora's] self',[8] and as a figure for the living truth which 'echoes and reinforces the truth Aurora claims for herself.'[9] But Marian is also, emphatically, a sister, and the often repeated term carries a nearly modern connotation of a liaison against the rules. Aurora does not find a real sister; she makes a sister of the lost other woman. The moral and political intrepidity of this act is part of the point, not only of Aurora's story, but also of Barrett Browning's new poetics. These are no longer a poetics of the daughter, but of the woman; and of a woman conscious of her imagination's responsibility towards her sex: 'it is exactly because pure and prosperous women choose to *ignore* vice, that miserable women suffer wrong by it everywhere.' Aurora seeks out Marian with the urgency, not only of a poet seeking her last muse, but of a woman making political amends for the oppression of her sex. Aurora does, in fact, succeed where Romney, the philanthropist, fails. Her imagination marries with the other, fallen woman, and does so with much more conviction and desire. ' "Come with me, sweetest sister," I returned.'

Once found, Aurora follows her sister Marian home with the dogged pertinacity of one for whom it has become a matter of life and death:

> Then she led
> The way, and I, as by a narrow plank
> Across devouring waters, followed her,
> Stepping by her footsteps, breathing by her breath,
> And holding her with eyes that would not slip . . .
> (6.500–4)

It is interesting that, although Aurora takes the philanthropist Romney's place in her relation to Marian, it is really Marian who finally saves *her*. 'The way' she takes leads significantly over the 'devouring waters', as if to say, that only by holding firm to this new sister of the present will Aurora escape the past's overwhelming message of grief. The quest for Marian is a quest to go on living and writing, in spite of and even,

7. Virginia Steinmetz, 'Images of "Mother-Want" in Elizabeth Barrett Browning's *Aurora Leigh*', *Victorian Poetry*, 21 (1983), 351–67, p. 359.
8. Dolores Rosenblum, 'Face to Face': Elizabeth Barrett Browning's *Aurora Leigh* and Nineteenth-Century Poetry', *Victorian Studies*, 26 (1983), 321–38, p. 333.
9. Nina Auerbach, 'Robert Browning's Last Word', *Victorian Poetry*, 22 (1984), 161–73, p. 169.

now, careless of, the seductive, haunting memories of the dead. The 'disinherited' Victorian daughter has become a woman and a poet in her own right, and the figure of Marian is the muse of her new direction and purpose on the imagination's desert plains.

Thus *Aurora Leigh* is the culmination of Barrett Browning's lifelong search for a poetics which will express her imaginative intentions as a Victorian and as a woman. Her ambition to be faithful to the 'age' and to find 'poetry *everywhere*' is realised in this epic which goes 'rushing into drawing-rooms and the like'. Its contemporaneity is achieved, however, through a hard, slow but total dispossession of the father. Aurora's progress towards a political and imaginative commitment to the age is a progress over graves. The sense of the father's inevitable and necessary death was always, from her earliest poems, the condition of Barrett Browning's bid for poetic power. But in *Aurora Leigh* that death is realised as an imaginative disinheritance which finds the father, not only lost, but also irrelevant. The rear expressed in *Casa Guidi Windows* of being 'orphaned' and 'disinherited' *even* of 'the Dead' is a fear which *Aurora Leigh* brilliantly and unsparingly realises.

However, in doing so it permits the fulfilment of a different quest. Marian Erle, the unmentionable, fallen other woman of Victorian society is the object of this quest and the muse of this 'unscrupulously epic' poem. While all Barrett Browning's earlier figures for the muse—her father, mother, brother, and even lover—remain absent and unanswering in her poems, Marian answers Aurora's 'desperate' call, and alone returns from the regions of 'the Dead' to make the desert place bearable. She *is* the answer to Barrett Browning's call for a new, contemporary, transgressive woman's poetry which will not 'be dumb and die'.

Meanwhile, such poetry has been written. 'I'm a woman, sir' (8.1130), Aurora a little impatiently reminds Romney at the end. This 'epic of the literary woman',[1] which has also been grandly called a 'feminist hymn',[2] insists from beginning to end on the fact of its female authorship. 'I write', Aurora announces at the beginning, and at the end she once more reminds the reader that this is the story of writing as well as of loving: 'I have written day by day' (9.725).

Not only does *Aurora Leigh* connect with fine insouciance the high and the low, the epic and the domestic, the poetic and the banal; it also connects the writing of poetry with the cause of the silenced woman. The presiding muse of this woman's poem is precisely that outlawed figure of the sexually fallen woman, who, jointly with her sister poet, dares nonetheless to speak. 'I'm a woman, sir' is a statement made on behalf of all women, whether fallen or unfallen, working-class or middle-class, illegitimately mothers or illegitimately poets. It is this shared,

1. Ellen Moers, *Literary Women* (London, The Women's Press, 1978), p. 40.
2. Nina Auerbach, *Woman and the Demon: The Life of a Victorian Myth* (Cambridge, Mass., Harvard University Press, 1982), p. 151.

confrontational, emancipatory right to language which marks Barrett Browning's sense of herself, at the height of her powers, as a woman poet, and as a poet speaking for women.

# DEIRDRE DAVID

## From *Intellectual Women and Victorian Patriarchy*†

* * *

When Barrett Browning looked for female poetic ancestors, she found none, and declared that before the work of Joanna Baillie, the late eighteenth-century Scottish dramatist and poet, there was no such thing in Britain as a 'poetess': 'England has had many learned women, not merely readers, but writers of the learned languages in Elizabeth's time and afterwards—women of deeper acquirements than are common now in the greater diffusion of letters, and yet where were the poetesses. . . . I look everywhere for grandmothers and see none'. She looked, of course, in those places that were available to her, in what we now term the canon. Had she looked in the uncanonised actuality, there were many women whom she could have claimed as female literary ancestors, but the fact that an extremely well-read woman poet could discover so few female poetic ancestors testifies to the canonised dominance of male poets. In her experienced absence of a sustaining female ancestry, in her very real isolation as a woman intellectual denied the regular companionship of other intelligent women, she attached herself to an androcentric line of poetic descent.

Moreover, despite her lyrics and justly famous sonnets, she also affiliated herself with a traditionally masculine genre: the epic. As a consequence of her Classical education, early in her career she apprenticed herself to this genre. In her maturity she revised the genre to write a major poem tracing Aurora Leigh's Odyssean quest for poetic identity and a home in the world and positing the proper political and social function for a poet in national life. In discussing the profession of literature for women, Dinah Craik tellingly praised *Aurora Leigh* for its successful competition with male poetry—women can be 'acute and accurate historians, clear explanators of science, especially successful in imaginative works', she declares, but Barrett Browning's poem proves that 'we can write as great a poem as any man among them all' (*A Woman's Thoughts about Women*, pp. 50–1). Epic poetry is androcentric in its thematic concern with heroes and war, indeed with arms and

† From *Intellectual Women and Victorian Patriarchy* by Deirdre David (London: Macmillan, 1987), 103–13. Reprinted by permission of the publisher. The author's notes have been deleted.

the man, and with elucidating the ways of God (or gods) to man, rather than with those ways of God to that part of man which is woman. Barrett Browning's self-termed 'novel-poem' *Aurora Leigh* is a formal hybrid that attempts to fit the explosive material more often to be found in the social novels of the 1840s to the traditional, male form of the epic; Barrett Browning chooses as the subject of her epic poem matters more usually represented by the genre dominated by women writers in the nineteenth century, namely the novel.

The plot of *Aurora Leigh* traces the development of its heroine from her Florentine childhood to eventual marriage to her cousin Romney. The orphaned child of an English father and Italian mother, she is sent to England to live with an aunt who trains her in the conventional accomplishments of young ladies and for marriage to her cousin. At the age of twenty Aurora refuses his proposal, inherits a small income on the death of her aunt, and moves to London determined to become a poet. Some ten years later, having achieved a modest recognition for her work, she learns that the Christian socialism favoured by Romney which she had scorned as insufficient to remedy social evil, has taken the form of intended marriage to a working-class girl, Marian Erle. In a stunningly visual depiction that calls to mind Hogarthian London, rich and poor meet at St James's Church where Romney vainly awaits his bride. Marian never arrives having been persuaded to leave for Australia by the woman who wants Romney for herself. Duped by the maid of this voluptuous aristocrat (Lady Waldemar) and drugged in a French brothel, Marian is raped. Aurora learns her story two years later when she spots Marian, now the mother of a baby boy, in a Paris flower market; she takes mother and child to Italy where they live happily together in the countryside of Aurora's childhood. Believing Romney to have married Lady Waldemar, Aurora is astonished to see him arrive on her porch one summer evening. The last two books of the poem are devoted to an extended dialogue between Romney and Aurora about the need to unify spiritual and material remedies for social ills, Aurora having at last realised that Romney has been blinded by an injury received in the fire that destroys his utopian socialist community. The poem is punctuated by Aurora's lengthy meditations upon art; it contains an arresting amount of violent imagery; and by the time of Barrett Browning's death in 1861 it had gone through five editions. In the broadest terms, Barrett Browning attempts a reconciliation of female and male: the poet/heroine is married to her cousin, private art is wedded to public politics, intellectual ambition united with the social good, and novel joined to poem.

The essential subjects of *Aurora Leigh* are Victorian society and the Victorian poet. Addressing itself to the ways in which poetry can remedy such evils as the rape of a working-class girl, the sexual lasciviousness of the aristocracy, and the provincial narrow-mindedness of the gentry, *Aurora Leigh* attempts to find function and meaning for poetry in the modern world. To be sure, a poetic self-consciousness that examines the function and meaning of poetry is hardly new to the nineteenth century, but what is remarkable about Barrett Browning's novel-poem, and her work in general, is an interrogation of whether there is a place and function for the poet at all in a society undergoing rapid alteration in all things. *Aurora Leigh* participates in the aesthetic discourse that examined the function of the artist in society, a discourse formed, for example, by Tennyson's 'Palace of Art', Arnold's 'Resignation' and Browning's 'How it Strikes a Contemporary'. *Aurora Leigh* was also conceived at an interesting moment in literary history, in the 1840s, when the Romantic poets were all dead. Wordsworth in his decline, Tennyson barely known, and the novel a vigorous form that dominated the popular market. The composition of the novel-poem spans a crucial decade of changes in English literary taste: most intensively worked on in the early 1850s (Books 1–6 were finished by March 1856), when it was completed in October 1856, Tennyson, Browning, and Longfellow had, at least, revitalised the English appetite for reading poetry, even if the novel remained sovereign with the reading public.

*Aurora Leigh* evokes poetry as balm for the wounds inflicted upon society by the materialistic values represented and questioned by the social novels of the 1840s. Barrett Browning admitted from the start of composition of the poem in 1844 that she wanted to write something of a 'new class', rhetorically asking 'where is the obstacle to making as interesting a story of a poem as of a prose work . . . Conversations and events, why may they not be given as rapidly and passionately and lucidly in verse as in prose'. Robert Browning thought there was no obstacle at all. When she wrote to him some two months after asking the above questions of Mary Russell Mitford, declaring her intention to write a poem that meets 'face to face and without mask the Humanity of the Age', he enthusiastically responded that such a 'fearless fresh living work [is] the *only* Poem to be undertaken now by you or anyone that *is* a Poet at all, the only reality, only effective piece of service to be rendered God and man'.

It is important to remember that when Barrett Browning articulated these plans for *Aurora Leigh*, the poem that was going to upset conventions, take a combative, confrontational stance in the English drawing room, she had barely been out of the house for two years and before that had lived an extremely secluded life at Hope End and Torquay. As I have already suggested, what Barrett Browning knew best was literature: immersed in text from the earliest moments of her writing life, she was spurred to write a confrontational poem in reading about what needed to be confronted. A veritable textual matrix of homage and literary allusion, *Aurora Leigh* is a discourse about society composed from other discourse. It is a novel-poem, a poetic art-novel, written by a woman who had been tutored, literally and figuratively, by patriarchal Classicists, who figured poetic creation through conventionally male, sometimes sexual, imagery, who literally had no experience of the society she set out to represent, and who made the subject of her formal hybrid female intellectual ambition.

What I am emphasising here is that Barrett Browning's literary practice was almost exclusively textual; that is to say, she held no salons, attended no dinners, and until her marriage travelled virtually nowhere. I do not mean this merely in terms of male literary dining out, the sort of activity welcomed by Robert Browning who was always walking backwards and forwards from Camberwell to London as a sought-after dinner guest. Despite their ambiguous social status, George Eliot and George Henry Lewes constantly entertained, dined out, and journeyed on the Continent; if her account is to be trusted, Harriet Martineau was only at home in the mornings, writing about what she did the rest of the time; Elizabeth Gaskell, productive social novelist, ran a busy Manchester household; Barbara Leigh Bodichon, Eliot's close friend, was a highly visible figure on the London intellectual scene. These women and the thousands of others who were active in English intellectual life saw the world in ways that Barrett Browning did not. What she did see was society represented by various forms of writing: what she insisted the poet saw was a privileged vision of a better society than the one she encountered in her extensive reading.

If, then, Barrett Browning, as a highly self-referential writer concerned with the role of the poet, deliberately produces a work she terms a novel-poem, it is certainly relevant to consider why she did not attempt to write a novel. The answer is two-fold: she believed that poetry was privileged over fiction and that the poet was a gifted being, called to the practice of poetry in ways the novelist was not elected to the practice of fiction. Consistently elaborating these values in her poetry, letters, and other writings, she consciously performed as a member of an aesthetically advantaged élite, mythologising herself as a member of that clerisy of poets described by Samuel Coleridge, whose poetic function is redefined in a secular community. That she was, in person, kind, modest, sincerely sensitive to the needs of her friends and remarkably forgiving of her father's tyrannical behaviour, is undeniable. Her personality and her manner do not indicate an unsympathetic élitism. Yet her performance as intellectual poet is strongly governed by explicit and implicit beliefs that the poet works in the highest aesthetic form, that the poet is chosen by, rather than chooses his vocation, and, in the terms of the cultural theory which has informed my readings of nineteenth-century women intellectuals, that the poet is a traditional, rather than organic intellectual. Bearing in mind Gramsci's foremost categories for traditional intellectuals (the clergy and the teaching profession), it is possible to construct a conjunctive paradigm in Barrett Browning's work linking form, vocation, and intellectual definition: the privileged poet produces poetry designed as a solace, sometimes cure, for the ills suffered by a materialistic society, and poetry also designed as an education in superior cultural values.

Understood from this perspective, the novel becomes the form of the organic intellectual, embraced by a writer such as Dickens whose work he, himself, would have been the last to characterise as culturally privileged. Dickens's business was to represent the teeming, secular world of the social class that produced him as organic intellectual, and, in ways that we now find thoroughly ambiguous, to present fictive remedies for the social malaise he describes. And bearing in mind the dominance of the genre by women writers in the nineteenth century, one can also define women's intellectual/literary practice primarily in the terms associated with the function of the organic intellectual: ratification of the influential ideas which are consented to by individuals in society, rather than imposed upon them by coercion. As I have shown, Harriet Martineau not only embraced her organic function as populariser of dominant ideologies, she also implicitly aligned that function with the subaltern role of Victorian women as it was designated by her culture.

Barrett Browning may very well have been incapable of writing a novel, but the point I want to emphasise here is that she had absolutely no desire to do so. Her close friend Mary Russell Mitford related that to fool her physician Barrett Browning had a small edition of Plato 'so bound as to resemble a novel' (*Recollections of a Literary Life*, p. 270), a strategy richly suggestive of her views of fiction. By implication, she rejects both the role of organic intellectual and the form that may be associated with it, choosing instead a model of literary production associated more with male than with female authors and, in Gramscian terms, with traditional intellectual function. In her view the novel was an inferior genre, all very well for Dickens whose celebrity was to her a curious marvel and who she believed would 'pass away, with all his "coarse caricatures", in the period of a *lifetime*'. If Dickens had any merit at all, she believed he owed it to reading Victor Hugo (and French novels remain exempt from her condemnation of the genre; crafted in ways that English novels were not, their authors possessed superior 'faculty of composition').

'The taste for fiction is a thing distinct from the taste for literature' she wrote to R. H. Horne and reading novels was low on her hierarchy of intellectual tasks, self-indulgence in the pleasure of listening to stories, a gratification which is a 'pleasant accompaniment to one's lonely coffee-cup in the morning. . . . After breakfast we have other matters to do—grave "Business matters", poems to write upon Eden, or essays on Carlyle, or literature in various shapes to be employed seriously upon'.

In Barrett Browning's 1843 poem 'upon Eden', 'A Drama of Exile', she places herself with some trepidation with those poets destined to write about the Fall with the majestic presence of Milton looming over them. While the regal reputation of *Paradise Lost* in English literary history has created numerous anxieties of influence for male poets, for a woman poet to write in the shadows of Milton creates multiple anxiety, rebellion and revision, as Sandra M. Gilbert and Susan Gubar have convincingly demonstrated. For Barrett Browning, it is her first exercise in poetry as witness to a transcendent, instructive order.

Beginning the Preface to 'A Drama of Exile' by saying that 'the subject of the Drama rather fastened on me than was chosen', she ambiguously proceeds to establish herself as both a passive and an active poet. Feeling that Eve's part in the Fall has been 'imperfectly apprehended hitherto' and that it is 'more expressible by a woman than a man', she will now undertake to give Eve a voice. The oscillation between being subjugated agent of a momentous poetic theme and autonomous spokeswoman for Eve becomes clearer as she elaborates her relationship to Milton: 'I had promised my own prudence to shut close the gates of Eden between Milton and myself, so that none might say I dared to walk in his footsteps. He should be within, I thought, with his Adam and Eve unfallen or falling,—and I, without, with my *EXILES*,—I also an exile! It would not do. The subject, and his glory covering it, swept through the gates, and I stood full in it, against my will, and contrary to my vow,—till I shrank back fearing, almost desponding; hesitating to venture even a passing association with our great poet before the face of the public' (2:143–4). She chooses to exile her fallen poetic self from the paradise of patriarchal poetic power, knowing in her dutiful prudence that she cannot walk there, has no licence by virtue of her sex and poetic immaturity to venture on Milton's ground. Yet the force of that power is so strong that it sweeps through the gates so that she stands 'full in it', against her will and against her vow. Electing to place herself in an inferior position to Milton *because* he is so powerful, Barrett Browning is consequently overwhelmed by his power. And the implication here, too, must be that she, the mortal poet outside Eden, is subject to the same power that Milton himself is subject to as he composes *his* epic, the power of God, of divine inspiration, just as, in a sense, Aurora as poet is subject to a power vastly greater than her own.

In 'The Drama of Exile', then, Barrett Browning as poet is made twice passive, by Milton and by God. A significant registration of her difference from Milton (putting aside all questions of qualitative difference between her poem and his) is that she chooses the form of verse drama with no poetic voice, in contrast to Milton's epic which begins with those lines (wanting no repetition here) invoking the poetic muse. Milton speaks as poet, as epic singer: as dramatist, Barrett Browning effaces herself from her text, secreting herself behind the mask of her 'masque'. Unlike Harriet Martineau, for whom Milton's verse was a source of consolation not of emulation and who relished work of auxiliary usefulness not of propitiatory revision, Barrett Browning must hide herself in her poem, shield herself from charges of misplaced ambition. Her own Eve declares herself 'twice fallen' from 'joy of place, and also right of wail'. She is given right of wail by Barrett Browning, who hopes to correct an incorrect emphasis upon Eve that sees her 'first in transgression' but not also '*first* and *deepest* in the sorrow'. Through her Eve, Barrett Browning wanted to voice that 'peculiar anguish [which is] the fate of woman at its root'.

Adopting an assertive interrogative style which implies the power she once possessed, and relishing the asking of questions to which she obviously knows the answers, Barrett Browning's Eve forwardly articulates her own sin and guilt:

> . . . The lady of the world, princess of life,
> Mistress of feast and favour? Could I touch
> A rose with my white hand, but it became
> Redder at once? Could I walk leisurely
> Along our swarded garden, but the grass
> Tracked me with greenness? Could I stand aside
> A moment underneath a cornel-tree,
> But all the leaves did tremble as alive,
> With songs of fifty birds who were made glad
> Because I stood there?
>
> (2: lines 1238–47)

The shameful misery she feels is intensified by her knowledge of having chosen, even willed, such a state: 'And is not this more shame,/To have made the woe myself, from all that joy?/To have stretched my hand, and plucked it from the tree,/And chosen it for fruit?' (lines 1253–56). The woman who emphasises her power in bewailing her loss, who could redden roses with her touch, who could improve upon nature and make a tree sing with pleasure for her presence, continues, in a sense, to dwell upon herself as she laments her undoing. Where Adam consistently speaks of 'our' fall and the fate 'we' share, Eve consistently employs the first person pronoun, and her speeches repeat such typical phrases as 'Alas, me alas,/Who have undone myself', a linguistic emphasis that does not escape the notice of Lucifer, always a figure preternaturally alert to narcissistic preoccupation. 'Boast no more in grief' he tells her, 'your grief is but your sin in rebound.' Taunted by various earth spirits who resent the post-lapsarian misery they share with Eve and Adam, Barrett Browning's first parents are consoled by a phantasmal Christ who instructs Adam in disciplining Eve to her future role as 'First woman, wife and mother', sanctified to work and devotion. A poem inspired by Barrett Browning's desire to give utterance to Eve's (and woman's) 'peculiar anguish', becomes a silencing of Eve's expressive voice. From a lengthy self-abnegation that serves to intensify her former power and actually gives her *more* power as a vital speaker, Eve moves to a dignified, noble acceptance of her Miltonic destiny. She finally becomes silent and acquiescent to her suffering—the Marian prototype obedient to Christ's will. Although Eve's eventual destiny is ineradically inscribed for Barrett Browning, the disciplining of Eve by Christ and Adam and the implicit disciplining of the female poet by one of her poetic fathers which Barrett Browning describes in her preface to 'A Drama of Exile', become significant in analysis of her developed ideology of the poet intellectual. Impeded by the absence of a positive female tradition, chastened by the presence of patriarchal power, to have a poetic voice, it would seem that an intellectual woman poet must dedicate her talent to conservative, androcentric ideals.

*Poems of 1844* also included 'A Vision of Poets', a lengthy homage to poets of the far and recent past: 'God's prophets of the Beautiful/These poets were.' More significant in terms of Barrett Browning's ideology of the poet intellectual than this mystical fantasy, consisting of three hundred tercets whose rhyme and metre tax the reader's attention, is Barrett Browning's explanation of the genesis of the poem: it originated in her desire to express 'the mission of the poet', a mission obscured by the materialism of her society as she perceived it. The Victorian poet 'wears better broad-cloth, but speaks no more oracles . . . the evil of this social incrustation over a great idea is eating deeper and more fatally into our literature than either readers or writers may apprehend fully' (2:147). The ideal poet performs oracular functions, is the cultural agent between a troubled society and ideal values which are encrusted, obscured by materialism. The poet's mission is remedial, he is empowered through his vocation to reveal the organic connections between God, man, society and culture obscured in a secular world. And even though Barrett Browning always emphasises the poet's craft, she also believes in the necessity of certain attributes for the poet which cannot be acquired: 'Without the essential thing, the genius, the inspiration, the insight . . . the most accomplished verse-writers had far better write prose, for their own sake's as for the world's'.

Barrett Browning's belief in 'the essential thing' governs all her aesthetic views, whether articulated in her letters or in her poetry. For example, Aurora Leigh's meditations on the meaning of poetry explore 'the inspiration, the insight' which Barrett Browning believed all poets *must* possess. Aurora insists that the poet unifies 'Natural things/and spiritual, – who separates those two/in art, in morals, or the social drift,/ Tears up the bond of nature and brings death,/Paints futile pictures, writes unreal verse,/Leads vulgar days, deals ignorantly with men,/Is wrong, in short, at all points' (7.763–9). In linking 'natural things/and spiritual', the poet displays possession of the fourth element of genius which Barrett Browning accorded the finest poets in 'An Essay on Mind': Association follows Invention, Judgment, and Memory. As Aurora Leigh explains it, the poet is enabled to perform this associative function by virtue of a privileged vision: 'Art's the witness of what Is/Behind this show . . . For we stand here, we,/If genuine artists, witnessing, for God's/Complete, consummate, undivided work' (7.834–9). The poet, then, by virtue of possessing 'the essential thing, the genius, the inspiration, the insight', links through an associative faculty, the 'natural' and the 'spiritual'.

In itself, Barrett Browning's preoccupation with the function of the poet is hardly noteworthy. Examination of the ways in which poets figure their relationship to God, man, society, and culture has long been a central critical enterprise, and Barrett Browning's beliefs are derived from a wealth of poetic self-examination locating the poet in an inspired, yet subjugated position. However, this well-established examination is given particular meaning by Barrett Browning in two ways: she participates in the well-documented Victorian endeavour that seeks to recover a lost social and cultural unity (which is, of course, mythical), and she adopts for her own career a governing model traditionally associated with male poets. Moreover, she implies, if the poet's visionary power, his special insight, could be enjoyed by all men, then society would transcend its degenerate, materialistic condition:

> . . . If a man could feel,
> Not one day, in the artist's ecstasy,
> But every day, feast, fast, or working-day,
> The spiritual significance burn through
> The hieroglyphic of material shows,
> Henceforward he would paint the globe with wings,
> And reverence fish and fowl, the bull, the tree,
> And even his very body as a man –
> Which now he counts so vile, that all the towns
> Make offal of their daughters for its use.
>
> (7.858–66)

It would seem, then, that Barrett Browning's ideal world is one where all men are poets, a concept that has certain revolutionary implications. If all men felt all the time as poets do in their ecstasy, then they would no longer be alienated from society, culture, or work. They would lose that consciousness of self which Carlyle in 'Characteristics' identifies as symptomatic of a diseased society, would no longer be so driven by his 'cash-nexus' that they sell their daughters as 'offal' in the streets (one of the several references to prostitution in *Aurora Leigh* which scandalised the critics). If the poet's mission is to instruct all men to feel and see as he does, then eventually he will no longer *be* privileged, will possess no mission, have no special insight. This is a revolutionary, apocalyptic vision, the 'New Jerusalem' invoked at the end of *Aurora Leigh*, and here figured as an end to self-awareness and an end to art. This view implies, of course, that art is symptomatic of a fallen society in the sense that representation signalises mediation between man and his world. Barrett Browning calls for a direct connection. Instructed by the poet, man will discover his Edenic self, a self lost in the post-lapsarian world of commercial individualism given demonic vitality by Carlyle in *Signs of the Times*—'We remove mountains, and make seas our smooth highway; nothing can resist us. We war with rude Nature; and, by our resistless engines, come off always victorious, and loaded with spoils' (pp. 34–5). Implying that poets are empowered to save man from destruction by his own creation, those 'resistless engines', Aurora declares that they are 'The only teachers who instruct mankind/From just a shadow on a charnel-wall/To find man's veritable stature out/ Erect, sublime' (1.865–8). The imagery of obfuscation is similar to that employed by Barrett Browning in her Preface to the *Poems of 1844*, where she describes the genesis of 'A Poet's Vow': the 'great idea' of the oracular function of the poet has become encrusted, obscured by a morally and culturally degenerate society. She will strip away the darkening layers.

If one considers, then, the principal motifs of Barrett Browning's definition of poetic function, those of privileged insight, instruction, and consolation, it is clear that to be a poet is to be a traditional intellectual in the sense that Gramsci defines such a function: it is to minister to those members of society who are troubled by the mounting domination of English life by secular, materialistic, middle-class values; it is to elevate oneself as superior to the organic intellectuals generated by the middle class, and to create oneself as the restorer of a legendary, lost unity which not only existed in terms of a coherent society, but also in terms of the relationship between nature and the artist. In common with many other Victorian poets and social thinkers, Barrett Browning constructs a pre-industrial Eden, the topos of benign authority, of joyful obedience, and of poetry, where the artist tends to copy order, rather than to create it. This is not the topos of the novel, which inclines to representation of conflict between authority and the individual and to the imposition of fictive order upon a disjunctive world. Avidly reading in her seclusion, Barrett Browning became intensely familiar with the social incoherence given form and sometimes resolution in the nineteenth-century novel, and she decided to fit the disturbing material of this genre to a revised epic form. Undertaking to instruct fallen man in his possession of that essential sublimity obscured by the ideologies welcomed and elaborated by organic intellectuals such as Harriet Martineau, she implicitly affiliates herself with the land-owning classes whose power was in decline. Through her heroine, Aurora Leigh, she aligns sex, gender and vocation in a female poetics and a sexual politics which dedicate woman's art to the realisation of a conservative ideal.

# MARJORIE STONE

## Genre Subversion and Gender Inversion: *The Princess* and *Aurora Leigh* †

Whereas Tennyson unsettles conventional genre and gender distinctions in *The Princess* only to uncover or reconstitute those he sees as fundamental, Elizabeth Barrett Browning is more subversive in *Aurora Leigh*. Tennyson ultimately respects stylistic and sexual decorum, but Barrett Browning is defiantly indecorous. As early as 1845, she had conceived the work as "a sort of novel-poem, . . . running into the midst of our conventions, & rushing into drawing-rooms & the like 'where angels fear to tread'; & so, meeting face to face & without mask the Humanity of the age, & speaking the truth as I conceive of it, out plainly."[1] As her term "novel-poem" implies, Barrett Browning does not merely mingle genres; she fuses them together to form a new whole. *Aurora Leigh* combines a verse bildungsroman or spiritual epic like *The Prelude*, tracing the growth of a woman poet's mind, with a treatise on poetics (including a survey of poetic genres) and a heavily plotted novel in the manner of George Sand, Charles Dickens, and Charlotte Brontë—all enlivened by liberal dashes of racy social satire in the manner of Byron's *Don Juan*.

This fusion of genres entails a fusion of genders since Victorians viewed epic, philosophic, and racy satiric poetry as male domains, but thought the novel more suited to female writers. Beyond associating the skills of the novelist with the supposedly female virtues of the heart, Victorians found the writing of novels by women more acceptable than attempts in the major poetic genres because, as Gilbert and Gubar observe, novels did not require or display the knowledge of classical models barred to most women, novelists did not aspire to be priestly or prophetic figures interpreting God and the world to their fellows, and the novel was less subjective than the prevalent lyric and confessional poetic forms and therefore more congruent with the self-effacing role prescribed for Victorian women (pp. 545–549). Precisely these features of the major poetic modes—the imitation of classical models (above all, the epic), prophetic aspirations, and confessional subjectivity—are the most prominent in *Aurora Leigh*. Yet Barrett Browning's subversion of conventional gender expectations goes further than that effected through her blending of novelistic and poetic conventions. She employs some of the same types of gender inversion as Tennyson does in *The Princess*, but more consistently. And along the way, she appropriates, revises, and

† Reprinted by permission from *Victorian Poetry* 25, no. 2 (Fall 1987): 115–27.

1. In *The Letters of Robert Browning and Elizabeth Barrett Browning 1845–1846*, ed. Elvan Kintner (Cambridge, Massachusetts, 1969), 1, 31.

satirizes many of the actions, situations, and speeches in Tennyson's medley, often by inverting them.

Although Kaplan emphasizes the parallels between *The Princess* and *Aurora Leigh*, the differences are more immediately apparent (p. 27). Indeed, nothing could be more unlike Tennyson's medley with its elaborate frame, multiple narrators, and continuously interrupted narrative than the narrative speed, suspense, and first-person immediacy of *Aurora Leigh*. In Tennyson's poem, the male poet remains shadowy and anonymous. In Barrett Browning's, the poet-heroine, though a woman, is constantly in the foreground speaking of her experience and her aspirations in an assertively epic manner matching Wordsworth's "egotistical sublime":

> I who have written much in prose and verse
> For others' uses, will write now for mine,—
> Will write my story for my better self.

Thus Aurora begins, emphasizing twice not only that she *will* write (as opposed to the simple future "I shall"), but also that she writes *for* herself. If *The Princess* reveals what some critics have seen as Tennyson's lack of narrative ability, *Aurora Leigh* reveals Barrett Browning's considerable ability to construct a suspenseful story—a difference that is not a little ironic considering the impression created in the frame of *The Princess* that storytelling is a male activity. Finally and most importantly, Ida's assertion of women's rights remains safely enclosed in a timeless world of romance with no fixed local habitation or name and no real economic pressures—the Princess and her students are "lapt/In the arms of leisure" (2.151–152). In contrast, Aurora's defiance of conventional gender distinctions is presented in a contemporary English context and followed by action as she refuses her cousin Romney's proposal of marriage and sets off for London to live as a writer in "a room of her own." Aurora's insistence in Book 5 that the sole work of artists is to represent their age—"Their age, not Charlemagne's" (l. 203)—can in part be viewed as Barrett Browning's corrective response to Tennyson's failure to do so in his "fairy tale," *The Princess*.[2] In keeping with Aurora's credo, Barrett Browning presents a detailed and cutting satire of the kind of education genteel young women actually received in Victorian England as opposed to Tennyson's depiction of a Utopian educational experiment in a "fairy tale" world of romance.

Aurora's curious double education—first in Italy at the hands of her father, and then in England at the hands of her father's sister—provides a context for some of the most noticeable gender inversions in *Aurora Leigh*. For her aunt, Aurora learns a smattering of facts and acquires

2. EBB described the work that was to become *The Princess* as a blank verse "fairy tale" on first hearing of it in January 1846, and expressed her amazement that such a work could be written in a world that was so "old & fond of steam." See *Letters*, I, 427.

the usual "accomplishments." More importantly, her aunt attempts to indoctrinate her with the ideology of true womanhood:

> I read a score of books on womanhood
> To prove, if women do not think at all,
> They may teach thinking. . .
> —books that boldly assert
> Their right of comprehending husband's talk
> When not too deep, and even of answering
> With pretty "may it please you," or "so it is"—
> . . . . . . . . . . . . . . . . . . . . . . . . . . . . . . . . . .
> — their angelic reach
> Of virtue, chiefly used to sit and darn,
> And fatten household sinners,—their, in brief,
> Potential faculty in everything
> Of abdicating power in it. (1.427–442)

Aurora is able to resist the stunting effects of this typical female education because she was nurtured in her Italian childhood by her scholarly father, who taught her "The trick of Greek/And Latin . . . as he would/ Have taught me wrestling or the game of fives" (1.714–716). Aurora observes:

> Thus, my father gave;
> And thus, as did the women formerly
> By young Achilles, when they pinned a veil
> Across the boy's audacious front, and swept
> With tuneful laughs the silver-fretted rocks,
> He wrapt his little daughter in his large
> Man's doublet, careless did it fit or no. (1.722–728)

Inverting a well-known classical image of gender inversion, Barrett Browning subverts the traditional focus of the epic on male heroic exploits through a doubly transvestite simile relating Achilles—whom Gilbert describes as the "paradigmatic warrior male"—to a young girl and her education (p. 216).

Browning's wrestling metaphor and the comparison of the young Aurora to the young Achilles suggest that the education Aurora's father gives her is wholly male. In fact, however, the poem constantly emphasizes that the most vital thing he teaches her is not "The trick of Greek and Latin," but the importance of Love. In other words, the "large/ Man's doublet" he uses to make his daughter his double is itself double in nature, symbolizing both the wisdom of the Heart and the wisdom of the Head. Aurora rejects the conventional alignment of women with the heart and men with the head when she scorns Romney's assumption that heartache is "the woman's special, proper ache" (1.113), just as Barrett Browning does in "To George Sand, A Desire" when she addresses the French novelist as "Thou large-brained woman and large-hearted man." Aurora's father may have a "heavier brain" than her mother and therefore love his child "not as wisely, since less foolishly" (1.61–63), but still he can love and nurture her, whereas in *The Princess* Tennyson focuses only on mothers as nurturing figures. Moreover, as Barrett Browning implies in her depiction of Romney's humanitarian obsessions, some men have a compulsive desire as well as the ability to nurture. Romney comes to recognize this desire in himself and describes it in a series of similes that are conspicuously female:

> I, who felt
> The whole world tugging at my skirts for help,
> . . . . . . . . . . . . . . . . . . . . . . . . . . . . . . . . . . . . . . . . . .
> I beheld the world
> As one great famishing carnivorous mouth,—
> A huge, deserted, callow, blind bird Thing,
> With piteous open beak that hurt my heart. (8.370–398)

Although Barrett Browning's exploration of the head/heart dichotomy is generally less conventional than Tennyson's, she seems to imitate rather than revise his use of gender inversion in *The Princess* in her depiction of Aurora and Romney. Thus, just as Tennyson presents a girlish hero and an Amazonic heroine, she presents a heroine whom some reviwers criticized as excessively masculine and a hero criticized as a "decided milksop"—though at least Romney does not faint like Tennyson's Prince or like the hero in Barrett Browning's reverse-Cinderella poem "Lady Geraldine's Courtship." Yet Browning does not dwell on the physical appearance of her characters as Tennyson does; nor does she present transvestite scenes that paradoxically call attention to male and female differences. More important, she reverses the roles of the two major characters in *The Princess* by substituting a male Utopian reformer for Tennyson's feminist reformer. Just as Ida's dreams of establishing a women's college eventually lie in ruins about her, so Romney's dreams of turning his estate into a socialist phalanstery eventually lie in ruins about him. Browning is rather more severe in her treatment of Romney's socialism that Tennyson is in his treatment of Ida's feminism. Romney not only fails in his socialist schemes but also is made to ridicule his own failure in a grotesquely mock-heroic figure of speech that again calls attention to his desire to nurture. With others of his age, he puts up "Hostelry signs" of "Some red colossal cow with mighty paps/A Cyclops' fingers could not strain to milk," only to offer in the end no more than a "saucerful/Of curds" (8.847–852). Yet Barrett Browning does not allow the reader to rest with this mock-heroic impression of Romney for in the same scene Aurora insists that if aimed too high, still "The gesture was heroic" (l. 787). Like Tennyson, Barrett Browning combines the heroic and the mock-heroic in an unsettling balance, at one minute emphasizing Romney's nobility, at the next his histrionic folly. Thus she appropriates Tennyson's "strange diagonal" but reverses its slant. What we hear in *Aurora Leigh* is not a story about a woman's idealistic ventures told by a number of men and "dressed up" by a male poet, but a story in part about man's idealistic ventures told by a woman.

Barrett Browning also echoes and revises speeches and actions appearing in *The Princess*, most notably in Romney's initial proposal to Aurora. After dismissing Aurora's aspirations to become an artist and asserting that no woman can be a Christ or a great poet, Romney invites Aurora to "come down" to him and be his dutiful helpmate in his work (2.385–387). Aurora is associated in this section and elsewhere with images of mountain height reminiscent of those surrounding Ida and the "maid" in "Come down, O maid." But her response to Romney's invitation to "come down" and to allow her woman's heart to "melt" in passion is very different from Ida's final response to the Prince. In terms reminiscent of Jane Eyre's spirited rejection of St. John Rivers, she rejects Romney's bid for "A wife to help your ends,—in her no end" (2.403). When Romney further presses her and tries to flatter and reduce her with flowery comparisons, she responds with one of the many images conveying female strength and power running through *Aurora Leigh* even more insistently than images of male strength and power run through *The Princess:* "certain flowers grow near as deep as trees,/And, cousin, you'll not move my root" (2.848–849). In fact, the reverse eventually occurs as, toward the close of the poem, we find Romney confessing that Aurora has written poems "Which moved me in secret, as the sap is moved/In still March branches, signless as a stone" (8.593–594). Additional reversals occur at this point, as Romney finally comes *up* to Aurora in her villa overlooking Florence and arrives just when she is musing on the terrace of her "tower" and struggling to resist the erotic fantasy of "passionate desire" that makes her long not just to "come down" to Romney, but

> to leap and plunge
> And find a sea-king with a voice of waves,
> And treacherous soft eyes, and slippery locks. (8.40–42)

Aurora, finally, does not need to resist the temptation represented by this male siren because the fantasized "sea-king" with the "treacherous soft eyes" gives way to the blinded and enlightened Romney. Romney no longer threatens Aurora's artistic identity but affirms it, and so finally she does "come down" to him, though significantly she does so at Marian's invitation and not at his own.

Earlier, however, in the garden scene in Book 2 that echoes *Paradise Lost* in ending with an expulsion—though an expulsion determined by Aurora's fiat and not by God's, as Romney later suggests (8.320–323)—Romney is not so benign a figure, and Aurora must resist him in other ways as well. Thus, after she rejects his proposal, she also rejects his attempts to endow her with economic assistance, triumphantly tearing up the document that would make him her benefactor:

> I tore
> The paper up and down, and down and up
> And crosswise, till it fluttered from my hands,
> As forest-leaves, stripped suddenly and rapt
> By a whirlwind on Valdarno, drop again,
> Drop slow, and strew the melancholy ground
> Before the amazèd hills . . . why, so, indeed,
> I'm writing like a poet, somewhat large
> In the type of the image, and exaggerate
> A small thing with a great thing, topping it:—
> But then I'm thinking how his eyes looked, his,
> With what despondent and surprised reproach! (2.1162–73)

Recalling this incident seven years later when she is a successful author living on her own in London, Aurora checks herself as she dilates into a full-fledged epic simile because she shrewdly realizes that her poetic hyperbole is a cover for her repressed feelings for Romney. Here the interrupted epic simile manifests the "dialogized," multi-layered consciousness that Bakhtin finds characteristic of novelistic discourse, discourse permeated with irony and self-parody, and semantically open-ended because of its contact with an ongoing reality. Yet the final impact of this passage is more than ironically self-mocking. Aurora undercuts her own epic pretensions, but perhaps a "large" image is in fact well-suited to the apparently trivial gesture by which she frees herself from any economic dependence upon Romney's patriarchal legacies, since in tearing up the document she gains the independence that Tennyson's Princess conspicuously lacks in her reliance on her father's summer palace for her university. Aurora later theorizes that the poet's task is to discern the heroic in contemporary actions and characters that seem unheroic: "every age/Appears to souls who live in't (ask Carlyle)/Most unheroic" (5.155–157). Certainly, in the larger perspective of her own history or the history of women writers collectively, Aurora's act assumes a momentous significance, though in her case as in Romney's Barrett Browning delicately balances the mock-heroic and the heroic. She is not by any means suggesting that by tearing up the bonds of economic dependence women like Aurora can also tear up the bonds of emotional dependence. Hence the wry irony that the interruption in Aurora's epic flight springs from the love for Romney that she cannot yet articulate or accept.

In rejecting economic dependence on Romney, Aurora also insists that she does not need his aid to keep her or her honor, and that no one's honor—"Nor man's nor woman's"—can be deputed to another (2.1056). She will not depute hers, she emphasizes, to father or brother or, given the absence of those in her case, to her male cousin. This rejection again involves a revision of *The Princess* where Ida and little Lilia both call on knights to defend their honor or their cause. Moreover, Barrett Browning further subverts this convention of chivalric romance by underscoring the gender inversion brought about by the Victorian cult of true womanhood. As Aurora ironically points out, self-sacrifice and self-denial in the cause of helping others is so much a part of correct "womanly behaviour" in her age that it has become not man's but

woman's trade
To suffer torment for another's ease.
The world's male chivalry has perished out,
But women are knights-errant to the last. (7.222–225)

Nevertheless, part of the complexity of Barrett Browning's exploration of gender and the generic conventions of romance is that she unsettles and questions even her own generalizations. No character in *Aurora Leigh* is more intent on suffering torment to ease others than the Quixotic Romney. Aurora describes him in a simile drawn from Greek tragedy as a "male Iphigenia," but one who is "self-tied" (2.778–779). In a later more complex reversal, Marian Erle compares Romney's tender voice to "the ointmentbox broke on the Holy feet/To let out the rich medicative nard" (3.1222–23)—a comparison that puts Marian, who subsequently becomes a Madonna figure, in the position of Christ, and Romney, a would-be Christ figure and her self-appointed saviour, in the position of the woman who anointed the Messiah's feet with nard.[3]

Aurora's reflections on the "womanly trade" of self-sacrifice are called forth by her thought that she might have "saved" Romney by marrying him, thereby obstructing the schemes of the rich, duplicitous Lady Waldemar—though only at the cost of renouncing her artistic ambitions. She successfully resists the subtle temptation, however, and her success leads her to muse on her unusual nature: "It seems as if I had a man in me" (7.213). In Book 7 Aurora frequently mentions the "man" within her, or the "man" that she can be if she chooses. For instance, she tells herself she can go on despite her futile love for Romney: "I'm not too much/A woman, not to be a man for once" (ll. 984–985). Conversely, men can also be women in the way they behave: "Note men!—they are but women after all" (l. 1017). At this point, Aurora also nostagically recalls the time in childhood before she fell into consciousness of gender and division—the time when the child sits among earth's creatures in "fellowship and mateship, . . . /Before the Adam in him has foregone/ All privilege of Eden" (ll. 1088–91). And subsequently, prompted by the androgynous features of Marian's child, Aurora muses, "We're all

3. It is difficult to determine which version of the Biblical narrative Barrett Browning is referring to; see Matthew 22.6–12, Mark 14.3–7, Luke 7.36–50, and John 12.1–8.

born princes"—not, as Tennyson would have it, princes and princesses (8.15). Statements such as these, like the suggestion that Romney has a woman's heart within him, indicate that gender is not the ultimate reality for Barrett Browning that it is for Tennyson; and evidently such thinking leaves its mark on Aurora's other writings as well as on the spiritual epic she writes about her own artistic and moral development. In Book 3, where Aurora reviews her reviewers, we learn of the critic Stokes who objects: "Call a man John, a woman Joan . . . /And do not prate so of *humanities*" (ll. 81–82).

The "man within" Aurora sometimes takes the form of a male muse whom she variously describes as "my angel of the Ideal" and "My Phoebus Apollo, soul within my soul" (2.797, 5.414). Faithful to this muse, she continues to dedicate herself to her art. Indeed, in a reversal of the usual Victorian domestic contract, Romney finally dedicates himself to the service of her art as well: asking Aurora to "work for two," he vows that he "for two, shall love"; "press the clarion on thy woman's lip," he urges, as he describes the revelation she can bring (9.911–912, 929). As the poem closes, Aurora not only speaks the last word; she also speaks in the words of the prophet of Revelation. Very different this from the Prince's last word to Ida in Tennyson's backward-looking finale: "Lay thy sweet hands in mine and trust to me."

The text of *Aurora Leigh* is the most notable result of Aurora's dedication to her art as, like her creator in this respect as well as others, she centers her most ambitious work on her own development as an artist and woman. Barrett Browning's boldly self-assertive presentation of a portrait of the artist as young woman indicates that the bildungsroman was not necessarily "a recalcitrant form" for all nineteenth-century writers, as Jane McDonnell implies in an analysis of *The Mill on the Floss*. Aurora's conflict bears out McDonnell's suggestion that there is generally a "conflict between the values of self-determination and personal development found in the bildungsroman, and the ideals of renunciation and self-sacrifice so often demanded of nineteenth-century woman."[4] But Barrett Browning does not deal with this "gender-genre conflict" as evasively and conservatively as George Eliot does in *The Mill on the Floss*. Indeed, she directly counters interconnected prejudices about gender and genre as she first satirizes the young Romney's disparagement of Aurora's poetic aspirations and then portrays her heroine's increasingly ambitious attempts in genres traditionally viewed as male preserves. Romney repeatedly suggests that, like other "literary ladies," Aurora can at best write escapist "happy pastorals" of "meads and trees" to provide facile young people with "innocent distraction" (2.1201, 4.1117); moreover, her work will be judged by the critics as "mere woman's work" (2.234). To a degree, Aurora acknowledges an

4. " 'Perfect Goodness' or 'The Wider Life': *The Mill on the Floss* as Bildungsroman," *Genre*, 15 (1982), 379.

element of truth in this charge when she describes her apprenticeship years in London in Book 3. She did write facile pastoral verse, she confesses—"pretty, cold, and false" (5.131). Yet in Book 3 and again in Book 5, Aurora also describes how she went on to try her hand at ballads and sonnets as well as pastorals, as she prepared to reach for what Gosse calls the "great solid branches of poetry" in her attempt at an epic of the present age, in the low mimetic rather than the high mimetic mode. This work, the "long poem" in manuscript that she considers selling to help finance her trip to Italy (5.1213) and that so impresses Romney and both Vincent Carrington and his wife when it is published, is also evidently an urban epic like *Aurora Leigh*, with its city scenes in London, Paris, and Florence. Like Dickens, Aurora finds a romance even in the realism of London fog (3.195–198), and later, exploring Paris, she pledges to confront "the coarse town-sights" rather than be drawn back through a "love of beauty" into pastoral seclusion (6.138–139). Before her apprenticeship years in London, Aurora had been even more ambitious but less successful as she poured her adolescent enthusiasm "Along the veins of others" and wrote "lifeless imitations" of classical odes, bucolics, didactics, elegiacs, and "counterfeiting epics." Very strange, Aurora muses, that "nearly all young poets should write old"—but so they do: thus Pope at sixteen writes like a man of sixty and "beardless Byron" is "academical" (1.973–1014).

Aurora's development from a young poet who writes "old" to a mature poet forging her own forms and her own poetics closely parallels Barrett Browning's own progression from writing imitations of classical epic verse like the juvenile "Battle of Marathon" to achieving success in minor verse forms such as ballads like "The Rhyme of the Duchess May" to attempting the novel-epic *Aurora Leigh*. What Barrett Browning does not depict in any detail in her epic künstlerroman, however, is her own growth from a young woman who writes male to a mature poet who writes female: a poet who shifts from imitating male genres, identifying with male protagonists, and addressing her "brothers," to addressing her "sisters," depicting female protagonists, and adapting genres previously defined in male terms. This development, more complex than Tennyson's shift from female to male protagonists, is too convoluted to trace here. But *Aurora Leigh*, with its bold confounding of gender and genre partitions, is its most notable outcome and one thoroughly in keeping both with the theory of organic form expressed by its heroine in Book 5 and with the general tendency of woman writers to create new hybrid forms.

In mixing epic and philosophic verse with a female bildungsroman, Barrett Browning may have been attempting both to capitalize upon the success of women in the genre of the novel and to defeat the gender-genre double-bind whereby this female achievement was repeatedly devalued. Critics might be able to rationalize the success of women novelists by reformulating the characteristics of the genre in female terms, but could they do the same with a novel that was also an epic? Some did, of course, by insisting that *Aurora Leigh* was only a novel after all, and a woman's novel at that. Thus William Bell Scott observed, "It is only a novel à la Jane Eyre, a little tainted by Sand" (cited by Hayter, p. 159). Others acknowledged the obviously hybrid quality of the work without, however, giving very much attention to Barrett Browning's epic aspirations. Thus, the reviewer in *Blackwood's* objected to the mixing of "splendid bursts of poetry" with the prosaic vulgarity of the mob's riot at Romney's planned wedding to a daughter of the people, insisting that "all poetical characters—all poetical situations, must be idealised. . . . Therein lies the distinction between a novel and a poem" (pp. 34–35). Similarly, in the *Revue des Deux Mondes*, Emile Montégut objected to the "mêlée" of the "vulgar and the ideal"; the novel alone can express "the vulgarity and decadence" of the modern age, he argued, because it is "the epic of an age without heroism, without an ideal."[5] Such criticisms disregard Barrett Browning's poetic credo, articulated in *Aurora Leigh*, that no age is without heroism and that the poet's task is to reveal the ideal at the heart of the real, the heroic in the midst of the apparently unheroic present. "The critics say that epics have died out," Aurora notes; but she declares,

> I'll not believe it, I could never deem,
> . . . . . . . . . . . . . . . . . . . . . . . . . . . . . . . . . . . .
> That Homer's heroes measured twelve feet high.
> They were but men:—his Helen's hair turned grey
> Like any plain Miss Smith's who wears a front;
> And Hector's infant whimpered at a plume
> As yours last Friday at a turkey-cock.

Thus "every age,/Heroic in proportions . . . claims an epos" (5.139–155).

Although Barrett Browning's contemporaries did not view her mixing of genres as an unqualified success or explore its connections with her mixing of genders, they did on the whole assume her to be a major author engaging in a significant experiment. Indeed, the *Westminster Review* thought that "the attempt to write a *novel*—which shall also be a *poem*—is a daring one" and that the general success of the attempt was "remarkable" (p. 220). In our own time, Barrett Browning's fusion of the epic with the novel has received much less attention than Tennyson's epic treatment of domestic and personal concerns in *The Princess* and *In Memoriam*, George Eliot's experimentation with a "home epic"

5. Cited by Roy E. Gridley, *The Brownings and France: A Chronicle with Commentary* (London, 1982), p. 182.

in *Middlemarch*, Thackeray's mixture of epic features with the historical romance in *Henry Esmond*, or, to take the most obvious example, Robert Browning's novelization of the epic in *The Ring and the Book*, the work that Chesterton called the "epic of free speech." Until the recent surge of feminist interest in *Aurora Leigh*, modern critics tended either to decry the generically polyglot nature of the work, or to insist, like some of Barrett Browning's contemporaries, that it is only a novel after all. Alethea Hayter, for instance, remarks that Barrett Browning "was writing a novel in verse, emphatically not an epic. She intended it as a novel, and as a novel it must be judged. . . . A great pity, because any judgement of *Aurora Leigh* as a novel must recognize it as a failure" (p. 163).

Hayter overlooks the obvious epic qualities of Barrett Browning's "novel-in-verse": the numerous epic similes and allusions, the division into nine books, the in media res narrative order, the epic catalogues (including catalogues of genres), and above all Aurora's (and by implication her creator's) explicitly epic aspirations. "Never flinch," Aurora tells herself,

> But still, unscrupulously epic, catch
> Upon the burning lava of a song
> The full-veined, heaving, double-breasted Age. (5.213–216)

The phrase "unscrupulously epic"—not, as one might expect, "scrupulously"—sums up the daring manner in which Barrett Browning both simulates and mocks epic conventions, making *Aurora Leigh* a particularly striking example of what Bakhtin terms the "novelized" epic. Bakhtin notes three "constitutive" features of the epic as genre: its subject is a national epic past; its source is national tradition as opposed to "personal experience and the free thought that grows out of it"; and, most important, an "absolute epic distance" created through a "monologic" style, tone, and manner separates the epic world from contemporary reality. When the epic is novelized, the world it depicts is brought into a "zone of maximal contact with the present"; its style becomes "dialogized," reflecting a "multilanguaged consciousness" that disrupts epic stylization with parody and self-parody; and reverence for a valorized, past world of national heroes is replaced by familiarization and laughter (pp. 7–15).

All of these effects result from Barrett Browning's unscrupulous use of epic conventions in *Aurora Leigh*. Thus, epic similes are introduced only to be interrupted in mid-flight, revised by gender reversals, or converted into mock-heroic similes. A satiric catalogue of the "accomplishments" taught to young ladies replaces the catalogues of ships or warriors. The division into nine books and the apocalyptic tone of the ending become self-reflexively parodic when Aurora breaks the seals on letters sent to her from critics and observers: "A ninth seal;/The apocalypse is drawing to a close" (3.98–99). The "monologic" style of the epic is replaced by a rapidly shifting blank verse that ranges from prophetic loftiness to tender lyricism to prosaic satire, satiric verse showing, as Martha Shackford has noted, that Barrett Browning "had read Langland, Chaucer, Pope and Byron to some purpose" (cited by Hayter, p. 162). The heroic exploits of male "characters in action" are replaced by action with the mind of a female character as Aurora takes "for a worthier stage the soul itself" in emulation of the new drama she calls for to replace the mask and buskin, "Boards, actors, prompters, gaslight, and costume" (5.339–340). Finally, the in media res construction takes us not into a past world of gods and heroes "twelve feet high" and founding fathers, "walled off absolutely" from the present age, as Bakhtin notes of the epic, but into the personal past and the spontaneous recollections, meditations, and occasional outbursts of a contemporary young woman whose past is still vitally connected to her present experience as she begins to write at the age of twenty-seven.

This parodic adaptation of epic convention is accompanied by a similar parodic revision of other genres—most notably, a revision of the gender and genre conventions of chivalric romance so conspicuous in Tennyson's *The Princess*. If *Aurora Leigh* is "only a novel," then, it is so not in any conventional sense but in Bakhtin's sense of the term. "Parodic stylizations of canonized genres and styles occupy an essential place in the novel," Bakhtin observes. The novel is "by its very nature, not canonic. It is plasticity itself. It is a genre that is ever questing, ever examining itself and subjecting its established forms to review. Such, indeed, is the only possibility open to a genre that structures itself in a zone of direct contact with developing reality" (pp. 7, 39). Barrett Browning brings the epic and romance into this familiar zone. Setting up a dialogue of genres to reinforce her dialogue of genders, she challenges the "violent order" of gender and genre hierarchies: turning men into compulsive nurturers and women into knights-errant, substituting Aurora for Achilles, bringing plain Miss Smith face to face with Homer's Helen and Homer's heroes. What she said of her experimentation with rhyme can also be said of her free-wheeling questioning of gender and genre distinctions. "If I deal too much with licences, it is not because I am idle, but because I am speculative for freedom's sake."[6]

6. Letter to Hugh Stuart Boyd, cited by Gardner Taplin, *The Life of Elizabeth Barrett Browning* (New Haven, 1957), p. 134.

# HELEN M. COOPER

## [Structure and Narrative in *Aurora Leigh*] †

* * *

The structure of *Aurora Leigh* is significant as a representation of Aurora's transformation. Castan[1] established the narrative time scheme of the poem: through Book 5 Aurora is twenty-seven years old, narrating her life story on the evening she decides to leave England and return to Florence; by the end of Book 5 the "youthful confident" Aurora has caught up with the "sadder" narrator who, unlike those in *Jane Eyre* and *Great Expectations*, does not know the outcome of her story, and therefore is not fully reliable; in Books 6–9 the "story has caught up with the narrator and till the end of the poem they stay together."

I want to extend these observations: the later books resemble journal entries in that Aurora records events as they occur. Her readers, thereby, experience the denouement as Aurora does, rather than mediated by her mature knowledge. The tightly structured plot is as important as the narrative time sequence: the events recorded in Books 1–4 are repeated in reverse order in Books 6–9, dividing the poem into two parts:

Written in England:

1. Aurora's parents' marriage, her childhood in Italy, adolescence in England, birth as a poet.
2. Romney's proposal on Aurora's twentieth birthday.
3. Aurora as a writer in London, introduction of Lady Waldemar, Marian Erle's story.
4. Marian's story continued, the abortive wedding.
5. A pivotal book: Aurora's meditation on Art, Lord Howe's party, Aurora's decision to leave England for Italy.

Written in Paris and Italy:

6. Aurora's discovery of Marian in Paris, Marian's explanation of the abortive wedding, Marian's second story.
7. Marian's story continued, the journey to Italy, letters to Lord Howe and Lady Waldemar.
8. Romney's arrival in Florence, his and Aurora's reassessment of the discussion that took place on her twentieth birthday.
9. Marian's refusal to marry Romney, Aurora's union with Romney, her rebirth as a poet.

† From *Elizabeth Barrett Browning: Woman and Artist* by Helen M. Cooper (Chapel Hill: U North Carolina P, 1988), 153–55.  The author's notes have been deleted.

1. C. Castan, "Structural Problems in the Poetry of *Aurora Leigh*," *Browning Society Notes* 7, no. 3 (December 1977): 73–81 [*Editor*].

Aurora repeats, in the last four books, the experiences of the first four, but engages in them very differently. Whereas Book 1 records the union of Aurora's parents, Book 9 celebrates the union between Romney and Aurora. Book 2 records Romney's proposal and Aurora's rejection of it, whereas Book 8 contains the cousins' reinterpretation of that day. Books 3 and 7 tell of the attempted and actual rape of Marian, whereas Book 4 records the abortive wedding and Book 6 gives Marian's explanation for her failure to appear at it. The poem describes a narrative return that can be schematized:

| ENGLAND | | ABROAD |
|---|---|---|
| 1 | Union | 9 |
| 2 | Romney and Aurora, her twentieth birthday | 8 |
| 3 | Marian's story | 7 |
| 4 | Marian's story, the wedding | 6 |
| 5 | Art | |

Whereas the first books offer a mediated though unfinished autobiography, the last four demonstrate in episodic fashion the stages in Aurora's integration of woman and poet, her transformation from being the object of Romney's gaze to being the subject of her own vision. The *National Review* had an inkling of this in its assessment of the poem's controversial ending:

> She learns the error of her life,—that she had striven to be an artist instead of a woman, rather than been content to be a simple woman, and let her art spring from that true basis; and the truth, which is the deepest moral of the work, overwhelms her with its sudden conviction, that great as is art, greater is the human life of the artist; and greatest, love, which is the centre of that life and of all life— . . . As the theme deepens, and the faulty artist forgets herself in the true poet, the verse runs smooth and clear.

The transformation of the "faulty artist" into the "true poet" is effected by Aurora's refusal to identify "artist" as "man." Whereas the relationship of Aurora to her father and his books informs the first half of the narrative, Marian Erle's experience controls the second half; Aurora's story resolves the conflicts between the male literary and female cultural economies to which Barrett Browning was heir.

* * *

# DOROTHY MERMIN

## [The Idea of the Mother in *Aurora Leigh*] †

* * *

While the plot which had haunted Barrett Browning's imagination from early childhood is so relentlessly discredited, moreover, a similar plot intersects and displaces it: the daughter's quest for the mother. Here women are both subject and object, men little more than distractions. Except for some obscure images of alienation and betrayal, Barrett Browning had had little to say about mothers, babies, feeding, and eating: having "breasts/Made right to suckle babes" is proof of being a woman (6:1183–84). All the women except Aurora herself, as well as such personifications as Nature, Italy, and the modern Age, are conceived primarily as mothers, good or bad, and filial perspectives are augmented by maternal ones.

The mother whose early death filled the world with the "mother-want" (1:40) that suffuses the poem was, like Barrett Browning's own, an ambiguous figure, simultaneously encouraging and quelling, of whom Aurora recalls only six words: "Hush, hush—here's too much noise!"—an ominous legacy to a poet-daughter, but for the fact that as she spoke them "her sweet eyes/Leap[t] forward, taking part against her word/In the child's riot" (1:17–19). She died when Aurora was four, and her death seems to have been somehow (not in any obvious way) a consequence of love. Like Mary Moulton-Barrett, she was too womanly and tender: "She was weak and frail;/She could not bear the joy of giving life,/The mother's rapture slew her" (1:33–35). Or, in an even more elliptical formulation: Aurora's father looked at her, "he loved./And thus beloved, she died" (1:91–92). It is not surprising that a portrait painted from her dead face haunts her daughter as an image of perplexing ambivalence:

> Ghost, fiend, and angel, fairy, witch, and sprite,
> A dauntless Muse who eyes a dreadful Fate,
> A loving Psyche who loses sight of Love,
> A still Medusa with mild milky brows
> All curdled and all clothed upon with snakes
> Whose slime falls fast as sweat will; or anon
> Our Lady of the Passion, stabbed with swords
> Where the Babe sucked; or Lamia in her first
> Moonlighted pallor, ere she shrunk and blinked
> And shuddering wriggled down to the unclean.
> (1:154–63)

† From *Elizabeth Barrett Browning: The Origins of a New Poetry* by Dorothy Mermin (Chicago and London: Chicago University Press, 1989), 190–96. Reprinted by permission.

These are images of virtue and power thwarted, self-contradiction and defeat, even though we know that love will return to Psyche and our Lady will ascend to heaven. Teaching that women are bound to sorrow, the mother appears to her daughter as both tender and malign. She becomes the shifting embodiment of everything the daughter "read or heard or dreamed" (1:148) about women, the object of worship, desire, repugnance, and fear. The milk that streams through the poem in an astonishing flood of imagery, signifying love, flows first from the slime of Medusa's snaky hair.

The first substitute for the lost maternal presence is nature, a familiar symbolic equivalence that here becomes unflinchingly literal. Aurora's father takes her to live in the mountains, "Because unmothered babes, he thought, had need/Of mother nature" (1:112–13) and of "Pan's white goats, with udders warm and full/Of mystic contemplations" (1:114–15). But at the moment of her departure the maternal hills of Italy withdraw from her, as her mother had withdrawn into death: from the ship taking her to England she looks back and sees

> The white walls, the blue hills, my Italy,
> Drawn backward from the shuddering steamer-deck,
> Like one in anger drawing back her skirts
> Which supplicants catch at.
>
> (1:232–35)

She returns to Italy, years later, still yearning for maternal love.

> And now I come, my Italy,
> My own hills! Are you 'ware of me, my hills,
> How I burn toward you? do you feel to-night
> The urgency and yearning of my soul,
> As sleeping mothers feel the sucking babe
> And smile?
>
> (5:1266–71)

Put so literally, Aurora's question can have only one answer: "Nay" (5:1271).

Into the vacancy left by her mother's death her father pours (all he has to give) a boy's education in the classics. But he dies when she is thirteen—at puberty, when gender distinctions come inexorably into play—and she is inducted into femininity by the unaffectionate aunt who represents not the nurturing mother of infancy but the one who betrays her daughter by inculcating subservience of men. Under her aunt's supervision she receives the lessons proper for a girl: music, drawing, dancing, and needlework, formalistic and inhumane religious instruction, a little French and German and a bit of mathematics, treatises on the inferiority of women, and a variety of disconnected facts (1:392–455). She performs without pleasure but without complaint the social duties that had galled Elizabeth Barrett when her own aunt imposed them. Her aunt tries to consummate her education in feminine subordination by persuading her to marry Romney, telling her (the most painful lesson of all, being true) that she is in love with him. But at this point—she is twenty now, her adolescence over—Aurora asserts her own will, and the aunt dies and leaves her to go her own way.

The composite maternal image in the portrait then splits into two opposite figures: virtuous Marian Erle and wicked Lady Waldemar, the victimized innocent and the predatory sophisticate, the good mother and the bad. They retain traces of mythic doubleness, their oxymoronic names linking them to nature and the preternatural: *Marian Erle,* virgin mother of Christ and pagan fairy, Lady *Waldemar* (wald-e-mar), the forest and the sea. And while Marian eventually becomes a mother herself, virgin in spirit if not in fact, she first appears as a daughter, the object of repeated maternal betrayals—the definitive ones being, like the aunt's attempt to give Aurora to Romney, sexual. Her mother tries to sell her to a man; and Lady Waldemar, the "woman-serpent" (6:1102) whose beautiful milk-white breasts are bared only for display (5:619–27), hands her over under the pretense of maternal affection to a still more depraved woman who in turn delivers her to a Parisian brothel. All this, says Marian, is "only what my mother would have done, [. . .] A motherly, right damnable good turn" (7:9–10).

As a mother herself, however, Marian becomes the object of Aurora's hunger and quest, "Whom still I've hungered after more than bread" (6:454). Having fled to Paris to escape from Lady Waldemar, the false mother she thinks Romney is going to marry, Aurora catches sight of Marian's face, which rises into her consciousness like that of a drowned person rising to the surface of the water—"a dead face, known once alive" (6:239), charged with the contradictions of the mother's portrait: "old" and "new" (6:240), familiar and fantastic, spectral and real, innocent and apparently (since she is holding a child) sexually impure. This momentary vision inaugurates a dreamlike, directionless search through the streets of Paris that is Aurora's version of a knightly quest. When she finds Marian, she immediately offers her "a home for you/And me and no one else" (6:458–59), as if proposing marriage.

Her attempt at rescue is more effective than any of Romney's, since it does not imply domination, and it is not punished like his. It does not work, however, quite as she plans. First she escorts Marian in proper knightly fashion, "As if I led her by a narrow plank/Across devouring waters" (6:482–83); but Marian wants to go home to her child, and so in turn (repetition stressing the reversal) "she led/The way, and I, as by a narrow plank/Across devouring waters, followed her,/Stepping by her footsteps, breathing by her breath" (6:500–503), like a child following her mother. The "home for you/And me and no one else" must have room for a baby, for although Marian is indeed a loving mother, Aurora is neither her husband nor her child. And insofar as Aurora thinks that she is pursuing the bad mother rather than the good, hoping to save a fallen woman (a favorite preoccupation of Victorian men and a charitable activity engaged in my many Victorian women, including Christina Rossetti), she is thwarted by the discovery that Marian did not acquiesce in—was not even conscious of—her sexual violation and is therefore not morally "fallen" at all. They settle down together in a little house in Italy, but she remains outside the charmed circle of mother and child into which she had hoped "to creep [. . .] somewhere, humbly" (7:392). Marian cannot satisfy her restless longing, and the vision of the sea king that summons Romney replaces Marian's drowned face as subaqueous object of desire.

Marian is the last and most benign of the large company of rejecting mothers who crowd the pages of the poem: Aurora's mother and aunt, Marian's mother, Lady Waldemar and her agent, as well as Marian's friend Lucy's horrible grandmother and the various passing sights, voices, and images that stain the fabric of the text with the colors of maternal cruelty. When Lucy dies her grandmother "Scream[s] feebly, like a baby overlain" (4:63)—as if she were simultaneously an evil mother and an abused child—to avoid being mistaken for the corpse. Among the proletarian guests at Romney's wedding Aurora sees "babies, hanging like a rag/Forgotten on their mother's neck,—poor mouths,/Wiped clean of mother's milk by mother's blow/Before they are taught her cursing" (4:576–79). She hears a woman describe herself as "tender": "I never banged a child at two years old/And drew blood from him, but I sobbed for it" (4:821–23). At the other end of the social scale, Lady Waldemar talks of "babes [stretching] at baubles held up out of reach/By spiteful nurses" (5:991–92), and Romney says bitterly that "things went smoothly as a baby drugged" (8:922). Marian generalizes: "God, free me from my mother, [. . .] These mothers are too dreadful" (3:1063–64), and "When mothers fail us, can we help ourselves?" (6:1229). Like Aurora, Marian received parental love among the hills, from nature, and is forced to leave them by a sexual awakening; when her mother tries to sell her to a man, the hills become tainted and terrifying, like the mother, and she cannot return. In the most dreadful of all the images of maternal corruption, Aurora compares natural innocence to "babes/Found whole and sleeping by the spotted breast/Of one a full day dead" (4:1064–66). Nurture is most typically imagined, as in Aurora's dream of Italy, in terms of breasts and milk—"mother's breasts/Which, round the newmade creatures hanging there,/Throb luminous and harmonious" (5:16–18). The imagery defines the quest for the mother as a yearning for the paradise of infancy (or perhaps one should say, makes explicit what lost Edens in poetry are apt to mean): a quest that by definition has to fail.

The representation of motherhood and the loss of Eden is marked as a woman's not only by its extreme literalness but also by the extraordinary balancing of the rejected child's pain on the one side by maternal ambivalence on the other: impulses of exceeding tenderness, and fear that motherhood costs a woman, figuratively or literally, her life. "Our Lady of the Passion" is "stabbed with swords/Where the Babe sucked" (1:160–61). "The mother's rapture slew" Aurora's mother (1:35). Pregnancy makes Marian an outcast, and after her child is born she is dead to everything but him. "I'm nothing more/But just a mother" (6:823–24). "This ghost of Marian loves no more/[. . .] except the child" (9:389–90). A fine emblematic set-piece shows mother and child in the Florentine garden: Marian knelt,

> And peeled a new fig from that purple heap
> In the grass beside her, turning out the red
> To feed her eager child (who sucked at it
> With vehement lips across a gap of air
> As he stood opposite, face and curls a-flame
> With that last sun-ray, crying "Give me, give,"
> And stamping with imperious baby-feet,
> We're all born princes).
>
> (8:8–15)

The kneeling mother and haloed child are like figures in a Florentine painting, a "madonna of the fig," but the child's imperious demand to suck what the mother withholds (a fig instead of a breast) gives an odd turn to the sacred story. Even Marian, who gives everything, does not give enough.

Visions of filial tyranny (inspired partly, no doubt, by the poet's own experience, although the more lurid version in "The Runaway Slave" precedes the birth of Pen) occur much less frequently than those of maternal hostility. Nevertheless, they are obviously interdependent, and they reinforce Aurora's resistance to marriage. While daughters without exception suffer from maternal withdrawal or treachery, male children (like Marian's, or a male poet to whom Aurora compares herself [5:524], or the prospective suitor who is "a good son [. . .] To a most obedient mother" [5:883–84]) command maternal attention—they all seem to have "the master's look" that provoked the runaway slave to murder her infant son. Aurora thinks that children are "given to sanctify/A woman" (6:728–29)—that is, to make her perfect in self-sacrifice. And like the speaker in "Bertha in the Lane" she assumes that children demand their mother's lives, if not their deaths as well.

Had she married Romney when he first asked, she thinks after she has been in London for a while,

> I might have been a common woman now
> And happier, less known and less left alone,
> Perhaps a better woman after all,
> With chubby children hanging on my neck
> To keep me low and wise. Ah me, the vines
> That bear such fruit are proud to stoop with it.
> The palm stands upright in a realm of sand.
> (2:513–19)

She is "a printing woman who has lost her place/(The sweet safe corner of the household fire/Behind the heads of children)" (5:806–8). She takes for granted that if she had children she would not write, but she regrets the children she does not have. Her delight in Marian's son is like Barrett Browning's extravagant baby-worship. While she was writing *Aurora Leigh*, Barrett Browning's friendship with the great singer Adelaide Kemble Sartoris, who had retired from the stage when she married, showed her precisely the predicament that Aurora fears. "The artist has revived in the woman," Barrett Browning reported in 1854, and "the domestic life, though perfectly happy, seems narrow for the soul. She tells me that she feels like a healthy person whose feet & hands are tied—& she suffers yearnings towards her great lost public career, even under the eyes of her beautiful youngest child who has the face of an angel."[1]

The traditional metaphor that poets give birth to poems holds no solace for a woman racked by doubts about maternity: quite the contrary. Aurora is the murderous poet-mother of stillborn children.

> I ripped my verses up,
> And found no blood upon the rapier's point;
> The heart in them was just an embryo's heart
> Which never yet had beat, that it should die.
> (3:245–48)

When she felt something greater burning within her, she could not give it birth (3:251–60), although later she "felt/[Her] heart's life throbbing in [her] verse to show/It lived" (3:338–40). Later still, however, she compares herself with Niobe (5:413–20), all her poem-children dead. Images of creativity as failed maternity are part of her more general realization that metaphorical satisfactions cannot replace real ones, just as the satisfactions of art do not suffice for life.

1. EBB to Anna Jameson, 17 October 1854, English Poetry Collection, Wellesley College Library.

# ALISON CASE

## Gender and Narration in *Aurora Leigh* †

* * *

What begins to emerge from *Aurora Leigh*, then, are two different kinds of story, which have in turn two different kinds of narration. The first, which corresponds roughly with the first four books of the poem, is the *Kunstlerroman*. It is told as a fully-conceived, retrospective narrative: as the reviewer says, "she had it all in her mind at that moment." The form and subject here complement each other, the reader's sense of the narrator's conceptual control of her story, her authority over it, contributing as much to a belief in the tale's telos—successful authorship—as the events of the story itself. If we are aware of a potential counter-narrative in her relations with Romney, it remains a dormant or subordinate one—precisely because of the narrator's conviction that it is tangential to the most important trajectory of her life: her development as an artist.

In Book Five, the novel shifts both its subject matter and its mode of narration. At the opening of this book, Aurora makes her most forceful and coherent statement of what Art in her age can and should be. She chides fellow poets for preferring a romanticized distant past to the heroism and beauty of the everyday present, speaking as someone confident both of her abilities and of her right to judge her fellow-artists. Unsurprisingly, this section of the poem is frequently cited as Barrett Browning's own poetic manifesto. Thus, while Aurora expresses frustration with the shortcomings of her own artistic efforts, complaining that "what I do falls short of what I see" (5.345), it is clear that this is the frustration of the accomplished artist, who cannot be satisfied with anything less than unattainable perfection. Indeed, even these frustrations, as they force Aurora to "set myself to art" (5.351), eventually issue forth in a work which Aurora implies is the long-awaited masterpiece: "Behold, at last, a book" (5.352).

But if Aurora's position as an artist is now as self-assured as it can be without casting doubt on her perfectionism, her emotional state is much more unclear. And as Aurora makes explicit in her discussion of her fellow-poets, Graham, Belmore, and Gage, the reasons for this have to do with the conflicts between her gender and her role as artist. While Aurora insists that she "never envied" these male poets for their "native gifts" or "popular applause" (5.505–517), she confesses to envying them for the adoring women who provide emotional support for their work and fill out the void in their personal lives: Belmore has a girl who,

† Reprinted by permission from *Victorian Poetry* 29, no. 1 (Spring 1991): 25–32.

hearing him praised, "Smiles unaware as if a guardian saint/Smiled in her" (5.523–524); Gage's mother murmurs wonderingly, " 'Well done,' " at each "prodigal review" of his new work, as unthinkingly proud of his poetry now as she was of his "childish spelling-book" years before, while Graham has "a wife who loves [him] so,/She half forgets, at moments to be proud/Of being Graham's wife" (5.525–537).

Aurora herself suggests that the emotional lack she feels is that of orphanhood, but it is hard to see how either Aurora's silencing mother—whose only remembered words are "Hush, hush—here's too much noise" (1.17)—or her melancholic intellectual father could provide the kind of self-effacing, unconditional adoration these male poets receive from mother, lover, or wife. The passage points rather to Aurora's frustration at the gap her gender creates between artistic and emotional self-fulfillment between the happy ending of a *Kunstlerroman* and that of a love story. Indeed, in case we miss the connection, Aurora immediately shifts to a forcedly casual mention of the fact that she has "not seen Romney Leigh/Full eighteen months . . . add six, you get two years" (5.572–573). The passage thus makes an appropriate transition from one tale to the other—from the quest for artistic achievement and recognition to that for emotional fulfillment. The quest will lead her (unwittingly) first to Marian Erle, who with her "doglike" (4.281) devotion seems a potential stand-in for the adoring women Aurora feels the lack of, and finally to Romney Leigh.

The discussion at the opening of Book Five not only marks the transition in subject matter from *Kunstlerroman* to love story, it also, significantly, marks the switch to a different mode of narration. The peculiar account of time in the passage quoted above—with the poet apparently noting with ellipses a lapse of six months during which the manuscript had been abandoned literally mid-line—suggests a more immediate relation between the narrator and her tale. Immediately afterward, Aurora refers to "tonight['s]" events, and from here until the end of the novel her narration approximates most closely to that of a journal, written, as she says at the end, "day by day," sometimes in the immediacy of strong emotion—as when, after discovering Marian in Paris, she has to break off writing because her "hand's a-tremble" (6.416)—and sometimes with a degree of calm retrospection. Just as the retrospective narrative of the previous portion of the novel/poem exemplifies the artistic control the acquisition of which it recounts, so here Aurora's more fragmented narrative reflects a certain lack of control and an absence of conscious purpose appropriate to her problematic relation to the love plot.

Of course, the division between narrative modes is not absolute. As I have mentioned, there are buried strains in the early account of Aurora's dealings with Romney. The tensions between romantic involvement and artistic control show themselves in other ways with the introduction of Marian Erle and Lady Waldemar in Books Three and Four. From the beginning of Book Three, in which the narrator lapses briefly into present tense to hint at her unhappiness—claiming that she has grown "cross" and "pettish" (3.35–36) for reasons she does not elaborate—Aurora's artistic self-confidence and determination begin to run parallel with an emotional dissatisfaction and even a certain self-distrust—as when she chides herself for failing to warn Romney and Marian about Lady Waldemar. This loss of control takes its most interesting artistic toll in the form of some curiously misused metaphors in Book Four. In the first, Aurora attempts to account for her feeling of awkwardness with Romney by comparing them to two clocks:

> Perhaps we had lived too closely, to diverge
> So absolutely: leave two clocks, they say,
> Wound up to different hours, upon one shelf,
> And slowly, through the interior wheels of each,
> The blind mechanic motion sets itself
> A-throb to feel out for the mutual time. (4.420–425).

But, she goes on, "It was not so with us, indeed: while he/Struck midnight, I kept striking six at dawn" (4.426–427). The point of the metaphor seems to be to demonstrate its inapplicability to herself and Romney, as if its very inappropriateness would account for her discomfort.

Later, Aurora attempts to comfort Romney after Marian's disappearance by assuring him that Marian, " 'however lured from place,/ Deceived in way, keeps pure in aim and heart/As snow that's drifted from the garden bank/To the open road' " (4.1068–71). Romney is quick to point out the flaw in her comparison:

> 'The figure's happy. Well a dozen carts
> And trampers will secure you presently
> A fine white snow-drift. Leave it there, your snow:
> 'Twill pass for soot ere sunset' (4.1072–75).

In both instances, Aurora introduces a comparison which seems curiously at odds with her intention, as each points to an end—reunion with Romney, or defilement for Marian—which is the direct opposite of the situation it is intended to illuminate. Interestingly, the "mistake" in each metaphor lies not in the initial comparison but in the ending assigned to its implicit "plot": the clocks which should align themselves remain discrepant; the snow remains pure in a place where in fact it would be defiled. What is most significant about these mistaken metaphors is not simply the unconscious desires they presumably reveal (desires which the novel goes on to fulfill), but the fact that such desires should reveal themselves precisely in a lapse of artistic control—of the poet's power to make metaphors.

The metaphors hence provide brief hints of a narrator not fully conscious of her own ends. This pattern becomes more pronounced once the retrospective portion of the narrative stops. The relation of events to error—can no longer be signaled authoritatively by Aurora herself, as she now writes from a position of immersion in events rather than of confident hindsight. Instead, Aurora as narrator is continually revealed as unreliable, in error, both through her conspicuous repressions and denials regarding her feelings for Romney, and through the reversals in her dealings with Marian, in which she must confess to her own hasty misjudgments.

The best example of the former is Aurora's prolonged attempt to come to terms with Romney's (supposed) new engagement to Lady Waldemar, news of which she has picked up at Lord Howe's evening party. This section is apparently written immediately after her return—the party is referred to as having occurred "tonight"—and it shows Aurora in the very process of assessing and resolving her feelings by writing about them. Her reflections continually change direction, as she recognizes the significance of what she has already written, and then pauses to redirect her thoughts. She opens, for example, with an effort to attribute her unhappiness after the event to a general discomfort with such occasions—"It always makes me sad to go abroad" (5.579)—but by the end of her poetic reproduction of the evening's conversation it has become clear to her that the real source of discomfort is Lady Waldemar: "The charming woman there—/This reckoning up and writing down her talk/Affects me singularly" (5.1041–43). Aurora goes on to attribute this to what she sees as Lady Waldemar's genius for social torture, but eventually pauses again to reflect: "And after all now . . . why should I be pained/That Romney Leigh, my cousin, should espouse/This Lady Waldemar?" (5.1064–66). From here she launches into an elaborate series of reflections on marriage, men, and Romney in particular, in an attempt to confront this "pain" and resign herself to the marriage. In the course of these, she examines and rejects every possible ground for objecting to Romney's marriage except the one which naturally presents itself to a reader—personal jealousy. That her attempt at resignation has ultimately failed is made clear by the broken, halting tone of her conclusion—

> And then at worst,—if Romney loves her not,—
> At worst—if he's incapable of love,
> Which may be—then indeed, for such a man
> Incapable of love, she's good enough.
> For she, at worst too, is a woman still
> And loves him . . . as the sort of woman can. (5.1120–25)

—and by her sense of physical irritation and discomfort at the close: "My loose long hair began to burn and creep,/Alive to the very ends, about my knees" (5.1126–27).

The repression and confusion which this passage reflects, the alternating suggestion and denial of romantic interest in the man being discussed, make the narration here closest to that of the heroines of epistolary novels. As innocent girls, such narrators are expected to be unable to hide or repress their tender feelings; as well-bred young women, however, they are not supposed to acknowledge, or even be fully conscious of, romantic feelings which are not (yet) reciprocated or approved. To the extent that (like Richardson's Clarissa) they are being presented as morally serious and intelligent, such heroines often go through the kind of elaborate self-questioning and efforts at resignation that we see here, but as in Aurora's case, these reflections are often at least as significant for what is not recognized or acknowledged as for what is.

Such a narrator necessarily has a fundamentally different relation, to her story and to a reader, from the authoritative retrospective narrator to whom we were initially introduced. In essence, we are asked to read against her more than with her. Instead of trusting the narrator to signal the shape his/her own life is to take, we focus on the gap between narrator and implied author, and trust the author to make the narrator betray herself, to signal the novel's telos between the lines of her own ignorance. And with the loss of the power of narrative ordering, Aurora comes too to seem less the shaper of her own fate, and more its passive object—it is no coincidence that the end of the novel sees such a concentration of accidental misunderstandings, missed meetings, and other twists of fate. Inevitably, the novel's satisfactory resolution comes to seem more the doing of the author acting as *deux ex machina* than of the narrator.

Herein lies one of the most recalcitrant discomforts of *Aurora Leigh*. Even after its sources and purposes have been traced, the contradiction between Aurora's initial "I loved him not, nor then, nor since, nor ever" and her later "I loved you always" remains as unsettling to modern feminist readers as it was to that early reviewer, for it points to a deeper contradiction between Aurora's self-confident, bitingly insightful argument for her right to vocational self-determination, and her abject retroactive repudiation of that right after her reunion with Romney. Barrett Browning puts this repudiation in a context which ensures that it is materially irrelevant to Aurora's fate, since it is matched (after she has made it) by Romney's own implicit disavowal of the right he earlier claimed to "use" Aurora for his own ends. Indeed, it is now he, moved by the power of her poetry, who will provide the kind of full-time emotional support for her work he once asked her to provide for his: " 'work for two,' " he tells her, " 'As I . . . for two, shall love!' " (9.911–912). I do not wish to underestimate the power and importance of this final vision of a non-hierarchical union between a man and a woman. But this balance is not Aurora's compromise. While Barrett Browning's plot balances, against Aurora's unconditional self-abasement to Romney,

Romney's own change of heart, her artist/narrator cannot reaffirm, in the face of romantic fulfillment, her right to have held out for that balance—calling instead for women to "believe in love" as a power to overcome the romantic/vocational contradictions she has experienced. The shift from the story of Aurora's artistic achievement to that of her romantic fulfillment is accompanied by a shift to a narrative mode which distances Aurora from the shaping of her own fate. Yet, significantly, the same narrative shift is what allows her earlier affirmation to remain within the novel-poem in all its original force, in the form of Aurora's initial retrospective narrative.

Nancy Miller suggests that "implausibilities" of plot in many women's novels represent efforts to express an " 'ambitious wish,' " a "fantasy of power" whose expression is impossible within the patriarchal conventions of the novel, because those conventions permit to female heroines only plots based on erotic wish-fulfillment. "The inscription of this power," she writes, "is not always easy to decipher," because it is necessarily covert:

> When these modalities of difference are perceived, they are generally called implausibilities. They are not perceived, or are misperceived, because the scripting of this fantasy does not bring the aesthetic "forepleasure" Freud says fantasy scenarios inevitably bring: pleasure bound to recognition and identification, the "agrément" Genette assigns to plausible narrative.[1]

Miller's argument about the conventions which govern "plausible" plots could be extended to cover those which govern "consistent" narration, for, as we have seen, the narrative improprieties of *Aurora Leigh* served to fold into the work a plot of female ambition. Barrett Browning could not, given the conventions she had taken on in writing a novel-poem, throw away altogether the idea of marriage as the required telos of a young woman's story—nor even fully subordinate it to a "higher" aim of artistic achievement. But the mixed narration of *Aurora Leigh* did allow her to create a kind of double teleology for the novel, in which the struggle toward artistic independence and success, the plot of poetic "ambition," could be kept relatively isolated from the undermining influence of the traditional lovestory, with its emphasis on female passivity and lack of emotional or sexual self-knowledge, its insistence on loving self-abnegation as the proper "end" of female existence.

1. Nancy K. Miller, "Emphasis Added: Plots and Plausibilities in Women's Fiction," *PMLA* 96 (1981): 41–42.

# JOYCE ZONANA

## "The Embodied Muse": Elizabeth Barrett Browning's *Aurora Leigh* and Feminist Poetics†

* * *

Angela Leighton avoids the patriarchal (and heterosexist) presumptions of Jungian anima-animus psychology when she persuasively argues that Aurora, after her "emancipation" from "the long shadow of the father muse" (p. 140), takes the female Marian to be her liberating sister muse of "contemporaneity and commitment" (p. 154). Leighton's argument is compelling, even exhilarating, particularly when she suggests that Aurora's mature voice no longer speaks a "poetics of the daughter, but of the woman" who daringly allies herself with her fallen sister (p. 154). But Leighton stops just short of an even more emancipatory vision of female poetic authority: that the poet finds her voice within herself, that the muse as well as the poet is liberated from her status as object to become a fully empowered subject.

If Aurora's identification with Marian is to be the radically feminist act Leighton (I think correctly) takes it to be, then Marian must cease to be an object to Aurora. And if she is the muse, then she must be a new kind of muse, one who is fully integrated with the poet, a subject in her own right. Aurora moves from her rediscovery of Marian in Paris to her discovery of her self in Italy. Marian helps her along her path, for she is, as Leighton, Cooper, Rosenblum, and others have shown, an essential mirror in Aurora's process of self-discovery. But it is trivializing Marian to see her only as an "instrument" of Aurora's growth. If Marian teaches anything to Aurora, it is that all individuals must be perceived as subjects, never as objects in other people's social schemes or literary representations. Thus, in the final pages of the poem, Marian vanishes from the narrative, for Barrett Browning refuses to place her in any position in relation to Aurora. Aurora must speak her own truth, affirming—and naming—a muse (the dawn) who is nothing less than her very self.

The reluctance of feminist critics to read *Aurora Leigh*'s concluding lines as a portrayal of Aurora as muse is understandable. To regard the female poet as a muse appears to be a denial of her subjectivity, a negation of her quest to be a poet rather than the object or inspirer of male poetry. Yet such conclusions are necessary only if we are confined to the traditional, Christian and patriarchal, conception of the "heavenly"—and "otherly"—female muse. We might be persuaded otherwise

† Reprinted by permission from *Tulsa Studies in Women's Literature* 8, no. 2 (Fall 1989): 243–59.

if we could see that Elizabeth Barrett Browning began the process (which has perhaps reached its apex in the recent work of Mary Daly) of reclaiming the muse as a powerful image of female divinity, creativity, and sexuality—for women as well as for men. Aurora is an earthly not a heavenly muse: what enables her to function as a muse is her full subjectivity, her radical embodiment, her complete acceptance of herself as woman and artist. Elizabeth Barrett Browning abandons the idealization and objectification of the female that have been a part of the Western tradition of the muse since the overlay of Christian neoplatonism on ancient Greek myth, offering instead a corporeal muse who has "herself a sort of heart" (9.27). Aurora is not a transcendent, disembodied, heavenly figure who can only be apprehended by a poet who has closed his senses to earthly temptations and distractions. Nor is she a Victorian Angel in the House, the nineteenth century's version of Milton's Urania. Instead, she is an immanent, embodied, earthly woman who teaches that the only "way" to heaven is through a complete valuation of "the despised poor earth,/The healthy, odorous earth" (9.652–53).

The proper conceptualization and function of both poet and muse is a focus of much of Barrett Browning's poem. Beginning with Aurora's celebrated analysis of her mother's portrait, the term "Muse" is introduced early in Book 1, and it recurs throughout the poem, reminding us that we are in an epic environment where one might legitimately expect to encounter muses. As Hesiod had observed in the *Theogony*, at the opening of the Western tradition of epic, the Muses had instructed him "always to put [them] at the beginning and end of my singing," and so most male poets had complied.[1] But in Barrett Browning's "unscrupulously epic" work (5.214), the poet and the reader must learn to "let go conventions" (1.852). Aurora meditates:

> What form is best for poems? Let me think
> Of forms less, and the external. Trust the spirit,
> As sovran nature does, to make the form;
> For otherwise we only imprison spirit
> And not embody. (5.223–27)

Aurora may refer to the Muses but only in ways that will "embody" rather that "imprison" her poetic spirit.

Thus there are no explicit invocations to the muse in the poem. At the outset of her nine-book epic, Aurora begins with a brash self-confidence: "I . . . /Will write my story," she proclaims, "for my better self" (1.2–4). She has no need for a muse because she is writing of what she knows; muses had primarily functioned as guarantors of poetic truth for poets writing about historical or cosmic subjects for which they required authoritative witnesses. Milton places his trust in a muse that "from the

1. Hesiod, *Theogony,* trans. Richmond Lattimore (Ann Arbor: University of Michigan Press, 1959), 1.34. Subsequent references are cited parenthetically in the text.

first/Wast present"; Homer appeals to muses who "know all things"; and Virgil calls on goddesses who "remember" and can tell."[2] In contrast to these epic singers, Aurora is her own authority, and she places herself at the beginning and end of her epic. In doing so, she goes even further than her recent precursor Wordsworth in a romantic revision of classical tradition, for Wordsworth, also writing an autobiographical epic, nevertheless maintained his dependence on the "correspondent breeze" in *The Prelude,* and in his "Prospectus" to the *Excursion* he called on a muse "greater" than Milton's Urania.

In another contrast with her male predecessors, particularly in the English tradition, Aurora is content to sing from a vantage point on earth. Not only does she not require an external muse for authoritative knowledge, she also does not ask to fly or be raised as both Milton and Wordsworth had requested. Rather, she deliberately insists that to write effectively and authentically, she must stand—or at times even lie—on the earth.

Aurora's full acceptance of her position as an earthly singer comes late in the poem. At first, following the patriarchal tradition she has imbibed in her father's books, she envisages inspiration as elevation and transcendence of the senses, imagining that Zeus's eagle has ravished her

> Away from all the shepherds, sheep, and dogs,
> And set me in the Olympian roar and round
> Of luminous faces for a cup-bearer. (1.921–23)

A moment later, however, she "drop[s] the golden cup at Herè's foot" and "swoon[s]" back to earth, where she finds herself "face-down among the pinecones, cold with dew" (1.929–31). Eventually Aurora will not have to fall but will choose to lie among the pine cones.

Aurora's vision of inspired flight recalls Eve's dream in *Paradise Lost;* she has moved up to the realm of the gods too quickly, failing to recognize what Romney will later emphasize:

> "You need the lower life to stand upon
> In order to reach up unto that higher;
> And none can stand a-tiptoe in the place
> He cannot stand in with two stable feet." (4.1207–10)

Or, as Aurora herself puts it,

> No perfect artist is developed here
> From any imperfect woman. Flower from root,
> And spiritual from natural, grade by grade

2. John Milton, *Paradise Lost, Complete Poems and Major Prose,* ed. Merritt Y. Hughes (Indianapolis: Odyssey, 1957), 1.19–20; Homer, *The Iliad,* trans. Richmond Lattimore (Chicago: University of Chicago Press, 1951), 2.485; Virgil, *The Aeneid,* trans. Allen Mandelbaum (Berkeley: University of California Press, 1981), 9.702.

In all our life. A handful of the earth
To make God's image! (9.648–52)

Heaven is to be gained not by abandoning but by embracing earth. As Milton expressed it in *Paradise Lost,* humans can only "put on" divinity through a full acceptance of their mortal limits. Yet while this is the thematic import of the action in *Paradise Lost,* the epic narrator needs to soar, "upheld" by Urania, in order to report that truth properly. In contrast, Aurora moves closer to the earth, deeper into her own embodied spirit, as her poem articulates its own transforming truth, "which, fully recognized, would change the world/And shift its morals" (7.856–57).

Before considering some aspects of the process by which Aurora arrives at the full knowledge of her "truth" and her muse, it may be helpful to examine briefly some of the central tenets of her philosophy and their implications for her poetics. Most simply stated, Aurora's mature message, presented in Book 7 of the poem, is that "a twofold world/Must go to a perfect cosmos" (7.762–63). The material and spiritual worlds are so intimately and necessarily intertwined, she claims, that "who separates those two/In art, in morals, or the social drift,/Tears up the bond of nature and brings death" (7.764–66). For Aurora, it is the division of spirit and flesh, not disobedience to Reason or God, that constitutes the Fall, bringing death into the world. As she states, to "divide/This apple of life"—"The perfect round which fitted Venus' hand"—is to destroy it "utterly as if we ate/Both halves" (7.769–73).

Aurora condemns both those who value only spirit and those who believe that only the material is real. Yet while the world is twofold, spirit and flesh inextricably intermingled, epistemologically and developmentally the material is primary. One cannot apprehend spirit except through flesh. Thus, the artist "holds firmly by the natural, to reach/The spiritual beyond it" (7.779–80). And hence Aurora's epic will be grounded in the "natural" world of the poet's life; she will tell a story of contemporary experience, and she will rely on highly concrete "woman's figures" (8.1131) to communicate her twofold truth that

Without the spiritual, observe,
The natural's impossible—no form,
No motion without sensuous, spiritual
Is inappreciable,—no beauty or power. (7.773–76)

That an embodied, visible muse will preside over the work of a poet with such a message and such a technique should not surprise the reader.

* * *

Beginning with the garden scene in Book 2, Aurora identifies herself as a disembodied, spiritual muse or Psyche, teaching truths to a world led astray by materialism. Though she rejects Romney's attempts to make her into the angel in his house, she becomes an angel all the same—the Angel in the House of poetry. While Romney, with what he later calls "male ferocious impudence" (8.328), insists on the importance of attending to mankind's material needs, Aurora aligns herself with a purely spiritual principle, the Victorian poet's "feminine ideal." As E. L. Bryans was to put it some fifteen years later, the Victorians believed that women more than men possess "natural gifts particularly adapted" for the production of poetry: pity and love, and the capability of "dwelling on the unseen."[3] It is not so much "unfeminine" to be a poet as it is "unmasculine"; in choosing to be a poet, Aurora does not so much challenge her century's gender rules as confirm them.

Thus, though Helen Cooper has argued that after Book 2 Aurora imagines herself as male, I would claim rather that she continues to see herself as a woman, but as a disembodied, spiritual woman—the "heavenly" female whose guises include the Christian muse and the Victorian angel. Cooper believes that because Romney scorns women's poetry, Aurora, to maintain her identity as poet, must redefine herself as male. Cooper reads Aurora's quest in the second half of her poem as the reclaiming of her female identity. Aurora, however, never abandons her female identity; she simply focuses on one aspect of the female (or any human) self—the spiritual. Her quest is to reclaim the material as an integral aspect of her already female, "heavenly" being.

Romney in the garden does not simply argue against "women's verses" (2.831); he questions the value of any commitment, poetic or feminine, to spiritual truths. He insists that his allegiance as a man is to the earth and to other men:

> "But I, I sympathize with man, not God
> (I think I was a man for chiefly this),
> And when I stand beside a dying bed,
> 'T is death to me.
> And I, a man, as men are now and not
> As men may be hereafter, feel with men
> In the agonizing present." (2.294–97; 302–04)

Romney's view of "man" is that he is a virile actor in the world. In the face of Romney's gendered commitment to the material, Aurora makes an equally gendered choice for the spiritual. As Romney chooses the male path of the body and Aurora the female path of the spirit, each divides and destroys the twofold "apple of life." Here in the garden is Elizabeth Barrett Browning's version of the Fall, the division between spirit and flesh, female and male, heaven and earth that will be "restored" in Books 8 and 9 when Romney and Aurora acknowledge their love and the "twofold" nature of reality.

3. E. L. Bryans, "Characteristics of Women's Poetry," *Dark Blue*, 2 (1871), 484.* * *

Because by her own and her culture's definition, poetry is a "feminizing," "angelic" pursuit, Aurora moves, as a poet, towards an excruciatingly disembodied experience of herself. Her contemporaries address her as the Muse and she does not contradict them.[4] She visualizes the landscape of the muse as a "melancholy desert" (1.1021), and she takes this desert to be her home, seeing herself as a "palm" that "stands upright in a realm of sand" (2.519) and feeling "the wind and dust/And sun of the world beat blistering in my face" (5.421–22). In imagining the muse's (and her own) realm as a desert, Aurora does violence to the memory of her mother, who had "drowned" (1.70) and "flooded" (1.68) Aurora's father with passion. The classical Muses too had always been associated with water, singing, as Hesiod tells us, "by the dark blue water/of the spring" (*Theogony*, II.3–4). Aurora goes further than her male precursors in making the muse a disembodied, infertile female figure. She must exaggerate the myths of patriarchy in order finally to free herself from them.

As Aurora becomes a disembodied muse/Psyche, so she perceives the other women in her life as each representing separate aspects of the once composite image. Her English aunt becomes a deadening Medusa, Lady Waldemar a threatening Lamia ("that woman-serpent"—6.1102), and Marian a suffering Madonna. Each of these categorizations allows Aurora to distance the other women she encounters to see them as different from, and potentially destructive to, her own "spiritual" essence as Psyche or muse. Yet eventually she discovers that she has in herself, as her mother's daughter—as a woman—the very qualities she has denied and projected onto others.

In Book 5, she is startled to discover her hair beginning "to burn and creep,/Alive to the very ends" (5.1126–27); she is beginning to recognize herself as a Medusa that has transfixed Romney, even as she repressed her desire for him. To escape this perception, she flees to Italy, only to encounter in France Marian Erle (a lower-class woman who had been betrothed to Romney but who fled from him when she became persuaded that he was marrying her out of charity rather than love). To some extent, she begins to identify with Marian, insisting that together they will be "two mothers" (7.124) for Marian's unnamed fatherless child. At the same time, however, she distances Marian by making of her a Madonna:

> And in my Tuscan home I'll find a niche
> And set thee there, my saint, the child and thee,
> And burn the lights of love before thy face,
> And ever at thy sweet look cross myself
> From mixing with the world's prosperities. (7.126–30)

4. See, for example, III, 363; III, 77; V, 796; and IX, 26.

In setting up Marian as a saint, Aurora promises to strengthen her already well-developed alienation from her physical self and from her world.

Aurora's final maturation as woman and poet comes when she acknowledges and articulates her love for Romney, the "sea-king" (8.60) risen from the depths of her desire. Significantly, Romney appears on a night when Florence appears to Aurora as "flooded" (8.37) and "drowned" (8.38) in shadows. Aurora is no longer in an arid desert; the muse is returning to her source. In the course of admitting to herself and to Romney the nature of her feelings, Aurora unites herself with the women she had previously distanced:

> Now I know
> I loved you always, Romney. She who died
> Knew that, and said so; Lady Waldemar
> Knows that;. . . and Marian. I had known the same,
> Except that I was prouder than I knew,
> And not so honest. (9.684–89)

The Medusa, the Lamia, and the Madonna all know the muse better than she knows herself; Aurora does not so much penetrate beneath the "masks" of womanhood as incorporate them into herself. Muse, Medusa, Madonna, Psyche, and Lamia need no longer be opposed as conflicting aspects of the female. The muse can be both spirit and flesh, heavenly and earthly, taking on a role not merely as the mediator between two realms but as their manifold embodiment.

Aurora offers an especially striking image of the "twofold" union of spirit and flesh in Book 5 during her meditation on her goals as a poet. Articulating her desire to "speak" her poems "in mysterious tune/With man and nature" (5.2–3), Aurora enumerates various aspects of the world she hopes her art will express. Among these are "mother's breasts/Which, round the new-made creatures hanging there,/Throb luminous and harmonious like pure spheres" (5.16–18). The poet seeks to "tune" her verse, not to the harmony of the inaccessible heavenly spheres, but to the music of these very earthly, tangible, and visible spheres of the female body. In just three lines of concentrated imagery, Barrett Browning offers a compelling alternative to the centuries-long tradition of cosmic harmony associated with disembodied and ethereal muses. The idea and the image are echoed when, joined in an embrace with Romney, Aurora feels "the old earth spin,/And all the starry turbulence of worlds/Swing round us in their audient circles" (9.838–40). Through physical passion the female Aurora is suddenly surrounded by the harmony once considered accessible only to males who had transcended their fleshly, mortal limits.

Intimately related to Aurora's ability to hear celestial harmony in mothers' breasts and through her own passion is her linking of the rhythm of blood with the rhythms of her verse—again, a radical alteration of tradition. She reports that, as a young woman, her "pulses set themselves/For concord," that the "rhythmic turbulence/Of blood and brain swept outward upon words" (1.896–98). Later as she articulates her mature poetic theory, she insists, while

> (glancing on my own thin, veined wrist)
> In such a little tremor of the blood
> The whole strong clamor of a vehement soul
> Doth utter itself distinct. (7.818–21)

Aurora here espouses what contemporary feminists have defined as a poetics of the body, and she takes this poetics to its extreme when, dropping her head on the "pavement" of an Italian church, she prays that God

> would stop his ears to what I said,
> And only listen to the run and beat
> Of this poor, passionate, helpless blood—And then
> I lay, and spoke not: but He heard in heaven. (7.1269–72)

Aurora, the poet, silences her voice, allowing her blood to speak.

The reader may object: Aurora's God may hear the beat of her blood, but can a reader? The poetics of the body seems to be a poetics of silence, Aurora's denial of her ambition to speak, a return to the dumbness imposed on women by patriarchy. But in its context, this is an expressive silence, signifying far more than what Aurora elsewhere calls the "full-voiced rhetoric of those master-mouths" (4.1108), the "pregnant thinkers of our time" (4.1098). Aurora's silence in the church recalls the "green silence of the woods" (4.164), the silence of nature that she hears "open like a flower" (1.683). It is a silence actively opposed to the noise of the "master-mouths," a writing with white ink that articulates the truths of what we perhaps should call "mistress-bodies."

In her espousal of silence, Aurora, prostrate on the floor of an Italian church, mimes the prostration of other women (legendary and contemporary) she has referred to throughout the poem. Specifically, she recalls her own allusions to descriptions of rape victims, whether they be the mortal women figuratively ravished by Zeus or the mortal woman—Marian—literally subjected to "man's violence" (6.1226). These problematic descriptions and associations force us to ask if Aurora (and through her Elizabeth Barrett Browning) in fact associates poetic inspiration with sexual possession or, indeed, rape by a male muse. In several discussions of art and the artist, Aurora pointedly refers to two classical rape stories, that of Danae and the shower of gold and of Io and the gadfly. While each story appears at first to suggest that Aurora imagines her inspirer to be a male divinity—or even, perhaps, her male lover-to-be Romney—closer analysis, supplemented by a consideration of Marian's rape, reveals that Aurora's comparisons of herself to these ravished maidens may lead us to see the female body itself—not the male-divinity—as the ultimate source of poetic truth and power.

The first story of divine rape is that of Danae. The painter Vincent Carrington introduces it into the narrative when he asks Aurora to help him judge two new sketches:

> "A tiptoe Danae, overbold and hot,
> Both arms aflame to meet her wishing Jove
> Halfway, and burn him faster down; the face
> And breasts upturned and straining, the loose locks
> All glowing with the anticipated gold.
> Or here's another on the self-same theme.
> She lies here—flat upon her prison-floor,
> The long hair swathed about her to the heel
> Like wet seaweed. You dimly see her through
> The glittering haze of that prodigious rain,
> Half blotted out of nature by a love
> As heavy as fate." (3.122–33)

The passage is resonant with echoes and anticipations of other significant moments and images in the poem. The "tiptoe" Danae may remind us of the Aurora who sought in Book 1 to fly up to heaven, the same Aurora who would later hear Romney insisting that "none can stand a-tiptoe in the place/He cannot stand in with two stable feet" (4.1209–10). Other aspects of the passage strike other chords, revealing the centrality of the Danae figure to Aurora's understanding of herself as woman and artist.

Both Carrington and Aurora prefer the second sketch. Carrington because it " 'indicates/More passion' " (3.134–35), Aurora because

> Self is put away,
> And calm with abdication. She is Jove,
> And no more Danae—greater thus. Perhaps
> The painter symbolizes unaware
> Two states of the recipient artist-soul,
> One, forward, personal, wanting reverence,
> Because aspiring only. We'll be calm,
> And know that, when indeed our Joves come down,
> We all turn stiller than we have ever been. (3.135–43)

Aurora's preference for the second sketch is unsettling, suggesting a passivity that ill accords with the determined activity we know to be necessary for the fulfillment of her "vocation." Yet the Danae "half blotted out of nature by a love/As heavy as fate" recalls the "dauntless Muse who eyes a dreadful Fate" in the mother's portrait. The Danae overcome by

Jove is transformed; she has what the figure in the first sketch can only aspire to. Divinity burns—and drowns—her, making her into a resonant image of the "twofold world" Aurora wants her art to reveal. In Carrington's Danae we literally see "the spiritual significance burn[ing] through/ The hieroglyphic of material shows" (7.860–61). Danae is the artist/ muse who embodies the truth of her art.

The "prodigious rain" that falls on the prostrate Danae has affinities with other "rains" in Aurora's narrative. In Book I she recalls how once, Romney "dropped a sudden hand upon my head/Bent down on woman's work, as soft as rain—/But then I rose and shook it off as fire" (1.543–45). Romney's hand is alternately rain and fire, a fragmented version of the fiery rain that will be Jove. But Aurora will not allow Romney's hand to "calm" her; she awaits, not her mortal lover, but her Jove. And, as Romney later tells her, her Jove has come down, entering into her poetry and finally into him:

> "this last book o'ercame me like soft rain
> Which falls at midnight, when the tightened bark
> Breaks out into unhesitating buds
> And sudden protestations of the spring.
> . . . . . . . . . . . . . . . . . . . . . . . . . . . . . . . . . . . . . . .
> in this last book,
> You showed me something separate from yourself,
> Beyond you, and I bore to take it in
> And let it draw me." (8.595–98; 605–08)

Aurora becomes the vehicle for a truth that transfigures Romney just as Jove transfigures Danae. Aurora herself becomes the "prodigious," fertilizing rain that, in the ancient myth, generates the hero Perseus. It is Perseus who kills the Medusa, whose blood, transformed into Pegasus, ultimately gives rise to Hippocrene, the spring that sustains the Muses.

Of course the most dramatic echo of Danae "flat upon her prison floor" is the moment, already referred to, when Aurora flattens herself on the pavement of the Italian church, no longer striving, no longer reaching up to God, but submitting in silence to the "run and beat" of her own blood. As we have noted, this is a passive Aurora, who has finally given in to the impulses of her own body; the impulses of desire and love. She does not give in to Romney's desire, for at this point she believes him to be married to Lady Waldemar. Rather, she accepts and acknowledges her own passion, taking it to be, finally, divine. Her "blood," then, becomes the equivalent of Danae's "Jove." This is the divinity to which she submits, not to any male within or without. And it is a divinity that has been "in" her all along.

The point is made more explicitly earlier in Book 7 when Aurora uses the story of Io and Jove to figure her experience as an artist. She explains that she has felt the "truth" expressed in her poetry to "hound" her

through the wastes of life
As Jove did Io; and, until that Hand
Shall overtake me wholly and on my head
Lay down its large unfluctuating peace,
The feverish gad-fly pricks me up and down. (7.829–33)

The gad-fly image indicates that the truth Aurora has perceived (of the "twofold world") has tormented her into expression. The "Hand" she awaits seems to promise the reconciling stillness of death. But the Hand is the gadfly transformed, the "truth" deepened to a fuller experience:

When Jove's hand meets us with composing touch,
And when at last we are hushed and satisfied,
Then Io does not call it truth, but love. (7.895–97)

Aurora equates the "truth" that has pursued her with "love," the very experience her father had insisted on in his last words: " 'Love—'/'Love, my child, love, love!' " (1.211–12). Similarly, Jove's hand recalls her father's hand, the hand that as a young woman she had longingly remembered: "O my father's hand,/Stroke heavily, heavily the poor hair down" (1.25–26). Romney had attempted to replace the father, and Aurora had rejected him. But the father's hand itself is a poor substitute for the dying mother's kiss, and the "love" the father had urged on Aurora was only what his wife had taught him. The imagery of a male muse/raptor that seems to pervade Aurora's figure of Jove as gad-fly/hand resolves into its female substrate, the love made manifest by Aurora's mother. And so we may also speculate about why Barrett Browning, who knew her classics well, apparently mistakes the identity of the gad-fly. In the story of Io as told by Ovid and others, the gad-fly is not Jove at all but a creature sent by the jealous Juno to torment her husband's latest mortal mistress. By conflating male and female divinities, Barrett Browning—or her Aurora—appears to signal that the gender of the divinity is less important than its truth—a corporeal/spiritual love that makes manifest the divinity inherent in the body.[5]

It is in Book 7 in the passages just discussed that Aurora offers the fullest articulation of her aesthetic, theological, and social message. Significantly these passages, as numerous critics have noted, occur after Aurora's reunion with Marian Erle. While Aurora first wrote these truths into the manuscript completed before leaving England (at the end of Book 5), the presentation of these ideas after Aurora's reunion with Marian suggests that for the reader if not also for Aurora the full understanding of them is contingent on knowledge of what has happened to

5. Io herself was, in the nineteenth century, identified as the moon, a priestess of Hera, or a form of Hera herself, the earth. "The nymph is an epithet of the goddess," wrote Thomas Keightley in his popular *The Mythology of Ancient Greece and Rome*, 2nd ed. (London: Whittaker, 1838), p. 408. Thus we may discern an even more compelling reason for Aurora's identification with Io and for her appropriation of the gad-fly/hand as an image of love.

Marian. Marian has experienced complete profanation of the human body and shows what can and will occur to a woman when the body is treated purely as body, divorced from spirit. To exalt pure spirit (as Aurora had in her disembodied pursuit of poetry's "spiritual" truth) or to embrace the material to the exclusion of spirit (as Romney had in his utilitarian attempt to improve society) is to create the conditions that caused Marian's rape. It is precisely because of the separation of spirit and flesh that, as Aurora puts it, "the towns/Make offal of their daughters," and both Aurora and Romney are guilty of that separation. Even Marian's rape can be described as a consequence of Aurora's willful denial of her own body and Romney's stubborn denial of his own spirit because their denial kept Aurora and Romney apart leading Romney to choose Marian and Aurora initially to abandon her. Marian's rape serves as a crucial counterweight to Aurora's idealized visions of divine rape and must be considered in any attempt to understand them. Marian too is both Danae and Io, though her Jove is certainly no god.

Marian experiences two devastating betrayals in her life, one when she is sold to a man by her mother, the second when lady Waldemar's former servant sells her to male desire. The first experience, a near-rape, identifies Marian with Danae; the second, an actual rape, links her with Io. Aurora reports how "one day" Marian's mother,

> snatching in a sort of breathless rage
> Her daughter's headgear comb, let down the hair
> Upon her like a sudden waterfall,
> Then drew her drenched and passive by the arm
> Outside the hut they lived in. (3.1044–48)

"Blinded" by "that stream/Of tresses," Marian finds herself confronted by a man "with beast's eyes" (3.1049–50),

> That seemed as they would swallow her alive
> Complete in body and spirit, hair and all,—
> And burning stertorous breath that hurt her cheek,
> He breathed so near. (3.1051–54)

Characterized in terms that recall Carrington's second Danae, Marian flees from this horribly material "Jove," whose heavy breath seems a parody of the longed-for "breathings" of a muse.

In her next encounter with female betrayal and male lust, Marian cannot escape:

> "Hell's so prodigal
> Of devil's gifts, hunts liberally in packs,
> Will kill no poor small creature of the wilds
> But fifty red wide throats must smoke at it,
> As HIS at me . . . when waking up at last . . .
> I told you that I waked up in the grave." (6.1213–18)

Drugged and raped, she finds herself "half-gibbering and half-raving on the floor" (6.1232), reduced like Io to the life of a beast. And like Io she takes to the road, "hunted round/By some prodigious Dream-fear at my back" (6.1266–67), imagining as well "some ghastly skeleton Hand" (6.1243) pursuing her through the landscape.

Marian's experiences of literal rather than figurative rape show Aurora that her own figures but weakly represent the truth she came to perceive. Marian teaches in her own body the terrible cost of separating spirit and flesh—a lesson that Aurora claims to have known before, but only, we must admit, a lesson that Aurora claims to have known before, but only, we must admit, in her spirit. Through her experience with Marian she comes to know and acknowledge this truth fully in her body, submitting to "the run and bear/Of this poor, passionate, helpless blood."

Marian moves from being treated as pure body to spiritual redemption effected by her maternity, "God's triumph" (7.331). For Marian, utter physical abasement results in spiritual elevation, just as Aurora's spiritual elevation, as disembodied muse/artist, requires her descent to the level of her own blood. The two women are necessary counterparts of one another, graphically illustrating through their complementary experiences and language the "twofold" world Aurora and her creator seek to make manifest. The stories of divine rape are completed by the reality of human rape, something that would not occur if the earth, the body, and woman were valued as both material and spiritual. Similarly, the story of human or earthly rape is completed by the stories of divine rape: Marian comes to the experience of divinity on earth through the birth of her child. She speaks of being "beaten down/ . . . into a ditch" (6.676–67) where she awakes to find "bedded in her flesh/ . . . some coin of price" (6.679–81). She reports that God tells her: "I dropped the coin there: take it you,/And keep it,—it shall pay you for the loss" (6.683–84). Marian's "coin of price" figure echoes the Danae imagery used earlier by Aurora. Yet what Marian calls God's "coin" is the product of woman's normal biological capacity. It is Marian's female physiology, her "blood," that becomes her token of divinity.

Rather than reifying or valuing the male muse/raptor, then, Aurora's figures of Danae and Io finally show that any "earthly" woman is, in herself, divine. She has no need of an external source of poetic or spiritual power but contains it within herself. This is the "truth" ("Love") that inspires Aurora, the truth she utters and embodies as both poet and muse.

To read Aurora as the muse—for Barrett Browning, for herself, for Romney, and, ultimately, for the reader—is, finally, to be in a better position to understand why Romney "had to be blinded . . . to be made to see."[6] Modern critics, following the lead of Barrett Browning's con-

6. Elizabeth Barrett Browning, *Letters*, ed. Frederic G. Kenyon (New York: Macmillan, 1897), 2.242.

temporary Anna Jameson, persist in reading Romney's blinding as analogous to (and perhaps even modeled on) Rochester's blinding in *Jane Eyre*, a "punitive equaliser" insuring that this powerful Victorian man cannot "reassert" his "dominant functions."[7] Such a reading ignores Barrett Browning's protest that she was not thinking of Charlotte Brontë's novel when she wrote her poem.[8] More importantly, it fails to take account of a far older cultural archetype that would have been present to Barrett Browning's imagination: the classical stories of a conflict between a mortal singer and the immortal Muses.

One of the most dramatic of such stories is the tale of Thamyris's blinding. As Homer tells the story in *The Iliad*, the poet Thamyris had "boasted that he would surpass" the "very Muses': "these in anger struck him maimed and the voice of wonder/they took away, and made him a singer without memory."[9] Early in *Aurora Leigh*, Romney rejects the transfiguring potential of poetry, claiming that he intends to "impress and prove" that "nature sings itself,/And needs no mediate poet, lute or voice,/To make it vocal" (2.1204–06). Romney assumes the role of Thamyris, claiming that the material world—without any spiritual dimension to it—can sing. Later, of course, after the failure of his schemes and after his blinding, he admits that he was wrong to view

> Our natural world too insularly, as if
> No spiritual counterpart completed it,
> Consummating its meaning, rounding all
> To justice and perfection, line by line (8.617–20)

Romney admits that the poetry of earth can only emerge, "line by line," if one believes that the material is infused with the spiritual. No mortal can sing without a muse who embodies the union of heaven and earth. Romney's blinding is his punishment, not for being a Victorian man, but for his presumption in challenging a goddess. At the conclusion of the poem he accepts Aurora as muse, a woman who will, in Aurora's terms, both "be and do" (5.367). This goddess, unlike her precursors in the poetry of men, is made of earth and committed both to living upon it and transforming it.

7. Cora Kaplan, Introd., *Aurora Leigh and Other Poems*, ed. Cora Kaplan (London: The Woman's Press, 1978), p. 24. See also Elaine Showalter, *A Literature of Their Own: British Women Novelists from Brontë to Lessing* (Princeton: Princeton University Press, 1977), p. 24, and Mermin, "The Damsel," p. 80.
8. *Letters*, 2.246; see also Julia Bolton Holloway, "*Aurora Leigh* and *Jane Eyre*," *Brontë Society Transactions*, 17 (1977), 130–33.
9. *The Iliad*, 2.597–600.

# HOLLY A. LAIRD

## *Aurora Leigh*: An Epical Ars Poetica †

* * * In *Aurora Leigh*, Browning's central *aesthetic* choice and worry appears to be between the Wordsworthian advocacy of a solitary songster inspired by the deep urgings of nature and the Carlylian demand for a didactic writer with urban concerns that he records through rhetorical narratives. Of course, Wordsworth and Caryle actually developed somewhat more complex scenarios than this, such that, paradoxically, we see Wordsworth finding solace both in the visions that come when he is alone and in the prospect of extending this vision to a larger community; while Carlyle's outspoken hero is often depicted as a wandering and visionary outcast who acquires stature and influence in the present age only through the written word. But neither Wordsworth nor Carlyle was able to urge this particular set of opposed possibilities with equal fervor. Browning confronts the choice quite directly, and she comes up with a poem and a poetics to embrace both.

Her poetic hero is a Carlylian character with the power to teach, persuade, and prophesy.

> poets should
> Exert a double vision; should have eyes
> To see near things as comprehensively
> As if afar they took their point of sight,
> And distant things as intimately deep
> As if they touched them. (5.183–87)

yet is also soulful, vulnerable, sensitive, and capable of a long, gradual growth of the mind: "And take for a worthier stage the soul itself" (5:340). Her hero poet lives both in country and city, indulges in both ethical discussion and ecstatic inspiration, is keen both to aesthetic beauty and to social truth, and is both personally interested in events around her and cautious to see them from more than one side. Her story takes form both as a mimetic narrative and an expressive poem (Browning called it a "novel-poem"[1] as well as unscrupulously epic" [5:214).] Later in the poem, Aurora summarizes its character as both an "imitation" of nature and "archetypal" in its symbolism (7:835–43). In short, this is a poetics that gives equal weight to action and character, to mimesis and expressive form, to the double aim to teach and to delight. Why and how the poem achieved aesthetic success in having it both ways is

† From *Writing the Woman Artist: on Poetics, Politics and Portraiture* by Holly A. Laird (Philadelphia: University of Pennsylvania Press, 1991), 357–63. Reprinted by permission of the publisher.

1. *The Letters of Robert Browning and Elizabeth Barrett Browning* (London, 1899), vol. 1, p. 31.

not something I have space to explore in this essay except to note that it was addressed to an audience happily alive to the appeal of large, multipurposed poems; many readers in *Aurora Leigh*'s Victorian audience responded to the formal aspects of the poem, to its richly imaginistic lyricism and large-spirited narrative, with great enthusiasm.

While this concern with a double vision deeply informs Aurora's professed poetics and is, as I will further argue below, its most distinctive feature, the discourse on poetry in Book 5 officially begins, like previous classic defenses of poetry, with a more specific issue likely to concern all writers of her time: the question whether she was living in an age in which heroical epic poetry could be written. She addresses the problem convincingly and wittily, first by cutting the classics down to the size of the present:

> The critics say that epics have died out
> With Agamemnon and the goat-nursed gods;
> I'll not believe it. I could never deem,
> As Payne Knight did . . .
> . . . . . . . . . . . . . . . . . . . . . . . . . . . . . . . . . . . . .
> That Homer's heroes measured twelve feet high.
> They were but men:—his Helen's hair turned grey
> Like any plain Miss Smith's who wears a front;
> And Hector's infant whimpered at a plume
> As yours last Friday at a turkey-cock. (5.139–50)

Second, she appeals to the possibility for heroism in any age and time:

> All actual heroes are essential men,
> And all men possible heroes: every age,
> Heroic in proportions, double-faced,
> Looks backward and before, expects a morn
> And claims an epos.
> Ay, but every age
> Appears to souls who live in't (ask Carlyle)
> Most unheroic. Ours, for instance, ours: (5:151–47)

Finally, she places the responsibility for recognizing heroism squarely with the poet: "the poets abound/Who scorn to touch [the age] with a finger-tip" (5:158–59). Browning joins another common debate of her age in arguing that the poet's subject should be the present rather than Carlyle's fabled past, and she argues that this is a noble subject against his tendency to see the present primarily as an object for satire. The task of seeing the age in this way remains with the poet: whether the age is great or not depends on whether or not its poets can see from two perspectives at once, see the world small and see it large.

In the course of this general argument, Aurora also indicates, indirectly, where to find epic battlegrounds in the present. The great battles of the age are waged, as Aurora's must be waged, in verbal debate:

Nay, if there's room for poets in this world
A little overgrown (I think there is),
Their sole work is to represent the age,
Their age, not Charlemagne's,—this live, throbbing age,
That brawls, cheats, maddens, calculates, aspires,
And spends more passion, more heroic heat,
Betwixt the mirrors of its drawing-rooms,
Than Roland with his knights at Roncesvalles.
. . . .
. . . King Arthur's self
Was commonplace to Lady Guenever;
And Camelot to minstrels seemed as flat
As Fleet Street to our poets. (5: 200–13)

Browning is humorously, yet correctly, specific about where epic debates predominantly occurred: in the social arena of women's drawing rooms and in the bookshops of Fleet Street. Although she does not reiterate them here, the rest of her poem is devoted to the social issues most debated: between the classes, between the sexes, between poetry and social science, between belief and agnosticism. These, in addition to her aesthetic choices, are the proper subject of her poem.

Nonetheless, her avowed aim is not finally to dramatize or announce the victory of any one side of these various issues over the other. Her key terms—as resonant for her as Arnold's "disinterestedness," Wordsworth's "feeling," or Aristotle's "mythos"—are the "twofold," "double vision," and "double-faced." Her use of these terms anticipates the obsession of twentieth-century criticism with the terminology of irony, double perspective, binary opposition, *différance.* In contrast to New Critical irony and structuralist binarism, whose self-cancellations enable the critic to achieve a transcendent detachment, and in contrast to Derridean *différance* with its endlessly radicalizing erosions, Browning's terminology enacts embrasure, enfolding possibilities, multiplying choices, permitting alternatives. Browning's usage in particular of "twofold" and "double vision" anticipates a number of contemporary feminist theorists, who have adopted the vocabulary of "doubleness" to call for a similarly syncretic criticism. A notable difference here is that contemporary feminists tend to use such terms to indicate the difficult dilemmas in which they find themselves, to indicate, for example, the necessity for women to see as men but also as women, to see as women but also as different women—as African-Americans, lesbians, Third-World women—to see as women but also beyond gender, or to see from within an experience but also from without. Browning adopts yet another term, expressive of difficulty, but she again translates it into a word for conciliated opposites. More provocative than "twofold" is the conventionally duplicitous "double-faced," which Browning transforms by continually placing the term in contexts in which it is redefined and revalued as an expression for empathetic vision. For Browning, to see with a "double vision" does not, however, occur without struggle: it is to be able, in another of her formulations, to stand "face to face" with the world, confronting and accepting, opening oneself to and recognizing all that is other to oneself.

Browning's terms receive very various applications in Aurora Leigh's hands. The age is "double-faced" in the citation above, in that, while inhering in the present moment, it looks into both the past and the future. More important, Browning believed that to lead others to a larger vision, she must meet "face to face & without mask the Humanity of the age."[2] and "exert a double vision" (5:184) by seeing both near and far. The artist must strive for a "twofold" life ("O sorrowful great gift/ Conferred on poets, of a twofold life,/When one life has been fond enough for pain!" [5:380–82]); that is, she must both be and see, to "stand up straight as demigods" (5:384). Rearticulating these premises in Book 7, Aurora Leigh sums up in an impressive monologue:

> a twofold world
> Must go to a perfect cosmos. Natural things
> And spiritual,—who separates those two
> In art, in morals, or the social drift,
> Tears up the bond of nature and brings death
> . . . . . . . . . . . . . . . . . . . . . . . . . . . . . . . . . . . . . . . .
> We divide
> This apple of life, and cut it through the pips:
> The perfect round which fitted Venus' hand
> Has perished as utterly as if we ate
> Both halves, Without the spiritual, observe,
> The natural's impossible—no form,
> No motion: without sensuous, spiritual
> Is inappreciable,—no beauty or power:
> And in this twofold sphere the twofold man
> (For still the artist is intensely a man)
> Holds firmly by the natural, to reach
> The spiritual beyond it,—fixes still
> . . . man, the twofold creature, apprehends
> The twofold manner, in and outwardly,
> And nothing in the world comes single to him,
> A mere itself,—cup, column, or candlestick (7:762–805)

Even in her twofold nature, then, the poet does not in fact transcend her fellow creatures, but remains "man, the twofold creature." To be fully "twofold" may be extraordinary, but it can be achieved by anyone with enough will and aspiration; thus, at the end of the poem, even Aurora's hitherto antivisionary cousin Romney, who has devoted his life

2. Ibid.

to everyday problems and practical reforms, can—though as blind as Milton—see with a poet's vision the New Jerusalem.

But the thorniest dialectic of all in this poem is the twofold *gender* of "man." Without the intense, personal experience of writing always in relation to men—in conflict with Romney's desire for a wife, in the shadow of his prejudices about women poets, and in competition with the great male poets of past and present—Aurora's (and Browning's) "twofold" philosophy might never have emerged. Aurora's struggle and ambition as a female animates all the other issues in the poem, most obviously in what she sees as possible "near" and "far" for herself and other women. The poem's feminism clearly has fueled the controversy surrounding it—Browning's gender carried much of the blame for flaws perceived by critics of her day—and most feminist scholars consider the gender issue to be the most distinctive feature of Aurora/Browning's aesthetics. A woman artist is the subject of this poem, and her gender is her major obstacle in setting out on a career. Aurora's speculations about gender literally surround the poetics of Book 5, constituting its narrative frame: her thoughts are most directly focused on gender when she is struggling with the fact of being female in her world, but being female is also her most recurrent worry when trying to write.

Even so, whether as a personal, sociological, or aesthetic problem, femaleness is seen by Aurora as a provisional, man-made obstacle that can be overcome. Aurora dedicates herself unhesitatingly to writing as well as any male ever wrote:

> Measure not the work
> Until the day's out and the labor done,
> . . . . . . . . . . . . . . . . . . . . . . . . . . . . . . . . . . . . . . .
> And, in that we have nobly striven at least,
> Deal with us nobly, women though we be,
> And honor us with truth if not with praise. (5:77–83)

Every artist has a gender (since the artist is "intensely a man"), but writes both in and beyond gender. Aurora does not see herself (and neither, of course, did Browning) as writing exclusively for or about women. She writes as a literate and thoughtful woman for and about both men and women. Speaking in anger to Romney, she makes her position clear,

> 'You misconceive the question like a man,
> Who sees a woman as the complement
> Of his sex merely. You forget too much
> That every creature, female as the male,
> Stands single in responsible act and thought
> As also in birth and death. Whoever says
> To a loyal woman, "Love and work with me,"
> Will get fair answers if the work and love,
> Being good themselves are good for her—

. . . . . . . . . . . . . . . . . . . . . . . . . . . . . . . . . .
But *me* your work
Is not the best for,—nor your love the best,
Nor able to commend the kind of work
For love's sake merely. . . .
For me,
Perhaps I am not worthy, as you say,
Of work like this: perhaps a woman's soul
Aspires, and not creates: yet we aspire,
And yet I'll try out your perhapses, sir,
And if I fail . . . why, burn me up my straw
Like other false works—I'll not ask for grace;
Your scorn is better, cousin Romney. I
Who love my art, would never wish it lower
To suit my stature.' (2:434–94)

Her poetics could not, then, be seen as an "alternative" poetics exclusively for women: it is a poetics for everyone, feminist in that it sees everyone as gendered, and everyone as in need of re-education about women's capacities.

The poem thus to some extent provides its own theoretical context for its celebrated imagery of childbearing women—imagery that forces us literally to see Aurora's ambitions for the female artist, and to see physical femaleness as twofold, sometimes grotesque, sometimes ennobled, and capable of the most diverse symbolism. At the climax of her speech about the possibility for a contemporary epic, she depicts the age itself as female:

Never flinch,
But still, unscrupulously epic, catch
Upon the burning lava of a song
The full-veined, heaving, double-breasted Age:
That, when the next shall come, the men of that
May touch the impress with reverent hand, and say
"Behold,—behold the paps we all have sucked!
This bosom seems to beat still, or at least
It sets ours beating. This is living art,
Which thus presents and thus records true life." (5:213–22)

Aurora does not argue for a gender-free art but for an art that is great with life, and women may represent (flesh out) that life quite literally.

Aurora's epic poetics would not slip easily, however, into a standard anthology of "The History of Criticism" because, of course, it is embedded in a narrative context. *Aurora Leigh* is an extensive *ars poetica*, and although its poetics appears to emerge primarily from a (male) Aristotelian tradition, its *ars* emerges from the modern (woman's) novel. Aurora's theory of art and the artist in Book 5 takes place while she is writing her books, philosophizing about them, trying to make a living, and suffering from solitude. A nonwriter reading the entire poem could glean from it an accurate description of a successful writer's life, of a lengthy career struggle, of writer's blocks, of postwriting depression, and of a writing woman's solitude, courage, selfdoubt, and lucky chances. It is precisely through this contextualization that Browning's poetics works for and, in my view, reaches her most far-flung goals. Browning places her theory in action; she refuses to divorce philosophical rationalization from practical contexts; hers is meant to be a "living " word.

* * *

# ANGELA LEIGHTON

## [Men and Women: Poetry and Politics] †

* * *

As a poet, she [Elizabeth Barrett Browning] learned early to distrust the iconic postures of romance in favour of a socialised and contextualised account of desire. She perceives love, not as a conclusive emotional absolute, but as a mixture of lust, ambition, rhetoric, fear and, above all, conventionality. Hers is thus an essentially politicised poetry, not because politics is its dominant subject matter and not because she shows herself in any sense a political radical (as some critics have complained), but because the tensions between desire and fact, between the individual and the system, can be felt in it. Those tensions were missing in the work of de Staël, Hemans and L.E.L., whose sense of morality was identical with the claims of the heart, but Barrett Browning found them in the novelist who, in a sense, provided her with a much needed counterbalance: George Sand.

Elizabeth lighted on 'the new French literature' comparatively late, in 1842, but thereafter was a confirmed devotee, who tried to convert both Miss Mitford and Robert Browning, though she kept her French enthusiasms secret from her increasingly puritanical father. In particular it seems to have been, as Patricia Thomson points out, not so much the *Corinne*-like *Consuelo* which drew her admiration, but Sand's novels about class and politics. 'Such a colossal nature in every way—', she exclaimed to Robert, 'with all that breadth & scope of faculty which women want—magnanimous, & loving the truth & loving the people'. When she visited Sand in Paris in 1852 she was struck, above all, by the novelist's indifference to appearances: 'A scorn of pleasing she evidently

† Reprinted by permission from *Victorian Women Poets: Writing Against the Heart* by Angela Leighton (Hemel Hempstead: Harvester, 1992), 102–09. The author's notes have been deleted.

had; there never could have been a colour of coquetry in that woman. Her very freedom from affectation and consciousness had a touch of disdain. But I liked her'. After the narcissistic monumentalism of *Corinne*, the sheer emotional and political variety of Sand's writing must have seemed like an opening into that 'experience of life & man' which Elizabeth herself so much craved. The story of *Aurora Leigh*, her long epic poem about the development of the woman poet, contains, among other things, the drama of Barrett Browning's own imaginative emancipation from the self-centred sensibility of de Staël's romance into the 'breadth & scope' of vision she envied in George Sand. Such an emancipation is achieved through sceptically reproducing many of the old figures of female sensibility: the myth of Italy, the figurative anatomisation of the woman's body, the interlocking of the narratives of love and fame, but such devices are now put in the context of a diminishing and sometimes discrediting reality.

As Ellen Moers has shown, the crowning scene in the garden of Book 2 is a prolonged, literary in-joke about the Corinne myth. Aurora, on her twentieth birthday, persuades herself of her poetic vocation by playing the part of Corinne at the Capitol, and crowning herself poet in her aunt's garden. She is then caught in the classic pose of a statue by the unexpected audience of her sceptical and disdainful cousin, Romney:

> I stood there fixed, –
> My arms up, like the caryatid, sole
> Of some abolished temple, helplessly
> Persistent in a gesture which derides
> A former purpose. Yet my blush was flame,
> As if from flax, not stone.
> (2.60–5)

In this moment of triumph turned silly, Barrett Browning seems to be enjoying a joke against all the Corinnes whose art consisted of standing in attitudes. 'Her arms were transcendently beautiful; her figure tall', de Staël wrote. At the end of 'A History of the Lyre', L.E.L. reproduced the same posture:

> There was a sculptured form; the feet were placed
> Upon a finely-carved rose wreath; the arms
> Were raised to Heaven, as if to clasp the stars . . .

But instead of a tragic funerary monument, Aurora looks like a useless 'caryatid', whose hands are empty and whose arms carry nothing. Purposeless and pretentious, her moment of triumph has the opposite effect to Corinne's, for Romney is not impressed. The temple of the old poetic goddesses has been 'abolished', and the 'former purpose' of uplifted arms, if there ever was one, has somehow been forgotten. Barrett Browning takes the classical imagery of the myth and turns it into an imagery of purely archaeological interest. Aurora's vocation is to be a poet, not a statue.

Yet it is interesting that, in the argument which follows, Romney tries to recuperate the myth for his own domestic purposes. He tells Aurora:

'Keep to the green wreath,
Since even dreaming of the stone and bronze
Brings headaches, pretty cousin, and defiles
The clean white morning dresses.'
(2.93–6)

The ' "green wreath" ' of leaves represents, for Romney, an Aurora who will stay ' "pretty" ' and ' "clean" ' in her ' "white morning dresses" ', and thus be a more picturesque and pleasing wife. Like Gilfillan, who praised Hemans for saving him from 'the ludicrous image of a double-dyed Blue . . . sweating at some stupendous treatise', Romney treacherously advises Aurora to avoid the ' "headaches" ' and dirty dresses of real work, and to keep to the pose of creativity which shows her person off to more advantage. To stand still in a wreath is thus turned back into the attitude, not of solitary poetic triumph as Aurora had fantasised, but of sexual and domestic appeal. It is as if Barrett Browning has found out the ideology behind her old favourite novel. By putting a man in the scene, she entirely changes its meaning. It is Romney's eye which both devalues Aurora's pose and then cunningly re-evaluates it in terms of its domestic propriety. The old double purpose of sensibility is thus exposed as Barrett Browning hints that, in the long run, it is Romney, not Aurora, who desires to play at statues. It is he who justifies, but only in his own terms, this standing about in a 'white' dress. Through such a deft reversal, which comments on the whole critical reception of women's poetry, she points out that, in fact, Romney's appreciation is worse than his scorn, for it traps the aspiring poet in the same formulas of romance as her predecessor, who sang to implore 'the protection of a friend'.

However, it is at this point that Aurora makes her break with the whole debilitating collusion of work and love which *Corinne* had encouraged. She tells Romney that she would rather be dead,

'than keep quiet here
And gather up my feet from even a step
For fear to soil my gown in so much dust.
I choose to walk at all risks.'
(2.103–6)

To rise and walk is a gesture full of defiance, not only of all the self-conscious statuary of the myth, but also of all the men in Elizabeth's own life, her father, brothers and Mr Hunter, who had a vested interest in her not 'daring to tread in the dust'. Aurora, instead of being rejected, herself rejects the cousin who offers her a wreath as a plaything or an ornament, and goes in search of the real one with all its 'headaches'. *Aurora Leigh* is Barrett Browning's poem of escape, both from the marital home and the Palace of Art (the two often subtly confused by critics) where, as a woman, she risks becoming a permanent fixture, whether angel or art work. In order not to be a Galatea but a Pygmalion, she must ' "walk at all risks" '. Her declared aesthetic aim of rejecting 'togas and the picturesque' (5.209) in order to capture her own 'live, throbbing age' (203) is connected with this rejection of an iconic poetic identity which ultimately only justifies the condescensions of male praise.

The scene of reunion between Aurora and Romney in Book 8 intriguingly parallels this first garden scene. But although it is June again, the place is Italy, Aurora has achieved fame in her writing and Romney is blind. This change is driven home in an image which crucially reverses the old roles:

> he, the man, appeared
> So pale and patient, like the marble man
> A sculptor puts his personal sadness in . . .
> (8.1099–101)

Now it is Romney who is the art object, the statue, and Aurora who walks free. Her reward at the end is not a triumphal crowning in public, but, almost its opposite: an invisibility which the darkness of the garden and the blindness of the man both emphasise. 'He had to be blinded, observe, to be made to see', Barrett Browning explained. Romney, who voices many of the prejudices and epigrams of the men Elizabeth knew and of the reviewers she had read, is deprived of the sense which lies behind the whole aesthetic of sensibility: the sense of sight. The eye of Phaon, for whom Sappho supposedly killed herself, the eye of Oswald, for whom Corinne paraded her art round Italy, the eye of Lockhart, which dissolved in tears at the frontispieces of women's poems, the eye of Mr Hunter, dogmatically fixed on women as clouds, and the eye of Romney himself, who once preferred Aurora to stand prettily in a garden rather than labour in the dust of the real world, are all forms of a controlling, external viewpoint, which turns women's art into a sight for men. Where Hemans and L.E.L. had played to a double audience, encoding a message to other women through their ritual appeals for one man's love, Barrett Browning, characteristically, exposes the contradiction. By blinding Romney, she attacks the whole sexually appreciating voyeurism of the literature she inherits.

To read this episode as part of a developing aesthetics rather than as a crude revenge of the plot is to avoid the embarrassment, either of Aurora seeming to be thus proved 'right' or of her seeming to be thus turned into another of Milton's daughters. Her triumphant invisibility at the end is, instead, a sign that she has freed herself from the applause of the

Capitol. She has learned to write of something other than herself, and Romney's praise, which was once only praise of her looks, is now honest praise of her work. ' "But, in this last book,/You showed me something separate from yourself" ' (8.606), he tells her. To gaze 'on Self apart', as George Eliot puts it in 'Erinna', is to have achieved the artist's necessary breadth and scope of feeling. Romney's blindness is Aurora's sight, in a symbolic disequilibrium which runs through Victorian women's writing. Aurora has learned to see precisely because she has learned the insignificance of being seen; she has learned to write because she has learned the insignificance of being loved. She gets both love and fame in the end, but only because she has found them to be separate and different, each with her own requirements and their own rewards. Furthermore, she has learned the 'hard & cold thing', that love may be only an elaborate convention of feeling or a flattering fantasy of power. *Aurora Leigh* thus continues the work of the ballads in rescuing the woman from the thrall of being seen, or rather not seen, for all the angels, clouds and statues of men's eyes. It offers a drastic revision of the terms of romance, even if it is a revision for which Romney pays a high and somewhat obvious price.

It is this sceptical awareness of the sexual politics of sensibility which marks out Barrett Browning's poetry from that of her predecessors. Love, in her work, is not a sacred ideal, removed from the contingencies of the world, but is dragged in the dust of that reality which was itself so hard-won an experience and a theme for her. The facts of power and money, which are so singularly absent from the works of de Staël, Hemans and L.E.L., give Barrett Browning an imagery for the larger system of things, which increasingly, in her work, undermines and disproves the inherited sanctities of the heart. If *Aurora Leigh* contains the story of this development, it is in some of Barrett Browning's lesser known political poems that the power of the system makes itself felt.

## *The Systems of Man*

'None of all these things
Can women understand. You generalise
Oh, nothing, – not even grief! Your quick-breathed hearts,
So sympathetic to the personal pang,
Close on each separate knife-stroke, yielding up
A whole life at each wound, incapable
Of deepening, widening a large lap of life
To hold the world-full woe. The human race
To you means, such a child, or such a man,
You saw one morning waiting in the cold,
Beside that gate, perhaps. You gather up
A few such cases, and when strong sometimes

Will write of factories and of slaves, as if
Your father were a negro, and your son
A spinner in the mills.'

(*AL:* 2.182–96)

These criticisms, which Barrett Browning puts into the mouth of Romney, are not simply to be dismissed as examples of male prejudice. His attack on the narrowness, sentimentality and ultimate self-centredness of women's verse is one which, at the moment of her humiliation in the garden, Aurora takes to heart. An article in the *Edinburgh Review* for 1841, which discussed some works by Lady Morgan and Mrs Ellis among others, had made similarly confident assertions about the law of sexual difference. Women, it claimed, 'are inferior in the power of close and logical reasoning. They are less dispassionate . . . They have less power of combination and generalization. They are less capable of steady and concentrated attention'. The 1839 *Works of Mrs. Hemans* carried a prominent review by Lord Jeffrey, which proposed that women are 'incapable of long moral or political investigations' since they are by nature 'averse to long doubt and long labour'. In 1833 a reviewer of L.E.L. had asked, scornfully in her defence, if women could be supposed 'to write of politics or political economy' instead of love. Such comments, which appear continuously throughout the century, must have impressed the weight of their assumptions on the consciousness of women poets. Even Elizabeth, though only in secret to Robert, fell into such comparisons. She comments, for instance, on a note she has received from one of Felicia Hemans' sons, 'which quite touched me', and then, as if there were some connection, she ventures a comparison between men and women: 'there *is* a natural inferiority of mind in women—of the intellect'. A little later, however, she points to the one exception which might disprove the rule: 'George Sand'. As so often in her writings, Barrett Browning takes her bearings from other women. Hemans and Sand subconsciously represent for her the difference between a woman's writing which is 'naturally' inferior and one which may be equal to men's in power and scope.

However, as the reader discovers, the criticisms which Romney issues are only the other side of an even more disabling praise. He concludes his devastating assessment of women's capacity to write with the exclamation:

'Women as you are,
Mere women, personal and passionate,
You give us doating mothers, and perfect wives,
Sublime Madonnas, and enduring saints!
We get no Christ from you, – and verily
We shall not get a poet, in my mind.'

(2. 220–5)

In a singularly self-contradicting article on 'The rights of women' in the *Quarterly* for 1845, the writer asserts: 'We hope—nay, we proudly believe—that the honourable freedom of our women may long be made to rest on those only foundations which can keep it secure against change—the purity, the harmony, the genial brightness of our English homes'. In fact it is not 'freedom' but 'women' who must be kept at home, 'secure against change'. The word 'home', which sums up a peculiarly English combination of wifeliness and property, and which de Staël used in its English form in *Corinne* because she could find no French equivalent, appears rarely in Barrett Browning's poetry. When Aurora finally admits her love for Romney, it is a love specifically free of homes, stately or otherwise. None the less, the ideological swindle in the myth of ' "doating mothers, and perfect wives" ' is a powerful one, particularly because it invokes a religious fervour hard to disavow. In 1883, Eric S. Robertson pointed to the hidden implication of such a myth. 'The trustfulness that is so characteristic of woman's views of existence may be one great cause of her comparative lack of imagination', he asserts. The double-handedness of his reasoning is like Romney's. The age needs women to be saints not poets. Men in particular need it, for, as Robertson neatly summarises: 'Faith is woman-like, doubt is man-like'. What he does not consider is the extent to which faith and doubt are qualities of reading as well as of writing, and therefore the extent to which male readers will look to women's writing, as they look to women themselves, for a reassuring statement of faith in a world beset by doubts. Aurora has to contend, not only with Romney's doubt of her poetic abilities, but also with his faith in her as one of the ' "Sublime Madonnas" ' and, if possible, a perfect wife.

* * *

## *Poetry and Politics: A Double Vision*

'*Marriage in the abstract*', Elizabeth wrote in 1846, when she was contemplating marriage in actuality, 'has always seemed to me the most profoundly indecent of all ideas'. She could be as scornful on the subject as the notorious anti-matrimonialist, George Sand. A dream recorded in her *Diary* when she was 25 suggests a temperamental aversion as well: 'I dreamt last night that I was married, just married; & in an agony to [procure] a dissolution of the engagement'. Years later, when she read *In Memoriam*, she wished away 'the marriage hymn at the end'. Throughout her life she held to the opinion that 'marriage is more necessary for a man than a woman' and, in Rome in 1853, she was intrigued by the 'house of what I call emancipated women', consisting of the sculptress Harriet Hosmer and the novelist and translator of George Sand, Matilda Hays. In the years which followed her own marriage, Barrett Browning wrote her epic novel poem about two unmarried women: Aurora the poet and Marian Erle the fallen woman. The delayed 'sistering' of the two is a powerful emotional event in the text, and points to an alternative love story, full of pastoral images of flowers and animals by comparison with which Romney's marital cravings seem obsessively money-minded. None the less, it is this sense of money and power, everywhere underlying the romance story of *Aurora Leigh*, which represents Barrett Browning's emancipation from that 'superabundance of sensibility' in her precedessors.

After the wreath crowning in Book 2, Romney adds to his many criticisms of Aurora's poetry the final insult of a marriage proposal. He reminds her that, if she marries him, she will legitimately inherit her part of the family fortune which her father had forfeited by marrying an Italian. Legally, of course, she would still not inherit her money because the first Married Women's Property Act, for which Elizabeth herself collected signatures in Paris and which, according to Mary Howitt, was spoken of 'as the petition of Elizabeth Barrett Browning, Anna Jameson, Mary Howitt, Mrs. Gaskell', had not yet been passed. The language of Aurora's refusal clearly brings out the connection between the terms of Romney's proposal and his economic power:

> 'At least
> My soul is not a pauper; I can live
> At least my soul's life, without alms from men . . .'
> (2.680–2)

The sense of that money, which ought also to be her own, if it were not for the 'master-right' of English inheritance laws, gives Romney's love a buying quality which irks Aurora:

> If I married him,
> I should not dare to call my soul my own
> Which so he had bought and paid for . . .
> (2.785–7)

George Eliot, who read *Aurora Leigh* at least three times and felt a deep 'sense of communion' with its author, puts many of Aurora's arguments against marriage into the mouth of her own artist heroine, the opera singer, Armgart:

> I will not be
> A pensioner in marriage. Sacraments
> Are not to feed the paupers of the world.
> If he were generous – I am generous too.

Marriage, for women, is a state of sentimental pauperism, of continuing gratitude to the charity of men. Both Aurora and Armgart reject the offer of security which is, in fact, a kind of blackmail, though it is interesting that, while Aurora holds out to the end and gets both fame and money of her own, Armgart's pride and power are broken and she accepts, after the loss of her voice, an almost Hemansesque fate of humble usefulness, teaching music in a small town. George Eliot punishes, not her heroes but her heroines, in an anxious swerve away from the female triumphalism of Barrett Browning's poem.

In the parallel garden scene at the end of *Aurora Leigh* there is a curious repetition of this exchange. Romney arrives in Florence and tries to make amends to Marian Erle by once again proposing marriage. The episode is one of those narrative doublings which run through the poem and seem intended to decentre the status of the romance. Romney, in the course of the poem, makes four proposals, two to each of the heroines. Whether this is narrative clumsiness or emotional realism, it is certainly quite different from the simple high peaks of individual faithfulness or betrayal in Hemans and L.E.L. Furthermore, the guilt which evidently motivates Romney's second proposal to Marian suggests another slippage or doubling: between himself and her unknown rapist. In terms of the plot, Romney can have no responsibility for Marian's escape and rape; it was she, after all, who left him on the wedding day. However, his offer of marriage at the end is riddled with subconscious self-justification. Her answer, like Aurora's in Book 2, resoundingly exposes and rejects the system of values which underpins his somewhat dubious good intentions. 'Here's a hand shall keep/For ever clean without a marriage-ring' (9.431–2), she tells him. Even though Romney is now property-less and blind, she can still make moral and emotional beggars of women. With the offer of ' "a marriage-ring" ', he can seem to purchase moral cleanness for both himself and Marian, though neither seems to have committed any sin. Her refusal typically rejects the short-cut of his reasoning: he is responsible neither for her fall nor for her rehabilitation. Above all, the etiquette of a marriage-ring is shown up as a form of male power which, even without money to justify it, assumes the pauperising generosity of the powerful and the moneyed.

Romney's sexual assumption of power is thus even more deep-rooted than his actual economic status. In one place near the beginning, Aurora mimics the terms of his proposal. He might as well have said outright:

> 'Come, sweep my barns and keep my hospitals,
> And I will pay thee with a current coin
> Which men give women.'
>
> (2.539–41)

The ' "current coin" ' is, politely, marriage. But the bareness of the phrase ' "Which men give women" ' loudly hints at the thing which is not always given within marriage:

'What, what, . . . being beaten down
By hoofs of maddened oxen into a ditch,
Half-dead, whole mangled, when a girl at last
Breathes, sees . . . and finds there, bedded in her flesh
Because of the extremity of the shock,
Some coin of price! . . .'

(6.676–81)

Marian's angry, articulate description of her rape uses an image of violence which recurs throughout Barrett Browning's work. Male power, whether of gods or men, is very often described as an animal trampling, and thus, even where it is meant as an attitude of mind, it develops the potently physical connotations of rape. It is interesting that, in one of her outbursts against the odious Mr Hunter, Elizabeth explains his constant reproofs of her as 'a sort of masculine rampancy which wd. have a woman under the feet of man'. In *Aurora Leigh*, the classical gods are invoked, as Dorothy Mermin has shown, as figures both of rape and inspiration. Danaë, in Vincent Carrington's picture, is 'Half blotted out of nature' (3.132) by the golden rain of Jove. In 'The Runaway Slave' even the Christian God himself seemed to condone the treading down 'to clay' of a whole race. Individual acts of violence are thus associated with the idea of masculinity itself.

Marian Erle points to this larger system of exploitation, when, in a speech which already repudiates the ' "marriage-ring" ' of the moral law, she asserts her mother-rights according to the other prevailing law of brute power:

'Mine, mine,' she said. 'I have as sure a right
As any glad proud mother in the world,
Who sets her darling down to cut his teeth
Upon her church-ring. If she talks of law,
I talk of law! I claim my mother-dues
By law, – the law which now is paramount, –
The common law, by which the poor and weak
Are trodden underfoot by vicious men,
And loathed for ever after by the good.'

(6.661–9)

Her self-defence consists in making a deliberate connection between the church law of marriage and, punningly, the ' "common law" ' of oppression, between legalisation of motherhood in a ' "church-ring" ' and legalisation of poverty in an established system. As ' "law" ' thus comes to seem, throughout the passage (as well as throughout the poem), less of a moral absolute and more of a social commodity affordable by the rich, the very nature of what is lawful and unlawful blurs. According to the common law of power, 'masculine rampancy' prevails. Thus Marian's own rape, ' "being beaten down/By hoofs of maddened oxen into a ditch" ', is equated with this moral general beating ' "underfoot" ' of a whole class of ' "the poor and weak" '. Barrett Browning's occasional tendency to portray Marian Erle as a sublime Madonna is counteracted by this secularising and socialising connectiveness in her imagery. Rape is part of a system of law which has little to do with wedding rings, but which does have something to do with class, power and specifically with ' "men" '.

Marian's rape thus gathers a cluster of images of violence, masculinity and money, which send small shocks in many directions through the poem. But it is above all the image of the coin which conveys the social as well as physical reality of the rape itself:

> 'and finds there, bedded in her flesh
> Because of the extremity of the shock,
> Some coin of price! . . .'

This last phrase brilliantly slides away from the expected biblical 'pearl of price', which is the more conventional conclusion. Instead, the image of the coin keeps its reference to the market—literally, the market of prostitution or, figuratively, of sexuality in general—and refuses the usual Christian argument that the purity of the child 'pays for' the sin of the mother. Hester Prynne's child, Pearl, in *The Scarlet Letter* (Hawthorne, 1850), which Barrett Browning had probably recently read, is a 'pearl of price'. This ' "coin of price" ', however, keeps its stark connotations of the actual (unpaid) prostitution Marian has experienced: ' "it shall pay you for the loss" ' (6.684), she imagines a good man saying. Barrett Browning's 'coined' phrase seems to drive the sexual and monetary argument home, as it were—literally into the woman's flesh—while keeping the hard, unmetaphorical, unchanged meaning of the coin awkwardly and harshly present. ' "Some coin of price" ', far from being a polite circumlocution, insists on the physical facts of conception, and resists transformation of those facts into moral or emotional compensations. It is, unambiguously, still ' "bedded in her flesh" '.

However, yet another meaning can be heard here. The coin recalls, at a distance of several books, the terms of Romney's proposal to Aurora. The narrative doubling between Aurora and Marian, which the plot repeatedly exploits, is emphasised by this imagery. Aurora is offered the ' "current coin" ' of marriage; Marian gets a crueller ' "coin of price" '. But both actions are represented, if subconsciously, as parts of a monetary transaction—a paying for or a paying off—in which both women are victims. Everywhere in this poem sexual relations, whether kind or violent, the aristocrat's or the rapist's, are part of a larger and interrelated economics of power. The Danaë myth, in which the raping god appears in the form of money itself, provides an association deeply and guiltily embedded in the Victorian subconscious. In *Aurora Leigh* the meaning of the 'coin' can be tracked down, through all its social ramifications, in race, class, family and birthright, to the lowest denominator of what ' "men give women" '.

Thus symbolising all the other economic legacies in the poem (and there are many), the coin traffics freely between the love story and the rape story, between romance and sexual power, between literary metaphor and social fact. It deliberately breaks down the differences between them. In the poem's market exchange of meaning, it shifts from one signification to another, thus introducing a relativity of meanings which cannot easily be separated out into good and bad, pure and impure, protected and unprotected. But these shifts are not gratuituous or purely playful. Rather, they are part of a larger story, a larger system of violence and money, which shadows the emotional and poetic progress of Aurora's creative self-realisation. That self-financed journey to Italy, unlike the aristocratic, self-advertising tourism of Corinne, ultimately leads towards an art which disproves Romney's criticisms, and shows the poet's capacity to write a love story whose ' "personal pang" ' is everywhere connected, through a mesh of images, to the impersonal reality of ' "the world full woe" '. Aurora's romance, unlike that of her performing predecessors, is tainted through and through by this 'coin' of socialisation which goes to 'the heart' (or even more literal organ) of love. *Aurora Leigh* is the epic of the woman poet who finds love, not in unique and tragic isolation on a cliff, but in the dust of the real world where it is rarely clean of double standards, power, crime and suffering.

For all her faults, Barrett Browning has succeeded in this poem in turning the woman's lyre of private feeling into an instrument of public conscience, and her improvised epithets of the body into a sexual complexity of desire which denies neither the claims of the body nor the claims of the work of art. All the poured, burning hearts of Hemans and L.E.L., which flowed from them so easily, are transformed by her, in a famous passage in Book 5, into a statement of her own distinctive aesthetics: into a lava-flow which is not fluent and univocal, but awkward and 'double' in its commitment both to 'song' and to 'true life', as well as to the differences between them:

> Never flinch,
> But still, unscrupulously epic, catch
> Upon the burning lava of a song
> The full-veined, heaving, double-breasted Age:
> That, when the next shall come, the men of that
> May touch the impress with reverent hand, and say
> 'Behold, – behold the paps we all have sucked!
> This bosom seems to beat still, or at least
> It sets our beating: this is living art,
> Which thus presents and thus records true life.'
> (5.213–22)

Yet it is true that, on the level of its plot, *Aurora Leigh* also plays out a struggle between politics and poetry in which poetry wins, hands down. Barrett Browning distrusted socialism, and Romney's socialistic experiments of setting up a 'phalanstery' in his ancestral home are made to look foolish. In 1848, in the midst of ferment and revolution on the continent, Elizabeth expressed her worries to Miss Mitford:

> As to communism, surely the practical part of *that* . . . is attainable simply by the consent of individuals . . . who may try the experiment of associating their families in order to the cheaper employment of the means of life . . & successfully in many cases. But make a government-scheme of *even so much*, & you seem to trench on the individual liberty – All such patriarchal planning in a government, issues naturally into absolutism.

Such language suggests that memories of her own experience of the small patriarchy of Wimpole Street are still colouring her views. 'I love liberty so intensely that I hate Socialism', she writes elsewhere. But although she ultimately shows up Romney's socialistic experiments as another patriarchal scheme, her cherishing of individuality is not to the exclusion of the general good, but remains discrepantly and sceptically juxtaposed with it. In Book 5, such a 'marriage' of perspectives becomes, explicitly, a poetic theory:

> But poets should
> Exert a double vision; should have eyes
> To see near things as comprehensively
> As if afar they took their point of sight,
> And distant things as intimately deep
> As if they touched them.
>
> (5.183–8)

In Barrett Browning's best poems such a 'double vision' involves, not so much an easy equivalence of the near and far, the personal and the general, the poetic and the political, as a sense of the difference between them, of the stress and tension of making the two match.

## MARGARET REYNOLDS

## [Allusion in the Verse-Novel: Experimental Bricolage] †

> "I am inclined to think that we want new *forms*, as well as thoughts. The old gods are dethroned. Why should we go back to the antique

† From *Aurora Leigh*, ed. Margaret Reynolds (Athens, OH: Ohio UP, 1992), 49–54. Reprinted by permission of the Ohio University Press.

moulds . . classical moulds, as they are so improperly called? . . . Let us all aspire rather to *Live* . . ."[1]

> "What form is best for poems? Let me think
> Of forms less, and the external. Trust the spirit,
> As sovran nature does, to make the form";[2]

One of the most striking characteristics of *Aurora Leigh*, an aspect of the verse-novel much overlooked, largely because of a critical focus upon the supposed autobiographical and experiential nature of the poem, is the *literariness* of the work. When the poem opens with the announcement of Aurora's intention to write she not only claims a right to speak as a woman, but she draws attention to the character of the verse-novel as a self-conscious text which examines the processes of writing and reading. That the work itself was conceived (as was the ideal book which Aurora writes) as a crossbreed verse-novel, androgynous in its appropriation of the feminine subjective and the masculine objective, is one reason for its obsessive artfulness and introspection, but the ways in which that literary enterprise of textual self-examination are effected are diverse in character.

One result of this formal enterprise is an intertextuality which uses allusion to widen its scope of reference. That *Aurora Leigh* employs allusion as a formal device promoting "philosophical dreaming and digression"[3] is a fact ignored by critics who (often unwittingly) downgrade the achievement of poetry written by women. Since the poem's first appearance, the story which was created for *Aurora Leigh* has been condemned by some as a patchwork of plagiarism, George Sand and Charlotte Brontë being the most regularly noticed influences. Other sources have been variously listed as Eugene Sue (especially his *Mystères de Paris*), Balzac, Charles Kingsley, Elizabeth Gaskell's *Ruth*, Clough's *Bothie of Tober-na-Vuolich* and, most persuasively, Germaine de Stael's *Corinne, or Italy*. If reductive source-hunting is the end, then the constituents of the plot of *Aurora Leigh* are an easy target for criticism. But this approach to the techniques of allusion betrays a critical doublethink, which essentially trivializes the reading process where the reader is a woman: novel-reading for her is a vice or a relaxation and the woman reader is excessively susceptible of influence because of her imitative nature.

Cora Kaplan offered a positive description of the plot as "an elaborate collage of typical themes or motifs of the novels and long poems of the 1840's and 1850's," and much has been made since the fact that *Aurora Leigh* is a dense work of textual and cultural reference, offering telling reinterpretations of familiar tropes, archetypes, myths, and literary texts. Thus *Aurora Leigh* becomes not a plagiarized would-be novel, but a

1. EBB to RB, 20 Mar. 1845, *RB/EBB Letters* 1:42.
2. *Aurora Leigh* 5.223–25.
3. 30 Dec. 1844, *EBB to MRM* 3:49.

poetic framework for suggestion and reference which foreshadows the constructive uses of fragmentation found in such later productions as Virginia Woolf's *Between the Acts*, or Angela Carter's art of *bricolage*. And this magpie form, which steals fragments of a tradition or language from which women have been alienated, to rewrite or invert them, can be defined in itself (though practiced in modernist and postmodernist works by both women and men) as culturally feminine.

Yet while the very form of the bastard verse-novel might express, in its diffuseness, the sense of female exclusion and marginalization both in and from a patriarchal culture, the example of *Aurora Leigh* shows how secret that femaleness has to be—in part, precisely because of the nineteenth-century woman author's acceptance of the ideology which excludes her. The most significant sources forming an allusive background to the poem were the works of Sand, Brontë and de Stael. Yet in *Aurora Leigh*, while the list of names or works cited include those of Aeschylus, Wordsworth, Carlyle, Keats, Browning, and Rousseau, not one woman author is named or quoted directly. Barrett Browning's experience of a personal anxiety of influence or rather, authority, meant that while allusions to the works of male writers are explicit, those to the works of female writers are implicit.

As the techniques of allusion break up formal constrictions, responding to the challenge of a new form, so the verse-novel recommends a program of exchange between text and reader which similarly breaks up conventional literary order. The very length of the verse-novel, the changing narrative methods, the palindrome of the plot, the repetition and modification of dominant images, the use of "round" time and the shuffling of tenses, provide scope for reflection and revision in the reader's experience of the poem—and the narrative form of *Aurora Leigh* insists that the reader participate in that process. A model for this procedure is included in the account of an ideal poetics as Aurora imagines an active reader-response which would allow her to convey ideas to "thrilling audient and beholding souls/By signs and touches which are known to souls" (7.849–50).

Barrett Browning's acknowledged aim in adopting formal methods which demanded the participation of the reader was related to her belief that the poet's art should live; taking God as the ultimate model for the artist, and God's art as the living world (5.434–35). Thus Aurora lives before the reader, all mistakes and confusions included, and we are expected to adjust assessment and judgment accordingly. In 1845 Robert Browning and Elizabeth Barrett had agreed that the dramatic poet should realize fictional characters before the eyes of the reader,[4] and

4. "And what easy work these novelists have of it! a Dramatic poet has to *make* you love or admire his men and women,—they must *do* and *say* all that you are to see and hear—really do it in your face, say it in your ears, and it is wholly for *you*, in *your* power, to *name*, characterize and so praise or blame, *what* is so said and done . . if you don't perceive of yourself, there is

Barrett Browning included this necessity in her exposition of Aurora's poetic theory, "The rulers of our art" (5.307);

> . . . conceive, command,
> And, from the imagination's crucial heat,
> Catch up their men and women all a-flame
> For action, all alive and forced to prove
> Their life by living out heart, brain, and nerve . . .
> (5.309–13)

It is of course the metaphor of writing which provides the first and most fully realized range of allegories on the theme of reader participation. In the central reverie of *Aurora Leigh* (book 5) the author presents, through her poet-heroine, the principles of poetry which have motivated both the book composed by the fictional author (5.352, 1213, 1263–64) and *Aurora Leigh* itself. The circumstances of production are the same for both books, and at the conclusion of the verse-novel Romney Leigh acts as the incarnation of Barrett Browning's ideal reader, able to read and comprehend all Aurora's poem, delivered though it is in shadowing "signs and touches" (8.265–69, 283–88, 605–13). Thus, a circular displacement is enacted as Barrett Browning writes a verse-novel which dramatizes the autobiography of a fictional woman writer who herself, within the poem, writes a verse-novel which mirrors the form, scope, and proposed achievement of the actual poem, *Aurora Leigh* itself. And this very circularity suggests the living quality of the vision Barrett Browning's work attempts, which is not static and clearly seen but subject to interference and variety—as in Aurora's own vision at the climax of the poem:

> His breath against my face
> Confused his words, yet made them more intense,
> (As when the sudden finger of the wind
> Will wipe a row of single city-lamps
> To a pure white line of flame, more luminous
> Because of obliteration)
> (9.743–48)

In addition to writing/reading images, *Aurora Leigh* employs a number of images where visual art, particularly the portrait, is invoked as an artifact powerfully suggestive to the viewer (or reader). Thus the narrator declares her intention to write her story in these terms (1.4–8), and each of the many portraits cited in the work is used, through the reactions of the viewer (usually Aurora herself), to reflect or emphasize some aspect

---

no standing by, for the Author, and telling you: but with these novelists, a scrape of the pen—out blurting of a phrase, and the miracle is achieved—'Consuelo possessed to perfection this and the other gift'—what would you more." RB to EBB, 10 Aug. 1845, *RB/EBB Letters* 1:150. EBB replied "there can be no disagreeing with you about the comparative difficulty of novel-writing & drama-writing." EBB to RB, 13 Aug. 1845, *RB/EBB Letters* 1:155.

of Aurora's personal narrative. The portrait of Aurora's mother is the medium which the child invests with capacity to represent all forms of feminine incarnation (1.145–63), and the reflexive suggestion of the portrait is developed as each incarnation is reenacted through the female characters in the poem: Aurora plays the part of the "dauntless Muse who eyes a dreadful Fate" (1.155) and the "loving Psyche who loses sight of Love" (1.156); her aunt, repressed and damaging, whose eyes are imaged as knives (1.327–330) represents Medusa; Marian, suffering virgin and mother, merges with "Our Lady of the Passion, stabbed with swords/Where the Babe sucked" (7.126–32); while Lady Waldemar becomes, in Aurora's imagination, the "woman-serpant" Lamia (6.1100–1101; 7.144–74).

In book 3, Aurora's status as a poet, alternately aspiring and quiescent awaiting inspiration, is mirrored in the two pictures of Danae which the artist Vincent Carrington sends to her (3.122–35), and in which Aurora recognizes an implied application to her own situation (3.135–42). The irony of Carrington's portrait of Kate Ward, which shows her in a cloak of Aurora's pattern, holding in complimentary reverence the poet's latest book, is not lost upon Aurora, who at that point has lost all faith in her own literary capability (7.705–7). Even Romney's decisive attachment to the portrait of their shared ancestor Lady Maud (8.955–59), is not so much a device for facilitating Romney's tragedy as another mirror of Aurora's destiny—for the picture resembles Aurora herself, and Romney's rescuing it leads obliquely to their reunion.

Like the process of allusion, which steals a language appropriate to the woman author (both Aurora and Barrett Browning) who at once accepts and resists her marginalization, the metaphoric emphasis upon images derived from writing/reading and painting/being viewed suggest the besieged ambivalences of the nineteenth-century woman writer. Aurora shows herself (like Barrett Browning) to be conscious always of her dual role as active subject and passive object (artist/woman, writer/text, individual/portrait), and she takes that self-consciousness into her text by introducing other objects (literary texts, the idea of the book and the picture, mirror characters), against which to measure herself as subject. Her poetic language, a woman's language growing out of her oblique relation to cultural and literary order, cannot employ any positive terms but works, initially at least, through resistance and difference while it attempts a new language and form. Using this language, the woman poet (Aurora/Barrett Browning) adopts a poetic method which returns continually to herself and her difference, playing endlessly between the two—thus her experience of cultural marginalization (rather than any biological essence or authenticity) yields her both a subject and a form.

To read Barrett Browning's verse-novel in the light of feminist theory is to acknowledge that there can be no jubilant and whole recovery of women's writing of the nineteenth century. When Barrett Browning looked for "grandmothers" and found only "poetesses," when she admired Robert Browning's masculine and objective method over her own subjective manner, when she attempted a synthesis of the two in the experimental form of the verse-novel, when she marshaled there metaphors, mirrors, and narrative procedures which relied upon difference and opposition, then Barrett Browning revealed her beleaguered position as a disinherited or bastard girl-child of the culture which fathered her. Her own awareness of that position was obvious to her only fitfully, but its effects can be clearly read from our perspective—and the results of that potential for disintegration can be positive.

Barrett Browning's (conscious and unconscious) recognition of difference promoted the strengths of experiment, subversion, and challenge both in the subjects tackled in *Aurora Leigh* and in the narrative and literary forms adopted there. And even when Aurora achieves the full integration into the nineteenth-century ideal of human individuality (that is, through marriage), she attempts strenuously to escape the (conventional platitudes of the) feminine which would lead to resolution/dissolution and silence. Instead of accepting the stereotype that to be a woman writer is to be unsexed and to be forced to make a choice between love and art, Aurora forcefully claims both.

*Aurora Leigh* is a woman's book; as the story of a woman poet told by a woman poet, its subjects and their treatment, its narrative and poetic form, are all dictated by that fact. Too frequently, however, that fact has been read not in relation to the historical context and cultural assumptions which produced the verse-novel but in the light of other, unexamined, ideological assumptions about what constitutes a woman's book. In these repeated, but diverse, erroneous readings lies the reason for the variety of critical reaction to *Aurora Leigh*. Always perceived as a woman's book, it was consequently valued—as a gospel by sympathetic nineteenth-century readers, as an authentic record of female experience by twentieth-century feminist readers—and dismissed—as shrill and unwomanly by nineteenth-century reviewers, as chaotic, uncontrolled, and sloppy by twentieth-century humanist critics.

*Aurora Leigh* has never been admitted to the canon of literature; women's texts are only permitted to appear there provided they are not read as women's texts. When *Aurora Leigh* can be included in the canon, recognized as of human and therefore generally significant interest *because* of its overriding address to the theoretical (and practical) questions of the cultural and literary formation, exclusion, and prohibition of women in writing, then its significance as a primary text of the nineteenth century might be acknowledged.

# Elizabeth Barrett Browning: A Chronology

1806 Born March 6 at Coxhoe Hall, the first child of Edward Moulton-Barrett and his wife, Mary Graham-Clarke. Edward was a gentleman, and heir to vast plantation estates in Jamaica. Mary was the daughter of a wealthy merchant, and Edward's guardian at first opposed the match on the grounds of his youth (19; Mary was 24), but at length declared, "I hold out no longer—she is far too good for him." They were married May 14, 1805.

1807 EBB's brother Edward, usually called "Bro," born June 26. On this occasion Edward Moulton-Barrett suggested that the slaves on his Jamaican plantations be given a holiday.

1809 After much searching, Edward Moulton-Barrett purchases Hope End, an estate of 475 acres in Herefordshire. The original Queen Anne house is converted into stables and offices, and work begins on a new and sumptuous mansion in the Turkish manner. Henrietta is born March 4, 1809. Mary is born in 1810, but dies in childhood. The other Moulton-Barrett children, twelve in all, are: Samuel (b. 1812), Arabella (b. 1813), Charles John "Stormie" (b. 1814), George Goodin (b. 1816), Henry (b. 1818), Alfred Price "Daisy" (b. 1820), Septimus James "Sette" (b. 1822), and Octavius Butler (b. 1824).

1814 EBB writes "On the Cruelty of Forcement to Man."

1815 The Battle of Waterloo (June 18). EBB and her parents travel to Paris on October 17 and return in November.

1817 Daniel McSwiney is engaged to tutor Bro, and EBB successfully petitions to join his Greek and Latin lessons. Madame Gordin teaches the other children. EBB studies French with her.

1820 George III dies. George IV succeeds.

1820 On March 6, EBB's first book, *The Battle of Marathon*, an epic in twelve books, is privately printed in an edition of 50 copies, only 5 of which are extant.

1821 In April, EBB and her sisters are ill. They recover, but EBB worsens, and in June is sent to the Spa Hotel Gloucester for medical treatment. Modern diagnoses have not satisfactorily located the cause of her illness. It might have been tubercular in origin, but anorexia, lack of exercise, and the severity of her treatments exacerbated the condition. At this time EBB was first prescribed opium, and some of her symptoms (poor appetite, insomnia, constipation, headaches, euphoria followed by lethargy) are attributable to her resulting addiction. In May, EBB's "Stanzas, Excited by Some Reflections on the Present State of Greece" are published in *The New Monthly Magazine* 2nd ser. 1, 523. In July, "Thoughts Awakened by Contemplating a Piece of the Palm Which Grows on the Summit of the Acropolis in Athens" published in *The New Monthly Magazine* 2nd ser. 2, 59. In September, EBB's mother warns her against placing too much faith in Mary Wollstonecraft's "system"; EBB has been reading *Vindication of the Rights of Woman*.

1822 EBB returns to Hope End around May.

1824 EBB's "Stanzas on the Death of Lord Byron" are published on June 30 in the London *Globe and Traveller*. The verses are anonymous, but Mary Moulton-Barrett guesses EBB to be the author.

1826 EBB's *An Essay on Mind with Other Poems* published on March 25 by James Duncan in London. In October, EBB begins her acquaintance with Uvedale Price, the scholar and writer on the picturesque.

1827 EBB begins a correspondence with Hugh Stuart Boyd, a blind Greek scholar living nearby at Malvern.

1828 EBB begins to study Greek and Hebrew with Hugh Stuart Boyd. EBB's mother dies on October 7 at Cheltenham, where she had gone to take the waters. She was suffering from general debilitation.

1830 George III dies. William IV becomes king. EBB's paternal grandmother, Elizabeth Moulton, dies, leaving £4000 to EBB.

1832 Reform Bill passed in June. In February, EBB translates Aeschylus's *Prometheus Bound*. Around June, Hope End Estate is sold, the Moulton-Barretts having lost a lawsuit over the Jamaican estates and Edward Moulton-Barrett's debts being called in. In August, EBB and most of her family leave Hope End and settle in Sidmouth. Hugh Stuart Boyd later moves to Sidmouth also.

1833 EBB's translation of *Prometheus Bound* published by Valpy. In August, Parliament votes to abolish slavery.

1835 In September, EBB's "Stanzas Addressed to Miss Landon and Suggested by Her 'Stanzas on the Death of Mrs Hemans' " published in *The New Monthly Magazine*. In December, EBB and her family move to 74 Gloucester Place, London.

1836 On May 27, John Kenyon introduces EBB to Mary Russell Mitford. EBB's "The Romaunt of Margret," "The Seaside Walk," and "The Poet's Vow" published in various magazines.

1837 William IV dies; Victoria succeeds. In July, EBB publishes two poems on Victoria in *The Athenaeum*. In December, EBB's uncle Sam dies in Jamaica, leaving her shares in a merchant ship called the "David Lyon" and several thousand pounds.

1838 EBB's "A Romance of the Ganges" published in *Finden's Tableaux*. In April, EBB and family move to 50 Wimpole Street. On June 6, EBB's *The Seraphim and Other Poems* published by Saunders and Otley. In August, EBB removes to Torquay under medical advice.

1840 In February, EBB's brother Sam dies in Jamaica. In July, EBB's brother Bro dies in a sailing accident in Tor Bay. As he had stayed in Torquay for EBB and against their father's wishes, EBB suffers guilt and undergoes a severe illness lasting many weeks.

1841 In September, EBB returns to Wimpole Street.

1842 EBB's essay "Some Account of the Greek Christian Poets" is published as a series of four articles in *The Athenaeum*. Her review and essay "The Book of the Poets" also published in *The Athenaeum*.

1843 EBB still composing and publishing numerous poems in magazines. In October, Richard Hengist Horne tells EBB his plans for *A New Spirit of the Age*, and she agrees to contribute.

1844 *A New Spirit of the Age* published in March. Contributions by Robert Browning (RB) also appear in it. August 13, *Poems by Elizabeth Barrett Barrett* published by Edward Moxon. It includes "Lady Geraldine's Courtship," and in December, EBB writes to Mary Russell Mitford that she would like one day to write a "longer poem of a like class."

1845 RB's first letter to EBB (January 10). She replies the next day, and soon afterward describes the germ of her idea for *Aurora Leigh* (not under that title). She begins writing in a notebook given to her by her brother. This notebook is now at Wellesley College and includes a clear false start, which might date from this time. RB's first visit to EBB at Wimpole Street (May 20).

1846 On September 12, EBB marries RB secretly. A week later they leave for Italy by way of France. EBB takes her manuscript notebooks with her and has the rest sent on by her sister. In spite of many attempts at reconciliation on EBB's part, her father breaks off all communication.

1847 In March, EBB has her first miscarriage. In April, EBB and RB move from Pisa to Florence.

1848 In May, EBB and RB settle at Casa Guidi in Florence.

1849 On March 9, Robert Wiedemann Barrett Browning ("Pen") is born. In September, EBB witnesses the entry of the occupying Austrian army into Florence.

1850 In July, EBB experiences her fourth and most serious miscarriage and is ill for some time. Publication of *Poems* (November), which includes "Sonnets from the Portuguese," which was written during 1845–46 and which EBB first showed to RB in 1849.

1851 *Casa Guidi Windows* is published in May. From July to September, EBB, RB, and Pen visit London. In September, they settle in Paris, where EBB meets George Sand. In December, the Brownings witness Louis Napoleon's coup d'etat.

1852 The Brownings remain in Paris until July, then visit London until October; they return to Casa Guidi in November.

1853 In March, EBB begins work on *Aurora Leigh* while living in Rome, Bagni di Lucca, and Casa Guidi in Florence. RB works on *Men and Women*.

1854 RB tries to arrange for American publication of both their books.

1855 EBB is ill in January. She has written 4,500 lines of *Aurora Leigh*, in the first draft copy (now at Wellesley). In March, she describes her new poem to John Kenyon. In June, the Brownings set out for England. EBB does not work on her poem again until December, when they settle in Paris and she begins to transcribe the work into the fair copy that she later will send to the printer. RB makes an agreement with the American publisher C. S. Francis for *Aurora Leigh*. RB's *Men and Women* published.

1856 In February, RB reads *Aurora Leigh* for the first time and annotates the fair copy manuscript (now at Harvard) with his reading dates. By March, EBB has transcribed six books into fair copy and begins composing the last three books.

In April, EBB corrects *Casa Guidi Windows* for inclusion in a new edition of *Poems*. The Brownings travel to London in June, and EBB completes the transcribing into fair copy in July and sends it to the printers in early August. The Brownings correct one set of proofs and two sets of revises during August and September while traveling to visit friends in Britain. The second set of revises (corrected) is sent to C. S. Francis in October.

On October 17, EBB writes the dedication to John Kenyon. On October 21, EBB writes a note to C. S. Francis, giving him exclusive American rights. On October 30, the Brownings arrive back in Casa Guidi. On November 15, *Aurora Leigh* is published simultaneously in London by Chapman and Hall and in New York by C. S. Francis. On December 2, the Brownings receive their first copy in Italy. RB refuses to allow EBB to correct the poem for the second edition and sends word that Chapman should "print tomorrow," as the first edition has sold in a fortnight.

Reviews begin to appear in November and December.

John Kenyon dies on December 4, leaving EBB £4,500 and RB £6,500, which makes them financially stable.

1857 "Second" edition of *Aurora Leigh*, a reprint without corrections, is published in January. "Third" edition, another reprint, is published in March. Edward Moulton-Barrett dies unreconciled on April 17.

1858 The Brownings set out for Le Havre in July, and RB offers Chapman a "fresh doing up of *Aurora Leigh*." EBB's photograph is taken in Le Havre and engraved for inclusion in a new edition. In October, EBB begins revising *Aurora Leigh* by marking up a copy of the first edition (now in the Bodmeriana). They return to Florence and then winter in Rome.

1859 The Brownings are sent proofs in January, which are corrected and kept by them (now in the Lilly Library, Indiana) while they return a list of corrections to Chapman (now in the J. Pierpont Morgan Library, New York). The last corrections were sent in March. The revised, "fourth" edition of *Aurora Leigh*, with the photograph frontispiece, is published on June 11. EBB later makes a list of thirteen corrections (whereabouts unknown; a photocopy is in the British Library) and corrects four errors in a copy presented to Isa Blagden (now at Yale). EBB is ill again. Winter in Rome.

1860 *Poems Before Congress* published in March by Chapman and Hall. In June, a "fifth" edition of *Aurora Leigh* is published. It is a reprint of the "fourth" and does not include any of EBB's late corrections. Also in June, the Brownings return to Florence from Rome. In November, EBB's sister Henrietta dies.

1861 Winter in Rome. EBB weak and often unable to go out. In June, the Brownings return to Florence. On June 6, Italian revolutionary statesman Cavour dies. EBB is moved and distressed by this. On June 29, EBB dies. On July 1, EBB is buried in the Protestant cemetery in Florence. A tomb by Frederic Leighton is later erected over her grave. On August 1, RB and Pen leave Florence for England.

1862 EBB's *Last Poems* published in March.

# Selected Bibliography

This bibliography does not include those works from which the excerpts above have been taken. The place of publication is London unless otherwise stated.


## 1. EDITIONS OF *AURORA LEIGH*

*Aurora Leigh*. 1857.
*Aurora Leigh*. New York and Boston, 1857.
*Aurora Leigh*. With an introduction and notes by Charlotte Porter and Helen A. Clarke. 1902.
*Aurora Leigh and Other Poems*. Introduced by Cora Kaplan. Women's Press facsimile reprint. 1978.
*Aurora Leigh*. Introduced by Gardner Taplin. Facsimile reprint. Chicago, 1979.
*Aurora Leigh*. A critical edition by Margaret Reynolds. Athens, OH, 1992.
*Aurora Leigh*. Edited by Kerry McSweeney. Oxford, 1993.

## 2. LETTERS OF ELIZABETH BARRETT BROWNING AND ROBERT BROWNING

*Twenty-Two Unpublished Letters of Elizabeth Barrett Browning and Robert Browning Addressed to Henrietta and Arabella Moulton-Barrett*. New York, 1935.
Browning, Robert Wiedemann Barrett, ed. *The Letters of Robert Browning and Elizabeth Barrett Barrett*. 2 vols. 1899.
DeVane, William Clyde, and Kenneth Leslie Knickerbocker. *New Letters of Robert Browning*. 1951.
Heydon, Peter N., and Phillip Kelley, eds. *Elizabeth Barrett Browning's Letters to Mrs David Ogilvy, 1849–1861*. London, 1974.
Huxley, Leonard, ed. *Elizabeth Barrett Browning: Letters to Her Sister*. 1929.
Kelley, Philip, and Ronald Hudson, eds. *Diary by EBB: The Unpublished Diary of Elizabeth Barrett Barrett, 1831–1832*. Athens, Ohio, 1969.
Kelley, Philip, Ronald Hudson, and Scott Lewis, eds. *The Brownings' Correspondence, 1809–1846*. Vols. 1–11. Winfield, KS, 1984–93.
Kenyon, Frederic, ed. *The Letters of Elizabeth Barrett Browning*. 2 vols. 1897.
———. Typescript of transcriptions for *The Letters of Elizabeth Barrett Browning* (edition listed above). BM Add. MS, 42228–42231. 4 vols.
Kintner, Elvan. *The Letters of Elizabeth Barrett Barrett and Robert Browning, 1845–1846*. 2 vols. Cambridge, MA, 1969.
MacCarthy, Barbara P., ed., *Elizabeth Barrett to Mr Boyd: Unpublished Letters of Elizabeth Barrett Browning to Hugh Stuart Boyd*. London: John Murray, 1955.
Raymond, Meredith B., and Mary Rose Sullivan, eds. *The Letters of Elizabeth Barrett Browning and Mary Russell Mitford, 1836–1854*. 3 vols. Winfield, KS, 1983.

## 3. SECONDARY SOURCES

Blake, Kathleen. *Love and the Woman Question in Victorian Literature: The Art of Self-Postponement*. Brighton, 1983.
———. "Elizabeth Barrett Browning and Wordsworth: The Romantic Poet as Woman." *Victorian Poetry* (Winter 1986): 387–98.
Borg, James Mitchell. "The Fashioning of Elizabeth Barrett Browning's *Aurora Leigh*." Ph.D. diss. Northwestern University, 1979.

Byrd, Deborah. "Combating an Alien Tyranny: Elizabeth Barrett Browning's Evolution as a Feminist Poet." *Browning Institute Studies* 15 (1987): 23–42.

Castan, C. "Structural Problems in the Poetry of *Aurora Leigh*." *Browning Society Notes* 7 (December 1977): 73–81.

Cooper, Helen. "Working into Light: Elizabeth Barrett Browning." In *Shakespeare's Sisters: Feminist Essays on Women Poets*, ed. Sandra Gilbert and Susan Gubar. Bloomington and London, 1979.

David, Deirdre. " 'Art's a Service': Social Wound, Sexual Politics, and *Aurora Leigh*." *Browning Institute Studies* 13 (1985): 113–36.

Diehl, Joanne Fiet. " 'Come Slowly—Eden': An Exploration of Women Poets and Their Muse." *Signs* 3 (Spring 1978): 572–87.

Donaldson, Sandra. "Elizabeth Barrett Browning's Poetic and Feminist Philosophies." Ph.D. diss. University of Connecticut, 1976.

———. " 'Motherhood's Advent in Power': Elizabeth Barrett Browning's Poems About Motherhood." *Victorian Poetry* 18 (1980): 51–60.

Friewald, Bina. "Elizabeth Barrett Browning's *Aurora Leigh*: Transcendentalism and the Female Subject." In *Proceedings of the Tenth Congress of the International Comparative Literature Association, Vol. 2, Comparative Poetics*, ed. Anna Balakian et al. New York, 1985: 414–20.

———. " 'The Praise Which Men Give Women': Elizabeth Barrett Browning's *Aurora Leigh* and the Critics." *Dalhousie Review* 66 (1986): 311–36.

Gelpi, Barbara Charlesworth. "*Aurora Leigh*: The Vocation of the Woman Poet." *Victorian Poetry* 19 (Spring 1981): 35–48.

Gilbert, Sandra M. "From Patria to Matria: Elizabeth Barrett Browning's Risorgimento." *PMLA* 99 (March 1984): 194–211.

Hickok, Kathleen. " 'New Yet Orthodox': The Female Characters in *Aurora Leigh*." *International Journal of Women's Studies* 3 (September–October 1980): 479–89.

———. *Representations of Women: Nineteenth-Century British Women's Poetry*. Westport, CT, and London, 1984.

Holloway, Julia Bolton. "*Aurora Leigh* and *Jane Eyre*." *Brontë Society Transactions* 17 (1977): 126–32.

Holmes, Alicia E. "Elizabeth Barrett Browning's Construction of Authority in *Aurora Leigh* by Rewriting Mother, Muse, and Miriam." *Century Review* 36, no. 3 (Fall 1992): 593–606.

Homans, Margaret. *Women Writers and Poetic Identity: Dorothy Wordsworth, Emily Brontë, and Emily Dickinson*. Princeton, NJ, 1980.

Hudson, Gladys. *An Elizabeth Barrett Browning Concordance*. 4 vols. Chicago, 1973.

Kelley, Philip, and Ronald Hudson. *The Brownings' Correspondence: A Checklist*. New York: The Browning Institute, 1978.

Kelley, Philip, and Betty Coley. *The Browning Collections: A Reconstruction*. Winfield, KS, and London, 1984.

Leighton, Angela. " 'Stirring a Dust of Figures': Elizabeth Barrett Browning and Love." *Browning Society Notes* 17 (1987–88): 11–24.

———. " 'Because Men Made the Laws: The Fallen Woman and the Woman Poet." In *New Feminist Discourses: Critical Essays on Theories and Texts*, ed. Isobel Armstrong. 1992.

Lewis, Linda M. "The Artist's Quest in Elizabeth Barrett Browning's *Aurora Leigh*." In *Images of the Feminine Identity*, ed. Kathryn Banzel et al. Lewiston, 1992.

Lupton, M. J. "The Printing Woman Who Lost Her Place." In *Woman: A Journal of Liberation* 2 (1970): 2–5.

McNally, James. "Touches of *Aurora Leigh* in *The Ring and the Book*." *Studies in Browning and His Circle* 14 (1986): 85–90.

Marxist-Feminist Literature Collective. "Women's Writing: *Jane Eyre, Shirley, Villette*, and *Aurora Leigh*. In *1848: The Sociology of Literature*, ed. Francis Barker et al. University of Essex, 1978.

Mermin, Dorothy. "The Female Poet and the Embarrassed Reader: Elizabeth Barrett Browning's *Sonnets from the Portuguese*." *English Literary History* 48 (1981): 351–67.

———. "Elizabeth Barrett Browning." *Victorian Poetry* 21 (Autumn 1983): 277–81.

———. "Barrett Browning's Stories." *Browning Institute Studies* 13 (1985): 99–112.

———. "Gender and Genre in *Aurora Leigh*." *Victorian Newsletter* (Spring 1986): 7–11.

———. "The Damsel, the Knight, and the Victorian Woman Poet." *Critical Inquiry* 13 (Autumn 1986): 64–80.

———. "Elizabeth Barrett Browning Through 1844: Becoming a Woman Poet." *Studies in English Literature, 1500–1900* 26 (1986): 713–36.

Moi, Toril. *Sexual/Textual Politics: Feminist Literary Theory*. 1985.

Montefiore, Jan. *Feminism and Poetry: Language, Experience, and Identity in Women's Writing*. 1987.

Raymond, Meredith B. "Elizabeth Barrett's Early Poetics: The 1820s: 'The Bird Pecks Through the Shell.' " *Browning Society Notes* 8 (1978): 3–7.

———. "Elizabeth Barrett Browning's Poetics: 1830–1844: 'The Seraph and the Early Piper.' " *Browning Society Notes* 9 (1979): 5–9.

———. "Elizabeth Barrett Browning's Poetics, 1845–1846, 'The Ascending Gyre.' " *Browning Society Notes* 11 (1981): 1–11.

Reynolds, Margaret. "Aurora Leigh: 'Writing Her Story for Her Better Self.' " *Browning Society Notes* 17 (1987–88): 5–11.

Ridenour, Georgé. "Robert Browning and *Aurora Leigh*." *Victorian Newsletter*, no. 67 (Spring 1987): 26–32.

Rosenblum, Dolores. "Face to Face: Elizabeth Barrett Browning's *Aurora Leigh* and Nineteenth-Century Poetry." *Victorian Studies* 26 (Spring 1983): 321–38.

———. "Casa Guidi Windows and *Aurora Leigh*: The Genesis of Elizabeth Barrett Browning's Visionary Aesthetic." *Tulsa Studies in Women's Literature* 4 (Spring 1985): 61–68.

Steinmetz, Virginia V. "The Development of Elizabeth Barrett Browning's Juvenile Self-Images in *Aurora Leigh*." Ph.D. diss. Duke University, 1980.

———. "Beyond the Sun: Patriarchal Images in *Aurora Leigh*." *Studies in Browning and His Circle* 9 (Fall, 1981): 18–41.

———. "Images of 'Mother-Want' in Elizabeth Barrett Browning's *Aurora Leigh*." *Victorian Poetry* 21 (1983): 351–67.

Stephenson, Glennis. *Elizabeth Barrett Browning and the Poetry of Love*. Ann Arbor, 1989.

Stone, Marjorie. "Taste, Totems, and Taboos: The Female Breast in Victorian Poetry." *Dalhousie Review* 64 (Winter 1984–85): 748–70.

———. *Elizabeth Barrett Browning*. New York and London, 1992.

Sutphin, Christine. "Revising Old Scripts: The Fusion of Independence and Intimacy in *Aurora Leigh*." *Browning Institute Studies* 15 (1987): 43–54.

Taplin, Gardner Blake. *The Life of Elizabeth Barrett Browning*. 1957.

Taylor, Beverly. " 'School-Miss Alfred' and 'Materfamilias': Female Sexuality and Poetic Voice in *The Princess* and *Aurora Leigh*." In *Gender and Discourse in Victorian Literature and Art*. Ed. Anthony H. Harrison and Beverly Taylor. DeKalb, IL, 1992.

Todd, Janet. *Feminist Literary History*. Oxford, 1988.

Turner, Paul. "Aurora Versus the Angel." *Review of English Studies* 24 (July 1948): 227–35.

Weinstein, Mark. *W. E. Aytoun and The Spasmodic Controversy*. Yale Studies in English 165. New Haven, 1968.

Whiting, Lilian. *The Brownings: Their Life and Art*. Boston, 1911.

Wilsey, Mildred. "The Composition of *Aurora Leigh*." Master's thesis. Yale University, 1938.

———. "Elizabeth Barrett Browning's Heroine." *College English* 6 (November 1944): 75–81.

Wing-Sheung, Leung J. "The Poet in Elizabeth Barrett Browning's *Aurora Leigh*." M.Phil. thesis. Oxford, 1981.

Woolf, Virginia. *A Room of One's Own*. 1929.

Woolford, John. "Elizabeth Barrett Browning: The Natural and the Spiritual." *Browning Society Notes* 8 (April 1978): 15–19.

———. "Elizabeth Barrett Browning: Woman and Poet." *Browning Society Notes* 9 (December 1979): 3–5.